Consumer Choice in Historical Archaeology

Consumer Choice in Historical Archaeology

Edited by
SUZANNE M. SPENCER-WOOD
University of Massachusetts
Boston, Massachusetts

Plenum Press • New York and London

Library of Congress Cataloging in Publication Data

Consumer choice in historical archaeology.

   Bibliography: p.
   Includes index.
   1. United States – Antiquities. 2. Archaeology and history – United States. 3. Con-
sumers' preferences – United States – History – Sources. I. Spencer-Wood, Suzanne M.
E159.5.C67   1987   930.1   87-2569
ISBN 0-306-42318-9

© 1987 Plenum Press, New York
A Division of Plenum Publishing Corporation
233 Spring Street, New York, N.Y. 10013

Printed in the United States of America

To my father, Willis Avery Wood,
and to the memory of my mother,
Alice Jane Spencer Wood

Contributors

Sherene Baugher ☐ New York Landmarks Preservation Commission, 20 Vesey Street, 11th Floor, New York, New York

Mark C. Branstner ☐ Department of Anthropology, Wayne State University, Detroit, Michigan

Lynn Clark ☐ Department of Anthropology, State University of New York, Binghamton, New York

Constance A. Crosby ☐ Department of Anthropology, University of California, Berkeley, California

Lu Ann De Cunzo ☐ CLIO Group, 3961 Baltimore Avenue, Philadelphia, Pennsylvania

Amy Friedlander ☐ Louis Berger & Associates, 1819 H Street N.W., Washington, D.C. 20006

Patrick H. Garrow ☐ Garrow & Associates, 4000 DeKalb Technology Parkway, Suite 375, Atlanta, Georgia

Paul M. Heberling ☐ Department of Sociology and Anthropology, Juniata College, Huntingdon, Pennsylvania

Scott D. Heberling ☐ Heberling Associates, Route 4, Box 20, Huntingdon, Pennsylvania

Susan L. Henry ☐ Heritage Resources Branch, Fairfax County Office of Comprehensive Planning, 2855 Annandale Road, Falls Church, Virginia

Cheryl A. Holt ☐ Analytical Services for Archaeologists, 900 Cameron Street, Alexandria, Virginia

Terry H. Klein ☐ Louis Berger & Associates, 100 Halsted Street, East Orange, New Jersey

Charles H. LeeDecker ☐ Louis Berger & Associates, 1819 H Street N.W., Washington, D.C. 20006

Mark P. Leone □ Department of Anthropology, University of Maryland, College Park, Maryland

Terrance J. Martin □ Anthropology Section, Illinois State Museum, Springfield, Illinois

Kim A. McBride □ Museum and Department of Anthropology, Michigan State University, East Lansing, Michigan

W. Stephen McBride □ Museum and Department of Anthropology, Michigan State University, East Lansing, Michigan

Charles E. Orser, Jr. □ Department of Geography and Anthropology, Louisiana State University, Baton Rouge, Louisiana

Elizabeth J. Reitz □ Department of Anthropology, University of Georgia, Athens, Georgia

Steven Judd Shephard □ Alexandria Archaeology, Box 178, City Hall, Alexandria, Virginia

David A. Singer □ 187 Thacher Street, Milton, Massachusetts

Suzanne M. Spencer-Wood □ Department of Anthropology, University of Massachusetts, Boston, Massachusetts

Robert W. Venables □ American Indian Community House, 842 Broadway, New York, New York

Foreword

Historical archaeology has made great strides during the last two decades. Early archaeological reports were dominated by descriptions of features and artifacts, while research on artifacts was concentrated on studies of topology, technology, and chronology. Site reports from the 1960s and 1970s commonly expressed faith in the potential artifacts had for aiding in the identifying socioeconomic status differences and for understanding the relationships between the social classes in terms of their material culture. An emphasis was placed on the presence or absence of porcelain or teaware as an indication of social status. These were typical features in site reports written just a few years ago. During this same period, advances were being made in the study of food bone as archaeologists moved away from bone counts to minimal animal counts and then on to the costs of various cuts of meat.

Within the last five years our ability to address questions of the relationship between material culture and socioeconomic status has greatly expanded. The essays in this volume present efforts toward measuring expenditure and consumption patterns represented by commonly recovered artifacts and food bone. These patterns of consumption are examined in conjunction with evidence from documentary sources that provide information on occupations, wealth levels, and ethnic affiliations of those that did the consuming. One of the refreshing aspects of these papers is that the authors are not afraid of documents, and their use of them is not limited to a role of confirmation. Despite what some have contended, historical archaeology is not in danger of being bastardized by the use of documents. In reality, its full potential will not be realized unless all resources are brought into play and are reflected against each other, as they are in these papers.

The models and approaches offered here are efforts toward a fuller understanding of the relationship between people and material culture, and represent strides toward a fuller realization of the interpretive potential of archaeology. They all represent approaches to the data that have been developed in the last five years. Several of these models have great promise and potential as tools for the interpretation of archaeological assemblages. Given the rate at which our knowledge and sophistication is developing, it is clear that, in another five years, some of these approaches will probably seem simplistic and naive. No doubt, in some cases, the models will be expanded and improved by the authors who are presenting them in this volume. This is an exciting time in historical archaeology because the boundaries of our knowledge are rapidly expanding and we are beginning to deal with broad questions of the relationship between people and their material culture.

To some observers, it may seem that the development of historical archaeology is slow because they focus on the distance to be covered rather than the
progress that has been made. This reminds me of the plea made by the English
potter Richard Champion when petitioning Parliament for the renewal of his
patent for making of hard-paste porcelain in 1774. His success in bringing
porcelain to production during the first patent was limited, and in stating his
case for renewal of the patent, he asked for Parliament to recognize his limited
success and to have faith in the potential of what he was undertaking. Champion summed up his case as follows:

> It is therefore presumed that the Legislature will distinguish between over-sanguine
> Hopes, in Point of Time, of an Invention, which however has, at length Succeeded,
> and those visionary Projects which deceive for ever. (Wedgwood 1775:9)[1]

Some of the models presented in this volume will succeed in becoming important tools for the interpretation of artifact assemblages, whereas others will be
superceded by systems and approaches yet to be developed.

GEORGE L. MILLER

---

[1] Wedgwood, Josiah, 1775, *Papers Relative to Mr. Champion's Application to Parliament for the Extension of the Term of a Patent,* No publisher listed.

Preface

The challenge facing historical archaeologists is to contribute insights into the past beyond those available from the historical record. The goal of this volume is to explain household variations in historic consumer behavior through combined analyses of archaeological and documentary data. Comparing the different data available from documentary and archaeological sources provides more information than can be gained from either source alone. The primary hypothesis of this volume is that socioeconomic stratification significantly affects certain consumer behaviors, involving choices to acquire, and later archaeologically deposit, relatively expensive versus inexpensive goods. Such consumer choices are inferred primarily from quantitatively measured patterns in archaeological data. Through comparative site analyses, household variations in these patterns are explained through documented variations in socioeconomic status and/or other factors affecting consumer behavior

This volume is not a haphazard collection of available research on a general topic. It developed out of my research interests and the recent growth of similar research in historical archaeology, facilitated by the development of price scaling indices for ceramics and fauna. All chapters are concerned with explaining consumer behavior, and were specifically written with the shared framework of "consumer choice." This framework was developed to combine the analysis of variables affecting the selective acquisition of goods with archaeological models of selective discard. Chapters draw on theory, concepts and research from economics, sociology, anthropology, and history to synthesize cultural frameworks that relate patterns in archaeological data to economic, social, and political factors in consumer behavior. In the aggregate, the chapters in this volume offer a comparative data base for assessing the conditions under which patterns of archaeologically deposited data were affected by socioeconomic consumer behaviors, and/or other behaviors.

This volume and my research in it could not have reached successful completion without the conscientious work, support, and enthusiasm of many professional colleagues and individuals. I am grateful to a number of colleagues both for their contributions to this volume and for assisting me in developing my research so that I could contribute to and edit this volume. While it is impossible to acknowledge individually all those who made this volume possible, I would like to express my thanks here to those who made unusual contributions to this effort.

The staff at Plenum Press have played a major part in the publication of this volume. From my first contact, Eliot Werner, senior editor at Plenum, encouraged and supported me in organizing and editing this volume. Eliot

Werner's professional advice on innumerable details, and his patience with the inevitable delays, were a great blessing. I am also grateful to production editors Kenneth Wishnia, and especially Daniel Spinella, for their painstakingly detailed work in professionally publishing this volume. Other individuals at Plenum, including Peter Strupp, associate managing editor, gave me assistance on many details. My warmest thanks to all the professionals at Plenum who made this volume possible.

Over the course of two years, colleagues freely sent me conference papers, from which I proposed this volume. Authors of every chapter in this volume completed the time-consuming tasks, both of comparative multisite archaeological and documentary research, and of rewriting and revising manuscripts to include the framework of consumer choice. Mark Leone not only contributed an insightful epilogue, but his enthusiastic support encouraged me in editing this volume. For inspiration, thoughtful comments, and support for my own research, I am especially grateful to Mark Leone and George Miller.

I have been privileged to see a number of graduate and undergraduate students develop professionally in the process of assisting in my research. Foremost among these is Scott Heberling, who, as a graduate student, contributed professional-quality research and writing to our coauthored chapter.

Finally, I am grateful to my father for sharing his love of science, nature, and music with me. I am thankful that my mother and father always actively encouraged and supported my intellectual and personal growth.

SUZANNE M. SPENCER-WOOD

Contents

Introduction

SUZANNE M. SPENCER-WOOD

This linkage between ideas and observations, which suggests that ideas be evaluated by objective means, pinpoints the need in any science for developing such means, and further emphasizes the *fact* that the testing of theory is dependent upon the availability of robust methods. I have designated the development of such means as "middle range research." It is not middle range because it is unimportant. Quite to the contrary, it is middle range because it links observations and experiences as to what the world is like to ideas—theories (if you will) that seek to tell us why the world is the way it appears to be. Middle range research results in the production of knowledge and understanding that may grow, serving as the research-based paradigmatic underpinning of science. (Binford 1982:128–129)

SCOPE

The purpose of this volume in historical archaeology is to present current research investigating the relationship of archaeological data to consumer behavior distinctions among and within American socioeconomic groups. The purpose of compiling this research in one volume is to gain more information from the whole than is available from any individual chapter. Considered together within a comparative framework, the book chapters suggest some systematic connections between patterns in the archaeological data and patterns of participation in consumer behaviors of cultural subgroups. In the aggregate, this volume demonstrates that, although archaeological patterns often can be related to social stratification, such relationships are not uniform and cannot be taken for granted. Considered as a whole, this volume begins to differentiate those situations in which archaeological patterns can be related to socioeconomic status behaviors and those situations in which other behaviors may be more strongly related to the archaeological patterns. By using a systems-theory framework, the effects of other behaviors on archaeological patterns have been considered, resulting from differences in market access, ethnicity, household structure and life cycle, and biases in the archaeological and documentary records.

In this book archaeological data have been related primarily to socioeconomic behaviors, both for theoretical and for practical reasons. Over the eighteenth and nineteenth centuries the critical transformation was made from a

Suzanne M. Spencer-Wood ☐ Department of Anthropology, University of Massachusetts, Boston, MA 02125.

mercantilistic to a capitalistic market economy, with the accompanying development of a social stratification system corresponding to capitalistic relations of production. Research in anthropological archaeology and on twentieth-century consumer behavior both find strong relationships between economic roles, social stratification, and types of material culture owned by households, or excavated from sites (Becker 1973; Hoffman 1974:36; Laumann and House 1970:327–328: Leone 1977; Millon 1974; Pires-Ferreira and Winter 1976; Rathje and McCarthy 1977; Reissman 1959:145–164; Renger 1971; Sabloff and Rathje 1975; Warner *et al.* 1960:123: Wasson 1969). The strength of these connections is assessed in this volume with data from American sites from the eighteenth century through the early twentieth century because the most documentation of social and economic status is available in this time span. In most cases, the documentary data permit researchers to go beyond inferences from the archaeological data. Site-specific documentary and archaeological data have been compared and contrasted in order to infer behavioral variations between and within cultural subgroups. The degree to which variation among sites in documented status corresponds with variation in archaeological patterns indicates the strength of the relationship between the archaeological patterns and status-related consumer behaviors. This volume describes the current state of development of this emerging research area, and suggests further research needed to determine those situations in which socioeconomic status relates most to archaeological patterns.

The basic site unit of excavations and analyses reported in this volume is the land or house lot associated with a domestic structure and outbuildings. Although a few artifacts could be lost in the yard by visitors to a house, the vast majority of the artifacts excavated from primary deposits in a house yard that is well fenced or otherwise clearly separated are usually assumed to have been deposited by house residents who controlled the yard space and artifact deposition there (Deagan 1982:161). The archaeological data associated with one structure usually cannot be divided to correspond with smaller economic or social units that may be housed in that structure, such as multiple families, servants, or boarders. Therefore, the archaeological meaning of a household, as used in this volume, corresponds to all of the residents of a domestic structure that could have created primary deposits of artifacts in the house yard in one time period. Archaeological analyses of these artifacts represent the combined acquisition and deposition behaviors of all residents in a house structure, and possibly these behaviors for some visitors to the house site as well. Formation processes for sites occupied by a number of residents over time may or may not yield archaeological stratigraphic deposits that form a chronological sequence of layers which can be related to developmental cycles in the sequence of archaeological households occupying the site (Beaudry 1984; De Cunzo this volume; LeeDecker *et al.* this volume; McManamon 1984).

In the eighteenth and nineteenth centuries, most consumer goods were probably acquired through the market economy (either wholesale, retail, or second-hand markets), with the exception of gifts or heirlooms that are usually less likely to be discarded than everyday items bought in the market economy. Some of the goods acquired by house residents would be selectively discarded or lost in the house yard, and some of these would later be recovered by archaeologists. This process permits some connection between patterns in archaeological assemblages associated with a house site and the residents' aggregate market acquisition behavior, distorted by archaeological biases of partial artifact deposition and recovery. The primary concern of this volume is the relationships between site residents' socioeconomic status and their acquisition of goods available at different prices in the market, with the possibility of other variables being important under certain conditions. If the values of other major variables are controlled, such as market access and ethnicity, the research in this volume indicates that the types of goods selectively acquired and discarded by households are strongly influenced by socioeconomic status. Although they can not usually be quantified, the effects of biases in the archaeological and documentary records are also considered. The archaeological data are always an incomplete and biased sample due to site formation processes such as selective discard, and methods of archaeological sampling (Gould 1978; Schiffer 1972, 1976; South 1978). The documentary record is biased by selective and incomplete recording methods.

This book contributes to both history and to anthropology. In history, the book offers information concerning seldom recorded behaviors within different American social strata from the eighteenth through the early twentieth centuries. Archaeological data, in conjunction with the documentary data, provide insights into lifeways within social and economic strata, especially the poorly recorded working class. In anthropology and archaeology, this volume indicates connections between archaeological patterns and inferred behavior patterns among cultural subgroups. Using a systemic consumer-choice framework, situations were identified in which patterns of archaeological data have good correspondence or fit with documented house residents' participation in the cultural system of socioeconomic stratification. Equally important were those recurring situations with patterns of poor fit between the archaeological and documentary data.

Differences between observed archaeological patterns and those expected on the basis of site residents' documented socioeconomic status may be due to inadequate theory, methods, and/or data, and their interconnections (Binford 1972:249). The theoretically hypothesized relationship of archaeological patterns to status may be incorrect, methods may inadequately measure status and/or archaeological patterns, and/or the data may be biased. At the theoretical level, the consumer-choice framework includes behavioral variables besides socioeconomic status that, in some situations, account for deviations from the expected relationships between patterns in archaeological data and documentary indications of socioeconomic status. Two major possible situations of poor fit involve biases in the archaeological and/or documentary records, corresponding to processes such as differential discard, other site formation processes, and selective documentation. Some suggestions of systematic bias can be made by aggregating the findings of individual chapters in this volume. A comparison of book chapters indicates a need for standardized methods in this research area to develop the large comparative site data base needed to establish connections between widely recurring site patterns in archaeological data and consumer behaviors within cultural subgroups, whether social, economic, political, or ethnic.

Taken as a whole, research in this volume suggests some substantive generalizations about variations in consumer goods deposited on sites of house residents participating in different socioeconomic cultural strata. In some cases it appears that wealthy house residents bought and discarded not only more expensive goods but also more inexpensive goods than less wealthy households (Spencer-Wood). Inexpensive goods, including food remains, found at the site of an elite resident may represent food preparation vessels, foodways behaviors, and/or goods used by servants or boarders. Studies by Spencer-Wood and Heberling, and Baugher and Venables indicate that, in general, expensive goods were handled more carefully, and broken and discarded less frequently, than were inexpensive goods. Therefore, it may be difficult archaeologically to distinguish the wealthy from the middle-class sites. Archaeological data in some cases indicate more about the selective discard behaviors of socioeconomic strata than they do about their acquisition behaviors. Archaeological data from working-class sites, possibly due to less selective discard, seem to give better indications of acquisition behaviors related to status than do data deposited by wealthier groups.

Research in this volume on working-class sites has begun to distinguish patterns in archaeological data corresponding to occupational strata with different socioeconomic statuses. For example, goods owned and later discarded by households headed by merchants or political leaders usually have been distinguished from those discarded by factory workers and laborers (McBride and McBride). It is inferred that merchants have more expensive goods not only because of their higher socioeconomic status than factory workers and laborers, but also because of their higher market access (Spencer-Wood and Heberling). Differences in status for specific occupations among industrial or factory workers are sometimes reflected in site-specific distinctions in archaeological data (De Cunzo; Heberling). Consumer behaviors are also differentiated archaeologically within socioeconomic status groups (Branster; Garrow; Martin; Singer). Baugher and Venables consider the interaction of political status and events with socioeconomic status, and their connections to house site archaeological patterns. Some researchers find that house residents' behaviors due to ethnic group membership (Clark; Henry) or household structure and life cycle (De Cunzo; LeeDecker et al.) affect the types of goods acquired and discarded by house site residents in conjunction with, and sometimes more than, socioeconomic status. An emergent finding from this volume is that it may only be possible to connect archaeological patterns to socioeconomic status for those sites with residents who participated in or emulated behaviors of socioeconomic groups forming the stratification system of the Anglo ethnic majority of the population.

THEORY OVERVIEW

Meanings are carried by concepts and arguments, and the archaeological record contains only arrangements of matter. We assign concepts to different arrangements of matter or offer arguments regarding the sources or conditions that brought into being particular arrangements of matter. (Binford 1982:129–130)

A problem intrinsic to archaeology is to relate archaeological data to the behaviors in a living culture that produced the archaeologically recovered material remains. In 1948, Taylor addressed this problem by suggesting that archaeologists shift from defining cultures as trait lists and types of artifacts to the use of the "conjunctive approach." This approach "aims at drawing the completest possible picture of past human life" from "the elucidation of cultur- al conjunctives, the associations and relationships, the 'affinities,' within the manifestation under investigation" (Taylor 1948:95–96). Binford (1962, 1967) carried this approach further by suggesting that lifeways be reconstructed by using archaeological patterns to test hypotheses of expectations generated from ethnographically derived cultural constructs. Binford advocated the use of scientific methodology to connect archaeological patterns with behavioral correlates (Binford 1968:13–14). Many archaeologists, including some contributors to this volume, have followed Binford's lead by using the scientific method of hypothesis testing in historical archaeology (Fritz and Plog 1970; Plog 1973; South 1977; Watson, LeBlanc, and Redman 1971), although others have found this type of explanation often unsatisfactory (Flannery 1973; Renfrew 1982). To further the development of theory in historical archaeology, Leone, in this volume's epilogue, suggests the use of middle range theory, based on Binford's most recent use of middle range theory in prehistoric archaeology.

Leone suggests that historical archaeologists use documentary data as Binford has used ethnographic data to construct an organizational framework of cultural behavior. By considering the documentary and archaeological records as two independent data sets, discrepancies between the expected and actual archaeological pattern can be used to generate a more complete organizational model of cultural behavior than is possible from either the documentary record or the archaeological record alone. By using middle range theory, discrepancies between archaeological and documentary data are not just explained by site-specific idiosyncratic behavior, but are used instead to generate a more sophisticated organizational model of behavior of cultural subgroups. In this volume, disparities between site comparisons of archaeological patterns and documentary indications of socioeconomic status are, in some cases, accounted for by being correlated with behaviors of other cultural subgroups, such as ethnic foodways (Henry) or style preferences (Clark). In other cases, discrepancies at a single site that cannot be related to a cultural subgroup behavior pattern are explained by circumstances at individual house sites (Baugher and Venables; Garrow).

A related problem in giving life and meaning to archaeological data is the degree of confidence in the connections between excavated material culture and different types of cultural behavior. Binford classified attributes as functioning primarily in technomic, sociotechnic, or ideotechnic spheres (1962). The highest confidence accompanies analyses of technomic function, with confidence decreasing in proportion to the amount of symbolic meaning interpreted from material culture. For those objects with dual functions, such as a sacred chalice, the technomic function can be inferred with some confidence, while the ideotechnic function may be lost forever, unless it is recovered in an identifiably religious context.

This volume contributes to our understanding of the sociotechnic content of attribute patterns symbolizing socioeconomic status by focusing on eighteenth through early twentieth century America, when, in general, the most site-specific documentary data are available indicating socioeconomic status of site residents. Comparative site analyses, in conjunction with documented price scales for consumer goods, permit archaeologists to distinguish, with some degree of confidence, which artifacts and attributes most strongly symbolize status. For example, documented status distinctions were found to correspond more with decorative types of cups and saucers than with groups having more combined technomic and sociotechnic functions, such as plates and bowls that include both tableware and kitchenware (Miller 1984; Spencer-Wood this volume). The continued strong relationship, in most cases, between documented house residents' status and cup and saucer decoration contrasts with historic generalizations about the declining importance of the tea ceremony (Miller 1984:47). A possible hypothesis resolving this apparent contradiction is the use of teaware simply for status display on shelves, without using it in a tea ceremony. Many people today collect expensive teaware and display it on shelves without using it for its intended foodways function.

At the most generalized level, this volume is concerned with the differential distribution of goods within state-level market economies. In anthropological archaeology, theories and research concerned with market economies have connected the unequal distribution of goods among sites to economic and social differentiation within the society (cf. Adams 1966, 1974; Fried 1967; Hodder and Orton 1979:183–195; Rathje 1971; Sabloff and Rathje 1975). Economic anthropologists and archaeologists both consider social status differences that are related to economic roles as one of the major factors in unequal access to goods (Clark 1969:217; Douglas and Isherwood 1979:25; Morris 1978; Pires-Ferreira and Winter 1976). Current consumer behavior research has established the highest correlations between occupation, social class, and types of consumer goods selected by house residents from the market (Kahl and Davis 1955; Laumann and House 1970; Reissman 1959:145–64; Warner et al. 1960). The term "socioeconomic status" indicates a connection between economic role and social status made by many anthropologists. Most theories in anthropological archaeology concerned with state-level market economies relate social stratification to economic differentiation (Adams 1966; Childe 1951; Redman 1978). Many anthropologists have connected economic division of labor to sociopolitical hierarchy (Fried 1960; Flannery 1972; Sahlins 1958; Service 1962).

Archaeologists have been increasingly concerned with relating social stratification to artifact patterns. In 1962, Binford stated:

> I would consider the study and establishment of correlations between types of social structure classified on the basis of behavioral attributes and structural types of material elements as one of the major areas of anthropological research yet to be developed. (Binford 1962:219)

Since then, an increasing amount of archaeological research has been concerned with artifact patterns related to social stratification and its connections to economic roles. Prehistoric archaeologists have differentiated social strata on the basis of grave goods, house size, and furnishings (Flannery and Coe 1968; Hill 1970; Hoffman 1974; Sanders and Webster 1978; Watson 1978).

A growing body of research in American historical archaeology has been concerned with relating archaeological patterns to behavioral distinctions among socioeconomic strata (Deagan 1982:164–165; Drucker 1981; Geismar 1982; Mudar 1978; Otto 1984; Paynter 1982; Poe 1979; Schulz and Gust 1983; Singer 1985). Social and economic historians also have been concerned with the lifeways of historic American social and economic strata (Bushman 1970; Fogel and Engerman 1971; Johnson 1978; Wallace 1978). Taken together, the chapters in this volume demonstrate some connections in eighteenth- and nineteenth-century American culture between social and economic stratification and site patterns in artifact attributes. Artifact attributes strongly affected by socioeconomic status were chosen for analysis. At the same time, the use of a systems theory framework led to the consideration of some other behavioral variables that could also affect the artifact attributes analyzed.

Within anthropological archaeology, a major problem is the disjunction between macrocultural theory and site-specific archaeological data. Many theoretical statements in archaeology are general and abstract, without offering any scientific methodology for testing them. At the same time, the site-specific variations in the archaeological record usually require much qualification and overgeneralization to connect them to macrocultural theory (Redman *et al.* 1978:7). Binford (1965) has suggested that archaeologists shift from the "normative" approach of associating change in shared cultural behaviors with changes in "typical" classes of artifacts, to a consideration of variations in archaeological patterns indicating differential participation in culture. This volume is concerned with relating site archaeological patterns to patterns of house residents' participation in behaviors of cultural subgroups, especially social and economic classes. Comparative site analyses permit description of the range of variation in documented status of site residents, and an assessment of the degree of correspondence between variations in status and variations in relative cost of consumer goods selectively deposited at sites.

In anthropology and archaeology, there is a disparity in scale between culture systems level theory and site-specific archaeological data (Dincauze 1984; Meltzer 1979:654). A similar difference in scale between theory and data in ecology led to the development of niche theory, to relate the general evolutionary principles of natural selection and competition to their manifestations at the level of specific field observations (Diamond 1978:323; Hutchinson 1975). It has been suggested "that a theory of change in household organization can bridge the existing 'mid-level theory gap' in archaeology" (Wilk and Rathje 1982:617). Recently the development of household-level theory has been suggested in historical archaeology in order to connect the household level of recovery and analysis of archaeological and documentary data to pancultural theories (Beaudry 1984; Deetz 1982; Mrozowski 1984).

The household is a primary unit in theoretical models and research in anthropology (cf. Arnould and Netting 1982; Friedman 1980; Horne 1982;

Sahlins 1972; Yanagisako 1979), prehistoric archaeology (cf. Flannery and Winter 1976; Hill 1970; Longacre 1970; McManamon 1984; Reid and Whittlesey 1982; Yesner 1984), and historical archaeology (cf. Beaudry 1984; Bowen 1975; Deetz 1977; Drucker 1981; Dyson 1982; Moran *et al.* 1982; Mrozowski 1984; Otto 1984; Saitta 1984; South 1977; Spencer-Wood 1984; Starbuck 1984; Worrell 1980). Although relationships between concepts of "household," "family," and social or economic units have been debated, archaeological data recovered from the yard of a house usually can be related only to the aggregate behavior of all residents of the house in one time period, and not to any subdivisions of economic or social units within a house (McManamon 1984). The residents living in one structure may be composed of one or more families, servants, and/or borders who may form one or more economic and social units. In some cases the economic and social relationships among such a household's members can be determined from documents. However, artifact deposits from a house yard cannot usually, with any confidence, be separated into groups belonging to different families or boarders living in the same house at one time period. Therefore, in order to make inferences of status-related consumer behavior, documentary indications of socioeconomic status for all site residents, to the extent that these can be determined, need to be related to archaeological patterns.

Theoretically and methodologically, this volume addresses the basic archaeological problem of relating site-specific archaeological data, biased by site formation processes and data recovery methods, to cultural behavior, sometimes hypothesized from incomplete documentary records. Research has been conducted both at the household level and at the scale of household participation in behavior patterns of social and economic groups. The consumer-choice framework applies a systems-theory multivariate approach at the household scale. This permits consideration of the importance of other variables to evidence of consumer behavior, such as market access, ethnicity, household structure and developmental cycle, and the unavoidable biases in archaeological and documentary data. The household is the most appropriate analytical unit because it relates most directly to the site-specific archaeological and documentary data that are usually available. Household-scale socioeconomic consumer behavior is indicated by comparing and contrasting site-specific archaeological and documentary data. The documentary data sometimes indicate house residents' memberships in socioeconomic and other cultural subgroups. Site artifact pattern variations may be connected with house residents' participation in shared cultural behavior patterns related to economic and social stratification. Intersite comparisons are used to assess the range of variation in household participation in shared socioeconomic group behaviors. Recurring relationships at the household scale between site-specific artifact patterns and documented cultural subgroup membership also permit inferences of shared acquisition and deposition behaviors in such groups. Comparative methods permit connections between site-specific archaeological patterns, house residents' behaviors, and their participation in consumer behavior of social and economic groups. In this way, this volume attempts to bridge the gap between pancultural systems theory and site-specific data. Documentary data are used to assess household participation in socioeconomic group behaviors and to formulate resulting expected patterns in the archaeological data. This volume contributes analyses relating archaeological patterns to cultural behaviors at the household, neighborhood, and cultural subgroup levels.

SOME ASPECTS OF PARADIGMS

A paradigm is a frame of reference that does not itself explain phenomena, but provides a conceptual construct and principles used to generate hypotheses explaining them (Binford 1982:126). According to Kuhn (1970:182–186), a paradigm defines the set of questions or research problems addressed by a community of researchers, and the appropriate data and methods used to address them. It involves language, concepts, models, and values shared by a community of researchers. For Clarke (1972), a paradigm is a framework model, with a conceptual and methodological approach, used to research and explain a particular set of observations. Many paradigms may coexist within a discipline at the same time in order to facilitate different interpretations being made from different aspects of data (Clarke 1972:6–7). Clarke (1978) developed a systems theory paradigm that subsequently has been used and expanded by a number of archaeologists (cf. Cooke and Renfrew 1979; Doran 1982; Hosler *et al.* 1978; Kristiansen 1982; Redman 197C; South 1977; Tuggle *et al.* 1972). Within the systems paradigm, the economic subsystem has been studied in relationship to the social subsystem (cf. Adams 1966; Fried 1967; Redman 1978). In this volume, aspects of the American market economy, including socioeconomic stratification, market access, ethnicity, and household size and structure, have been considered within the consumer-choice framework.

The Consumer-Choice Framework

In this volume the shared framework is the consumer-choice systemic model. Its principal application lies in explaining why goods of differing quality or price were selected for acquisition and archaeological deposition by different cultural subgroups in a market economy. While types of goods, such as food types, ceramic, glass, or house forms, and site location may have primarily technomic, utilitarian functions in subsistence and foodways, variations within these utilitarian categories in sociotechnic attributes of quality and price of goods can be explained primarily by their functions in social group behaviors. The market-oriented consumer-choice framework provides a theoretical basis for hypothesizing connections between site-specific archaeological data and levels of cultural behavior from the household to cultural subgroups and the national market. It forms a conceptual bridge between archaeological recovery and cultural behavior. In addition the possibility of using the consumer-choice framework as a conceptual bridge relating archaeological patterns to other frameworks is illustrated in two book chapters. Orser has developed a connection between an historical materialist approach and the consumer-choice framework. De Cunzo has viewed consumer choices as mechanisms of adaptation to industrialization and urbanization, within an ecological framework.

Anthropological archaeology has a tradition of deriving theory from other disciplines, such as the archaeological application of systems theory from cybernetics (Clarke 1978). The consumer-choice framework draws theoretically from anthropology, archaeology, economic anthropology, consumer behavior theory, economic theories of interaction within capitalistic market economies, and theories in economic geography dealing with market economies in the spatial dimension. This framework involves the application of systems theory at the level of the household to organize the multivariate consideration of factors involved in consumer behavior. This orientation is similar to multidimensional research by prehistoric archaeologists, which relates archaeological patterns to social as well as economic aspects of cultural behavior (Binford 1972; Flannery 1976). Economic anthropology considers the many factors involved in differential distribution of goods within the market economy (Douglas and Isherwood 1979). Economic theory is the source of the supply–demand dynamic used in the consumer-choice framework (Heilbroner 1970; Peterson 1977). Economic geography models are concerned with the spatial distribution of goods along transportation networks from manufacturers to distributors to consumers (Chorley and Haggett 1967; Haggett 1972; Lloyd and Dicken 1972; Lowe and Moryadas 1975). Archaeologists have applied theoretical models from economic geography in analyzing the distributions of artifacts (Hodder and Orton 1979:60–77; 183–195). In this volume, the importance of availability of consumer goods, or market access, has been considered in explaining some differences in site deposits of consumer goods (Baugher and Venables; McBride and McBride; Spencer-Wood and Heberling).

This volume is concerned with eighteenth and nineteenth century America, when most consumer goods would have been acquired from the market economy, although a few would have been gifts or inherited items. Consumer behavior theory is concerned with the complex interaction of economic, cultural, social, and psychological factors involved in the process of consumer decisions to acquire one particular item rather than another. Although the process of shopping or decision making cannot be reconstructed archaeologically, artifacts in a market economy predominantly represent goods that were first acquired and then lost or discarded. Household goods mostly acquired from the market are selectively discarded or lost at the house site, and then partially recovered archaeologically.

The consumer-choice systemic framework is appropriate for this volume because it is concerned with factors affecting individual selections of goods in the context of the supply–demand interactions of a market economy. While the primary behavioral variable considered in consumer demand is socioeconomic status, the systems theory approach is apparent in some book chapters considering locational variations in market supply, termed *market access,* variations in behavior due to political status, ethnicity, household size and structure, and functional utility of goods. Some historical archaeologists have been concerned with supply-side variables in analyzing the market access of different site locations (Miller and Hurry 1983; Riordan and Adams 1985; Spencer-Wood 1979). Archaeological data also have been used to analyze a number of variables affecting consumer demand, including socioeconomic status (Miller 1980; this volume), ethnicity (Clark this volume; Henry this volume; Otto 1984; Schuyler 1980; Spencer-Wood and Heberling this volume), household size and composition (De Cunzo this volume; Henry this volume; LeeDecker *et al.* this volume), and political status (Baugher and Venables this volume; McBride and McBride this volume). The consumer choice model relates archaeological data to such market factors, as well as biases of discard and recovery.

The use of a consumer-choice framework expands our ability to explain the archaeological record. It permits inferences of household behaviors by relating archaeological and documentary data. The model is the basis for hypotheses connecting documented participation of households in socioeconomic, ethnic, political, family life cycle, or other cultural subgroups, with archaeological data in order to gain information about selective acquisition and deposition behaviors that produced the archaeological data. Individual or household-level consumer behavior research corresponds to site-specific documentary and archaeological information sometimes available in historical archaeology. Differentiations among qualities of consumer goods by class categories forms the basis for analyzing relationships between archaeological data and documentary indications of socioeconomic status. Archaeologists' use of occupation as the primary status indicator is supported by research establishing that occupation is the single most highly correlated objective measure of social class (Engel *et al.* 1978:116). Although the concept of class is a complex combination of socioeconomic status, political status, values, and perceptions, economic position is the basis for class distinctions in American society (Edwards 1939; Reissman 1959; Warner *et al.* 1960). Most of the chapters in this volume consider economic position in society as the primary aspect of social status.

Although this book is mainly concerned with relationships between archaeological attribute patterns and socioeconomic status, many chapters consider the importance of other variables as well. For me the theoretical framework has developed from a consideration of one variable while holding some other variables constant, to systemic analyses of two or three variables. The consumer-choice framework relates archaeological data to a number of behavioral variables, including socioeconomic status, market access, foodways functions, ethnicity, household size and composition, and political status. These variables previously have been individually investigated as separate research problems. In addition to relating individual variables to the archaeological data, a systemic approach permits exploration of their interrelationships with each other and how their dynamic interactions may affect archaeological patterns. The multivariate systems model can be used to assess the relative significance to archaeological patterns of alternative variables such as status and ethnicity through correlations, multiple regressions, or factor analysis (Henry this volume; Spencer-Wood this volume). In some cases ethnicity (Henry) or market availability (Miller and Hurry 1983) have been found to be more important than socioeconomic status in determining the types of consumer goods deposited at particular sites. Some studies have related ethnicity both to archaeological patterns and to socioeconomic status (Clark this volume; Otto 1984; Spencer-Wood and Heberling this volume).

A conceptual shift is involved in transforming separate univariate approaches into the multivariate framework of consumer choice. Many research problems have been concerned with connecting the value of one variable, such as market access, or social status (class), or ethnicity to one measurement of an aspect of the archaeological data. A growing number of prehistoric archaeologists have recently developed multidimensional or multivariate explanations of archaeological data (Binford 1972; Flannery 1976; Thomas 1972; Wobst 1974; Zubrow 1971). The consumer-choice framework is concerned with relating archaeological patterns to socioeconomic status and its interaction with other variables when they strongly affect selections of goods from those available in the market, and their later deposition on a site. For archaeologists, an additional important subsystem in this framework includes the biases of discard and loss transforming consumer goods from the cultural system into the archaeological system (Schiffer 1976). As research continues using the systemic consumer-choice framework, situations may be analyzed in which additional behavioral variables can also be related to archaeological patterns.

Historical Materialism

Historical materialism precedes consumer behavior theory as a framework used to analyze relationships between aspects of production represented by occupational roles, and variations in archaeological patterns. The consumer-choice framework links production, through occupation and market price, to consumption patterns. Orser uses the historical materialistic analysis of relations of production to make distinctions among classes that lead to differences in income and ability to consume more expensive versus inexpensive goods. Historical materialist theory relates consumer choices to the degree of alienation of work, due to differences in extent of ownership of means of production between owners and producers. This framework has been used to analyze material culture correlates of dualistic oppositional relationships such as those of planter and slave, landowner and laborer, or factory proprietor and worker. Parts of the theory could be used to compare more complex sets of interrelationships among occupational groups (Orser this volume). Degree of ownership of means of production does generally increase from laborers on the bottom of the socioeconomic occupational scale, to craftsmen, farmers, and proprietors at the top of the scale. Ownership of the means of production adds an explanation for income differentials of occupations, which are most highly correlated to consumer choices. Historical materialism as well as the consumer-choice framework support the connection between occupation, as the primary indicator of a person's economic and social position in American society, and consumer behavior. The historical materialist framework fits the book's theme of consumer choice and socioeconomic status because it is concerned primarily with explaining economic differentiations in terms of relations of production, and consequent political and ideological dialectics.

Biases in Archaeological and Documentary Data

The consumer-choice systemic framework relates archaeological data not only to socioeconomic status but to other variables that may be at least as important in certain situations. Two major aspects of cultural behavior, intervening in the connection between archaeological data and socioeconomic status, include cultural deposition processes of selective discard and loss, and archaeological processes of recovery and analysis. Schiffer has developed theoretical connections between cultural transformation processes and the archaeological record (1972, 1976, 1983). Deposition and environmental processes, recovery biases, and analysis methods each affect results in tests of hypotheses connecting archaeological data with status, as well as other variables.

Most of the chapters in this volume consider the effects of archaeological biases on research results, although it is seldom possible to quantify them. Archaeological data can be conceptualized as a sample of goods that were once predominantly acquired in some way, and then either lost or selected for discard. Archaeological samples are most representative of goods with short use-lives, such as dietary fauna, that are usually unselectively discarded together in a dump. Archaeological samples of goods with relatively long use-lives, such as ceramics and glass, usually are more biased by socioeconomic and individual differences in frequency of use, breakage, loss, and discard of each artifact type. Archaeological bone samples are biased by problems of preservation and identification more often than ceramics or glass, and all archaeological data may suffer destruction by the environment, animals, or collectors. The different discard biases for ceramics, glass, and bones indicate the informational advantages to be gained by analyzing more than one type of consumer good and comparing these results with documentary indications of status (Branstner and Martin; Garrow; Heberling; Henry). The exigencies of differential discard and archaeological recovery must always be considered in archaeological analyses, and in some cases have been determined to form a major bias in the archaeological data (Baugher and Venables; Spencer-Wood and Heberling).

Both the archaeological and documentary records are biased by the many different processes involved in creating these two types of records, as well as the different methods of recovering and analyzing them. For example, in probate inventories, unusually valuable material culture is often recorded in more detail than common items, while selective discard often results in more

---

common than expensive items in the archaeological record. A probate inventory records those items remaining in the house after an individual's death, while the archaeological data left by that individual represent items discarded or lost before death. The different types of information available in documentary and archaeological records are often complementary and seldom redundant. Therefore most of the chapters in this volume are concerned with establishing recurring relationships between archaeological patterns and documentary indications of socioeconomic status, and sometimes other variables. In a few cases, information in the documentary and archaeological records has permitted some assessment of the biases involved in the formation of whichever record is less complete (Baugher and Venables; Spencer-Wood and Heberling).

Comparisons among book chapters suggest some systematic biases in the archaeological and documentary records that may be useful in further advancing research on historic consumer behaviors among and within cultural subgroups. The quality of archaeological and documentary data varies systematically with socioeconomic stratification. For the lower socioeconomic strata, or working classes, the documentary data are often incomplete and sketchy. Due to economic limitations, few, if any, expensive goods could be acquired from the market economy. Since the cheapest types of goods would mostly be acquired, little selectivity in discard is expected. In these cases the archaeological record may often yield better information about household consumer behavior than the documentary record. For the middle and upper classes, as wealth increases, more expensive goods are usually acquired from the market (Herman *et al.* 1973:59–63; Massachusetts Bureau of Statistics of Labor 1875). Chapters in this volume about sites of elite households demonstrate the unusually good documentation for these households. Yet greater wealth is related to more selective discard at the house sites of the middle and upper classes than for those of the lower classes. As a result, documentation of the upper classes often yields more accurate information about consumer behavior than the archaeological record, due to less frequent use and discard of expensive goods compared to inexpensive ones. The high quality of documentation for sites of elite households researched in this volume resulted in added information concerning relationships between discard behavior and socioeconomic status (Baugher and Venables; Spencer-Wood and Heberling). Taken as a whole, the research reported here suggests that selectivity of discard increases with increasing socioeconomic status. As a result, it may be archaeologically difficult to distinguish between the consumer behavior of middle- and upper-class households.

METHODOLOGY

Theory and methods are interdependently related in the scientific process (Binford 1982:128). In comparing sites to discern sociocultural subgroup patterns, the need not only for a shared theoretical approach, but also for appropriate standardized methods, becomes apparent. The book deals with theory and method for relating archaeological patterns to cultural behavior basically at two interrelated scales: the household, and its participation in cultural sub-group behaviors. Among the chapters in this book, methodology varies from explicit scientific hypothesis testing to inductive formulation of generalizations. Methods of quantifying archaeological patterns permit explicit tests of hypotheses or propositions (Redman 1978:13). Some chapters use the scientific methodology of holding other variables constant in order to determine degree of variation in artifact patterns accounted for by socioeconomic status variations (McBride and McBride; Spencer-Wood). In other chapters, no variables could be held constant and site archaeological patterns are compared and contrasted with documentary indications of socioeconomic status (Branstner and Martin; Garrow; Heberling; Shephard; Singer). In some cases, the relative importance and/or interrelationships of two or three behavioral variables are considered in accounting for variations in site artifact patterns (Baugher and Venables; Clark; De Cunzo; Henry; LeeDecker *et al.* Orser; Rietz; Spencer-Wood). The consideration of multiple behavioral variables in relationship to variability in particular site-artifact patterns is an advance over the consideration of one variable at a time, since an artifact pattern may be produced by the systemic interaction of many cultural variables simultaneously (Binford 1972:264–287).

Sociotechnic Attributes Selected for Analysis

Within a systems theory approach to lifeways, Binford (1962) related different artifact attributes to technomic, sociotechnic, and ideotechnic cultural functions. Food types and ceramic forms are technic attributes carrying information about dietary selections and methods of food processing and preparation. Such foodways behavior may vary among ethnic and socioeconomic groups (cf. Baker 1980; Otto 1984). Because this volume is concerned primarily with the relationships between archaeological data and socioeconomic status, sociotechnic attributes of artifacts that can be expected to relate to status are analyzed. It also relates socioeconomic status to sociotechnic attributes of archaeological samples of ceramics, glass, fauna, gravestones, and architecture. Within fauna available in the market economy, the different prices of types and cuts of fauna are related to the economic ability to afford them, and may occasionally involve display of status to dinner guests (Branstner and Martin; Garrow; Henry; Reitz; Singer). Within a given ceramic or glass form serving a foodways function, the quality of the vessel, its decoration, and its price are related to economic ability to afford them and to their use in displaying social status to guests at social functions such as tea or dinner (all chapters in this volume except Clark; Orser; Reitz; Singer). Size and location of dwelling are also related to status, both in this volume (De Cunzo; Heberling) and in research on American social classes (Warner *et al.* 1960). Price differences affect the quality of consumer goods that can be afforded by households, resulting in acquisition behaviors related to socioeconomic status.

By using a systems theory framework, some contributors to this volume have considered the possibility that some types of artifacts may have primarily utilitarian foodways functions (Shephard; Spencer-Wood; Spencer-Wood and Heberling), or be chosen for use in ethnic behaviors rather than for socioeconomic status behaviors (Clark; Henry). For example, low-quality ceramics or food would probably be used by high status families in situations not related to socioeconomic status, such as kitchenware for food preparation, and servants' food. My research suggests a stronger relationship of status to cup and saucer than to plate or bowl decorative types because of the mixed status and utilitarian functions of plates and bowls, that include tableware and kitchenware, while the function of tea- and coffeeware appears to be primarily status display. Shephard's analyses of ceramic vessel variety in form found less differentiation among social strata than in quality and quantity of ceramics because of the large number of common ceramic forms among most households. Ethnic preferences could also result in household goods not reflecting the highest quality that could be afforded. However, ethnic groups attempting to be assimilated into a socioeconomic group can be expected to emulate that group's status buying behaviors (Clark). Price differences affect the quality of consumer goods that can be afforded by households, which are therefore related to socioeconomic status.

Methods Overview

Theory and methods are interdependent and integral parts of the scientific process. It should be possible to test a theory with appropriate methods and data. It is in comparing theoretically expected results with actual results to determine situations of agreement and disagreement that new knowledge and insight are gained. While the primary hypotheses tested in this volume concerned connections between socioeconomic status related behaviors and patterns in attributes of archaeological data, the use of systems theory encouraged investigation as well of those conditions in which variables other than status were important determinants of variability in artifact patterns.

In this volume, a number of different methods are used in relating socioeconomic status to archaeological data. Reitz considers possible relationships between fauna, status, ethnicity, and environment. Price-scaling indices are applied to white ceramics and fauna. Singer develops a price scale for fish, and Henry developed a ceramic price scaling index for late nineteenth through early twentieth century whiteware. Clark relates gravestone styles to aspects of interrelationships between socioeconomic status and ethnicity. A number of different methods are used in relating ceramics to socioeconomic status. Shephard analyzes ceramic quality using Miller's indices, quantity using percentages, and variety using another ratio measure. McBride and McBride relate price indices for decorative types of whiteware sherds to socioeconomic status. Spencer-Wood finds socioeconomic status correlate better with cup and saucer vessel ceramic indices than with indices for other vessel shapes or sherds. Baugher and Venables relate ceramics not only to socioeconomic status but also to political status and events. One way of dealing with the limitations of one method of relating one sociotechnic attribute pattern to status is to relate a number of different classes of artifacts to socioeconomic status. Branstner and Martin, and Garrow analyze both faunal remains and whiteware. LeeDecker *et al.* analyze fauna, ceramics, and glass in relationship not only to socioeconomic status but also to family life cycle. Henry considers the relative importance of status, ethnicity and family life cycle in relationship to archaeological remains of fauna and whiteware. De Cunzo discusses relationships between status, ethnicity and bottles, ceramics, household structure and settlement pattern. Heberling analyzes architecture, settlement pattern, glass, and ceramics to infer the spatial social structure of a poorly documented iron-working village. Most authors consider the limitations of documentary and archaeological records as well as problems with archaeological methods. The choice of analytical methods may be limited by comparative site-recording methods (Reitz) and the condition of recovered artifacts, including the degree of faunal preservation and degree to which ceramic or glass vessels can be reconstructed. Some archaeological deposits can be tightly dated and identified with a particular well-documented household, but more often, deposits can only be loosely dated and associated with more than one household, or a neighborhood. The chapters in this volume indicate the amount of status information that can be gained at a number of different scales of survival and recovery for both documentary and archaeological data. Although some sites yield more information than others, even poorly documented sites with small archaeological samples have permitted the analysis of relationships between consumer choices and socioeconomic status, as well as some other variables.

The Need for Standardized Methods

In order to generate the amount of comparative site data needed to establish characteristic archaeological patterns corresponding to behavioral differences among cultural subgroups, standardized methods are needed. Although each book chapter compares a number of sites, most express the need for more comparable data to establish conclusively correspondences between attribute patterns and socioeconomic status, or complex interrelationships among additional behavioral variables. Standardized methods would permit the accumulation of the large data base needed to control intervening variables such as time period, market access due to site location, and ethnicity. Standardization would create an as yet unrealized opportunity for historical archaeologists to share research results more fully, generating a powerful data base to significantly test more broadly applicable hypotheses.

Comparisons need to be separated by the scale of available data, whether household or neighborhood, and short- versus long-time period analyses. Short-term deposits are best, although some information can still be gained with deposits covering a half century. Archaeological strata need to be excavated separately and identified, if possible, with particular households whose occupations, incomes, household size, and ethnicity are documented. Sites also need to be separated into different scales of analysis depending on amount of documentary data available.

At present, many researchers use slightly different methods, as exemplified by chapters in this volume. Some methods are roughly comparable, others are not, and in many studies published outside this volume the methods are not even discussed. It would be useful, especially for those in contract archaeology, to have minimum standards in field methods to serve as a baseline for calculating time and cost of work to be contracted. It seems to me that production of useful data requires excavation of features and cultural deposits by cultural strata, with screening for artifacts using at least a 3/8-inch mesh, if not 1/4 inch. Sociotechnic artifact attributes also need to be recorded in artifact catalogues and reports, so data can be related to socioeconomic status.

Many authors consider which analytical methods measure artifact patterns that can be related most consistently to documentary indications of socioeconomic status. In most cases, analyses by the marketed unit are best for relating household socioeconomic status to calculated value of a given class of goods. For example, in most cases ceramic vessel counts yield more consistent results than sherd counts, and meat cuts are a better analytical unit than counts of bones or minimum numbers of individuals. The chapters in this volume have also demonstrated that in some cases sherd counts or minimum numbers of fauna can be related to socioeconomic status (Branstner and Martin; Garrow; Heberling; McBride and McBride). If vessel or meat cut counts are not available it may be possible to relate these other measures to socioeconomic status differences. However, in this volume, vessel counts and meat cut counts are most often related to socioeconomic status. After comparing and contrasting the results in this volume, it also seems best to use as much of the relevant archaeological data as possible, such as ceramic vessel counts of all whiteware decorative types, or meat cut counts of all types, with the best estimate of cost if possible, rather than discarding data that may significantly alter the assessed relative value for the class of goods analyzed. Discarding a decorative type or a meat cut type may distort or destroy the existing relationship between the archaeological artifact attribute patterns and documentary indications of socioeconomic status and other behavioral variables.

ORGANIZATION OF THE VOLUME

The chapters in this volume have been organized into three time periods in the development of the American market system, involving locational as well as temporal changes in the supply of, and demand for, consumer goods. The American economy grew in size and complexity as population, accompanied by a sequence of economic activities, spread inland over time from the East Coast into the South and Midwest, and finally to the Far West. In each region and area, at different times, the economy grew in a sequence starting with agriculture, commerce, and crafts, followed by the development of industry and urbanization. American social and economic stratification became increasingly complex as the economy diversified both in agricultural and industrial production. Commercial agriculture for the national market increased, and national scale industry developed first in the Northeast, and later in the South and the old Midwest. Throughout the nineteenth century, an increasing variety and quantity of consumer goods became available as economies of scale and technological innovations decreased the costs of production and distribution to more different locations within the growing national market. The greater range of consumer goods available at relatively low, as well as higher, prices offered more choices to the increasing number of socioeconomic subgroups within the American economy.

Each section covers a time range that includes different regional developments due to the spread of the American economy from East to West. Each section has a brief introduction providing a general overview of the American market economy, with major national and regional developments, which form the context for its chapters. The contributions made by each chapter are also briefly summarized. Some information that can be gained through comparisons of chapters is also discussed. Chapters in each of the three sections are concerned with aspects of socioeconomic stratification in different American site locations and regions within a time range.

Although the time ranges of the volume sections were defined to include distinctions among the chapters, both in time period and development of the American economy, some chapters include time ranges spanning more than one section. There was no mutually exclusive way to organize the chapters into groups with shared characteristics. Therefore, chapters were placed in the section corresponding to the earliest predominant time period of the research. Those also dealing with later time periods were placed toward the end of the section because of their relevance to the time period(s) of the following section(s). This organization facilitates comparisons between chapters with overlapping temporal ranges. Overall, the temporal organization of the volume offers perspectives on a cross section of the progressive sequence of developments in different regions of the American market economy.

The section introductions briefly outline the major developments in the American market economy that form the context of the specific chapter studies. The first section, from the eighteenth century through the early nineteenth century, is concerned with an American economy dominated by agriculture, commerce, and craft-scale industry. The second section is concerned with factors affecting house site archaeological patterns, predominantly in the mid-nineteenth century, when the South, Midwest, and West specialized in different types of commercial agriculture, while the Northeast developed the most industrial factories and largest urban aggregations in cities. The third section, from the second half of the nineteenth century into the twentieth century, is concerned with archaeological patterns and socioeconomic status in the context of complex urban-industrial social stratification systems.

Following the three temporal sections is the epilogue, suggesting a next step in this area of research, and in the development of theory in historical archaeology. An epilogue in a novel deals with the future of the characters. In this epilogue, Leone suggests future directions in theory to expand the ability

of historical archaeologists to contribute to our knowledge about the organization of behavior in historic cultural subgroups.

REFERENCES

Adams, Robert McC., 1966, *The Evolution of Urban Society: Early Mesopotamia and Prehispanic Mexico,* Aldine, Chicago.

Adams, Robert McC., 1974, Anthropological Perspectives on Ancient Trade, *Current Anthropology* 15:239–258.

Arnould, E., and Netting, R. McC., 1982, Households: Changing Form and Function, *Current Anthropology* 23:571–575.

Baker, Vernon G., 1980, Archaeological Visibility of Afro-American Culture: An Example from Black Lucy's Garden, Andover, Massachusetts, in: *Archaeological Perspectives on Ethnicity in America* (R. L. Schuyler, ed.), Baywood Publishing, Farmingdale, New York, pp. 29–37.

Beaudry, Mary C., 1984, Archaeology and the Historical Household, *Man in the Northeast* 28(1):27–38.

Becker, M. J., 1973, Archaeological Evidence for Occupational Specialization Among the Classic Period Maya at Tikal, Guatemala, *American Antiquity* 38:396–406.

Binford, Lewis R., 1962, Archaeology as Anthropology, *American Antiquity* 28:217–225.

Binford, Lewis R., 1965, Archaeological Systematics and the Study of Culture Process, *American Antiquity* 31:203–210.

Binford, Lewis R., 1967, Smudge Pits and Hide Smoking: The Use of Analogy in Archaeological Reasoning, *American Antiquity* 32(1):1–12.

Binford, Lewis R., 1968, Archaeological Perspectives, in: *New Perspectives in Archaeology* (S. R. Binford and L. R. Binford, eds.), Aldine, Chicago.

Binford, Lewis R., 1972, Model Building—Paradigms, and the Current State of Paleolithic Research, in: *An Archaeological Perspective,* Seminar Press, New York, pp. 244–294.

Binford, Lewis R., 1982, Objectivity–Explanation–Archaeology, 1981, in: *Theory and Explanation in Archaeology* (C. Renfrew, M. J. Rowlands, and B. A. Segraves, eds.), Academic Press, New York, pp. 125–138.

Bowen, J., 1975, Probate Inventories: An Evaluation from the Perspective of Zooarchaeology and Agricultural History at the Mott Farm, *Historical Archaeology* 9:11–25.

Bushman, Richard L., 1970, *From Puritan to Yankee,* W. W. Norton, New York.

Childe, V. Gordon, 1951, *Social Evolution,* World Press, Cleveland.

Chorley, Richard J., and Haggett, Peter (eds.), 1967, *Socio-economic Models in Geography,* Methuen, London.

Clark, Grahame, 1969, *Archaeology and Society,* Barnes & Noble, New York.

Clarke, David L., 1972, Models and Paradigms in Contemporary Archaeology, in: *Models in Archaeology* (D. L. Clarke, ed.), Methuen, London, pp. 1–60.

Clarke, David L., 1978, *Analytical Archaeology,* Methuen, London.

Cooke, K. R., and Renfrew, C., 1979, An Experiment on the Simulation of Culture Changes, in *Transformations: Mathematical Approaches to Culture Change* (C. Renfrew and K. R. Cooke, eds.), Academic Press, New York, pp. 327–348.

Deagan, Kathleen, 1982, Avenues of Inquiry in Historical Archaeology, *Advances in Archaeological Method and Theory* 5:151–178.

Deagan, Kathleen, 1983, *Spanish St. Augustine: The Archaeology of A Colonial Creole Community,* Academic Press, New York.

Deetz, J. F., 1977, *In Small Things Forgotten: The Archaeology of Early American Life,* Doubleday, New York.

Deetz, J. F., 1982, Households: A Structural Key to Archaeological Explanation, *American Behavioral Scientist* 25:717–724.

Diamond, J. M., 1978, Niche Shifts and the Rediscovery of Interspecific Competition, *American Scientist* 66:322–331.

Dincauze, Dena F., 1984, The Paradigm Trap, or Horatio's Blindspot: Comments Freely Offered in Advance of the Meeting, *Man in the Northeast* 27:17–20.

Douglas, Mary, and Isherwood, B., 1979, *The World of Goods,* Basic Books, New York.

Doran, J., 1982, A Computational Model of Sociocultural Systems and Their Dynamics, in: *Theory and Explanation in Archaeology* (C. Renfrew, M. J. Rowlands, and B. A. Segraves, eds.), Academic Press, New York, pp. 375–388.

Drucker, Leslie M., 1981, Socioeconomic Patterning at an Undocumented Late 18th Century Lowcountry Site: Spiers Landing, South Carolina, *Historical Archaeology* 15(2):58–68.

Dyson, S. L., 1982, Material Culture, Social Structure, and Changing Cultural Values: The Ceramics of Eighteenth- and Nineteenth-Century Middletown, Connecticut, in: *Archaeology of Urban America: The Search for Pattern and Process* (R. S. Dickens, Jr., ed.), Academic Press, New York, pp. 361–80.

Edwards, Alba M., 1939, *A Social Economic Grouping of the Gainful Workers of the United States,* U.S. Government Printing Office, Washington, D.C.

Engel, James F., Blackwell, Roger D. and Kollat, David T., 1978, *Consumer Behavior,* Dryden Press, Hinsdale, Illinois.

Flannery, Kent V., 1972, The Cultural Evolution of Civilizations, *Annual Review of Ecology and Systematics* 3:399–426.

Flannery, Kent V., 1973, Archaeology with a Capital S, in: *Research and Theory in Current Archaeology* (C. L. Redman, ed.), Wiley, New York, pp. 47–53.

Flannery, Kent V. (ed.), 1976, *The Early Mesoamerican Village,* Academic Press, New York.

Flannery, Kent V., and Coe, Michael D., 1968, Social and Economic Systems in Formative Mesoamerica, in: *New Perspectives in Archaeology* (S. R. Binford and L. R. Binford, eds.), Aldine, Chicago, pp. 103–142.

Flannery, Kent V., and Winter M. C., 1976, Analyzing Household Activities, in: *The Early Mesoamerican Village* (K. V. Flannery, ed.), Academic Press, New York, pp. 34–47.

Fogel, Robert W., and Engerman, Stanley L. (eds.), 1971, *The Reinterpretation of American Economic History,* Harper & Row, New York.

Fried, Morton H., 1960, On the Evolution of Social Stratification and the State, in: *Culture in History* (S. Diamond, ed.), Columbia University Press, New York.

Fried, Morton H., 1967, *The Evolution of Political Society,* Random House, New York.

Friedman, H., 1980, Household Production and the National Economy: Concepts for the Analysis of Agrarian Formations, *Journal of Peasant Studies* 7:158–183.

Fritz, J. M., and Plog, F. T., 1970, The Nature of Archaeological Explanation, *American Antiquity* 35:405–412.

Geismar, Joan H., 1982, *The Archaeology of Social Disintegration in Skunk Hollow, A Nineteenth-Century Rural Black Community,* Academic Press, New York.

Gould, R., 1978, The Anthropology of Human Residues, *American Anthropologist* 80:815–835.

Haggett, Peter, 1972, *Geography: A Modern Synthesis,* Harper & Row, New York.

Heilbroner, Robert L., 1970, *The Economic Problem,* Prentice-Hall, Englewood Cliffs, New Jersey.

Herman, Lynne L., Sands, John O., and Schecter, Daniel, 1973, Ceramics in St. Mary's County, Maryland, During the 1840's: A Socioeconomic Study, *The Conference on Historic Site Archaeology Papers* 8:52–93.

Hill, James N., 1970, *Broken K. Pueblo: Prehistoric Social Organization in the American Southwest,* University of Arizona Press, Tucson.

Hodder, Ian, and Orton, Clive, 1979, *Spatial Analysis in Archaeology,* Cambridge University Press, Cambridge, England.

Hoffman, M. A., 1974, The Social Context of Trash Disposal in an Early Dynastic Egyptian Town, *American Antiquity* 39:35–49.

Horne, L., 1982, The Household in Space: Dispersed Holdings in an Iranian Village, *American Behavioral Scientist* 25:677–685.

Hosler, D., Sabloff, J. A., and Runge, D., 1978, Simulation Model Development: A Case Study of the Classic Maya Collapse, in: *Social Process in Maya Prehistory* (N. Hammond, ed.), Academic Press, New York, pp. 553–590.

Hutchinson, G. E., 1975, Variations on a Theme by Robert MacArthur, in: *Ecology and Evolution of Communities* (M. L. Cody and J. M. Diamond, eds.), Harvard University Press, Cambridge, Massachusetts, pp. 492–521.

Johnson, Paul E., 1978, *A Shopkeeper's Millennium,* Hill & Wang, New York.

Kahl, Joseph A., and Davis, James A., 1955, A Comparison of Indexes of Socio-economic Status, *American Sociological Review* 20:317–325.

Kristiansen, K., 1982, The Formation of Tribal Systems in Later European Prehistory: Northern Europe, 4000–5000 B.C., in: *Theory and Explanation in Archaeology* (C. Renfrew, M. J. Rowlands, and B. A. Segraves, eds.), Academic Press, New York, pp. 241–280.

Kuhn, Thomas S., 1970, *The Structure of Scientific Revolutions,* University of Chicago Press, Chicago.

Laumann, Edward O., and House, James S., 1970, Living Room Styles and Social Attributes: The Patterning of Material Artifacts in a Modern Urban Community, *Sociology and Social Research* 54:321–342.

Leone, Mark P., 1977, Foreword in: *Research Strategies in Historical Archaeology* (S. South, ed.), Academic Press, New York, pp. xvii–xxi.

Lloyd, Peter E., and Dicken, Peter, 1972, *Location in Space: A Theoretical Approach to Economic Geography,* Harper & Row, New York.

Longacre, W. (ed.), 1970, *Reconstructing Prehistoric Pueblo Societies,* University of New Mexico Press, Albuquerque.

Lowe, John C., and Moryadas, S., 1975, *The Geography of Movement,* Houghton Mifflin, Boston.

Massachusetts Bureau of Statistics of Labor, 1875, Public Document Number 31: Sixth Annual Report of the Bureau of Statistics of Labor, Wright & Potter, State Printers, Boston.

McManamon, Francis P., 1984, Methods of Description and Interpretation in the Archaeology of Households: An Afterword on Saitta's Paper, *Man in the Northeast* 28.1:9–10.

Meltzer, D., 1979, Paradigms and the Nature of Change in American Archaeology, *American Antiquity* 44:644–657.

Miller, George L., 1980, Classification and Economic Scaling of 19th Century Ceramics, *Historical Archaeology* 14:1–41.

Miller, George L., 1984, George M. Coates, Pottery Merchant of Philadelphia, *Winterthur Portfolio* 19:37–49.

Miller, George L., and Hurry, Silas D., 1983, Ceramic Supply in an Economically Isolated Frontier Community: Portage County of the Ohio Western Reserve, 1800–1825, *Historical Archaeology* 17(2):80–92.

Millon, R. (ed.), 1974, *Urbanization at Teotihuacan,* Volume 1, University of Texas Press, Austin.

Moran, G. P., Zimmer, E. F., and Yentsch, A. E., 1982, *Archaeological Investigations at the Narbonne House, Salem Maritime National Historic Site, Massachusetts,* Cultural Resources Management Study 6, Division of Cultural Resources, North Atlantic Regional Office, National Park Service, Boston.

Morris, Craig, 1978, The Archeological Study of Andean Exchange Systems, in: *Social Archaeology: Beyond Subsistence and Dating* (C. L. Redman, W. T. Langhorne, Jr., M. J. Berman, E. V. Curtin, N. M. Versaggi, and J. C. Wanser, eds.), Academic Press, New York, pp. 315–328.

Mrozowski, Stephen A., 1984, Prospects and Perspectives on an Archaeology of the Household, *Man in the Northeast* 27:31–50.

Mudar, K., 1978, The Effects of Socio-cultural Variables on Food Preferences in 19th Century Detroit, *The Conference on Historic Sites Archaeology Papers* 12:323–391.

Otto, John S., 1984, *Cannon's Point Plantation, 1794–1860: Living Conditions and Status Patterns in the Old South,* Academic Press, New York.

Paynter, R., 1982, *Models of Spatial Inequality,* Academic Press, New York.

Peterson, Willis L., 1977, *Principles of Economics: Micro,* Richard D. Irwin, Homewood, Illinois.

Pires-Ferreira, Jane W., and Winter, Marcus C., 1976, Distribution of Obsidian among Households in Two Oaxacan Villages, in: *The Early Mesoamerican Village* (K. Flannery, ed.), Academic Press, New York, pp. 306–311.

Plog, F. T., 1973, Laws, Systems of Law and the Explanation of Observed Variation, in: *The Explanation of Culture Change: Models in Prehistory* (C. Renfrew, ed.), Duckworth, London, pp. 649–662.

Poe, C., 1979, The Manifestation of Status in 18th Century Criollo Culture in Colonial St. Augustine, paper presented at the Society for Historical Archaeology Meetings, Nashville, Tennessee.

Rathje, William L., 1971, The Origin and Development of Lowland Classic Maya Civilization, *American Antiquity,* 36(3):275–285.

Rathje, William L. and McCarthy, Michael, 1977, Regularity and Variability in Contemporary Garbage, in: *Research Strategies in Historical Archaeology* (S. South, ed.), Academic Press, New York, pp. 261–286.

Redman, Charles L., 1978, Mesopotamian Urban Ecology: The Systemic Context of the Emergence of Urbanism, in: *Social Archeology: Beyond Subsistence and Dating,* Academic Press, New York, pp. 329–347.

Redman, Charles L., Curtin, Edward, Versaggi, Nina, and Wanser, Jeffrey, 1978, Social Archeology: The Future of the Past, in: *Social Archeology: Beyond Subsistence and Dating,* Academic Press, New York, pp. 1–36.

Reid, J. J., and Whittlesey, S. M., 1982, Households at Grasshopper Pueblo, *American Behavioral Scientist* 25:687–703.

Reissman, Leonard, 1959, *Class in American Society,* Free Press, New York.

Renfrew, C., 1982, Explanation Revisited, in: *Theory and Explanation in Archaeology* (C. Renfrew, M. J. Rowlands, and B. A. Segraves, eds.), Academic Press, New York, pp. 5–24.

Renger, J., 1971, Notes on Goldsmiths, Jewelers and Carpenters of Neobabylonian Eanna, *Journal of American Oriental Society* 91:495–503.

Riordan, Timothy B., and Adams, William H., 1985, Commodity Flows and National Market Access, *Historical Archaeology* 19(2):5–18.

Sabloff, J. A., and Rathje, W. L., 1975, The Rise of a Maya Merchant Class, *Scientific American* 233:72–82.

Sahlins, M. D., 1958, *Social Stratification in Polynesia,* University of Washington Press, Seattle.

Sahlins, M. D., 1972, *Stone Age Economics,* Aldine, Chicago.

Saitta, D. J., 1984, The Archaeology of Households: Alternative Approaches, *Man in the Northeast* 28.1:1–8.

Sanders, William T., and Webster, David, 1978, Unilinealism, Multilinealism and the Evolution of Complex Societies, in: *Social Archaeology: Beyond Subsistence and Dating* (C. L. Redman, W. T. Langhorne, Jr., M. J. Berman, E. V. Curtin, N. M. Versaggi, and J. C. Wanser, eds.), Academic Press, New York, pp. 249–302.

Schiffer, M. B., 1972, Archaeological Context and Systematic Context, *American Antiquity* 37:156–165.

Schiffer, M. B., 1976, *Behavioral Archaeology,* Academic Press, New York.

Schiffer, M. B., 1983, Toward the Identification of Formation Processes, *American Antiquity* 48:675–706.

Schulz, Peter D., and Gust, Sherri M., 1983, Faunal Remains and Social Status in 19th Century Sacramento, *Historical Archaeology* 17(1):44–53.

Schuyler, Robert L. (ed.), 1980, *Archaeological Perspectives on Ethnicity in America,* Baywood Publishing, Farmingdale, New York.

Service, Elman, 1962, *Primitive Social Organization: An Evolutionary Perspective,* Random House, New York.

Singer, David A., 1985, The Use of Fish Remains as a Socio-Economic Measure: An Example from 19th Century New England, *Historical Archaeology* 19(2):110–113.

South, Stanley, 1977, *Method and Theory in Historical Archaeology,* Academic Press, New York.

South, Stanley (ed.), 1978, Pattern Recognition in Historical Archaeology, *American Antiquity* 43:223–230.

Spencer-Wood, S., 1979, The National American Market in Historical Archaeology: Urban Versus Rural Perspectives, in: *Ecological Anthropology of the Middle Connecticut River Valley* (R. Paynter, ed.), Research Report 18, Department of Anthropology, University of Massachusetts, Amherst, pp. 117–128.

Spencer-Wood, S., 1984, Status, Occupation, and Ceramic Indices: A Nineteenth-Century Comparative Analysis, *Man in the Northeast* 28.1:87–110.

Starbuck, D. R., 1984, The Shaker Concept of Household, *Man in the Northeast,* 28.1:73–86.

Taylor, Walter W., 1948, A Study of Archaeology, *American Anthropological Association Memoir* (No. 69).

Thomas, David H., 1972, A Computer Simulation Model of Great Basin Shoshonean Subsistence and Settlement Patterns, in: *Models in Archaeology* (D. L. Clarke, ed.), Methuen, London, pp. 671–704.

Tuggle, D. H., Townsend, A. H., and Riley, T. J., 1972, Laws, Systems and Research Designs: A Discussion of Explanation in Archaeology, *American Antiquity* 37:3–12.

Wallace, Anthony F. C., 1978, *Rockdale: The Growth of an American Village in the Early Industrial Revolution,* W. W. Norton, New York.

Warner, W. Lloyd, with Meeker, Marchia, and Eells, Kenneth, 1960, *Social Class in America: A Manual of Procedure for the Measurement of Social Status.* Harper & Row, New York.

Wasson, Chester R., 1969, Is it Time to Quit Thinking of Income Classes? *Journal of Marketing* 33:54–57.

Watson, P. J., 1978, Architectural Differentiation in Some Near Eastern Communities, Prehistoric and Contemporary, in: *Social Archaeology: Beyond Subsistence and Dating* (C. L. Redman, W. T. Langhorne, Jr., M. J. Berman, E. V. Curtin, N. M. Versaggi, and J. C. Wanser, eds.), Academic Press, New York, pp. 131–158.

Watson, P. J., LeBlanc, S. A., and Redman, C. L., 1971, *Explanation in Archaeology: An Explicitly Scientific Approach,* Columbia University Press, New York.

Wilk, R. R., and Rathje, W. L., 1982, Household Archaeology, *American Behavioral Scientist,* 25:617–640.

Wobst, H. Martin, 1974, Boundary Conditions for Paleolithic Social Systems: A Simulation Approach, *American Antiquity* 39:147–178.

Worrell, J., 1980, Scars Upon the Earth: Physical Evidence of Dramatic Change at the Stratton Tavern, in: *Proceedings of the Conference on Northeastern Archaeology* (J. A. Moore, ed.), Research Report 19, Department of Anthropology, University of Massachusetts, Amherst, pp. 133–145.

Yanagisako, S. J., 1979, Family and Household: The Analysis of Domestic Groups, *Annual Review of Anthropology* 8:161–206.

Yesner, D. R., 1984, The Structure and Function of Prehistoric Households in Northern New England, *Man in the Northeast* 28.1:51–72.

Zubrow, Ezra B. W., 1971, Carrying Capacity and Dynamic Equilibrium in the Prehistoric Southwest, *American Antiquity* 36:127–138.

Eighteenth-through Early Nineteenth-Century Commercial Agricultural Economy

I

In the eighteenth to early nineteenth century, major sectors of the American economy included agriculture, commerce, crafts, and a few larger-scale industries. Starting in the colonial period, wealth was accompanied by high social status, whether the wealth was inherited or gained through employment as a merchant, craftsman, or farmer (Bining and Cochran 1964:122, 227–228). In this period, most of the population were farmers, either southern planters or smaller family farmers who commonly traded labor power, oxen, and plows with neighbors in order to harvest their crops. Most farms also engaged in home manufacture of items such as cheese, butter, cider, wool, cotton, and/or linen cloth, and some furniture (Gruver 1972:303; Tryon 1917). Southern plantations, more widely spaced on the landscape because of their large size, were more self-sufficient than smaller farms. Sometimes plantations included some small mills and crafts, and planters often ordered goods directly from manufacturers rather than buying from country stores, peddlers, or merchants. Villages with general stores and small crafts and mills were more widely spaced in the South than in the North. Because of the slowness of transportation overland and by water, most towns included traditional craftsmen such as blacksmiths, wheelwrights, coopers, cobblers, and potters. Gristmills and sawmills were first established on small watercourses, to be followed in the early nineteenth century by fulling mills and carding mills. Most villages were established near a small watercourse where these mills operated, often forming a small industrial center with the craftsmen. Many mills and crafts were often conducted on a part-time basis by farmers (Gruver 1972:95–100). Country store merchants were also often farmers. Craftsmen, millers, merchants, and farmers often exchanged their products and services on a barter rather than cash basis because of the scarcity of specie. Country stores sold products both locally and to more distant markets, from which such extralocal manufactures as British ceramics, silverware, European wines, New England table glass, and other products were imported for the community (Bining and Cochran 1964:114–115, 274; Danhof 1969:14, 29–30). By the early nineteenth century, only a few regional scale factories were established, principally for textiles, glass, and iron manufacture. Cities developed along the Eastern seaboard as trade entrepots that exported principally American raw materials, foodstuffs, and some processed goods such as flour, and imported principally manufactures and nonlocal foods, such as sugar and molasses (Bining and Cochran 1964:67–93, 98–99, 235–240, 273; Ratner et al. 1979:52–56, 89–91; Robertson, 1973:63–70).

As the American population increased through immigration and high birth rates, settlement spread to the Midwest and the central South in the early nineteenth century. Westward migration and commerce were first facilitated by turnpikes around the turn of the century, followed by canals in the first half of the nineteenth century, and railroads starting in the East in the 1830s, and spreading to the interior progressively over time (Bining and Cochran 1964: 150–200; Robertson 1973:113–123, 137–151). In the Far West, early Spanish settlement began to be displaced by English colonists in the mid-1840s. Land speculation, overinvestment in ventures such as canals and railroads, decreasing European prices, and overextension of credit resulted in the Panics of 1819 and 1837, when the federal government required payment for land in specie (Gruver 1972:313–320, 320–321, 382–383). These economic depressions decreased the ability of many families to afford consumer goods, and led many to migrate west (Bining and Cochran 1964:212, 216–219).

Household selections of consumer goods, later discarded on sites in this period, were affected not only by socioeconomic status, but by factors limiting market access. Goods became less readily available as the population spread to less accessible inland areas. Political events constrained trade, starting with British restrictions on the development of colonial industries and independent trade, and including disruptions in the flow of consumer goods from England to America during the Revolutionary War, Jefferson's Embargo, and the War of 1812. In between and after these constraining situations, the English dumped on the American market their overproduction of outdated goods, including ceramics, iron goods, and textiles. In order to promote American manufacturing against such foreign competition during the early decades of the Republic, a number of tariffs imposed increasing duties on imported textiles, iron products, and many other manufactures and commodities. In 1828 the tariffs reached the highest levels attained in the first half of the nineteenth century. Due to pressure from southern states, tariffs were thereafter gradually decreased towards the compromise goal of no duties above 20 percent by 1842 (Bining and Cochran 1964:244–247). In Part I of this volume, Baugher and Venables, Spencer-Wood and Heberling, Singer, and Reitz consider the effects of site location or market access, as well as socioeconomic status, on the types of archaeological data recovered from sites. In analyzing sites from the Revolutionary period, Baugher and Venables are particularly concerned with the effects of political status and events on ceramic discard.

The chapters in this section analyze materials from urban and rural sites in both the North and the South, and a few comparative sites from the Western frontier. Within the context of the developing American economy, the research presented demonstrates contrasts between high, medium, and low status households in some of the consumer goods residents selected for consumption and discarded or lost on their house sites. A number of methods are used to analyze the quality and quantities of types of ceramics and fauna in archaeological assemblages. These artifact measurements are related to socioeconomic statuses ranging from elite Tory landowners, plantation owners, and merchants to craftsmen, laborers, and slaves. Using the systemic framework of consumer choice, relative value of types of ceramics or fauna are considered in relationship not only to socioeconomic status, but also to political status, ethnicity, and market access. Most chapters also deal with biases of artifact deposition that affect archaeologists' ability to use archaeological assemblages to infer historic consumption patterns and relate them to economic, social, and political circumstances.

In the first chapter, Baugher and Venables analyze ceramics from seven eighteenth century sites to determine the relative importance of market access, documentary indications of social, economic, and political status of site residents, and site-specific historic events, to site differences in quality and quantity of ceramics. At two sites, marked disparities were found between the documented wealthy elite status of the resident families and the few porcelain or other expensive ceramics recovered archaeologically. This is a somewhat surprising pattern, given the expected greater frequency of use and discard of expensive ceramics, such as porcelain and white salt-glazed stoneware, by the wealthiest families in the colonies, compared with middle-class families. Documents indicated the possibility that, due to the Revolutionary War, ceramics from these Tory households were removed and not discarded at these sites. In contrast, a high-status house that burned yielded more high-quality ceramics. The authors conclude that such site-specific documented events need to be determined whenever possible because they strongly condition the quantities of ceramic decorative types that archaeologists may find to relate to status, especially for upper-class sites practicing selective discard.

In the second chapter, Spencer-Wood and Heberling contrast whiteware ceramic indices for a merchant in Windsor, Vermont, with those from ten other early nineteenth century sites that include a range of occupational statuses. Cups and saucers and total vessel indices usually could be related to socioeconomic status behaviors, usually in conjunction with market access and ethnicity. In contrast, plate and bowl indices often could not be related to status, possibly because they combine utilitarian food preparation vessels and tableware, while tea- and coffeeware were used primarily for status display. In addition, a quantitative comparison of whiteware from a probate inventory and an archaeological assemblage, forming different partial records of the Greens' household ceramics, indicated the selective discard of less porcelain than inexpensive ceramics by this rural elite household. The fact that the rank order of Green site ceramic indices for cups and saucers, and all vessels, did correspond to its occupational status rank order, indicates that selective discard may affect most middle to upper-class sites (if not destroyed by fire), resulting in comparable ceramic indices that are all lower than they would be if the total white ceramic inventory were used. This pattern indicates that small differences in ceramic index value may correspond to larger actual status differences among middle- and upper-class households.

In the third chapter, Singer develops and applies a price-scaling index for fish species. Mean prices of fish species, and to some extent cuts, in archaeological assemblages indicated relative status distinctions among site residents in different occupations, and among residents within the same occupational category. Singer suggests another avenue of research in historical archaeology that may permit status-buying behaviors to be related to differences in the average value of archaeological fish remains deposited at sites. Singer found that mean value of fish assemblages indicated status distinctions between two craftsmen in eighteenth-century Portsmouth, New Hampshire, and between two nineteenth-century sites in Boston. Comparable availability and cost of fish types were expected at all four sites because they were located in New England coastal cities. One site was occupied from the first half into the second half of the nineteenth century by laborers participating in mid- to late nineteenth-century urbanization and industrialization of the East Coast. Singer notes the need for further research on possible locational and temporal variations in fish prices.

Reitz's chapter is concerned with the possibility of relating socioeconomic status to archaeological faunal assemblages from plantations. Reitz explores the possibility of differentiating a number of slave versus planter faunal assemblages with alternative measurements, including number of taxa, relative frequencies of body parts that indicate butchering cuts for pig and cow, and relative frequencies of wild versus domestic animals, pig versus cow, and caprine versus chicken. With this large site sample, differences between slaves and planters do not form a universal pattern, possibly due to intervening variables such as differential availability of wild fauna due to site environment, or biases of discard, recovery, identifiability, and analytical methods for bones. Reitz works towards delineating the different site situations and conditions affecting the acquisition, deposition, and analysis of faunal remains.

Orser's chapter compares and contrasts antebellum and postbellum plantations, forming a temporal bridge to the next part of the book. Orser contrasts Otto's approach with an historical materialist approach to identifying plantation socioeconomic statuses. Plantation status distinctions are contrasted with postbellum status variations among tenant farmers due to different degrees of ownership of the means of production. When slaves are replaced on postbellum plantations by wage laborers or tenants at different status levels, rapid turnover in site residents with different statuses may make it impossible to differentiate among them from analyses of the archaeological record. Although Orser, and to some extent Reitz, consider status in postbellum as well as antebellum plantations, basic continuities in plantation social structure resulted in the inclusion of these chapters in the context of the early agricultural and commercial American economy.

Taken together, these chapters create a site-comparative framework for assessing the complex relationships between some attributes of archaeological assemblages and, not only socioeconomic status, but political status, ethnicity, market access, and patterns of differential artifact deposition among status levels. By comparing and contrasting data from a number of sites, different situations begin to emerge in which status accounts for variation in archaeologically deposited consumer goods, and situations in which other variables, such as market access due to site location, ethnicity, or site-specific historical events, have at least as much influence on consumption patterns and their archaeological remains.

REFERENCES

Bining, Arthur C., and Cochran, Thomas C., 1964, *The Rise of American Economic Life,* Charles Scribner's Sons, New York.

Danhof, C. H., 1969, *Change in Agriculture: The Northern United States, 1820–1870,* Harvard University Press, Cambridge.

Gruver, Rebecca B., 1972, *An American History,* Volume 1, to 1877, Addison Wesley, Reading, Massachusetts.

Ratner, Sidney, Soltow, J. H., and Sulla, R., 1979, *The Evolution of the American Economy,* Basic Books, New York.

Robertson, R. M., 1973, *History of the American Economy,* Harcourt, Brace, Jovanovich, New York.

Tryon, Rolla M., 1917, *Household Manufactures in the United States, 1640–1860,* University of Chicago Press, Chicago.

2

Ceramics as Indicators of Status and Class in Eighteenth-Century New York

SHERENE BAUGHER AND ROBERT W. VENABLES

INTRODUCTION

This chapter analyzes three major factors which affected eighteenth-century archaeological ceramic assemblages in New York. Seven sites were studied. Four are rural. Three are in lower Manhattan, the location of colonial New York City and the colony's major port. The following were considered:

1. Market access
2. Socioeconomic status
3. The specific historic events which occurred at each site

In addition, three other factors will be briefly discussed in the historical section: colonial material culture, including "fashion"; the broad historic trends and circumstances which had effects on all sites; and ethnicity.

The archaeological and documentary data both indicated an availability of fine ceramics in rural areas and on the frontier as well as in New York City. Status, not location, was the significant factor when a colonist chose ceramic wares. However, both middle and upper classes sought similar ceramic wares, although the upper classes could obviously afford more of the same wares. European ethnicity evidently did not strongly affect ceramic choices, but a pervasive colonial culture and fashion, largely shaped by the trade restrictions of imperial Britain, did affect these choices by limiting what ceramics could be most readily purchased (i.e., primarily British, Chinese, and some German). We conclude that market access is primarily determined by class and by economic and political factors. Spatial considerations are negligible. In addition, we asked under what circumstances are ceramics reliable indicators of status. We noted that the proportions of expensive wares to inexpensive wares found in an archaeological assemblage are not necessarily indicative of class. Nor does the presence of high-quality and/or expensive wares in a ceramic assemblage necessarily permit the differentiation between middle- and upper-class sites. Our discussion of social class and its relationship to status in

Sherene Baugher ☐ New York City Landmarks Preservation Commission, 20 Vesey Street, 11th Floor, New York, NY 10007. **Robert W. Venables** ☐ American Indian Community House, 842 Broadway, New York, NY, 10003.

eighteenth-century North America is framed within definitions and theoretical perspectives, primarily from the field of history rather than anthropology. We hope that this chapter presents a model that can be used and
tested on other sites.

Historical Perspectives

This section is divided into the following subsections: trade networks,
settlement patterns and market access, and socioeconomic status and class.

Trade Networks

A review of colonial trade indicates the different ways goods reached each
class of colonists. To obtain finer goods, affluent colonials might occasionally
buy from shopkeepers catering primarily to the other classes. Usually, however, colonial aristocrats would contact, as individuals or in a group, a representative or agent in Britain who also conducted most of their other business
affairs for them abroad. The aristocrats might also agree to invest together—
to subscribe—in order to place a major order from Britain. Local arrangements might be made for these transactions through an exchange of correspondence or at a meeting, especially at a gathering at a prestigious coffee
house (Schlesinger 1968 (1917):23–32, *passim;* Bridenbaugh 1955:160–162).

Whatever their other incomes, one or more among any gathering of aristocrats was likely to be a merchant. Historian Jackson Turner Main defined a
merchant as "one who imported and who characteristically sold at wholesale,"
noting how Samuel Johnson's eighteenth-century *Dictionary* distinguished the
roles of merchants and shopkeepers: "a merchant was 'one who trafficks to
remote countries' whereas a shopkeeper was 'a trader who sells in a shop; not a
merchant who deals only by wholesale'" (Main 1965:86). In acquiring their
goods, the middle and lower classes, as well as the occasional aristocrat, had a
number of options. There were, of course, the shopkeepers. There were also
individual street sellers. The street or open markets, not unlike their medieval
predecessors, were yet another source (Bridenbaugh 1955:77–83, 272–280).

Trade items coming from Britain, Europe, Asia (via Britain), and Africa
(primarily direct) were targeted principally at the elite and middle classes.
(The exceptions were those goods, of a wide range of quality, imported for the
Indian fur and deerskin trades: cf. Corkran 1967; Jacobs 1950; Norton 1974;
Phillips 1961.) The lower (laboring) class, the poor, and the slaves were at the
tail end of the Atlantic trade network because of their relative inability to buy
into it. Catering to these classes, as well to anyone else who would buy, were
the peddlers. The peddlers were at the bottom of the business hierarchy. They
were frequently young, too ill for farm labor, and/or lacking a limb. In 1772,
twenty-two were licensed by the colony of New York, and many more peddled
without a license. Of eighteen peddlers of whom there is a detailed record in
the colony of New York, eight traveled by foot, six had one horse apiece, and
only four had carts (Greg 1750–1755: *passim;* and Main 1965:84–85).

Unfortunately, there are few surviving documentary records of the lower strata of colonial society—and even fewer archaeological records. Lower-class, poor, and slave families could acquire at best a few treasured items, although they could also obtain the castoffs of their superiors by scavenging, and occasionally receive an item as a gift. Of course, there were always families that had seen better days, and they might cherish an object from a previous generation which had a monetary and aesthetic value far beyond the family's current ability to purchase such items. An expensive object could also be stolen, a *modus operandi* equally open to the middle and upper classes. The theft factor should also be extended to include—again, applicable to all classes—looting during war.

Settlement Patterns and Market Access

A major reason it is not unusual to find the widespread distribution of the same high-quality goods among the aristocrats and middle class of both country and city is that most of colonial America was *country*. Consequently, more aristocrats lived in the country, or both in the country and in the city, than exclusively in the city.

"Market access" is not synonymous with "proximity." Distances from markets is thus not a major issue in colonial trade patterns. If a product could be shipped 3,000 miles across the Atlantic (Boatner 1974:49), it was relatively easy to get that product to any aristocratic or middle-class colonist living in the colonies, almost all of whom lived on or close to a major river (Adams 1927:3; Boorstin 1958:107). Market access, in fact, had less to do with spatial circumstances than with economic and political situations (McCusker and Menard 1985:303). Finally, in considering the spatial relationship of the 3,000-mile ocean route to the colonies, it is especially significant to note that, even by 1775, the colonies had spread inland less than 250 miles from the Atlantic coast, and that all *legal* white settlements were located east of that frontier (Cappon 1976:22–25). *Personal* isolation from an urban center should not be equated with *commercial* isolation. Merchants and other distributors moved their goods regularly over longer, time-consuming distances, expecting to cope with such spatial considerations in the ordinary course of doing business. In summary, if a colonist could afford to buy it, someone was ready, willing, and able to ship it.

Throughout the colonies, more than 95 percent of the population lived in the countryside. In the colony of New York, 87 percent lived outside New York City. In 1770, the entire colony numbered 162,920, only 21,000 of whom (13 percent) lived in New York City. In 1775, the thirteen colonies had a population of approximately 2.6 million. There were only sixteen cities (that is, urban areas with three thousand or more people). These sixteen cities totaled 132,105 (5.1 percent). Of the top five cities, Philadelphia ranked first with 23,739. In 1775, New York was the thirteen colonies' second most populous city, with 22,000, followed by Boston with 16,000, Charleston with 14,000, and Newport, Rhode Island, with 9,209. Within the framework of the British empire, when

London numbered 700,000, it is no wonder that European visitors to American colonial cities such as New York remarked on how beautifully pastoral their settings were. Because Britain forbad extensive heavy industry in the colonies, for example, there was little industrial smoke rising in the sky (Bridenbaugh 1955:3, 216–217; Cappon 1976:97–98, 103–107; Kalm 1966 ([1770–1771]:130–136, *passim;* Morris 1982:648).

Transport along the trade routes was primarily by water, beginning, of course, with the voyage across the Atlantic. During the colonial period, an Atlantic voyage took about eight weeks from England to America but, because of the westerly winds, about four weeks from America to England (Boatner 1974:48). Thus, to both merchant and customer, the few additional days during which the goods were shipped up a river or across a bay were truly the easy part of a trip. Librarian of Congress Daniel J. Boorstin (1958:295) notes that "it was easier to travel a thousand miles by water than a hundred by land." Thus an area like Staten Island, just across the bay from the major entry port of New York and surrounded by easily accessible water, was hardly isolated. Furthermore, the major trade route to central New Jersey and the land route to Philadelphia put Staten Islanders right on the eastern end of a major trade network that ferried goods by water to Elizabeth, Perth Amboy, and various New Jersey rivers and streams near Staten Island (Levitt 1981:7–44). The extensive trade along the Hudson River kept that valley in constant communication with New York City. The Mohawk Valley frontier depended upon market access: its Indian fur trade and its colonial agricultural commodities were both important because they had access to New York City via the Mohawk and Hudson Rivers (Venables 1967:15–17, 23–24, *passim*).

The affordability of goods in the interior depended, of course, on the ability of the peripheral, interior agricultural products to reach core markets, thus creating the profit (income) needed to purchase goods. As historians John J. McCusker and Russell R. Menard (1985:302–303) make clear in their summary of markets in colonial America:

> Conventional wisdom suggests that high transport costs severely limited farmers' access to markets and that the "tyranny of distance" kept many farmers isolated, forcing them into a subsistence mode of production. Again, there is evidence that such a formulation is misleading, that it overestimates the costs and underestimates the sophistication of interior transportation, and that it thus misjudges the distance which farmers were willing and able to haul their products.
>
> The isolation of farmers has been much exaggerated.

Our own research confirms this. The account book and papers of a Mohawk Valley trader-shopkeeper from 1769 to 1775 demonstrate how interior farmers had access to markets and to finished goods from England. The Mohawk Valley was part of Tryon County, colonial New York's westernmost frontier county. Living at Caughnawaga on the Mohawk River, Jelles Fonda (Jane's ancestor) coordinated trade for many of the county's white inhabitants as well as carrying on trade with Mohawk, Oneida, Tuscarora, and other Indians (especially through representatives at Fort Stanwix—now Rome, New York— at the western boundary of the county). Fonda's imports included Irish linen, lace, calico, fine clothing, silk handkerchiefs, pewterware, mirrors, and women's worsted hose (Fonda 1771–1773:94–184; cf. Fonda 1769–1775).

There is a major reason why upper and middle classes throughout British North America sought similar goods. Superficially, this reason is apparent as "fashion." But behind "fashion" were subtler components. One was psychological, the other was economic, and both were tied to the imperial context of Britain's colonial America.

The strongest sense of isolation among colonists was not between coastal colonist and frontier farmer. Rather, it was the isolation brought by the trans-Atlantic abyss between the European homeland and America. James Thomas Flexner (1975:33), the eminent scholar of American art and culture, detects among the American colonists, isolated by an ocean from Britain, an actual "twinge of guilt felt by the colonists at the realization that they were separated from traditional culture" in London and Britain. Aristocrats might feel the need to compensate for this isolation even more strongly than other classes simply because they could afford it, and because their access to the latest news from Britain in their various businesses made them all the more aware of what they were missing on the London scene. Flexner (1975:10), however, sees a "colonial attitude" that pervades all American colonial life:

> The colonial mind . . . does not seek the new, but rather wishes to reproduce the institutions and the society of the mother country. Deviations, however strongly forced by a different environment, are regarded as provincial mannerisms that will eventually be overcome and should in the meantime not be stressed.

One of the subjects of this paper, Sir William Johnson, was a self-made aristocrat living on the frontier. Flexner's description goes far in explaining some of the psychological reasons Johnson established an English country estate in the Mohawk Valley (cf. Flexner 1979:295–311).

Richard L. Bushman has defined the common elements in the arts and architecture that were patronized by the upper and middle classes in all the colonies as "the diffusion of genteel culture." But he notes that, while America looked to England for its culture and fashion, England was also looking to other European nations for cultural inspiration, even as it created its own (Bushman 1984:352–364, 367, 373). This European factor may have mitigated the cultural identity among non-British colonists. Colonial British America included many ethnic groups not from the British Isles (Cappon 1976:96–100). Ethnicity among these non-British colonists survived most successfully in personal, family, and religious customs as well as in these groups' locally produced arts and crafts. However, a sense of ethnic identity for non-British colonists was difficult to maintain in imported material culture because imports from a particular non-British homeland were constricted (though not eliminated) by an overwhelmingly significant factor in colonial life: the system of trade itself.

The colonial ties to England were not just cultural and spiritual—they were also economic. British goods were not just the fashion, they were often "the only." The British empire was organized so that the 2.6 million colonists supplied raw materials to, and consumed the finished products of, the 8 million who lived in the British Isles. Because the British monarchy since the eighteenth century had belonged to the German House of Hanover, a German connection was included in this trade network, evident in the German ceramics found at the sites. Through an economic system called "mercantilism" (which has its modern counterpart in what economists now call "protectionism"), the colonists were forced to "buy British" (McCusker and Menard 1985:35–88, *passim*). Such a policy, of course, was most easily implemented when it voluntarily encouraged the colonial passion for things English. Thus, colonial aspirations to mimic London fashions were both a phenomenon of the colonial mind-set and a method by which London could perpetuate its imperial economic goals (Schlesinger 1968 [1917]:31). The result of this policy was that, by the 1760s, there was clearly a complicated, unfavorable balance of trade from the colonial point of view (McCusker and Menard 1985:36–39). However, since English liberties in the colonies were usually broader than other European nations, and certainly more liberal than those in the neighboring French and Spanish colonies, the English model was not intrinsically distasteful. When rebellion finally came in 1775, it is well to remember that for more than a year the Patriots proclaimed that they were fighting for the rights of Englishmen, not independence (cf. Bailyn 1967:94–143, 273–313).

Socioeconomic Status and Class

In addition to colonial trade, this chapter focuses on the material manifestations of class in eighteenth-century British North America. It is important to note that class history in America is a complex topic. Especially since the seminal work by Jackson Turner Main, *The Social Structure of Revolutionary America,* published in 1965, specific examinations of class have increased so that class history in colonial British North America has now accumulated a historical literature as challenging and varied as that of, for example, Frederick Jackson Turner's frontier thesis. While there is an enormous literature on the subject, a major difficulty arises from examining a colonial preindustrial society from a postindustrial perspective—that is, from a perspective at least twice removed from the colonial era. Colonial society had more in common with the lifestyles, values, and class structure of Renaissance Europe than with industrial nineteenth- and twentieth-century America. No more dramatic set of statistics demonstrates the difference than those available for comparing the very rich in colonial New York City with those of New York City in 1860. In colonial New York City, there was indeed a disparity between rich and poor, but the rich did not control the overwhelming amount of wealth in the colonial period as they did in 1860. More or less constantly, between 1695 and 1789, the top 10 percent of New York City taxpayers owned 45 percent of the wealth. Yet by 1860 the top 5 percent owned 70 percent of the wealth (Henretta 1984:277–279).

The following checklist was developed by the authors to outline major points of reference which archaeologists can use to determine a colonist's status. The checklist is intended to emphasize the point that, in any study of class and status in colonial society, it would be misleading for archaeologists and historians to rely on economic status alone. The checklist is applicable to whites, blacks, and Indians. The more the following apply to an individual, the higher that individual's status in the eyes of fellow colonists; the fewer, the lower. (Caveat: By no means is this or any other list inclusive, for each individual colonist had unique characteristics and circumstances which contributed to success or failure.)

1. Annual income
2. Annual expenditures
3. Amount of land holding(s)
4. Franchise rights
5. Number of servants
6. Number of slaves
7. Number of tenant farmers and/or urban tenants
8. Capital, including inheritances and investments, especially investments in land speculations and trade enterprises such as shipping
9. Size, architectural style, and location of homes
10. Political offices
11. Military offices
12. Lineage
13. Number of generations in America
14. Marriage(s)—especially useful in indicating social, political, and business alliances, and in tracing movements up and down the social ladder
15. Degree of name recognition in a European capital such as London
16. Material details such as possession of carriages, membership in libraries or societies
17. Religion
18. Ethnicity
19. Friends
20. Enemies
21. Physical appearance and health
22. Personal behavior (e.g., gracious, rude, alcoholic)

In considering the above (and other factors), it is important to note that the colonists accommodated their society's belief systems to their own individual personalities and characters. Thus, an aristocrat who was an alcoholic might be regarded with low esteem (i.e., low status) even as that aristocrat is recognized as a member of the upper class. Generalizations must also allow for individual perceptions, initiatives, and idiosyncrasies.

There were firm class roles and a class structure during the colonial period, although there were no firm classes (Kammen 1972:154; Main 1965:219; 1973:29–36). This seeming contradiction actually incorporates two realities in colonial America: while there was more class *mobility* than in Europe—that is, the ability to move up (or down) the social ladder—there were definite expectations within each class (Adams 1927:56–112; Main 1965:165–239). That is, while a person was on a particular rung of the social ladder, certain social dictates applied. One of the ways a person could demonstrate a change in status was to acquire higher quality goods. (It should be noted, however, that even the richest colonial aristocrat could not have competed with the upper crust of either the hereditary aristocracy or the *nouveau riche* in Britain.)

A Note on Ethnicity

Sir William Johnson was born in Smithtown, Ireland, yet he emulated English fashions. This emulation was not unusual in the colonies (or in Ireland, an older English colony). There are different ethnic backgrounds among the families at, specifically, all four of the rural sites. But there is no difference in the ceramic choices made by the occupants:

1. Sir William Johnson, born in Smithtown, Ireland
2. Robert R. Livingston, great-grandson of a Scot (Robert Livingston) and a colonial Hollander, Alyda Schuyler
3. Christopher Billopp, grandson of an Englishman (Christopher Billopp)
4. Jacob Rezeau, grandson of a French Huguenot, René Rezeau (Davis 1926; Gerlach 1964:314; Hopkins 1964:504, 576; Leng and Davis 1930)

While ethnicity may have been demonstrated in other ways, the ceramic assemblages at the four rural sites studied were not indicative of the ethnicity outlined above.

Summary

The British ethos created a substantial homogeneity in British colonial America, despite the pluralistic components of its colonists. The economics of the British empire were integrated with its politics and political philosophy, and both were intertwined with aspects of British fashion and culture, all impacting on the colonial state of mind. In a colonial world of many national backgrounds, material culture and the aspirations which prompted its acquisitions served as a social glue.

Given all of these historical perspectives, an archaeologist should expect to find a tremendous similarity in the goods unearthed at city and country sites of people of the same socioeconomic status. Furthermore, the difference between goods owned by members of the middle and upper class should be a quantitative difference, not a qualitative difference. To test these ideas, we have analyzed data from rural and city sites, and artifacts discarded by middle- and upper-class families.

ARCHAEOLOGICAL SOURCES AND METHODS

To test our hypotheses, our criteria was to choose sites that had ceramic assemblages that could be linked to a specific family with a documented history. The family could be either from the upper or middle class in colonial New York (mid- to late eighteenth century). We also selected sites that were excavated in a similar manner so that field methodology did not account for differences in the assemblages. The four sites were: the Conference House and the Voorlezer House sites on Staten Island, and Clermont and Johnson Hall in upstate New York (see Figure 1 for site locations).

The two eastern upstate New York sites, Johnson Hall and Clermont, are both state historic sites and also include original eighteenth-century homes.

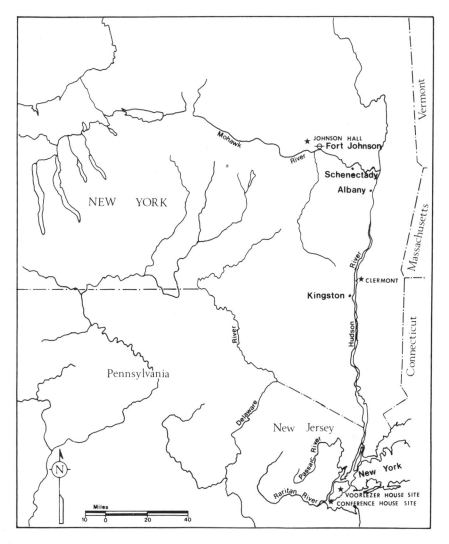

Figure 1. Map showing the location of Clermont, the Conference House, Johnson Hall, and the Voorlezer House. Map adapted from "Iroquois Frontier 1768–1780" Plate 78 in James Truslow Adams's *Atlas of American History*. Map drafted by Louise DeCesare.

Both are managed as State Historic Parks. The excavation of these two sites was sponsored by the New York State Historic Trust and the Bureau of Historic Sites. The staff of the archaeology unit within the Bureau of Historic Sites excavated these two sites, with Lois Feister (1981) authoring the Clermont report and Rich Goring (1981) writing the Johnson Hall report.

The excavation of the two Staten Island sites represent a cooperative research endeavor between the New York City Landmarks Preservation Commission and each of the buildings' museum boards and directors. Funding for the excavation and laboratory work was shared by the museums and the Landmarks Commission and was aided by grants. The two sites were excavated by Baugher and a small team of graduate and undergraduate students from local colleges. The Voorlezer House site report was written by Baugher, Judith Baragli, and Louise DeCesare (1985), and the Conference House report is under preparation by Baugher, Baragli, and DeCesare.

The four sites, Clermont, Conference House, Johnson Hall, and Voorlezer House, were excavated for the same purpose: to sample the site prior to construction work. All four excavations were confined to areas of the property that were going to be destroyed by construction projects. In all cases, the construction work was postponed to allow time for an archaeological excavation. The artifacts from the four sites were sheet scatter deposits in the yard area alongside the homes. No artifacts were from features. The ceramic assemblages from each site were fairly similar in size. The artifacts were from sites that contained a clearly documented use and ownership. The artifacts can be attributed to specific families.

The following is a brief historical sketch of each of the four rural sites chosen for the primary analysis.

The Conference House is located at the southern tip of Staten Island, eighteen miles from Manhattan. Christopher Billopp, one of the most affluent landowners in eighteenth-century New York, owned the Conference House, at that time known as Bentley Manor. Billopp was a staunch Loyalist during the American Revolution. In the twentieth century, the name Conference House was given to Bentley Manor to commemorate the famous but unsuccessful peace conference held at the house in 1776 between British and Patriot negotiators, including Benjamin Franklin and John Adams (Davis 1926; Zavin 1980).

The Voorlezer House is located in the heart of Richmondtown, the eighteenth-century county seat of Staten Island. In 1705, a French family, the Rezeaus, purchased the property and resided on this land until 1872. Documentary evidence shows that Jacob Rezeau was a cooper, farmer, slave owner, and public official who lived in the present Voorlezer House from 1740 until 1789 (Baugher, Baragli, and DeCesare 1985).

Clermont is located in the Hudson River Valley between the towns of Tivoli and Germantown, fifty miles south of Albany and about one hundred miles north of the colonial city of New York. In 1782, the Livingston family built the mansion at Clermont upon the ruins of a 1730 house that was also owned by the Livingstons (Feister 1981:39). The most famous resident of Clermont was Robert Livingston, a member of the committee that drafted the Declaration of Independence, a minister to France responsible for the Louisiana Purchase in 1803, and a partner with Robert Fulton in their successful steamboat venture, the *Clermont,* in 1809 (Boatner 1974:642–643; Hopkins 1964:576; Launitz-Schurer 1980:28–32, 158–159).

Robert Livingston was rivaled in wealth and power by Sir William Johnson. Johnson's home, Johnson Hall, is located in Johnstown (near the Mohawk River) thirty-eight miles from Albany and about one hundred and forty miles from Manhattan. Sir William Johnson, colonial Superintendent of Indian Affairs, built his Georgian house in 1763. This home in the Mohawk Valley was on New York's colonial frontier (Flexner 1979).

To address the question of whether site location affected market access to colonial New York, we compared the data from our four rural sites to information from three sites in lower Manhattan (see Figure 2). The three Manhattan excavations considered in this paper were directed by Bertram Herbert and Terry Klein (the Barclays Bank site), by Nan Rothschild and Arnold Pickman (7 Hanover Square site), and by Nan Rothschild and Dianna Rockman (the Stadt Huys site). They were conducted as public archaeology projects monitored by the New York City Landmarks Preservation Commission. Site reports have not been completed on these three sites, although research and report preparation is underway.

The Manhattan artifacts were unearthed from colonial backyards and basements which were buried underneath buildings from the nineteenth and twentieth centuries. On all three sites, many of the eighteenth-century structures were destroyed by an 1835 fire. The later nineteenth-century buildings covered, and thus protected, a few of the eighteenth-century building foundations, backyards, and their associated artifacts. These three sites had been parking lots immediately prior to the archaeological excavation, but now skyscrapers are rising upon them.

The Manhattan data were used to illustrate the presence or absence of material in the Port of New York. None of the Manhattan sites contained ceramic assemblages that could be linked to a specific family. The three Manhattan sites had various problems: (a) the time range for the levels was too broad; or (b) they lacked supportive documentary evidence; or (c) there were too many varied uses of a property to link the archaeological data to a particular occupant. Thus the Manhattan sites only revealed generalized and broad chronological sweeps for the eighteenth century rather than era-specific, quantifiable data linked to specific families.[1]

The Manhattan archaeological data were used in tandem with historical data: the records of an eighteenth-century colonial merchant, Frederick

[1]After the completion of this chapter, we were informed by Terry Klein, principal investigator of the Barclays Bank site, that his staff had identified a late eighteenth-century archaeological deposit that could be associated with a known family. Unfortunately, the historical and archaeological analysis of this material is still in process, therefore there was no information available for inclusion in this chapter.

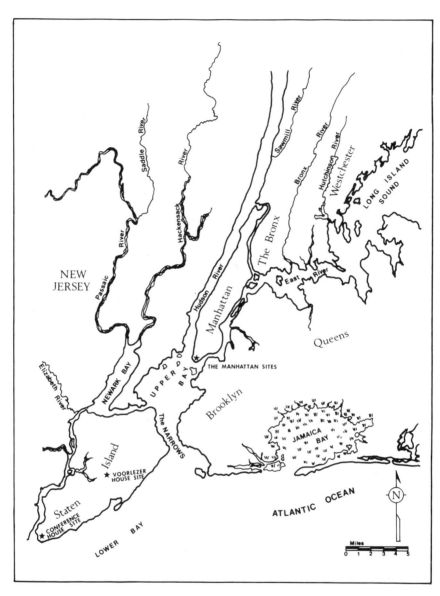

Figure 2. Map showing the location of the Conference House and the Voorlezer House in relation to the Port of New York. Map adapted from "New York (City) in 1776" Plate 70 in James Truslow Adams's *Atlas of American History*. Map drafted by Louise DeCesare.

Rhinelander, who specialized in ceramics. The New York Historical Society contains the papers (twenty-five volumes) of Frederick Rhinelander, proprietor of a china, glass, and earthenware store in Manhattan from 1770 to 1786. Ceramic historian Arlene Palmer Schwind's (1984) lengthly article detailed all of the ceramic types (and their prices) that were imported by Rhinelander. Thus we were able to document the range of goods available in the colonial capital of New York. The archaeological data were compared with documentary evidence listing the exact types of wares that were being imported into the Port of New York during the 1770s and 1780s.

Schwind (1984) notes that, in the 1770s and 1780s, the fashionable wares were Chinese porcelain, creamware, pearlware, white salt-glazed stoneware, and some decorated delft. Delft and white salt-glazed stoneware were at the height of fashion in the mid-eighteenth century; the Rhinelander papers demonstrate that this style of wares continued to be popular into the late eighteenth century (Schwind 1984:26–27). One of the lower-status wares was Nottinghamware. The documentary records show that within each ware type there is a diversity in vessel shape, design, and price. For example, enameled, white salt-glazed stoneware cups and saucers were four times more expensive than the undecorated white salt-glazed cups (Schwind 1984:26).

After reading the Rhinelander data, it is clear that there are problems in the way archaeologists record the data from eighteenth-century sites. Site reports usually present the number of sherds within each broad category. However, if we are to use ceramics as status indicators, then we need to know the specific information about vessel shape and style of decoration. If two sites contain the same number of creamware sherds, but one site had undecorated creamware from a chamberpot, and the other had enamel-painted designed creamware tea cups, this difference in vessel form and decoration would certainly indicate a difference in the cost of the objects. It is recommended that future site reports provide a more detailed presentation of ceramic data. For the current cross-site research, the comparisons had to be made within the broad categories of ware type.

Hypothesis: Site Location Did Not Affect Market Access in Colonial New York

The general hypothesis that site location on waterways eliminates market access as an important variable affecting eighteenth-century consumer choices, has been tested using seven sites in colonial New York. Ceramic assemblages from our four rural sites (Clermont, Conference House, Johnson Hall, and Voorlezer House) and three urban sites (from Manhattan) were examined to determine the type and diversity of wares present at both urban and rural sites. During the eighteenth century, no difference was found in the quality and diversity of the imported wares found on Manhattan, on Staten Island, and in upstate New York. The similarity of the range and quality of the artifacts found on the Staten Island sites, the upstate sites, and on those sites in Manhattan therefore suggests that social class and economic wealth, not geographic location, determined what a colonial New Yorker obtained.

As stated earlier, no site reports exist for the three Manhattan sites. This study, though, incorporates the findings from the very thorough research undertaken by archaeologist Meta Janowitz of the ceramic assemblages from all three Manhattan sites (personal communication, 1985). After the Voorlezer House site and Conference House site ceramic assemblages had already been studied by Baugher and Baragli (1985, 1987), Janowitz was asked to review the ceramic artifacts and to note the similarities and differences between the Staten Island artifacts and Manhattan ceramic assemblages. Janowitz confirmed that the imported wares on Staten Island were similar to those unearthed in Manhattan. Thus Staten Island was not an isolated, peripheral area in terms of trade, and it had access, just as did Manhattan, to British goods. For example, the Staten Island and Manhattan families were using fine-quality white salt-glazed stoneware and creamware dishes and cups from England. Their porcelain tea sets were imported, via England, from China to both Manhattan and Staten Island. Delftware bowls, mugs, and dishes—with both designed and plain motifs—were being brought from England and distributed both on Manhattan and Staten Island. These families were drinking tea and thereby participating in a fashionable English custom that was far from a necessity. As the Revolutionary era dawned, on Staten Island and Manhattan, the families who could afford it were also purchasing the fashionable new Wedgewood dishes.

Janowitz did not review the assemblages from the two upstate sites. Baugher analyzed the ceramic assemblages from the two Staten Island sites and compared this material to the data from the thorough site reports on Clermont (Feister 1981) and Johnson Hall (Goring 1981). The reports show similar artifacts being unearthed at these upstate sites. These sites were similar to the downstate sites in that they contained porcelain, white salt-glazed stoneware, creamware, delftware, and pearlware—the status wares from the mid- to late eighteenth century.

The difference in the Manhattan, Staten Island, and upstate New York artifacts is not in the high-status table wares, but in the inexpensive kitchen wares. Local potters throughout the Northeast were producing a variety of utilitarian wares, from mixing bowls to baking dishes. Meta Janowitz noted that the two Staten Island sites contained both local redwares and stonewares not found in the Manhattan sites, as well as some wares similar to those from the Manhattan sites. Even though Staten Island had clay deposits that could have been used for redware and stoneware, there were no known eighteenth-century potters on Staten Island (Charles L. Sachs, Chief Curator, Staten Island Historical Society, personal communication, August 1984). New Jersey had abundant clay deposits, and the documentary record clearly identifies potters and potteries operating during this period. The question is therefore raised: Were the utilitarian wares used on Staten Island imported from New Jersey, or were they made by a Staten Island potter whose name and location has been lost?

A hint to the answer lies in the motifs. Some of the decorations on this pottery can be attributed to particular potteries and/or cities beyond Staten Island. Pottery from Philadelphia and from Cheesequake near Perth Amboy, New Jersey, have been uncovered at other Staten Island sites (Baugher and Venables 1985). All one can say is that the pottery found on the two Staten

Island sites was made by a New York or New Jersey potter.[2] Thus the evidence indicates that kitchenware used by the families studied on Staten Island was "imported" from the nearby colonies of New Jersey and Pennsylvania or from New York. Such a distribution seems probable, given the trade routes by water and by land from Philadelphia across New Jersey that converged at Staten Island on their way to Manhattan. Furthermore, because of the relatively low colonial population of Staten Island—at most a few thousand—a local Staten Island full-time potter might not have been able to survive economically. Yet there is another possible explanation for the existence in Staten Island archaeological sites of what looks to be New York and New Jersey pottery. It is possible that, even though there is no record of a Staten Island redware potter, the potter may have existed, copying designs known to be popular with potters in New York and New Jersey. The potter may have been a part-time potter, who survived economically through another occupation, such as full-time farming.

American-made pottery also was unearthed at Johnson Hall and Clermont in upstate New York. Given the ubiquitous nature of American redware manufacturing, more likely than not, this redware was made locally rather than being shipped from Manhattan or New Jersey.

During the eighteenth century, no difference was found in the quality and diversity of the imported wares found on Manhattan, on Staten Island, and in upstate New York. The similarity of the range and quality of the artifacts found on the Staten Island sites, the upstate sites, and on those sites in Manhattan therefore suggests that social class and economic wealth, not geographic location, determined what a colonial New Yorker obtained.

Hypothesis: Ceramics Can Be Used as Indicators of Status on Eighteenth-Century Sites

Was socioeconomic status a major factor in determining eighteenth-century consumer choices? If so, then we would expect that both upper- and middle-class colonial families owned some of the same status wares. The difference in their possessions would not be in the quality of their wares but in the quantity of these wares. Four rural sites (Clermont, Conference House, Johnson Hall, and Voorlezer House) are used here to test this hypothesis.

---

[2]An analysis needs to be made of the clay from the extant clay pits in New York and New Jersey to see if there are any differences in this clay. If noticable differences exist, then samples of the clay body from sherds from New York and New Jersey sites need to be tested. This work has not been done. However, Professor Alan Gilbert from Fordham University has just received a grant to undertake this study. In fall 1985, Professor Gilbert took clay samples from pottery from archaeological sites on Staten Island. Dr. Gilbert will be taking clay samples from clay pits on Staten Island and in New Jersey, as well as taking samples from pottery from Manhattan and New Jersey archaeological collections. He will be working with the curatorial staff of Staten Island Historical Society to locate local colonial clay pits. This work should answer some questions about colonial trade in local pottery.

The archaeological data were compared with documentary evidence of the exact types of wares that were being imported into the Port of New York during the 1770s and 1780s.[3] Schwind (1984) notes that, in the 1770s and 1780s, the fashionable wares were Chinese porcelain, creamware, pearlware, white salt-glazed stoneware, and some decorated delft.

For the quantitative study of ceramics from the four sites, the data was divided into two broad categories, expensive and inexpensive wares. Within each broad category, the material was divided into ware types; for example, porcelain, creamware, and pearlware (see Table 1). The category of utilitarian stoneware encompassed both American and European stoneware, and because of the Rhinelander data, Nottinghamware was included in this group.

All four sites contain a similar diverse selection of quality tablewares and kitchenwares. The artifact types found at all four sites were the same kinds of wares that were being imported by Frederick Rhinelander. No differences were found in the quality of ceramics at these sites. A comparison of the ceramic assemblages of the middle-class site on Staten Island with the aristo-cratic site of Clermont, however, confirms the obvious: middle-class colonists could not afford the quantity of high-quality wares that the aristocrats could. There is, instead, some archaeological evidence of a middle-class emulation of the aristocratic taste—what the eighteenth century referred to as aping one's betters. Thus, traces of a few of the highest-quality goods were found at the middle-class site. The Rezeau family had porcelain tea bowls, but porcelain comprised only 4.2 percent of their collection, whereas it comprised 14 percent of the Livingston collection. The Livingstons had more than three times as much creamware, and almost twice as much delft. Predictably, the proportions are reversed when comparing archaeological assemblages of utilitarian wares, with the Rezeaus having the higher proportions of these kitchenwares. The Rezeaus had three times as much redware, four times as much stoneware, and twice as much buff earthenware as the Livingstons.

From the perspective of only a quantitative study, ceramics indicated that the Johnsons of Johnson Hall, the Billopps of the Conference House, and the Rezeaus of the Voorlezer House were all middle class, and that only the Livingstons of Clermont were aristocrats. In fact, we know from the documen-tary record that the Johnsons and the Billopps were aristocrats like the Liv-ingstons, and that only the Rezeaus were middle class. Why are ceramics accurate status indicators at the middle-class Voorlezer House and the upper-class Clermont site, while they are not reliable at the upper-class sites of Johnson Hall and the Conference House? A study of the documentary record, especially of military events, sheds light on this question, if only to suggest possible rather than absolute answers.

[3]George Miller (1980), in his excellent article on economic price scaling of nineteenth-century ceramics, has provided archaeologists who work on nineteenth-century sites with a very useful reference and method for analyzing their ceramic assemblages. At present, there is no price-scaling index for eighteenth-century ceramics. Schwind's (1984) study is a very useful report for archaeologists to begin to analyze price differentiation for eighteenth-century ceramics.

Table 1. A Comparison of Ware Types from Four New York State Sites[a]

Type of ware	Voorlezer House sherds		Clermont sherds		Conference House sherds		Johnson Hall sherds (1)		(2)	
	Percentage	Number	Percentage	Number	Percentage	Number	Percentage	Number	Percentage	Number
Porcelain	4.2	10	14.0	10	3.7	8	3.4	3	3.3	16
Creamware	11.8	28	37.0	26	14.4	31	48.9	43	39.1	188
Pearlware	12.2	29	11.0	8	7.0	15	23.9	21	43.0	207
White salt-glazed stoneware	5.9	14	10.0	7	1.9	4	2.3	2	2.5	12
Delft	5.0	12	4.0	3	16.3	35	1.1	1	1.7	8
Buff earthenware	23.9	57	13.0	9	10.7	23	—	—	1.0	5
Redware	24.8	59	7.0	5	26.0	56	12.5	11	7.5	36
Other stoneware	11.8	28	3.0	2	17.2	37	2.3	2	1.9	9
Whiteware	0.4	1	—	—	2.8	6	5.7	5	—	—
Total	100.0	238	100.0	70	100.0	221	100.0	88	100.0	481

[a]Table 1 provides *only* the eighteenth-century ceramic component of the Voorlezer and Conference House site assemblages. The majority of the ceramics from these two sites (not shown on this chart) date from the mid-nineteenth century to the early twentieth century. The one whiteware sherd from the Voorlezer House represents slippage due to water problems during the last day of the dig. The whiteware sherds from the Conference House can be attributed to soil disturbance (a modern drain pipe disturbed a small portion of the levels at the southern edge of two of the squares). There are two archaeological assemblages from Johnson Hall; the first collection was gathered in 1969 (481 sherds) and the second collection was retrieved in 1976 (88 sherds).

Hypothesis: Political Factors Can Affect Artifact Deposition on Nonmilitary Sites

This time, we are suggesting effects on colonial sites that were not common due to class, cultural aspirations, or a common imperial trade network. Rather, we are noting an uncommon factor—a unique circumstance—that is not self-evident archaeologically. The clues and even confirmation of the evidence will be primarily, if not exclusively, documentary. This circumstance is the military impact on a civilian site. We are focusing on military impacts on four civilian sites to suggest the array of historical evidence and trends that archaeologists need to consider before making judgments.

The artifact assemblages indicated that three sites were middle class and only one site was aristocratic. Yet the documentary evidence proves the opposite: three sites were aristocratic and only one site was middle class. Since all four sites were impacted by British and/or Patriot military activities during the American Revolution, we want to suggest ways in which those military activities may have altered the sites.

At Johnson Hall there is a small percentage of porcelain (3.4 percent) versus the percentage found at Clermont (14 percent). Yet Sir William Johnson and Robert Livingston were near-equals in terms of wealth and power. Rich Goring (1981:34) writes that the documentary records show that "Sir William did indeed possess a very large portion of porcelain." Goring (1981:34) adds that the "1774 inventory shows a creamware to porcelain ratio of 2:1 while the archaeological test pit ratio is 14:1." From Rhinelander's accounts, it is known that porcelain was the most expensive ware being imported to New York. Families, as well as their servants and slaves, would have been more careful in handling their expensive vessels than with their everyday wares. Rich Goring (1981:34) comments on the presence and use of porcelain and creamware by Sir William:

> English gentlemen of the eighteenth century such as Johnson may have valued
> porcelain for its aesthetic appeal and value and as a symbol of status. That cream-
> ware was the more utilitarian ware is also suggested by the fact that all but one of
> the creamware items in the inventory are included in the "Butlers room, Kitchen,
> etc.," and these areas do not include any porcelain.

At Livingston's Clermont, a single military event may have had a significant impact on the archaeological assemblage. In 1777, Sir Henry Clinton attempted to aid General John Burgoyne during the British campaign to conquer the entire colony of New York. Clinton moved up to the Hudson Highlands and then dispatched a flotilla of seventeen hundred men under General John Vaughan and Sir James Wallace to strike further north along the river. These seventeen hundred troops burned Kingston, New York, and then continued northward until, some fifty miles south of Albany, they burned Clermont. It is possible that the burning of Clermont by the British army caused a higher rate of ceramic destruction, and that this is why the percentage of high-status ceramic wares is greater at Clermont than at the two other aristocratic sites, Johnson Hall and the Conference House. But it is also possible that military events at Johnson Hall and at the Conference House had the accumulative effect of lowering the percentage of high-status ceramic wares in the assemblages there.

The historical record offers other possible answers in the matter of Johnson Hall's seemingly scant and unrepresentative ceramic assemblage. During the lifetime of the house prior to the American Revolution (1763–1774), the house was occasionally the scene of visits by delegations of American Indians and of whole conferences of Indian delegations that utilized the immediate grounds. This higher-than-normal traffic of visitors (unmatched until the tourist traffic of the twentieth century) may have resulted in heavy disturbances—not the least of which would have come with any "clean-up" detail following a meeting (again, a parallel might be made with twentieth-century tourists, as the grounds crew can testify). There is yet another factor to consider with regard to Johnson Hall which, as evidence will later demonstrate, may also apply to the Conference House site as well. This is the possible impact of the inhabitants' flight, as refugees, from Johnson Hall during the American Revolution. The Loyalists of the Mohawk Valley faced extreme Patriot pressures. On May 13, 1776, Sir John Johnson, son of the late Sir William, assembled 170 of his loyal tenants (including whole families) and fled northward to Canada through the Adirondacks. Under the circumstances, high-quality goods were removed, abandoned, or hidden. But Sir John left his wife Mary behind because she was four months pregnant. A few days later, as the party trudged through the woods, an Indian messenger caught up with Sir John and told him that Lady Johnson had been taken hostage by the Patriots. She had been removed from Johnson Hall and taken to Albany (she later escaped to New York City). Unfolding from this dramatic episode are three questions for the historical archaeologist to consider: What disturbance to the grounds occurred if—and the historical record is not helpful—some household goods were buried before the flight? What effect did the sudden assembly and flight of 170 refugees have on the grounds? And what exactly happened to the interior goods of Johnson Hall when Lady Johnson was seized by zealous Patriots? Because the historical record is again incomplete, the questions are circumstantial. However, while the answers to these questions are only speculative regarding Johnson Hall, the evidence is firm in understanding similar circumstances at the Conference House.

The Conference House site poses other problems. When a comparison is made between the ceramics found at the Conference House and Voorlezer House, there are marked similarities. One could conclude, based on the quantitative study, that the occupants of these two sites were both from the middle class. However, the documentary records show just the opposite: Christopher Billopp was the most affluent man living in eighteenth-century Staten Island. The lack of many high-status wares at the Conference House becomes more understandable after reading the documentary records. Historian William T. Davis (1926:159–169) researched British war records and found that Christopher Billopp, a Loyalist, petitioned the crown to recover £4,441 lost. These losses were due to both British confiscation and Patriot looting, for example:

1. In 1776, Hessian and British troops confiscated goods and food from Billopp amounting to £1,441.
2. Also, on several occasions between 1776 and 1780, rebel troops looted Billopp's house and property, taking horses, cows, furniture, bedding, and other household goods amounting to £1500. lt is important to note that Billopp states that the goods were "carried off," not destroyed.
3. During the war, Billopp obtained another house, probably in Manhattan, and moved his family and some possessions to the other house. The expense of moving his family and possessions to a safer location while he maintained his residence (in the service of the government) at the Conference House amounted to £1500.

Thus, the lack of status indicators at the Conference House are possibly due to: theft by rebel troops, confiscation by British troops, and intentional removal by Billopp.

Finally, it should be noted that, from 1776 to 1783, the town in which the Voorlezer House is located, Richmondtown, was occupied by British troops who manned a fortification on the heights above the town (Leng and Davis 1930:Volume 1). There is also documentary evidence that at least one soldier in the British forces—a Hessian mercenary—was quartered in the Voorlezer House and lived with the civilian Rezeau family—a practice not unusual during times of war in the colonial period. What impact did the military occupation of Richmondtown and the quartering of a soldier have on the Voorlezer House site's assemblage?

All these situations should raise a red flag to archaeologists. Ceramic assemblages should not be used as a sole or even a certain indicator of economic status. There are many factors, such as the military occupation of a civilian site, that can affect the archaeological deposits. A quantitative study of ceramics can reveal some patterns, but such studies, when used in conjunction with the historic record, may raise questions that will require still more detailed research.

CONCLUSION

A major conclusion demonstrated by the ceramic assemblages analyzed in this study suggests its application to all colonial sites: The buying power of a colonist, not the individual's proximity to a colonial city, determined what (and how much) the individual purchased. The colonial settlement patterns and trade networks exploited river transportation, thus individuals in the hinterland could share the same taste and market access for fashionable ceramics as their city counterparts. Furthermore, to the best of its ability, the middle class imitated the fashions of the upper class. Significantly, if obviously, the imperial context of the colonial era meant that these fashions were really not colonial fashions, but rather the fashions of the imperial capital, London, of Britain, and/or of Europe.

This study also demonstrates that ceramic assemblages are not dependable as the sole or primary indicator in determining the status of the site's residents. The percentage and variation of archaeological artifacts surviving at a site may not accurately reflect the quality and quantity of ceramics used by the past residents. Ceramic patterns can raise questions for further historical research. When available historical records are vague or contradictory, ceramics may be useful as significant evidence to lend credence to one interpretation over another or to provide new insights. The interaction and cooperation of archaeologists and historians from the very start of a project is thus sure to enrich both disciplines. Lastly, this study is meant to be a starting point, not an end. The hypotheses that were presented and tested in this study should be tested at other colonial sites.

ACKNOWLEDGMENTS

We appreciate the efforts of the hardworking and thorough field and laboratory crews who worked on the Conference House and the Voorlezer House excavations. Special thanks go to Judith Baragli, Sandra Famolare, and Louise DeCesare for their meticulous and diligent laboratory work. We wish to thank Meta Janowitz for generously sharing her data on the Stadt Huys, 7 Hanover Square, and the Barclays Bank ceramics assemblages. Meta Janowitz's observations and comments on the differences between the redware and stoneware found on Manhattan and Staten Island were very helpful. We are grateful to Louise DeCesare for drafting the maps used in this chapter. For help in typing drafts of this article, we wish to thank Louise DeCesare.

REFERENCES

Adams, James Truslow, 1927, *Provincial Society, 1690–1763,* MacMillan, New York.
Adams, James Truslow, 1943, *Atlas of American History,* Charles Scribner's Sons, New York.
Bailyn, Bernard, 1967, *The Ideological Origins of the American Revolution,* Harvard University, Cambridge, Massachusetts.
Baugher, Sherene, and Venables, Robert W, 1985, Trade Networks and Archaeology: Colonial and Federal Period, research report for an exhibit, *Staten Island Trade Networks: A Study of Community History Through Archaeology,* at the Staten Island Museum (March through August 1985), on file in the archives of the Staten Island Institute of Arts and Sciences.
Baugher, Sherene, Baragli, Judith, and DeCesare, Louise, 1985, The Archaeological Investigation of the Voorlezer House Site, Staten Island, New York, report on file in the archives of the Staten Island Historical Society.
Baugher, Sherene, and Baragli, Judith, 1987, Archaeological Investigation of the Conference House Site, Staten Island, New York, manuscript in preparation, New York City Landmarks Preservation Commission.
Boatner, Mark Mayo, III, 1974, *Encyclopedia of the American Revolution,* bicentennial ed., David McKay, New York.
Bonomi, Patricia U., 1971, *A Factious People: Politics and Society in Colonial New York,* Columbia University Press, New York.
Boorstin, Daniel J., 1958, *The Americans: The Colonial Experience,* Random House, New York.

Bridenbaugh, Carl (ed.), 1948, *Gentleman's Progress: The Itinerarium of Dr. Alexander Hamilton, 1744,* University of North Carolina Press, Chapel Hill.

Bridenbaugh, Carl, 1955, *Cities in Revolt: Urban Life in America 1743–1776,* Oxford University Press, New York.

Bushman, Richard L., 1984, American High-Style Vernacular Cultures in: *Colonial British America: Essays in the New History of the Early Modern Era* (Jack P. Greene and J. R. Pole, eds.), Johns Hopkins Press, Baltimore.

Cappon, Lester J., Petchenik, Barbara Bartz, and Long, John Hamilton (eds.), 1976, *Atlas of Early American History: The Revolutionary Era, 1760–1790,* the Newberry Library and the Institute of Early American History and Culture, Princeton University Press, New Jersey.

Corkran, David H., 1967, *The Creek Frontier, 1540–1783,* University of Oklahoma Press, Norman.

Davis, William T., 1926 *The Conference or Billopp House, Staten Island, New York,* Staten Island Historical Society, Staten Island, New York.

Feister, Lois M., 1981, Archaeological Testing at Clermont State Historic Park, Town of Clermont, Columbia County, for a Proposed Telephone–Electric Line, *The Bulletin and Journal of Archaeology for New York State* 83 (Fall):39–45.

Flexner, James Thomas, 1975, *The Face of Liberty: Founders of the United States,* Amon Carter Museum of Western Art, Fort Worth, Texas, and Clarkson N. Potter, New York.

Flexner, James Thomas, 1979, *Lord of the Mohawks: A Biography of Sir William Johnson,* revised ed., Little, Brown, Boston.

Fonda, Jelles, 1769–1775, The Fonda Family Papers, Manuscript Division, New-York Historical Society.

Fonda, Jelles, 1771–1773, Account Book, Manuscript Collection, Fort Johnson, Fort Johnson, New York.

Gerlach, Don R., 1964, *Philip Schuyler and the American Revolution in New York, 1733–1777,* University of Nebraska Press, Lincoln, Nebraska.

Greg, Robert, 1750–1755, Account Book, 1750–1755, Manuscript Collection, New-York Historical Society.

Goring, Rich, 1981, An Archaeological Testing Project at Johnson Hall State Historic Site, Johnstown, New York, *The Bulletin and Journal of Archaeology for New York State,* 82 (Fall):25–38.

Henretta, James A., 1984, Wealth and Social Structure, in: *Colonial British America: Essays in the New History of the Early Modern Era* (Jack P. Greene and J. R. Pole, eds.), Johns Hopkins Press, Baltimore, pp 262–289.

Hopkins, Joseph G. E. (ed.), 1964, *Concise Dictionary of American Biography,* Charles Scribner's Sons, New York.

Jacobs, Wilbur R., 1950, *Wilderness Politics and Indian Gifts: The Northern Colonial Frontier, 1748–1783,* Stanford University Press, Palo Alto, California.

Kalm, Peter, 1966 (1750), *The America of 1750: Travels in North America by Peter Kalm,* Volumes 1 and 2, revised from the original Swedish and edited by Adolph B. Benson (1937, 1964), Dover Publications, New York.

Kammen, Michael, 1972, *People of Paradox: An Inquiry Concerning the Origins of American Civilization,* Alfred A. Knopf, New York.

Launitz-Schurer, Leopold S., Jr., 1980, *Loyal Whigs and Revolutionaries: The Making of the Revolution in New York, 1765–1776,* New York University Press, New York.

Leng, Charles W., and Davis, William T., 1930, *Staten Island and Its People: A History, 1609–1929* (5 volumes), Lewis Historical Publishing, New York.

Levitt, James H., 1981, *For Want of Trade: Shipping and the New Jersey Ports, 1680–1783,* New Jersey Historical Society, Newark.

Main, Jackson Turner, 1965, *The Social Structure of Revolutionary America,* Princeton University Press, New Jersey.

Main, Jackson Turner, 1973, *The Sovereign States, 1775–1783,* New Viewpoints, Franklin Watts, New York.

McCusker, John J., and Menard, Russell R., 1985, *The Economy of British America, 1607–1789,* University of North Carolina Press, Chapel Hill.

Miller, George L., 1980, Classification and Economic Scaling of 19th Century Ceramics, *Historical Archaeology* 14:1–40.

Morris, Richard B. (ed.), 1982, *Encyclopedia of American History,* 6th ed., Harper & Row, New York.

Norton, Thomas Elliot, 1974, *The Fur Trade in Colonial New York, 1686–1776,* University of Wisconsin Press, Madison.

Phillips, Paul Chrisler, with Smurr, J. W., 1961, *The Fur Trade,* University of Oklahoma Press, Norman.

Schlesinger, Arthur M., 1968 (1917), *The Colonial Merchants and the American Revolution, 1763–1776,* reprint ed., Atheneum, New York.

Schwind, Arlene Palmer, 1984, The Ceramic Imports of Frederick Rhinelander, New York Loyalist Merchant, *Winterthur Portfolio* 19(1):21–36.

United States Bureau of the Census, 1976, *Bicentennial Statistics, Reprinted from Pocket Data Book, USA 1975,* United States Bureau of the Census, Washington, D.C.

Venables, Robert W., 1967, Tryon County, 1775–1783: A Frontier in Revolution, Ph.D. dissertation, Vanderbilt University, Nashville, Tennessee.

Zavin, Shirley (ed.), 1980, The Conference House, Staten Island, New York, report on file in the archives of the Staten Island Institute of Arts and Sciences.

3

Consumer Choices in White Ceramics

A Comparison of Eleven Early Nineteenth-Century Sites

SUZANNE M. SPENCER-WOOD AND
SCOTT D. HEBERLING

INTRODUCTION: THEORETICAL CONTEXT, PREVIOUS RESEARCH, AND HYPOTHESES

Social and economic stratification have long been interrelated by anthropologists and archaeologists (Adams 1966; Clark 1970:217, 221; Sahlins 1958). Since Binford stated that archaeological research on social structure was "one of the major areas of anthropological research yet to be developed" (Binford 1962:219), prehistoric archaeologists have increasingly studied social stratification, often in relation to economic stratification (Flannery and Coe 1968; Hill 1968; Hoffman 1974; Sanders and Webster 1978; Watson 1978). Historical archaeologists have recently developed new methods for measuring attributes of artifact assemblages that may be related to socioeconomic status (Miller 1980; Schulz and Gust 1983; Singer 1985). Within the context of reconstructing past lifeways (Binford 1968:12), this research investigates the possibility of distinguishing patterns of early nineteenth-century socioeconomic stratification among eleven United States archaeological sites on the basis of differences in the relative mean value of whiteware decorative types found at those sites, measured with Miller's ceramic indices (1980).[1] Ceramic indices were used to form a scale of sites ranked according to relative mean value of whiteware assemblages. Relative site positions on this scale were then contrasted and compared with documentary indications of socioeconomic status of

This chapter is an updated and expanded version of an article entitled Ceramics and Socioeconomic Status of the Green Family, Windsor, Vermont, by Suzanne M. Spencer-Wood and Scott D. Heberling, published in *Northeast Historical Archaeology*, Volume 13, 1984: 33–52.

[1]Miller's "ceramic" indices are concerned specifically with nineteenth-century white ceramics, termed *whiteware*.

Suzanne M. Spencer-Wood ☐ Department of Anthropology, University of Massachusetts, Boston, MA 02125. **Scott D. Heberling** ☐ Heberling Associates, Route 4, Box 20, Huntington, PA 16652.

site residents, in order to determine the relationship between value of white ceramics and social stratification. Relationships were also considered between relative mean value of household whiteware decorative types and market access, utilitarian foodways functions, and ethnicity.

Ceramic attributes have many functions that can be classified according to Binford's (1962) three categories of technomic, sociotechnic, and ideotechnic. Technomically, ceramics carry information about manufacturing techniques within the ceramic industry. Ceramic marks and patterns that can be traced to manufacturers permit delineation of the ceramic distribution system, resulting in site location differences in availability of goods. In their forms, ceramics yield information about their uses in food processing, preparation, consumption, and other aspects of foodways behavior. Within the basic limits of use, the same ceramic form could have different foodways functions in households with different ethnic food processing, preparation, or consumption patterns. Within a given ceramic form, decorative types, through price and fashion distinctions, convey information about social stratification. Some decorative types could only be afforded by the very wealthy, while more moderately priced ceramics could be acquired by all but the poorest among the working class and the unemployed. If some households did not use ceramics for status display, there may be a lack of correspondence or fit between a household's ceramic decorative types and its socioeconomic status. For example, although the English teaware imported to the United States carried status display information (Miller 1984:47), some Americans, for example, in non-English ethnic groups, might not display status through the decorative type and price of their teaware. Some particular ceramic decorations or forms may also convey ideology, possibly through the content of some scenes depicted in transfer prints, for example. These alternative meanings of ceramics were considered, and whiteware decorative types were chosen for analysis because of their hypothesized relationship to socioeconomic status (Miller 1980:11).

In the nineteenth century, the market economy, through the mechanism of ceramic prices, was a major cultural subsystem affecting household acquisition of ceramics, as well as the frequency of use and selective discard of ceramics. Most nineteenth-century households acquired most of their ceramics from those available in the market economy, although some may also have been received as gifts or heirlooms, or acquired through some form of secondary recycling. Some disenfranchised groups, such as slaves, did not directly purchase ceramics but were supplied with ceramics by the planter, who may have handed down old ceramics and/or purchased new ones for the slaves. In most cases, consumer selections of ceramics purchased from the range available in the market economy, are among the major cultural formation processes responsible for the archaeological record (Schiffer 1977). Ceramics are used in households for food processing, preparation, and eating, for status display, and possibly sometimes as ideological statements. Some of the ceramics used by a household may be lost or discarded in the yard around the house, while some ceramics may be deposited elsewhere by a household. Some ceramics may remain in the cultural system of the household for long periods or be passed to other locations in the cultural system through recycling mechanisms, such as inheritance within an extended family, gift giving, barter, or resale. Schiffer (1977) has considered theoretically the types of cultural formation processes affecting the relationships between the archaeological record and material culture in the cultural system.

The archaeologically recovered ceramics discarded or lost by a household on their site represent a partial sample of the ceramics used by the household. Selective household discard patterns and unavoidable biases due to whatever archaeological methods were used (since total recovery is never possible), result in partial and biased archaeological samples of ceramics. To some extent it may be possible to assess the representativeness of an archaeological ceramic sample from a house site by contrasting it with complementary documentary data, such as an extremely detailed probate inventory recording the non-archaeologically-deposited portion of the same household's ceramics. Since the documentary record is not necessarily less biased than the archaeological record, the different biases in each type of data may be determined to some extent by contrasting comparably detailed partial documentary and archaeological records of the same household's ceramics. More complete documentary data for some ceramic types may indicate lack of discard of these types in the archaeological record, while more complete archaeological data for other ceramic types may indicate less documentation and/or more discard of these types. For the primary research site of the Green Mansion, the archaeological whiteware assemblage was compared and contrasted with an unusually detailed probate inventory, both representing whiteware from the same household and time period. The pattern of correspondence, or fit, between these two complementary sources of data indicated some different, possibly systemic, types of bias in probate inventories, as contrasted to archaeological whiteware assemblages.

Establishing the relationship between whiteware decorative types in archaeological assemblages and socioeconomic status was the primary research objective. Whiteware decorative types were analyzed because they are related to price and therefore to socioeconomic status (Miller 1980:10–11), considered as the combination of the ability of afford certain decorative types, and the social status symbolized by the decorative types owned by a household. At the same time, the possibility was considered that ceramics could be acquired by a household simply for their utilitarian foodways functions, and not for their indications of status. It was hypothesized that ceramic forms with primarily utilitarian functions would not be of expensive decorative types. These ceramic forms that served primarily to display status were expected to include the household's most expensive ceramic decorative types. However, the possible relationships of whiteware assemblages to utilitarian foodways functions, to market access, and to ethnicity were also considered. For the Green site, the effects of selective discard on the archaeological whiteware assemblage were also considered. Other aspects of cultural behavior that may affect ceramic assemblages, such as religious or political affiliation, education, and personal preference could not be considered because they were unknown for most of the sites analyzed.

Archaeological samples of ceramics recovered on historic sites are the results predominantly of consumer choices of goods available in the market economy, and loss and selective discard patterns of the past inhabitants of those sites. Consumer selections of decorative types within a given ceramic form are influenced by an indeterminate number of interrelated factors, including site location and the availability of goods, occupation, ethnicity, economic level, social status, family size, religious and political affiliation, as well as individual preferences. The complex interaction of these and other factors affecting consumer decisions makes it difficult to understand fully the role of each variable. The problem is central to historical archaeology, since a major goal of the discipline is to reconstruct the lifeways of past societies on the basis of the material artifacts that they left behind, and to use this information to make general statements about cultural processes (Binford 1968). Consumer decisions are among the cultural formation processes responsible for the archaeological record (Schiffer 1977). Until more is known about the many factors that influence consumer behavior and the kinds of artifacts deposited and excavated, sophisticated archaeological interpretation is difficult.

In attempting to explain the reasons for variations among site archaeological assemblages, considered as partial biased samples indicating consumption patterns, most investigators have chosen to focus on only one or two variables. With this approach, the role of each variable can be determined as far as possible before a complex systemic model incorporating all of them is devised (Clarke 1978). The most desirable strategy is to hold factors such as site location constant while exploring the effect of one variable, such as socioeconomic status (cf. Spencer-Wood 1984). However, because of a scarcity of comparable studies, this is seldom possible. A frequent strategy is to isolate one variable for study and then delineate a pattern among sites. Once such a pattern is demonstrated, the roles of other factors can be addressed.

Major factors affecting consumer choices of goods later deposited at archaeological sites include ethnicity, market access, and socioeconomic status. Several studies have focused on the effect of ethnicity on ceramic and faunal consumption patterns indicated by archaeological data (Baker 1980; Baugher 1982; Greenwood, 1980; Langenwalter 1980; Otto, 1977, 1984; Schuyler 1980a). Others have been concerned with the effect of site location on market access and the availability of goods (Adams 1976; Miller and Hurry 1983; Riordan and Adams 1985; Schuyler 1980b, Spencer-Wood 1979). A few studies have explored the importance of family size and structure to consumer choices partially indicated by archaeological data (De Cunzo this volume; LeeDecker et al., this volume). However, a growing number of archaeologists have focused on the closely related variables of income, occupation, and social status and their effects on archaeologically indicated patterns of consumer behavior (De Cunzo 1982; Dyson 1982; Felton and Schulz 1983; McBride & McBride 1983;

Spencer-Wood 1984). The primary hypothesis of this research is that the mean value of archaeologically sampled whiteware is most strongly affected by socioeconomic status, despite other variables that could not be held constant.

The terms "status" and "class" are ambiguous and can be defined in many ways. Status is defined here as "the location of the behavior of individuals or the social positions of individuals themselves in the structure of any group. It is a defined social position located in a defined social universe" (Warner et al. 1949:253). Although the two concepts are not synonymous, there is a high degree of correlation between an individual's economic position and his ranked status within the society (Warner et al. 1949:39). Some archaeologists and other anthropologists have long related social status to economic division of labor (Clark 1970; Kaplan and Manners 1972:94–101). Studies in the United States found that status is best indicated by occupational category, followed by quality of house and residential area, in a factor analysis of nineteen status-related variables (Kahl and Davis 1955). If an individual's economic position can be determined, it usually is possible to predict his social status because occupation forms the basis of income, social interaction, leisure time, shared knowledge, and values of a social group (Barth and Watson 1967:394). Historians (Hershberg and Dockhorn 1976:60–68; Katz 1972:85, 87), economists (Engel et al. 1978:116; Martineau 1958) and sociologists (Hodges 1964:95; Reissman 1959:144) have considered occupation to be the most objective indicator of socioeconomic status, supporting this use by archaeologists.

A number of historical archaeologists have related archaeological ceramic assemblages to occupational status (De Cunzo 1982; Felton and Schulz 1983; Heberling 1985; Henry this volume; McBride and McBride, 1983; Morenon et al, 1982; Otto 1984; Raffa 1983; Shephard this volume; Spencer-Wood 1984). At some sites, ceramics have been analyzed in order to infer the status of site inhabitants whose occupations were poorly documented (Dyson 1982; Geismar 1982; Heberling this volume). A major objective of this study is to determine the possibility of using Miller's ceramic index to indicate status when insufficient documentation exists, by establishing a scale relating the relative value of whiteware assemblages and occupations documented for eleven early nineteenth-century sites.

Several studies have established strong relationships among occupation, income, wealth, and amount of consumer expenditure for durable goods and ceramics in both the twentieth and nineteenth centuries. Some economic anthropologists (cf. Douglas and Isherwood 1979:25, 116–119) consider wealth, usually determined by occupation, as a major factor in consumer selections of goods. Keynsian economic models, supported by twentieth-century data, espouse a directly proportional relationship between income and amount of consumer spending versus saving (Dunsenberry 1971; Heilbroner 1970:230). Recent research has established that income has a significantly nonrandom relationship to many consumer choices (Myers and Mount 1973). Living room furniture in its status display aspects was found to have high correlations with income, occupation, and education followed by lower correlations with other variables such as religion, ethnicity, and political affiliation (Laumann and

House 1970). For 1926 data, expenditures on dishes and glassware gradually increased with increasing income, although this expense formed a decreasing proportion of income after it reached the $1,800 to $2,100 range (Nystrom 1929:394). In Massachusetts during the 1870s, an "intimate" relationship was found between occupational income and degree of expenditure on necessities versus luxuries (Massachusetts Bureau of Statistics of Labor 1875:355). In the Boston area, correspondences were found between average probate inventory values of durable goods and total personal estate by occupational category in Quincy during the 1870s (Spencer-Wood and Riley 1981), and between average value for personal estates and total estates for six occupational categories in Quincy 1870–1900 (Spencer-Wood 1984). Research on probate inventories from the 1840s in St. Mary's County, Maryland, established that, although ceramics formed only a small percentage of total expenditures, the amount did increase proportionately with the value of movable goods, until this reached $1,500. After this "saturation point" for movable goods, ceramic values level-led off and no longer increased in proportion to increasing total inventory values (Herman *et al.* 1973:59–63). The concept of "saturation point" is called decreasing marginal utility by economists (Peterson 1977). These studies indi-cate strong relationships among occupation, income, wealth and consumer choices of durable goods, including ceramics.

The above studies suggest that other variables do not usually affect con-sumer choices as strongly as socioeconomic status. These studies support the use of ceramics from archaeological sites to indicate status. The importance of ceramics is due to their abundance on historic sites, their durability, and their role as status indicators (Deetz 1977:46; Miller 1980:10–11, 1984:47; Miller and Stone 1970:100; Stone 1970). The research discussed above indicates that individuals of higher economic and social status would usually have invested more of their economic resources in expensive ceramics than would indi-viduals of lower status. However, some wealthy families, particularly in oc-cupations such as farming, might choose to invest less than would be expected in ceramics due to competing investments in land and other goods. On the other hand, since both nineteenth- and twentieth-century studies indicate that investment in ceramics forms only a small proportion of total wealth, and the smallest proportion for the wealthy, it can reasonably be expected that most wealthy families could afford to make this small investment. In only a few cases is it expected that individual preferences or overextended investments in other goods would result in ceramic choices that are not related to occupational status.

In order to assess relationships between relative mean values of archae-ological whiteware assemblages and occupational status, the possible effects of differential discard must be considered. Although individual variation in discard behavior always affects the archaeological record in unpredictable ways, some patterns can be expected for different status levels. Discard of expensive whiteware is, in general, expected to increase with status due to larger numbers of these ceramics and their greater frequency of use with increased status. At the same time, in comparison to inexpensive whiteware, households are expected to discard fewer expensive ceramics, such as porcelain, due to the greater care expected in the less frequent use of expensive versus inexpensive whiteware. The less frequent discard of expensive whiteware, particularly by moderate- and low-status households, may result in ceramic index values differentiated more by relative quantities of moderate- and low-priced whiteware than by amounts of expensive whiteware. As wealth increases, it is expected that more ceramics of all kinds would be bought and discarded, resulting in more porcelain than moderate-status households, and more less expensive whiteware as well. However, the proportion of discarded expensive ceramics in the total assemblage, usually of whiteware, is expected to increase with wealth.

The research is concerned with relating the mean relative value of archaeological whiteware assemblages to variables affecting ceramic consumer choices. It is hypothesized that the variation in value among site ceramic indices can be accounted for by variations in occupational status, influenced in some cases by ethnicity and market access. The primary analysis involved comparing socioeconomic status and relative mean values for the whiteware assemblage from the Green site in Windsor, Vermont, excavated in 1983 by students at the University of Massachusetts at Boston, under the direction and supervision of the authors. In the next section, the Green family's socioeconomic status is first assessed through documentary analyses. Then the archaeological data and methods of analysis are described. In order to assess the relationship between occupational indications of status and Miller's ceramic price-scaling indices, eleven sites, including the Green site, are rank ordered by ceramic index. The ceramic index site rank order is compared and contrasted to the accompanying rank order of sites by residents' occupations, in order to assess the degree of correspondence or fit between the archaeological and documentary data. Secondarily, ceramic index site rank orders are compared with ethnicity and market access of site residents to determine the extent to which these variables also affect the mean values of archaeological whiteware assemblages. Market access, foodways utilization of ceramics, and ethnicity were considered as variables explaining possibly recurring conditions of disparity between the mean value of whiteware expenditures and occupational indications of status. These three variables are considered in this analysis because of their importance to consumer selections of ceramics. Although other variables might also be significant, their values are not available to be compared for all the sites. The variable of time is controlled within the short, twenty-two-year time span of 1824 to 1846, but other variables could not be controlled for the available comparative sites, although this is desirable and may be possible as more sites are analyzed.

The major methodological research problem is concerned with expected differential discard patterns for whiteware decorative types. For the Green site, it was possible to quantify some biases in the archaeological and documentary records by comparing and contrasting percentages of decorative whiteware types recovered archaeologically with percentages recorded in Isaac Green's unusually detailed probate inventory. For archaeological data, less discard of expensive than inexpensive whiteware was hypothesized. At the same time it was expected that the probate inventory would record expensive whiteware in more detail than inexpensive whiteware. Finally, the effect on ceramic indices of alternative methods of quantifying archaeological ceramics was also assessed.

THE GREEN FAMILY'S SOCIOECONOMIC STATUS

The Green Mansion site possessed an ideal combination of extensive documentation and a large whiteware assemblage in order to relate Miller's ceramic price-scaling indices to socioeconomic status. The elite socioeconomic status of the Green family is well documented in local histories, town meeting minutes, probate and land records, newspapers, tax lists, personal letters, and manuscript census schedules, which also were used to construct a mid-century economic profile of Windsor, Vermont, as the context for assessing the family's position in the community. The Green family maintained a fairly constant socioeconomic level, providing a control over this variable in relation to their ceramic consumer choices.

The Green Mansion site was located in Windsor, Vermont, a key market crossroads town with ready access to the national market. Further, Isaac Green was a dry-goods merchant with high access to ceramics at lower cost than that at which he sold them to his neighbors. Therefore the family's ability to acquire goods probably was limited only by their needs, their income, and their personal preferences, rather than by the availability of consumer items.

Isaac Green was a physician and dry-goods merchant who moved to Windsor from Leicester, Massachusetts, in 1788. He built the original section of the mansion in 1791, although additions were constructed in the following two decades and in the late 1840s. Within a short time, Green had firmly established himself among the local economic and social elite. Although he devoted much of his attention to his thriving dry-goods business, he was very active in a variety of business ventures; he served as director of both the Bank of Windsor and the Cornish Bridge Company, which operated the covered bridge across the Connecticut River between Windsor and Cornish, New Hampshire. He gradually accumulated a considerable amount of land in and around the town, much of which he acquired for speculative purposes or leased to tenants. Green served as a selectman seven times and held numerous other major and minor public offices as well. He was nominated for several state offices, and he was instrumental in the lobbying effort to bring the new Vermont State Prison to Windsor in 1807. He was related by marriage to Samuel Barrett, a leading Boston merchant, and to the artist John Singleton Copley. Among the furnishings in the Green Mansion were a Chippendale secretary, currently in Boston's Museum of Fine Arts, and two Copley portraits.

Isaac Green died in 1842, and at the death of his wife in 1847, the property passed to their son George. George B. Green began his career as a dry-goods merchant but retired in 1835 to devote his energy to farming and the raising of fruit. In the late 1840s, at the same time that he came into possession of the family home, he began to manufacture and market a popular brand of patent medicine, Oxygenated Bitters, which was sold at least as far away as Boston. He was not as active in public life as his father had been, but he, too, accumulated a large amount of real estate in Windsor. He also was a pillar of the local Congregational church.

Several years after George Green's death in 1866, the property passed to his daughter Ann, who owned it until her death in 1922. Except for a period of six years, when she was married, Ann Green lived alone in the house. For the next forty years, the property was used only as a summer residence by her two nieces, until it finally passed from the family in the late 1950s (Heberling 1985).

There is no doubt that the Greens were members of Windsor's economic elite. According to the federal census records, the average Windsor resident owned only $2,810 worth of property in 1860, and $2,718 worth in 1870, and in each year only 5 percent of the work force owned property worth at least $10,000. An additional 6 percent owned property valued at between $5,000 and $10,000 in 1860, while 11 percent fell within that range in 1870. Windsor's economic hierarchy was highly stratified, with the wealthiest ten men (comprising only 2.5 percent of all adult males) owning about 35 percent of the town's total property. At the bottom of the scale were those individuals owning less than $1,000 worth of property—53 percent of all adult males in 1860 and 57 percent in 1870. In both 1850 and 1860, George Green was the second largest landowner in town, with real estate valued at $18,000 and $23,500, respectively, and in the latter year he ranked third in the combined value of his real and personal property (United States Census Bureau 1850–1870).

At George Green's death in 1866, he owned at least $9,143 worth of property, although his cash apparently was not inventoried (Windsor Probate Records, 29:504). Isaac Green's estate was inventoried at $6,174.77 in 1844, and Ann Green owned property worth $21,957.90 at her death in 1922 (Windsor Probate Records 17:141, 74:563). All three family members can be placed near the top of the local socioeconomic hierarchy. The census and probate records indicate that they chose to invest the bulk of their economic resources in land rather than in tangible forms of personal property. Household goods accounted for 29 percent ($1,476), 18 percent ($1,395), and 12 percent ($1,298) of the combined value of real estate and personal property in the inventoried estates of Isaac, George, and Ann Green, respectively. These dollar amounts are close to the $1,500 value, after which the value of movable goods leveled off in St. Mary's County, Maryland, in the 1840s (Herman *et al.* 1973:59–60). Ceramics comprised 4.5 percent ($66.10) and 3.6 percent ($49.83) of the value of the household goods owned by Isaac and George Green (Windsor Probate Records 17:141, 29:504, 74:563). These seem high percentages for one of the wealthiest families in town, possibly because, as merchants, Isaac and George Green had unusually high access to ceramics. These data supported the expectation that the archaeological ceramic index would correspond to the Green family's relatively high status.

DATA AND METHODS

Data

The data included documented occupations and ceramic indices for eleven comparative sites. Besides the Green Mansion, these sites included a privy deposit, circa 1842–1850, of Manuel Diaz, a prominent merchant in Monterey, California (Mean Ceramic Date [MCD] 1846.5; Felton and Schulz 1983:3–13, 69–71); sites of the planter's kitchen, an overseer's house, and a slave cabin at Cannon's Point Plantation, St. Simon's Island, Georgia, 1793–1860 (MCDs 1815–1824; Otto 1980:5–7); Black Lucy's Garden, an indigent freed slave, 1815–45 (Baker 1980:31–32; Felton and Schulz 1983:77); the Skunk Hollow, New Jersey, Cluster B deposit dating circa 1798–1829 from the house of a freed black laborer and later a minister (Geismar 1982:17, 23–24, 47–51, 71, 186); the Franklin Glass Factory and Glassworker's house sites, Portage County, Ohio, 1824–1832; the Jonathan Hale Cabin, Summit County, Ohio, built by squatters in 1810, and occupied by the Hale farm family until 1830; and a circa 1800–1840 deposit from the Moses Tabbs tenant farm house in St. Mary's County, Maryland (Miller 1980:35–36; Miller and Hurry 1983:89–90). Although the amount of socioeconomic information varied, occupations were available for all of the site residents. Thus the ceramic index site rank orders were first compared and contrasted with corresponding occupational status site rankings. Because data were also available on variations in ethnicity and site location, indicating market access, the relationships of these two variables to ceramic indices and socioeconomic status was also considered. The analysis year was 1824 for all of the sites except Black Lucy's Garden and the Green Mansion, both 1833, and the Diaz merchant site, 1846. In this research, occupation and ceramic indices were determined for the Green Mansion, and ceramic indices were calculated for the Cannon's Point Plantation sites from Otto's dissertation (1975:205–217). The other data were drawn from the publications cited.

The primary research at the Green house site is concerned with the analysis of an archaeological sample of ceramics deposited in sheet refuse adjacent to the foundation of a large house in the small town of Windsor, Vermont. It is assumed that the ceramics were discarded or lost by the household living in the house and controlling its yard. This assumption seems warranted since there was only one neighboring structure, a dwelling that served as a school during part of the first half of the nineteenth century. The house was located on a hill, with a long set of stairs to the front door, a steep bank behind the house, a cemetery on the south side and a dwelling, or school, to the north. Thus the limited difficult access to the site argues against deposition on the site by nonhousehold members, who would have to make a special effort to do so. The archaeologically recovered ceramics, as in other cases, represent a partial sample of some of the ceramics used and discarded or lost predominantly by the household. The archaeological sample suffers from the normal biases of selective discard and archaeological recovery techniques that can never recover all deposited data. Given these normative archaeological conditions, the ceramics represent a partial and biased sample of the Green household's ceramics that were probably predominantly acquired through the economic system, particularly since the head of household was a merchant.

The ceramics analyzed from the Green Mansion site were recovered from twenty excavation units, each three feet square, located near the surviving structures on the site. The surviving house structure, historic maps, and ethnographic information on recent and planned land alterations all afforded information affecting the stratification of the site into areas with different archaeological potential. Those strata with highest potential and most threatened by future land alterations were sampled first, supplemented by additional units when heavy sheet refuse deposits were located. The sampling strategy was designed within the constraints of time and manpower to provide a maximum ceramic sample, most probably discarded by the household.

The vast majority of the ceramics were found in ten excavation units placed along the foundation of a structure dating to the 1840s, an area which was the location of a large deposit of building debris and household refuse. Other units were placed around a small addition dating to about 1810. The Mean Ceramic Date of the assemblage was 1821.1, corresponding well with the median date of 1828.5 for the most intensive occupation of the Green site between 1791 and 1866. After 1866 the Green house never was occupied by more than one or two individuals at any time. Further, these individuals apparently were extremely fastidious about the appearance of the property, and were unlikely to have disposed of refuse in close proximity to their home (Carroll 1983). In contrast, Isaac Green was the head of a family of six and George Green of a family of seven, and boarders and servants lived in the households of both men between 1791 and 1866. Therefore, it was expected that the ceramic assemblage recovered during excavation would date primarily to the early nineteenth century. This expectation proved to be warranted, since the vast majority of ceramic sherds are creamware and pearlware. In addition, observation of the artifacts indicate that most of the ceramics were of types, designs, and colors manufactured in the early nineteenth century.

The possibility that all the ceramics could have been discarded or lost by Isaac Green's family is supported by Isaac's probate inventory, which lists most of the types of ceramic discarded, including stone china. In addition, since George Green probably inherited his father's ceramics, it is likely that many of his discarded ceramics actually represented earlier purchases by Isaac Green. This possibility is supported by some listings of the same ceramic types in Isaac and George Green's inventories, with smaller quantities in George's than Isaac's inventory. Since Miller's index values are relative prices of ceramics, they pertain to acquisition date rather than discard date. The archaeological and documentary evidence indicates that most of the ceramics in the archaeological assemblage are of types acquired and owned by Isaac Green, as indicated in his probate inventory. It is also possible that George Green could have acquired and discarded some of the same kinds of ceramics owned by his father, particularly some of the ironstone or stone china excavated (Collard 1984:125–126). Since the ceramics were not segregated into strata that could be temporally distinguished by artifact type frequencies as belonging to George rather than Isaac Green's family, it was necessary to treat the entire assemblage as a single unit. Although Isaac and George Green's time span of seventy-five years could be considered rather long for the accurate application of Miller's indices, all of the ceramics could have been acquired in the early nineteenth century, so the ceramic assemblage could not be subdivided into smaller groups corresponding to the occupation period of each owner.

Methods

The relationship between the mean value of archaeological whiteware assemblages and socioeconomic status was assessed by comparing and contrasting the rank order for eleven site ceramic indices (Miller 1980) with their accompanying occupational status rankings. Through research into nineteenth-century English whiteware prices, Miller developed three ceramic price-scaling indices for calculating the relative value of cups and saucers, plates, and bowls in archaeological whiteware assemblages. Miller's indices are based on the value of various whiteware decorative types relative to the value of the cheapest ware available, undecorated creamware, in specific years in the nineteenth century. For each year with price data, ratios were calculated of the price of each decorative type to the price of undecorated creamware, the cheapest whiteware. Ratio values were calculated for three types of forms: plates, bowls, and cups and saucers. An index was calculated for each form by multiplying the vessel number for each decorative type by its ratio value to creamware. Then the total product for all decorative types was divided by the total vessel count to calculate a weighted mean ratio value index for each ceramic form. A combined vessel form index was also calculated by adding the total products for the three indices and dividing by the combined vessel number. Because Miller's ceramic indices are weighted mean ratios, determination of the significance of a site's index requires its comparison with indices at other sites to establish the scale for each index. Site occupations need to be documented in order to assess the possible correspondence between the ceramic index value scales and socioeconomic status. Miller's ceramic indices are potentially valuable tools for inferring social stratification by comparing the relative values of whiteware assemblages from different sites.

The relative value of the Greens' whiteware was assessed from the rank order of the site's ceramic indices compared to ten other sites. Sites were rank-ordered first by the ceramic index value representing the mean value of cups and saucers, plates, and bowls combined. Ceramic index site rank orders were compared with the resulting occupational site rank order to determine whether variations in the ceramic index values could be accounted for by site differences in socioeconomic status. In a second analysis, sites were rank-ordered according to their cup and saucer ceramic index values because these were found to correspond best to the occupational status site rank order. The effects of differential market access and black ethnicity were secondarily considered in relationship both to socioeconomic status and intersite variations in ceramic index values.

The methods of ceramic index calculation varied among sites, but are basically comparable. For the Green site, pearlware was categorized as white-glazed (Miller 1980:32), while for most other sites it was grouped with creamware, sometimes due to lack of differentiation in data recording (Felton and Schulz 1983:74–80; Otto 1975:205–217). In a test on five Boston area sites, calculation of ceramic indices with pearlware classified either as white-glazed or creamware caused very little variation (at the .01 level) in the weighted mean value. Thus these different recording methods probably do not significantly affect the index values. Felton and Schulz calculated ceramic indices for the Cannon's Point Plantation, Diaz, and Black Lucy sites, excluding ironstone, porcelain, and other types when values were not available in the index year. Recalculation of the three Cannon's Point site indices, including these ceramic types with the value available nearest to the index year, resulted in some changes in ceramic index values but little change in site rank orders. At most, the different calculations resulted in a shift of two positions in a given ceramic index rank order. Because ceramic indices are weighted means, differences in quantities of decorative types must be quite large to result in any substantial variation in the mean. Thus, despite minor differences in data base, such as the inability to separate all platters from plates for the Cannon's Point sites (Otto 1975:205–217), or the differentiation of handled and un-handled cups from the Diaz Privy (Felton and Schulz 1983:76), the ceramic index values for all eleven sites are considered comparable. The sites were also basically comparable in terms of time period. The scale values for 1824 were applied to the whiteware from eight of the eleven sites, while 1833 values were used at two sites and 1846 values in one case.

Although the documented median date of intensive occupation for the Green site is 1829, Miller does not provide ceramic scale values for that year. The closest years for which scale values are provided are 1824 and 1833, and it was decided to use the 1833 values since these would be more effective in taking into account the site's continued light occupation after 1866. For decorative types without assigned relative values for 1833, the value for the year closest to 1833 is used. For example, it is necessary to use 1858 scale values for ironstone bowls because 1858 is the earliest year for which such values are provided. In some cases, the decorative type values used for cups and saucers and for plates were averages of two or three years representing possible acquisition dates before or after 1833. These methods seem preferable to the ceramic index distortion produced by simply excluding wares for which index values are not provided in the appropriate year. Several other adjustments have been made to Miller's technique. First, since most of the vessels are far too fragmentary to indicate their original dimensions, the scale values for the various sizes of plates have been averaged for each decorative type to produce a single plate value. Similarly, it is usually impossible to determine whether or not a cup originally possessed a handle, so the values of each decorative type for cups—handled, not handled, and not given—as well as saucer values, have been averaged to produce a single cup and saucer value. Despite these limitations, the Green site yielded a large sample of whiteware, increasing the reliability of the ceramic indices calculated.

Since relatively few vessels could be reconstructed from the Green site assemblage, two methods of vessel counting were used in two ceramic index analyses. First, vessels were counted on the basis of distinctive rims. Second, distinctive vessels were determined from both rims and body sherds that represented different vessels from any of the rims, due to distinct shape, glaze, and/or design color. Ceramic indices were calculated from each vessel count to determine whether the more complete vessel count based on both distinctive rims and body sherds would yield a substantially different index value than that calculated from rims alone. An average ceramic index value was calculated by each method from the combined cup and saucer, plate and bowl indices. The total vessel index, calculated by each method, included shapes such as pitchers and unidentifiable vessels that fit into none of Miller's categories, but could be related to status as much as cups, plates, or bowls. For these other vessel shapes, an index value was calculated from the mean whiteware decorative type values for cups and saucers, plates and bowls. This index value for other shapes was then averaged with the index values for cups and saucers, plates, and bowls to yield the total vessel index. In the last analysis, the mean whiteware decorative type values for cups and saucers, plates, and bowls were used to calculate the Green site ceramic index from sherd counts. The sherd index was compared and contrasted with the vessel indices to determine differences to be expected using these alternative methods.

The last analysis was a comparison of the percentages of decorative whiteware types recovered archaeologically with percentages of identified and quantified types in Isaac Green's unusually detailed inventory. This analysis indicated some of the different biases in the archaeological and documentary records. This comparison was undertaken because the decorative types recovered were the same ones listed in Isaac Green's inventory, indicating that they could have been acquired by his family. Although some of the whiteware could have been acquired by George Green, the lack of detail in most of his inventoried ceramic listings makes this impossible to determine. A few of the itemized ceramics in George Green's inventory suggest the inheritance and discard of ceramics acquired by Isaac's family. A listing of 2½ dozen custard cups in Isaac Green's inventory is paralleled by the unusually detailed listing for George Green's inventory of 1⅓ dozen custard cups, suggesting some additional discard by George's family. Other similar listings found in both inventories include one chamber set, a fruit dish, three ewer and basin listings, and a number of stone jars and churns. It is also possible that these similar listings represent different items bought by each family. George Green's inventory does list two pairs of vases and CC chambers that are not listed in Isaac Green's inventory. The lack of detail in George Green's inventory does not permit an assessment of the whiteware decorative types his family acquired. Because the Mean Ceramic Date of 1821.1 and artifact examination indicate that all of the ceramics could have been acquired by Isaac Green's family, decorative type percentages in Isaac's probate inventory were contrasted with archaeological percentages in order to assess discard and recording biases.

Results

Figure 1 represents the rank order of eleven early nineteenth century sites based on the average index value for cups and saucers, plates, and bowls combined. Although in some cases documentation on the sites' inhabitants is not very complete, their relative status can be basically inferred from their occupations. Among site average ceramic indices, the Green Mansion site ranks near the top of the scale, surpassed only by the Cannon's Point planter site and the Diaz merchant site. The Cannon's Point planter and Manuel Diaz were individuals of documented high socioeconomic status, as were Isaac and George Green. The sites with scale values falling below that of the Green site were occupied mainly by slaves, free blacks, and whites of relatively low occupational status. The position of the Green site on the scale is where it was expected to be, based on the documentary evidence. The average ceramic index scale generally corresponds with the occupational status rankings, indicating

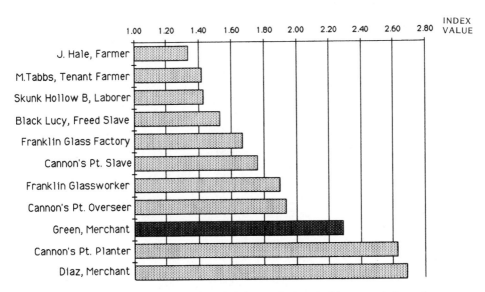

Figure 1. Vessel ceramic indices for eleven sites ranked by mean index value.

a strong relationship between the relative mean value of site assemblage decorative types and socioeconomic status.

The mean index value of a whiteware assemblage is more influenced by the cup and saucer index value than by the plate or bowl index values. This is due to the significantly higher values for all decorative types of cups and saucers, compared with plates or bowls. Since the amount of ceramics, including cups and saucers, increases with wealth, the more tea- and coffeeware owned by a household, the higher its value, and therefore, the more its value influences the mean whiteware value. Another possible factor in higher ceramic indices with more cups and saucers is sample size. Larger archaeological samples, being more representative than small samples, should usually yield more expensive, highly decorative types in proportion to low-valued whiteware. Four of the five highest ranking sites have sample sizes of between 94 and 211 vessels, while the sample sizes of the lower-ranked sites generally decline with their ranking. However, low ceramic index values are produced for low-status sites with moderate as well as small samples, since little status ware is present at these sites. In addition, the highest ranked Diaz merchant had a sample size of 74, indicating the representativeness of this sample size.

Figure 2 is based on a ranking of ten sites by the ceramic index values of their cups and saucers, shown in black. The Cannon's Point slave site has been eliminated from this figure because of its similarity to the overseer ceramic indices, and its non-status-related methods of ceramic acquisition. Cup and

Figure 2. Indices for cups and saucers, plates, and bowls at ten sites rank-ordered by cup and saucer index.

saucer indices were used to rank-order the sites because they corresponded most with occupational status rankings. The higher the economic level of a household, the more tea- and coffeeware it could afford of expensive and decorated types. In contrast, plates and bowls more often served utilitarian than status display functions. It will be noted that, among the ten sites, the ceramic index values for bowls have a narrow range of variation ranging from 1.18 for Skunk Hollow cluster B, to 1.68 for the Diaz merchant. Since the index values are so similar, mainly falling between 1.18 and 1.37, the relative value of bowls in an assemblage does not seem to be an accurate status indicator. The index values for plates exhibit a greater range of variation, from 1.23 for the Hale Cabin, to 2.69 for the Cannon's Point planter. Both extremes appear to be unusual, since the remaining assemblages all have plate indices falling between 1.46 and 1.99. By far the greatest range is in cup and saucer index values, which vary from 1.44 for the Tabbs House, to 3.59 for the Diaz Privy. The ranking of sites is similar to that in Figure 1, but there is a much wider gap between the two extremes, and the scale conforms more to what the documentary record indicates about the status of the inhabitants. The latter point is illustrated by Table 1, which ranks all eleven sites by the scale values for each vessel form. While the ranking of sites by cup and saucer indices corresponds in most cases to documented occupational status differences, ranking by plate or bowl indices is much less satisfactory. These results indicate that most plates and bowls have a primarily utilitarian function, while the primary status display function of cups and saucers yield index site rankings that often correspond to their occupational status.

In contrast to other sites, the Cannon's Point Plantation site ceramic indices did not all correspond well with their occupational status differences. The particular relationships among these sites offer an explanation for their unusual indices. The exceptionally high cup and saucer index for the Cannon's Point slave is due to whiteware handed down from the planter and/or overseer, as indicated by shared patterns and types of ceramics, including porcelain. The unusually high cup and saucer, and plate index values for both the overseer and the slave are due in part to shared transfer printed patterns from the planter's site (Otto 1975:162–173). Similarly, all three sites have unusually low bowl index values. The apparent contradiction between the planter's top rank order among plate indices, and his third rank order among cup and saucer indices may be due to the effects of the variable of site location. Felton and Schulz (1983) pointed out that, because the planter lived in a rural environment, he may have been more likely to invite guests for complete meals rather than for tea alone, and this may have caused him to invest in expensive flatware instead of tea- and coffeeware. Individuals living in more urban environments, such as Manuel Diaz and the Green family, may have tended to invest in tea- and coffeeware because of their different social needs. Felton and Schulz suggest that "the Diaz vessel pattern (high average values of tea and coffee wares relative to other vessel forms) represents status spending" and is indicative of high economic position (Felton and Schulz 1983:83), although it should be added that this may be true only for urban and semiurban

Table 1. Rank Order of Sites by Ceramic Index for Each Vessel Form and Their Average

Site, occupation, state	Index year	Ceramic index average value	Total number of vessels
Average ceramic index rank order			
Diaz, merchant, CA[a]	1846	2.69	74
Cannon's Pt., planter, GA	1824	2.63	211
Green, merchant, VT	1833	2.29	94
Cannon's Pt., overseer, GA	1824	1.94	105
Franklin Glass Factory, worker, OH[b]	1824	1.90	94
Cannon's Pt., slave, GA	1824	1.76	92
Franklin Glass Factory, OH[b]	1824	1.67	62
Black Lucy, freed slave, MA[a]	1833	1.53	58
Skunk Hollow B, black laborer, NJ[c]	1824	1.43	64
M. Tabbs, 2, tenant farmer, MD[b]	1824	1.42	16
J. Hale, farmer, OH[b]	1824	1.34	45

Site, occupation, state	Cup and saucer ceramic index values	Number of vessels
Cup and saucer ceramic index rank order		
Diaz, merchant, CA[a]	3.59	35
Green, merchant, VT	3.04	40
Cannon's Pt., planter GA	2.78	77
Cannon's Pt, slave, GA	2.36	22
Cannon's Pt., overseer, GA	2.24	35
Franklin Glass Factory, worker, OH[b]	2.15	33
Franklin Glass Factory, OH[b]	2.11	21
Black Lucy, freed slave, MA[a]	1.68	17
Skunk Hollow B, black laborer, NJ[c]	1.53	11
J. Hale, farmer, OH[b]	1.45	17
M. Tabbs, tenant farmer, MD[b]	1.44	3

Site, occupation, state	Plate ceramic index value	Number of vessels
Plate ceramic index rank order		
Cannon's Pt., planter, GA	2.69	121
Cannon's Pt., overseer, GA	1.99	51
Diaz, merchant, CA[a]	1.92	34
Cannons's Pt., slave, GA	1.90	36
Franklin Glass Factory, worker, OH[b]	1.86	44
Green, merchant, VT	1.83	35
Black Lucy, freed slave, MA[a]	1.61	25
Skunk Hollow B, black laborer, NJ[c]	1.51	36
Franklin Glass Factory, OH[b]	1.47	33
M. Tabbs, tenant farmer, MD[b]	1.46	8
J. Hale, farmer, OH[b]	1.23	20

Table 1. (*Continued*)

Site, occupation, state	Bowl ceramic index value	Number of vessels
	Bowl ceramic index rank order	
Diaz, merchant, GA[a]	1.68	5
Green, merchant, VT	1.59	19
Franklin Glass Factory, worker, OH[b]	1.54	17
Franklin Glass Factory, OH[b]	1.37	8
J. Hale, farmer, OH[b]	1.36	8
M. Tabbs, tenant farmer, MD[b]	1.29	5
Black Lucy, freed slave, MA[a]	1.24	16
Cannon's Pt., overseer GA	1.23	19
Cannon's Pt., planter, GA	1.23	13
Cannon's Pt., slave, GA	1.23	34
Skunk Hollow B, black laborer, NJ[c]	1.18	17

[a]Felton and Schulz 1983:3–13, 74–77
[b]Miller 1980:35–37.
[c]Geismar 1982:17, 23–24, 44–51, 71, 186.

sites. In addition, the higher cup and saucer index value for the Diaz site compared to the Cannon's Point planter is due to the greater amounts of transfer printed tea- and coffeeware at the Diaz site, and its effect on the ceramic index. The Green family's whiteware exhibit many of the characteristics of the "Diaz vessel pattern." The similarities between the two assemblages may well be a result of the inhabitants' similar positions as successful merchants belonging to the local social and economic elite living in semiurban settings.

Although the variation in archaeological ceramic index values, particularly for cups and saucers, corresponds most to variations in socioeconomic status, in some cases the variables of ethnicity and market access are related both to occupational status and to ceramic consumer behavior. The low status of the black ethnic sites is evident in occupational status as well as ceramic index values. For these cases, ethnicity strongly influences socioeconomic status and its relationship to mean values of archaeological whiteware assemblages. In the case of the Cannon's Point Plantation slave site, unusually high cup and saucer and plate indices are due to handed down whiteware from the planter, and do not represent ceramics chosen from the market on the basis of the slaves' ability to afford them.

Socioeconomic status, rather than market access, accounts for most of the variation among site ceramic index values. Most of the sites had relatively high market access, due to nearby water transportation to either the East or West Coast cities where English ceramics were imported into the United States. In the cases of the Green and Diaz sites, higher market access accompanies the occupation of merchant, permitting these individuals to obtain high-status whiteware at a lower cost than people with other occupations.

High values, both for market access and socioeconomic status, reinforce each other, producing two of the highest ceramic index values. In contrast, in the case of the Jonathan Hale site, documentary research has established that the residents' social status and wealth in land was not reflected in whiteware because of the difficulty of market access from Ohio to the East Coast and England before the Erie Canal was constructed across the Allegheny mountain barrier in 1825 (Miller and Hurry 1983). In addition, because Hale site residents were farmers, they probably had less need for status display through ceramics than did the merchant and planter occupations that were highly ranked. In most cases, occupational status accounts for the variation among site ceramic index values. Black ethnicity is related both to low-status occupations and low mean ceramic index values, while high market access reinforced the high status and ceramic indices of the two merchants (Table 1, Figures 1 and 2).

The possibility was considered that the application of scale values for years other than 1833 might alter the position of the Green assemblage in the ranking. To explore this possibility, assemblage scale values for five different years have been calculated. Again, if values for certain decorative types were not provided by Miller for a given year, the figures for the nearest year were used. As can be observed in Table 2, the use of different scale years has a noticeable effect on the resulting scale values, but it does not alter the relative position of the Green assemblage in the site ranking. The steady decline in value, as successively later index years are used, is quite interesting and seems to be attributable almost completely to the declining value of the plate group. As Table 2 demonstrates, the relative values of other forms remain very stable, regardless of the index year used. The decline of the plate group is due to the declining relative values of its three most common types: edged, transfer-printed, and ironstone. The decline in the relative value of plates over time and the stability of other vessel forms should be remembered when applying the index to assemblages containing large numbers of plates, since the selection of appropriate index years would seem to be particularly important in these cases. In this instance, the different assemblage values, obtained by the use of different scale years, do not change the Green site's ranking among

Table 2. Green Mansion Ceramic Index Values, 1814–1870

	Number of vessels	1814	1824	1833	1846	1870
Bowls	19	1.59	1.58	1.59	1.59	1.53
Plates	35	1.99	1.85	1.83	1.68	1.41
Cups and saucers	40	3.04	3.04	3.04	3.01	2.89
Other	11	1.85	1.83	1.83	1.78	1.76
Average value for bowls, plates, and cups and saucers	94	2.35	2.30	2.29	2.22	2.06
Average value for all vessels	105	2.30	2.25	2.25	2.18	2.05

the eleven sites for any of the indices except for plates, due to the rapid decrease in this index value over time. Therefore, the comparison of the Green site assemblage to assemblages that have been scaled by 1824 or 1864 index values does not seem to present a serious problem.

For the Green site, all methods of calculating a minimum vessel count generated similar ceramic indices and the same site rank (Table 3). A minimum combined vessel count for cups and saucers, plates, and bowls, based strictly on rim types, yielded a minimum of 94 vessels and a ceramic index of 2.29, compared with the count for rims and distinctive sherds of 107, and an index of 2.32. Although a vessel count derived from the use of the first method is used here for the purpose of intersite comparison, ceramic indices were calculated using other methods of vessel counting, and a sherd count, in order to determine whether the use of different techniques would produce significantly different results in assemblage index values. Average vessel indices were calculated for all distinct vessels, including other or unidentifiable forms as well as cups and saucers, plates, and bowls, using the average scale values for Miller's three indices. The count of all vessels based on 105 rims produced a scale value of 2.25, while the vessel count based on distinctive rims and body sherds (127) resulted in a value of 2.24. Although a little variation in the average ceramic index was produced by alternative methods of vessel counting, the Green site's rank order remained the same.

In contrast, when a ceramic index is calculated from a sherd count, the resulting index value is 1.65, which would have placed the assemblage far down the scale, between Black Lucy's Garden and the Franklin Glass Factory. This low sherd index is due to the high proportion of 75 percent of the total 4,551 sherds in the assemblage that were creamware or pearlware, in contrast to the 16 percent of sherds that were ironstone. In contrast, of the total vessel count, 24 percent was ironstone and only 17 percent creamware or pearlware, resulting in the higher vessel indices. This low sherd index is due to the higher number of plain sherds per vessel of creamware or pearlware compared to ironstone. This is due both to the larger number of small sherds produced by creamware and pearlware than ironstone vessels, and the fact that some decorated pearlware and creamware vessels, such as shell edged, yielded many more plain pearlware sherds than edged sherds. The differences between sherd and vessel ceramic index values indicate that they should not be compared with each other. In addition, the disparities between relative frequencies of decorative types of sherds versus vessels may yield a site rank order for sherds that is not related to socioeconomic status to the same extent as are vessel indices.

Biases in the archaeological and documentary records are indicated by comparing and contrasting percentages of archaeological versus inventoried whiteware (Table 4). A comparison of Isaac Green's inventory with the whiteware assemblage indicates that his family was careful with its porcelain, discarding little of the numerous sets recorded in his inventory. However, there is a large difference between the ceramic index values of low- to moderate-status versus high-status occupations, supporting the hypothesis that

Table 3. Green Mansion 1833 Ceramic Index Calculations

Form	Type	Index years used	Vessel count A[a]			Vessel count B[b]		
			No.	× Value =	Product	No.	× Value =	Product
Cups and saucers	CC	1814, 1802	2	× 1.22 =	2.44	2	× 1.22 =	2.44
	White-glazed	1814	2	× 1.67 =	3.34	2	× 1.67 =	3.34
	Sponged	1871	3	× 1.17 =	3.51	5	× 1.17 =	5.85
	Painted	1814, 1824	6	× 1.70 =	10.20	7	× 1.70 =	11.90
	Printed	1814, 1824	9	× 3.22 =	28.98	11	× 3.22 =	35.42
	Ironstone	1856, 1858, 1881	12	× 3.98 =	47.76	13	× 3.98 =	51.74
	Porcelain	1824, 1857, 1875	6	× 4.20 =	25.20	7	× 4.20 =	29.40
Subtotal for cups and saucers			40		121.43	47		140.09
Mean value of cups and saucers				3.04			2.98	
Bowls	CC	1833	7	× 1.00 =	7.00	7	× 1.00 =	7.00
	Dipped	1833	1	× 1.29 =	1.29	2	× 1.29 =	2.58
	White-glazed	1814	2	× 1.60 =	3.20	2	× 1.60 =	3.20
	Sponged	1855	–		–	1	× 1.10 =	1.10
	Painted	1833	1	× 1.71 =	1.71	1	× 1.71 =	1.71
	Printed	1833	1	× 2.57 =	2.57	2	× 2.57 =	5.14
	Ironstone	1858	6	× 2.00 =	12.00	6	× 2.00 =	12.00
	Flow	1855	1	× 2.40 =	2.40	1	× 2.40 =	2.40
Subtotal for bowls			19		30.17	22		35.13
Mean value of bowls				1.59			1.60	

	Dates	Count	Vessel Count A[a]		Count	Vessel Count B[b]	
Plates							
CC	1833	5	× 1.00 =	5.00	5	× 1.00 =	5.00
Edged	1833, 1824	9	× 1.34 =	12.06	9	× 1.34 =	12.06
Printed	1833, 1824	8	× 2.86 =	22.88	11	× 2.86 =	31.46
Willow	1833, 1836	1	× 2.20 =	2.20	1	× 2.20 =	2.20
Ironstone	1858, 1861	12	× 1.82 =	21.84	12	× 1.82 =	21.84
Subtotal for plates		35		63.98	38		72.56
Mean value of plates			1.83			1.91	
Other							
CC		2	× 1.07 =	2.14	4	× 1.07 =	4.28
Printed		1	× 2.88 =	2.88	2	× 2.88 =	5.76
Painted		1	× 1.88 =	1.88	6	× 1.88 =	11.28
Edged		2	× 1.34 =	2.68	2	× 1.34 =	2.68
Flow		3	× 2.40 =	7.20	4	× 2.40 =	9.60
Underglaze-lined		2	× 1.69 =	3.38	2	× 1.69 =	3.38
Subtotal for other		11		20.16	20		36.98
Mean value of other			1.83			1.85	
Total for assemblage		105		235.74	127		284.76
Mean value of assemblage			2.25			2.24	
Total cups and saucers, plates, and bowls		94		215.58	107		247.78
Mean ceramic index value			2.29			2.32	

[a] Vessel Count A is determined by rim decoration.
[b] Vessel Count B is determined by presence of demonstrably different types, regardless of presence or absence of rims.

wealthier households would discard relatively more porcelain than lower-status households. It is interesting that, in the case of the Greens, this higher level of discard still represented much less frequent discard of porcelain than of less expensive whiteware. The archaeological ceramic index values are lower than was expected from Isaac Green's probate inventory, principally because only a few porcelain vessels and relatively few porcelain sherds were excavated, compared to the relatively large quantity and high value of stone china listed in the inventory. Of the excavated whiteware, porcelain comprised only 6 percent of the vessel count and 0.6 percent of the sherd count, in contrast to 24 percent porcelain among the inventoried whiteware. Even taking into consideration that some inventoried ceramics were not counted or identified, this large discrepancy between excavated and inventoried proportions of porcelain indicates that the Greens were taking better care of porcelain than other whiteware, and discarding a smaller proportion of porcelain than they owned. The 24 percent ironstone vessels in the archaeological assemblage indicates much more discard of the 13 percent stone china vessels listed in Isaac Green's probate inventory (Table 4). Ironstone was probably used every day, resulting in more breakage and discard in contrast to the probably less used and discarded porcelain. Another possible explanation for this disparity is that not all the vessels owned were properly identified and counted. This may explain the difference between the 21 percent archaeological transfer-printed vessels and the 8 percent inventoried. Because stone china was relatively expensive, indicating status, it is more likely to be specified in the inventory than the less expensive transfer-printed, edged, and undecorated wares. Several listings of "blue," "green," and "brown" dishes could have been transfer-printed, but were not so specified. In contrast, the archaeological percentage of creamware is a little smaller than the inventoried percentage, indicating relatively less discard of this inexpensive ware than the expensive stone china. The apparently low discard of creamware also could be due to the standard archaeological method of making minimum vessel counts, in which sherds that cannot be visually distinguished are counted as the same vessel when they could be from matching vessels.

Table 4. Percentages of Archaeological and Inventoried Ceramics from the Green Mansion

Ceramic type	Isaac Green's inventory		Archaeological assemblage	
	Percentage	Vessel no.	Percentage	Vessel no.
Porcelain	24	162	6	7
Ironstone	13	90	24	31
Creamware	20	141	14	18
Printed	8	57	21	27
Other whiteware	35	239	35	44
Total	100	689	100	127

Table 5. Value of Archaeological and Inventoried Ceramics from the Green Mansion

Ceramic type	Isaac Green's inventory		Archaeological assemblage	
	Percentage	Value	Percentage	CI Value[a]
Porcelain	24	$17.82	10	29.40
Ironstone	43	$31.15	30	85.58
Creamware	9	$ 6.75	7	18.72
Printed	4	$ 3.03	28	79.98
Other whiteware	20	$14.45	25	71.08
Total value of ceramics	100	$73.20	100	284.76

[a]CI Value (Ceramic Index Value) = the product of the frequency of each ceramic decorative type multiplied by the value of that type used in calculating the ceramic index (Table 3). Each ceramic decorative type's CI Value is divided by the total value of ceramics to produce the percent of the archaeological assemblage's total value.

A second comparison was made between percentages of decorative type values contributing to the total vessel ceramic index, versus the total value of inventoried whiteware. Compared to the numerical relative frequencies, there is less difference between the percentage contributions of porcelain, ironstone, and creamware to the sum of value products in the total vessel ceramic index, and to the total value of inventoried whiteware. Although the archaeological porcelain is still a smaller proportion of the ceramic index than of the inventoried whiteware, the difference is smaller. The proportional contribution of ironstone to the ceramic index is less than its percentage of the total inventoried white ceramic value, while the percentage of creamware is nearly the same. The greater contribution of transfer-printed to the ceramic index value than to the inventoried white ceramic value may be due to underrecording of this type in the inventory. This comparison indicates that the Green site ceramic indices are lower than is indicated by the inventoried whiteware (Table 5).

CONCLUSIONS

This analysis has demonstrated that relative economic status can be indicated in most cases by calculating Miller's price-scaling ceramic index for cups and saucers alone. This indicates a primary status display function for tea- and coffeeware, in contrast to the combination of possibly status-related tableware and more utilitarian kitchenware plates and bowls that function in food processing and preparation. The ranking of sites by cup and saucer indices seems to be much more accurate than ranking them by plate or bowl indices, and even more accurate than ranking them by total assemblage indices, although the cup and saucer values strongly influence the relative value of the combined assemblage ceramic index. Even in the case of the Cannon's Point planter, with higher ceramic index values for plates than for cups and saucers, the latter index value identifies him as a person of comparatively high economic status in relation to the other site inhabitants. The results of this research suggest a strong relationship between occupation and archaeological assemblages of whiteware decorative types, particularly for cups and saucers. This relationship may often permit the inference of the relative socioeconomic status of site residents from the relative value of whiteware assemblages, especially cups and saucers, when documentary data are not available.

It has been demonstrated that the relative socioeconomic position of the Green family could have been determined, in the absence of extensive documentation, by applying Miller's ceramic price-scaling indices to their archaeologically recovered whiteware. Although the Greens chose to invest the bulk of their economic resources in land, they still spent a relatively high proportion of their income on ceramics. A high degree of correspondence was found between the mean value of the Green's archaeological whiteware assemblage and documentary data on their relative wealth.

The results of this research are particularly interesting because they indicate that, in many instances, the variation in archaeological ceramic index values can be accounted for by variations in occupational status that are not contravened by differences in market access and ethnicity, although these variables may act in conjunction. Only at the Jonathan Hale site was market access more important than socioeconomic status in limiting the mean value of an archaeological whiteware assemblage. This type of recurring circumstance can be identified, as well as sites representing groups that are not choosing their ceramics from the market, such as the Cannon's Point Plantation slaves. In this case, the archaeological evidence of the same decorative patterns at the planter and slave sites indicated some recycling of whiteware from the planter to the slaves. Further research may establish those recurring conditions in which market access and other variables have more effect than socioeconomic status on the types of decorative whiteware archaeologically recovered from domestic sites.

Alternative methods of analysis were shown to affect ceramic index values to some extent. At the Green site, alternative methods of vessel counting resulted in small variations in ceramic index values. Calculations using different index years produced very little variation in cup and saucer, and bowl ceramic index values, and a decline in plate indices and average ceramic index values. The Green site rank order remained the same for different index years and methods of vessel counting. In contrast, a significantly lower ceramic index value was produced by using sherd counts from the Green site. This indicates that sherd and vessel ceramic indices do not necessarily yield comparable results for early nineteenth-century sites.

The Green site also permitted a case study in the quantification of archaeological and documentary biases. Comparison of percentages of porcelain, ironstone, creamware, and transfer printed whiteware in the archaeological assemblage with those in Isaac Green's detailed probate inventory indicated that a very small proportion of porcelain was discarded in contrast to a relatively large proportion of ironstone. In the probate inventory, underrecording of transfer-printed, edged, and other inexpensive types was apparent (Table

4). One possible explanation for the smaller proportion of archaeological versus inventoried creamware is the standard archaeological method of making minimum vessel counts, in which sherds that cannot be distinguished are considered as one vessel, when they could be from matching vessels. In contrast to percentages of decorative types of vessels in the archaeological and documentary records, the proportional contributions of porcelain, ironstone, and creamware values to the total vessel ceramic index value were more similar to the percentages these wares contributed to the total value of inventoried whiteware (Table 5).

Miller's ceramic price-scaling indices will be more useful when there are a large number of sites for which scale values have been calculated by comparable methods, for this will greatly enhance its predictive and interpretive capability. In the present case, it was possible to gather comparable data on only a relatively small number of sites, all of which were similar chronologically but were scattered from Massachusetts to Georgia, Ohio, Michigan, and California. This geographic scattering may introduce variables unrelated to the socioeconomic status of the inhabitants, and makes the sites less than ideal for comparison. It would be best to compare sites for which variables such as time period, geographic location, and ethnicity are identical. The development of a ceramic index ranking scale for a large number of thoroughly documented site assemblages, with greater variable control in all parts of the United States and Canada, would greatly increase understanding of the relationship between archaeological whiteware assemblages, socioeconomic status, and other variables.

Nonetheless, the primary finding of this research was a correspondence, in most cases, between rank orders for occupational status and for both cups and saucers, and total vessel ceramic indices. Although site locations ranged across the United States, the research results indicate that relative mean values of archaeologically sampled whiteware decorative types are usually more strongly related to socioeconomic status than to market access, in some cases because of similar access due to analogous site locations. Market access was seldom more of a limiting factor in the value of whiteware than was socioeconomic status. The highest ceramic indices were generated for site residents with both high socioeconomic status and high market access. The effect of ethnicity is apparent in occupational status and is therefore largely incorporated in this variable. The conjunctive effect of two variables often reinforced similar decorative type choices. A large difference in ceramic index values for moderate- versus high-status households was found to correspond to expected differential discard patterns. This large difference also suggests the possibility of aggregating sites into status groups indicated by relative value of archaeologically recovered whiteware decorative types as Miller's ceramic indices are applied to more sites.

ACKNOWLEDGMENTS

The authors would like to thank Larry Bowser and Holly Taylor for enthusiastically facilitating the excavation of their property, the Green Mansion site. Thanks also to the students of the University of Massachusetts field school, who provided most of the data for this research. Laura Genberg deserves special thanks for her continued assistance in every phase of the project. Particular thanks also to Windsor residents Emma Carroll and Katherine E. Conlin for their invaluable historic information on the Green family.

REFERENCES

Adams, Robert McC., 1966, *The Evolution of Urban Society: Early Mesopotamia and Prehispanic Mexico,* Aldine, Chicago.

Adams, William H., 1976, Trade Networks and Interaction Spheres—A View from Silcott, *Historical Archaeology* 10:99–112.

Baker, V. G., 1980, Archaeological Visibility of Afro-American Culture: An Example from Black Lucy's Garden, Andover, Massachusetts, in: *Archaeological Perspectives on Ethnicity in America* (R. L. Schuyler, ed.), Baywood Publishing, Farmingdale, New York, pp. 29–37.

Barth, Ernest A. T., and Watson, Walter B., 1967, Social Stratification and the Family in Mass Society, *Social Forces* 45:392–402.

Baugher, S., 1982, Hoboken Hollow: A 19th Century Worker's Housing Site, *Northeast Historical Archaeology* 11:26–38.

Binford, Lewis R., 1962, Archaeology as Anthropology, *American Antiquity* 38:217–225.

Binford, Lewis R., 1968, Archaeological Perspectives, in: *New Perspectives in Archaeology* (Sally R. Binford and Lewis R. Binford, eds.), Aldine, Chicago, pp. 5–32.

Carroll, Emma, 1983, personal communication.

Clark, Grahame, 1970, *Archaeology and Society,* Barnes & Noble, New York.

Clarke, David L., 1978, *Analytical Archaeology,* Columbia University Press, New York.

Collard, E, 1984, *Nineteenth Century Pottery and Porcelain in Canada,* McGill-Queen's University Press, Montreal.

De Cunzo, Lu Ann, 1982, Households, Economics and Ethnicity in Paterson's Dublin, 1829–1915: The Van Houten Street Parking Lot Block, *Northeast Historical Archaeology* 11:9–25.

Deetz, James F., 1977, *In Small Things Forgotten: The Archaeology of Early American Life,* Anchor, New York.

Douglas, M., and Isherwood, B., 1979, *The World of Goods,* Basic Books, New York.

Dusenberry, J. S., 1971, Income–Consumption Relations and their Implications, in: *Readings in Macroeconomics* (M. G. Mueller, ed.), Holt, Rinehart & Winston, New York, pp. 61–76.

Dyson, S. L., 1982, Material Culture, Social Structure, and Changing Cultural Values: The Ceramics of Eighteenth- and Nineteenth-Century Middletown, Connecticut, in: *Archaeology of Urban America* (R. S. Dickens, Jr., ed.), Academic Press, New York, pp. 361–380.

Edwards, Alba M., 1939, *A Social Economic Grouping of the Gainful Workers of the United States,* U.S. Government Printing Office, Washington, D.C.

Engel, James F., Blackwell, Roger D., and Kollat, David T., 1978, *Consumer Behavior,* Dryden Press, Hinsdale, Illinois.

Felton, D. L., and Schulz, P. D., 1983, *The Diaz Collection: Material Culture and Social Change in Mid-Nineteenth Century Monterey,* California Archaeological Report 23, California Department of Parks and Recreation, Sacramento.

Flannery, Kent V., and Coe, Michael D., 1968, Social and Economic Systems in Formative Mesoamerica, in *New Perspectives in Archaeology* (S. R. Binford and L. R. Binford, eds.), Aldine, Chicago, pp. 103–142.

Geismar, J. H., 1982, *The Archaeology of Social Disintegration in Skunk Hollow, A Nineteenth-Century Rural Black Community,* Academic Press, New York.

Greenwood, Roberta S., 1980, The Chinese on Main Street, in: *Archaeological Perspectives on Ethnicity in America* (R. L. Schuyler, ed.), Baywood Publishing, Farmingdale, New York, pp. 113–123.

Heberling, Scott D., 1985, "All the Earthenware Plain and Flowered": Socio-economic Status and
    Consumer Choices in Ceramic on Early Nineteenth Century Historic Sites, unpublished M. A.
    thesis, University of Massachusetts, Boston.
Heilbroner, R. L., 1970, *The Economic Problem,* 2nd ed, Prentice-Hall, Englewood Cliffs, New
    Jersey.
Herman, Lynne L., Sands, John O., and Schecter, Daniel, 1973, Ceramics in St. Mary's County,
    Maryland During the 1840's: A Socioeconomic Study, *The Conference on Historic Site Archae-
    ology Papers* 8:52–93.
Hershberg, Theodore, and Dockhorn, Robert, 1976, Occupational Classification, *Historical Meth-
    ods Newsletter* 9:59–98.
Hill, James N., 1968, Broken K. Pueblo: Patterns of Form and Function, in: *New Perspectives in
    Archaeology* (S. R. Binford and L. R. Binford, eds.), Aldine, Chicago, pp. 103–142.
Hodges, Harold M., Jr., 1964, *Social Stratification: Class in America,* Schenkman Publishing,
    Cambridge, Massachusetts.
Hoffman, M. A., 1974, The Social Context of Trash Disposal in an Early Dynastic Egyptian Town,
    American Antiquity 39:35–49.
Kahl, Joseph A., and Davis, James A., 1955, A Comparison of Indexes of Socio-economic Status,
    American Sociological Review 20:317–325.
Kaplan, David, and Manners, Robert A., 1972, *Culture Theory,* Prentice-Hall, Englewood Cliffs,
    New Jersey.
Katz, Michael B., 1972, Occupational Classification in History, *Journal of Interdisciplinary Histo-
    ry* 3:63–88.
Langenwalter, Paul E., II, 1980, The Archaeology of 19th Century Chinese Subsistence at the
    Lower China Store, Madera County, California, in: *Archaeological Perspectives on Ethnicity
    in America* (R. L. Schuyler, ed.), Baywood Publishing, Farmingdale, New York, pp. 102–112.
Laumann, Edward O, and House, James S., 1970, Living Room Styles and Social Attributes: The
    Patterning of Material Artifacts in a Modern Urban Community, *Sociology and Social Re-
    search* 54:321–324.
Martineau, Pierre, 1958, Social Classes and Spending Behavior, *Journal of Marketing* 23:121–
    130.
Massachusetts Bureau of Statistics of Labor, 1875, *Public Document Number 31: Sixth Annual
    Report of the Bureau of Statistics of Labor,* Wright & Potter, State Printers, Boston.
McBride, K. A., and S. W. McBride, 1983, An Examination of Status from Two Perspectives, in:
    Oral Historical, Documentary and Archaeological Investigations of Barton and Vinton, Mis-
    sissippi: An Interim Report on Phase II of the Tombigbee Historic Townsites Project (C. E.
    Cleland and K. A. McBride, eds.), submitted by Anthropology Division, Michigan State Uni-
    versity, to National Park Service, Mid-Atlantic Region, Philadelphia.
Miller, George L., 1980, Classification and Economic Scaling of 19th Century Ceramics, *Historical
    Archaeology* 14:1–41.
Miller, George L., 1984, George M. Coates, Pottery Merchant of Philadelphia, *Winterthur Portfolio*
    19:37–49.
Miller, George L., and Hurry, Silas D., 1983, Ceramic Supply in an Economically Isolated Frontier
    Community: Portage County of the Ohio Western Reserve, 1800–1825, *Historical Archae-
    ology* 17(2):80–92.
Miller, J. Jefferson, and Stone, Lyle M., 1970, Eighteenth-Century Ceramics from Fort
    Michilimackinac: A Study in Historical Archaeology, *Smithsonian Studies in History and
    Technology* 4.
Morenon, P. E., Cook, L., Callahan, K., Huntington, J., Kroian, C., LaCroix, D., and Stachiw, M.,
    1982, *Archaeological Excavations at the Jere Tabor House Site, Triverton, Rhode Island,*
    Public Archaeology Program at Rhode Island College, Occasional Paper in Anthropology and
    Geography 9.
Myers, James H., and Mount, John F., 1973, More on Social Class vs. Income as Correlates of
    Buying Behavior, *Journal of Marketing* 38:71–73.
Nystrom, Paul H., 1929, *Economic Principles of Consumption,* Ronald Press, New York.
Otto, John S., 1975, Status Differences and the Archaeological Record—A Comparison of Planter,

Overseer, and Slave Sites from Cannon's Point Plantation (1794–1861), St. Simons Island, Georgia, unpublished Ph.D. dissertation, University of Florida.

Otto, John S., 1977, Artifacts and Status Differences: A Comparison of Ceramics from Planter, Overseer and Slave Sites on an Antebellum Plantation, in: *Research Strategies in Historical Archaeology* (S. South, ed.), Academic Press, New York, pp. 91–118.

Otto, John S., 1980, Race and Class on Antebellum Plantations, in: *Archaeological Perspectives on Ethnicity in America* (R. L. Schuyler, ed.), Baywood Publishing, Farmingdale, New York, pp. 3–13.

Otto, John S., 1984, *Cannon's Point Plantation, 1794–1860: Living Conditions and Status Patterns in the Old South,* Academic Press, New York.

Peterson, Willis L., 1977, *Principles of Economics: Micro,* Richard D. Irwin, Homewood, Illinois.

Raffa, Joan H., 1983, Ceramics and Status: The Critical Links, 1832–1872. A Study in Historical Archaeology, unpublished M.A. thesis, University of Massachusetts, Boston.

Reissman, Leonard, 1959, *Class in American Society,* Free Press, New York.

Riordan, Timothy B., and Adams, William H., 1985, Commodity Flows and National Market Access, *Historical Archaeology* 19(2):5–18.

Sahlins, Marshall, D., 1958, *Social Stratification in Polynesia,* University of Washington Press, Seattle.

Sanders, William T., and Webster, David, 1978, Unilinealism, Multilinealism and the Evolution of Complex Societies, in: *Social Archaeology: Beyond Subsistence and Dating* (C. L. Redman, W. T. Langhorne, Jr., M. J. Berman, E. V. Curtin, N. M. Versaggi, J. C. Wanser, eds.), Academic Press, New York.

Schiffer, Michael B., 1977, Toward a Unified Science of the Cultural Past, in: *Research Strategies in Historical Archaeology* (S. South, ed.), Academic Press, New York, pp. 13–40

Schulz, Peter D., and Gust, Sherri M., 1983, Faunal Remains and Social Status in 19th Century Sacramento, *Historical Archaeology* 17(1):44–53.

Schuyler, Robert L., 1980a, *Archaeological Perspectives on Ethnicity in America,* Baywood Publishing, Farmingdale, New York.

Schuyler, Robert L., 1980b, Sandy Ground and Archaeology of a 19th Century Oystering Village, in: *Archaeological Perspectives on Ethnicity in America* (Robert L. Schuyler, ed.), Baywood Publishing, Farmingdale, New York, pp. 48–59.

Singer, David A., 1985, The Use of Fish Remains as a Socio-Economic Measure: An Example from 19th Century New England, *Historical Archaeology* 19(2):110–113.

Spencer-Wood, S., 1979, The National American Market in Historical Archaeology: Urban Versus Rural Perspectives, in: *Ecological Anthropology of the Middle Connecticut River Valley* (R. Paynter, ed.), Research Reports 18, Department of Anthropology, University of Massachusetts, Amherst, pp. 117–128.

Spencer-Wood, S., 1984, Status, Occupation, and Ceramic Indices: A Nineteenth Century Comparative Analysis, *Man in the Northeast* 28:87–110.

Spencer-Wood, S., and Riley, Julian A., 1981, The Development of an Urban Socio-economic Model for Archaeological Testing, *Northeast Historical Archaeology* 10:41–51.

Stone, Garry W., 1970, Ceramics in Suffolk County, Massachusetts, Inventories, 1680–1775, *Conference on Historic Sites Archaeology Papers* 3:73–90.

United States Census Bureau, 1850–1870, Manuscript Population Schedules for Windsor, Vermont, for the Seventh, Eighth and Ninth Censuses of the United States, U. S. Government Printing Office, Washington, D.C.

Warner, W., Lloyd, Marchia Meeker, and Eells, Kenneth, 1949, *Social Class in America: A Manual of Procedure for the Measurement of Social Status,* Science Research Associates, Chicago.

Watson, Patty Jo, 1978, Architectural Differentiation in Some Near Eastern Communities, Prehistoric and Contemporary, in: *Social Archaeology: Beyond Subsistence and Dating* (C. L. Redman, W. T. Langhorne, Jr., M. J. Berman, E. V. Curtin, N. M. Versaggi, J. C. Wanser, eds.), Academic Press, New York.

Windsor, Probate Records, 1842–1922, Bound Volumes in Windsor County Probate Court Office, Woodstock, Vermont.

4

Threshold of Affordability

Assessing Fish Remains for Socioeconomics

DAVID A. SINGER

INTRODUCTION

Numerous historical and zooarchaeological studies have focused upon food-ways, butchering, marketing, and their connections to status (Anderson 1971; Davidson 1982; Honerkamp 1981; Lyman 1977, 1979; Miller and Lewis 1977; Reitz 1984; Rothenberg 1980). More general dietary studies have been based upon probate inventories (McMahon 1980). Bowen (1978) has integrated probate analysis with zooarchaeology and agricultural history; Graffam (1982) has synthesized the historical and archaeological evidence of food acquisition, preparation, storage, and consumption. Singer (1982a) has integrated probate, accounts, and archaeological data to produce coastal and inland patterning in fish consumption.

Fish remains can be adversely affected by sampling techniques and recovery biases (see Casteel 1972, 1976). During an experimental study in recovery techniques, the author noted that a minimum of 75 percent of all herring-sized bones were lost using one-quarter-inch mesh screen, a factor that can greatly affect the interpretation of the importance of fish in diet.

The scope of this research is to demonstrate that fish remains may be used to indicate socioeconomic status. This assessment is based upon the development of weighted mean rank values that allow identified species of fish to be assigned a fractional dollar value, expressed as a threshold of affordability. A lower threshold is indicative of a lower socioeconomic level.

The statement of research is a discussion of the importance and goals of this study. This is followed by a terse presentation of consumer theory, and the variables that affect consumer choices. The documentary data and methods section presents a replicable format through which data collection and analytical methodology may be reproduced. The section on archaeological methods includes a discussion of butchering pattern and skeletal ratio analysis. The archaeological data from each of four sites is briefly described and analyzed, and socioeconomic evaluations of the assemblages follow each site. A summation of the success, advantages, limitations, and need for further research concludes this study.

David A. Singer ☐ 187 Thacher Street, Milton, MA 02187.

STATEMENT OF RESEARCH

The apparent high rate of success, in many dietary studies, in indicating status supports both the applicability and accuracy of the use of faunal remains as a reliable indicator of socioeconomic status. Deetz (1977) noted that foodways of social classes had significant differences. It is therefore feasible that, as in the case of mammalian remains, fish remains may also be used to indicate economic status.

A cursory study on this subject has been recently introduced, and has had promising results (Singer 1985). The present study is an expansion and refinement of the previous work, and appears to support the contention that fish remains may be useful for indicating socioeconomic levels.

Socioeconomic evaluations are based upon accurate identifications of fish present, and observations of butchering marks found on skeletal elements. The presence or absence of specific species or cuts of fish may increase the visibility of an existing pattern, and may allow individual, group, or class distinctions to be made. The presence of butchering marks is an important parameter for distinguishing the various forms in which fish were acquired or prepared. When butchering data is integrated with the array of skeletal elements present or absent from the archaeological assemblage, it may be determined whether a fish was acquired as a portion or purchased whole and subsequently prepared as a cut. The distinction may be significant because, oftentimes, when fish were purchased as cuts (i.e., steak), costs were higher per pound (one cent) than whole fish.

It is logical to hypothesize a relationship between income, status, and foods. Faunal materials are relatively steadfast indicators of socioeconomic status in that food prices may oscillate but seldom decrease. Furthermore, food remains are unlikely items for use in the display of status. These items have little status visibility, and as such, should reflect income more closely. Conversely, ceramic wares have high-status visibility. A household may overextend its financial resources on occasion to acquire fanciful items; ceramics have a considerable lifespan. However, it is not possible for that same household to overextend its income level to continuously consume food products that are beyond its threshold of affordability. Again, unlike ceramics, food is a necessary daily expense, one that can only be sustained within the limits of household finances. While luxurious food items may appear in the diet of a lower-status household, these occurrences will be infrequent. The threshold of affordability, therefore, is a proposed measure of food expenditures. It is defined as the average price per pound that a household can afford to spend.

CONSUMER THEORY

Central to the function of pricing is the ability to measure product values and reflect consumer preferences through various stages of marketing systems. The quantity of goods purchased is affected by changes in market variables—number of buyers, income levels, personal preferences, price, availability, and quality. A study of market prices provides a window through which consumer preferences and economic trend can be viewed.

Expenditures change as incomes change. Consumers will purchase more goods at a lower price than at a higher one. It is not necessarily true that an increase in income will result in the purchase of more expensive goods, but possibly only more lower-priced goods. For example, McCoy (1972) noted that hamburger may be considered an inferior product by people of higher income, who would probably eat less of it if their income were to increase. However, people with lower incomes would probably increase hamburger consumption if their income were to increase.

The difficulty in assessing socioeconomic status from food items arises when unobservable changes occur in one or more market variables. From the list of variables cited above, the only change that can be uniformly observed and documented is price. Fortunately, given price, we may make a number of assumptions or inferences regarding the other variables. For example, if the price of a food item is low, we may infer that the product is widely available, the number of buyers moderate to high, and income levels are sufficient to bring the product within reach of most consumers. However, a low price may also reflect some degree of indifference towards the product (no preference), and may raise some questions regarding quality. Generally, a low price is designed to reach a large target population. A high price, on the other hand, may indicate a scarcity of the product, higher production costs, higher quality, and/or fewer buyers with higher income levels. For example, the high cost of caviar is not a reflection of product scarcity; it is designed to appeal to an elite target population. The market is apparently sufficient to produce high profits. One's income level need only be conducive to its acquisition, assuming one has a personal or social preference for it. For those who can afford it, quality is an important issue; a lower-grade pressed roe may be purchased for, say, $230 per pound, while premium Beluga must be purchased for $350 per pound. But to the uninitiated, quality is not an issue because prices are nearly prohibitive in either grade category. These same expenditures could procure 50 to 100 pounds of choice-quality beef, veal, or pork. This example illustrates that consumer choices are a function of many variables, although the most important determining factor is probably income level.

Those who attempt to assign socioeconomic values to zooarchaeological assemblages should work within a framework of culturally derived norms. Once normative values have been established, lower, or higher deviations will be more apparent. A valid approach to value measurement is indexing. Livestock management studies use this system to measure and predict the behavior of market variables (McCoy 1972). If we treat zooarchaeological materials as extensions of a price index network, more accurate information can be extrapolated from these remains, and interpreted values can be distributed to the originators of the assemblages. By producing methods by which we may measure and explain consumer behavior, we may be in a better position to evaluate the varied manifestations of socioeconomic status.

Documentary Data and Methods

The documentary data upon which this study is based consisted of nineteenth century wholesale and retail market prices in the Northeast. Over 120 newspapers from this region, primarily representative of the Boston market during the 1832–1887 period, were examined (Singer 1983). Each species of fish listed in the market quotations was noted and arranged in a descending order, thus creating a ranking scheme based upon price per pound (Table 1). While actual prices fluctuated within the period of study, the position of the various species relative to one another within the index framework remained more or less stable. Only in a few instances were juxtapositions noted, and these were of little apparent significance. Frequently, price per pound was listed within a range (i.e., salmon $.50–$.70); each occurrence of this type of listing was assigned a mean price.

Modifications based upon the relative rank market index have produced a more refined measure of market ranking. The weighted mean index (Table 2) is the product of fractional dollar values per pound. These values are interpreted as the threshold within which a household can afford to expend for food items. Values are calculated by multiplying cost per pound by the quantity of fish of that species producing a subtotal. Subtotal calculations are figured for each species, which are then summed and divided by the total

Table 1. Relative Rank Market Index of Fish in the Northeast, 1832–1887

High (.20–.70)	
Salmon	Lake trout
Spanish mackerel	Pickerel
Brook trout	
Middle (.10–.19)	
Black bass	Eel
Striped bass	Shad
Mackerel	Tautog
Halibut	Freshwater perch
Whitefish	Bluefish
Swordfish	Sturgeon
Low (.01–.09)	
Herring	Hake
Scup/porgy	Pollack
Cod	Flounder
Cusk	Saltwater perch
Haddock	Smelt

Table 2. Weighted Mean Index for Fish in the Northeast, 1832–1887

Fish	Mean value	Fish	Mean value
Salmon	.60	Freshwater perch	.11
Spanish mackerel	.50	Bluefish	.10
Brook trout	.47	Sturgeon	.10
Lake trout	.22	Herring	.09
Pickerel	.21	Scup/porgy	.08
Black bass	.18	Cod	.07
Striped bass	.16	Cusk	.07
Mackerel	.15	Haddock	.06
Halibut	.15	Hake	.06
Whitefish	.15	Pollack	.06
Swordfish	.13	Flounder	.05
Eel	.13	Saltwater perch	.02
Shad	.12	Smelt	.01
Tautog	.11		

number of fish and/or cuts in the collection. For example, in an assemblage containing 4 shad and 3 bluefish, a weighted mean value of .11 is obtained:

$$\frac{4(.12) + 3(.10)}{7} = .11$$

The threshold of affordability is then compared with the relative rank market index to provide an interpretation of this economic level of expenditure, which in this instance is middle class.

While a random examination was made of eighteenth-century newspapers, these yielded no economic data that could be used in the construction of an index. In the absence of documentary prices for this period, it was assumed that, while actual prices were certainly different from those of the nineteenth century, rank order would be comparable. This assumption is subjected to testing in the economic analysis of fish remains from two eighteenth-century sites.

Differential pricing of cuts within a species have been noted in the nineteenth century (viz., whole cod at $.06 per pound; cod steaks at $.07 per pound). Similar occurrences have also been noted for halibut fins and napes. Prices for fish heads were not documented. However, an investigation of current prices for cod and haddock heads yielded a range of $.25 for a small-to-medium-size head and $.50 for a large one. When these prices are contrasted with that for flesh ($3.99 per pound), it is evident that heads are valued at approximately 12 percent of that for flesh. When considering the relatively low price for cod and haddock in the nineteenth century, 12 percent of this value, to estimate the cost of heads, seemed unwarranted; indeed, this figure would be negligible. Heads were therefore generously allotted a value of two cents, or approximately 30 percent flesh value. During a recent study by the author, it was noted that a large head could yield approximately 1 to 3 pounds of flesh.

Threshold analysis can also be applied to a range of food items, and can be compared and contrasted to assess the stability of food expenditures within a household through time, on an intersite or intrasite level. Calculated values for one form (fish) may be used to predict values for other forms; predicted values can then be converted into actual food items with corresponding values, and tested archaeologically.

Archaeological Methods

Butchering Patterns

Butchering practices can oftentimes be noted on fish bones. The various forms in which fish were acquired and prepared can be discerned by an examination of these marks, in conjunction with the presence or absence of specific skeletal elements. Culinary practices can become altered through time, with the change in availability of particular fish, fluctuating prices, or personal taste. These practices also differ with the size, thickness, and shape of the fish, frequently dictating the methods in which the fish is to be butchered or prepared. Different cuts of fish can further determine the manner in which the fish is to be cooked. For example, small fish may be bought, prepared, and pan-fried whole, while medium-sized fish may be acquired as fillets for baking, and large fish as steaks for broiling.

A fish acquired in steak form would produce an assemblage of relatively large trunk or caudal vertebrae only. The first few anterior vertebrae will not be present, as they are postcranial attachments to the unaccompanying head. The acquisition and preparation of whole fish in steak form would produce an assemblage of cranial and postcranial elements. In both cases, the vertebrae may display a dorso–ventral steaking cut at the point of knife or cleaver impact. The discard of fish that had been acquired whole or drawn would contain cranial and postcranial elements. Fish purchased dressed would produce vertebrae only, as head, tail, and fins were removed previously. These vertebrae may exhibit two dorsal cranio–caudal dress cuts, along either side of the neural spine or fin ray, where the fin has been cut away from the body. Fish acquired whole and subsequently dressed might be distinguished by the presence of cranial and postcranial elements; vertebrae may also exhibit the dress cut. Fish purchased whole and prepared as fillets would produce an assemblage of cranial and postcranial elements. In addition, the vertebrae may display a dorsal, cranio-caudal, primary fillet incision where the fillet was prepared by a split along the top of the backbone; vertebrae may also exhibit a lateral cranio–caudal secondary fillet mark where the fillet has been cut away from the fish. Forms acquired as heads only, for stews or chowders, would produce an assemblage exclusively of cranial and pectoral elements, supplemented by few anterior trunk vertebrae. Vertebrae of this form would not display any butchering marks, save a lateral dorso–ventral heading cut at the locus where the head was severed from the body. Splitting a fish for the purpose of broiling will result in a ventral, cranio–caudal split on the vertebrae.

The use of the butchering unit as the analytic unit, rather than the minimum number of individuals (MNI) count, produces a more accurate assessment of meat yields, and further provides a method for which socioeconomic evaluations can be made. Generally, a household will acquire a cut rather than a unit, as the former offers least cost and least mass.

Skeletal Ratio Analysis

Portions of fish may be discerned by noting differences between cranial and postcranial elements (Singer 1982b). The total number of cranial elements can be contrasted against the number of vertebrae a species of fish is known to possess. In fishery studies, pleomerism is the correlation of the number of vertebrae a fish possesses to its body length. This correlation has been confirmed, with little deviation, in the Atlantic mackerel (MacKay and Garside 1969). Lindsey (1975) has stated that this tendency occurs among related species.

By adapting these studies for archaeological use, it becomes a simple matter to count the cranial elements and compare these with known vertebral counts for various species (see Lindsey 1975). It is then possible to produce a standardized ratio of cranial to postcranial elements in known species of fish. By quantifying these ratios in archaeological materials, we may assess whether whole fish or portions of fish are present, based upon a harmonious or discordant representation. For example, one may utilize fourteen paired cranial and pectoral elements as a source for comparison, yielding twenty-eight elements for the standard ratio. Should haddock be the species undergoing analysis, we are provided with a mean vertebral count of fifty-four. These figures then become the standard ratio (1:2) for comparison with archaeological materials (haddock). If an assemblage is determined to contain six haddock, a skeletal ratio analysis should reveal that 168 cranial/pectoral and 324 vertebrae can be expected, if each fish is represented by whole individuals, and preservation, sampling techniques, and recovery biases are not factors for loss or error. In this example, fifty-two cranial and seventeen vertebral elements are present. When the expected numbers are compared with the actual numbers, the archaeological remains are seen to constitute only 31 percent of the cranial and 5 percent of the vertebral elements (3:1). The question of how many individuals must be re-posed. In our traditional way of thinking, establishing an individual count of six may be correct; that is, six right elements document six distinct fish. However, whether these fish are whole individuals or parts of individuals needs to be further explored. In actuality, these six individuals most probably represent fish heads.

Fish remains from historical assemblages have undoubtedly undergone erroneous analyses, similar to the example given above. The limited amount of research in this area is due to lack of knowledge of it. It is important that future analyses take into account these methodologies to prevent inflating or deflating the importance of this item, projected biomass, and assessing socioeconomic levels. In the previous example, six haddock would reflect a .06 threshold of affordability. Heads may have been acquired for probably less than two cents each. Recalculation of the weighted value produced a .03 threshold. Although in both cases these ratings reflect a low socioeconomic level, a .03 rating may be interpreted as one of meager existence.

This form of analysis has potential as a method for relating fish consumption to economic status. Its use and applicability in conjunction with noted butchering data can provide much needed information on material representation, butchering patterns, and socioeconomic evaluations. For fish, the butchering unit appears to have superior value to the traditional MNI count. It provides more information and is better equipped to yield accurate socioeconomic data.

ARCHAEOLOGICAL DATA ANALYSIS

Fish remains recovered from four archaeological assemblages, dating from circa 1730–1885, were identified and analyzed. The identification of fish fauna was made on the basis of contemporary comparative materials in the author's collection. Assemblages consisted of both identifiable and unidentifiable bone counts; subassemblages pertain to identifiable materials only. All percentages refer to subassemblages. Two collections originated from Portsmouth, New Hampshire, and two from Charlestown, Massachusetts.

Rider-Wood Site

The Rider-Wood House site, located in Portsmouth, New Hampshire, was excavated in 1981 under the direction of Gray Graffam. This excavation was part of an ongoing educational research program sponsored by Strawberry Banke, a Portsmouth, New Hampshire firm. The assemblage was an accumulation of material with a date range of 1830–1840, and was attributed to a widow residing in an economically depressed area (Graffam 1981). The collection of fish remains was recovered from an estimated 10 percent sampling of a wood-lined privy. Archaeological materials were water-sorted through window screen, resulting in the recovery of small bones and seeds. The biological materials were in an excellent state of preservation due to water saturation of the privy.

The collection comprised 261 fish bones, of which 54 percent (140) were identifiable to a family or species level. One family of fish was identified, *Gadidae*. This family contained *Melanogrammus aeglefinus* (haddock), *Gadus morhua* (Atlantic cod), and *Gadidae* species.

Haddock constituted 52 percent (73) of the collection. Diagnostic elements were sorted, and MNI was established based upon either paired or unpaired cranial and pectoral elements, whichever of the two proved to be greater. It was determined that the collection contained six individuals. Skeletal analysis revealed a significantly discordant ratio. Had whole fish been acquired, a ratio of 168 : 324 (1 : 2) would have been expected. This subassemblage revealed a ratio of 52 : 17 (3 : 1). The relative dearth of vertebrae was attributed to the probability that five of the fish represented the acquisition of fish heads, rather than whole fish. This conclusion is further supported by the absence of fillet marks on those few vertebrae that were found, and an absence of caudal vertebrae.

Atlantic cod constituted 5 percent (7) of the collection. MNI was established by the presence of four upper-right portions of cleithria. This subassemblage was quite puzzling, as only cleithria and one supracleithrium represented this species. Cranial elements and vertebrae were absent. It was presumed that this subassemblage comprised a collection of postcranial scraps that would be used for a stew or chowder.

Cod species constituted 44 percent (62) of the collection. This species was represented by vertebrae only. Diagnostic attributes were examined, resulting in the formation of two distinct groupings based on size, thus indicating the presence of two distinct individuals. The first group of vertebrae indicated a fish of medium size, while the second grouping indicated a much larger fish. The absence of cranial and pectoral elements suggested that these were acquired headed. Vertebrae of the first group exhibited deeply incised, secondary fillet marks, documenting the manner in which this fish was butchered. Based upon vertebral measurements (thickness, width, and length), the larger fish had a conjectured length of 1,066 millimeters (41.9 inches). This fish was represented by few posterior caudal vertebrae, indicating the acquisition of a tail-portion steak.

The analysis of the fish remains from the privy deposit indicated a MNI count of 12. Skeletal ratio and butchering pattern analyses indicated that this collection was overwhelmingly represented by cuts of minimal value: five heads, one caudal steak, scrap, and one whole fish. With the exception of the filleted specimen, all discernible portions were suitable for use in stews or chowders.

Weighted mean analysis produced a .06 value, based upon MNI. It has been demonstrated that by, far, portions outweighed individuals. Thus any assessment of socioeconomic levels incorporating MNI must be obviated. In consideration of this factor, mean values were recalculated accordingly. Assuming the five heads could be acquired for $.02 each, one whole haddock for $.06 per pound, one whole cod species for $.06 per pound, and a caudal steak and scrap for $.03:

$$\frac{5(.02) + 2(.06) + 1(.03)}{8} = .03$$

A comparison of this value with the relative rank market index indicated that the fish consumed by this household fell within the lowest economic level, one of relative poverty.

Each of the methodological forms of analyses indicated that this was a household of the lowest economic level, which sustained itself only by the barest necessities. Historically, we know that the head of the household was a widow residing in an economically depressed neighborhood occupied by a predominant laborer class. Based upon this information, one could anticipate that archaeological assemblages originating from this neighborhood would, most likely, reflect a relatively low economic level. The analysis of fish remains from one residence in this area has documented that a small segment of that population subsisted at minimal levels.

Deer Street Tavern

The Deer Street Tavern, located in Portsmouth, New Hampshire, was initially excavated by Steven Pendery in 1981 (Cox *et al.* 1981). Later that same year, further work was undertaken by Aileen Agnew (Agnew 1981). The archaeological assemblage was attributed to a tavern privy, and had a tentative date range of 1845–1885. During this period, the area underwent a class shift, with increasing numbers of laborers occupying the neighborhood. The collection of fish remains recovered from the excavation were in an excellent state of preservation.

The collection comprised 249 bones, 82 percent (205) of which were identifiable to a family or species level. Two families of fish were identified, *Gadidae* and *Bothidae*. *Gadidae* was represented by two species, *Melanogrammus aeglefinus* (haddock) and *Gadus morhua* (Atlantic cod). *Bothidae* was represented by one unidentifiable flounder.

Haddock constituted 42 percent (105) of the collection. Diagnostic elements were sorted, and MNI was established based upon the presence of thirteen left cleithria. Skeletal ratio analysis indicated that a portion of the collection represented heads rather than whole fish. While a ratio of 364 : 702 (1 : 2) was expected, the subassemblage was found to reflect a ratio of 53 : 49 (1 : 1). These figures indicate that perhaps as many as six individuals are represented by heads, and that the remaining seven fish were whole acquisitions. Butchering marks were notably absent. Heads may have been baked or boiled for use in stews or chowders, and whole fish may have been baked or broiled.

Atlantic cod constituted 31 percent (78) of the collection. The MNI was determined to have been 4, based upon the presence of four right cleithria. Skeletal analysis produced a ratio of 17 : 35 (1 : 2). This ratio indicated that these fish were probably acquired whole. As with the previous subassemblage, vertebrae lacked evidence of butchering, providing no additional information regarding preparation, save that they were possibly cooked whole.

Flounder constituted 8.8 percent (22) of the collection. One individual was noted present, and was represented by vertebrae only. The absence of cranial elements indicated that this fish was acquired headed. A mean vertebral count for flounder (38) contrasted against the archaeological count (22) supports the MNI. As the head of this fish would have offered little food value, it would have been expedient to market this fish dressed (less head, fins, and tail). The absence of caudal and pectoral fin rays supports the conjectured form of this acquisition. Vertebrae lacked butchering marks, indicating that this fish may have been baked or broiled whole.

It is noteworthy that, of the forty-four unidentifiable bones (vertebrae), seven exhibited fillet marks. Since these can not be assigned with certainty to any of the forementioned species, their value is limited. In all probability, these belong to either one or both of the cod species previously identified. They are cited here only in support for the probable methods of butchering whole fish.

The analysis of the fish remains from the Deer Tavern privy indicated an MNI count of 18. Skeletal ratio and butchering pattern analyses suggested that this collection was represented by six cuts (heads) and twelve whole fish. Some of the whole fish had been filleted.

Weighted mean analysis produced a .06 value, based upon MNI. Recalculation of the value, taking portions into consideration, produced:

$$\frac{6(.02) + 7(.06) + 4(.07) + 1(.05)}{18} = .05$$

The threshold of affordability for the Deer Tavern assemblage is one of lower status, and may be typical of a laborer-craftsman household. It may not be surprising that a commercial establishment catering to a laborer clientele would reflect a lower status. However, when studying communal deposits, there is always a concern for a blending of individual economic characteristics; these may result in a collective mosaic of behavior. The implications of such a mosaic could be as small as inflating or deflating economic patterns peculiar to individuals, or as significant as producing an inexplicable array of diverse patterns. In this instance, the collective mosaic was a true reflection of the individual; economic patterning remained autonomous.

Maudlin Street Archaeological District

Feature 32

The Maudlin Street Archaeological District was part of the large-scale Charlestown Central Artery Project, located in Charlestown, Massachusetts. Excavation was conducted by Steven Pendery in 1984, under contract with the Peabody Museum, Harvard University. During the seventeenth and eighteenth centuries, the district was occupied by members of the working class. The collection of fish remains was recovered from a trash pit that dated from 1730–1750, and was attributed to a craftsman of lower status.

The fish remains from Feature 32 consisted of 900 bones, of which 30 percent (272) were identifiable to a family or species level. Three families of fish were represented by five species. *Gadidae* included *Melanogrammus aeglefinus* (haddock), *Gadus morhua* (Atlantic cod), and *Gadidae* species. *Sparidae* was represented by *Stenotomus chrysops* (scup). *Bothidae* was represented by flounder. The preservation of fish bones was excellent, even though the assemblage contained a large quantity of bone fragments.

Haddock constituted 57.3 percent (156) of the collection. MNI was established based upon paired cranial elements, and was determined to have been 8. Skeletal analysis revealed a ratio of 122 : 23 (5 : 1), and reflected a dominance of head cuts. Perhaps as many as seven of these specimens were acquired in this form for presumable use in stews or chowders. Few vertebrae exhibited fillet marks, concluding that at least one of these fish was acquired whole and subsequently prepared as fillets.

Atlantic cod constituted 4 percent (11) of the collection. MNI was determined to have been two fish, as evidenced by the identification of two left dentaries. Skeletal analysis revealed a ratio of 6 : 5 (1 : 1), indicating that these fish probably represented head cuts. The absence of butchering marks on vertebrae tends to support this conclusion, as does the scant number of vertebrae representing two individuals.

Cod species constituted 37.8 (103) of the collection. MNI was determined to have been 3. Skeletal analysis revealed a ratio of 23 : 59 (1 : 3), suggesting that these fish represented whole acquisitions. Butchering marks were notably absent from vertebrae, which may be an indication of baking or broiling.

Scup and flounder both constituted less than 1 percent of the collection, each being represented by one element (occipital and vertebra, respectively), thus establishing an MNI of 1 each. Since scup are generally small fish, it may be presumed that this element represents a whole fish rather than a portion. The presence of a flounder vertebra may similarly indicate a whole fish, since butchering techniques peculiar to flatfish are usually limited to fillets.

The analysis of the fish remains from this feature indicated an MNI count of 15. Skeletal and butchering analyses suggest that this collection is represented by nine cuts (heads) and six whole fish. Some of the whole fish had been prepared as fillets, while others may have been baked or broiled in whole form. Weighted mean analysis produced:

$$\frac{9(.02) + 4(.06) + 1(.08) + 1(.05)}{15} = .04$$

The threshold of affordability for this assemblage is one of a lower status household. The historical data revealed that the occupant of the site was, as was much of the neighboring community in which he lived, a craftsman of lower status. The economic assessment of the fish remains from the craftsman's privy has supported this conclusion.

Feature 34

Feature 34 was a trash pit that was excavated during the course of the Charlestown Central Artery project. Part of the same district, this feature dated to 1730–1750, and was attributed to a craftsman of somewhat higher status than his counterpart, discussed earlier.

The fish remains from Feature 34 consisted of 344 bones, of which 68.9 percent (237) were identifiable to a family or species level. Two families of fish were identified, *Gadidae* and *Percidae*. *Gadidae* included *Melanogrammus aeglefinus* (haddock), *Gadus morhua* (Atlantic cod), and *Gadidae* species. *Percidae* was represented by *Perca flavescens* (yellow perch). MNI was determined to have been 7.

Haddock constituted 38.4 percent (91) of the collection. MNI was determined to have been 3. Skeletal analysis revealed a ratio of 22 : 69 (1 : 3), suggesting that these specimens were acquired as whole fish. Vertebrae exhibited both primary and secondary fillet marks, documenting the manner in which these fish were prepared.

Atlantic cod represented 23.2 percent (54) of the collection. MNI was determined to have been 2. Skeletal analysis revealed a ratio of 5 : 49 (1 : 10). The high vertebral ratio indicated that perhaps three fish may have been present. Some vertebrae exhibited fillet marks; one displayed a steaking cut. The differences in butchering marks indicated that one or both fish were acquired whole and subsequently prepared as fillets; the cod steak was an additional acquired form.

Cod species constituted 38.3 percent (90) of the collection. Based upon paired and unpaired cranial and pectoral elements, MNI was established at 1. Skeletal analysis revealed a ratio of 11 : 89 (1 : 8). A vertebral count in excess of fifty-four documented that the collection contained a minimum of two fish. Butchering marks were absent from these vertebrae, which may be an indication of baking or broiling whole fish. The erroneously established MNI (1) was the result of a failure to take into account the acquisition of headed portions. In this instance, one fish probably reflects a whole form, and the second, a headed form.

Yellow perch constituted less than .1 percent (2) of the collection. MNI was determined to have been 1. This fish was represented by one cranial and one vertebral element (1 : 1), and suggests that perch represented a whole form. This conclusion is supported by the generally small size attained by this species. This fish may have been pan-fried, baked, or broiled whole, as butchering marks were not noted on the vertebra.

The analysis of fish remains from this feature indicated an MNI count of 7. Skeletal and butchering analyses indicated that this collection was comprised of one steak, eight whole fish, and perhaps as many as four headed fish. Some of the whole fish had been prepared as fillets; others were presumably cooked whole.

Weighted mean analysis produced:

$$\frac{3(.06) + 2(.07) + 2(.06) + 1(.11) + 1(.08)}{13} = .07$$

The threshold of affordability for this feature is one of a lower-status household. As in the previous analysis, historical data documented that the occupant of the site was a craftsman of lower status. It was also known that the economic status of this craftsman was higher than the one that produced Feature 32. The statement has been supported through the analysis of the fish remains, which indicates a 75 percent higher threshold of affordability.

CONCLUSION

The present study has demonstrated that fish remains may be used to indicate socioeconomic levels. The results of the various forms of analysis have formed a complementary approach to this form of economic measure. In each archaeological sample, the fish remains have supported general historical information regarding the individual or community economic level. Based upon the four test studies, the use of fish remains appears to accurately reflect economics. It was expected that lower-status households would contain lower-priced fish, and this was indeed the case. Furthermore, differential levels within the lower level were noted in two instances from the Charlestown material.

In assessing socioeconomic status, fish remains offer analysts an advantage not found in material culture studies: a data resource that has little status visibility and a more accurate reflection of income. A possible limitation to the application of this method of economic analysis may be geographical region. In each of the four case studies presented, all were coastal sites. On inland sites, fish consumption may be different. In addition, market size, as well as location, may greatly affect the results of such analyses. Documentary and archaeological analyses of riverine and lacustrine markets and sites may provide comparative data for future use. Undoubtedly, the types of fish available in different areas may not be applicable to the Boston market index, however, the methods employed in this paper can be replicated for these other regions and other fish so that construction of a similar indexing system is practical. As for the New England coastal region, additional assemblages need to be analyzed so that threshold studies can be further tested and refined, or modified as needed.

REFERENCES

Agnew, Aileen Button, 1981, Preliminary Report of the Deer Street II Archaeological Project, Portsmouth, New Hampshire, manuscript on file at Strawbery Banke, Inc., Portsmouth, New Hampshire.
Anderson, Jay, 1971, A Solid Sufficiency: A Ethnography of Yeoman Foodways in Stuart England, Ph.D. dissertation, University of Pennsylvania.
Bowen, Joanne, 1978, Probate Inventories: An Evaluation from the Perspective of Zooarchaeology and Agricultural History at Mott Farm, in: *Historical Archaeology: A Guide to Substantive and Theoretical Contributions* (Robert L. Schuyler, ed.), Baywood Publishing, New York, pp. 149–159.
Casteel, Richard W., 1972, Some Biases in the Recovery of Archaeological Faunal Remains, *Prehistoric Society Proceedings* 38:382–388.

Casteel, Richard W., 1976, Comparison of Column and Whole Unit Samples for Recovering Fish Remains, *World Archaeology* 8(2):192–196.

Cox, Stephen, Lettieri, Ronald, Pendery, Steven, and Vaughan, James, 1981, Historical and Archaeological Assessment and Data Recovery Program for Deer Street Site, Portsmouth, New Hampshire, manuscript on file at Strawbery Banke, Inc., Portsmouth, New Hampshire.

Davidson, Paula Edmiston, 1982, Patterns in Urban Food Ways: An Example from Early Twentieth-Century Atlanta, in: *Archaeology of Urban America* (Roy S. Dickens, Jr., ed.), Academic Press, New York, pp. 381–398.

Deetz, James, 1977, *In Small Things Forgotten*, Anchor Press, New York.

Graffam, Gray, 1981, Preliminary Site Report of the Rider-Wood House Site, manuscript on file at Strawbery Banke, Inc., Portsmouth, New Hampshire.

Graffam, Gray, 1982, The Foodways of Harvard Students, 1651–1674: The Archaeological Evidence, M.A. thesis, Cooperstown Graduate Programs, New York.

Honerkamp, Nicholas, 1981, Social Status as Reflected by Faunal Remains from an Eighteenth Century British Colonial Site, *The Conference on Historic Site Archaeology Papers* 14:87–115.

Lindsey, S. C., 1975, Pleomerism, the Widespread Tendency among Related Fish Species for Vertebral Number to be Correlated with Maximum Body Length, *Journal of Fisheries Research Board Canada* 32(12):2453–2469.

Lyman, H. Lee, 1977, Analysis of Historic Faunal Remains, *Historical Archaeology* 11(2):67–73.

Lyman, H. Lee, 1979, Available Meat from Faunal Remains: A Consideration of Techniques, American Antiquity 44(3):536–546.

MacKay, K. T., and Garside, E. T., 1969, Meristic Analyses of Atlantic Mackerel from the North American Coastal Populations, *Journal of Fisheries Research Board Canada* 26(9):2537–2540.

McCoy, John H., 1972, *Livestock and Meat Marketing*, AVI Publishing, Connecticut.

McMahon, Sarah F., 1980, Provisions Laid Up for the Family: Toward a History of Diet in New England, 1650–1850, paper presented at the Workshop in Economic History, Harvard University.

Miller, Henry M., and Lewis, Lynne G., 1977, Zoocultural Resource Utilization at a Low Country South Carolina Plantation, *The Conference on Historic Site Archaeology Papers* 12:250–265.

Reitz, Elizabeth J., 1984, Urban/Rural Contrasts in Vertebrate Fauna from the Southern Coastal Plain, paper presented at the 17th Annual Meeting of the Society for Historical Archaeology, Williamsburg, Virginia.

Rothenberg, Winnifred B., 1980, The Marketing Perimeters of Massachusetts Farmers, 1750–1855, paper presented at the Workshop in Economic History, Harvard University.

Singer, David A., 1982a, Fish in Foodways Systems—Data Integration and Patterning, *Northeast Historical Archaeology* 11:39–47.

Singer, David A., 1982b, Ichthyofauna as an Interpretive Tool in Historic Sites Archaeology, M.A. thesis, University of Massachusetts, Boston.

Singer, David A., 1983, *Perspectives in Newspaper Advertisements: A Kitchen Prices Current*, Data Publishing, Massachusetts.

Singer, David A., 1985, The Use of Fish Remains as a Socio-Economic Measure: An Example from 19th Century New England, *Historical Archaeology* 19(2):132–136.

5

Vertebrate Fauna and Socioeconomic Status

ELIZABETH J. REITZ

INTRODUCTION

One of the problems that can be addressed through analysis of data from an archaeological deposit is the identification of the socioeconomic status of the site's previous occupants. Since many historic sites lack information on the identity of the previous occupants, reliance must be placed upon the excavated remains themselves for clues of socioeconomic status. Consequently archaeologists have been delineating characteristics that will serve to identify the socioeconomic status of the former occupants from archaeological data. To define status markers from faunal remains, it is necessary to recognize that the contents of trash deposits have been subjected to a variety of biasing influences. However, in historical archaeology little attention has been paid to factors that influence faunal deposits other than socioeconomic status. In a discussion of socioeconomic status and faunal assemblages, variables that affect the deposition and survival of bones, as well as those that influence the human choices that produced those deposits, should be considered. These variables may be roughly divided into those that affect the survival of bones, those that affect the recovery and interpretation of faunal deposits, and those that affect choice of foodstuffs. When data available from plantations on the Atlantic coastal plain are studied with these variables in mind, it can be seen that more work needs to be done before the influence of socioeconomic status can be determined from vertebrate faunal remains.

RESEARCH DESIGN

In this paper, the characteristics used to identify socioeconomic status from vertebrate faunal collections are examined with reference to materials from plantations on the Atlantic coastal plain. First, variables that influence the interpretation of faunal deposits are reviewed. These include cultural and taphonomic processes that alter the faunal record prior to and during deposi-

Elizabeth J. Reitz ☐ Department of Anthropology, University of Georgia, Athens, GA 30602.

tion as well as excavation, identification, and analytical factors that influence the interpretation of faunal assemblages. It can be seen that some of the characteristics that are used to determine socioeconomic status from faunal remains may reflect these factors instead. Variables that influence choice are reviewed next. These include ethnicity, cost, temporal factors, environment, and site function. Some of these may have little to do with status but may influence the faunal assemblage. Criteria that may be used as status markers include documentary and nonfaunal archaeological materials, butchering patterns, element distribution, disposal patterns, species used, and diversity. As the archaeological evidence for socioeconomic status is reviewed, it can be seen that much of the evidence for socioeconomic status extracted from zooarchaeological data is unclear.

VARIABLES THAT INFLUENCE THE INTERPRETATION OF FAUNAL DEPOSITS

Many of the characteristics found in faunal assemblages from Atlantic coast plantations may be attributed to variables that influence the survival of bones. It is as difficult to assess the extent of this bias for historic faunal remains as it is for prehistoric samples. In the case of all twenty-one samples reviewed for this paper, it is not possible to determine how they came to be a part of the archaeological assemblage. Differential disposal is probably an important bias, but one that cannot be assessed in these samples. It is clear that most of the bones were recovered from areas where pre- and postdepositional activity could have disturbed them. Taphonomic variables such as differential rates of bone weathering, adverse soil chemistry, mechanical disturbances, differential destruction or disturbances of skeletal elements by carnivores and burrowing animals, and the character of bone must be considered before attributing a described pattern to status. Biases that are introduced during deposition include: inaccurate representation of certain taxa in relation to others; skewed relative frequencies of skeletal elements within a taxon; and introduction of noncultural remains into the faunal record. Many of the fragments identified are from durable elements that taphonomic studies have shown have a good chance of surviving in the archaeological record (Lyman 1984). In many cases the bones that are lacking are those that taphonomic studies show are least likely to be recovered archaeologically, without regard to human input, let alone status differences (Brain 1981:22).

Variables that influence the recovery and analysis of faunal remains are also important factors in the development of these data. Many of the collections were recovered during excavations that focused on architectural features. Since many sites had experienced occupations by diverse status groups within a short period of time, archaeological control over mixed deposits was limited in most cases. Documentary information about activity areas on the plantation was generally not available to guide archaeologists in placing units in locations more suitable for recovering subsistence information. Screen size generally was ¼ inch; however, no screen was used for recovery of faunal remains from the three tidewater Virginia collections.

Control over mixed deposits was limited in most cases since most of the sites had experienced multiple occupations, some within a short period of time. All of the Kings Bay Plantation faunal remains were superimposed upon an extensive aboriginal deposit (Johnson 1978; Smith *et al.* 1981). This is important in interpreting historic subsistence because historic deposits in this region differ from prehistoric deposits primarily with the addition of domestic animals (Reitz 1985, 1986). The Colonel's Island (Singleton 1978) and Campfield Settlement (Zierden and Calhoun 1983) freedman deposits were probably mixed with slave deposits from which they were difficult to distinguish. Fauna recovered from deposits associated with planter kitchen deposits at Bray Plantation (Barber 1976), Cannon's Point (Otto 1975), Sinclair (Moore 1981), Kings Bay (Smith *et al.* 1981), and Pike's Bluff (Moore 1981) contain foods consumed by household slaves. Bray's well apparently served as a repository for both household garbage and carrion (Barber 1976). Only the deposits from Stafford Plantation (Ehrenhard and Bullard 1981), slave and overseer deposits at Cannon's Point Plantation (McFarlane 1975; Otto 1975), Jones Creek Settlement (Moore 1981), the Sinclair domestic slave cabin (Moore 1981), and Butler Island (Singleton 1980) are from contexts that might not contain deposits from several status groups. With the exception of the overseer's deposits at Cannon's Point, all of these are associated with slaves. Of these deposits, the largest is from the Jones Creek Settlement (Moore 1981), which contained 145 individuals.

It is apparent that the samples vary considerably in size (Tables 1, 2; Figure 1). Samples from many collections are so small that the data available from them are highly questionable (Grayson 1978, 1981). Only a few collections from Atlantic coast plantations have over 100 individuals; none have over 200. These small samples may be due to limited depositional activity, poor survival rates, limited field time, or limited time for laboratory analysis. A further problem is that some of the samples are reported in such a form that cross-site comparison is restricted (Ascher and Fairbanks 1971; Fairbanks 1974; Singleton 1980).

It is important to recognize that identifiability is clearly a factor in these samples. Some species have either more elements, or more identifiable elements, than others. For example, a pig's tooth can be identified from a very small fraction of the entire tooth, while many bird elements must be essentially complete to be identified. Ribs and vertebra are more difficult to identify than are most carpals, tarsals, or metapodials. As a result, some taxa and some elements stand a much better chance than others of being identified in large numbers.

Several other analytical biases exist in the samples. The problems of primary quantification measures such as bone weight and bone count have been extensively reviewed (Grayson 1979; Perkins 1973; Wing and Brown 1979). Derived measures such as minimum numbers of individuals (MNI), edible meat weight, and usable meat weight are even more problematical

Table 1. Summary of Sites

Site	Location	Date[a]	Occupant
Bray Plantation	Kingsmill, VA	1770–1790	planter
Butler Island	Darien, GA	1804–1861	slave
Campfield Settlement	Georgetown Co., SC	1865–1900	slave/freedman
Cannon's Point	St. Simon's Is., GA	1794–1866	s. slave
Cannon's Point	St. Simon's Is., GA	1794–1866	n. slave
Cannon's Point	St. Simon's Is., GA	1794–1866	overseer
Cannon's Point	St. Simon's Is., GA	1794–1866	planter
Drayton Hall	near Charleston, SC	MCD 1787	planter
Jones Creek (Hampton)	St. Simon's Is., GA	1801–1870s	slave
Kings Bay, outbuilding	Camden Co., GA	1790–1840	slave
Kings Bay	Camden Co., GA	1790–1840	slave
Kings Bay	Camden Co., GA	1790–1840	planter
Kingsley	Ft. George Is., FL	1831–1850	slave
Parland Plantation	Colonel's Island, GA	1830–1880	planter
Parland Plantation	Colonel's Island, GA	1860–?	freedman
Pettus Plantation	Kingsmill, VA	17th century	planter
Pike's Bluff	St. Simon's Is., GA	1827–1857	planter
Rayfield Plantation	Cumberland Is., GA	1834–1865	slave
Sinclair	St. Simon's Is., GA	1790–1820	slave
Sinclair	St. Simon's Is., GA	1790–1820	planter
Stafford Plantation	Cumberland Is., GA	1800–1865	slave
Utopia Cottage	Kingsmill, VA	17th century	tenant

[a]Dates are approximate.

Table 2. Summary of Data

Site	MNI	Taxa
Bray Plantation, planter	135	42
Butler Island, slave	na[a]	17
Campfield Settlement, slave	11	8
Cannon's Point, s. slave	55	23
Cannon's Point, n. slave	69	29
Cannon's Point, overseer	42	26
Cannon's Point, planter	181	39
Drayton Hall, planter	78	31
Jones Creek (Hampton), slave	145	34
Kings Bay, outbuilding/slave	110	41
Kings Bay, slave	26	19
Kings Bay, planter	60	34
Kingsley, slave	na	na
Parland Plantation, planter	70	24
Parland, freedman	46	22
Pettus Plantation, planter	50	14
Pike's Bluff, planter	68	24
Rayfield, slave	na	na
Sinclair, planter/slave	151	45
Stafford, slave	16	14
Utopia Cottage, tenant	71	20

[a]Data are not available.

(Bobrowsky 1982; Casteel 1978; Grayson 1973, 1979; Reitz and Cordier 1983; Reitz, Quitmyer, Hale, Scudder, and Wing, 1987; Stewart and Stahl 1977; Wing and Brown 1979). While it does not appear possible at this time to avoid the problems associated with these methods, we should remain aware of their significance for interpretation of faunal remains. In analysis of the plantation data, there were numerous inconsistencies in the application of these methods that made intersite comparisons difficult. This was especially the case for the calculation of edible or usable meat from the bones. More work needs to be done on the methodologies involved. One bias common to historic faunal analysis was avoided, however. Unlike some cases where the emphasis was just on the domestic fauna, the entire faunal spectrum was identified for each collection. This made it possible to compare use of wild and domestic taxa.

✳ Variables That Influence Choice

Choice may be based upon such variables as ethnicity, cost, time period, environment, and site function in addition to status. Many of these factors are interrelated or will individually produce faunal patterns that resemble those produced by other variables. Thus a similar faunal pattern may be produced by several factors. During this discussion it is important to realize that, in the antebellum South, not all blacks were poor slaves, nor were all whites rich slave owners (Craven 1930:16–18; Genovese 1974:24, 63, 533; Morgan 1982; Zierden and Calhoun 1982:22–23).

Ethnic differences may be reflected in faunal remains, apart from status or the economic ability to make choices. In a multiethnic community, social status and ethnicity are interwoven and, in some instances, ethnicity may become confused with a culture of poverty.

Cost is another factor that is multifaceted. Cost includes time, effort, the expense of the technology, and opportunity. Species that can be captured with greatest efficiency will be more heavily exploited, though less valued, than species that are more difficult to obtain (Jochim 1976). The resources requiring great effort, involving high risk, but providing large yields will be more prestigious. A human population can support energetic extravagances only if basic nutritional requirements are being met through more efficient and less costly mechanisms. Even in a wealthy household, the primary goal may be to obtain necessary foods and raw materials while keeping the cost/risk/effort factor low (Jochim 1976). A wealthy household, however, could afford risks more than a poor one could. High caloric cost to obtain and process an animal may therefore correlate with high social status.

Temporal period is a variable that may influence choice but that may not be related to status. Most of the plantation materials are from a similar time period (Table 1). All of the plantations were occupied from the late eighteenth century to the mid-nineteenth century, with the exception of Pettus Plantation and Utopia Cottage, which were occupied in the last quarter of the seventeenth century (Miller 1979:161), and the Bray Plantation, at which the well

was backfilled at the end of the eighteenth century (Barber 1976). A Mean
Ceramic Date (MCD) of 1787.8 and a *terminus post quem* of 1820 were obtained for the Drayton Hall deposits (Miller and Lewis 1978:251). The Campfield Settlement cabin (Zierden and Calhoun 1983) and the Parland freedman
cabin (Singleton 1978) were occupied during the antebellum period, but the
deposits analyzed were probably from postbellum occupations. The Kings Bay
Plantation outbuilding (Johnson 1978) was probably occupied somewhat after
the slave cabin on the same plantation (Smith *et al.* 1981:264).

The environmental zone in which the site is located is a component in food
selection, and hence is important for interpreting socioeconomic status from
animal remains. Environmental availability is a function of opportunity, technological capacity, marketing opportunities, and personal freedom. Environment, for example, apparently has influenced the use of sheep, pigs, or cattle
in certain regions (Gray 1933). Environmental variables probably are the
basis for regional food preferences.

Most of the plantations were located on sea islands or the immediately
adjacent mainland areas on the Georgia coast (Figure 1). Therefore the resources available to each of the plantations were generally similar. There were
five exceptions. Pettus, Utopia (Miller 1979), and the Bray Plantation (Barber
1976) were located in tidewater Virginia, which is a slightly different environment; Drayton Hall was located twelve miles inland of Charleston, South
Carolina (Miller and Lewis 1978); Campfield Settlement was located on the
upper reach of a tidal creek draining into Winyah Bay, eight miles north of
Georgetown, South Carolina (Zierden and Calhoun 1983).

Rural and urban conditions are a special form of environmental variable
to be considered. It has been found that, on the Atlantic coastal plain, there is
a strong correlation between the diet at a site and the location of the site in an
urban or rural location (Reitz 1986). At rural sites, wild animals were probably
both more common and more easily captured, thereby encouraging a greater
degree of self-sufficiency among rural households than among urban ones.
Self-sufficiency may also have been a virtue born of necessity. This could have
been due to a shortage of livestock at rural locations, combined with difficulties in receiving shipments of meat.

Two other variables influence subsistence decisions. In studying faunal
deposits, it is important to recall that characteristics of the faunal deposit, as
well as differences among sites, will probably reflect the type of activity that
occurred in the excavated area of the site. Also, the larger economic unit,
within which the excavated area functioned, influenced subsistence decisions.
While most of the plantations functioned as agricultural production units,
Drayton Hall was used primarily as an entertainment center rather than as a
residence. Some differences might be expected between the fauna from the
Drayton Hall deposits and the deposits of owners who lived more permanently
on their lands.

From this review, it can be seen that a variety of factors influence choice
aside from status, and these must be considered before attributing to socioeconomic status characteristics found in an archaeological deposit. There

Figure 1. Location of sites.

can be little doubt that the food remains deposited at a historic site reflect the status of the household living there, but the selection, processing, consumption, and disposal of food was also influenced by a variety of additional factors. Socioeconomic status should be inferred from deposits only with due consideration to these factors.

CRITERIA FOR SOCIOECONOMIC STATUS

Criteria that could be used to identify status from the vertebrate faunal record are therefore not independent of the same site formation processes that influence other data classes. In spite of this, some characteristics remain that may indicate the status of a site's occupant(s).

Documentary Evidence

Some evidence for the socioeconomic status of a site's former occupant may be available from documentary and nonfaunal archaeological evidence.

Most historic sites, however, do not have adequate documentation. Even where documents do exist, the use of documentary evidence to identify a faunal deposit's status is not without problems. Architectural and material culture collaboration should be sought in addition to documentary evidence.

Documentary evidence is not available for many of the plantation collections. There was no documentary evidence to support the identification of the Kings Bay Plantation outbuilding excavated as a slave cabin, although analysis of the materials recovered from the site suggests that it was occupied by a low-status individual (Johnson 1978). Documentation was also lacking for what is called a kitchen/wash house and a second possible slave deposit at Kings Bay (Smith *et al.* 1981:180). The cabins on Colonel's Island (Singleton 1978), Campfield Settlement (Zierden and Calhoun 1983), and Utopia Cottage (Miller 1979) were not well documented either. Archaeological evidence indicates that they were first occupied by freedmen, then by slaves, again by freedmen, and finally by tenants who were neither slaves nor freedmen. Some of the planter-associated materials from Parland Plantation were collected from the tidal flats off what was interpreted to have been the plantation's administrative center (Singleton 1978). Control over these data was very weak. In some cases, however, standing architectural features assisted in associating the deposits with a status group. The remaining collections were identified as slave, overseer, or planter samples through correlations between field surveys and documentary evidence.

Butchering Marks

The presence of unmodified bones, burned bones, hacked bones, or sawed bones may be evidence of socioeconomic status. Status differences also have been inferred from the archaeological record by the identification of what are presumed to have been valued portions of an animal. Valued portions are generally identified as those cuts that contain the largest portions of meat. While subtle variations in butchering patterns, food preparation techniques, and disposal of animal remains may be associated with ethnicity or status, it is important to recall that, in the absence of documentary evidence, such inferences may be in error. The recovered elements were influenced by the taphonomic, disposal, recovery, and analytical factors summarized earlier, and may not be an accurate reflection of the original diet or original deposit. Deposits of bones from nonmeaty cuts, such as carpals, tarsals, metapodials, and phalanges, could be refuse from meat butchered for consumption by the planter; it could be refuse from slave consumption; it could be that these bones are all that survived deposition; or it could be that the planter family also ate pigs' feet.

Data on butchering marks have been inconsistently reported and rarely quantified. From Kingsley (Fairbanks 1974) and Rayfield (Ascher and Fairbanks 1971), no information is available. The bones from the slave cabin at Stafford Plantation were highly fragmented. Some of the cow phalanges and a cow astragalus were sawed, and most of the pig bones were chopped (Ehrenhard and Bullard 1981:48–49, 53). Butchering marks identified from the Kings Bay Plantation showed that, while cut and hack marks were common at the planter's house, and slave cabin, only one bone had been sawed (Smith *et al.* 1981:256). Bones recovered from the Kings Bay Plantation outbuilding/slave cabin (Reitz 1978a) showed evidence of sawing on twenty-six deer, cow, and pig bones as well as on an opposum humerus. There were also numerous cut and hack marks. No data are available from the Parland Plantation or the Colonel's Island freedman's cabin (Reitz 1978b). Many of the bones recovered from Butler Island were so badly burned that this was the reason Singleton decided to weigh rather than count them (Singleton 1980:169–170). Sawed bones were identified at the Couper's kitchen on Cannon's Point Plantation, but not at the north slave cabin or the overseer's cabin (Otto 1975:357) or in the south slave cabin area (McFarlane 1975:166). Burned, hacked, and cut bones were identified from both Cannon's Point slave cabins as well as from the overseer's cabin (McFarlane 1975:166; Otto 1975:357). No data on butchering marks were provided for Pike's Bluff, Sinclair, or Jones Settlement (Moore 1981), although a cormorant identified from Pike's Bluff might have been skewered during preparation (Moore 1981:114). At Campfield Settlement (Reitz 1983:83), bones showed evidence of burning, hacking, and cutting, but no sawed bones were identified. No information is offered on butchering marks from Drayton Hall (Miller and Lewis 1978). Sawing as well as other butchering marks were found on cattle in the Bray Plantation well, but in general there was a low frequency of butcher marks (Barber 1976). None of the Pettus Plantation or Utopia Cottage bones had been sawed, although some animals had been butchered with axes or cleavers (Miller 1979:168).

Elements Identified

Status may also be reflected in the cuts of meat used. Sometimes the relative costs of cuts can be determined from documentary sources (Schulz and Gust 1983) and correlated with the archaeological materials. Since retail meats from different portions of an animal carcass have different market values, it should be possible to identify status from the value of the meat cuts represented in the faunal assemblage. Once that is done, the cuts can be ranked following the retail meat prices of the time period and correlated with the status of the household. Use of prices is, of course, restricted to areas where prices are known, which is not the case for the Atlantic coastal plain. Peter Schulz and Sherri Gust have shown that there is change over time in the value of meat cuts (Gust 1983:346; Schulz and Gust 1983:48). There may have been regional differences as well. Therefore associating cuts of meat with prices is risky without access to local, contemporary records or some other type of supporting evidence. It is also important to remember that people may chose to display their status in ways other than expensive cuts of meat. Just as a wealthy family may decide to spend their money on land rather than on ceramics (Heberling and Spencer-Wood 1985), they may choose not to buy expensive food either. Studies that depend upon correlations between documentary evidence on the prices of cuts of meat and the recovered bones assume that there was extensive utilization of retail meats, which was perhaps not the case on plantations. It also remains to be seen that the patterns of elements recovered from these sites could not be the result of differential disposal practices, taphonomic factors, and identification biases.

Information on elements identified and, by inference, the cuts of meat used, is generally commonly reported, although rarely in quantified form. When the data that have been provided in quantified form are summarized, it can be seen that the elements recovered from all sites are very similar, regardless of status (Tables 3 and 4). While there are considerable differences between the types of elements identified between pigs and cows, within each taxon there is not very much difference between sites in the types of elements identified.

For pigs, most of the elements identified were from the head, followed generally by fragments from the body and the lower leg (Table 3). While most of the samples are fairly small, these data do not demonstrate any major differences between deposits of different social strata. The lowest frequency of head elements was identified in the samples from Pettus Plantation, Utopia Cottage (Miller 1979), Campfield Settlement (Reitz 1983), and the Stafford slave cabin (Ehrenhard and Bullard 1981). The first two sites are the earliest of the plantation materials to be examined, and are also from a different environmental zone. More work needs to be done in the Virginia tidewater region before these differences can be attributed to temporal change, environmental differences, recovery methods, ethnicity, or status. The Campfield Settlement sample is so small that sample size bias cannot be eliminated as a source of error. The Stafford collection is also small, but may be an indication that, on the Stafford Plantation, slaves ate more pork from the body and lower legs of pigs than they did from the head. It is also possible that the skulls and mandibles were disposed of elsewhere, either before or after consumption of meat, brains, or tongue. Elements from the body were more common than elements from the lower leg in every case except at Drayton Hall, where leg elements were somewhat more common.

More variation is present in the fragments identified from cattle (Table 4). Unfortunately, the differences do not seem to correlate with status. The materials from Pettus Plantation and Utopia Cottage are similar to one another, as Miller pointed out (1979), but they differ substantially from the other plantation samples. This may be an indication of temporal or environmental differences. Two other collections are also similar to one another: those from the Stafford slave cabin (Ehrenhard and Bullard 1981) and those from the Kings Bay outbuilding/slave cabin (Reitz 1978a). Since one of these collections is undoubtedly from a slave cabin, and the other is probably from a low-status area, the data might be interpreted as evidence that slaves consumed more meat from the heads of cattle than did higher-status groups. A contradiction to this interpretation is found in the collection from the Kings Bay slave cabin (Smith *et al.* 1981:257), which is very similar to that from most of the planter deposits. It is interesting that, in spite of an apparent tendency for low-status

Table 3. Elements Identified from Pig

Site	Head		Body		Lower leg		Total
	Number	Percentage	Number	Percentage	Number	Percentage	
Stafford, slave cabin	9	39.1	7	30.4	7	30.4	23
Kings Bay, outbuilding	151	63.2	45	18.8	43	18.0	239
Kings Bay, slave	23	85.2	3	11.1	1	3.7	27
Kings Bay, planter	63	86.3	6	8.2	4	5.5	73
Parland Plantation	41	75.9	11	20.4	2	3.7	54
Parland, freedman	24	80.0	5	16.7	1	3.3	30
Drayton Hall[a]	263	82.0	19	6.0	39	12.0	321
Campfield Settlement	1	20.0	—	—	4	80.0	5
Pettus Plantation[a]	124	55.0	88	39.0	14	6.0	226
Utopia Cottage[a]	148	64.0	77	33.0	7	3.0	232

[a]These values are reconstructed from the published form (adapted from Miller 1979; Miller and Lewis 1978).

Table 4. Elements Identified from Cattle

Site	Head		Body		Lower leg		Total
	Number	Percentage	Number	Percentage	Number	Percentage	
Stafford, slave cabin	46	75.4	7	11.5	8	13.1	61
Kings Bay, outbuilding	334	77.1	65	15.0	34	7.9	433
Kings Bay, slave	4	36.4	2	18.2	5	45.5	11
Kings Bay, planter	6	37.5	2	12.5	8	50.0	16
Parland Plantation	32	38.6	20	24.1	31	37.4	83
Parland, freedman	—	—	3	100.0	—	—	3
Drayton Hall[a]	101	44.7	51	22.6	74	32.7	226
Campfield Settlement	—	—	—	—	3	100.0	3
Pettus Plantation[a]	85	21.0	219	54.0	101	25.0	405
Utopia Cottage[a]	117	21.0	256	46.0	183	33.0	556

[a]These values are reconstructed from the published form (adapted from Miller 1979; Miller and Lewis 1978).

deposits to contain more head elements from cattle than high-status deposits, this did not mean that high-status deposits contained more elements from the body. Instead, the high-status deposits contain about the same quantity of body elements as low-status deposits, but high-status deposits contain more fragments from the lower leg than do low-status deposits. Clearly, more work needs to be done in this area.

✷Species Used

Just as value is associated with different cuts of meat from a carcass, different values are placed upon the taxa being consumed. This is a marker that must be used with caution. Use of exclusively or primarily domestic taxa may not be a good indicator of high status, but rather an indicator of low status. The use of rare, mobile, or otherwise costly taxa may also be indicators of status. If diversity was prized, and expensive to obtain, than it can be expected that high-status diets might have both a greater diversity of domestic taxa, as well as a greater diversity of wild taxa.

In some cases, it is possible to evaluate the species used for status differences. Differences in the use of wild or domestic taxa might reflect status differences (Table 5). It should be noted that it is probable that meat from

Table 5. Comparison of Wild and Domestic Animal Use

Site	Percentage MNI		Total MNI
	Domestic taxa	Wild taxa	
Bray Plantation, planter	36.3	63.7	135
Butler Island, slave	na[a]	na	na
Campfield Settlement, slave	45.5	54.6	11
Cannon's Point, s. slave	20.0	80.0	55
Cannon's Point, n. slave	12.5	87.5	96
Cannon's Point, overseer	8.9	91.1	45
Cannon's Point, planter	8.7	91.3	195
Drayton Hall, planter	32.1	68.0	78
Jones Creek (Hampton), slave	31.3	68.7	147
Kings Bay, outbuilding/slave	24.6	83.0	110
Kings Bay, slave	23.1	76.9	26
Kings Bay, planter	13.3	86.7	60
Kingsley, slave	na	na	na
Parland Plantation, planter	37.1	62.7	70
Parland, freedman	21.7	78.3	46
Pettus Plantation, planter	76.0	24.0	50
Pike's Bluff, planter	36.8	63.2	68
Rayfield, slave	na	na	na
Sinclair, planter/slave	31.3	68.7	150
Stafford Plantation	29.4	70.6	17
Utopia Cottage, tenant	64.8	35.2	71

[a]Data are not available.

domestic animals provided a larger share of the diet than the MNI values
indicate. Although it was anticipated that collections from the more northerly
sites (Drayton Hall, Campfield Settlement, Bray Plantation, Pettus Plantation, and Utopia Cottage) would demonstrate differences in the use of wild
taxa due to environmental factors, only those from Pettus Plantation and
Utopia Cottage noticeably differ from the general pattern for wild taxa to
dominate the individuals utilized. The main difference between the collections
from Pettus and Utopia is that the collection from Utopia contained more fish
species and individuals than did the one from Pettus (Miller 1979). The two
collections were very similar in most respects, however. Domestic individuals
comprised 24 percent of the individuals in Georgia coastal slave deposits and
23 percent of the individuals in planter deposits. Nonetheless, there does appear to be a slight tendency for planter deposits to contain somewhat more
wild individuals than do slave deposits.

Use of specific types of domestic animals may provide some evidence of
status differences (Tables 6 and 7). Pigs are consistently more common than
cattle when MNI is used, but beef is far more common than pork. In terms of
individuals, pigs form a major part of the collection only in the Pettus and
Utopia samples. Pigs are less common than cows in half of the slave collec-

Table 6. Comparison of Pig and Cow

Site	Percentage MNI		Percentage meat weight	
	Pig	Cow	Pig	Cow
Bray Plantation, planter	8.2	5.2	12.8	59.7
Butler Island, slave	na[a]	na	31.5	67.7
Campfield Settlement, slave	18.2	9.1	4.3	24.5
Cannon's Point, s. slave	10.9	5.5	na	na
Cannon's Point, n. slave	4.4	4.4	18.2	33.2
Cannon's Point, overseer	4.8	2.4	24.8	29.5
Cannon's Point, planter	2.8	2.2	8.1	42.2
Drayton Hall, planter	14.1	10.3	20.0	67.6
Jones Creek (Hampton), slave	12.8	14.2	8.0	11.5
Kings Bay, outbuilding/slave	8.2	24.6	16.8	65.8
Kings Bay, slave	11.5	7.7	10.0	22.3
Kings Bay, planter	5.0	5.0	12.8	10.1
Kingsley, slave	na	na	na	na
Parland Plantation, planter	18.6	14.3	1.2	8.2
Parland, freedman	15.2	4.3	0.4	0.5
Pettus Plantation, planter	42.0	26.0	28.1	66.0
Pike's Bluff, planter	11.8	16.2	9.7	16.2
Rayfield, slave	na	na	na	na
Sinclair, planter/slave	9.3	11.3	6.7	14.1
Stafford Plantation	5.9	11.8	na	na
Utopia Cottage, tenant	31.0	22.5	24.5	67.1

[a]Data are not available.

Table 7. Comparison of Caprine and Chicken

Site	Percentage MNI		Percentage meat weight	
	Caprine	Chicken	Caprine	Chicken
Bray Plantation, planter	12.6	10.4	12.8	0.9
Butler Island, slave	x[a]	na[b]	x	0.8
Campfield Settlement, slave	9.1	9.1	2.5	0.2
Cannon's Point, s. slave	1.8	1.8	na	na
Cannon's Point, n. slave	2.9	4.4	9.1	1.9
Cannon's Point, overseer	x	2.4	x	0.4
Cannon's Point, planter	2.8	1.7	9.5	0.3
Drayton Hall, planter	5.1	2.6	3.4	0.1
Jones Creek (Hampton), slave	x	4.1	x	1.0
Kings Bay, outbuilding/slave	x	1.8	x	0.1
Kings Bay, slave	x	3.8	x	0.05
Kings Bay, planter	x	3.3	x	0.5
Kingsley, slave	na	na	na	na
Parland Plantation, planter	x	4.3	x	0.02
Parland, freedman	x	2.2	x	0.01
Pettus Plantation, planter	6.0	2.0	0.98	0.03
Pike's Bluff, planter	1.5	7.3	1.7	1.8
Rayfield, slave	na	na	na	na
Sinclair, planter/slave	x	1.3	x	0.3
Stafford, slave	5.8	5.8	na	na
Utopia Cottage, tenant	8.5	2.8	2.0	0.05

[a]Taxon was not identified in the collection.
[b]Data are not available.

tions, two of the planter collections, and one of the tenant/freedmen collections. Cows equaled pigs in two of the planter and one of the slave collections. In terms of meat, beef contributed the bulk of the meat in every instance, except in the collection from the Kings Bay Plantation outbuilding/slave cabin. Although a wide range of methods was used in calculate meat weight in these samples, nonetheless, there does not appear to be a strong difference among the samples along status lines. There does appear to be some tendency for beef to be more prominent in the collections from the Virginia area and Drayton Hall.

The use of exotic taxa might also be a marker of status. No truly exotic taxa appear in any of these collections (Gibbs *et al.* 1980; Reitz 1986; Reitz *et al.* 1985), however, caprines may be a rare species on sea island plantations (Table 7). While caprines are identified in both slave and planter deposits, they are far more likely to be found in tidewater Virginia collections than in ones from coastal Georgia. Among the more southerly plantations, caprines have been identified from only Cannon's Point and Stafford Plantation. They were more common at Cannon's Point than at Stafford. It could be that "status" in this case refers to the plantation as a whole, rather than to subgroups. Perhaps Cannon's Point was a very successful, large plantation, with both slaves and planters enjoying goods obtained by this success.

Diversity and Equitability

Diversity might be another marker of status; however, statistical faunal diversity and equitability was not calculated due to small samples. Clearly, the number of taxa are associated with the number of individuals identified. Small collections are less diverse than large ones. There appears to be some evidence, however, that planters used a slightly wider range of wild taxa than did slaves (Reitz 1986; Reitz *et al.* 1985).

Conclusions

This review of vertebrate data for evidence of differences in subsistence due to socioeconomic status has failed to demonstrate convincingly that any such differences exist. All deposits indicated a varied diet that included both wild and domestic taxa. Wild species generally contributed more individuals to the diet than did domestic taxa, although the reverse probably held true for dietary contributions. Generally the most common wild taxa were estuarine fishes. All of the sites generally showed similar use of the same major domestic animals: pigs and cattle. Cattle were generally more significant in the diet than pigs regardless of status. There appears to be some evidence that diversity was a valued dietary characteristic, but this conclusion must be tentative until the influence of the samples sizes is resolved. In terms of self-sufficiency, fishes and other local resources were perhaps more dependable and less expensive than imported meats, and both groups used such local resources extensively. At the moment, it is difficult to assess the contribution of imported meats to the diet, or to know if these would have been more expensive than locally raised foods.

So far, it appears that taphonomic, environmental, and temporal variables, as well as archaeological and analytical decisions, could account for most of the differences observed. For example, the heavy use of pigs' heads and lower legs may be nothing more than a combination of a high survival rate plus enhanced identifiability. It is possible, of course, that slaves and planters living in the same environment did, in fact, have a very similar diet. Access to purchased foods could have been so restricted for both groups that locally available wild foods, cattle herds, and local hogs were the resources upon which both groups depended, and that there were few differences in the way these foods were prepared.

Still, there should be some differences that can be attributed to socioeconomic status. In order to delineate those differences, several areas need to be given more attention. Success in our efforts to delineate status markers in vertebrate faunal assemblages will depend upon studies of well-collected and carefully identified samples that are large in size. One hopes there will be good documentary support, as well as collaboration from other data classes. During analysis, it will be necessary to remember that taphonomic and archaeological variables can influence the sample. In addition, ethnic affiliation, the local environment, and temporal factors should be considered. More research is needed into the impact of meat processing on preserved meats, and efforts should be made to acquire documentary evidence on the costs of seventeenth-century through early nineteenth-century cuts of meat. Discussions of the elements found in collections should be more extensive, and we need to develop a better way to present the data. It is also probable that there are other criteria that will serve to distinguish between deposits of different social strata better than the ones considered here. If attention is paid to these factors, it should be possible, in the next several years, to identify status markers from plantation collections.

ACKNOWLEDGMENTS

The above review is not written to be critical of the archaeologists who have been engaged in plantation archaeology. They have been pioneers in the study of historic subsistence strategies. It is because of their contributions that it is possible to evaluate where we stand in determining socioeconomic status from vertebrate remains. I acknowledge gratefully their contribution in this area, and hope that we can continue to build upon their work.

REFERENCES

Ascher, Robert, and Fairbanks, Charles H., 1971, Excavations of a Slave Cabin: Georgia, U.S.A., *Historical Archaeology* 5:3–17.

Barber, Michael, 1976, The Vertebrate Fauna from a Late Eighteenth Century Well: The Bray Plantation, Kingsmill, Virginia, *Historical Archaeology* 10:68–71.

Bobrowsky, Peter T., 1982, An Examination of Casteel's MNI Behavior Analysis: A Reductionist Approach, *Midcontinental Journal of Archaeology* 7(2):171–184.

Brain, C. K., 1981, *The Hunters or the Hunted?: An Introduction to African Cave Taphonomy*, University of Chicago Press, Chicago.

Casteel, Richard W., 1978, Faunal Assemblages and the "Wiegemethode" or Weight Method, *Journal of Field Archaeology* 5(1):71–77.

Craven, Avery O., 1930, Poor Whites and Negroes in the Antebellum South, *Journal of Negro History* 15:14–25.

Ehrenhard, John E., and Bullard, Mary R., 1981, Stafford Plantation, Cumberland Island National Seashore, Georgia: Archaeological Investigations of a Slave Cabin, Southeast Archaeological Center, National Park Service, Tallahassee.

Fairbanks, Charles H., 1974, The Kingsley Slave Cabins in Duval County, Florida, 1968, *Conference on Historic Sites Archaeology Papers* 7:62–93.

Genovese, Eugene D., 1974, *Roll, Jordon, Roll*, Pantheon Books, New York.

Gibbs, Tyson, Cargill, Kathleen, Lieberman, Leslie Sue, and Reitz, Elizabeth J., 1980, Nutrition in a Slave Population: An Anthropological Examination, *Medical Anthropology* 4:175–262.

Gray, Lewis C., 1933, *History of Agriculture in the Southern United States to 1960*, Carnegie Institute, Washington, D.C.

Grayson, Donald K., 1973, On the Methodology of Faunal Analysis, *American Antiquity* 38(4): 432–439.

Grayson, Donald K., 1978, Minimum Numbers and Sample Size in Vertebrate Faunal Analysis, *American Antiquity* 43(1):53–65.

Grayson, Donald K., 1979, On the Quantification of Vertebrate Archaeofaunas, in: *Advances in Archaeological Method and Theory*, Volume 2 (Michael B. Schiffer, ed.), Academic Press, New York, pp. 199–237.

Grayson, Donald K., 1981, The Effects of Sample Size on Some Derived Measures in Vertebrate Faunal Analysis, *Journal of Archaeological Science* 8:77–88.

Gust, Sherri M., 1983, Problems and Prospects in Nineteenth Century California Zooarchaeology, in: *Forgotten Places and Things: Archaeological Perspectives on American History* (Albert E. Ward, ed.), Center for Anthropological Studies, Contributions to Anthropological Studies No. 3, Albuquerque, pp. 341–348.

Heberling, Scott, and Spencer-Wood, Suzanne, 1985, Ceramics and the Socio-economic Status of the Green Family, Windsor, Vermont, 1788–1956, paper presented at the 18th Annual Meeting of the Society for Historical Archaeology, Boston.

Jochim, M. A., 1976, *Hunter-Gatherer Subsistence and Settlement: A Predictive Model,* Academic Press, New York.

Johnson, Robert E, 1978, Archaeological Excavations of 9Cam167 and 9Cam173 at Kings Bay, Camden County, Georgia, manuscript on file, Department of Anthropology, University of Florida, report prepared for the Department of the Navy.

Lyman, Lee, 1984, Bone Density and Differential Survivorship of Fossil Classes, *Journal of Anthropological Archaeology* 3:259–299.

McFarlane, Suzanne, S., 1975, The Ethnoarchaeology of a Slave Community: The Couper Plantation Site, unpublished M.A. thesis, Department of Anthropology, University of Florida, Gainesville.

Miller, Henry M., 1979, Pettus and Utopia: A Comparison of the Faunal Remains from Two Late Seventeenth Century Virginia Households, *Conference on Historic Site Archaeology Papers 1978* 13:158–179.

Miller, Henry M., and Lewis, Lynne G., 1978, Zoocultural Resource Utilization at a Low Country South Carolina Plantation, *Conference on Historic Site Archaeology Papers 1977* 12:250–265.

Moore, Sue Mullins, 1981, The Antebellum Barrier Island Plantation: In Search of An Archaeological Pattern, Ph.D. dissertation, University of Florida, University Microfilms, Ann Arbor.

Morgan, Philip D., 1982, Work and Culture: The Task System and the World of Lowcountry Blacks, 1700–1880, *William and Mary Quarterly* 4(39, Series 3):563–599.

Nöel Hume, Audrey, 1978, *Food,* Colonial Williamsburg Archaeological Series No. 9, Williamsburg, Virginia.

Otto, John S., 1975, Status Differences and the Archaeological Record—A Comparison of Planter, Overseer, and Slave Sites from Cannon's Point Plantation (1794–1862), St. Simons Island, Georgia, Ph.D. dissertation, University of Florida, University Microfilms, Ann Arbor.

Perkins, Dexter, 1973, A Critique on the Methods of Quantifying Faunal Remains from Archaeological Sites, in: *Domestikationsforschung und Geschichte der Haustiere* (J. Matolosi, ed.), Adademiai Kiado, Budapest, pp. 367–369.

Reitz, Elizabeth J., 1978a, Appendix B—Faunal Remains from a Coastal Georgia Plantation (KBS-12), with Reference to KBS-8, in: Johnson, R., Archaeological Excavations of 9Cam167 and 9Cam173 at Kings Bay, Camden County, Georgia, report for the Department of the Navy, manuscript on file, Department of Anthropology, University of Florida, Gainesville, pp. 116–151.

Reitz, Elizabeth J., 1978b, Report on the Faunal Material Excavated from Colonel's Island, Georgia, in: Cultural Evolution and Environment of Colonel's Island, Georgia, (K. Steinen, ed.), manuscript on file, Department of Sociology and Anthropology, West Georgia College, Carrollton, Georgia, pp. 135–162.

Reitz, Elizabeth J., 1983, Zooarchaeological Analysis of Vertebrate Fauna from Campfield Settlement, Greenfield Plantation, South Carolina, in: Zierden, Martha, and Calhoun, Jeanne, An Archaeological Assessment of the Greenfield Borrow Pit, Georgetown County, *The Charleston Museum Archaeological Contributions* 4, pp. 70–88.

Reitz, Elizabeth J., 1985, A Comparison of Spanish and Aboriginal Subsistence on the Atlantic Coastal Plain, *Southeastern Archaeology* 4(1):41–50.

Reitz, Elizabeth J., 1986, Urban/Rural Contrasts in Vertebrate Fauna from the Southern Coastal Plain, *Historical Archaeology* 20(2):47–58.

Reitz, Elizabeth J., and Cordier, Dan, 1983, Use of Allometry in Zooarchaeological Analysis, in: *Animals in Archaeology: 2. Shell Middens, Fishes and Birds* (C. Grigson and J. Clutton-Brock, eds.), BAR International Series 183, London, pp. 237–252.

Reitz, Elizabeth J., Gibbs, Tyson, and Rathbun, Ted A., 1985, Archaeological Evidence for Subsistence on Coastal Plantations, in: *The Archaeology of Slavery and Plantation Life* (T. A. Singleton, ed.), Academic Press, New York, pp. 163–191.

Reitz, Elizabeth J., Quitmyer, I. R., Hale, H. S., Scudder, S. J., and Wing, E. S., 1987, Application of Allometry in Zooarchaeology, *American Antiquity* 52(2):in press.

Schulz, Peter D., and Gust, Sherri M., 1983, Faunal Remains and Social Status in 19th Century Sacramento, *Historical Archaeology* 17(1):44–53.

Singleton, Theresa Ann, 1978, Report on the Historic Excavations, Colonel's Island, Glynn County, Georgia, in: The Cultural Evolution and Environment of Colonel's Island, Georgia (K. Steinen, ed.), manuscript on file, Carrollton, Georgia, Department of Sociology and Anthropology, West Georgia College, pp. 70–133.

Singleton, Theresa Ann, 1980, The Archaeology of Afro-American Slavery in Coastal Georgia: A Regional Perception of Slave Household and Community Patterns, Ph.D. dissertation, University of Florida, University Microfilms, Ann Arbor.

Smith, Robin L., Braley, C. O., Borremans, N. T., Reitz, E. J., 1981, Coastal Adaptations in Southeast Georgia: Ten Archaeological Sites at Kings Bay, manuscript on file, University of Florida, Department of Anthropology, Gainesville, prepared for the Department of the Navy.

Stewart, F. L., and Stahl, P. W., 1977, Cautionary Note on Edible Meat Poundage Figures, *American Antiquity* 42(2):267–270.

Wing, Elizabeth S., and Brown, Antoinette B., 1979, *Paleonutrition: Method and Theory in Prehistoric Foodways,* Academic Press, New York.

Zierden, Martha A., and Calhoun, Jeanne A., 1982, Preliminary Report: An Archaeological Preservation Plan for Charleston, South Carolina, *The Charleston Museum Archaeological Contributions* 1.

Zierden, Martha A., and Calhoun, Jeanne A., 1983, An Archaeological Assessment of the Greenfield Barrow Pit, Georgetown County, *The Charleston Museum Archaeological Contributions* 4.

Plantation Status and Consumer Choice

A Materialist Framework for Historical Archaeology

CHARLES E. ORSER, JR.

INTRODUCTION

In all of American history, the southern plantation stands alone as unique. Caused mainly by the presence of slaves before 1865, and tenancy after that date, this distinctiveness has intrigued scholars for many years. Although American archaeologists have been slower to study plantations, research on plantations has been growing recently (Fairbanks 1984; Orser 1984). Nonetheless, even though great strides have been made in illustrating the material culture used at plantations, fewer archaeologists have been willing to confront the more difficult problems associated with plantation social position, economic ranking, and consumer choice. These deficiencies are unfortunate because an understanding of these sociological questions is consistent with the goals of anthropological historical archaeology.

In this chapter, the sociological questions of plantation life are considered, and a framework for examining plantation status and consumer choice on the southern cotton plantation from 1800 to 1930 is presented. The transformation of the southern plantation during this period incorporated major changes in the status and consumer choices of the plantation's inhabitants. The best framework within which to examine these changes is historical materialism, an approach that holds great promise for historical archaeology.

HISTORICAL MATERIALISM AND HISTORICAL ARCHAEOLOGY

Briefly, historical materialism maintains that society is constantly changing, and that social life is divided into three interconnected spheres: economic, political, and ideological (Kohl 1981:109). Although not invented by Karl Marx, today's historical materialism largely derives from his analysis of it (Matsumae 1975; Rattansi 1982; Thalheimer 1936). The literature on Marx's

Charles E. Orser, Jr. ☐ Department of Geography and Anthropology, Louisiana State University, Baton Rouge, LA 70803-4105.

historical materialism is voluminous (see, for example, Marx 1904, 1967, 1971; Marx and Engels 1970), and because much of what Marx wrote is ambiguous, a number of scholars, both sympathetic and unsympathetic, have examined his work in detail (for some examples, see Barnett and Silverman 1979; Dumont 1977; Gandy 1979; Leacock 1972; Mayo 1960; among many others). Out of the controversy that arose from this scrutiny, the proponents of historical materialism have often faced the Herculean task of explaining what Marx really meant (see, for example, Cole 1934).

Although complex, two main tenents of Marx's historical materialism concern the organization of social life and the conflictual nature of human social history. For Marx (1904), social life consists of an economic base, a political superstructure, and ideologies. These spheres of life coexist as simultaneous "moments" that collectively characterize human history. Although simultaneous, primacy is given to production over the relations of individuals, society, and consciousness (Dumont 1977:135). However, Marx's position is clearly not economic determinism (Genovese 1984:315–353). A second tenent of historical materialism, that social life is maintained through conflict rather than by agreement, underlies Marx's model of social organization. This conflict, described as dialectical, characterizes human history.

Scholars in many disciplines have borrowed Marx's ideas, and archaeologists are no exception. The logic of materialism is well suited to archaeological research because of the nature of the information collected. As a result, materialist approaches in archaeology are as old as the discipline itself (Kohl 1981:90).

Recently, more archaeologists have reexamined the explicit Marxist writings of V. Gordon Childe (1946, 1947, 1951, 1956, 1964, 1979) as well as those of ethnologists (Bloch 1975, 1985; Godelier 1977; O'Laughlin 1975), and have turned to historical materialism (Hodder 1982; Spriggs 1984a). Nonetheless, within archaeology, prehistorians have had some difficulty using historical materialism because of Marx's imperfect understanding of the preliterate world (Bloch 1985: 16–20). Historical archaeologists, on the other hand, have had a somewhat easier time because of their concentration on those social organizations that Marx knew best: modern, literate, capitalist societies. These societies contained the people Marx wrote about, and if one accepts the proposition that "historical archaeology has always been about capitalism" (Handsman 1985:2), then the union of historical archaeology and historical materialism seems natural. Although many historical archaeologists are turning to historical materialism, the most erudite supporters of this approach have been Russell G. Handsman (1980, 1981, 1982, 1983, 1984, 1985) and Mark P. Leone (1981, 1982a,b, 1983, 1984).

Although different kinds of historical materialism have been pursued, none seems more appropriate for historical archaeology than that proposed by the Polish social philosopher Leszek Nowak (1983). Nowak's historical materialism, called "non-Marxian," is suited to archaeological research because of its explicit nonsocialist character. The concern over linking archaeology and politics, particularly socialism, too closely with materialism, has been voiced by Leone (1982b:757), who has received sharp criticism for this position (Spriggs 1984b:7n). Leone's stance, however, is consistent with Nowak's (1983) and with Childe's (1947:71–72). Although it may be true, as Engels said at Marx's graveside, that "Marx was before all else a revolutionary" (quoted in Foner 1983:39) and that "divorced from its revolutionary practice the materialistic theory of history would be lifeless" (Thalheimer 1936:185), materialist historical archaeology is revolutionary but not of a revolution. Every kind of archaeology is related to politics in some fashion (Trigger 1984), but as scholars, historical archaeologists would gain nothing by tying themselves to a socialist program, regardless of their personal views. However, it may be difficult, as Childe discovered, to maintain this intellectual detachment at all times (Green 1981).

Nowak's (1983:32) historical materialism is meant to be used as a "weapon against the new forms of oppression that have risen in societies calling themselves socialist ones and using Marx's theoretical faults to cover their inhuman nature." For Nowak, the issue is not to discern what Marx really meant, but rather to use and improve his good ideas and discard the rest. According to Nowak, serious Marxist scholars should not hide social inequality and class oppression as socialist Marxists have done (see Aronowitz 1981 for a similar call). Marx's failure, for example, to consider sexual division of labor is a serious omission that should not be ignored by modern scholars, regardless of how much they might revere Marx (Rattansi 1982:197).

Although Nowak's (1983) message is a complex one, his basic premise is that historical materialism represents the best way to study historical and cultural processes, but that Marx's historical materialism must not be blindly followed. Accordingly, Nowak argues that Marx's historical materialism is ambiguous and inconsistent in his view of the conflicts in society between, on the one hand, direct producers and owners, and on the other, the forces of production and the relations of production. Orthodox historical materialists, such as V. I. Lenin, have solved this ambiguity by ignoring it; praxistic historical materialists, such as Georg Lukacs, have solved it by stressing the idea of class struggle at the expense of the immutable laws of historical motion; and nomological historical materialists, such as Karl Kautsky, have solved it by stressing historical laws relating to the contradiction between production and political economics at the expense of the class struggle (Nowak 1983:18–33).

Nowak's alternative is to construct a historical materialism that is neither nomological nor praxistic, but that combines the idea of class struggle with a socioeconomic formation that is consistent with historical process. As a result, this historical materialism is well suited to historical archaeology because it provides an excellent theoretical and historical framework within which to study capitalist societies. As such, Nowak's historical materialism rests on research and scholarship rather than on dogma and rhetoric.

Nowak's (1983) model of society draws heavily from Marx in that he stresses the presence of three "momentums" in society: economic, political, and ideological. Within each moment, a basic class struggle exists. In the economic moment, this struggle separates direct producers from owners; in the political moment, it separates rulers from citizens; and in the ideological mo-

ment, it separates priests from faithful. Although ideally distinct, the reality
is much more complex even though the conflicts operate in a theoretically
identical manner. Thus, the disposal of the means of repression is analogous to
the disposal of the means of production, even to the point of incorporating
social relations, social institutions, and social consciousness (Nowak
1983:137). This point is a significant one, because in Nowak's mind, the theory
of power was "the weakest point of Marxian social theory" (1983:137). Nowak's formulation of this body of thought is significant and provides an excellent and enlightening framework for plantation archaeologists.

The Plantation: Racial or Economic Institution?

One of the major research questions pursued by modern scholars concerns
the role of slaves in both plantation and southern societies. Because America's
slaves were black, the racial basis of American slavery, and thereby of the
American plantation, has been studied extensively. Some researchers, who
have regarded skin color as of paramount importance (Thompson 1939), have
remarked on the castelike qualities of southern society (Park 1928; Warner
1936, 1941). Others, however (Cox 1942, 1945, 1948; Dumont 1967; Kahl 1957;
Leach 1967; Simpson and Yinger 1953), have convincingly argued against the
application of the caste model for the American South, and have pointed to
other factors that helped stratify that society.

Those who have applied the caste model to the South (see, most particularly, Moore and Williams 1942 and Warner 1936, 1941; also see Ball 1837:
286–287 for a contemporary comment) have viewed southern society as consisting of two endogamous castes, black and white, that have incorporated
individual class structures. The white caste contained four classes defined on
the basis of slave ownership: large planters, small planters and commercial
farmers, nonslaveholding yeomen, and poor whites. The classes in the black
caste were based on legal status and plantation labor position: free blacks,
house servants, and field hands (Moore and Williams 1942:344).

This caste model continues to be used by many scholars (Davis *et al.* 1941;
Dollard 1957; Flynn 1983; Myrdal 1944; Powdermaker 1968), and in historical
archaeology, it has been used most extensively by John Solomon Otto (1975,
1977, 1980, 1984). Otto's model closely follows that of Warner (1936, 1941) and
Moore and Williams (1942), and contains "ethnic" (i.e., color) castes and "social" (i.e., occupational) classes. Within this color–caste model, even though
poor whites lacked property, economic security, and dignity, they were still
"nominal members of the more prestigious ethnic caste" (Otto 1975:14).

Otto's model, however, deviates from the earlier color–caste models in
that a third caste, composed of free, urban blacks, also existed. This third caste
was not a true color caste because its membership was based on legal status
rather than skin color.

The creation of this third caste demonstrates a basic problem with the archaeological application of the caste model, and the identification of ethnicity as a major criterion for plantation status has been a significant stumbling block for historical archaeologists who have followed Otto's lead. The use of the color–caste model is inappropriate for plantation studies because its user must make the assumption that skin color was the single most important element of plantation organization. Such an assumption is quickly violated by the presence of the occupational classes, which rest, not on ascribed characteristics, but on achieved ones. The use of skin color obscures the economic function of southern plantations and turns the focus away from the main reason plantations existed. In fact, Otto's often repeated statement that "many black slaves may have had better housing, possessions, and foods than some poor whites" (1975:14, 1980:4, 1984:12) suggests that something other than skin color was a driving force in structuring plantation society. This driving force was occupation and its concomitant status structure.

Status, usually defined as a person's position in a given social situation that incorporates a collection of rights and duties, is a dynamic relationship that is difficult to understand in living societies (Goodenough 1965). This difficulty is compounded when archaeological data are used. As an extremely personal attribute, status cannot be abstractly applied to entire plantation groups, such as "planters," "overseers," and "slaves," because a nineteenth-century plantation slave, for example, could have held a number of statuses, including, for instance, "Alice's son," "carpenter's helper," "runaway," and "Baptist." To the plantation owner, the status "Baptist" might be fairly unimportant, whereas the status "runaway" would have great significance. On the other hand, to an itinerant preacher, "Baptist" could have more meaning than "runaway." Similarly, a female field hand who had recently given birth would experience a change in standing from "field hand" to "suckler," even though she would still be a slave. In the strict plantation context, the statuses "black" and "slave" have little real meaning. Clearly, the slaves' occupational statuses are analytically more important because they reflect the reasons slaves were held in bondage.

The plantation, although part of southern society, was not southern society, and its primary function was as an economic institution meant to increase the planter's wealth. Most free southerners in 1860 had no connection with slavery (Stampp 1956:29–30), and most were not plantation owners (Owsley 1949). However, even though planters were accorded prestige in antebellum society by the number of slaves they owned (Stampp 1956:385–386), they did not generally buy slaves solely to increase their status or in the hopes that the slaves would add a certain cultural ambience to their estates. Planters bought slaves to work. Cultural interaction was obviously an important outgrowth of plantation existence (Blassingame 1979; Thompson 1939), but it was not the reason planters owned slaves. (For the controversy over the profitability of slavery, see Conrad and Meyer 1958; David et al. 1976; Fogel and Engerman 1974; Genovese 1967; Gutman 1975; and others.)

A plantation ranking based on occupation was not unknown to nineteenth-century plantation observers. In this regard, the comments of Daniel R. Hundley (1860:351–352) are particularly important:

> [The slaves'] chief ambition is to become master's waiting-man, or *valet;* or, in case of a female, lady's maid; next they would prefer to act as housekeeper, chambermaid, steward, dining room servant, or groom, or better still, carriage-driver. This last is considered a post of great honor. . . . Even to be a wagoner, to drive the plantation mules and oxen, often becomes a fruitful source of rivalries and ill-feeling. But the chief ambition of a field hand, or plantation slave, is to become a headman.

As Hundley (1860:358) further notes, the failure to work at the level expected by the owner often meant a work demotion: "seamstresses and weavers, in particular, seem to fade [from work] soonest, and masters are constrained oftentimes to send such out into the field, to labor with the field hands for the benefit of their health, which is always recruited greatly thereby." Here, occupation was clearly viewed as a major criterion for status assignment.

Still, the racial and social aspects of plantation life cannot be ignored, because the plantation was a social place as well as an economic one, and because whites were not slaves (Genovese and Fox-Genovese 1983:127). Blacks were accorded lower social positions in southern society because of ascribed characteristics, but on the plantation they were also accorded different occupational positions based on ability. Nonetheless, black slaves were still victimized by the "enforced personal feeling of inferiority" (DuBois 1935:9) that was brought to them by way of the prevailing racist ideology of southern society. Blacks were probably mistreated because of their skin color but this mistreatment might be impossible to discern in archaeological contexts. Planters and slaves are known to have lived on plantations, and all that is necessary to identify these "statuses" is to identify their readily obvious homesites (Orser 1985; Orser and Nekola 1985). Clearly, a better method of analysis is needed for plantation archaeologists to explain why these homesites are so identifiable.

PLANTATION STATUS AND CONSUMER CHOICE

A general framework for examining plantation status and consumer choice can be constructed using the principles outlined by Nowak (1983). Unfortunately, space does not permit the evaluation of this framework here.

Antebellum

The antebellum plantation was a restrictive institution that was a slave's main sphere of experience. Although many factors operated to stratify the antebellum South (Cairnes 1862; Helper 1860; Hundley 1860; Wolfe 1860), the plantation was largely stratified in terms of occupation. The southern plantation contained its own social hierarchy composed of two basic economic groups: direct producers, with the general status "slaves," and owners, with the general status "planters." These groups formed the antithesis between the producer and the owner of the means of production (Marx 1967:3:383–384). (Overseers held an ambiguous position in this scheme as wage laborers who worked directly for planters.)

Although this antebellum arrangement may have many archaeological correlates that are as yet unknown, the clearest evidence for the economic aspects of the plantation appears in settlement pattern (Adams and Orser 1984; Orser and Nekola 1985). On small plantations and slave-owning farms, slaves worked and lived alongside their white masters (Stampp 1956:35). On larger plantations, even though selected slaves lived in the master's house in order to render special services, such as tending the fire at night or emptying the chamber pot (Genovese 1974:327–441), the overwhelming majority of slaves lived in the "quarters" some distance from the plantation big house. Even though at least one writer (Le Page du Pratz 1975:381) states that the "proper distance" for the placement of the quarters was based on the needs of surveillance and freedom from the "smell which is natural to some nations of negroes," the social relationships of the plantation have long been regarded as having clear spatial correlates (Blassingame 1979:223; Thompson 1975:32; Wolf 1959:136–137). From an economic standpoint, antebellum plantation settlement was a function of the mode of production, and slaves were housed close to their work places in order to decrease transportation time.

Theoretically, property in a slave society is appropriated according to two values: the surplus value—that value produced by the direct producers but that goes to the owners—and the variable capital—that value that falls to the slaves (Nowak 1983:35). The owners used the surplus value to purchase more luxuries as a means of consolidating and symbolizing their power and position according to planter ideology. This partially accounts for the construction of large mansions as a form of conspicuous consumption in the richer portions of the Old South. However, when planters increased their supply of luxury goods, the needs of the direct producers were not met, and the economic gap between the producers and the owners increased. This gap, called the "alienation of work" (Nowak 1983:36–37), signifies the difference between the level of the direct producers' needs and the variable capital that falls to them. The economic struggle that is waged between planters and slaves becomes more intense when the needs of the direct producers far outweigh the variable capital. When this happens, short, violent slave revolts and long, less violent slave desertions occur (Aptheker 1964, 1968; Cheek 1970).

As members of a primary consumer group, a small group of people who communicate regularly on a face-to-face basis (Block and Roering 1979:155), plantation slaves did not have free access to consumer goods, but rather only received them on special occasions, during infrequent trips to towns, or directly from the planter or overseer as gifts or by theft. As the alienation of work increased, the access of slaves to consumer goods proportionately decreased.

This dialectical opposition between plantation owners and direct producers was not the only struggle that took place. In fact, a relationship similar to that in the economic sphere occurred in the political sphere, where a dialectical relationship also existed between the rulers—those who disposed the forces of coercion—and the citizens—those who felt these forces (Nowak 1983:141). The rulers—in this case, those with the status "owner" rather than "planter"—attempted to increase their regulatory powers over the citizens—in this case, those with the status "slave" rather than "field hand," "carpenter," or "housemaid." In this sphere, the alienation that occurs is a civic alienation that increases as the citizens (i.e., nonrulers) realize how powerless they are. Thus, the slave plantation society is an economically and politically totalitarian one where the "planters-owners" consolidate their productive and coercive power over the "direct producers-slaves." Throughout, however, the plantation system is upheld by the prevalent "plantation ideology."

Postbellum

The situation on southern plantations changed after 1865 as the United States entered what Marx (Marx and Engels 1937:277) calls the "revolutionary period." Legally, this change was a radical one because former slaves became emancipated members of society. However, certain other aspects of plantation life did not change so dramatically.

Immediately after the war, the reestablishment of plantation agricultural production was prompted by exceptionally high cotton prices (Vance 1929; Zeichner 1939). Southern planters with experience in cotton culture and some capital were interested in these potentially high profits, and sought to devise ways of finding willing laborers. These attempts represent a complex historical sequence that is outside the scope of this paper (but see Orser and Holland 1984:112–116). However, in essence, planters, who now held the status of "landlord," hired agriculturalists with the statuses of "wage hand," "sharecropper," "share renter," "standing renter," and "cash tenant." All of these plantation agriculturalists could contemporaneously live at the same plantation (Woofter *et al.* 1936:10) because each made his own arrangement with the landlord. Also, each arrangement was based, not on color, but on economics, and are examples of Marx's "ground" and "labor" rent, where the landlord is paid, in money or labor, for the use of his land, buildings, implements, and so forth (Marx 1967:3:618, 790).

The wage laborer was simply a person who was paid a wage to perform plantation labor. In many cases, they were freed slaves who continued to perform their antebellum tasks, even to the point of living in the former slave quarters (Brooks 1914:18). The wage system, although disliked by former slaves, existed on many plantations until the mid-1870s (Prunty 1955:472). On the "agricultural ladder" (Spillman 1919:29), a hierarchy that ranked agriculturalists according to their economic situation, wage laborers were on the lowest rung.

In the sharecropping arrangement, the landlord supplied the land, housing, tools, animals, animal feed, and one-half of the fertilizer. The crop produced did not belong to the sharecropper, and at harvest, it was equally divided between the landlord and the sharecropper, who was the direct producer.

In the share renting arrangement, the landlord supplied the land, housing, and either one-quarter or one-third of the fertilizer costs, and the share renter supplied the labor, animals, animal feed, tools, seed, and the remainder of the fertilizer. The crop was divided so that each party received a portion equal to the amount of fertilizer he had supplied. Obviously, the exact distribution relied on the renter's ability to buy fertilizer.

In the cash renting arrangement, the landlord supplied the land and housing, while the farmer supplied everything else needed to produce the crop. The landlord received a fixed rent per acre in either cash or cotton (Boeger and Goldenweiser 1916:7; Orser and Holland 1984:115). The cash renter was directly below the independent owner-operator on the agricultural ladder.

In each arrangement, both the alienation of work and the civic alienation diminished as one moved up the agricultural ladder. The wage laborer was unconcerned about the plantation crop, as had been the slave before him, and because he was a paid employee, he had little free time to enjoy himself (see Maguire 1975:43). The power and domination of the landlord over the wage laborer was strong, and wage laborers generally viewed their work status as temporary. According to one observer, "the dream of the wage-earner is to become at least a renter" (Dillingham 1896:201). The sharecropper had some interest in the crop, but because he did not own the means of production, he was not deeply concerned about it. Also, because sharecroppers bought most of their material items on credit from a merchant who charged mark-up rates, often as high as 140 percent (Mann 1984:418; Shannon 1945:91; White and Leonard 1915:107–108), they were not even close to owning the means of production. Caught in this endless cycle of debt peonage (Ransom and Sutch 1977:149–170), many sharecroppers who wanted to climb the agricultural ladder found it impossible.

The true ownership of the means of production by the direct producers occurred in the standing and cash renting arrangements. However, the standing renter did not receive the full benefit of his crop, and so did not have autonomy from the landlord. Only in the cash renting arrangement was the plantation tenant finally somewhat autonomous from the landlord (Boeger and Goldenweiser 1916:7; Brannen 1924:30–31, 34). Still, black cash renters suffered the indignities of racial prejudice even though they had gone far up the agricultural ladder.

Even though racial prejudice cannot be overlooked in the study of the postbellum plantation, the most important variable to be considered by archaeologists is the ownership of the means of production. Historical information suggests that cash renters were materially better off than were other postbellum plantation agriculturalists, due to the greater return of fixed-rent tenancy to the direct producers (Higgs 1974:478). Surveys conducted among twentieth-century plantation tenants reflect the material hierarchy of the agricultural ladder. For example, in their study of the Yazoo–Mississippi Delta, Boeger and Goldenweiser (1916:1) found that the average annual income of sharecroppers was $333, of share renters $398, and of cash renters $478. Another survey conducted twenty years later produced similar results (Woofter *et al.* 1936:86–87).

This material difference, reflecting the amount of variable capital that fell to each kind of plantation agriculturalist, should have clear archaeological correlates because it will directly demonstrate the tenant's ability to purchase consumer goods (Orser and Holland 1984:116–118). Although the tenant's consumer group grew larger after he had moved his family away from the plantation nucleus, his purchasing power was not great because of the constraints placed upon him by low wages, high rates of credit, and prejudice. More often than not, tenants were left at the end of the year with no "cash after settling." This amount was the difference between the value of the tenant's part of the crop and the amount he owed for supplies (called "furnishings"), advances made by the landlord, and interest (Woofter et al. 1936:86–87). The "cash after settling" did not greatly differ between black and white tenants, except that black tenants may have been cheated more regularly.

The unequal treatment received by black and white tenants has been reported at length and is hard to ignore (Maquire 1975; Rosengarten 1974). Census documents from the 1930 agricultural survey provide an index of this unequal treatment (United States Department of Commerce 1932). Records compiled from eleven counties in the Mississippi Delta (Bolivar, Coahoma, Humphreys, Issaquena, Leflore, Quitman, Sharkey, Sunflower, Tallahatchie, Tunica, and Washington), an area with a long plantation tradition, indicate that black tenants generally fared worse than white tenants in income and possessions (Table 1). In fact, the greater overall values held by white cash renters over black owners both in land and buildings, and in implements and machinery suggests that skin color, and by extension, a racist ideology, did indeed affect the distribution of wealth in these eleven Mississippi counties. This finding lends support to the ethnic basis for the unequal distribution of wealth on the postbellum plantation. A closer examination, however, reveals that white sharecroppers fared worse than white cash renters when compared

Table 1. Distribution of Wealth in Eleven Mississippi Counties in 1930[a]

	Number	Total (dollars)		Each (dollars)	
		L/B[b]	I/M[c]	L/B	I/M
Owners					
White	2,317	27,455,810.00	3,479,371.00	11,849.72	1,501.67
Black	1,918	6,110,487.00	425,562.00	3,185.86	221.88
Cash renters					
White	1,826	8,977,204.00	924,564.00	4,916.32	506.33
Black	5,508	13,860,432.00	725,879.00	2,516.42	131.79
Sharecroppers					
White	7,547	14,931,239.00	413,776.00	1,978.43	54.83
Black	54,272	93,787,111.00	3,345,488.00	1,728.09	61.64

[a]United States Department of Commerce (1932).
[b]Land and buildings.
[c]Implements and machinery.

with black sharecroppers versus black cash renters. In terms of both land and buildings, and implements and machinery, white sharecroppers reported less than half of the values that white cash renters did, and black cash renters had greater property values than white sharecroppers. This unequal distribution suggests that factors other than purely racial ones also affected the relations between direct producers and owners. The equal relative difference between white owners and white tenants, and black owners and black tenants provides strong evidence of the primacy of economic factors overall, although the difference between white owners and black owners is striking.

Identifying Plantation Status and Consumer Choice

When examining the consumer choices and statuses of the southern plantation from an archaeological perspective, a number of factors must be kept in mind. These factors, because of the special nature of nineteenth-century plantation history, are different for the antebellum and postbellum periods.

Antebellum

In the antebellum period, a major factor is production. Archaeologists must learn, through historical research, how much agricultural produce the direct producers made for the planter. This figure will fluctuate, depending upon the number of slaves, the amount of rainfall, and the skill and interest of the overseer. However, this figure will provide an index for slave alienation and exploitation levels that will relate to consumer opportunities. Another important index concerns the severity of slave punishments and the number of slave desertions from the plantation. The occurrence of slave revolts in the immediate plantation area is also significant. Finally, archaeologists must develop an index of the luxury items the planter's family owned. Here, the integrative powers of historical archaeology become most important, because archaeologists must rely both on documents—probate inventories, bills of lading, and sales records—and excavation results.

Although it has been fashionable recently for plantation archaeologists to shun the excavation of plantation big houses in favor of the excavation of slave quarters (Orser 1984:3–5), big houses cannot be ignored because they will contain tangible evidence for the possession of luxury items by planter families. Plantation archaeologists can compare the big houses with the slave quarters as another measure of alienation. During periods of plantation prosperity, the enlargements and refinements made to planters' homes did not carry over to the slave quarters. Only by examining all of these variables, will plantation archaeologists develop some idea about the consumer choices available to plantation labor groups.

The consumer choices open to plantation owners were, of course, more extensive than those of their slaves, and rested more on the plantation's proximity to major cities and the efforts of the planter's urban agent. Because planters were not restricted to their plantations by coercion, their consumer choices were wider and more varied, and their buying power was vastly superior to that of other plantation groups.

Postbellum

When studying the postbellum plantation, archaeologists are required to consider a number of factors not present on the antebellum plantation. Again, production is most important, but only in light of the kinds of agriculturalists employed on the estate. Obviously, the proportion of sharecroppers to cash renters is significant, because this relationship will bear on the landlord's income, but here the emphasis shifts from the slaves, as a primary group of consumers, to individual tenants, as single consumers who make up a secondary group, or a group that has less interpersonal contact than the primary group (Block and Roering 1979:155). This individualism develops largely because the tenants are, more or less, on their own, and because they have spread their houses throughout the plantation lands (Barrow 1881).

However, one important process of the postbellum period makes the archaeological analysis of postbellum plantation socioeconomics and consumer choice extremely difficult. This process, called "shifting," referred to the habit of tenant farmers to move frequently. Shifting was a problem throughout the United States, and most tenants moved approximately every three years (Ely and Galpin 1919; Schuler 1938). Shifting represents a significant problem for archaeologists because the houses of the tenants belonged to the landlord, who decided who lived in them. As a result, one particular house might have been inhabited by a sharecropper one year, a cash tenant for the next two, and a share renter after that. This kind of occupation sequence makes the identification of socioeconomic status on postbellum plantations extremely difficult, at best.

CONCLUSION

The identification of plantation socioeconomic status and consumer choices is difficult because of the changing nature of the nineteenth-century plantation. Historical materialism, by concentrating on those elements of culture that present the greatest tangible archaeological evidence, provides a realistic and enlightening way to examine plantation phenomena. Still, historical archaeologists must learn to examine the plantation situation carefully, and avoid using outdated and inefficient means of analysis, such as the caste model. This purely ethnic model obscures our view of the social processes that, at one time, operated to establish the socioeconomic positions and consumer opportunities of a great number of American agriculturalists. Historical materialism provides an exciting and enlightening way in which to identify and study these processes.

REFERENCES

Adams, William H., and Orser, Charles E., Jr., 1984, The Evolution of Plantation Settlement Systems in the Southeast During the 19th Century, unpublished manuscript prepared for *Archaeological Perspectives on Farm Tenancy in the Eastern United States* (William H. Adams and Stephanie H. Rodeffer, eds.).

Aptheker, Herbert, 1964, Negro Slave Revolts in the United States, 1526–1860, in: *Essays in the History of the American Negro,* International Press, New York, pp. 1–70.

Aptheker, Herbert, 1968, Slave Guerrilla Warfare, in: *To Be Free: Studies in American Negro History,* International Press, New York, pp. 11–30.

Aronowitz, Stanley, 1981, *The Crisis in Historical Materialism: Class, Politics, and Culture in Marxist Theory,* Praeger, New York.

Ball, Charles, 1837, *Slavery in the United States: A Narrative of the Life and Adventures of Charles Ball, A Black Man,* John S. Taylor, New York.

Barnett, Steve, and Silverman, Martin G., 1979, *Ideology and Everyday Life: Anthropology, Neomarxist Thought, and the Problem of Ideology and the Social Whole,* University of Michigan Press, Ann Arbor.

Barrow, David Crenshaw, 1881, A Georgia Plantation, *Scribner's Monthly* 21:830–836.

Blassingame, John W., 1979, *The Slave Community: Plantation Life in the Antebellum South,* rev. ed., Oxford University Press, New York.

Block, Carl E., and Roering, Kenneth J., 1979, *Essentials of Consumer Behavior,* 2nd ed., Dryden Press, Hinsdale, Illinois.

Bloch, Maurice (ed.), 1975, *Marxist Analysis and Social Anthropology,* Malaby Press, London.

Bloch, Maurice, 1985, *Marxism and Anthropology,* Oxford University Press, Oxford.

Boeger, E. A., and Goldenweiser, E. A., 1916, A Study of the Tenant Systems of Farming in the Yazoo–Mississippi Delta, United States Department of Agriculture Bulletin 337.

Brannen, C. O., 1924, Relation of Land Tenure to Plantation Organization, United States Department of Agriculture Bulletin 1269.

Brooks, Robert Preston, 1914, The Agrarian Revolution in Georgia: 1885–1912, Bulletin of the University of Wisconsin 639.

Cairnes, J. E., 1862, *The Slave Power: Its Character, Career, and Probable Designs, Being an Attempt to Explain the Real Issues Involved in the American Contest,* Carleton Press, New York.

Cheek, William F., 1970, *Black Resistance Before the Civil War,* Glencoe Press, Beverly Hills, California.

Childe, V. Gordon, 1946, Archaeology and Anthropology, *Southwestern Journal of Anthropology* 2:243–251.

Childe, V. Gordon, 1947, *History,* Cobbett Press, London.

Childe, V. Gordon, 1951, *Man Makes Himself,* Mentor, New York.

Childe, V. Gordon, 1956, *Society and Knowledge,* Harper & Brothers, New York.

Childe, V. Gordon, 1964, *What Happened in History,* Penguin Books, Baltimore.

Childe, V. Gordon, 1979, Prehistory and Marxism, *Antiquity* 53:93–95.

Cole, G. D. H., 1934, *What Marx Really Meant,* Victor Gollancz, London.

Conrad, Alfred H., and Meyer, John R., 1958, The Economics of Slavery in the Antebellum South, *Journal of Political Economy* 66:95–130.

Cox, Oliver Cromwell, 1942, The Modern Caste School of Race Relations, *Social Forces* 21:218–226.

Cox, Oliver Cromwell, 1945, Race and Caste: A Distinction, *American Journal of Sociology* 50:360–368.

Cox, Oliver Cromwell, 1948, *Caste, Class, and Race: A Study in Social Dynamics,* Doubleday, New York.

David, Paul A., Gutman, Herbert G., Sutch, Richard, Temin, Peter, and Wright, Gavin, 1976, *Reckoning With Slavery: A Critical Study in the Quantitative History of American Negro Slavery,* Oxford University Press, New York.

Davis, Allison, Gardner, Burleigh B., and Gardner, Mary R., 1941, *Deep South: A Social Anthropological Study of Caste and Class*, University of Chicago Press, Chicago.

Dillingham, Pitt, 1896, Land Tenure Among the Negroes, *Yale Review* (o.s.) 5:190–206.

Dollard, John, 1957, *Caste and Class in a Southern Town*, 3rd ed., Doubleday Anchor, New York.

DuBois, W. E. B., 1935, *Black Reconstruction*, Harcourt, Brace & World, New York.

Dumont, Louis, 1967, Caste: A Phenomenon of Social Structure or An Aspect of Indian Culture? in: *Caste and Race: Comparative Approaches* (Anthony de Reuck and Julie Knight, eds.), J. and A. Churchill, London, pp. 28–38.

Dumont, Louis, 1977, *From Mandeville to Marx: The Genesis and Triumph of Economic Ideology*, University of Chicago Press, Chicago.

Ely, Richard T., and Galpin, Charles J., 1919, Tenancy in an Ideal System of Landownership, in: Papers on Tenancy, Office of the Secretary of the American Association for Agricultural Legislation, Bulletin 2, University of Wisconsin, Madison, pp. 39–71.

Fairbanks, Charles H., 1984, The Plantation Archaeology of the Southeastern Coast, *Historical Archaeology* 18:1–14.

Flynn, Charles L., Jr., 1983, *White Land, Black Labor: Caste and Class in Late Nineteenth-Century Georgia*, Louisiana State University Press, Baton Rouge.

Fogel, Robert W., and Engerman, Stanley L., 1974, *Time on the Cross: The Economics of American Negro Slavery*, Little, Brown, Boston.

Foner, Philip S. (ed.), 1983, *Karl Marx Remembered: Comments at the Time of His Death*, Synthesis Press, San Francisco.

Gandy, D. Ross, 1979, *Marx and History: From Primitive Society to the Communist Future*, University of Texas Press, Austin.

Genovese, Eugene D., 1967, A Note on the Place of Economics in the Political Economy of Slavery, in: *The Political Economy of Slavery: Studies in the Economy and Society of the Slave South*, Vintage Press, New York, pp. 275–287.

Genovese, Eugene D., 1974, *Roll, Jordon, Roll: The World the Slaves Made*, Pantheon Press, New York.

Genovese, Eugene D., 1984, *In Red and Black: Marxian Explorations in Southern and Afro-American History*, University of Tennessee Press, Knoxville.

Genovese, Eugene D., and Fox-Genovese, Elizabeth, 1983, *Fruits of Merchant Capital: Slavery and Bourgeois Property in the Rise and Expansion of Capitalism*, Oxford University Press, Oxford.

Godelier, Maurice, 1977, *Perspectives in Marxist Anthropology*, Cambridge University Press, Cambridge.

Goodenough, Ward, 1965, Rethinking "Status" and "Role": Toward a General Model of the Cultural Organization of Social Relationships, in: *The Relevance of Models for Social Anthropology* (Michael Banton, ed.), Tavistock Press, London, pp. 1–24.

Green, Sally, 1981, *Prehistorian: A Biography of V. Gordon Childe*, Moonraker Press, Bradford-on-Avon.

Gutman, Herbert G., 1975, *Slavery and the Numbers Game: A Critique of Time on the Cross*, University of Illinois Press, Urbana.

Handsman, Russell G., 1980, The Domain of Kinship and Settlement in Historic Goshen: Signs of a Past Cultural Order, *Artifacts* 9(1):2, 4–7, 9.

Handsman, Russell G., 1981, Early Capitalism and the Center Village of Canaan, Connecticut: A Study of Transformation and Separations, *Artifacts* 9(3):1–22.

Handsman, Russell G., 1982, The Hot and the Cold of Goshen's History, *Artifacts* 10(3):10–20.

Handsman, Russell G., 1983, Historical Archaeology and Capitalism, Subscriptions, and Separations: The Production of Individualism, *North American Archaeologist* 4:63–79.

Handsman, Russell G., 1984, Merchant Capital and the Historical Archaeology of Gender, Motherhood, and Child Raising, unpublished paper delivered at the Annual Meeting of the Council for Northeast Historical Archaeology, Binghamton, New York.

Handsman, Russell G., 1985, Thinking about an Historical Archaeology of Alienation and Class Struggles, unpublished paper delivered at the Annual Meeting of the Society for Historical Archaeology, Boston.

Helper, Hinton Rowan, 1860, *The Impending Crisis of the South: How To Meet It*, A. B. Burdick, New York.

Higgs, Robert, 1974, Patterns of Farm Rental in the Georgia Cotton Belt, 1880–1900, *Journal of Economic History* 34:468–482.

Hodder, Ian (ed.), 1982, *Symbolic and Structural Archaeology,* Cambridge University Press, Cambridge.

Hundley, Daniel R., 1860, *Social Relations in Our Southern States,* Henry B. Price, New York.

Kahl, Joseph, A., 1957, *The American Class Structure,* Rinehart, New York.

Kohl, P. L., 1981, Materialist Approaches in Prehistory, *Annual Review of Anthropology* 10:89–118.

Leach, Edmund, 1967, Caste, Class, and Slavery: The Taxonomic Problem, in: *Caste and Race: Comparative Approaches* (Anthony de Reuck and Julie Knight, eds.), J. and A. Churchill, London, pp. 5–16.

Leacock, Eleanor, 1972, Introduction, in: Engels, Frederick, *Origins of the Family, Private Property and the State,* International Press, New York, pp. 7–67.

Leone, Mark P., 1981, Archaeology's Relationship to the Present and the Past, in: *Modern Material Culture: The Archaeology of Us* (Richard A. Gould and Michael B. Schiffer, eds.), Academic Press, New York, pp. 5–14.

Leone, Mark P., 1982a, Childe's Offspring, in: *Symbolic and Structural Archaeology* (Ian Hodder, ed.), Cambridge University Press, Cambridge, pp. 179–184.

Leone, Mark P., 1982b, Some Opinions About Recovering Mind, *American Antiquity* 47:742–760.

Leone, Mark P., 1983, Method As Message: Interpreting the Past With the Public, *Museum News* 62(1):35–41.

Leone, Mark P., 1984, Interpreting Ideology in Historical Archaeology: Using the Rules of Perspective in the William Paca Garden in Annapolis, Maryland, in: *Ideology, Power, and Prehistory* (Daniel Miller and Christopher Tilley, eds.), Cambridge University Press, Cambridge, pp. 25–35.

Le Page du Pratz, A. S., 1975, *The History of Louisiana* (Joseph G. Tregle, ed. and trans.), Louisiana State University Press, Baton Rouge.

Maguire, Jane, 1975, *On Shares: Ed Brown's Story,* W. W. Norton, New York.

Mann, Susan A., 1984, Sharecropping in the Cotton South: A Case of Uneven Development in Agriculture, *Rural Sociology* 49:412–429.

Marx, Karl, 1904, *A Contribution to the Critique of Political Economy* (N. I. Stone, trans.), International Library, New York.

Marx, Karl, 1967, *Capital: A Critique of Political Economy,* International Publishers, New York.

Marx, Karl, 1971, *The Grundrisse* (David McLellan, ed. and trans.), Harper & Row, New York.

Marx, Karl, and Engels, Frederick, 1937, *The Civil War in the United States* (Richard Enmale, ed.), International Publishers, New York.

Marx, Karl, and Engels, Frederick, 1970, *The German Ideology, Part I* (C. J. Arthur, ed.), Lawrence and Wishart, London.

Matsumae, Shigeyoshi, 1975, *Materialism in Search of a Soul: A Scientific Critique of Historical Materialism,* Tokai University Press, Tokyo.

Mayo, Henry B., 1960, *Introduction to Marxist Theory,* Oxford University Press, New York.

Moore, Wilbert E., and Williams, Robin M., 1942, Stratification in the Ante-Bellum South, *American Sociological Review* 7:343–351.

Myrdal, Gunnar, 1944, *An American Dilemma: The Negro Problem and Modern Democracy,* Harper & Brothers, New York.

Nowak, Leszek, 1983, *Property and Power: Towards a Non-Marxian Historical Materialism,* D. Reidel, Dordrecht, Holland.

O'Laughlin, Bridget, 1975, Marxist Approaches in Anthropology, *Annual Review of Anthropology* 4:341–370.

Orser, Charles E., Jr., 1984, The Past Ten Years of Plantation Archaeology in the Southeastern United States, *Southeastern Archaeology* 3:1–12.

Orser, Charles E., Jr., 1985, What Good Is Plantation Archaeology?, *Southern Studies: An Interdisciplinary Journal of the South* 24:444–455.

Orser, Charles E., Jr., and Holland, Claudia C., 1984, Let Us Praise Famous Men, Accurately: Toward A More Complete Understanding of Postbellum Southern Agricultural Practices, *Southeastern Archaeology* 3:111–120.

Orser, Charles E., Jr., and Nekola, Annette M., 1985, Plantation Settlement from Slavery to
    Tenancy: An Example from a Piedmont Plantation in South Carolina, in: *The Archaeology of
    Slavery and Plantation Life* (Theresa A. Singleton, ed.), Academic Press, Orlando, pp. 67–94.
Otto, John Solomon, 1975, Status Differences and the Archaeological Record: A Comparison of
    Planter, Overseer, and Slave Sites from Cannon's Point Plantation, (1794–1861), St. Simons
    Island, Georgia, Ph.D. dissertation, University of Florida, University Microfilms, Ann Arbor.
Otto, John Solomon, 1977, Artifacts and Status Differences: A Comparison of Ceramics from
    Planter, Overseer, and Slave Sites on an Antebellum Plantation, in: *Research Strategies in
    Historical Archaeology* (Stanley South, ed.), Academic Press, New York, pp. 91–118.
Otto, John Solomon, 1980, Race and Class on Antebellum Plantations, in: *Archaeological Perspec-
    tives on Ethnicity in America: Afro-American and Asian American Culture History* (Robert L.
    Schuyler, ed.), Baywood Press, New York, pp. 3–13.
Otto, John Solomon, 1984, *Cannon's Point Plantation, 1794–1860: Living Conditions and Status
    Patterns in the Old South,* Academic Press, Orlando.
Owsley, Frank Lawrence, 1949, *Plain Folk of the Old South,* Louisiana State University Press,
    Baton Rouge.
Park, Robert E., 1928, The Bases of Race Prejudice, *The Annals of the American Academy of
    Political and Social Science* 140:11–20.
Powdermaker, Hortense, 1968, *After Freedom: A Cultural Study in the Deep South,* Atheneum
    Press, New York.
Pruty, Merle C., 1955, The Renaissance of the Southern Plantation, *Geographical Review* 45:459–
    491.
Ransom, Roger L., and Sutch, Richard, 1977, *One Kind of Freedom: The Economic Consequences of
    Emancipation,* Cambridge University Press, Cambridge.
Rattansi, Ali, 1982, *Marx and the Division of Labor,* Macmillan, London.
Rosengarten, Theodore, 1974, *All God's Dangers: The Life of Nate Shaw,* Vintage Books, New
    York.
Schuler, E. A., 1938, Social Status and Farm Tenure: Attitudes and Social Conditions of Corn Belt
    and Cotton Belt Farmers, United States Department of Agriculture, Farm Security Admin-
    istration, and the Bureau of Agricultural Economics, Social Research Report 4.
Shannon, Fred A., 1945, *The Farmer's Last Frontier: Agriculture, 1860–1897,* Farrar & Rinehart,
    New York.
Simpson, G. E., and Yinger, J. M., 1953, *Racial and Cultural Minorities,* Harper & Brothers, New
    York.
Spillman, W. J., 1919, The Agricultural Ladder, in: Papers on Tenancy, Office of the Secretary of
    the American Association for Agricultural Legislation, Bulletin 2, University of Wisconsin,
    Madison, pp. 29–38.
Spriggs, Matthew (ed.), 1984a, *Marxist Perspectives in Archaeology,* Cambridge University Press,
    Cambridge.
Spriggs, Matthew, 1984b, Another Way of Telling: Marxist Perspectives in Archaeology, in: *Marx-
    ist Perspectives in Archaeology* (Matthew Spriggs, ed.), Cambridge University Press, Camb-
    ridge, pp. 1–9.
Stampp, Kenneth M., 1956, *The Peculiar Institution: Slavery in the Ante-Bellum South,* Vintage
    Books, New York.
Thalheimer, August, 1936, *Introduction to Dialectical Materialism: The Marxist World-View*
    (George Simpson and George Weltner, trans.), Covici-Friede, New York.
Thompson, Edgar T., 1939, The Plantation: The Physical Basis of Traditional Race Relations, in:
    Race Relations and the Race Problem: A Definition and an Analysis (Edgar T. Thompson, ed.),
    Duke University Press, Durham, pp. 180–218.
Thompson, Edgar, T., 1975, The Plantation: Background and Definition, in: *Plantation Societies,
    Race Relations, and the South: The Regimentation of Populations, Selected Papers of Edgar T.
    Thompson,* Duke University Press, Durham, pp. 3–40.
Trigger, Bruce G., 1984, Alternative Archaeologies: Nationalist, Colonialist, Imperialist, *Man*
    (n.s.) 19:355–370.
United States Department of Commerce, 1932, *Agricultural Census of the United States: 1930,*

Agriculture, Volume II, Part 2, The Southern States, Government Printing Office, Washington, D.C.

Vance, Rupert B., 1929, *Human Factors in Cotton Culture,* University of North Carolina Press, Chapel Hill.

Warner, W. Lloyd, 1936, American Caste and Class, *American Journal of Sociology* 42:234–237.

Warner, W. Lloyd, 1941, Deep South: A Social Anthropological Study of Caste and Class, in: *Deep South: A Social Anthropological Study of Caste and Class,* (Davis, Allison, Gardner, Burligh B., and Gardner, Mary R., eds.), University of Chicago Press, Chicago, pp. 3–14.

White, E. V., and Leonard, William E., 1915, Studies in Farm Tenancy in Texas, University of Texas Bulletin 21.

Wolf, Eric R., 1959, Specific Aspects of Plantation Systems in the New World: Community Sub-Cultures and Social Classes, in: Plantation Systems of the New World, Pan American Union, Social Science Monograph 7, pp. 136–212.

Wolfe, Samuel M., 1860, *Helper's Impending Crisis Dissected,* J. T. Lloyd, Philadelphia.

Woofter, Thomas J., Jr., Blackwell, Gordon, Hoffsommer, Harold, Maddox, James G., Massell, Jean M., Williams, B. O., and Wynne, Waller, Jr., 1936, Landlord and Tenant on the Cotton Plantation, Works Progress Administration, Division of Social Research, Monograph 5.

Zeichner, Oscar, 1939, The Transition from Slave to Free Agricultural Labor in the Southern States, *Agricultural History* 13:22–32.

Mid-Nineteenth-Century Commerce and Industrialization

In the mid-nineteenth century, most Americans were farmers, and many were involved in commerce as merchants, jobbers, peddlers, craftsmen, and related occupations. Total farm production increased as much of America's growing population migrated west and used agricultural machinery to increase their production of staple crops for regional and national markets. Increasing numbers of people were being employed in regional-scale factories that were gradually replacing some of the earlier village crafts and mills, as well as home manufactures. As transportation innovations facilitated long-distance travel, and technological innovations facilitated larger-scale production, many farms and factories produced increasingly for regional, national, and sometimes international markets (Niemi 1975:94–96, 227). Some industries, for example, shoe manufacture, made the transition from craft to factory through the "putting-out" system, in which the raw materials, such as leather, were "put out" to craftsmen by entrepreneurs who paid low rates for the manufacture of shoes or other products by household labor. The entrepreneur or middleman marketed these home manufactures to larger regional and national markets than were available locally to craftsmen (Tryon 1917). In this process, many types of small mills and craftsmen once found in nearly every community were gradually replaced by larger-scale mills spaced at greater distances on the landscape (Robertson 1973:202–221, 326). The independent-artisan middle class was gradually reduced in socioeconomic status to factory employees. Attempts to organize factory workers against deteriorating wages and working conditions in the mid-nineteenth century failed in the panics and depressions of 1848, 1853–1854, and 1857–1859 (Ingle and Ward 1978:180–193).

In mid-nineteenth century America, first canals and then railroads facilitated distribution of goods between the East, the Midwest, and then the Far West. Regional specializations in production for the growing national market developed both in agriculture and industry. In the South, agricultural specializations in cotton, tobacco, and rice were primary (Bining and Cochran 1964:279–281). The Northeast specialized predominantly in the development of textile and other industries, with farms near cities raising primarily dairy, chicken, and market-garden products for rapidly growing urban populations (Niemi 1975:52; Russell 1982:218–222). Agricultural specializations in grain, beef cattle, and sheep spread in sequence to the West, as did mining (Bining and Cochran 1964:282–284; Gruver 1972:405; Ratner *et al.* 1979:148–151). The depression of 1857 was felt principally in the North, due to deflation in European demand for American foodstuffs after the Crimean War, and American overextension of railroad construction and land speculation in the Midwest and Northwest (Gruver 1972:520). In the mid-nineteenth century, some important industries developed in the Midwest, including some ceramics and glass manufacturers and coal, oil, and iron and steel industries in Pennsylvania and Ohio. Industrial production was predominantly small scale by modern standards, resulting in industrial villages such as that analyzed by Paul Heberling in this volume. While water and wood remained the dominant sources of power, the use of coal and steam power was starting to grow (Bining and Cochran 1964:239–241; Ratner *et al.* 1979:189–194, 283). With transportation innovations, larger-scale factories could distribute their products more widely, increasing market access to consumer goods for households in many different locations (Ingle and Ward 1978:178–181).

Part II also includes the major impact of the Civil War. The first chapter by McBride and McBride is concerned with social stratification in an interior, riverine, antebellum agricultural and commercial town. In the second chapter, Shephard analyzes status differences from antebellum urban site deposits in the predominantly commercial city of Alexandria, Virginia. In this study, numbers of slaves are one of the indications of wealth, as contrasted with the low socioeconomic status of freed blacks. The Pennsylvania iron-working village where social stratification is analyzed by Heberling, was started before the Civil War and may have contributed iron goods to the war. Garrow analyzes status, white ceramics, and fauna for antebellum deposits in Washington, D.C., and Wilmington, Delaware. LeeDecker and his associates' analyses of Wilmington sites include periods both before and after the war. While the occupations of the Wilmington and Washington, D.C., site residents predominantly involve commerce and local industry, De Cunzo analyzes the documentary and archaeological indications of status among different ethnic families predominantly employed in the larger-scale factories that became more frequent first in the Northeast, and later in the South, Midwest and Far West.

The first chapter in this section is concerned with sites in a small southern commercial town that existed at the same time as some of the later plantations and as the tenant-farming arrangements considered in the previous section by Reitz and Orser. The McBrides demonstrate a fairly close correspondence between documentary indications of the socioeconomic status of site residents and the relative values of their archaeological white ceramic assemblages. Occupations are principally used to indicate status, and a modification of Miller's ceramic price-scaling index is used to quantify relative value of archaeological whiteware sherd assemblages. The McBrides demonstrate the possibility of relating analyses of decorative types of sherds to status when vessel counts are not available. The status of site residents is also considered in the context of the distribution of property, and personal and real estate mean and median values for occupations of heads of household in the town area.

Shephard's chapter deals with the utility of alternative measures of ceramics for distinguishing middle-class whites from poor blacks in Alexandria, Virginia. Site assemblage ceramic quantity, quality, and variety are measured, and compared with documented indicators of site residents' class, including differences in household occupational rank, value of personal and real property, location, size and building material of house, size of household, number of slaves, and ethnicity. Shephard generates hypotheses and test implications of expected class differences in ceramics from the conjunctive use of consumer behavior theory and previous archaeological research. Shephard's results indicate that measures of site ceramic quality and quantity differentiated the middle- from lower-class sites as expected, while ceramic variety did not. This research distinguishes some measures of ceramic attributes that are related to status, and one that is not.

The third chapter in this section is concerned with status and settlement pattern in an iron-making village in Pennsylvania. In this case, very little documentation is available on the village and its residents. Through collaborative use of archaeological ceramics, glass, and architectural features in combination with a little documentation, Heberling reconstructs the social structure in the residential settlement pattern around the iron furnace where the villagers all worked. Methods are suggested for the analysis of glass and architectural attributes that may be related to socioeconomic status. Heberling demonstrates the utility of conjunctive analyses of three artifact classes, and of documentary data in delineating socioeconomic patterning within a settlement pattern.

Garrow compares and contrasts documented occupations for residents of city blocks in Washington, D.C., and Wilmington, Delaware, with relative value of site whiteware, evidence of ceramic sets, and faunal species and cuts. Possible temporal changes in socioeconomic status are considered in explaining disparities between the relative values of fauna and whiteware deposited by one household at its site. Biases due to selective discard of ceramics, differential preservation of faunal remains, and archaeological methods of data recovery and analysis are considered. This chapter demonstrates how documentary and archaeological data can be used conjunctively to gain more information about socioeconomic status than is available from either source of data by itself.

LeeDecker, Klein, Holt, and Friedlander consider the effect of family life cycle, as well as status, on the types of consumer goods acquired and deposited on household sites in Wilmington, Delaware. Relationships between Miller's ceramic index and occupational status are assessed through a temporal, comparative analysis of a number of sites in the eastern United States. Household composition, size (including number of boarders), and developmental stage are related to variations among lower- and middle-class site assemblages in architectural artifacts, types of bottles, fauna, and ceramics. Household composition is related to consumption patterns through analysis of artifact patterns in South's Kitchen and Architecture Groups. Site formation processes are analyzed and used with artifact dates to identify archaeological deposits with households and to infer methods of deposition. LeeDecker and his associates suggest interrelationships between socioeconomic status, household size and composition, and selections of consumer goods later deposited at house sites.

De Cunzo's chapter considers consumer choices as adaptations to industrialization and urbanization. The archaeological data analyzed include choice of household location and types of ceramics and glass deposited at household sites. Differences in types of consumer goods at house sites are related to factors affecting their acquisition, including socioeconomic status, household size, composition, degree of employment, and ethnicity. The formation of ethnic communities, household location and composition, work force participation, and selections of durable goods deposited at household sites are analyzed as methods of adapting to developments in urban industry. Another important aspect of this chapter is the separate consideration of biases in both the documentary and archaeological data. Biases are considered in the partial documentary data available on status of site residents, in the selective deposition of artifacts by households, in their partial recovery archaeologically, and in the methods of analysis. De Cunzo points out that, in order to determine relationships between aspects of archaeological data and socioeconomic status, other variables need to be controlled, a condition that can seldom be met in archaeology.

Chapters in this section consider social stratification and its changes under developing industrial and urban conditions in the mid-nineteenth century. In most cases, two or more measurements of archaeological data—including ceramics, glass, architecture, and fauna—are assessed in relationship to documentary indications of socioeconomic status. LeeDecker and associates, and De Cunzo also consider relationships between measurements of some archaeological attributes and family size, structure, life cycle, and ethnicity, as well as socioeconomic status. Most chapters also consider the effects of biases in the archaeological and documentary records. This section contributes to the conjunctive analysis of more than one artifact class in relationship to socioeconomic status, and furthers the consideration of additional factors within the multivariate framework of consumer choice.

REFERENCES

Bining, Arthur C., and Cochran, Thomas C., 1964, *The Rise of American Economic Life*, Charles Scribner's Sons, New York.

Gruver, Rebecca B., 1972, *An American History, Volume I, To 1877,* Addison-Wesley, Reading, Massachusetts.

Ingle, H. L., and Ward, James A., 1978, *American History: A Brief View Through Reconstruction,* Little, Brown, Boston.

Niemi, A. W., Jr., 1975, *U.S. Economic History: A Survey of the Major Issues,* Rand McNally, Chicago.

Ratner, Sidney, Soltow, J. H., and Sulla, R., 1979, *The Evolution of the American Economy,* Basic Books, New York.

Robertson, R. M., 1973, *History of the American Economy,* Harcourt, Brace, Jovanovich, New York.

Russell. Howard S., 1982, *A Long Deep Furrow: Three Centuries of Farming in New England,* University Press of New England, Hanover.

Tryon, Rolla M., 1917, *Household Manufactures in the United States, 1640–1860,* University of Chicago Press, Chicago.

7

Socioeconomic Variation in a Late Antebellum Southern Town

The View from Archaeological and Documentary Sources

W. STEPHEN McBRIDE AND KIM A. McBRIDE

INTRODUCTION

This paper looks at socioeconomic stratification as reflected in the distribution of material goods in a small, inland, antebellum community. Based on both archaeological and documentary resources, this sort of research represents one of the major strengths of historical archaeology in that it fosters comparison and integration of different types of data, allowing for a more complete picture of socioeconomic scaling and material wealth. The major goals of the paper are twofold: the first is methodological, comparing the results of artifactual and documentary approaches to the assessment of material culture consumption; and the second is more substantive, involving a general consideration of socioeconomic stratification, its nature in antebellum southern society, and relationships between social structure and material culture and its consumption.

Socioeconomic studies of the antebellum South have tended to focus on the two extremes of society—the wealthy planters and the slaves. This is true of studies both by historians and historical archaeologists (for example, Blassingame 1972; Fairbanks 1983, 1984; Genovese 1967, 1974; Orser 1984). While some research has dealt with the more moderate socioeconomic levels of southern society (such as Atherton 1949; Bonner 1944; Eaton 1961; Foust 1975; Hahn 1983; Owsley 1949; Scarborough 1984; Stewart-Abernathy 1980), these groups have received relatively little scholarly attention. The study of these people is important to archaeologists not only because they made up the majority of white southern society (Owsley 1949), but also because their standards of consumer behavior are the best baseline against which socioeconomic differences can be measured (Wise 1984:2). This lack of attention also pertains to southern urban places, except for the larger and more romantic centers such as

W. Stephen McBride and Kim A. McBride ☐ Museum and Department of Anthropology, Michigan State University, East Lansing, MI 48824. Much of the data for this study was collected by Michigan State University under contract with the National Park Service and the U.S. Army Corps of Engineers, and their support is gratefully acknowledged.

Richmond, Charleston, or New Orleans. The smaller inland towns, with their merchants, professionals, craftsmen, and resident planters, have received little attention, even though they played a crucial role in the cotton economy (Atherton 1949; Woodman 1968).

Material Culture and Wealth

As archaeologists, we are often left to build our cases upon the discarded and misplaced items of domestic material culture. Even when we can deal with more complete inventories, such as in exceptional archaeological assemblages or in probate documents, we still tap into a very small percentage of wealth. Jones's (1980:97) excellent study of colonial wealth suggests that all consumer goods accounted for only 8.1 percent of all physical wealth in 1774. While similarly detailed studies remain to be conducted for the mid-nineteenth century, a general study of the American standard of living in 1860 (Martin 1942) concluded that only between 5 percent and 10 percent of income was left to go to consumer goods after providing for the basics of housing, food, and clothing. However, this situation may actually work in favor of the archaeologist trying to study status and its relationship to material goods consumption, since such a small margin of wealth renders the variations in our samples more sensitive as indicators of status differences.

There may be important regional variations in the role of material culture in status maintenance, which the archaeologist should be sensitive to. For example, comparisons are sometimes made between the extravagant consumption of the antebellum South versus savings and investment in the North (Eaton 1961). However, this thesis, like most concerning southern society, focuses only on the extremely wealthy planters. It may be that lavish consumption was an important mechanism of status maintenance for some planters, although the basic generalization remains little tested for *any* socioeconomic level, let alone all of southern society. Calling again on Jones's study of colonial wealth, consumer goods made up only 8.6 percent of southern nonhuman physical wealth (excludes slaves). In comparison, consumer goods accounted for 12 percent of New England's, and 10 percent of the Middle Colonies' nonhuman, physical wealth. Unfortunately, there is a lack of antebellum wealth studies that isolate consumer goods as a percentage of wealth. We do, however, have antebellum regional comparisons of income, which could be an important first step in comparing its dispensation. Easterlin (1961:527) showed that 1840 and 1860 income levels for white southerners exceeded the national average and compared favorably with the Northeast.

Despite the fact that southern society was not exclusively a society of slaveholders—and, in fact, was quite the opposite, with only 26 percent of the free population holding slaves in 1860 (Moore and Williams 1942:343; Owsley 1949)—the goals of slaveholding and "planting" were strong enough that material wealth and status were disproportionately contingent upon possession of slaves and land (Eaton 1961; Moore and Williams 1942). This does not mean that consumer goods played only a minor role in status differentiation and maintenance in the South; in fact, we will show that they are good indicators of such. However, the point remains that the relationships between wealth and consumer goods on one hand, and status on the other, may not have been identical to such relationships in other regions.

Ceramics in Status Studies

Because they constitute an artifact group that is especially sensitive to "sociotechnic" dimensions (Binford 1962), refined ceramics are the most commonly used artifact type in status studies in historical archaeology. The quality and variety of ceramics found on a site are a good measure of relative economic level (Miller and Stone 1970:98). Other artifact types, such as drinking glasses, silverware, silverplate, and clothing items, have also been utilized in assessing socioeconomic level (Lewis 1978:110; South 1977:193). However, since these artifact types are relatively less common than ceramics in the archaeological record, they have not been used as frequently in status analyses.

The exact use of ceramics in status studies varies considerably. For eighteenth-century sites, many authors have used the presence of expensive Chinese-export porcelain, particularly in tea sets, as indicators of high socioeconomic status (cf. Lewis 1978:104; Miller and Stone 1970:98–100; Stone 1970:88). Other approaches include an examination of the overall quality and variety of ceramics (Lewis 1978:110; Miller and Stone 1970:98; South 1977:221), and the determination of purchasing practices, namely, whether ceramics were bought individually or in sets (Miller 1974). Two of the most innovative and commonly cited studies of socioeconomic status include Otto's comparison of ceramic decoration and vessel forms at slave, overseer, and planter sites at Cannon's Point, Georgia (1977, 1980) and George Miller's ceramic price-scaling analysis (1980).

Such endeavors are not without problems. There is not, of course, a perfect correlation between material culture and status. Further, in more complex societies, "there are a great variety of status differences which may produce patterning in the archaeological record" (Otto 1980:3), including such factors as the economic context of the site under investigation, the ethnicity of the occupants, and the types of artifacts utilized. Some of the complexities have been demonstrated recently by Miller and Hurry (1983) and Lees and Kimery-Lees (1984) in studies of frontier settlements in Ohio and Oklahoma, respectively. Both utilized Miller's (1980) price-scaling index for ceramics but concluded that the differences found between sites was due more to transportation and trade network differences than socioeconomic status. These studies stress the importance of a detailed knowledge of the economic context within which a settlement operated. In this light, we present a brief summary of the history and economic context of the Barton sites. As will be seen, Barton, the subject of this analysis, had ready access to consumer goods, and transportation constraints were minor, or at least equivalent, for all of the sites being compared.

Barton, Small Riverport Town

Barton townsite is located along the western bank of the Tombigbee River in Clay County, Mississippi (see Figure 1). Its history is not unlike that of many other extinct towns in northeastern Mississippi (see Adkins 1972). Its existence was relatively short, and inextricably linked with cotton marketing and transportation.

Barton was founded in 1848 by residents of the recently flooded town of Colbert. Barton's economy revolved around cotton, providing storage facilities and access to the Mobile steamers that shipped cotton down river and goods up for a hinterland of cotton producers. These steamers had been operating regu-

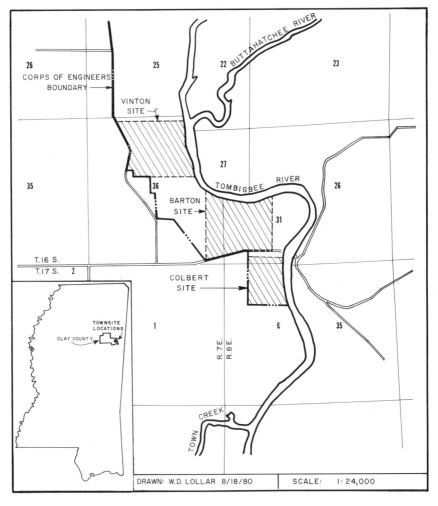

Figure 1. Tombigbee historic townsites and vicinity.

larly since the 1830s and their runs increased during the late 1840s and 1850s as cotton production in the Tombigbee Valley grew (Doster and Weaver 1981:67; Way and McBride 1983:51). Navigation was, however, subject to seasonal fluctuations of the river, a problem that eventually led to Barton's demise in the late 1850s, when rail service became available about ten miles away. During both periods, site residents had fairly reliable connections to the large shipping centers of Mobile and New Orleans, and to the many foreign and domestic goods coming through these ports.

The services provided at Barton are very typical of small, inland towns in the cotton South. Storekeepers in these towns, who often made up a sizable percentage of the population, acted as middlemen for farmers and small planters who did not produce enough cotton to deal directly with a port city factor. Cotton was either sold to the merchant for cash, or traded for goods, and merchants usually gave long-term credit to farmers so that goods were given out long before the cotton crop came in (Atherton 1949; Woodman 1968). Records from the Barton stores also indicate that merchants served to dispense cash to farmers. Complementary to their role in handling cotton, merchants at Barton also provided general merchandise for farmers and planters in the surrounding area, as well as for town residents. Other services at Barton are reflected in the presence of a tavern and hotel, a church, a school, a blacksmith shop, and a post office. Physicians, lawyers, carpenters, planters, and a hatter also lived in Barton. During its peak in the mid 1850s, Barton probably included fifteen to twenty households and from three to seven commercial enterprises (Way and McBride 1983). Because the local craftsmen, farmers, and small planters had low purchasing power, it was unwise for small stores to specialize, and most carried general merchandise (Adkins 1972:55; Atherton 1949:71). These stores did have some dealings with the wealthier members of the antebellum community, whose purchasing power was much greater, although these were not their main customers, and merchants often served them in the capacity of agent, handling the details of securing goods from factors rather than providing general merchandise from their own store.

This study focuses on six of the fourteen domestic sites located at Barton during Michigan State University Museum's Tombigbee Historic Townsites Project. These six sites were chosen for intensive investigation by the project because of their archaeological integrity, supporting documentary and oral historical information, and impending impacts (Minnerly 1983). Brief descriptions from McBride and McBride (1983) follow. Throughout the text, sites will be referred to by both their site numbers and their major occupants.

The first site is Site 5442, the McGowen site, which was occupied successively by two merchants and their families between 1849 and 1857, after which time it was occupied by the Futrell family, who were engaged in farming. Site 5443, the Barton hotel, served as a stopover for travelers, a boardinghouse, and, with its tavern, a central place in the community for socializing and the conducting of town business. It was owned by the Hanks from 1849 until 1857, after which it passed through the ownership of three successive individuals from the eastern bank of the river. It probably did little official business during these later years, and the main structure appears to have been removed by the mid- to late 1860s. Site 5444 was the residence of a clerk and later merchant, Benjamin Howorth, through most of the 1850. By 1860 it was the residence of an overseer, William Rodgers, and his family. Site 5445 was occupied by the merchant Peter Warren from 1849 until 1857, and was then sold to the merchant A. B. Duling, who resided there with his family for several years. Duling was also the mayor of Barton. Site 5447 was also strictly residential, although it is unique at Barton in that it was occupied by two professionals, first the physician Mathew Debrill, and then a lawyer, James Capshaw, and their families from 1851 until 1859. Further occupation is not documented. The final site of this analysis, Site 5448, was the home of one of Barton's most successful merchants, James Griswold, from the early 1850s until 1858, after which it was occupied for several years by the town minister Robert Ussery and his family.

Most of these sites had fairly complex occupational histories, despite their relatively short existence. The extreme geographical mobility demonstrated by the different birthplaces of children in these families (Way and McBride 1983) is typical of settlement patterns in the Old Southwest, although the intrasite mobility documented here has received less study. From 1848 to 1865, the mean length of occupation for these sites was 4.4 years, and for these six sites, there were seventeen different occupations. Together, these six sites form a good representation of the occupational and economic variation at Barton, including occupations by a number of merchants of varying prominence, two professionals, a clerk, and several families engaged in agricultural production.

Consumption at Barton

With this introduction, we move into the analysis of the distribution of consumer goods, and by inference, of wealth, at the antebellum town of Barton, Mississippi. This section will begin with the analysis of excavated ceramics from the six Barton sites, followed by an analysis of personal property records for these sites, and by broader examination of property holdings for the entire town of Barton and its hinterland.

Artifact Analysis

The first stage of analysis is based on ceramics recovered from these sites and utilizes Miller's (1980) investigation into price scaling and expenditures on refined ceramics. Miller defined four main price groups (Miller 1980:3–4). These are, from lowest to highest:

1. Undecorated cream-colored ware (equivalent to whiteware on mid-nineteenth-century sites)
2. Minimal decoration—shell edged, banded, stamped, sponged, or slipped

3. Hand-painted floral motif
4. Transfer-painted—from willow to flowed, increasing in cost

The price differentials between these groups can be considerable, with transfer-printed being up to five times as expensive as undecorated cream-colored ware (Miller 1980:30).

For sites occupied into the 1850s or later, a fifth group should be added. This is ironstone or white granite, which was generally undecorated and at a price equal to that of transfer-printed whiteware (Miller 1980:4). Unfortunately, the separation of ironstone or white granite from whiteware is difficult and not well described by archaeologists or by ceramic historians. The latter simply do not give enough objective criteria for identification, and most archaeologists combine them (cf. Lofstrom 1976; Price 1979; South 1974). This study uses criteria that have been suggested by Praetzellis (1980) and Cleland (1983). Praetzellis separates whiteware from what she calls opaque porcelain by the latter's harder, vitreous paste (1980:4–7). Cleland (1983) refers to the ironstonelike ceramics by the more etic term white-pasted stoneware, and defines them as having a nonporous paste and a glaze that does not readily craze (1983:43). Although not extremely precise, these criteria seem the best to date, and are used in the present study.

The reader may be surprised at the exclusion of porcelain from this analysis since it is often the basis for status studies on sites from the eighteenth century. Unfortunately, the exact cost of porcelain relative to other nineteenth-century ceramics is not well understood at present, although it is known to have been the most expensive ceramic (Miller 1980:4). Miller's price-index tables contain porcelain values for only one year for plates, three years for cups and saucers, and no years for bowls (1980:26, 30, 33). It is hoped that future research will allow for the inclusion of porcelain.

One deviation from Miller's (1980) analysis in the present study is the use of sherd counts rather than vessel counts. To adapt Miller's system to sherd counts, with vessel form unknown, the prices for plates, cups, and bowls were averaged. Although somewhat experimental, the adaptation of Miller's system to sherd counts has led to successful results in a number of studies (Cook 1982; Exnicious and Pearson 1985; Lees and Kimery-Lees 1984; Spencer-Wood 1984). It is hoped that this method can be tested more fully in the near future, and its discrepancies noted and adjusted (Heberling and Spencer-Wood 1985).

At Barton townsite, the ceramic price analysis was conducted for the hotel and five house sites whose occupational histories have already been described. All but two of these sites had only antebellum occupations, and their entire samples were used. Two sites (Sites 5442 and 5448) had longer occupational sequences, and only ceramics from the antebellum features and site areas were included. The results of the ceramic price indexing are given in Tables 1 and 2. Given that Miller's scale for 1855, the year used for this analysis, ranges from 1.00 to 2.50, these sites only represent a modest amount of variation (1.14 to 1.42). The use of sherd counts instead of vessel counts may in part account for this, since the larger number of undecorated fragments (some of which could be from decorated vessels) can have a lowering and homogenizing influence on the mean index value. Nevertheless, these slight differences seem to be meaningful compared to the documentary analysis and our knowledge of the sites' occupations, and the six sites can be roughly grouped into four levels as follows: (1) Site 5448 (index value 1.42), the home of the wealthy merchant James Griswold; (2) Site 5447 (index value 1.30), the home of the professionals Debrill and Capshaw; (3) Sites 5442, 5444, and 5445 (index values 1.19 to 1.24), the homes of two merchants and a clerk, later merchant; and (4) Site 5443 (index value 1.14), the Barton hotel. These levels suggest the relative socioeconomic positions of the sites' occupants at Barton, based on the patterns of ceramic consumption evident in the archaeological record.

Table 1. Determination of Ceramic Average Value

Site	Type	Count	1855 index value	Sum of counts × ind. value	Total count	Average value (sum ÷ total)
5442	1 undec.	341	1.00			
	2 min. dec.	52	1.16			
	3 painted	4	1.30	536.52	449	1.20
	4 printed	29	2.50			
	5 ironstone	23	2.50			
5443	1 undec.	1,459	1.00			
	2 min. dec.	216	1.16			
	3 painted	106	1.30	2,164.86	1,908	1.14
	4 printed	72	2.50			
	5 ironstone	55	2.50			
5444	1 undec.	291	1.00			
	2 min. dec.	17	1.16			
	3 painted	19	1.30	437.92	368	1.19
	4 printed	29	2.50			
	5 ironstone	12	2.50			
5445	1 undec.	1,869	1.00			
	2 min. dec.	456	1.16			
	3 painted	102	1.30	3,488.06	2,810	1.24
	4 printed	298	2.50			
	5 ironstone	85	2.50			
5447	1 undec.	315	1.00			
	2 min. dec.	43	1.16			
	3 painted	10	1.30	585.38	451	1.30
	4 printed	52	2.50			
	5 ironstone	31	2.50			
5448	1 undec.	408	1.00			
	2 min. dec.	72	1.16			
	3 painted	26	1.30	977.82	687	1.42
	4 printed	83	2.50			
	5 ironstone	98	2.50			

Table 2. Ranking of Sites by Ceramic and Documentary Analysis[a]

Ceramic ranking	Average value	Documentary ranking
Site 5448, Griswold	1.42	Site 5448, Griswold
Site 5447, Deb./Capshaw	1.30	Site 5447, Deb./Capshaw
Site 5445, Warren	1.24	Site 5442, McGowen
Site 5442, McGowen	1.20	Site 5445, Warren
Site 5444, Howarth	1.19	Site 5443, Hanks (hotel)
Site 5443, Hanks (hotel)	1.14	Site 5444, Howarth

[a]Correlation of the rankings yields a Spearman's correlation coefficient of .886, statistically significant at the .05 level.

Documentary Analysis

Just as archaeologically recovered artifacts can be seen as an index of consumption and of consumer choices, the personal property records document the same processes by providing a synchronic glimpse into certain categories of personal property for specific years. For this reason, they provide an alternative data source to complement the analysis based on the excavated materials. In and of themselves, they do not really tell us about overall socioeconomic scaling, in the way that some sort of variable like income is often used, but they do tell us about consumption patterns from which we can make inferences about socioeconomic status, distribution of wealth, access to material goods, and other related topics.

Probate or estate records, generally considered the superior source for such analysis, are scanty since the short life of Barton meant that few occupants died while in residence there. Personal property records, however, are extant for several years in the 1850s, and provide a good substitute. These records are not an enumeration of total material wealth, being confined to certain luxuries, such as pianos, gold and silver plate, guns, carriages, and so forth, as well as slaves, for taxation. However, they do provide some idea of relative wealth, and may, in fact, by focusing on "luxury items," be ideal for the study of status. These personal property rolls are also complemented by the 1860 United States Census Bureau report on population, which also estimated personal estate and real estate. The census assessment of property was generally much higher than the personal property rolls, reflecting the aim of the Census Bureau "to add the proper amount to the [tax] assessment, so the [census] return should represent as well the true or intrinsic value . . . [of the personal estate]" (United States Census Bureau 1866:294).

The ceramic assemblages we used resulted from sequential occupations at each house site, although it was not possible to discern separate depositional or occupational levels during excavation or analysis. A strategy was now needed to provide a similar summary of each sites' occupational history in our use of the documentary records. The procedure used, the results of which are presented in Table 3, was, first, to total the taxed nonhuman personal property for the

Table 3. Percentages of Personal Property for Barton Sites

Site	1852	1853	1857	1860	Mean percentage
5442	merchant	merchant	farmer	farmer	
	17.9	25.2	0.6	26.3	17.5
5443	hotel	hotel	hotel	hotel	
	0.6	0.6	17.5	5.3	6.0
5444	clerk	clerk	merchant	overseer	
	0.0	0.0	18.1	2.6	5.2
5445	merchant	merchant	merchant	farmer	
	14.1	1.4	0.0	26.3	10.5
5447	widow	lawyer	lawyer	farmer	
	0.0	22.3	43.3	?[a]	21.9
5448	merchant	merchant	merchant	minister	
	67.4	50.4	20.5	39.5	44.4

[a]This occupant was not located in the 1860 census.

six sites for a number of observation points. These observation points are 1852, 1853, and 1857 from the Personal Property rolls, and 1860 from the Census Bureau, the sample being determined by the contingencies of survival of these types of data. Next, the percentage of the year's total of nonhuman personal property that each individual occupant (site) controlled was calculated for each observation year. Percentages rather than the actual value of luxuries are used because the 1860 census assessments are not comparable to the other three years of tax assessments. Finally, each site's mean percentage of property controlled was calculated by averaging that site's percentages for each observation year (i.e., averaging across the rows in Table 3). This result served as the summary measure of the *relative* level of material goods consumption at that site, and the sites could then be ranked.

The final ordering of the six sites can be seen by comparing the values in the last column in Table 3, or by looking at Table 2, where this ranking from the documentary analysis is compared to the ranking from the ceramic analysis. Overall, the similarity of the ordering is striking, especially given the experimental nature of each analysis, the incomplete nature of the archival sources, and the less than simple occupational histories for each site. The orderings correspond not only with each other but also with our general knowledge of the sites' histories. For example, Site 5448, which appears to represent the highest level of consumption of material goods, was occupied by James Griswold and his family, Griswold being one of the most successful merchants in Barton, and his wife a member of the wealthy Young family associated with the nearby Waverly plantation and other extensive holdings (Adams 1981). The overall lower position of Site 5444 is consistent with its history of occupation by a young clerk, who did not have extensive property during most of his occupation at Barton, followed by an overseer and his family (Way and McBride 1983).

The only discrepancies are the reversal of Sites 5442 and 5445, for which the differences between mean percentages are not large, and the reversal of the bottom two sites, Sites 5444 and 5443. The reversal of Sites 5442 and 5445 may suggest that the ceramics from 5442 are associated with the lower-status Futrell occupation. Due to the postbellum occupation of this house site, only two deposits, a well and a trash pit, could be utilized in our analysis, in contrast to the use of widely spread and mixed sheet refuse for the other sites. The reversal of Sites 5444 and 5443 may well stem from the fact that Site 5443 was a hotel. In this case, ceramics, generally assumed in our analysis to be for household use and/or display, may not be as useful an indicator of consumption and socioeconomic status. Further discussion is reserved until we take a broader look at the town and region in which these occupations were situated.

Regional Comparisons

Although these results are striking, they are limited to only six sites, which need to be viewed in the context of the entire Barton community, and if possible, the broader regional context of Barton's economic hinterland. Unfortunately, the archaeological data for such extensive comparisons is not available, and would be quite costly to gather. However, some comparisons can be drawn from additional documentary data.

Table 4 below gives personal property information for the Barton–Vinton area during the 1850s and 1860. We have extended this analysis beyond Barton proper because of the proximity of the Vinton community and the difficulty in assigning the exact location of residents. The mean values of taxed personal property (1852–1857) and total personal property (1860) for the six excavated sites are given in Table 4. As can be seen, our six samples average much higher than the overall mean of the Barton–Vinton community before 1860. This is undoubtedly due to the heavy bias toward merchants at these sites until after 1858.

It is also clear from Table 4 that merchants in Barton, including those from the excavated sites, did control a disproportionate amount of the wealth, making up from 14 to 34 percent of the taxed household heads, but owning from 60 to 80 percent of the taxed nonhuman wealth, and from 20 to 45 percent of slaves. Although not presented here, previous analysis has shown that many Barton merchants also owned considerable land (Way and McBride 1983). Even in 1860, when most merchants had left for more favorable towns in which to conduct business, the holdings of the remaining merchant, W. E. Trotter, were so extensive that the category of merchants still dominated in the analysis of the Barton–Vinton community (Table 4). This was not the case for the only remaining merchant of the six excavated sites, A. B. Duling, after 1858. He fell well below the mean and was about equal to the median for the Barton–Vinton area in 1860, when he was, in fact, listed as a farmer in the census. The low values for the six sites overall in 1860 reflect the decline of Barton as a commercial and service center, and the higher percentage of small-scale agriculturalists at the excavated sites.

Table 4. Distribution of Property, Barton–Vinton Area

	1852	1853	1857	1860[a]
Number of households	26	29	38	22
Households, total value ($)	1,859	1,787	2,781	100,200
Households, mean value ($)	72	62	73	4,555
Households, median value ($)	1.67	5.00	4.50	1000
Mean value ($), households from excavated sites only	156.40	178.00	146.33	760.00
Total number of merchants	6	10	10	3
Merchants, total value ($)	1,032	1,398	1,745	61,000
Merchants, mean value ($)	172	140	174	20,333
Mean value ($), merchants from excavated sites only	259	178.33	113	1,000
Mean value, all nonmerchants ($)	41	20	37	2,063
Percentage of population, all merchants	23	34	26	14
Percentage value held by merchants	56	78	63	60
Total number of slaves	69	87	102	36
Mean number of slaves	2.6	3.0	2.6	1.6
Median number of slaves	1.0	2.0	2.0	3.5
Mean number of slaves, owned by merchants	2.3	3.3	3.2	3.7
Mean number of slaves, owned by nonmerchants	2.7	2.8	2.5	1.3
Percentage of slaves owned by merchants	21	38	31	31

[a]Value calculated from Personal Property rolls for all years except 1860, which is taken directly from the United States Census.

Since the sample from the six sites is biased toward merchants—who were, of course, a major part of Barton's population, given its function as a small port town—it becomes appropriate to ask how merchants were situated in the socioeconomic structure of the larger regional society and economy. It is interesting to note that in Jones's (1980) study of colonial wealth, southern merchants were less wealthy, and much less important in terms of the region's total capital, than merchants in the mid-Atlantic colonies or New England. The continued development of the southern factorage system through the eighteenth and nineteenth century, which bypassed local merchants in the marketing of cotton, meant that interior southern merchants retained this marginality relative to planters and larger farmers, and especially relative to merchants in other regions. Still, within towns such as Barton, merchants were relatively wealthy and were key figures. They provided much more than access to goods, their stores often serving as the post office, surrogate bank, and central gathering place (Atherton 1949; Eaton 1961; Woodman 1968). This was certainly true in Barton, where merchants often held key positions in town government or as elders of the church, and usually also served as post-master (Way and McBride 1983).

In order to get a larger perspective and a more reliable sample of southern society, we have presented in Table 5 real and personal property from the 1860

United States Census for Barton and its hinterland. This is essentially the western half of Lowndes County. We were forced to utilize the census instead of the personal property rolls for this analysis since the latter do not list occupation. This created somewhat of a problem for the six excavated sites since their higher-status occupants (largely merchants) had left after 1858, and thus the 1860 data do not give an exact representation of their main occupations, although the two points of observation are very close. One can only assume that during Barton's prime in the mid-1850s, its merchants and professionals were at relatively similar economic levels as persons of those occupations in the 1860 census.

One can see in Table 5 that, within the larger region, antebellum merchants were quickly outdistanced by planters in terms of both real and personal estate, being much more on the economic level of farmers and controlling a share of wealth almost identical to their size in the total wealthholding population. Planters, on the other hand, assume a position in the regional economy akin to that of merchants within the town of Barton, making up 11 percent of household heads but controlling 47 percent of real estate and 48 percent of personal estate. In the hinterland, professionals generally ranked slightly below merchants in real and personal estate. This is at slight variance with both the townsite of Barton, where the single occupation by professionals, Site 5447, fell above all merchant sites except for Site 5448, and with Bonner's (1944) findings.

Few studies of antebellum occupational differences in wealth exist with which to compare these results, Bonner's (1944) work being a time-tried and excellent exception. His study of Hancock County, Georgia in 1860 showed that merchants fell below planters, with farmers owning over $1,000 of realty, and professionals owning in terms of their average value of personal estate.

Table 5. Property Distribution 1860, Barton and Hinterland[a]

Occupation	N	Real property			Personal property		
		Total	Mean	Median	Total	Mean	Median
Planter	31	1,216,200	39,232	30,000	2,046,300	66,010	52,000
Farmer	60	597,480	9,958	1,500	949,600	15,826	8,000
Overseer	33	48,600	1,473	0	92,500	2,803	300
Merchants	27	241,025	9,826	3,000	416,400	15,422	7,000
Professional	20	157,825	7,891	2,500	216,900	10,845	4,000
Craftsmen	34	73,660	2,166	0	103,400	3,041	0
Laborers	4	0	0	0	200	50	0
Farm Laborer	1	0	0	0	0	0	0
Women as head of household	18	114,100	63,338	100	236,200	13,122	4,000
Other[b]	9	122,200	13,577	6,200	173,700	19,300	15,000
Total	237	2,571,090	6,230	—	4,232,200	17,870	—

[a]All calculations for heads of households, which are male except as indicated.
[b]Includes government or political employees, and miscellaneous.

Fifty percent of merchants owned real estate, 45 percent owned slaves, and 76 percent owned personal estate (at least as enumerated by the census). Bonner's presentation of average ages for various occupations suggests a life-cycle process to becoming a planter. The average age of merchants in his study was 33.5 years, that for the lowest and next lowest division of farmers was 44.9 and 45.8 years, respectively, and the average age for planters and the wealthier farmers was 49.7 years (Bonner 1944: Tables 1 and 2). This gives added support to the hypothesis that, although merchants were important members of the local community, the ultimate goal of many was probably planting.

DISCUSSION AND CONCLUSIONS

The above results from Bonner (1944) and western Lowndes County suggest a relatively moderate economic position for backcountry merchants and professionals in antebellum, white southern society. This conclusion is also supported by the brief census analysis of Moore and Williams (1942). Given this moderate socioeconomic status for merchants, it is then possible to make some tentative statements as to the relative statuses of the excavated sites' occupants and the significance of their associated ceramic price indexes.

Ceramics and Socioeconomic Levels at Barton

The ceramic index values for the merchants' sites (5442, 5445, 5448) are 1.20, 1.24, and 1.42, respectively, while the value for the single professional site (5447) is 1.30. It is therefore likely that if these site residents were typical for their occupational groups, this index range of 1.20 to 1.42 should represent a moderate socioeconomic level. It is evident, however, from documentary information (Way and McBride 1983), that the merchant James Griswold (Site 5448) was much wealthier than the typical merchants in the Barton–Vinton area. Therefore, the ceramic index value for this site (1.42) represents a fairly high socioeconomic level, and a range of 1.20 to 1.30 more closely approximates a moderate or middle socioeconomic level. Of course, we should remind the reader that these index values are from sherd counts only, and also do not include porcelain.

One of the stated goals of this paper was to evaluate the utility of the sherd count variation of Miller's ceramic price indexing, which seems quite good. The correspondence in ranking with the documentary records is close. It also appears that, although the variation in the ceramic index values is not great, it does have significance. The congruence between these two data sources suggests a definite relationship between ceramic consumption patterns and overall consumption of material goods, or at least of luxuries. This latter measure is commonly used as a marker of socioeconomic status within capitalistic societies (Bonner 1944; Douglas and Isherwood; Jones 1980; Wright 1978).

Through the investigation of documentary and archaeological sources within Barton, and documentary sources for its surrounding hinterland, an understanding has been gained of the socioeconomic status of the residents of the six sites and of backcountry merchants and professionals in general. The moderate economic position of the merchants and professionals in western Lowndes County in 1860 seems to parallel their relative position in other areas of the South during the late antebellum period (Atherton 1949; Bonner 1944; Moore and Williams 1942; Woodman 1968). The relative statuses of the sites' occupants during Barton's zenith were probably moderate for the region, with some slightly above and others slightly below this level. It is especially interesting to contrast the relatively higher status of merchants within the town of Barton, in comparison to their more diminished status when they are placed in the broader regional context. The economic and political power of these southern merchants did not extend into the countryside, as did that of many northern merchants or southern furnishing merchants in the postbellum period.

Further Thoughts on Material Culture and Status Studies

To conclude, we would at least like to raise several issues relating to the broader context of material culture studies, and how they may enable us to arrive at a deeper understanding of the society we study. Historical archaeology is a discipline with roots in prehistoric archaeology, and historical archaeologists often have not only that general heritage, but a good deal of training and practical experience on prehistoric sites. While this is not necessarily disadvantageous, it can create problems if we take for granted that material culture is an important guide to social structure without considering how and why material items are relevant. In not reflecting on our subject, and what we are trying to do in our studies, we are apt to transfer methodologies and assumptions appropriate to one setting but not another, to overlook relevant nonarchaeological historical data and studies, and to perpetuate the "prehistorian's game" (Cleland 1981) of pretending we know less about our subject than we really do, or could, know.

For example, we may need to broaden the ways in which we think about material culture to recognize that material goods, as material culture, have "an active role in forming and enforcing behavior" (Leone 1984:1). This means looking at objects, and the exchange of objects, as cultural events or communications, as in the work of Douglas and Isherwood (1979), and recognizing the powerful aspect of objects stemming from their physical nature. "Once it is produced, it [material culture] is part of the world in which people must function and to which they must adapt their behavior. That it can be *both* a physical and symbolic constraint gives material culture a particular power over human action" (Mukerji 1983:15).

We need to tailor the ways that we think about people and their relationship with material goods to the culture and era under investigation. In a very interesting article, Carr and Walsh (1980) show that, in one context in colonial Maryland, the quantity of ceramics seemed most indicative of socioeconomic status, but that in another it was variety that seemed the better marker. Recent scholarship on "mass consumption" or "consumer society" has been innovative and interesting, suggesting the heightened importance of material culture studies and new debates into which material culture specialists can enter. However, much of this literature has been restrictive in focusing on the late nineteenth century and the growth of modern advertising (Baudet and Meulen 1982; Ewen 1976; Fox and Lears 1981; Lears 1983; McKendrick, Brewer, and Plumb 1982; Williams 1982).

In contrast, Mukerji (1983) has hypothesized major cultural changes in the West beginning in the fifteenth century, culminating in a profound new emphasis on materialism. A major feature of this "materialism" was that material interests were no longer made subservient to other social goals, a point made also by Marshall Sahlins (1976). This emphasis on materialism is an important although little reflected upon assumption that offers support to historical archaeology's often exclusive use of material culture to study the position of individuals within a social system, or to our assumptions that social and economic status are inextricably linked, evidenced by the almost casual use of the term "socioeconomic status" within our discipline. But if it is the increasing importance and insularity of the economic that provides the best single characterization of capitalist class-divided society, which is generally our subject, as Giddens (1979) suggests, our focus and assumptions may be theoretically sound. Among the changes Mukerji cites, especially interesting to historical archaeologists, was the increasingly important role of fashion and taste in stimulating seventeenth- and eighteenth-century economic growth and expansion. Historical archaeologists have, as a major data source, one of the key areas in which these changes were implemented and can be documented—ceramics, presenting an opportunity to make important contributions to our understanding of the development of our own society, and, given its contact with and conquest of others, much of the modern world.

ACKNOWLEDGMENTS

We would especially like to thank Stephanie H. (Tef) Rodeffer for her encouragement. The thoughtful reading and comments provided by Dean L. Anderson, Charles E. Cleland, Kenneth E. Lewis, Russell K. Skowronek, and Suzanne Spencer-Wood have been extremely helpful and much appreciated.

REFERENCES

Adams, William H. (ed.), 1981, Waverly Plantation: Ethnoarchaeology of a Tenant Farming Community, report submitted to the Heritage Conservation and Recreation Service, Washington, D.C.

Adkins, Howard G., 1972, The Historical Geography of Extinct Towns in Mississippi, Ph.D. dissertation, University of Tennessee, University Microfilms, Ann Arbor.

Atherton, Lewis E., 1949, The Southern Country Store, 1800–1860, Louisiana State University, Baton Rouge.

Baudet, Henri, and van der Meulen, Henk (eds.), 1982, *Consumer Behavior and Economic Growth in the Modern Economy,* Croom Helm, London.

Binford, Lewis, 1962, Archaeology as Anthropology, *American Antiquity* 28:217–225.

Blassingame, John, 1972, *The Slave Community,* Oxford University Press, New York.

Bonner, James C., 1944, Profile of a Late Antebellum Community, *American Historical Review* 49:663–680.

Carr, Lois Green, and Walsh, Lorena S., 1980, Inventories and the Analysis of Wealth and Consumption Patterns in St. Mary's County, Maryland, 1658–1777, *Historical Methods* 13:81–104.

Cleland, Charles E., 1981, On the Development of Theory in Historical Archaeology, keynote address delivered at the Fourteenth Annual Meeting of the Society for Historical Archaeology, New Orleans, Louisiana, January 5, 1981.

Cleland, Charles, E. 1983, A Computer Compatible System for the Categorization, Enumeration, and Retrieval of Nineteenth and Early Twentieth Century Archaeological Material Culture: Manual of Identification and Classification, report submitted to the National Park Service, Mid-Atlantic Region, Michigan State University Museum.

Cook, Lauren, 1982, Adaptation of Miller's Economic Index for 19th Century Ceramics to the Jere Tabbor and Jullson House Sites, in: Phase II Study of the Jere Tabor House Site on the Mount Hope Interceptor in Tirerton, R.I., Public Archaeology Program, Rhode Island College, pp. 139–45, Appendix G.

Doster, James F., and Weaver, David C., 1981, Historic Settlement in the Upper Tombigbee Valley, report submitted by the Center for the Study of Southern History and Culture, University of Alabama to the Heritage Conservation and Recreation Service, Albuquerque.

Douglas, Mary, and Isherwood, Baron, 1979, *The World of Goods,* Basic Books, New York.

Easterlin, Richard, 1961, Regional Income Trends, 1840–1950, *American Economic History* (Seymour E. Harris, ed.), McGraw-Hill, New York, pp. 525–547.

Eaton, Clement, 1961, *The Growth of Southern Civilization, 1790–1860,* Harper Torchbooks, New York.

Ewen, Stuart, 1976, *Captains of Consciousness: Advertising and the Social Roots of the Consumer Culture,* McGraw-Hill, New York.

Exnicious, Joan, and Pearson, Charles, 1985, Nineteenth-Century New Orleans: Variability and Pattern in the Archaeological Record, paper delivered at the Annual Meeting of the Society for Historical Archaeology, Boston, Massachusetts, Janaury 12, 1985.

Fairbanks, Charles, 1983, Historical Archaeological Implications of Recent Investigations, *Geoscience and Man* 23:17–26.

Fairbanks, Charles, 1984, Plantation Archaeology in the Southeastern U.S., *Historical Archaeology* 18:1–14.

Foust, James D., 1975, *The Yeoman Farmers and Westward Expansion of U.S. Cotton Production,* Arno Press, New York.

Fox, Richard Wightman, and Lears, T. J. Jackson (eds.), 1981, *The Culture of Consumption: Critical Essays in American History, 1880–1980,* Pantheon Books, New York.

Genovese, Eugene, 1967, *The Political Economy of Slavery,* Vintage Books, New York.

Genovese, Eugene, 1974, *Roll, Jordan, Roll: The World the Slaves Made,* Vintage Books, New York.

Giddens, Anthony, 1979, *Central Problems in Social Theory,* University of California Press, Berkeley.

Hahn, Steven, 1983, *The Roots of Southern Populism: Yeoman Farmers and the Transformation of the Georgia Upcountry, 1850–1890,* Oxford University Press, New York.

Heberling, Scott, and Spencer-Wood, Suzanne, 1985, Ceramics and the Socio-Economic Status of the Green Family, Windsor, Vermont, 1877–1956, paper presented at the 1985 Annual Meeting of the Society for Historical Archaeology, Boston.

Jones, Alice Hanson, 1980, *Wealth of a Nation To Be: The American Colonies on the Eve of the Revolution,* Columbia University Press, New York.

Lears, T. J. Jackson, 1983, *No Place of Grace: Antimodernism and the Transformation of American Culture 1880–1920,* Pantheon Books, New York.

Lees, William B., and Kimery-Lees, Kathryn M., 1984, Regional Perspectives on the Fort Towson Sutler's Store and Residence, A Frontier Site in Antebellum Eastern Oklahoma, *Plains Anthropologist* 29:13–24.

Leone, Mark P., 1984, Material culture and the Georgian World, paper delivered at a conference. The Colonial Experience: The Eighteenth Century Chesapeake, Baltimore, September 13–14, 1984.

Lewis, Lynne G., 1978, *Drayton Hall: Preliminary Archaeological Investigation at a Low Country Plantation,* National Trust for Historic Preservation, University of Virginia Press, Charlottesville.

Lofstrom, Edward, 1976, An Analysis of Temporal Changes in a 19th Century Assemblage from Fort Snelling, Minnesota, *Minnesota Archaeologist* 35:16–47.

Martin, Edgar W., 1942, *The Standard of Living in 1860,* University of Chicago Press, Chicago.

McBride, W. Stephen, and McBride, Kim A., 1983, Phase III Mitigations: Site Summaries, in: Cleland, Charles E., and McBride, Kim A., Oral Historical, Documentary, and Archaeological Investigations of Barton and Vinton, Mississippi: An Interim Report on Phase III of the Tombigbee Historic Townsites Project, report submitted to the National Park Service, Mid-Atlantic Region, Michigan State University Museum, pp. 136–252.

McKendrick, Neil, Brewer, John, and Plumb, J. H., 1982, *The Birth of Consumer Society: The Commercialization of Eighteenth-Century England,* Europa Publications, London.

Miller, George L., 1974, A Tenant Farmer's Tableware: Nineteenth Century Ceramics from Tebb's Plantation, *Maryland Historical Magazine* 69:197–210.

Miller, George L., 1980, Classification and Economic Scaling of 19th Century Ceramics, *Historical Archaeology* 14:1–14.

Miller, George L., and Hurry, Silas D., 1983, Ceramic Supply in an Economically Isolated Frontier Community, *Historical Archaeology* 17:80–92.

Miller, J. Jefferson, II, and Stone, Lyle M., 1970, Eighteenth-Century Ceramics from Fort Michilimackinac: A Study in Historical Archaeology, *Smithsonian Studies in History and Technology* 4, Smithsonian Institution Press, Washington, D.C.

Minnerly, W. Lee (ed.), 1983, Oral Historical, Documentary, and Archaeological Investigations of Barton and Vinton, Mississippi. An Interim Report on Phase II of the Tombigbee Historic Townsites Project, report submitted to the National Park Service, Mid-Atlantic Region, Michigan State University Museum.

Moore, Wilbert E., and Williams, Robin M., 1942, Stratification in the Ante-bellum South, *American Sociological Review* 7:343–351.

Mukerji, Chandra, 1983, *From Graven Images: Patterns of Modern Materialism,* Columbia University Press, New York.

Orser, Charles E., Jr., 1984, The Past Ten Years of Plantation Archaeology in the Southeastern United States, *Southeastern Archaeology* 3:1–12.

Otto, John S., 1977, Artifacts and Status Differences—A Comparison of Ceramics from Planter, Overseer, and Slave Sites on an Antebellum Plantation, in: *Research Strategies in Historical Archaeology* (Stanely South, ed.), Academic Press, New York, pp. 91–118.

Otto, John S., 1980, Race and Class on Antebellum Plantations, in: *Archaeological Perspectives in Ethnicity in America* (Robert L. Schuyler, ed.), Baywood Publishing, New York, pp. 3–13.

Owsley, Frank, 1949, *Plain Folk of the Old South,* Louisiana State University Press, Baton Rouge.

Praetzellis, Mary, 1980, Ceramics, in: *Historical Archaeology at the Golden Eagle Site* (Mary Praetzellis, Adrian Praetzellis, and Marley R. Brown, III, eds.), Anthropological Studies Center, Sonoma State University, pp. 71–84.

Price, Cynthia R., 1979, 19th Century Ceramics in the Eastern Ozark Border Region, Center for Archaeological Research, Southwest Missouri State University, Monograph Series 1, Springfield.

Sahlins, Marshall, 1976, *Culture and Practical Reason,* University of Chicago Press, Chicago.

Scarborough, William Kaufman, 1984, *The Overseer: Plantation Management in the Old South,* the University of Georgia Press, Athens.

South, Stanley, 1974, Palmetto Parapets: Exploratory Archaeology at Fort Moultrie, S.C., 38CH50, Institute of Archaeology and Anthropology, University of South Carolina, Anthropological Studies 1.

South, Stanley, 1977, *Method and Theory in Historical Archaeology*. Academic Press, New York.

Spencer-Wood, Suzanne, 1984, Socio-economic Status and Boston Area Domestic Sites, paper presented at the Annual Meeting of the Society for Historical Archaeology, Philadelphia, January 8, 1984.

Stewart-Abernathy, Leslie C., 1980, The Seat of Justice: 1815–1830: An Archaeological Reconnaissance of Davidsonville, 1979, Arkansas Archaeological Survey Research Report No. 21, Fayetteville, Arkansas.

Stone, Garry W., 1970, Ceramics in Suffolk County, Massachusetts Inventories, 1680–1775: A Preliminary Study with Diverse Comments Thereon, and Sundry Suggestions, *The Conference on Historic Site Archaeology Papers, 1968* 3:73–90.

United States Census Bureau, 1866, *Report: Statistics, Eighth Census of the United States, Volume 4,* U.S. Government Printing Office, Washington, D.C.

Way, Winston W., and McBride, Kim A., 1983, The Study in Historical Perspective: A Narrative of Mid-Nineteenth Century Barton and Vinton, Mississippi, in: Oral Historical, Documentary, and Archaeological Investigations of Barton and Vinton, Mississippi: An Interim Report on Phase III of the Tombigbee Historic Townsites Project (Charles E. Cleland and Kim A. McBride, eds.), report submitted to the National Park Service, Mid-Atlantic Region, Michigan State University Museum, pp. 7–73.

Williams, Rosalind H., 1982, *Dream World: Mass Consumption in Late Nineteenth-Century France,* University of California Press, Berkeley.

Wise, Cara L., 1984, Choices: Consumer Behavior as an Approach to Urban Adaptation, paper delivered at the Annual Meeting of the Society for Historical Archaeology, Williamsburg, Virginia, January 5, 1984.

Woodman, Harold D., 1968, *King Cotton and His Retainers,* University of Kentucky Press, Lexington.

Wright, Gavin, 1978, *The Political Economy of the Cotton South,* W. W. Norton, New York.

8

Status Variation in Antebellum Alexandria

An Archaeological Study of Ceramic Tableware

STEVEN JUDD SHEPHARD

Studies of socioeconomic status using archaeological materials have proliferated in recent years. Although certain material correlates of social group membership have been identified, the patterning in the data has often proved to be fairly subtle.

This paper concerns the results of research into the material correlates of socioeconomic class membership utilizing three ceramic assemblages from Alexandria, Virginia (see Figure 1). These results are part of a dissertation (Shephard 1985) that concerns both identification of class affiliation and study of changing social structure through analysis of artifactual data. The theoretical framework developed in this study is presented briefly here, but is fully discussed in the dissertation. Documentary sources are used here to establish the socioeconomic standing of households in nineteenth-century Alexandria. Hypotheses that associate variation in the quantity, quality, and variety of ceramic assemblages with class membership are tested.

The theoretical framework will be presented first, along with the hypotheses and archaeologically testable implications. The methods used in the documentary research, field excavation, and artifact analysis will be discussed next. Research results will then be presented, followed by conclusions drawn from this research, a reconsideration of the theoretical modeling, and suggestions for further research.

It should be noted that the term "class" is used throughout this study to mean the equivalent of "socioeconomic group." This term is employed here in order to facilitate communication and is specifically defined by particular social and economic variables later in this chapter.

THEORETICAL FRAMEWORK

Previous archaeological research into the material correlates of social stratification has included studies focusing on skeletal remains (e.g., Buikstra

6

Steven Judd Shephard ☐ Alexandria Archaeology, Box 178, City Hall, Alexandria, VA 22313.

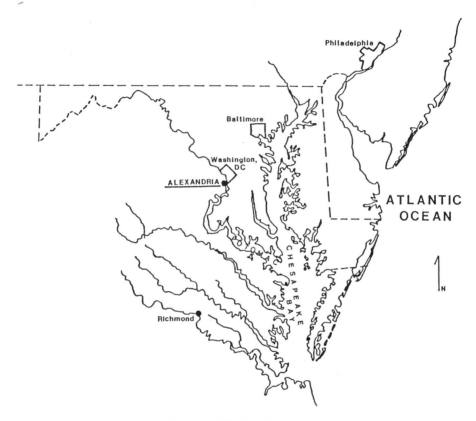

Figure 1. Mid-Atlantic region.

1976), grave location and contents (e.g., Peebles and Kus 1977), and residential patterning (e.g., Vogt 1956). Household material assemblages have also been investigated and related to social status but usually are secondary to another focus such as acculturation (e.g., Deagan 1974; Shephard 1983) or ethnicity (e.g., Baker 1980; De Cunzo 1982; Deetz 1977). Some studies have grappled specifically with the challenge of identifying socioeconomic status through household artifact assemblages associated with different classes (e.g., Friedlander *et al.* 1985; Otto 1977). None of these studies adopts, as its primary objective, the identification of general characteristics of household material culture that can be positively correlated with socioeconomic standing. This study strives for that objective in testing hypotheses that can be applied to state-level societies.

Development of a theoretical framework with broad social applicability requires conceptualization of social structure and dynamics in abstract terms. An appropriate conceptualization of stratification is offered by organizational and systems theory.

Various scholars have viewed human society as a system of interacting units with relationships among them (e.g., Chapple and Coon 1952; Levy 1942;

Miller 1978; White 1949). The interactions among these units involve a flow of matter and energy. Socioeconomic hierarchy serves as a means of facilitating exchanges of information, which control the flow of matter and energy in society (Adams 1975:141). Maintenance of status differences increases the probability of efficient information exchange and facilitates the successful functioning of society (Johnson 1978:101). At the finer level, the members of different socioeconomic classes participate in this system. The distinctive behavior that identifies the members of different classes is a concern of the present study in order to differentiate these classes through analysis of material culture. It is not, however, the symbols of socioeconomic class that account for the existence of classes or their persistence in society.

One form of behavior that has been identified as varying positively with class membership is consumer behavior (e.g., Levy 1966; Martineau 1958, 1961; Smelser 1963; Warner and Lunt 1950; Zimmerman 1936). The results of research in this area allow a bridge to be made from the theoretical conceptualization of socioeconomic structure and signaling of class membership, to the prediction of patterning in material culture.

By combining observations on the nature of individual social classes made by Margaret C. Pirie (1960:45–48) with the summary of class characteristics made by Engel, Kollat, and Blackwell (1968:287–295), class profiles conducive to building a class-consumption model may be developed. This synthesis provides the following class profiles:

1. *Upper Class:* ownership–management occupations, high-income professional and managerial occupations; goods often passed down through generations; maintain large residences (frequently multiple); have an abundance of possessions.
2. *Middle Class:* moderate income professionals, owners and executives of businesses, skilled workers; the upwardly mobile may engage in conspicuous consumption; are the most active class in the consumer market; are concerned with product quality.
3. *Lower Class:* low education–training, manual skill jobs; limited in social mobility; impulsive buying of new products with little evaluation of quality; more frequent small purchases rather than fewer larger purchases.

From this collection of attributes, it is necessary to extract those that apply to broad categories of household possessions and that are both discernable and measurable in the archaeological record. Three general variables satisfy these requiements. These are quantity, quality, and variety. The degree of expression of any of these variables in a material assemblage is governed by accessibility and preference. Accessibility, in this case, is the facility with which an object can be acquired by an individual or group. This ability usually depends on purchasing power (capital or other means of exchange), geographical proximity of the desired object(s), and/or social connections. Preference is reflected in the type of possessions that a person chooses to purchase. This is commonly referred to as "taste" and is a result of socialization processes and, thus, class membership (Martineau 1961:190).

In order to generalize the class-specific consumer characteristics given above for quantity, quality, and variety, Table 1 is presented. It illustrates the expected strength of the three variables within the three major classes. The signs indicate the relative strength of each variable within the material assemblage of each class: plus sign, a stronger manifestation; minus sign, a weaker manifestation.

Quantity, as used here, is the number of different items making up a material assemblage, or a category of items within a material assemblage. This is a reflection of the household's (1) wealth and income, (2) size, and (3) residential stability (Schiffer *et al.* 1981). In the mid-1800s, Ernst Engel observed that families with less money spent a higher portion of it on food than families with more money. In addition, families purchased necessities first while heavy spending or saving occurred only at higher income levels (Zimmerman 1936:51). It follows from this, that families with less money to spend on nonfood items buy fewer and/or less expensive items than families with more money. So in general, it is expected that the size of a material assemblage should range from the largest in the upper class to the smallest in the lower class. Household income is the strongest determinant of size of a material assemblage (Schiffer *et al.* 1981).

Household size also affects the number of items making up a material assemblage. A greater number of residents should, as a rule, possess a larger material assemblage when compared to a small family. Residential stability refers to the length of time a household remains at one residence, and the longer a household remains at a site, the more items it accumulates (Schiffer *et al.* 1981). Household size and residential stability crosscut class lines and so must be considered when interpreting any household assemblage.

Class-specific differences in discard behavior may also affect the interpretation of residential artifact assemblages. Due to the conservative nature of members of the upper class noted earlier, artifacts assemblages from these sites may prove less representative of total possessions than assemblages from lower-class house sites. Variations in rate of discard of items according to their rarity and costliness are also expected to occur.

Quality denotes the value of an item or items, usually expressed in mone-

Table 1. Manifestation of Quantity, Quality, and Variety by Class

	Upper class	Middle class	Lower class
Quantity	+++	++	−
Quality	+++	++	+ −
Variety	+++	+	−

tary terms. Value depends on the rarity of the item itself or the materials of which it is composed, combined with its desirability. As was noted in the class profiles presented earlier, higher-quality goods are purchased more frequently by the upper and middle classes. Members of the lower class are characterized as not making careful evaluation of quality for price, and often as purchasing impulsively. This is indicated by the presence of both a plus as well as a minus sign under quality for the lower class in Table 1. Coleman has noted, more specifically, that it is not always those with high incomes that purchase items of the highest quality, but members of the upper and upper-middle classes in general (1961:178).

Variety refers to the number of items within an assemblage that have differing, and usually specialized, functions. It is proposed that higher socioeconomic status households will possess a greater variety of objects when compared to households of lower status. Deetz (1977), for one, has recognized this relationship in variety, as well as quality, of the composition of household assemblages. He reasons that (a) households of modest means could not afford the more costly ceramics and that (b) the differing foodways of the other classes, would result in their having distinct ranges of forms of ceramic vessels (1977:51). It is understandable, then, that less affluent families would have basic utilitarian items with fewer "luxury" goods, while the more comfortable would have basic furnishings, as well as an assortment of nonnecessities. In addition, social observers in the nineteenth century (e.g., Tocqueville 1831; Veblen 1899) suggest that, in general, class-related patterns of consumption were similar to those of today.

The manifestation of each one of the three variables—quantity, quality, and variety—is influenced by *social* as well as economic factors. Lasswell has noted that consumer studies indicate that "Money alone does not seem to be enough to buy 'good taste'" (1965:243). Showing "good taste" in decorating a home is a matter of filling the house with furnishings that will elicit the admiration of one's peers.

It has been observed that families with the same annual income, but of different social classes, show a "radical difference in their ways of spending money" (Coleman 1961:176). This is a reflection of the socialization process through which the members of each class learn what kinds of possessions are highly desirable (even if unattainable), which items are proper and acceptable, and which are undesirable. Money is thus "translated into socially approved behavior and possessions" (Warner *et al.* 1949:22).

Possession of the material goods that are acceptable within one's class communicates class membership. These objects act as symbols of common perspective, or value system, which defines class membership (Burk 1968:75; Markin 1974:418; Martineau 1958:123) and serve to integrate family units into socioeconomic groups within society (Parsons and Smelser 1965:224; Wobst 1977:326).

It is proposed here, then, that quantity, quality, and variety are three variables of material assemblages that correlate with socioeconomic status. More specifically, the following general propositions, or hypotheses, are made in order to distinguish households of differing classes from one another, while controlling for household size and residential stability:

1. The higher the socioeconomic status of a household is, the greater the *quantity* of possessions composing its material assemblage will be.
2. The higher the socioeconomic status of a household is, the greater the *quality* of its material assemblage will be.
3. The higher the socioeconomic status of a household is, the greater the *variety*, or diversity, of items composing its material assemblage will be.

The very general nature of these hypotheses may seem to be such as to render them of insignificant value for testing, yet these hypotheses have not been tested before in an archaeological situation where status level is controlled. It is only through the testing of these hypotheses and their corresponding, though unstated, null hypotheses, that a basis for investigating change in socioeconomic structure may be obtained.

Furthermore, applicability of this model to any state-level society demands that generality be maintained. All societies have similar categories of possessions filling different human needs. Some goods, such as food, clothing, and shelter, are necessities, but the quantity, quality, and variety of these necessities vary according to the owner's socioeconomic position in society. The hypotheses stated above should obtain in any state-level society. Nineteenth-century Alexandria society certainly qualifies as a testing ground for these proposals. There existed a social hierarchy ranging from black slaves to wealthy planters and merchants, along with a consumer market offering the full range of material goods available at that time.

Testing the hypotheses in the Alexandria setting requires that archaeologically testable implications be deduced from the hypotheses. Measurement must be made of quantity, quality, and variety of household assemblages in terms meaningful to nineteenth-century Alexandria material culture. More specifically, one particular artifact category, household ceramics, is selected for analysis in this inquiry. A number of archaeological studies have focused on ceramic assemblages as a basis for investigating social organization (e.g., Deetz 1960; Hill 1966; Longacre 1964). Various scholars have observed that differences in socioeconomic status can be discerned through analysis of historic household ceramic assemblages (e.g., De Cunzo 1982; Deetz 1972; Miller and Stone 1970:100; South 1972:81). On the basis of these investigations, and assessment of the nineteenth-century Alexandria ceramics market, the following test implications are proposed (citations refer to studies supporting the statements).

Test Implication for Hypothesis 1: Quantity

1. Both middle-class assemblages will have a greater number of vessels (correcting for number of occupants and length of residence) as compared to the lower-class assemblage (Abbitt-Outlaw *et al.* 1977:10; Deetz 1972:20; Gill 1976:93; Herman *et al.* 1975:63).

Test Implications for Hypothesis 2: Quality

2a. Both middle-class assemblages will have a greater percentage of porcelain, transfer-printed ware, and ironstone (Fairbanks 1972:79; Gill 1976:95; Kingsbury 1974:169; Miller 1980:4; Stone *et al.* 1972:124) and a smaller percentage of undecorated and minimally decorated ware within the total ceramic assemblages, as compared to the lower-class assemblages, which will show the opposite pattern (Miller 1980:3; Otto 1977:98).

2b. Both middle-class assemblages will have a higher percentage of matched vessels within total transfer-printed ware, total porcelain, and total ironstone as compared to the lower-class assemblage (Gill 1976:95; Miller 1980:4; Otto 1975:173–174; Herman *et al.* 1975:66; Stone *et al.* 1972:124).

2c. Both middle-class assemblages will have higher ceramic-assemblage average values (Miller 1980), as compared to the lower-class assemblage (Abbitt-Outlaw *et al.* 1977:10; Deetz 1972:20; Gill 1976:94; Herman *et al.* 1975:63).

Test Implications for Hypothesis 3: Variety

3a. Both middle-class assemblages will have a smaller percentage of tableware and a larger percentage of storage ware and tea- and coffeeware within the total ceramic assemblage, as compared to the lower-class assemblage, which will show the opposite pattern (Miller 1980: 34; Otto 1975:219; Otto 1977:98,99).

3b. Both middle-class assemblages will have a larger percentage of serving flatware and a smaller percentage of serving bowls within total tableware, as compared to the lower-class assemblage, which will show the opposite pattern (Baker 1980:34; Otto 1977:99).

3c. Both middle-class assemblages will have a larger percentage of transfer-printed flatware and a smaller percentage of banded bowls and edged flatware within total tableware, as compared to the lower-class assemblage, which will show the opposite pattern (Fairbanks 1972: 77–78; Otto 1977:98).

3d. Both middle-class assemblages will have a larger ratio of number of different shapes to total number of vessels within the total ceramic assemblage, as compared to the lower-class assemblage (Abbitt-Outlaw *et al.* 1977:10; Drucker 1981:65; Otto 1977:116, 219; South 1972:99).

Definitions for Ceramic Categories Used in the Test Implications

1. *Minimally decorated ware:* edged, banded (annular), sponge-decorated, mocha, and common cable (finger-trailed slip) (Miller 1980:4)
2. *Tableware:* all plates, platters, bowls, mugs, and tureens (Otto 1975: 205–217)

3. *Storage ware:* jugs, jars, coolers, ink wells (Otto 1975:205–217)
4. *Tea- and coffeeware:* all cups and saucers, coffee cans, coffee pots, sugar bowls, and creamers (Otto 1975:205–217)
5. *Serving flatware:* plates, soup plates, and platters (Otto 1977:99)
6. *Serving bowls:* all individual-size bowls; "common bowl" shape as illustrated in Godden 1966:173 (Otto 1975:204)

ANALYTICAL METHODS

Documentary Records

In order to implement the research design developed in this study, techniques for both documentary and archaeological analysis are utilized. To begin with, the term "class" must be defined in a way such that an empirical determination of class membership may be made for the household under study. Class is defined here by the covariance of four variables: occupation, wealth (assessment of real property), condition of tenure, and ethnic background. These four variables are selected for defining class membership because they reflect both social and economic aspects of the stratification hierarchy. In addition, these variables have been recognized in other research studies (e.g., Engel *et al.* 1968; Goheen 1970; Hershberg and Dockhorn 1976; Kahl 1953; Pareto 1916; Parsons 1953; Warner 1949) and are measurable through documentary records.

A method was developed by John Stephens (1981a,b) while serving as historian for the Alexandria Regional Preservation Office, that produces a graphic representation of the socioeconomic structure of Alexandria using documentary data. A 15 percent sample is taken from the records for the entire population of the city for a particular year. The occupational rank of head of household, property tax assessment decile, condition of tenure (i.e., owner or renter), and ethnic background (i.e., Euro- or Afro-American) are recorded for each observation. The variable values are recorded as numerals: occupational rank has the values 1–6 from high to low (adapted from Hershberg and Dockhorn 1976); property tax assessment, 1–10 high to low (on a decile scale); condition of tenure, 1 (owner) or 2 (renter); and ethnic background, 1 (Euro-American) or 2 (Afro-American). The frequencies of every combination of variable values (e.g., 1-2-1-1) may then be tabulated and divisions made to delineate a range for upper, middle, and lower classes (see Shephard 1985:92–97). Rankings for any individual household may then be determined by placement of the household's four-digit combination of variable values in the overall city range of values for the same time period.

Stephens created socioeconomic scales for the years: 1790, 1810, 1830, 1850, 1870, 1890, and 1910. The documentary records used in this analysis were Alexandria and federal censuses, Alexandria city directories, Alexandria tax records, and Alexandria deed and will books.

Archaeological Excavation

The ceramic assemblages utilized in this study were recovered from three well-privy features dating to the nineteenth century. Two of the features were located on the Courthouse site, 500 block of King Street in Alexandria's commercial core (Cressey *et al.* 1982). The northwest quarter of this block was excavated in anticipation of urban renewal activities. This block was made up of combined commercial and residential structures. Excavations uncovered twelve brick-lined shafts—some as deep as eight meters—five sections of house walls, two trash pits, one basement, and one water filtration system (Beidleman 1979).

The two features of concern to this study were Feature 6, (located at 522–524 King Street (Lot 3), and Feature 7, located at 104 South St. Asaph Street (Lot 26). Feature 6 was located in one corner at the very back of the lot on which a brick, three-story house was built in 1812. Feature 7 was located in one corner at the extreme rear of Lot 26, where a smaller, two-story brick house was constructed in 1805. Both features were constructed of dry-laid rectangular bricks, set in circular stretcher courses, except for the final bottom courses, which were header laid. Feature 6 averaged approximately 2.14 meters in diameter and was 7.51 meters in depth. Feature 7 averaged approximately 1.16 meters in diameter and was 7.97 meters in depth.

The third assemblage was recovered from 916 Gibbon Street (Lot 18), located on the periphery of nineteenth-century Alexandria in an Afro-American neighborhood called "The Bottoms." Feature 5, which contained the ceramics, was situated at the rear of the lot where a one-story wood frame house had been built by 1810. It is probable that the feature had originally been constructed as a well. It was formed by three wooden, metal-hooped barrels placed one atop the other. Most of the top barrel was missing, while the lower two were fairly complete. The feature extended to a depth of 3.03 meters below ground surface. The average diameter of the shaft was eighty-seven centimeters.

Each of the well-privies was excavated in twenty-centimeter levels since natural levels could not be distinguished. Use of the features as privies was apparent through the presence of distinctive, odoriforous matrices and the remains of a two-hole privy seat in Feature 6. The soil matrices were generally dark brown to black claylike soil changing to mixed sterile sand and clay at the bottom of the feature. The soil from all these features was screened through ¼-inch mesh. Soil and flotation samples were collected from each level.

Each of the features contained thousands of artifacts, including ceramics, glass, wood, leather, seeds, faunal remains, and textiles. Of specific interest to this study were the ceramic sherds from the nineteenth-century components that analysis showed to represent 506 vessels in Feature 6, 629 in Feature 7, and 148 in Feature 5.

The artifacts from Feature 5 represent the only Afro-American assemblage recovered from an undisturbed well-privy context in Alexandria. The use of barrels as shoring for a shallow well sharply contrasts with the deep, bricklined shafts on King Street. Indeed, well or well-privy shafts are much more common in Euro-American core areas than in the lower socioeconomic black neighborhoods located in more peripheral areas (Cressey and Stephens 1982). It has been suggested that the scarcity of wells or privies on the house lots in "The Bottoms" area may indicate the use of public wells and privies for the bulk of the nineteenth-century Afro-American population, while excavations at one lot in "The Bottoms" have indicated the use of the ground surface as a privy (Henley *et al.* 1980).

Artifact Analysis

Establishing chronological components for each of the features was the first step in analyzing the artifacts in this study. In this way, groups of artifacts may be associated with documentary data relating to the occupants of each site.

Dating Methods

The dating of the artifacts in each of the three features just discussed, produced components or component groups that could be compared during two general time periods: circa 1820–1850 and circa 1850–1860. Artifact analysis was carried out comparing the ceramic assemblages from these two time categories, as well as from the assemblages as a whole (i.e., dating to circa 1820–1860). Table 2 illustrates the component dates of each of the three features.

In establishing chronological components for Features 6 and 7 on the 500 block of King Street, two complimentary techniques of ceramic analysis were used (Beidleman 1980). A seriation chart was created for each feature based on sherd counts. Component divisions were evident and an SAS average link cluster analysis program was employed as a cross-check on these results. This program indicated similar divisions within the assemblages. Manufacturing dates or date ranges were established for each component from datable maker's marks and certain datable transfer-print designs. In addition, the glass assemblages from Feature 6 were analyzed, with the result that the glass was contemporaneous with the ceramics in the later period but later than the ceramics in the early components (Magid 1980). The dates in Table 2 reflect this outcome.

A full analysis of Feature 7 glass was not undertaken, but preliminary analysis indicated that there was a lag between ceramic and glass manufacture dates similar to that found in the Feature 6 assemblages (Beidleman 1980:5). A revision of the *termini post quem,* even to the point of adding ten years to the date of both component groups, would not significantly affect the comparisons made in this study.

Because of the smaller quantity of ceramic wares recovered from the Gibbon Street well-privy (148 vessels as compared to 506 in Feature 6 and 629 in Feature 7), a seriation analysis based upon pearlware and whiteware and an evaluation of cross-mending of vessels between levels were sufficient to delineate three components (Magid 1980). Analysis of the glass from this feature,

Table 2. Component Dates for Features 6 and 7, King Street, and Feature 5, Gibbon Street

Level	Component	Component group	Date of manufacture	*Terminus post quem*
		Feature 6, King Street		
1–11	—	—	twentieth century	modern
12–14	F	III	c.1890–1897	1891
15–21	E	III	c.1860–1890	1855
22–27	D	II	c.1850–1860	1843
28–31	C	II	c.1833–1850	1833
32–36	B	I	c.1820–1835	1840
37–39	A	I	c.1793–1820	1820
		Feature 7, King Street		
1–10	—	—	twentieth century	modern
11–16	—	—	twentieth century	modern
17–19	G	III	c.1845–1856	1845
20–23	F	III	c.1845–1856	1845
24–26	E	II	c.1834–1854	1834
27–29	D	II	c.1834–1854	1834
30–33	C	I	c.1820–1840	1831
34–36	B	I	c.1810–1840	1828
37–41	A	I	c.1810–1840	1828
		Feature 5, Gibbon Street		
1–2	C	—	twentieth century	modern
3–6	B	—	c.1840–1862	1862
7–16	A	—	c.1820–1840	1840

however, indicated a difference between ceramic and glass *termini post quem*. The dating of the glass assemblages extended the *terminus post quem* of Component B later in time and reaffirmed the *terminus post quem* of Component A, the reverse situation to that of Feature 6.

This difference in date of manufacture between ceramics and glass within the same stratigraphic component is perhaps a result of nineteenth-century technology. As glass became less expensive and more available due to improvements in the manufacturing process, continued re-use became unnecessary. This seemed to be particularly true of bottles. In any case, the result of this analysis was that the ceramic date ranges were extended later in time, and the breaks between components set by ceramic dates were reaffirmed by the glass dates.

Analytical Techniques: Quantity and Quality

The methods employed in the analysis of the ceramic assemblages, using the categories presented in the test implications, were fairly standard. Frequencies of vessels for each analytical category were calculated, and significant difference was determined using the chi-square statistic at the .05 level of significance.

In the analysis of the quantity variable, it should be noted that three different ceramic-vessel totals were used for different comparisons (see Table 3). The Total Vessel Count, or TVC, is used in the calculation of quantity of ceramic vessels within the features, and in figuring percentages of porcelain, transfer-printed ware, ironstone, undecorated ware, and minimally decorated ware within the total ceramic assemblage.

The Identifiable Vessel Count, or IVC, is required in calculating the percentage of tableware, storage ware, and tea- and coffeeware within the total ceramic assemblage. IVC figures are also used in calculating percentages of serving flatware, serving bowls, transfer-printed flatware, banded bowls, and edged flatware within the total tableware assemblage. The variety of vessel forms within the total ceramic assemblage is also determined using the IVC figures.

The Miller Vessel Count, or MVC, is used in arriving at Miller Index values for the various ceramic-assemblage groupings. This total is the smallest of the three in that it includes only those vessels identifiable as to form and measurable plates and saucers. The scale year (or years) used for each assemblage in this analysis is that which is closest to the *terminus post quem* for the particular component, and which lists price indices for the ceramic types contained in that assemblage. The index years used are: Feature 7-1814 (Components A and B), 1824 and 1836 (C), 1824, 1836, and 1838 (D), 1824 and 1836 (E), 1846 and 1855 (F), 1846 and 1855 (G); Feature 6-1814 (Components A and B), 1824 and 1836 (C), 1824 and 1846 (D); Feature 5-1814, 1824, and 1833 (Component A), 1824 and 1846 (B). Porcelain vessels, for which Miller has few index values, are consistently assigned the index figure of the most expensive type of that form of vessel (i.e., plate, cup, etc.) for the particular index year. Where Miller does not have an index value for a certain ware type, a figure is assigned that approximates the value. For example, plates that measure either nine or eleven inches in diameter are given the index value for ten-inch plates, since values are not available for plates of either of these sizes.

Table 3. Total Vessel Counts, Features 6 and 7, King Street, and Feature 5, Gibbon Street

		Features		
Ceramic total	Abbreviation	5	6	7
All vessels, including those of unknown form	TVC	148	506	629
All vessels identifiable as to form	IVC	77	462	535
Measurable plates, cups, saucers, and bowls for Miller Index Analysis	MVC	36	302	258

In evaluating the results of the Miller Ceramic Price Index analysis, it must be decided what constitutes a *significant* difference between two average index figures. The total combined range of index values for the scale years utilized in this study—1814, 1824, 1833, 1836, 1838, 1846, and 1855—is 1.00 to 4.00. The level of significant difference used here is 5 percent; so on this scale, if the difference in index values is .20 or less, they are considered *not* significantly different.

In addition, one new analytical measure was developed. Because the three features utilized in this study varied in their diameters, depths, number of associated users, and length of time used by different households, an evaluative technique for making meaningful comparisons of quantity of vessels was required. This was accomplished by multiplying the average number of years of residence together, then dividing this figure by the total vessel count for that component. This yielded total number of vessels per person-year of residence for each component.

The results of the application of this technique and all others used in this study are reported in the next section.

ANALYSIS RESULTS

Identification of Class Affiliation

The class affiliation of the households associated with the three ceramic assemblages is determined according to the covariance of the four socioeconomic categories—occupation, property assessment, condition of tenure, and ethnic background—as described in the analytical methods section. These data and other pertinent documentary information available are presented in Table 4.

This documentary information places the households associated with Features 6 and 7 firmly in the Alexandria middle class according to the Socioeconomic Ranking Scales for Alexandria in 1810, 1830, and 1850 (Stephens 1981c; Terrie 1979). The Gibbon Street households are definitely ranked at the bottom of the lower class in Alexandria for the same years.

The middle-class standing of the Feature 6 and 7 households are evident from their occupations as merchants and small businessmen, their moderately low to moderately high property assessments, ownership of one or two slaves, and living in brick two- or three-story houses in the city's commercial and political core. In contrast, the occupants at the Gibbon Street site are free blacks with jobs as unskilled laborers, very low real and personal property assessments, living in a one story wood frame house on the periphery of the city.

The one area where the status pattern seems to break down is condition of tenure. The renters are the middle-class householders, while the owners are the free blacks. This is resolved, however, when it is understood that most of the 500 block residents are upwardly mobile, moving on to ownership or resi-

Table 4. Archival Data Summary

| | Date and site | | | | | |
| | Circa 1800–1849 | | | Circa 1850–1860 | | |
Variable	King St. / Lot 3, F.6	King St. / Lot 26, F.7	Gibbon St. / Lot 18, F.5	King St. / Lot 3, F.6	King St. / Lot 26, F.7	Gibbon St. / Lot 18, F.5
Average occupational rank for occupants (Scale: 1–6)	1.4 (ranks: 1, 2, 3, 4)	2.4 (ranks: 1, 3)	5 (rank: 5)	2.8 (ranks: 2, 3)	2 (rank: 2)	4 (ranks: 3, 5)
Average real property assessment (house and lot)	$3,307 ($1,000–$4,000)	$1,364 ($750–$2,200)	$198 ($100–$250)	$4,450 ($3,800–$5,500)	$1,885 ($1,500–$2,500)	$318 ($200–$500)
Real property decile	Bottom 20% (1810) Top 40% (1830)	Bottom 20% (1810) Bottom 30% (1830)	Bottom 10% (1810, 1830)	Top 30% (1850)	Bottom 40% (1850)	Bottom 10% (1850)
Average personal property assessment for occupant	$325 ($100–$500)	$357 ($150–$700)	None recorded	$400 ($400)	$525 ($300–$800)	$40 ($30–$50)
Aggregate property decile for occupant (real and personal)	Top 50% (1810) Top 30% (1830)	Top 50% (1810) Top 20% (1830)	Bottom 10% (1810, 1830)	Top 50% (1850)	Top 30% (1850)	Bottom 10% (1850)
Condition of tenure	Owned two years Rented all other years	Owned three years Rented all other years	Owned (ground rent paid 1827–1841)	Rented all years	Rented all years	Owned (ground rent paid 1850–1863)
Ethnic background	Euro-American	Euro-American	Afro-American	Euro-American	Euro-American	Afro-American
Average number of Euro-American occupants	4.75	4.7	0	8	3	0
Average number of Afro-American occupants	1.5 (slaves)	2 (slave)	4.3 (free blacks)	2 (slaves)	0	5 (free blacks)
Location of property	Commercial core	Commercial core	Periphery	Commercial core	Commercial core	Periphery
Building material of house	Brick	Brick	Wood frame	Brick	Brick	Wood frame
Number of stories of house	3	2	1	3	2	1
Socioeconomic class	Middle	Middle	Lower	Middle	Middle	Lower

dence in a more desirable dwelling, while the residents at Gibbon Street pass down ownership of the relatively low-value property from generation to generation.

While the middle-class households as a group are very different from the free black households, at a finer scale, status distinctions may be possible between the two middle-class samples. When the entire sixty-year period is considered, the heads of household associated with Feature 6 have a higher average occupational ranking, as well as a higher average real property assessment and decile rank than the households contributing to Feature 7. However, when average personal property assessments are compared, the Feature 7 households have higher assessments than the residents associated with Feature 6. Thus, it is difficult to reach a conclusion as concerns intraclass differences. Is average occupational ranking a stronger status indicator than real property assessment? Identification of the range of variation concerning these variables awaits accrual of a larger analytical sample.

Testing the Hypotheses

The results of testing the three hypotheses presented earlier are that quantity and quality increased with higher socioeconomic status, while variety did not. This is based upon the following data.

Hypotheses 1: Quantity

Quantity of ceramic vessels was measured by total number of vessels per average person-year of residence for each assemblage. Table 5 presents the results.

This table indicates that the quantity of vessels per average person-year is much higher for the middle-class households as compared to the lower-class households. This is consistently true for the total vessel counts, refined ware vessel counts, and coarseware vessel counts. It is interesting also that the figures for number of vessels per average person-year of residence are higher for refined vessels as compared to coarseware vessels for all features.

Thus the prediction that quantity of vessels would increase with higher socioeconomic status is borne out by this analysis. The middle class have over seven times as many total vessels, over six times the number of refined ware vessels, and over eight times as many coarseware vessels per average person-year of residence, compared to the lower class. All three features show a decrease in quantity of vessels in all categories through time.

Hypothesis 2: Quality

Quality is measured by evaluating three groups of data. First, the percentage of porcelain, transfer-printed ware, ironstone, undecorated ware, and minimally decorated ware within total ceramic wares is calculated using Total

Table 5. Comparison of Quantity of Ceramic Vessels to Average Person-Years of Residence, Features 7, 6, and 5

Feature	Component(s)	Average person-years of residence	Total refined vessels	Vessels/ person-year	Total coarse vessels	Vessels/ person-year	Total all vessels	Vessels/ person-year
Feature 7	I	21.5	243	11.3	131	6.1	374	17.4
	II, III	33.0	159	4.8	96	2.9	255	7.7
	I–III	20.7	402	19.4	227	11.0	629	30.4
Feature 6	I	15.5	210	13.6	67	4.3	277	17.9
	II	18.4	156	8.5	73	4.0	229	12.5
	I, II	17.0	366	21.5	140	8.2	506	29.8
Feature 5	A	30.9	83	2.7	12	.4	95	3.1
	B	50.0	29	.6	24	.5	53	1.1
	A, B	35.4	112	3.2	36	1.0	148	4.2

Vessel Count figures. Table 6 shows these data, which present some interesting patterns when the features are compared.

The percentages for the combined component group totals in both Features 6 and 7 are very similar except in the case of porcelain. The Feature 6 total assemblage has 18 percent porcelain, as compared to only 9 percent in Feature 7. Feature 5 has a little less than half the percentage of porcelain relative to Feature 6 (7 percent versus 18 percent), while having only a slightly smaller percentage than Feature 7 (7 percent versus 9 percent). The amount of transfer-printed ware in the Feature 5 assemblage is nearly half those in Features 6 and 7 (15 percent versus 30 percent and 35 percent). The percentage

Table 6. Counts and Percentages of Ceramic Type Categories within Total Vessel Count, Features 7, 6, and 5

Feature	Component(s)	Porc.	T.P.	Iron.	Un.dec.	Min.dec.	Total
Feature 7	A	30	59	0	29	7	125
	B	2	24	0	16	8	50
	C	9	50	0	12	11	82
	I	41	133	0	57	26	257
	Percentage in TVC (374)	11%	36%	0%	15%	7%	
	D	9	40	0	8	11	68
	E	5	17	2	12	14	50
	F	4	20	4	11	6	45
	G	0	12	3	8	5	28
	II, III	18	89	9	39	36	191
	Percentage in TVC (255)	7%	35%	4%	15%	10%	
	I, II, III	59	222	9	96	62	448
	Percentage in TVC (629)	9%	35%	1%	15%	10%	
Feature 6	A	21	26	0	18	8	73
	B	37	56	0	20	28	141
	I	58	82	0	38	36	214
	Percentage in TVC (277)	21%	30%	0%	14%	13%	
	C	17	33	2	9	13	74
	D	16	36	3	18	11	84
	II	33	69	5	27	24	158
	Percentage in TVC (229)	14%	30%	2%	12%	11%	
	I, II	91	151	5	65	60	372
	Pecentage in TVC (506)	18%	30%	1%	13%	12%	
Feature 5	A	5	22	0	21	11	59
	Percentage in TVC (95)	5%	23%	0%	22%	12%	
	B	5	0	0	15	10	30
	Percentage in TVC (53)	9%	0%	0%	28%	19%	
	A, B	10	22	0	36	21	89
	Percentage in TVC (148)	7%	15%	0%	24%	14%	

of minimally decorated ware is similar in all three assemblages, but Feature 5 has a greater amount of undecorated ware (24 percent versus 13 percent for Feature 6, and 15 percent in Feature 7). No ironstone vessels are present in the Feature 5 assemblage.

The second group of data examined in order to evaluate quality of the ceramic assemblages is matched sets of porcelain, ironstone, and transfer-printed ware. Vessels are designated as matching if they display the same decorative design, or, in a few cases of undecorated pieces (e.g., ironstone), the same shape. The calculations were compiled by Perry Swain (1983) from information on vessel catalog cards and from direct examination of the matching vessels. Table 7 summarizes these data.

The "Number of sets" column in Table 7 shows the number of matching groups, or "sets," for each ceramic type in each component group. The next column displays the total number of vessels matching in each category. "Average number of vessels/sets" presents the results of the number of vessels divided by the number of sets in each case. The last column displays the percentage of matching vessels within the Total Vessel Count for each ceramic category. The ceramic category "other refined wares" ("Other") includes undecorated ware, hand-painted ware, and minimally decorated ware.

It is immediately evident that Features 6 and 7 have an overwhelmingly greater number of matched vessels in comparison to Feature 5. The only comparison that demonstrates a similarity between these two features and Feature 5 is the area of matched "other refined wares." Very few of the vessels in this category match in any of the three assemblages, being only 6 percent in each. Feature 5 has only six matching vessels in a total refined-ware assemblage of 102 (6 percent), and these are three cases of two vessels matching each other.

The assemblages of the middle class, in contrast, contain large percentages of matching vessels: 113 out of 506 refined-ware vessels in Feature 6 (22 percent); 130 out of 350 refined ware vessels in Feature 7 (37 percent). The assemblages of porcelain and transfer-printed ware in both features have high percentages of matched pieces. Feature 6 has 46 percent matched transfer-printed vessels and 35 percent in porcelain, while Feature 7 has 38 percent matched transfer-printed vessels and 49 percent porcelain. The number of pieces per set is also high, with Feature 7 averaging about five per set for both transfer-printed and porcelain, while Feature 6 averages five per set for transfer-printed and six per set for porcelain. Notable also is the fact that Feature 7 includes a set of nine commemorative, blue transfer-printed plates, as well as twenty-one matched green-and-brown transfer-printed pieces ("Select Sketches" pattern), which include plates, cups, platters, a bowl, a serving dish, and a gravy boat. Similarly, the Feature 6, transfer-print assemblage includes thirteen matching pieces in the blue "Ponte Rotto" pattern and a group of twenty-seven green-and-black printed vessels in the "Continental Views" pattern (this is composed of plates, platters, serving dishes, and a soup bowl). In addition, Feature 6 contains part of a porcelain tea set, hand-painted with an urn

Table 7. Matching Ceramic Vessel Summary, Features 7, 6, and 5

Feature	Component(s)	Number of sets					Number of matched vessels					Average number of vessels/set					Percentage matching within type			
		T.P.	Porc.	Iron.	Other	Total	T.P.	Porc.	Iron.	Other	Total	T.P.	Porc.	Iron.	Other	Total	T.P.	Porc.	Iron.	Other
Feature 7	I	14	4	0	2	20	50	22	0	7	79	3.6	5.5	0	3.5	4.0	38	54	0	7
	II, III	5	2	1	2	10	34	7	5	5	51	6.8	3.5	5	2.5	5.1	38	39	56	6
	I–III	19	6	1	4	30	84	29	5	12	130	4.4	4.8	5	3.0	4.3	38	49	56	6
Feature 6	I	7	2	0	1	10	31	20	0	3	54	4.4	10.0	0	3.0	5.4	38	35	0	3
	II	6	3	0	3	12	38	12	0	9	59	6.3	4.0	0	3.0	4.9	55	36	0	10
	I, II	13	5	0	4	22	69	32	0	12	113	5.3	6.4	0	3.0	5.1	46	35	0	6
Feature 5	A	1	0	0	1	2	2	0	0	2	4	2.0	0	0	2.0	2.0	9	0	0	4
	B	0	0	0	1	1	0	0	0	2	2	0	0	0	2.0	2.0	0	0	0	10
	A, B	1	0	0	2	3	2	0	0	4	6	2.0	0	0	2.0	2.0	18	0	0	6

design in black, represented by fifteen pieces, including tea cups, saucers, and tea bowls.

Ironstone vessels are rare in any of the assemblages. There are five in Feature 6, nine in Feature 7, and none in Feature 5. In Feature 7, however, there are five undecorated molded bowls that match, and so result in a figure of 56 percent matching for this assemblage.

Feature 5 has only six matching pieces, which consist of a hand-painted, blue floral cup and saucer, a stenciled green-and-rose colored cup and saucer, and a blue transfer-printed saucer and serving bowl. These may relate to the serving of tea or coffee and so may indicate that the few matching pieces possessed by the residents at this house were used for special occasions.

The third evaluative technique for measuring the quality of the ceramic assemblages is the Miller Ceramic Price Index (Miller 1980). Perry Swain (1983) compiled the data presented in Table 8.

Comparison of the Miller indices for the total ceramic assemblage for each of the three features reveals a distinction between the King Street ceramics and those from Feature 5. There is a difference of .11 between Features 6 and 7, while Features 6 and 5 differ by .32, and Features 7 and 5 differ by .21. The indices for total plates, cups and saucers, and bowls are also consistently higher in the assemblages of the middle class, as compared to Feature 5. Only in the bowl category do the Feature 6 and 7 indices differ significantly, that is, by .32. It is interesting to observe also that, in each assemblage, the highest index values are for cups and saucers, then plates, and the lowest values are for bowls. Again, as noted in the evaluation of matching vessels, this suggests an emphasis on the status value of ceramics used in tea and/or coffee drinking. This pattern is not a function of cups and saucers being more expensive than plates, which were more expensive than bowls. All three types of vessels were available in cheaper and more expensive varieties. In the scale years used in the calculations, cups and saucers had an index value range of 1–4, plates 1–3.60, and bowls 1–3.

Table 8. Miller Ceramic Price Index Summary, Features 7, 6, and 5

Feature	Component(s)	Plates	Cups and saucers	Bowls	Average index
Feature 7	I	2.55	2.68	1.74	2.42
	II, III	1.92	3.05	2.33	2.31
	I–III	2.24	2.80	1.96	2.37
Feature 6	I	2.49	3.06	1.59	2.61
	II	2.35	2.48	1.69	2.31
	I, II	2.42	2.81	1.64	2.48
Feature 5	A	1.97	2.50	1.29	2.19
	B	1.13	2.19	0	1.98
	A, B	1.93	2.43	1.29	2.16

Hypothesis 3: Variety

The variable "variety" is measured through four sets of comparisons: (1) tableware, storage ware, and tea- and coffeeware within the total ceramic assemblage; (2) serving flatware and serving bowls within total tableware; (3) transfer-printed flatware, banded bowls, and edged flatware within total tableware; and (4) variety of vessel forms within the total ceramic assemblage. The calculations for these comparisons are all derived from the Identifiable Vessel Count. The first comparison is displayed in Table 9. These figures are the percentages of each ceramic grouping within total ceramics.

Perhaps the first pattern that is noticed in this table is that the percentages of tableware and tea- and coffeeware within the total identifiable vessel assemblage are very similar in all three features. There is, in contrast, a distinct difference in the percentages of storage ware in the Feature 6 and Feature 7 assemblages as compared to Feature 5. Storage ware accounts for 2 percent and 3 percent of the total ceramic assemblages in Features 7 and 6, respectively, while making up 20 percent of the Feature 5 assemblage. This is the reverse of the expected situation.

Evaluation of the proportion of serving flatware and bowls within the total ceramic assemblage for each feature as a measure of variety is presented in Table 10. Calculations were made as percentages within total tableware.

This comparison is interesting in that the total assemblage percentages of serving flatware and bowls are similar in all three features, yet Features 7 and 5 are the most similar. The Feature 7, serving flatware percentage is consistently lower than the Feature 6 percentage, while the figures for serving bowls are just the opposite.

The third evaluation of variety in the ceramic assemblages is a focusing of the previous comparison down to transfer-printed flatware, edged flatware, and banded bowls. The results are shown in Table 11. Calculations were made as percentages within total tableware.

It is immediately evident in the above table that the percentages of transfer-printed and edged flatware are greater in the Feature 6 and 7 assemblages, as compared to the Feature 5 assemblage. Banded bowls are only present in the Feature 7 assemblage when the expectation has been that Feature 5 should have a greater proportion of these vessels than either of the assemblages of the middle class. Overall, the assemblage of the lower class has very few of any of these categories of ceramics.

The final test of variety within the ceramic assemblages involves an evaluation of the range of forms, or shapes, of the vessels making up each assemblage. The figures are calculated using the Identifiable Vessel Count. Different sizes of plates, bowls, and saucers are counted as different vessel forms in keeping with the fact that differences in size relate to differences in use. Also, a variety of sizes may be an indicator of tableware sets, which have been associated with status ranking, as presented earlier in this study.

In order to compare the number of forms from one component to another, a figure is calculated for each by dividing the total vessel count by the number of

Table 9. Table, Storage, and Tea- and Coffeewares, Features 7, 6, and 5

Feature	Component(s)	Identifiable vessel count	Tableware	Percentage	Storage	Percentage	Tea and coffee	Percentage
Feature 7	I	374	139	37	9	2	82	22
	II, III	255	118	46	4	2	30	12
	I–III	629	257	41	13	2	112	18
Feature 6	I	277	114	41	3	1	75	27
	II	229	101	44	9	4	47	21
	I, II	506	215	43	12	3	122	24
Feature 5	A	95	45	47	11	12	26	27
	B	53	14	26	18	34	10	19
	A, B	148	59	40	29	20	36	24

Table 10. Serving Flatware and Bowls, Features 7, 6, and 5

Feature	Component(s)	Total tableware	Serving flatware	Percentage	Serving bowls	Percentage
Feature 7	I	139	72	52	39	28
	II, III	118	64	54	33	28
	I–III	257	136	53	72	28
Feature 6	I	114	73	64	25	22
	II	101	66	65	20	20
	I, II	215	139	65	45	21
Feature 5	A	45	30	67	9	20
	B	14	5	36	8	57
	A, B	59	35	59	17	29

forms. The closer the resulting number is to 1.00, the greater the proportion of forms to total vessels. The larger the number is, the fewer the proportion of forms, and hence the less variety. The results of this evaluation are presented in Table 12.

The number-of-vessels-per-form figures for the Feature 6 and 7 total assemblages are much higher than the figure for Feature 5 (13.05, 11.55, and 5.69, respectively). The Feature 6 and 7 total figures are very close in value while being approximately double that of Feature 5. Part, if not the majority, of this variation is a function of the much higher vessel counts for Feature 6 and 7, as compared to Feature 5, combined with the fact that there is a comparatively limited range of ceramic vessel forms. For this reason, this index figure may be more appropriate for within-feature, rather than between-feature, comparison.

Specific examination of the types of vessel forms in each feature contrasts with the calculations in Table 12. Examination of Table 13 reveals that the Feature 6 and 7 assemblages are very similar in their range of vessel forms, differing in only a few insignificant form types. The Feature 5 assemblage, in contrast, has a smaller variety of bowl and saucer sizes, as well as fewer specialized serving forms such as sugar bowls, creamers, gravy boats, and refined ware pitchers. Certain utilitarian ware forms present in the Feature 6 and 7 assemblages are absent from Feature 5, such as milk pans, jugs, and ewers. The contrast in total number of vessels between the assemblages of the middle class and those of the lower class, explains the unexpected results of this analysis. The range of forms commonly available at any given time is much more limited than the number of ceramic vessels that a household may possess. So even though the assemblage of the lower class contains fourteen fewer forms (mostly specialized forms) than are present in both Features 6 and 7, these features each have over three times as many vessels as Feature 5, and this results in skewed comparative vessels-per-form figures.

Table 11. Transfer-Printed Flatware, Banded Bowls, and Edged Flatware, Features 7, 6, and 5

Feature	Component(s)	Total tableware	Transfer-printed flatware	Percentage	Banded bowls	Percentage	Edged flatware	Percentage
Feature 7	I	139	45	33	3	2	21	15
	II, III	118	25	21	2	2	16	14
	I–III	257	70	27	5	2	37	14
Feature 6	I	114	37	33	0	0	22	19
	II	101	13	13	0	0	17	17
	I, II	215	50	23	0	0	39	18
Feature 5	A	45	6	13	0	0	6	13
	B	14	0	0	0	0	1	7
	A, B	59	6	10	0	0	7	12

Table 12. Vessel Form Summary, Features 7, 6, and 5

Feature	Component(s)	Identifiable vessel count	Number of forms	Number of vessels per form
Feature 7	I	316	39	8.10
	II, III	219	32	6.84
	I–III	535	41	13.05
Feature 6	I	254	38	6.68
	II	208	33	6.30
	I, II	462	40	11.55
Feature 5	A	95	21	4.52
	B	53	11	4.82
	A, B	148	26	5.69

Summary of Hypothesis Testing

In order to delineate which of the patterns presented above are significant, and to objectively evaluate the test implications, the chi-square statistic is utilized. Table 14 summarizes the results of testing Hypotheses 1 through 3. This table lists the number of each test implication and features/components being compared, the result of testing (rejection or retention of H_o), calculated x^2 value, tabled x^2 value at .05 level of significance, and outcome of testing (if the test result supported the hypothesis—symbolized by "+"; rejected the hypothesis because of lack of significant difference—symbolized by "x"; or rejected the hypothesis due to the figures being the opposite of those expected—symbolized by "*").

The testing results presented in Table 14 may be further condensed for discussion as is shown in Table 15. The overall result is that the null hypothesis is rejected in favor of differences between the ceramic assemblages associated with the middle and lower classes being significantly different. When the three hypotheses are considered individually, Hypotheses 1 and 2 concerning the quantity and quality of vessels are strongly supported, while the null hypothesis for 3, regarding variety, is retained. More important, however, is which measures of quantity, quality, and variety appear as strong or weak material correlates of social class membership.

Quantity of artifacts in this study corresponds very well to class affiliation in the manner predicted. All of the individual tests for evaluating this variable produce results that match expectations. The assemblages of the middle class contain a significantly greater quantity of refined ware vessels and coarseware vessels, as well as all vessels totaled, as compared to the lower-class assemblage.

In the area of quality, most tests produced the results predicted. The ceramic assemblage of the middle class does contain significantly more trans-

Table 13. Ceramic Vessel Forms, Features 7, 6, and 5

Form	Inches	Feature 7			Feature 6			Feature 5		
		Cp.Gp. I	Cp.Gps. II, III	Cp.Gps. I–III	Cp.Gp. I	Cp.Gp. II	Cp.Gps. I, II	Cp. A	Cp. B	Cps. A, B
Plate	6	X	X	X	X	X	X	X		X
	7	X	X	X	X	X	X	X		X
	8	X	X	X	X	X	X	X		X
	9	X	X	X	X	X	X	X	X	X
	10	X	X	X	X	X	X	X		X
	11	X	X	X		X	X			
Bowl	5	X	X	X	X	X	X		X	X
	6	X	X	X	X	X	X		X	X
	7	X	X	X	X	X	X			
	8	X	X	X	X	X	X			
	9	X	X	X	X	X	X			
	10	X	X	X	X	X	X	X		
	11	X		X	X	X	X			
Saucer	3	X		X	X	X	X			
	4	X	X	X	X		X	X		
	5	X	X	X	X	X	X			X
	6	X	X	X	X	X	X	X		
Soup plate		X	X	X	X	X	X	X		X

	39	32	41	38	33	40	21	11	26
Tea cup	X	X	X	X	X	X	X		X
Coffee cup	X	X	X	X	X	X	X	X	X
Coffee can	X	X	X	X	X	X	X		X
Tea bowl	X	X	X	X	X	X	X		X
Mug	X	X	X	X	X	X	X		X
Platter	X	X	X	X	X	X	X	X	X
Teapot		X	X	X	X	X			
Tea caddy	X	X							
Sugar bowl	X	X	X	X	X	X			
Creamer	X		X	X	X	X	X		X
Serving dish	X	X	X	X	X	X	X		X
Tureen	X	X	X	X	X	X	X		
Gravy boat	X	X	X	X	X	X			
Ref. pitcher	X	X	X	X	X	X			
Util. pitcher	X		X	X	X	X			X
Mixing bowl	X		X	X	X	X		X	X
Milk pan	X		X	X	X	X		X	
Jar	X	X	X	X	X	X	X	X	X
Jug	X		X	X		X		X	
Porringer	X		X						
Bottle							X	X	X
Shaving mug	X	X	X	X	X	X			
Chamberpot	X	X	X	X	X	X	X	X	X
Ewer	X	X	X	X	X	X		X	
Wash basin	X	X	X	X	X	X	X	X	X
Flowerpot	X	X	X	X	X	X	X		X
Totals	39	32	41	38	33	40	21	11	26

Table 14. Summary of Testing Hypotheses 1 through 3

Hypothesis/ test implication	Null hypothesis ret.	Null hypothesis rej.	x^2 Calcu. value	.05 Table value	Outcome[a]
1 (a) Ft. 7:30 avg.v./per.yr.	Ft. 6:30		Ft. 5:4 —	—	++
(b) Ft. 7:19 avg.v./per.yr.	Ft. 6:22		Ft. 5:3 —	—	++
(c) Ft. 7:11 avg.v./per.yr.	Ft. 6:8		Ft. 5:1 —	—	++
2a (a) Ft. 7, 5	x		.87	3.84	×
Ft. 6, 5		x	8.57	3.84	+
(b) Ft. 7, 5		x	13.47	3.84	+
Ft. 6, 5		x	8.23	3.84	+
(c) Ft. 7, 5 (7:1% 5:0)		x	—	—	+
Ft. 6, 5 (6:1% 5:0)		x	—	—	+
(d) Ft. 7, 5		x	4.73	3.84	+
Ft. 6, 5		x	8.04	3.84	+
(e) Ft. 7, 5	x		1.86	3.84	×
Ft. 6, 5	x		.44	3.84	×
2b (a) Ft. 7, 5		x	4.23	3.84	+
Ft. 6, 5		x	5.56	3.84	+
(b) Ft. 7, 5 (7:49% 5:0)		x	—	—	+
Ft. 6, 5 (6:35% 5:0)		x	—	—	+
(c) Ft. 7, 5 (7:56% 5:0)		x	—	—	+
Ft. 6, 5 (both: 0)	x		—	—	×

2c Miller Index values

	Plates	Cups and saucers	Bowls	Average index	
Ft. 7, 5, 7:	2.24	2.80	1.96	2.37	—
5:	1.93	2.43	1.29	2.16	++++
Ft. 6, 5, 6:	2.42	2.81	1.64	2.48	—
5:	1.93	2.43	1.29	2.16	++++

Hypothesis/ test implication	Null hypothesis ret.	Null hypothesis rej.	x^2 Calcu. value	.05 Table value	Outcome[a]
3a (a) Ft. 7, 6, 5	x		.19	5.99	××
(b) Ft. 7, 5		x	58.76	3.84	*
Ft. 6, 5		x	47.05	3.84	*
(c) Ft. 7, 6, 5	x		5.10	5.99	××
3b (a) Ft. 7, 6, 5	x		1.74	5.99	××
(b) Ft. 7, 6, 5	x		2.15	5.99	××
3c (a) Ft. 7, 5		x	5.15	3.84	+
Ft. 6, 5	x		3.44	3.84	×
(b) Ft. 7, 5 (7:2% 5:0)		x	—	—	*
Ft. 6, 5 (both:0)	x		—	—	×
(c) Ft. 7, 5	x		.20	3.84	×
Ft. 6, 5	x		1.20	3.84	×
3d Ft. 7, 5		x	10.07	3.84	*
Ft. 6, 5		x	7.59	3.84	*

[a] + as predicted; × no difference; * opposite predicted.

Table 15. Outcome of Hypotheses Testing

Hypothesis number	Total number of tests	Testing results[a]			Outcome
1	6	6+	0×	0*	H_o rejected
2	24	20+	4×	0*	H_o rejected
3	18	1+	12×	5*	H_o retained
1–3	48	27+	16×	5*	H_o rejected

[a] + as predicted; × no difference; * opposite predicted.

fer-printed ware, ironstone, matched porcelain, matched transfer-printed vessels, and fewer undecorated ware, as compared to the Gibbon Street assemblage. The value of the ceramic assemblages from King Street, as calculated using the Miller Pricing Index, are significantly higher in all categories than the assemblage representing the lower class. Testing indicates no significant difference between the proportion of minimally decorated ware among any of the assemblages. Calculations of the amount of porcelain and matched ironstone vessels both produce mixed results, allowing no clear conclusions to be drawn concerning these ceramic categories. The higher-than-expected proportions of porcelain and matched vessels on the lower-class site may be an indicator of hand-me-downs from employers to their household maids or laborers.

None of the test implications for the variety measure are supported (only one individual test result is as predicted). There is no significant difference between assemblages in proportions of tableware, tea- and coffeeware, serving flatware, serving bowls, or edged flatware. It was predicted that the assemblages of the middle class would have larger proportions of storage wares and larger ratios of number of shapes to total number of vessels, as compared to the assemblage of the lower class. Instead, it is the latter assemblage that has the larger figures.

A mixed result is evident in the categories of transfer-printed flatware and banded bowls. The assemblages of the middle class were expected to have a larger proportion of flatware and a smaller proportion of bowls, as compared to the Gibbon Street assemblage. Feature 7 yielded a larger proportion of both categories of vessels than either of the other two assemblages, while the Feature 6 figures were not significantly different from those derived from the assemblage of the lower class.

What is indicated as a result of testing the hypotheses designed to delineate material correlates of class membership is that the variables relating to quantity and quality of ceramic assemblages do show a fairly consistent pattern as hypothesized. The variety variable, however, does not vary with class differences in the manner expected. The only test for variety that does not correspond to predictions, is that the Feature 7 assemblage has a significantly larger quantity of transfer-printed flatware than the assemblage of the lower class. It should also be noted that comparison of vessel forms results in the assemblages of the middle class having fourteen more forms than the lower-class assemblage, thus supporting this hypothesis.

CONCLUSIONS

The primary conclusion drawn from the results of testing the hypotheses proposed in this study is that the quantity and quality variables are the strongest correlates of class membership evaluated in this study. Only two of the ceramic categories evaluated while investigating the variety of ceramics within the assemblages evidence a positive correlation with class differences. Testing these three variables with different data sets is required to determine the validity of these findings.

The results of testing the hypotheses provide descriptive profiles of the ceramic assemblages associated with middle-class and lower-class households during the first half of the nineteenth century. The profiles must be stated in relative terms. The following generalized descriptions of household ceramic assemblages are suggested:

1. *Middle-Class Ceramic Assemblage:* When compared to the lower class, middle-class households have a greater quantity of ceramic vessels per average person–year of residence on the site. The variety of specialized vessel forms, including such pieces as gravy boats, sugar bowls, and ewers, is greater. More expensive ceramic varieties and vessels of the latest ware, form, and/or pattern of decoration are present. The proportion of matched vessels is greater and the number of pieces in the sets is larger, as compared to the lower-class assemblage. In addition, the ratio of tableware to storage ware is greater, indicating an emphasis on material display in dining.

2. *Lower-Class Ceramic Assemblage:* Quantity of vessels is lower relative to the middle class. A somewhat narrower range of wares and decorative varieties are present in the lower-class assemblage, as compared to the middle-class assemblage. The number of expensive vessels is fewer. Certain specialized vessel forms do not occur that do appear in the middle-class assemblage. Matched sets are fewer and the number of matched pieces per set are fewer. The proportion of storage ware to tableware is greater. As stated earlier, these results differ from expectations in certain ceramic categories. Some of these discrepancies can be explained by reconsidering previous research.

One explanation for the discrepancy between expectations stated in the test implications and the outcome of testing is that many of the varibles used in the testing were derived from the studies of Otto (1977,1980) and Baker (1980), which concerned material correlates of status in rural contexts. Perhaps less pronounced dietary differences between the middle and lower classes in the urban setting account for the small number of observed differences in the proportions of the variety categories: tableware; tea- and coffeeware; serving, edged, and transfer-printed flatwares; and serving and banded bowls. The present study also indicates that the proportion of storage wares within household assemblages decreases with higher status rather than increases, as Otto (1977,1980) found in his plantation context. This also may reflect rural-urban dietary differences. Perhaps lower-class households depended more on growing and storing food than did middle-class households, which could more readily purchase goods from the market.

Besides these comparisons between the lower and middle classes, the present study allows intraclass comparisons to be made for the middle class. A few differences are observed, but the overall impression is one of similarity in ceramic assemblages. With the inclusion of the documentary variables, higher status is associated with the *Feature 7* assemblage average personal property assessments, aggregate property deciles percentage of matched ironstone vessels within total ironstone, and percentage of transfer-printed flatware within total tableware (Tables 7 and 11). However, higher status is associated with the *Feature 6* assemblage as compared to that of Feature 7 in average real property assessments, average real property decile, percentage of porcelain with total ceramics, and percentage of banded bowls within total tableware (Tables 6 and 11).

These differences are not significant when it is realized that there exists a range of variation within any class. The differences observed do not present a convincing pattern that suggests overall higher socioeconomic standing within the middle class for the occupants of one residential site over the other. True, the house fronting on King Street (Feature 7) was consistently assessed at a higher value than the house on the St. Asaph Street side of this same block (Feature 6), and the evidence suggests that the King Street residents had more porcelain on their table, but it also seems that these neighbors possessed a similar range and quantity of ceramics. It is probably reasonable to assume that their household possessions, in general, and their lifestyles were similar as well.

Finally, the question of the appropriateness of the theoretical framework developed here and the adequacy of the data must be reconsidered. What modifications are called for in the approach? What suggestions can be made for further research as a result of this study?

The results of this study indicate that differences in the composition of household ceramic assemblages are associated with differences in class affiliation of the households. Whether the members of the same class are consciously signaling group membership or are unconsciously conforming to peer-group behavior, an exchange of information as transmitted by household objects seems to be taking place. It seems reasonable to retain the model correlating differences in consumer patterns with socioeconomic class membership. The hypotheses generated from this model are stated in terms of general characteristics of material assemblages. With revised archaeologically testable implications, the hypotheses could be tested on other categories of historical materials, such as glass, faunal remains, items of personal adornment, standing architecture, as well as on assemblages of prehistoric materials.

The data used in this study fulfill the criteria for adequacy. Documentary records evidence that nineteenth-century Alexandria society was structured as a socioeconomic hierarchy. The records also clearly indicate the relative difference in class affiliation of the households associated with the ceramic assemblages compared. The archaeological features from which the artifacts were recovered were undisturbed, and they were dug in a manner that allowed proper dating of the ceramic vessels. Furthermore, the ceramic assemblages are able to be associated with documented households.

Documentation provides the strength of this study in providing identification of the class affiliation of households. Even without this information, there would be evidence indicating that the three assemblages compared here would represent households of differing socioeconomic status. The location of the wells-privies of the middle class in the commercial core of Alexandria, and the shaft construction and depth, would all indicate a higher status affiliation than the barrel well located in "The Bottoms." Analysis of the ceramics would indicate a definite similarity between the Feature 6 and 7 assemblages, as compared to the assemblage of Feature 5. Nevertheless, the strength of the analysis would be greatly weakened if the component groups of the assemblages could not be associated with households of known class affiliation. The consistency of the class membership of the occupants of the sites would be unsure without documentation. Analysis would more profitably take the form of broad comparisons between features.

Further research building upon or re-testing the results of this study could take various forms. One area of inquiry could be the distinction of ethnicity from the encompassing socioeconomic class variable. This study incorporates ethnic background, a variable associated with class membership, but does not specifically address the question of the role of ethnicity in social structure. The Gibbon Street site ceramic assemblage is associated with free blacks, but this assemblage is considered only in its general lower-class association. Research into the socioeconomic standing of the Gibbon Street site households within the Alexandria black community as a whole would provide a different perspective. The point to be made here is that further investigations using data from both Euro- and Afro-American households with the same class affiliation could begin to distinguish ethnic differences in material culture. Testing using comparable material assemblages from upper-class households, nonblack households of the lower class, and black households of the upper and middle classes are also called for. Changes in social structure could be determined for a wider range of socioeconomic groups as well.

Another area requiring definition, as mentioned earlier, is the question of rural and urban differences in class-related material culture. Perhaps the types of possessions and variations within particular material assemblages that are associated with individual classes, differ in the two contexts. Again, further testing using the same sets of variables for both contexts is the only means of discovering such patterns.

In conclusion, the real assessment of the theoretical framework and hypotheses generated from it awaits further testing. Preferably, the hypotheses can be tested as they are stated, using artifact assemblages representing other middle- and lower-class households from rural and urban contexts. The hypotheses are stated in terms to facilitate broad cross-cultural application. Ethnoarchaeological investigations could offer invaluable data for testing and modifying the hypotheses presented here.

The investigation of social stratification is both a rewarding and challenging endeavor, especially for the anthropological archaeologist. Advances in understanding the subject are achieved slowly. The results of hypotheses testing, after all, are only the current state of knowledge concerning any subject. The more data that are compiled supporting the propositions that are made, the greater the understanding of the subject there will be. In this, way it is hoped that this study has added to the fund of knowledge concerning the nature of human social structure.

ACKNOWLEDGMENTS

I would like to express my appreciation to the Alexandria Archaeological Commission and the City of Alexandria, Virginia, for making the Alexandria Archaeology artifacts and data available for me to study. In addition, the Virginia Historic Landmarks Commission is gratefully acknowledged for the funding of the Courthouse Site Project (Grant 51-09970). Finally, my sincere thanks go to the Alexandria Archaeology staff and to the volunteers who contributed so much to this study through their efforts in site excavation, artifact analysis, and archival research.

REFERENCES

Abbitt-Outlaw, Merry, Bogley, Beverly A., and Outlaw, Alain C., 1977, Rich Man, Poor Man: Status Definition in Two 17th Century Ceramic Assemblages from Kingsmill, paper presented at the 10th Annual Meeting of the Society for Historical Archaeology, Ottawa.

Adams, Richard N., 1975, *Energy and Structure: A Theory of Social Power,* University of Texas Press, Austin.

Alexandria Censuses, 1791, 1794–1797, 1799, 1800, 1808, 1810, 1816, 1830, Lloyd House Library, Alexandria.

Alexandria City Directories, 1834, 1860, 1876, 1888, Lloyd House Library, Alexandria.

Alexandria Deed Books, Volumes I, M, U-2, 13, 14, 18, Alexandria Courthouse.

Alexandria Tax Records, 1787–1790, 1796–1798, 1800–1855, Lloyd House Library, Alexandria, 1856–1900, Virginia State Library, Richmond.

Alexandria Will Books, Volumes 2, C, Alexandria Courthouse.

Anderson, Nels, 1971, *The Industrial Urban Community: Historical and Comparative Perspectives,* Appleton-Century-Crofts, New York.

Baker, Vernon G., 1980, Archaeological visability of Afro-American Culture: An Example from Black Lucy's Garden, Andover, Massachusetts, in: *Archaeological Perspectives on Ethnicity in America, Afro-American and Asian American Culture History* (R. L. Schuyler, ed.), Baywood Publishing, New York, pp. 29–37.

Beidleman, D. Katharine, 1979, The 500-Block King Street Excavation: Alexandria Archaeology's First "Test Square," paper presented at the 9th Annual Middle Atlantic Archaeology Conference, Rehobeth Beach, Delaware.

Beidleman, D. Katherine, Ax-1 Field Reports, on file, Alexandria Urban Archaeology Program, Alexandria.

Buikstra, Jane E., 1976, Hopewell in the Lower Illinois Valley: A Regional Study of Human

Biological Variability and Prehistoric Mortuary Behavior, *Northwestern Archaeological Program Scientific Papers 2*.

Burk, Marguerite, 1968, *Consumption Economics: A Multidisciplinary Approach*, Wiley, New York.

Chapple, E. D., and Coon, Carlton S., 1942, *Principles of Anthropology*. Henry Holt, New York.

Coleman, Richard P., 1961, The Significance of Social Stratification in Selling, in: *Marketing, A Maturing Discipline* (M. L. Bell, ed.), American Marketing Association, Chicago, pp. 171–184.

Cressey, Pamela J., and Stephens, John F., 1982, The City-Site Approach to Urban Archaeology in Alexandria, Virginia, in: *Archaeology in Urban America: A Search for Pattern and Process* (R. S. Dickens, ed.), Academic Press, New York, pp. 40–61.

Cressey, Pamela J., Stephens, John F., Shephard, Steven J., and Magid, Barbara H., 1982, The Core/Periphery Relationship and the Archaeological Record in Alexandria, Virginia, in: *Archaeology in Urban America: A Search for Pattern and Process* (R. S. Dickens, ed.), Academic Press, New York, pp. 142–173.

Deagan, Kathleen A., 1974, Sex Status and Role in the Mestizaje of Spanish Colonial Florida, Ph.D. dissertation, Department of Anthropology, University of Florida, University Microfilms, Ann Arbor.

De Cunzo, Lu Ann, 1982, Economics and Ethnicity, an Archaeological Perspective on Nineteenth Century Paterson, New Jersey, paper presented at the 15th Annual Meeting of the Society for Historical Archaeology, Philadelphia.

Deetz, James, 1960, An Archaeological Approach to Kinship Change in Eighteenth Century Arikara Culture, Ph.D. dissertation, Harvard University, University Microfilms, Ann Arbor.

Deetz, James, 1972, Ceramic from Plymouth, 1620–1835: The Archaeological Evidence, in: *Ceramics in America* (I. Quimby, ed.), University of Virginia Press, Charlottesville, pp. 15–40.

Deetz, James, 1977, *In Small Things Forgotten*, Anchor Press/Doubleday, New York.

Drucker, Lesley M., 1981, Socioeconomic Patterning at an Undocumented Late 18th Century Lowcountry Site: Spiers Landing, *Historical Archaeology* 15(2)58–68.

Engel, James F., Kollat, David T., and Blackwell, Roger D., 1968, *Consumer Behavior*, Holt, Rinehart and Winston, New York.

Fairbanks, Charles H., 1972, The Kingsley Slave Cabins in Duval County, Florida, 1968, *The Conference on Historic Site Archaeology Papers* 7:62–93.

Federal Census of Population, 1790–1900 (dicennial), National Archives, Washington, D.C.

Friedlander, Amy, Holt, Cheryl A., Klein, Terry H., and LeeDecker, Charles H., 1985, From House to Outhouse: A Study of 19th Century Household in Wilmington, Delaware, paper presented at the 18th Annual Meeting of the Society for Historical Archaeology, Boston.

Gill, Bruce G., 1976, Ceramics in Philadelphia, 1780–1800: An Indicator of Socioeconomic Status in a Major City of the New Nation, M.A. thesis, George Washington University, Washington, D.C.

Godden, Geoffrey, A., 1966, *An Illustrated Encyclopedia of British Pottery and Porcelain*, Crown, New York.

Goheen, Peter G., 1970, *Victorian Toronto 1850–1900: Pattern and Process of Growth*, Department of Geography, Research Paper No. 127, University of Chicago.

Henley, Laura A., Palkovich, Anne M., and Haas, Jonathan, 1980, The Other Side of Alexandria: Archaeology in an Enduring Black Neighborhood, paper presented at the 45th Annual Meeting of the Society for American Archaeology, Philadelphia.

Herman, Lynne L., Sands, John O., and Schecter, Daniel, 1975, Ceramics in St. Mary's County, Maryland during the 1840's: A Socioeconomic Study, *Conference on Historical Site Archaeology Papers* 8:52–93.

Hershberg, Theodore, and Dockhorn, Robert, 1976, Occupational Classification, The Philadelphia Social History Project, *Historical Methods Newletter* 9(2,3)59–98.

Hill, James N., 1966, A Prehistoric Community in Eastern Arizona, *Southwestern Journal of Anthropology* 22(1)9–30.

Johnson, Gregory A., 1978, Information Sources and the Development of Decision-Making Organizations, in: *Social Archaeology: Beyond Subsistence and Dating* (C. L. Redman, ed.), Academic Press, New York, pp. 87–112.

Kahl, Joseph, 1953, *The American Class Structure*, Rinehart, New York.

Kingsbury, Pamela, 1974, Staffordshire Transfer-Printed Ware from the Thayer Collection, *Antiques* 105:169–173.

Lasswell, Thomas E., 1965, *Class and Stratum: An Introduction to Concepts and Research,* Houghton Mifflin, Boston.

Levy, Michael J., Jr., 1952, *The Structure of Society,* Princeton University Press, Princeton.

Levy, Sidney J., 1966, Social Class and Consumer Behavior, in: *On Knowing the Consumer* (J. W. Newman, ed.), Wiley, New York, pp. 48–59.

Longacre, William A., 1964, Archaeology as Anthropology: A Case Study, *Science* 144:1454–1455.

Magid, Barbara H., 1980, unpublished artifact analysis notes and charts for AX-1, Features 6 and 7, and AX-8, Feature 5, on file, Alexandria Urban Archaeology Program, Alexandria.

Markin, Rom J., Jr., 1974, *Consumer Behavior: A Cognitive Orientation,* Macmillan, New York.

Martineau, Pierre D., 1958, Social Classes and Spending Behavior, *Journal of Marketing* 23:121–130.

Martineau, Pierre D., 1961, Social Class and Its Very Close Relationship to the Individual's Buying Behavior, in: *Marketing, a Maturing Discipline* (M. L. Bell, ed.), American Marketing, Chicago, pp. 185–192.

McKearin, George S., and McKearin, Helen, 1977, *American Glass,* Crown Publishers, New York.

Miller, George L., 1980, Classification and Economic Scaling of 19th Century Ceramics, *Historical Archaeology* 14(1)1–40.

Miller, J. Jefferson, and Lyle M. Stone, 1970, *Eighteenth-Century Ceramics from Fort Michilimackinac,* Smithsonian Institution Press, Washington, D.C.

Miller, James G., 1978, *Living Systems,* McGraw-Hill, New York.

Otto, John S., 1975, Status Differences and the Archaeological Record: A Comparison of Planter, Overseer, and Slave Sites from Cannon's Point Plantation (1794–1861), Ph.D. dissertation, University of Florida, University Microfilms, Ann Arbor.

Otto, John S., 1977, Artifacts and Status Differences: A Comparison from Planter, Overseer, and Slave Sites on an Antebellum Plantation, in: *Research Strategies in Historical Archaeology* (S. South, ed.), Academic Press, New York, pp. 91–118.

Otto, John S., 1980, Race and Class on Antebellum Plantations, in: *Archaeological Perspectives on Ethnicity in America* (R. L. Schuyler, ed.), Baywood Publishing, New York, pp. 3–13.

Pareto, Vilfredo, 1916 (1963), *A Treatise on General Sociology,* Dover Publications, New York.

Parsons, Talcott, 1953, A Revised Analytical Approach to the Theory of Social Stratification, in: *Class, Status and Power* (R. Bendix and S. M. Lipset, ed.), Free Press, Glencoe, Illinois, pp. 92–128.

Parsons, Talcott, and Smelser, Neil J., 1965, *Economy and Society,* Free Press, New York.

Pebbles, Christopher S., and Kus, Susan M., 1977, Some Archaeological Correlates of Ranked Societies, *American Antiquity* 42(3)421–448.

Pirie, Margaret C., 1960, Marketing and Social Classes: An Anthropologist's View, *Management Review* 49(9)45–48.

Schiffer, Michael B., Downing, Theordore E., and McCarthy, Michael, 1981, Waste Not, Want Not: An Ethnoarchaeological Study of Reuse in Tucson, Arizona, in: *Modern Material Culture: The Archaeology of Us* (R. A. Gould and M. B. Schiffer, eds.), Academic Press, New York.

Shephard, Steven J., 1983, The Spanish Criollo Majority in Colonial St. Augustine, in: *Spanish St. Augustine: The Archaeology of A Colonial Creole Community* (K. A. Deagan, ed.), Academic Press, New York, pp. 65–97.

Shephard, Steven J., 1985, An Archaeological Study of Socioeconomic Stratification Status Change in Nineteenth-Century Alexandria, Virginia, Ph.D. dissertation, Southern Illinois University—Carbondale, University Microfilms, Ann Arbor.

Smelser, Neil J., 1963, *The Sociology of Economic Life,* Prentice-Hall, Englewood Cliffs, New Jersey.

South, Stanley, 1972, Evolution and Horizon as Revealed in Ceramic Analysis in Historical Archaeology, *The Conference on Historic Site Archaeology Papers, 1971* 6(2)71–106.

Stephens, John F., 1981a, Geographical Methods in Urban Preservation Planning, *Alexandria Papers in Urban Archaeology,* Planning Series No. 2., Alexandria Urban Archaeology Program, Alexandria.

Stephens, John F., 1981b. Historical Methods in Urban Preservation Planning, *Alexandria Papers in Urban Archaeology,* Planning Series No. 3., Alexandria Urban Archaeology Program, Alexandria.

Stephens, John F., 1981c, Socioeconomic Ranking Scales for Alexandria, Virginia, 1790, 1810, 1830, 1850, 1870, 1890, 1910, on file at the Alexandria Urban Archaeology Program, Alexandria.

Stone, G. W., Little, II, Glenn, and Israel, Stephen, 1972, Ceramics from the John Hicks Site, 1723–1743: The Material Culture, in *Ceramics in America* (I. Quimby, ed.), University Press of Virgnia, Richmond, pp. 75–102.

Swain, Perry, 1983, unpublished Ceramic Analysis Notes and Charts for AX-1, Features 6 and 7, and AX-8, Feature 5, on file, Alexandria Urban Archaeology Program, Alexandria.

Terrie, Philip G., 1979, A Social History of the 500 Block in Alexandria, Virginia, on file, Alexandria Urban Archaeology Program, Alexandria.

Tocqueville, Alexis de, 1831 (1959), *Journey to America,* Yale University Press, New Haven.

Veblen, Thorstein, 1899 (1953), *The Theory of the Leisure Class: An Economic Study of Institutions,* Macmillan, New York.

Vogt, E. Z., 1956, An Appraisal of "Prehistoric Settlement Patterns in the New World," in: *Prehistoric Settlement Patterns in the New World* (G. R. Wiley, ed.), Viking Fund Publications in Anthropology No. 23, New York, pp. 173–182.

Warner, Lloyd W., and Lunt, Paul, 1950, *The Social Life of a Modern Community,* Yale University Press, New Haven, Connecticut.

Warner, Lloyd W., Meeker, Marchia, and Eells, Kenneth, 1949, *Social Class in America,* Science Research Associates, Chicago.

White, Leslie A., 1949, *The Science of Culture,* Grover Press, New York.

Wobst, Martin, H., 1977, Stylist Behavior and Information Exchange, *Anthropological Papers of the Museum of Anthropology, University of Michigan, No. 61,* Ann Arbor.

Zimmerman, Carle C., 1936, *Consumption and Standards of Living,* Van Nostrand, New York.

9

Status Indicators

Another Strategy for Interpretation of Settlement Pattern in a Nineteenth-Century Industrial Village

PAUL M. HEBERLING

The crumbling piles of masonry, which are old furnace sites, are so common in rural Pennsylvania that their significance is usually overlooked. Yet the charcoal iron industry reflected a remarkable episode in American history—a time when the personal touch of the craftsman was still part of the industrial product. At the same time, the industry was contributing profoundly to the sociocultural development of central Pennsylvania and, to a lesser degree, to the Middle Atlantic states. Among other things, it was influential in the final location of the Pennsylvania Canal, and subsequently, to the routing of the Pennsylvania Railroad.

The technological aspects of the iron industry have been thoroughly described in both contemporary and later literature (cf. Chapman 1889; Moldenke 1920; Overman 1850; Parrott 1921; Pearse 1876; Peters 1921; Seely 1980; Swank 1892).

There has been considerably less attention directed to the life-style of the people living in those villages generated by the furnace activity. Most information has come from a variety of anecdotal accounts (cf. Moore 1936; Pierce 1966), from historical sites guidebooks, and from a few focused chapters incidental to broader historical works, like Hartley (1957) and Bining (1938). Notable exceptions to this generalization have been Joseph E. Walker's (1966) semipopular but graphic description of Hopewell Village and William A. Sullivan's (1955) discussion of the conditions facing industrial workers in the hectic days of the first half of the nineteenth century.

Most reports dealing with iron-making towns have been generally consistent with each other in emphasizing isolation and self-sufficiency, hardship and poverty, and patriotic, proletarian communities (cf. Bining 1933), and have made little reference to status differences (except at the upper level) or to possible bases for distinctions among residential units. This might suggest

Paul M. Heberling ☐ Department of Sociology and Anthropology, Juniata College, Huntingdon, PA 16652.

that they were truly egalitarian settlements, but the persistence of formal or euphemistic neighborhood designations like Minersvillage, Stable Row, "Dog-town," or "Irish Alley," and the common pattern of widely spaced neighborhoods, leave that interpretation in doubt.

This study, spawned during a routine archaeological investigation, was concerned with the interpretation of settlement pattern and possible socioeconomic stratification in the village of Greenwood Furnace, one of forty-eight charcoal blast furnaces operating in Pennsylvania's Juniata Valley during the nineteenth century. Two counties in particular, Huntingdon and Centre, were rich in hematite, limestone, water power, and charcoal-producing forests, and constituted, as Zentmyer testified, "the principal iron-producing district in [America]" (Zentmyer 1916:19).

Because of especially favorable conditions, Greenwood did not go out of blast until December 1904. The five hundred residents and most of the ninety-odd structures disappeared within a year, and the area was converted to a tree nursery, thus protecting most of the site from destructive redevelopment. The sudden abandonment created a perfect ethnographic moment, and nearly established an absolute *terminus ante quem* for much of the village.

In 1976, there began an extensive survey of the central 1,800 acres of what had been a 40,000-acre establishment, as an effort to locate building sites, roads, charcoal hearths, and any industrial vestiges not already identified (cf. Heberling 1978). During the early years of the investigation, most of the stack, bellows room, cast house, and other features associated with the original (1833) cold blast furnace were excavated. (Greenwood is unusual in having ruins of cold blast and hot blast furnaces standing side by side.)

THE PROBLEM

During the early survey work at Greenwood, several conditions became apparent, and changed the research emphasis from the industrial area to the sociocultural pattern of the village itself.

1. Outside of the industrial area, the community did not appear to be nucleated; rather, identifiable house foundations occurred in rows. These rows appeared to be discrete units, sometimes separated from each other by distances of as much as a quarter mile. Some of these clusters occupied distinctly more favorable locations than others in terms of drainage, water supply, proximity to the furnace, or pollution probability. On all of the low-lying, marshy areas, the houses had been constructed on lots that were slag- and trash-fill from the furnace. In many cases, there had been little planned effort to top the slag with soil, though humus and charcoal dust had gradually filled in; the daily outlook must have been grim indeed. This raised the question of whether ecological variables might have been one of the bases for settlement pattern in the village.

2. Except for the access roads to various parts of the reservation, there were no discernable streets. Usually the house sites were not aligned on any

grid pattern, but those that did not front on an access road all seemed to face the furnace, regardless of their location in the settlement.

3. In three of the residential clusters, all houses had stone foundations; but not all were mortared. In one of these three neighborhoods, several houses had cellars; this was the only area where cellars occurred. In a third cluster, there were four house sites with no foundations; the wooden sill had apparently been laid directly on the ground.

4. Other observable structural characteristics, like brick or stone chimneys, el-shaped houses, and particular house sizes seemed to be correlated with different neighborhoods.

5. There was also an impression that surface-scattered artifacts varied in types, not between individual houses, but between neighborhoods. Controlled surface samples revealed what seemed to be marked differences in amounts of white earthenware (ironstone), transfer ware, stoneware, painted ware, and pressed glass. At the time of the survey, before any excavation, it was not clear whether style variables reflected temporal changes or consumer-choice differences.

These clusters of residences, with their discrete spacing and apparently shared characteristics, might suggest that there had been segregation, or at least some deliberate homogeneity. Whatever the basis, such a spatial configuration would not only be central to the reconstruction of the sociocultural patterns of this village, but might be prototypical of early iron-making communities. It seemed worth the effort to find out, but the research plan would have to address several questions progressively:

1. Are there cultural differences between any residential units that are archaeologically identifiable?
2. Are there cultural features that tend to distinguish one residential cluster from another?
3. Are neighborhood characteristics the functions of ethnicity, occupation, economic status, or company-imposed variables?
4. To what degree does the entire village settlement pattern (clustering, interhouse spacing, distance from furnace, environmental advantages) reflect social stratification?

As the research focus broadened from question 1 to question 4, it appeared that we would have to enter the archaeological never-never land of "status indicators," with all of the usual problems. There would not only be questions of definition and predictability, but assessment of differential discard patterns, exchange or "hand-me-down" practices, and, in a remote company town, the real possibility of restricted market access.

In planning the research strategy, these variables might have been constraining, but not critical, for they were to be simply tools; the central interest was settlement pattern and not status. The methodology was to be common and straightforward: documentation from court and company records matched against archaeological samples from each of the residence clusters.

From census records, deeds, tax maps and/or company records, we should learn who occupied some or all of the houses in each neighborhood. The census usually reports occupations, and we ought to be able to match these against specific or general wage scales and determine the economic level of each of the occupants. These data, traced temporally, would also tell how the community was settled at a given time, and how it changed through time. They should also show whether neighborhoods tended to be dominated by particular occupations, ethnic groups, or income levels.

It would obviously make a difference whether the residences were company-built and owned, whether all units in a cluster were built at the same time or by a common contractor, and, if they were tenant houses, it would matter how their use was assigned. A few houses were still standing or removed to other known locations. They were all modified to modern use, but important details still reflected their original architectural style. In addition, three of the company's functional structures (store, meat house, and mule barn), having a fair degree of integrity, remained.

As an ambitious final goal, a sample of houses from each neighborhood was to be excavated; this would have permitted the comparison of material collections with independent variables to test the "status indicators."

Coping with the Real World

To make a complicated story brief, we soon faced a situation that many archaeologists have known. Because of a realignment of state priorities and a drop in student and public participation, the opportunity for extensive excavation ceased. Worse, there were no company records to examine. The parent company had changed identity several times since 1904, and no data from the Greenwood operation are known to exist, either in public or private repositories. Not one of the workers survives to give testimony. Two nonagenarian former residents tried to be helpful, but their memories, even of their own childhoods, were fuzzy and contradictory.

The census, too, was a problem. It only began in this area in 1840, and the 1890 records were destroyed by fire. Listings are only by townships; Greenwood Furnace is never mentioned. In a township where there were twenty-four Dearments and twelve McCardles, never mind the Hunters and Wilsons and Troys, it's a real question which belong to Greenwood. Some occupations were indeed listed—colliers, miners, and founders, clear enough—but how does one pick out the teamsters, laborers, and blacksmiths who could be working anywhere?

Exercise in Improvisation

Well, once in a while, we have to remind ourselves that archaeology is a problem-solving discipline; that's what makes it fun. I was reminded sometimes of Richard Lee's article on the !Kung Bushmen, "What Hunters Do for a

Living, or, How To Make Out on Scarce Resources." What we had to do was, like the Bushmen, assess what we had and make the most of it. What we had was:

1. Some census data on 380 families over a sixty-year period
2. The archaeological record from the partial excavation of five houses
3. An extensive survey plot plan with (in 1981) 25 houses located
4. A fair delineation of six separate neighborhoods
5. A clear *terminus ante quem*
6. A dominant cultural influence (vernacular Victorian)
7. A well-preserved archaeological area with few intrusions

One should count his blessings.

Step 1 in the new strategy was to change perspective from long-term village life to short-term, focusing on the natural ethnographic moment, 1904, when the world suddenly came to an'end at Greenwood Furnace. This not only made it possible to relate interpretation generally to a single census, but to make surface artifacts a relevant standard; they would most likely be associated with the last (at least one or two) occupations.

We made what use we could of census information, considering that there were no addresses or even community identification for the residents. We were able to identify from informants the certain residence location of two workers, one from "suburbia" (Minersville) and one from "downtown" (Creek Row). We could then mentally follow the census-taker from house to house, and assume that we had some continuity, although it was not always clear where one neighborhood ended and another began.

For nearly a year, research consisted of tediously following out small leads: sorting out reminiscences of informants, systematic hand probing[1] for foundations in suggested places, a page-by-page review of four newspapers over a seventy-year period,[2] and of course title searches, where possible. This work resulted in the location of two more residence clusters, Viantown and Stable Row, both of which had been referred to in documents, but had never been pinpointed, and importantly, the identification of twenty-one occupants of specific houses as of 1900. Ten of these were confirmed by deeds associated with owners in Minersville, which, along with Viantown, has privately owned houses. By cross-referencing these known occupants with associations reported in newspapers and oral reflections, it was ultimately possible to identify a total of thirty-eight 1900–1904 householders generally with neighborhoods, although not necessarily with specific houses.

To complete the geographic pattern, a final survey involving probing, test pitting, logic, and chance, resulted in the physical record of settlement pattern shown on the line map (Figure 1). This includes forty-seven confirmed house

---

[1] A forty-inch steel probe was used, with soundings taken every twelve inches along two intersecting transects, and the findings were recorded on a graph.

[2] Huntingdon *Gazette*, 1832–1835; Huntingdon *Journal*, 1838–1904; *The Globe*, 1855–1905; *The Monitor*, 1870–1899, all of Huntingdon, Pennsylvania.

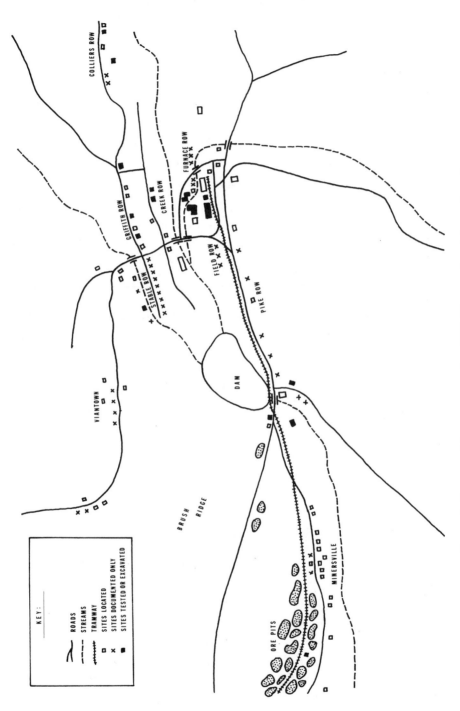

Figure 1. Greenwood furnace area, circa 1880. The map is not drawn to scale.

sites and twenty others that were somehow referenced (maps, newspapers, deeds, informants), but for which no structural evidence was found. No secure record has confirmed the number of houses associated with the old village; one hand-drawn map (Knepp 1929:6) shows 110, and Knepp himself (1929:7) lists 127 "in all," but both of these documents are difficult to validate. We certainly have not documented every structure that may have ever existed at Greenwood, but there is no reason to believe that there were more neighborhoods. Even our most confused informants think that this map is reasonably correct.

TESTING THE HYPOTHESES

Among the hypotheses that we considered prior to this study of settlement pattern were suggestions that the residence clusters may have been organized around ethnic identification, occupation and/or socioeconomic status.

Historically, the Greenwood area was settled heavily by Scots-Irish immigrants, and the census records suggested little change in the ethnic composition of the valley through 1900. Type names are overwhelmingly Scottish, Irish, or English, with Germans making up the remainder. Italian, French, Scandinavian, and African ancestries are extremely rare. Nowhere in written or oral comments was any reference made to racial or ethnic identity, and all of the common groups were represented at all occupational levels. To the extent that neighborhood families could be identified, there was no evidence of special ethnic dominance.

The occupational association of the thirty-eight known neighborhood residents in 1900 shows the following pattern:

- Minersville: ten miners, three colliers, two woodcutters
- Viantown ("Dogtown"): two sawmill workers, three laborers, one teamster, one store clerk, one woodcutter
- Creek Row: one blacksmith, one wagonmaker, one laborer
- Griffith Row: two teamsters, one keeper
- Pike Row: one foundryman, one miller, a "tavern"
- Stable Row: three teamsters, two laborers, (one bookkeeper)
- Furnace Row: (manager)
- Field Row and Colliers Row: none known

Although the "Bookkeeper's House" is adjacent to Stable Row, and the "Big House" is at the end of Furnace Row, neither was likely to have been perceived as part of those neighborhoods. The houses were the most pretentious in the village, and the occupants were usually referred to with some deference. In addition, the label of "Colliers Row," acquired from a later hand-drawn map (Knepp 1929:6), certainly sounds descriptive, and the house sites in that area differed from those in other neighborhoods (smaller floor plan, fireplace-heated), but there is no certain identification of any collier with that row. Because of the apparent special social and economic position of that occupation (low status, high income), it is very necessary to know where they fit in the settlement. Eric Sloane (1956), in his whimsical way, calls colliers "raggies," and implies that they were a sort of outcast. Interestingly, at Greenwood, three identifiable colliers lived on the extreme western edge of Minersville, in some isolation.

In general, the configuration shown suggests a tendency toward occupational clustering, but there is no evidence that it was a mandated pattern.

That note forces a discussion of the final variable, the economic status of the known workers, and the testing of the third suggestion in the possible hypotheses: settlement pattern may have been predicated upon economic differences. In the censuses, workers tend to be listed clearly enough as colliers, laborers, miners, or teamsters, and it is well known that, in the iron industry, incomes varied considerably among some trades, with founders and colliers earning twice as much as fillers or guttermen, and the latter commanding much more than the teamster or laborer. However, it is also true that wages tended to remain very stable, little affected by economic cycles (Walker 1966:260). Moreover, workers tended individually to negotiate their own wages, based entirely upon the quality of their work (Sullivan 1955:62). Collective bargaining, which never asserted itself in the iron industry until the late nineteenth century, apparently was never practiced at all at Greenwood, and worker threats against management were unheard of (Moore 1946:unpaged). There was considerable job shifting, however, and during periods of furnace shutdown, furnace men commonly became woodcutters; this flexibility was noted by Pierce (1966) at Batsto also.

A salient problem encountered in trying to correlate workers' economic positions with their residential neighborhoods was shown by Scott Heberling (1979) in a comparative study involving Greenwood Furnace. It was demonstrated that there was a great deal of mobility into and out of the iron industries in this region, making it possible that a given householder might remain there through several job changes, or that a number of workers with different occupations might live in a given house during a single census period. Thus, the occupational record alone might be very misleading if used as a predictive variable in explaining community organization.

Finally, there were no known official wage records surviving for this furnace, yet if there were to be any test of social stratification, there would have to be some kind of independent economic variable. The only reasonable option, recalling the tendency for wages within the industry to remain stable through time, was to create a relative standard from known wage scales of contemporary industries. From Stevens (1927) there was a complete scale for nearby Centre Furnace for the year 1858, which could be compared with that of Hopewell for 1853 (Walker 1966:261). These records were commensurate, and although the figures would not be identical at other places, there were enough anecdotal and unofficial references in literature and from informants to suggest that the *relative* positions of the occupations were similar at Greenwood. The probable conditions are shown in Table 1. Normally, wages were based on twelve-hour shifts and seven-day weeks. Colliers, miners, and woodcutters usually made their rate on piecework.

Table 1. Relative Wage Scale for Greenwood Furnace, Latter Part of the Nineteenth Century

Founder	$50 per month	Carpenter	$22 per month
Collier	$35 or more	Woodcutter	$21
Foundryman	$25–$30	Filler	$21
Miner	$25–$30	Gutterman	$20
Keeper	$25	Teamster	$12
Blacksmith	$25	Laborer	$12
Miller	$25		

Applying the wage standards to those workers whose occupations and residences were known (34 cases) produced the average income per neighborhood, as shown in Table 2. These are substantial economic differences for the day, although certainly, the sample is small and the record incomplete. There is a range of differences between households within neighborhoods, but it is difficult to ignore the contrast in average incomes within residential clusters. It is interesting to speculate on what effect the unknown data would have had on the actual averages, but there is nothing in the physical appearances of the unidentified house sites to suggest that they would be markedly different from their immediate neighbors.

ARCHAEOLOGICAL EVIDENCE

Limited as they are, the independent economic variables are fairly well established. The dependent variables would be primarily the archaeological ones. With the hope that we could identify some material correlates, if not predictors, a rough effort was made to scale the data that came from the ground.

When house excavations were done, they followed a sampling plan (Figure 2); the site selections in each locality were determined solely by accessibility, since most of the village area is today in heavy forest. Subsurface work began with the digging of two intersecting sondages to determine the site

Table 2. Average Income by Neighborhood

Minersville (miners, colliers, woodcutters)	$358 per year
Pike Row (foundryman, miller)	$330
Creek Row (blacksmith, laborer, wagonmaker)	$248
Griffith Row (teamsters, keeper)	$196
Viantown (laborers, teamster, clerk, woodcutter)	$166
Stable Row (teamsters, laborers)	$144
Collier Row (none known)	—
Furnace Row (no data)	—
Field Row (no data)	—

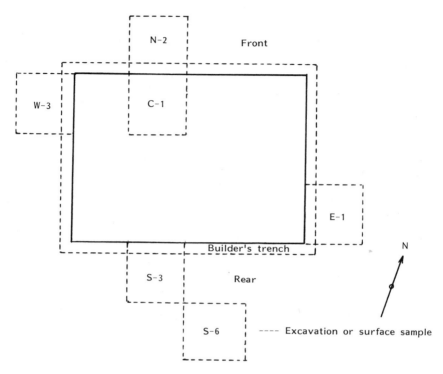

Figure 2. Typical residence excavation plan. Scale: 1/8 inch = 1 foot.

characteristics. Walls were traced by a twelve-inch exterior abutting trench to the base of whatever type foundation existed. Then six five-foot by five-foot squares (five exterior, one interior) were troweled by arbitrary three-inch levels to base clay, which was usually at ten to fourteen inches. Except for a 10 percent check sample, the spoil was unscreened.

Profiles were invariably diffused; soil accumulations during the seventy-year life of the village was mostly humus, charcoal dust, loess, and household refuse, mixed sometimes with a little water-borne clay. The vast majority of artifactual material occurred in the upper three-inch level; some of this may have been debris from the final destruction of the houses.

In 1981, when the research plan was altered, we were restricted to the five excavations already done, but it appeared that we could include controlled surface samples from four additional houses and two additional neighborhoods. The original excavation plan (Figure 2) was simply applied to the surface collection; it was clear that this technique could be employed only where the surface was relatively undisturbed and where the *terminus ante quem* was confidently established at that level. Of course, only the artifacts recovered from Level 1 excavation were comparable with the surface materials. The primary archaeological data were architectural and ceramic.

Architectural Variables

Without assuming status values, arbitrary statistical markers were created to grade five architectural features: floor space (square footage), foundation type, house elevation (stories), heating plant, and presence or absence of cellar.

Foundation Plan (Outside Dimensions)

a. Less than 280 square feet   Value: 1.00
b. 281–350   1.50
c. 351–500   2.00
d. 501 plus   2.50
e. El or addition   +.50

Foundation Type

a. None   Value: 1.00
b. Piers   1.50
c. Dry wall on surface   1.50
d. Dry wall in trench   2.00
e. Mortared wall   2.50

Elevation

a. One story   Value: 1.00
b. One and one-half stories   1.50
c. Two stories or more   2.50

Elevation was determined by foundation type and size alone, or by matching data with extant contemporary houses. For example, ground sills or piers never supported more than one story; a dry wall foundation supported no more than one and a half stories. Mortared foundations of more than sixteen-inch width were always associated with houses of two or more stories.

Heating Plant

a. Fireplace only   Value: 1.00
b. Stove, one flue   1.50
c. Stoves, two or more flues   2.00
d. Soft coal; hard coal   +.25; +.50

The type chimney was determined by the position and type of chimney pad, and in some instances, by the actual chimney fall-out. In "Colliers Row," the only unit associated with any house was a gable-end fireplace. It is possible that an iron stove could have been vented into the fireplace stack, but this could not be determined. Soft coal, hard coal, charcoal, or wood fuel could sometimes be determined either from the accumulation at the chimney site or from separate coal dumps.

Cellar

    a. Partial   Value: 1.50
    b. Full   2.00

This value would have been added to any type house where it might have been found, but it was associated with only three houses, all in the same neighborhood. An environmental constraint should also be noted: In Stable Row, Griffith Row, and Creek Row, cellars would not have been possible, due to the high water table.

In no case was evidence of a well or privy found in direct association with any house site. In three of the neighborhoods, there was what appeared to be a common well or spring.

Artifactual Inventory

The total artifactual inventory was collected according to the sampling plan described earlier. It represented the collection from the Level 1 excavation of five houses in three neighborhoods, and from the surface plot of four other houses and one additional neighborhood. In both excavation and surface collecting, the sampling pattern was identical.

The collection is essentially a pedestrian picture dominated by domestic ceramic and glassware, window glass, nails, a lesser number of buttons and clay pipes, and a few tools and toys—the marks of very simple households.

Ceramic (Redware, Stoneware)

No values were assigned to these materials, and only their average count per neighborhood was recorded (Table 3). It might be possible to make a case for stoneware's having a higher value or for suggesting that it is more sophisticated than common redware, but that is pretty tenuous, particularly since large stoneware potteries were established in both of the nearby towns of Lewistown and Huntingdon. The sharp differences in count by neighborhoods are interesting, however.

Refined Ceramics

Values were assigned to identifiable sherds according to the late nineteenth-century components of the Miller Ceramic Index (Miller 1980). In developing this now well-known technique, Miller determined from price lists the actual costs of different types of ceramic objects, and created a relative index based on common creamware (CC), the cheapest of the wares. The nineteenth-century listing was an extension of earlier indices for the seventeenth and eighteenth centuries, but as Miller emphasizes, many of the critical value

Table 3. Ceramic Inventory from Excavation or Surface Sample, with Average Value per Site

Location	Stoneware	Redware	Ironstone (1.69)	Edged (1.20)	Transfer (1.60)	Porcelain (5.83)	Sponge (1.10)	Other (various)	Average value
Stable Row									
Site S-41	12	3	14	7	2	0	3	3	1.47
Colliers Row									
Site Co-21	48	2	80	5	3	1		14	1.67
Site Co-22	0	0	12	4	4	0	0	4	1.63
Griffith Row									
Site G-1	51	125	152	28	40	0	3	7	1.62
Site G-2	12	72	143	15	21	8	5	21	1.74
Site G-5	23	4	17	4	0	0	0	0	1.60
Creek Row									
Site Cr-13	23	0	153	8	1	12	0	11	1.95
Site Cr-15	26	65	106	4	7	6	9	20	1.77
Pike Row									
Site P-31	56	271	285	24	28	7	3	47	1.74

differences are blurred by the popularizing of refined white earthenware (ironstone) after 1850.

Because price indices for the year 1900 are not available, the Greenwood ceramics were matched against the 1858 index for plain ironstone, against the 1857 index for porcelain, and against the 1855 listing for other refined ceramics such as shell-edged or transfer-printed ware (Miller 1980:26, 30, 33). Eighty-six percent of the inventory involved sherds too small to determine specific vessel type precisely, but by matching them against templates of contemporary local ware, the majority of fragments could at least be identified as plates, cups, or saucers; all flatware sherds were indexed as if they were from ten-inch plates.

The inventory was dominated at all sites by plain white earthenware, which was mostly "ironstone" (74 percent), followed by transfer ware (8 percent), shell-edged (8 percent), porcelain (3 percent), and all other types (7 percent). The relative values of the ceramic materials are shown by households in Table 3 and by neighborhoods in Table 4.

Glassware

We created some similar market values for domestic glassware, just to see what would happen. The criteria were dramatically less sophisticated than Miller's; we simply used the average price quotations from the 1897 Sears Roebuck Catalog (Israel 1968) and from the 1902 Sears Roebuck Catalog (1969), and indexed three types: clear pressed glass of eight patterns, pressed milk glass, and cut glass (by reference). This was a crude procedure, and no claim is made for the significance of the data, except to note that the economic standards represented are not incompatible with the architectural and ceramic standards. It is another possibility that may be worth pursuing.

Table 4. Comparison of All Indices by Neighborhood

	Stable Row	Colliers Row	Griffith Row	Creek Row	Pike Row
Architecture index					
Floor plan	1.50	1.25	1.68	2.25	2.50
Foundation type	1.50	1.50	2.00	2.50	2.50
Elevation	1.00	1.00	1.50	2.00	2.50
Heating	1.50	1.25	1.50	1.63	2.00
Cellar	—	—	—	—	+2.00
Average	1.37	1.25	1.67	2.09	2.87
Ceramic index	1.47	1.66	1.69	1.87	1.74
Glassware index	—	1.43	1.76	2.25	2.50
Indices average	1.42	1.45	1.71	2.07	2.37
Income rank	1.44	—	1.96	2.48	3.30
Stoneware average	12	24	29	25	56
Redware average	3	1	67	33	271

Analysis of Archaeological Data

The standards upon which the statistical data are based are consistent for all neighborhoods, but the samples themselves are not necessarily commensurate. In some instances, most of a neighborhood's data came from a single site, while two or three sites were tested in other neighborhoods. No archaeological fieldwork at all has been undertaken at Viantown or Minersville, for these are areas of private ownership. No material data have been gathered from Furnace Row or Field Row, for although their existence is thoroughly documented, no clear house sites have been located. From Colliers Row, four house sites have been found, and two have been sampled, but no residents have been identified, so the material cannot be correlated with occupation or income. These limitations are apparent in the summary tables, and keep this from being a complete community study. Nevertheless, the comparative record shows both individual household preferences and neighborhood consistency.

The central concern in this study has been neighborhood patterns. As attention returns to the residence clusters, it might be helpful to review some of the independent conditions, to the degree that they are known.

> *Stable Row:* Environment: Low terrain along a stream; adjacent to long row of animal sheds.
> Occupations: three teamsters @ $144 per year
> two laborers @ $144 per year
> Average income: $144
> *Colliers Row:* Environment: Hillside, one-half mile from furnace
> Occupations: None identified
> *Griffith Row:* Environment: Extremely rocky with little soil, or marshy with slag fill
> Occupations: two teamsters @ $144 per year
> one keeper @ $300 per year
> Average income: $196 per year
> *Creek Row:* Environment: Very marshy; slag fill; downwind from furnace
> Occupations: one blacksmith @ $300 per year
> one wagonmaker @ $300 per year
> one laborer @ $144 per year
> Average income: $248 per year
> *Pike Row:* Environment: Hillside terrain, parallel to road; upwind of furnace
> Occupations: one miller @ $300 per year
> one foundryman @ c. $300 per year
> Average income: $300 per year

The architectural, artifactual and economic indices were applied to each of the five residence clusters, with results as indicated in Table 4.

To the degree that any of these indices reflect affluence or status, or both, Pike Row is clearly at the highest level, while Stable Row is "the other side of the tracks." In each case, the average material index correlates directly with economic level based on occupational income. That observation may qualify for the "Golden Fleece Award," for it is hardly surprising. What is more interesting is the consistency with which the residential neighborhoods maintain their relative rankings. Even when taking into account all of the project's data limitations, arbitrary values, and substitute procedures, the archaeological data correlate well with the independent variables. Whether these are good enough to become predictors cannot be determined until they are tested on many more cases, at this or at other sites.

Conclusions

I am very much in agreement with George Miller's complaint (SHA meeting, Boston, 1985) that much of our work in historical archaeology falls short of good science, so I make no special claims for this little exercise. We have had many constraints imposed on our methodology, the most serious of which has been the paucity of documentary evidence against which we might match our index data; this forced the drastic change in strategy. Methodology should always be dictated by the research objectives, and even when the focus of a project is humanistic, as this one originally was, analytic techniques should be as rigorous as possible.

There is also a place for experimentation, particularly on sites that pose new problems, and where the methodology is sampling, rather than extensive excavation. Like it or not, the golden age of American archaeology is over, and for the next decade or two, contributions will come from small, question-oriented projects, often enough staffed by amateurs and volunteers. It will not be a time so much for intellectual arrogance as for imagination, testing, and sharing.

In part, the Greenwood Furnace project has become such an exercise in adaptability, and the work a labor of love—I think there is still room for that in archaeology. It has been interesting to apply some established assessment devices to new problems, and under duress, to create some other tests that might have an application to a macrocosmic site; time will determine how useful they might be.

We certainly know more about the life and times of one iron-making village than we knew before, and some conclusions can be drawn confidently. We now know what the houses, grounds, and natural environment looked like. Greenwood Furnace was poor, dreary, and unhealthy, and life there was probably grim. Both air and water were probably polluted. According to one report, there was nothing green, taller than a lilac bush, visible in any direction. It was a time of repeated economic depressions and business failures. The pittance that was a wage often failed to find its way into a pocket, for it usually took more than that to pay the debt to the company store. To try to structure significant status differences in this village would be to "make a silk purse from a sow's ear." The evidence certainly suggests that there were differences, but they were small ones, perhaps not so much social as circumstantial.

Whatever else might be fuzzy, the settlement pattern is now clear. There *were* identifiable neighborhoods, and they seem to have been influenced primarily by occupation, as opposed strictly to income; they apparently served to encourage proximity of workers to their main tasks. Where a laborer lived beside a foundryman, the laborer probably worked at the furnace also, rather than at the sawmill or the mines. The few personalized accounts suggest that workers' attitudes were generally democratic, that they had more of an identification with their furnace than with a specific job or trade, or even with income.

If Samuel Moore's comments (1936) are anything more than just an old man's nostalgia, then it appears that the alchemy that changed rock to metal was a very private experience. If it is ultimately confirmed that all of the houses in Greenwood Furnace Village faced the furnace, that pattern may be more than coincidental.

REFERENCES

Africa, J. S., 1883, *History of Huntingdon and Blair Counties, Pennsylvania,* Louis H. Everts, Philadelphia, pp. 54–56, 297–298.

Bining, A. C., 1933, The Iron Plantations of Early Pennsylvania, in: *Pennsylvania Magazine of History and Biography* 17:117–137.

Bining, A. C., 1938, *Pennsylvania Iron Manufacture in the Eighteenth Century,* Pennsylvania Historical and Museum Commission, Harrisburg.

Chapman, T. J., 1889, Early Iron Industry of Pennsylvania, in: *Magazine of Western History* 9:659–664.

Hartley, E. N., 1957, *Ironworks on the Saugus,* University of Oklahoma Press, Norman.

Heberling, P. M., 1978, Greenwood Furnace: An Archaeological Investigation of an Iron-Making Village, unpublished manuscript, Huntingdon, Pennsylvania.

Heberling, S. D., 1979, Work Force Stability and Occupational Mobility in the Charcoal Iron Industry of Central Pennsylvania, 1850–1900: Two Case Studies, unpublished manuscript, Newark, Delaware.

Israel, F. L. (ed.), 1968, 1897 Sears Roebuck Catalog (reprinted.), Chelsea House, New York.

Knepp, T. H., 1929, Greenwood Furnace: Yesterday and Today, unpublished manuscript, Huntingdon, Pennsylvania.

Lee, R. B., and DeVore I., 1968, *Man the Hunter,* Aldine Atherton, Chicago.

Miller, G. L., 1980, Classification and Economic Scaling of 19th Century Ceramics, in: *Historical Archaeology.* 14(1)1–40.

Moldenke, R., 1920, *Charcoal Iron,* Lime Rock, Connecticut, the Salisbury Iron Corporation.

Moore, S. T., 1936, Sketches of Greenwood, in: *The Valley and the Fort,* multilithed 1976, McAlevy's Fort, Pennsylvania.

Overman, F., 1850, *The Manufacture of Iron in All Its Various Branches,* Henry C. Baird, Philadelphia.

Parrott, R. D., 1921, *Cold Blast Charcoal Pig Iron Made at Greenwood, Orange County, New York, During the Civil War Period, 1861–65,* Flushing, New York, privately printed.

Pearse, J. B., 1876, *A Concise History of the Iron Manufacture of the American Colonies Up to the Revolution, and of Pennsylvania until the Present Time,* Allen, Lane and Scott, Philadelphia.

Peters, R. L. Jr., 1921, *Two Centuries of Iron Smelting in Pennsylvania,* Philadelphia.

Pierce, A. D., 1966, *Iron in the Pines,* Rutgers University Press, New Brunswick.

Sears Roebuck Catalog, 1902 (1969), Crown Publishers, New York.

Seely, B. E., Blast Furnace Technology in the Mid-19th Century: A Case Study of the Adirondack

Iron and Steel Company, in: *IA, The Journal of the Society for Industrial Archaeology* 7: 27–54.

Sloane, E., 1956, *American Yesterday*, W. Funk, New York.

Stevens, S. K., 1927, Centre Furnace: A Chapter in the History of Juniata Iron, unpublished M.A. thesis, the Pennsylvania State University, University Park.

Sullivan, W. A., 1955, *The Industrial Worker in Pennsylvania, 1800–1840*, Pennsylvania Historical and Museum Commission, Harrisburg.

Swank, J. M., 1892, *History of the Manufacture of Iron in All Ages and Particularly in the United States from Colonial Times to 1891*, Allen, Lane and Scott, Philadelphia.

Walker, J. E., 1966, *Hopewell Village: A Social and Economic History of an Iron-Making Community*, University of Pennsylvania Press, Philadelphia.

Zentmyer, R. A., 1916, *Early Ironworks of Central Pennsylvania*, Altoona *Tribune*, Altoona, Pennsylvania.

10

The Use of Converging Lines of Evidence for Determining Socioeconomic Status

PATRICK H. GARROW

INTRODUCTION

The trash deposits encountered within an historic site may be viewed as the end products of a series of purchase–use–discard incidents that took place during the occupation of that site. Under this approach, each step in this process represents distinct and measurable choices made by the individuals who generated the archaeological record under study. Each category of materials that entered the household (either by purchase or other means), that was used within the household, and that was subsequently lost or discarded (when no longer deemed useful), has the potential to reflect specific types of information about that household.

The goal of this paper is to explore dimensions of socioeconomic status that can be determined from the analysis of ceramic and faunal collections, and verified through the use of historical research. Ceramic and faunal collections have been chosen for this purpose since each represents a category of material that can be expected to have been purchased, used, and discarded within an archaeological site on an ongoing basis. Further, each category is made up of single items or clusters of items that could have been functionally replaced by goods of greater or lesser cost without affecting the survival potential of the household. It is also possible to gauge, in at least relative terms, the original purchase costs of ceramic collections (Miller 1980) and the desirability (and thus relative costs) of specific cuts of meat (Crader 1984; Schulz and Gust 1983).

There are a number of variables that should be controlled when conducting a study of socioeconomic position based on the original purchase costs of a ceramic collection. Access to markets for goods produced to exchange for manufactured items, such as ceramics, is certainly one variable. Miller and Hurry (1983) have recently pointed out that ceramic economic-scaling data presented by Miller (1980) on two sites in Ohio measured differential access to market

Patrick H. Garrow ☐ Garrow & Associates, 4000 DeKalb Technology Parkway, Suite 375, Atlanta, GA 30340.

(before and after the completion of the Erie Canal), and not true differences in socioeconomic status level. Although it may be argued that the economic scaling technique had accurately assessed the economic purchasing power of the earlier resident, it must be conceded that, in that case, purchasing power and social status were independent factors. A second variable that should be controlled is the ethnicity of the residents of the household under study. It may be assumed, for example, that a household occupied by slaves represented a unit of purchase–use–discard that had little or no control over the purchase of the goods used within that household (Wheaton, Friedlander, Garrow 1983). Further, cultural or subcultural differences between ethnic groups might influence the types of ceramics used within a household (Otto 1975).

Additional variables that should be controlled, when utilizing ceramic collections as reflectors of socioeconomic status, deal with specific attributes of the household unit under study. The underlying assumption of ceramic economic scaling studies is that households will purchase ceramics that are reflective of their relative socioeconomic level. That assumption may not always be valid. As an example, a blue-collar worker with a large family may be able to devote a smaller percentage of his disposable wealth to ceramic purchases than a person with the same occupation but a smaller family. Also, families may choose to display their wealth in a manner that does not include the purchase and use of more expensive ceramics. An additional factor is that the socioeconomic level of a family is not necessarily static. Level of wealth and level of income may be highly volatile factors that are subject to upward or downward changes over relatively brief spans of time. This means that use of ceramic socioeconomic scaling carries with it the inherent risk that relative value assigned to a collection could reflect the former, rather than the current, socioeconomic status of the household unit under study.

Recent studies conducted on antebellum plantation sites (Crader 1984; Otto 1975) have demonstrated that within small, hierarchically arranged groups, the members receive cuts of meat reflective of their standing in the hierarchy. That is, slaves receive cuts of meat for their consumption that represent the least desirable cuts, while plantation masters take the most desirable cuts for their own consumption. Schultz and Gust (1983), while discussing faunal materials retrieved from nineteenth-century contexts in Sacramento, demonstrated that it was possible to correlate socioeconomic class and the original purchase price of cuts of meat in an urban setting. The distribution of cuts of meats on antebellum plantations and the differential distribution of cuts predicated on purchase price in the case of the Sacramento example, each represent products of consumer choices. It is likely that many of the same variables that affect the utility of ceramic collections as reflectors of socioeconomic status also affect faunal collections. One variable can be omitted when studying faunal collections, however. Food bone discarded from a household should represent items purchased, used, and discarded over a very short span of time, and thus should reflect the purchasing power of the household under study at the time the faunal material was used and discarded.

There are factors that can effect the results of ceramic or faunal socioeconomic studies, that are independent of the shortcomings that might be inherent in these techniques. Those factors include selective discard of trash within the study site, differential preservation of faunal remains, methods of faunal recovery, and the size or method of selection of the excavation sample. Each of those factors should be controlled, or at least assessed, on a site-by-site basis.

The paper that follows discusses the use of ceramic economic scaling and specialized faunal analysis in concert to determine the relative socioeconomic standings of the investigated households. In each case, the results achieved from application of ceramic and faunal analysis techniques are compared with historical research data to test those results.

THE CASE STUDIES

The examples to be used in this paper were drawn from excavations and analyses conducted on the Washington Civic Center Project (Garrow 1982) in Washington, D.C., and the Wilmington Boulevard Project (Klein and Garrow 1984) in Wilmington, Delaware. Each project included historical research that was extensive enough to characterize the general socioeconomic status level of the site occupants. The faunal analysis conducted for the Washington Civic Center Project was somewhat superficial, and was designed to characterize the range and general composition of the faunal assemblages. The faunal analyses conducted for the Wilmington Boulevard Project was much more detailed, and a stated goal of the analysis was to study the relative socioeconomic status levels of the residents of the study blocks through study of cuts of meat that were presumed to have been served in the various households.

Field Methods

Similar field methods were used to excavate the sites used as case studies in this report. The Washington Civic Center field investigations were conducted in two phases. The initial phase involved excavation of backhoe trenches in an attempt to identify features and middens within the study lots. The context discussed in this paper (Area D1) was explored in the testing phase through placement of a single backhoe trench that intercepted an area of intense midden along the extreme rear of a lot line. The second phase of that investigation, data recovery, involved placement of four, hand-excavated, five-foot squares that were dispersed so as to test both the center and margin of the trash deposit. Approximately 19 percent of the dump was investigated, based on the estimated horizontal extent of the deposits. Excavation proceded in arbitrary ten-centimeter levels, and all excavated soils were dry-screened through quarter-inch mesh screen. The deposits in the dump varied from seventy to eighty centimeters thick (Garrow 1982).

Area A within the Wilmington Boulevard Project was explored under two methodological approaches. Part of the area had been heavily disturbed, and lacked intact midden deposits. That section was machine-stripped and searched for features. The remainder of the area was investigated in hand-excavated blocks placed in a checkerboard fashion. Fifty percent of the section with intact midden was explored in that fashion. Soil was excavated in levels and dry-screened through quarter-inch mesh screen. All encountered features were excavated. Excavations in Area H included two backhoe trenches followed by hand excavation of four ten-foot squares. The ten-foot squares were placed in a checkerboard pattern similar to that used in Area A. Midden deposits were found in Area H, but were found to be heavily disturbed. All encountered features were excavated, and all soils removed were dry-screened through quarter-inch mesh screen (Klein and Garrow 1984).

The areas explored on the Washington and Wilmington Boulevard projects were excavated under comparable methodologies. Each collection represents a tightly controlled assemblage of artifacts removed from an urban backyard setting. Further, each collection represents a "lot-specific" (Garrow 1984) collection, which means that the materials were generated and discarded by households resident on the study lots.

Analysis Methods

Consistent methods of ceramic analysis were applied to the collections from the Washington Civic Center and Wilmington Boulevard. Two ceramic analysis methods applied to those collections that are germane to this chapter were the Miller (1980) economic scaling technique and ceramic set analysis (Garrow 1982). Use of the Miller ceramic economic scaling technique first requires that a ceramic collection be organized into vessels by decoration and ware types. That was done in the cases of Washington and Wilmington by utilizing minimum vessel counts. Under the minimum vessel count approach, all sherds that can be cross-mended are organized together, and the remaining sherds are organized by vessel form, ware type, and decoration. Once that is completed, sherds of the same vessel form, ware, and/or decoration are studied in order to establish the *minimum* number of vessels present in the collection.

Once the minimum number of vessels by form, ware, and/or decoration is determined, the Miller (1980) index value for each form, ware, and/or decoration in the collection is applied. The index value chosen from Miller is the value for the year that most closely approximates the mean ceramic date or median date derived from other means for the study collection. There are gaps in a number of the Miller indices, and relative values for particular wares and/or decorative types are not available. In those instances, extrapolated values are used to fill those gaps. As an example, Miller (1980:30) does not present a value for plain, unhandled porcelain cups in his 1846 index. A value for unhandled, plain porcelain cups was extrapolated by observing that the "form unknown" porcelain cups in the 1857 index was valued at 51.6 percent above the value of printed unhandled cups in that year. The same percentage of value above unhandled printed cups for 1846 was applied, and a fixed value for unhandled porcelain cups was thus achieved. An important consideration applied to extrapolation of values on the Miller indices was that every effort was made to assign conservative values that would undervalue, rather than overvalue, specific ware and/or decorative types.

The second technique applied to ceramic analysis that has value for this study was ceramic set analysis. Ceramic set analysis simply consisted of grouping vessels of the same decoration together, and studying the range of forms present. Two types of sets were observed in the collections. Tea sets consisted of matched cups and saucers, and occasionally tea bowls and tea pots. Table sets were composed of plates, platters, cups, saucers, and a variety of food-service dishes. Table sets appear to have become available on a wide-spread basis by the 1840s (Miller 1980), and large and elaborate ceramic sets were available at modest prices by the end of the nineteenth century. The presence of table sets in contexts that date to at least the first half of the nineteenth century appears to have some value in describing socioeconomic status, as they seem to be absent in assemblages from households occupied by persons of low socioeconomic status (Garrow 1982; Klein and Garrow 1984).

The methods used to analyze the faunal collections from Washington and Wilmington were not consistent. The goal of the Washington faunal analysis was to determine the minimum number of individuals present in the collection by species, and no attention was given to the cuts of meat by species that were present. Observations were made during the Washington analysis concerning butchering techniques, culinary marks, and any other evident pre- and post-depositional modifications of the bones. Preservation of faunal material was excellent within context D1.

The faunal analysis of the Wilmington Boulevard collections was conducted under a research design that included study of the relative socioeconomic levels of occupants of the study blocks through time as a research priority. The faunal analysis for the Wilmington Boulevard Project was conducted by David T. Clark (1984:545–684), and his results were synthesized and interpreted by Cheryl A. Holt (1984:347–367). Holt employed a method developed by Schulz and Gust (1983:44) to rank the various cuts of meat present in the project sample by cost into high, medium, and low-cost cuts. She then employed the Z statistic to "test the null hypothesis that the proportions of ranked skeletal elements were the same between populations. Each classification of meat value was tested at the 0.5 confidence level" (Holt 1984:352). The analysis conducted by Holt resulted in establishing the relative purchase costs of the faunal collections from the nineteen "lot-specific" (Garrow 1984) contexts within that project. Holt's analysis did not establish absolute purchase prices for each assemblage, but the relative values achieved represented an excellent means for internal comparisons within that project, as well as a comparative base that can be used to compare the results of other projects utilizing the same methodological approach. Faunal preservation was excellent in each of the contexts discussed in this paper.

THE WASHINGTON CIVIC CENTER PROJECT

The Washington Civic Center Project (Garrow 1982) produced one context that was suitable for detailed socioeconomic studies. That context was a small, backyard, single-family trash dump (Area D1) that was deposited between circa 1844 and circa 1857. The historical research conducted for this project failed to identify the residents of the lot where the trash dump was deposited during the 1844–1857 period, but it did demonstrate that the block was occupied by artisans and white-collar workers during the period of interest. Identification of a single printer's type spacer within the collection from the dump led the investigators to speculate that the context had been generated from the household of one of the two printers who are known to have lived on the block at that time. At any rate, based on the occupations of the inhabitants known from the historical research for the period of interest, it was assumed that the socioeconomic status of the block residents was probably higher than laborers or other blue-collar workers, and that they enjoyed a moderate status level.

The analysis methods employed to study the faunal collections from the D1 trash make it difficult to extrapolate more than very coarse data concerning the socioeconomic status of the household that generated the trash dump based on the faunal evidence. Table 1 lists the species represented, the number of bones identified for each, and the minimum number of individuals (MNI) present by species.

Table 1 illustrates that the single-family trash dump contained a broad range of faunal materials, and yielded bones of both domesticated and wild animals. The presence of saw marks on many of the bones, combined with the general lack of skull and teeth elements, led to the conclusion that most, if not all, of the cuts of meat in the sample had been purchased from a professional butcher. This was apparently true even in the case of the deer bones, as several contained saw marks indicative of professional butchering. The two mustelid

Table 1. Faunal Material from Area D1, Washington Civic Center Project[a]

Species	Number of bones	Minimum number of individuals (MNI)
Chicken	63	6
Turkey	11	3
Pig	17	2
Cow	42	2
Sheep	10	2
Goat	5	1
Ovid	11	2
Artiodactyl	10	1
Deer	19	1
Squirrel	4	1
Mustelid	2	1
Opposum	4	1
Catfish	1	1
Clam	1	1

[a]From Garrow 1982:173, 177.

bones in the sample may have come from a *Martes pennanti* (fisher), which is generally not thought edible, but at least one of the two recovered bones did exhibit what appeared to be culinary marks.

It is unfortunate that the analysis of the Washington Civic Center dump did not include identification and quantification of the types of cuts present. A general impression that can be gained from the assemblage, is that the diet of the family that deposited trash in the dump was diverse, and that even some of the wild species present had been purchased from a professional butcher.

Application of the Miller (1980) ceramic economic scaling technique to the ceramics recovered from the single-family trash dump confirmed the impression of the socioeconomic status of the occupants that had been gained from the historical research. The ceramic collection from that context (Garrow 1982:74–91) totalled 2,575 sherds representative of twenty-three decorative or ware types and an estimated 240 vessels. The results of application of the Miller ceramic economic scaling technique to this collection are presented in Table 2. The results of the Miller analysis indicated that only bowls reflected a value of under two, while cups had a high average value of 2.87. The ceramic collection from this site was thus notable for its range of values from bowls to cups, but also (on the whole) exhibited a higher purchase price for the assemblage than any of the examples cited by Miller in his 1980 article.

Strong evidence for the presence of ceramic sets was identified during the analysis of the D1 collections. The ceramic sets present included two porcelain tea sets and portions of four table sets. The set evidence gained from this context was so strong that it was possible to trace the replacement of individual sets vertically through this deposit, which was a key factor in determining that the deposits had indeed originated from a single household. The sherds from each vessel were plotted within the trash deposit during this analysis, and the proveniences of each vessel at the sherd levels was studied. It was determined that only one table set and one tea set was in everyday use at a time. That determination was based on the assumption that the most often used ceramic sets will be the most vulnerable to breakage, and therefore those sets will be the most well represented in a trash deposit during its maximum period of use.

It is not possible to state uncategorically that the ceramic values reflected by the Washington Civic Center Project sample reflects occupation by a family that enjoyed a moderate status level. It is fair to state that the occupants who generated the study context did have more disposable wealth available for ceramic purchases than did the occupants of the sites presented in Miller's (1980) article, and that they had sufficient disposable wealth to be able to purchase ceramics in sets versus single pieces.

THE WILMINGTON BOULEVARD PROJECT

The Wilmington Boulevard Project (Klein and Garrow 1984) investigated portions of seven blocks in downtown Wilmington, Delaware. That project was

Table 2. The Miller Analysis for Plates, Cups, and Bowls from Area D1 of the
Washington Civic Center Project

	Scale: 1846	Number	Product
Plates			
Edged	1.13	8	9.04
Willow	2.63	2	5.26
Printed	2.63	14	36.82
Flow	2.63	3	7.89
Ironstone	2.63	15	39.45
Totals		42	98.45
Average value: 2.34			
Cups			
Sponged	1.23	4	4.92
	1.77	0	0
Painted	1.23	5	6.15
	1.77	0	0
Ironstone	2.45	1	2.45
	3.00	6	9.00
Printed	2.45	3	7.35
	3.00	6	18.00
Porcelain	4.55	9	40.95
Totals		31	88.82
Average value: 2.87			
Bowls			
CC ware	1.00	2	2.00
Dipped	1.20	10	12.00
Printed	2.80	1	2.80
Flow	2.80	2	5.60
Ironstone	2.80	2	5.60
Totals		17	28.00
Average value: 1.65			

conducted under a sophisticated research design that had a stated goal of investigating the historical development of the City of Wilmington from the perspective of the seven study blocks. This research perspective included intensive study of the socioeconomic character of the occupants of the study blocks, and how the socioeconomic "profile" of the area had changed through time. Study of the socioeconomic character of individual lot residents and of the study area at large was pursued through the use of historical research, application of the Miller (1980) ceramic economic scaling technique, and specialized faunal analysis as primary tools.

The historical research conducted for this project (Heite 1984; Heite and Friedlander 1984) indicated that the history of the seven study blocks (and the City of Wilmington) could be divided into weakly defined "preindustrial" and "industrial" periods. Further, the transition between the two periods was demonstrated to have taken place after the construction of the railroad into Wilmington in the late 1830s and between 1840 and 1850. The residents of the study area during the preindustrial period ranged from signers of the Constitution to manual laborers, and well-defined neighborhoods composed of individuals of similar socioeconomic status appeared to have been absent. Industrialization slowly changed that picture, and by the twentieth century, the study area primarily housed small shops and manual workers.

The Wilmington Boulevard archaeological excavations produced nineteen lot-specific contexts (Garrow 1984) that could be used for sophisticated artifact analysis. Those contexts included backyard middens and features that dated to both the preindustrial and industrial periods. Only four contexts, all features, of that larger sample yielded a suitable ceramic collection to support a Miller (1980) ceramic economic scaling analysis, however. The features that returned suitable collections for a Miller analysis included a cistern-privy from Area D, a cluster of three features from a single occupation in Area A, and a single feature from Area H dating from the industrial period.

It was anticipated that the occupants who generated the materials recovered from the cluster of three features in Area A enjoyed a higher socioeconomic standing than did the individuals who discarded the Area H artifacts. The three features in Area A were attributed to a mineral water manufacture operated by Joseph Dowdall from 1848 to 1852. The three features consisted of a trash lens, a filled barrel privy, and a shell-filled trench. Attribution of these features to the Dowdall occupancy was based on mean ceramic dates (Feature 17, 1849.7; Feature 15, 1849.8; and Feature 25, 1850.2), and the fact that marble chips and embossed mineral-water bottles (including examples embossed with Dowdall's name, but many more embossed with the names of his competitors) were recovered from the features. The presence of marble chips was an important clue in this case, as marble chips were used in the production of mineral water. The Area H feature consisted of a barrel privy that contained a cap of brick rubble overlying a stratum of fecal matter, ash, and artifacts. The underlying stratum was excavated in three arbitrary six-inch levels. Analysis of the contents of the arbitrary levels indicted that the lowest level returned a mean ceramic date of 1851.9, the middle level a date of 1854.3, and the upper level a date of 1859.9. Subsequent analysis established that the lowest two levels related to one occupation, while the upper level was deposited in a subsequent occupation. The residents of the investigated lot Area H at the time the materials were deposited in the barrel privy were determined from historical research to have been persons who were presumably of low socioeconomic status. Available historical data indicated Area A had either housed Joseph Dowdall or the manager of his mineral-water manufacture, and in either case it was anticipated that the resident would have enjoyed a higher socioeconomic status than the Area H residents.

The faunal assemblages from the Dowdall features and the Area H context (Feature 2) were similar in terms of the proportions of each species represented. Both collections included cow, pig, sheep, goat, chicken, turtle, and fish. The Dowdall features additionally yielded a single goose bone and numbers of oyster and clam shells. Despite the superficial similarities between the two collections, they proved to be quite different in terms of the cuts of meat present. Holt applied the Z statistic to preindustrial and industrial middens and features, and found that there were pronounced differences between the Dowdall features and the features of Area H. She concluded:

> The Dowdall contexts are believed to have been generated by persons of medium to high socio-economic level, while features 2 and 11 of Area H are believed to have been filled by households of low socio-economic standing. Those assumptions were indeed supported by application of the Z statistic. . . . The pronounced dissimilarities of the faunal assemblages from those areas suggests greater social distance between the Dowdall contexts and Features 2 and 11 of Area H than was observed between the pre-industrial and industrial assemblages of Area A alone. (Holt 1984:354)

The faunal analyses thus supported the historical data concerning the relative socioeconomic statuses of the occupants of the two lots, and demonstrated that there was considerable socioeconomic distance between the two sets of occupants.

It was assumed that the Miller (1980) ceramic economic scaling technique would reflect a relatively high index value for the ceramics recovered from the Dowdall deposits, and a low value for the Area H collections. Application of the Miller (1980) ceramic economic scaling technique to the ceramics from the Dowdall features produced the anticipated results. Table 3 presents the ceramic economic scaling data, and the results achieved.

The ceramic values derived from the Dowdall features cluster around 2.00, with plates and cups scaling an identical 2.11, and bowls slightly lower at 1.80. The values for plates and cups were lower than the plate and cup values (2.34 and 2.87, respectively) recorded for the Washington Civic Center example, but the Dowdall features returned a slightly higher value for bowls (1.8 versus 1.65).

As previously discussed, intensive analyses of the Area H feature (Feature 2) indicated that the artifacts in that feature were derived from two separate households. Tables 4 and 5 present the ceramic economic scaling data from the collections derived from those two distinct collections.

The ceramic economic scaling values derived for plates and bowls for the two analysis units within Feature 2 were relatively low, as anticipated. The cup value of Level 2A at 3.54 was extraordinarily high, while the cup value for Levels 2B and 2C was a moderately high 2.52. Quantified cross-mend analysis (Garrow 1982, 1984) had clearly demonstrated that while Levels 2B and 2C formed a single context with numerous crossmends, very few crossmends could be demonstrated to span from 2A to the other levels. The few crossmends that spanned Level 2A and 2B or 2C derived from minor disturbances within the feature, as well as the fact that the levels were arbitrarily derived during excavation.

Combined Levels 2B and 2C yielded a mean ceramic date of 1852.6, while the overlying Level 2A returned a mean ceramic date of 1859.9, a difference of 7.3 years. It appears that the barrel privy that constituted Feature 2 began receiving trash in the early 1850s (the property changed hands and was divid-

Table 3. Ceramic Economic Scaling Data for the Dowdall Features, Wilmington Boulevard Project[a]

	Scale: 1846	Number	Product
Plates			
Porcelain	4.29	1	4.29
CC ware	1.00	4	4.00
Ironstone	2.63	4	10.52
Edged	1.13	8	9.04
Painted	1.75	1	1.75
Flow blue	2.63	1	2.63
Printed	2.63	19	49.97
Sponged	1.13	1	1.13
Plain pearlware	1.00	1	1.00
Totals		40	84.33
Average value: 2.11			
Cups			
Porcelain	3.70	6	22.20
CC ware	1.00	4	4.00
Ironstone	2.45	7	17.15
Painted	1.23	8	9.84
Dipped	1.23	2	2.46
Flow blue	2.43	4	9.80
Printed	2.45	14	34.30
Sponged	1.23	4	4.92
Plain pearlware	1.00	1	1.00
Totals		50	105.67
Average value: 2.11			
Bowls			
CC ware	1.0	2	2.0
Painted	1.6	2	3.2
Dipped	1.2	4	4.8
Printed	2.8	5	14.0
Sponged	1.2	1	1.2
Totals		14	25.2
Average value: 1.8			

[a]From Klein and Garrow 1984:327.

ed into smaller lots around 1854), and that the artifacts in Levels 2B and 2C were discarded at that time. By the late 1850s (perhaps later), the initial trash deposit had settled, and the incorporated organics had decayed to the point that a void was left in the top of the feature. That void was apparently filled with trash at that time, and then capped with brick rubble. The artifacts in Level 2A were thus deposited later than those in Levels 2B and 2C, and, given the lack of similarity of the two collections, it is probable that they came from different households. This would mean that the household that generated the ceramics in Levels 2B and 2C was replaced by a household that contained even

Table 4. Ceramic Economic Scaling Data, Area H, Feature 2, Level 2A[a]

	Scale: 1858	Number	Product
Plates			
CC ware	1.00	1	1.00
Ironstone	1.80	1	1.80
Edged	1.00	1	1.00
Totals		3	3.80
Average value: 1.27			
Cups			
Ironstone	4.00	5	20.00
Painted	1.23	1	1.23
Totals		6	21.23
Average value: 3.54			
Bowls			
CC ware	1.0	3	3.0
Ironstone	2.0	3	6.0
Dipped	1.1	3	3.3
Totals		9	12.3
Average value: 1.37			

[a]From Klein and Garrow 1984: 328.

more costly tea wares (cups). That came at a time when the lot in question was inhabited by individuals with very low-ranking job classifications.

The problem of assigning an appropriate socioeconomic ranking to the late 1850s residents of this lot is increased by the presence of unanticipated Activities Group artifacts from Level 2A and from nearby Feature 11 (deposited on the same lot and at approximately the same time as Level 2A). Level 2A yielded two porcelain figurine fragments and two marbles, while Feature 11 contained a wooden chess piece, an ebony and mother-of-pearl inlay violin bow fragment, decorative glass rods, and a number of toys (a wooden whistle, a tin soldier, two porcelain doll fragments, and a lead-and-wood broadaxe). Level 2A further contained three glass syringe parts and a slate pencil, while Feature 11 contained a brass pen nib, a wooden pen holder, and 10 slate pencils. In comparison, Levels 2B and 2C yielded 10 toys (eight marbles, one bone domino, and one porcelain doll fragment) and nine slate pencils.

There are many potential explanations for the disparity in socioeconomic scaling derived from the various sources. One explanation is, of course, that the historical data and faunal analysis results could be in error, just as the results of the Miller (1980) ceramic economic scaling results could be spurious. That explanation does not seem to fit in this case, however, as consistent results were achieved in other instances within the Wilmington Boulevard Project, in which the three methods were used in conjunction. A second possible explanation is that the wrong index values were assigned to the various decorative-ware groups from Levels 2A and Levels 2B and 2C. That explanation could be valid if the features date much later than the assigned mean ceramic dates, but not if the features were earlier. It is possible that the ceramics could date to a later period than indicated by the mean ceramic date if the household had purchased and used out-of-date (and thus cheaper) ceramics. That is not a viable explanation in this case, as the other items recovered from this context were consistent with the assigned mean ceramic date. Use of earlier index values would have increased most of the average values, and made the disparity between the data sets even greater.

The simplest explanation for the disparity is that the historical research and faunal analysis correctly measured the socioeconomic status of the household that deposited the material in Level 2A and presumably Feature 11 at the time that material was deposited, while the Miller (1980) analysis did not accurately reflect their socioeconomic status at that point in time. This could mean that Level 2A and probably Feature 11 were deposited by a family in socioeconomic decline, and that the Miller (1980) analysis measured (at least in part) their former status level. That interpretation is supported by the presence of the chess piece and violin bow fragment in Feature 11, as well as the figurine fragments in Level 2A and the range of toys recovered from Level

Table 5. Ceramic Economic Scaling Data, Area H, Feature 2, Levels 2B and 2C, Wilmington Boulevard Project[a]

	Scale: Combined	Number	Product
Plates			
CC ware	1.00	1	1.00
Ironstone	1.50	2	3.00
Edged	1.25	3	3.75
Flow blue	2.50	2	5.00
Printed	1.50	12	18.00
Totals		20	30.75
Average value: 1.54			
Cups			
CC ware	1.00	1	1.00
Ironstone	3.60	7	25.20
Painted	1.23	4	4.92
Printed	3.60	3	10.80
Sponged	1.17	3	3.51
Totals		18	43.43
Average value: 2.52			
Bowls			
CC ware	1.00	3	3.0
Ironstone	2.00	1	2.0
Dipped	1.10	22	24.2
Totals		26	29.2
Average value: 1.12			

[a]From Klein and Garrow 1984:331.

2A and Feature 11. Those items are simply not the types of objects that would be expected to be present in a family of low socioeconomic status, at least in a family that had always had a low socioeconomic ranking. It is possible that the very high cup value derived for Level 2A reflects the last, surviving, high-priced ceramic items in the household.

Level 2A and Levels 2B and 2C contained weak evidence for the presence of ceramic sets. The individual vessels that could be linked into sets apparently represented set remnants. The Dowdall features, on the other hand, yielded strong evidence of two sets plus evidence of a set remnant. The relative set evidence extracted from those contexts appears to support the contention that the Dowdall features actually reflect a higher socioeconomic level for those residents than did Feature 2 in Area H.

CONCLUSIONS

Determination of relative socioeconomic status levels from historical and archaeological data is a difficult process that is sensitive to a number of potential variables. At present, it is possible to generate quantifiable data from the use of historical research, the Miller (1980) ceramic economic scaling technique, and specialized faunal analysis. Two of those methods involve measurements of consumer choices, while the third is a measurement based on occupation (job) ranking. The use of converging lines of evidence, as opposed to the use of one or even two of the techniques in question, should yield accurate statements concerning the relative socioeconomic status level of the household or group that generated the study collection.

Discrepancies among the three data sets may offer valuable insights into the individual or individuals under study. As an example, discrepancies among the data sets from Feature 2A on the Wilmington Boulevard Project suggested the interpretation that the household that generated that context was in socioeconomic decline at the time the study collection was being deposited. That small example indicates the dynamic nature of the period of industrialization in terms of socioeconomic class. Some families doubtless improved their socioeconomic position, while other families suffered financial reversals.

The use of converging lines of evidence, if they produce consistent results, can build a stronger case for assignment of a particular socioeconomic level. As an example, the historical, faunal, and ceramic data from the Dowdall features all supported a fairly high socioeconomic ranking for that occupation. Also, the historical data and ceramic economic scaling data from the Washington Civic Center example appeared to be consistent with generalized faunal observations, and supported an interpretation of a moderate status level for the household that generated that context.

The study of socioeconomic levels through combined historical and archaeological data is still a relatively new area of inquiry. Hopefully, the tools available for such studies will be refined in coming years, and new methods for producing replicable, quantifiable measurements will be devised. In the meantime, it is essential that the tools that are available be used in the most productive manner possible. The use of converging lines of evidence appears to have the potential for producing accurate, relative assessments of socioeconomic status, and should be considered for use on future projects.

REFERENCES

Clark, D. T., 1984, Faunal Data, in: *Final Archaeological Investigations at the Wilmington Boulevard Monroe to King Street Wilmington, New Castle County, Delaware*, (DELDOT Archaeology Series, Number 29, T. H. Klein and P. H. Garrow, eds.), Dover, New York, pp. 545–683.

Crader, D. C., 1984, The Zooarchaeology of the Storehouse and the Dry Well at Monticello, in: *American Antiquity* 49:542–558.

Garrow, P. H. (ed.), 1982, Archaeological Investigations on the Washington, D.C., Civic Center Site, report on file with the Historic Preservation Office, Department of Housing and Community Development, Government of the District of Columbia.

Garrow, P. H., 1984, The Identification and Use of Context Types in Urban Archaeology, *Southeastern Archaeology* 3:91–96.

Heite, L. B., 1984, History, in: *Final Archaeological Investigations at The Wilmington Boulevard Monroe to King Street Wilmington, New Castle County, Delaware*, (DELDOT Archaeology Series, Number 29, T. H. Klein and P. H. Garrow, eds.), Dover, New York, pp. 29–82.

Heite, L. B., and Friedlander, A., 1984, Project Area Block Histories, in: *Final Archaeological Investigations at The Wilmington Boulevard Monroe to King Street Wilmington, New Castle County, Delaware*, (DELDOT Archaeology Series, Number 29, T. H. Klein and P. H. Garrow, eds.), Dover, New York, pp. 410–446.

Holt, C. A., 1984, Dietary Pattern Analysis, in: *Final Archaeological Investigations at the Wilmington Boulevard Monroe to King Street Wilmington, New Castle County, Delaware*, (DELDOT Archaeology Series, Number 29, T. H. Klein and P. H. Garrow, eds.), Dover, New York, pp. 368–386.

Klein, T. H., and Garrow, P. H. (eds.), 1984, *Final Archaeological Investigations at the Wilmington Boulevard Monroe Street to King Street Wilmington, New Castle County, Delaware*, (DELDOT Archaeology Series, Number 29, Dover, New York.

Miller, G. L., 1980, Classification and Economic Scaling of Nineteenth Century Ceramics, *Historical Archaeology* 14:1–40.

Miller, G. L., and Hurry, S. D., 1983, Ceramic Supply in an Economically Isolated Frontier Community: Portage County of the Ohio Western Reserve, *Historical Archaeology* 17:80–92.

Otto, J. S., 1975, Status Differences and the Archaeological Record—A Comparison of Planter, Overseer, and Slave Sites From Cannon's Point Plantation (1794–1861), St. Simon's Island, Georgia, University Microfilms, Ann Arbor.

Schulz, P. D., and Gust, S. M., 1983, Faunal Remains and Social Status in 19th Century Sacramento, *Historical Archaeology* 17:44–53.

Wheaton, T. R., Friedlander, A., and Garrow, P. H., 1983, Yaughan and Curriboo Plantations: Studies in Afro-American Archaeology, report on file with the National Park Service, Atlanta.

11

Nineteenth-Century Households and Consumer Behavior in Wilmington, Delaware

CHARLES H. LeeDECKER, TERRY H. KLEIN, CHERYL A. HOLT, AND AMY FRIEDLANDER

INTRODUCTION

A recently completed historical and archaeological investigation of Block 1101 in Wilmington, Delaware, has provided important information concerning nineteenth-century urban households, primarily in the area of consumer behavior and household composition. The study block is one block away from Market Street and two blocks away from Front Street, the two primary corridors on which Wilmington's initial residential and commercial development occurred (Figure 1).

In Wilmington's core, nineteenth-century households practiced a range of income strategies, such as delaying the departure of children in order to retain their income within the household, taking in boarders to obtain supplemental income, and possibly using boarders as part of the labor force working for the head of household. Along with these different income strategies and forms of household composition, archaeological research revealed a range of variation in consumer behavior, in addition to some unexpected similarities.

Using only the occupation of the head of household, as is common in current historical archaeological research, the households examined in this study would have been categorized as upper, middle, or lower class/status. However, this study suggests that these socioeconomic categories have only limited utility for understanding consumer behavior. The study findings suggest that several factors other than occupation of the head of household seem to be linked to consumer choices in nineteenth-century households in Wilmington. These include the household income strategy, the size and composition of the household, and the household life cycle. There were also external

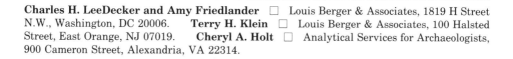

Charles H. LeeDecker and Amy Friedlander ☐ Louis Berger & Associates, 1819 H Street N.W., Washington, DC 20006. **Terry H. Klein** ☐ Louis Berger & Associates, 100 Halsted Street, East Orange, NJ 07019. **Cheryl A. Holt** ☐ Analytical Services for Archaeologists, 900 Cameron Street, Alexandria, VA 22314.

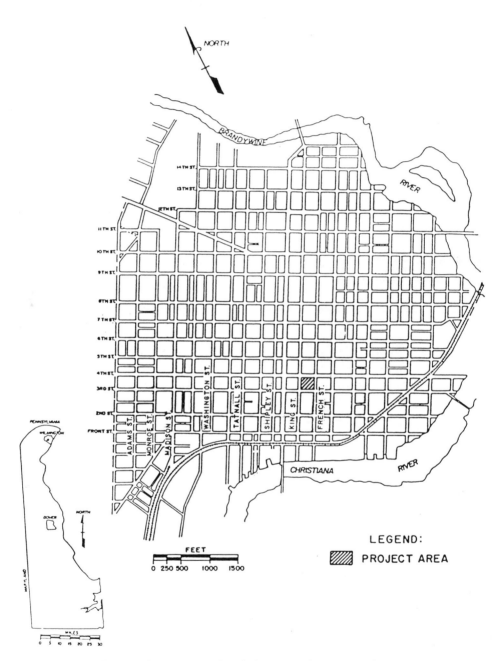

Figure 1. Location map for Block 1101, Wilmington, Delaware.

factors that acted upon the household and that reflected larger processes within Wilmington's historical development. One variable was the changing character of the marketplace whereby households of the city's core in the mid- to late nineteenth century had more equal access to goods. The process of migration into the city also had a major influence on the character of the household. In order to absorb these incoming populations within the already-small lots of the city's core area, there was an increase in the utilization of space, which was reflected by increased consumption and discard of architectural items.

The next section provides a discussion of the research problems addressed in this study, the broad theoretical context of this research, and the concepts and models from which hypotheses are derived for testing. This is followed by a description of the documentary and archaeological data and the analytical methods employed. The research findings are summarized in the "Results" section. The chapter concludes with a brief discussion of the significance of this study's research findings, within the broad context of archaeological research on consumer behavior.

This presentation is based on historical research and archaeological excavation conducted by the Cultural Resource Group of Louis Berger & Associates for the City of Wilmington, Delaware. The program was administered for the city by the Department of Planning, Department of Commerce. These investigations were performed in compliance with the National Historic Preservation Act (et al.), for an Urban Development Action Grant project. The program was accomplished through a series of three sequential contract phases: archival research, archaeological testing, and archaeological data recovery. The third phase was accompanied by additional historical research. All archival and field research was completed within the period from February 14 to April 7, 1984.

RESEARCH CONTEXT

Dimensions of Household Behavior

Taking the household as the principal unit of analysis, both the documentary and archaeological research focused on the relationship between consumption patterns and household composition and size, household income strategy, household life cycle, and socioeconomic class. Several issues associated with the rubric of consumer behavior were examined, including the choice of housing location, the selection of alternate income strategies to augment the earnings of the head of household, the consumption of dietary elements of varying quality and cost, and the purchase, use, and discard of different classes of material goods. It was assumed that the quality, quantity, and diversity of material goods and dietary elements recovered from the archaeological deposits directly reflects consumer choices made by the household; however, this assumption was upheld only after careful assessment of formation processes that had produced the excavated deposits.

In the most basic sense, the household may be defined as a group of individuals who share a common residence. Household groups are identifiable from the list of individuals enumerated by the census taker at a given address. Beyond common residence, however, members of the household group are normally bound together by kinship and economic relations. As a domestic unit, households include a network of social relations, a behavioral component that includes a set of activities to meet the economic needs of the household membership, and common use of a dwelling, activity areas, and possessions (Netting 1982; Wilk and Rathje 1982).

Various forms of household composition may be distinguished by the types of relationships, both economic and social, that exist between the members of the household group. The household types that were normally found in nineteenth-century urban American settings include the nuclear family household, the extended family household, the augmented family household, the boarding house, and the solitary individual household. The nuclear family household consists simply of a married couple and their children, while the extended family household consists of two or more nuclear families linked by kinship bonds such as between siblings or parent and child (Murdock 1949). Augmented family households are comprised of either a nuclear or an extended family in addition to other individuals who may be kin or nonkin, such as servants, boarders, or lodgers. The terms "boarder" and "lodger" will be used synonymously, referring to a nonkin member of the household who receives bed and meals in exchange for money. A servant is a nonkin member of the household who receives bed, meals, and wages in exchange for services rendered within the household. A boarding house represents the commercialization of the household; in addition to a number of boarders, a boardinghouse may or may not include a complete nuclear family unit. Finally, a solitary individual household includes a single person who lives alone.

The household income strategy refers to the set of activities by which income is brought into the household, including supplementing of the head of household's income by the participation of secondary wage earners in the labor market. The male head of household provided the primary source of income for late nineteenth-century urban households, but children frequently provided an important supplemental income. Also, the family could enhance the overall household income by the taking in of boarders. In addition to raising the overall household income by supplementing the earnings of the head of household, the inclusion of secondary wage earners within the household provided a means of support for the family during periods of difficult circumstances, such as illness or unemployment of the primary breadwinner (Goldin 1979; Modell 1978).

The life-cycle concept is used to describe the normal developmental sequence that accompanies changes in age, including marital status, residential circumstances, child rearing, and participation in the labor force (Goody 1971). Beginning with birth and culminating with death, the life cycle of the individual normally includes the succession of statuses of child, adult, spouse, and parent. A typical twentieth-century developmental cycle for the household may be defined, beginning with the formation of a new household by a married, childless couple, progressing through a nuclear family stage, and culminating in the "empty nest" stage after the children leave to form their own households.

Urban historians and anthropologists have demonstrated that the household income strategy and life cycle are closely linked to household composition. Moreover, household composition reflects urban migration processes, and there appear to be distinctive patterns of household composition and income strategies among various ethnic groups. Household composition also reflects cultural norms, and adherence to popular ideals or legally sanctioned forms of household organization may exhibit broad variation within a population. Given the significant economic dimension of household behavior, the household is therefore an excellent unit for the study of consumer behavior. A review of the current literature pertinent to household composition, income strategy, developmental cycles, and consumer behavior will define the research context for the present study.

Netting (1982) has examined the relationship between household size and wealth, using historical and contemporary populations from a variety of ethnographic settings. While his sample size was small, the examples show that larger households had not only greater total wealth but also greater wealth per capita, as measured from estate values and ownership of land and livestock. In some populations, there was also evidence of movement of people from less wealthy to more wealthy households where jobs were more plentiful. Netting (1982:657) concluded that wealthy households enhance their status and prestige by maintaining larger residential groups, and that social stratification is reflected in larger household size, regardless of the culturally preferred form of household composition.

Glasco (1977, 1978) has studied household structure, life cycles, and migration patterns in Buffalo, using the 1855 New York state census. Data from the entire city were coded to examine the passage of Irish, Germans, and native-born whites through the life-cycle stages of childhood, adolescence, marriage, childbearing, and retirement, as well as the household statuses of husband, wife, child, boarder, servant, and relative (Glasco 1977:123). Among men, there was similarity with regard to the timing of the various life cycle stages, but striking differences in their occupational characteristics. Native-born men filled the white collar and entrepreneurial positions, while the Irish were concentrated in the unskilled jobs, and the Germans dominated the crafts and construction industries. Differences in the life cycles were more apparent among the women, and the major differences occurred during the years of adolescence. German and Irish women tended to leave home at a much earlier age than their native-born counterparts, and they typically spent their adolescent years working as domestics in the households of native-born whites. German and Irish households showed a greater preference for the nuclear family household, as the native-born households were more likely to include boarders and relatives. Native-born households were established later than those of the German and Irish immigrants, and they tended to restrict their family size by limiting the number of children; German and Irish families, on the other hand, did not appear to regulate childbearing.

Glasco (1978) examined the interrelationship between migration and household composition, viewing migration from an internal American and regional perspective. He found that while recent migrants to Buffalo were primarily skilled young men who boarded with private families and in commercial hotels and boardinghouses, a significant number arrived as a member of a family group. Rather than being fragmented by migration, Glasco (1978:178) asserted that "the family and household institutions of migrants served as perhaps the key mechanism for their migration and adjustment to the city." His study has important spatial implications for the city as well, as he found that male boarders tended to cluster in the commercial core of the city. However, when they married and established their own households, they tended to move out of the central city. Similarly, acquisition of a home meant movement further from the central commercial district. Therefore, the character of mixed commercial-residential areas would have been predominantly male and highly transient.

Boarding was a widespread practice in the late nineteenth century, both in rural and urban settings. Modell and Hareven (1977) have examined the practice of boarding in American families and estimated that roughly one in five urban households took in boarders during the period from the 1860s to the 1920s. In its nineteenth-century urban manifestation, boarding was an adaptation of a traditional middle-class practice, however, it became associated with lower-class immigrants and, by the end of the nineteenth century, progressive moralists termed it "the lodger evil" as middle-class values tightened (Modell and Hareven 1977:165–166). In the context of chaotic urban housing markets, taking in boarders simultaneously provided housing and a surrogate family life for the influx of migrants, while providing a source of supplemental income for working- and middle-class families.

Several studies by urban historians (Glasco 1977, 1978; Goldin 1979; Modell 1978; Modell and Hareven 1977) have shown that the practice of boarding was also closely linked with the life cycles of the individual boarders, and with the life cycles of the households that took in boarders. In late nineteenth-century urban context, boarders were primarily young men who had recently left their parents' homes, while the families most likely to take them in were those whose children had recently left to establish their own households. The propensity to take in lodgers also appears to be linked to home ownership, which increased in the later life-cycle stages (Modell and Hareven 1977:178). The institution of boarding also allowed widows and single women in their 40s, 50s, and 60s to maintain their own household rather than live with kin (Modell and Hareven 1977:175–176).

Distinctive income strategies and patterns of consumer behavior have been identified for late nineteenth-century urban populations. Goldin (1979:111) has found that urban families in the late nineteenth century depended on the labor of children as their most important source of income after the male head of household. The higher the father's wage, the lower the probability of a child participating in the labor force. Since the wages of the working class tend to decrease with age, Goldin found that the older the father, "the more probable the labor force participation of children" (Goldin 1979:124). Also, the presence of boarders and working relatives tended to deter entry of daughters into the labor force. The taking in of boarders was a means of augmenting income for the middle class, for the elderly whose income declined, and for married and widowed women who did not wish to work outside the home (Goldin 1979:126).

Goldin (1979:127–128) also found that entry of daughters into the labor force varied with ethnic affiliation. Native-born Americans, in particular, tended to keep daughters at home, although the practice of taking lodgers was more prevalent among this group than among immigrant groups (see also Glasco 1977, 1978; Modell and Hareven 1977). Using family budget information gathered from 1874 to 1901, Modell (1978) has studied the consumption patterns for working-class families in the Northeast United States and has identified distinctive patterns of consumption and income strategy. Variations in income strategies included the higher frequency of boarders among native-American families and the tendency for immigrant, primarily Irish wives and children (both male and female) to work outside the home (Modell 1978). The critical factor, he found, was the income level of the head of household. Because immigrants tended to hold the lowest-paid positions, households headed by immigrants were compelled to find multiple sources of income. As wages of the head of household increased, immigrant households tended to approach the norm set by native-American workers (Modell 1978:325).

For both Irish and native-born white households, total expenditures varied widely over the family life cycle, and were closely linked to the changing demands of children. Modell also was able to discern patterns in various types of discretionary expenditures, which he termed expressive (charity, amusements, vacations), prudential (organizations, life insurance), and indulgent (alcohol, tobacco). Life-cycle analysis showed that expressive expenditures were highest in the earlier stages of the household life cycle and dropped significantly after all children had left the household, that is, the empty-nest stage. Prudential expenditures gained steadily through the life cycle. The most significant change in the level of indulgent expenditures occurred during the empty-nest stage (Modell 1978:236–237), when there was a marked increase in spending for alcohol and tobacco.

A number of studies of contemporary populations have also demonstrated the utility of the life-cycle concept for understanding consumer behavior. Wells and Gubar (1970) have reviewed the results of various marketing studies that have employed the life-cycle concept. While researchers have not employed a common definition the life-cycle stages, the criteria most often used include: marital status of the head of household (single–married), presence of children within the household, the distribution of children according to various age groups (under six/six-to-twelve/twelve-to-eighteen/eighteen or over), the age of the head of household (younger or older than forty or forty-five), and the occupational status of the head of household (working–retired).

The studies cited by Wells and Gubar (1970) show that the life-cycle stage is a better predictor than age for a wide variety of goods and services. Purchases of furniture are highest among newly married couples and among families whose children have just begun to date. The use of medicines is greatest among families with children under six, and second highest among the elderly. Consumption of luxury items (furs, jewelry, blended liquor, etc.) increases through the life cycle but decreases sharply with retirement.

The Reuse Project conducted at the University of Arizona revealed a number of findings concerning acquisition and disposal of goods that establish a linkage between consumer behavior and household life cycle, residential stability, and household income (Schiffer *et al.* 1981). While based on a contemporary population in Tucson, Arizona, a number of the project findings are particularly pertinent to the nineteenth-century households examined in the present study. First, the project demonstrated the widespread reuse of material goods, and that participation in reuse processes is, in a large measure, dependent on household income. Lower income households tended to own a greater percentage of used items and to participate in a greater variety of reuse processes. The "rest effect" was a term applied to the finding that the longer a household remains at a particular residence, the more items it accumulates (Schiffer *et al.* 1981:78). Finally, it was found that changes in status may result in the disposal of certain items, since some elements of the household inventory may not be perceived as appropriate for the individual's new status.

Class, Status, and Consumer Behavior

Even the most casual perusal of the current historical archaeological literature demonstrates a widespread use of the terms "class" and "status" in the study of material culture. Implicitly or explicitly, scholars have used these terms even in situations in which social ranking was not the object of the research. Such hierarchical groupings, whether motivated by Marxist, functionalist, or other theoretical frameworks, are inherent in all complex societies and are necessary in order to discuss collective behavior. Recently, historical archaeologists have shown great interest in the examination of relationships between consumer behavior, and socioeconomic status and class. Most of these works stem from Otto's study of a nineteenth-century plantation on St. Simon's Island, Georgia, in which a broad range of archaeological data sets were linked to differences in status (Otto 1977, 1984). Given the scope of the present study, some attention to these concepts is appropriate.

In 1936, Linton applied the term "status" to anthropological research, borrowing the concept from contemporary sociological investigations (Keesing and Keesing 1971:397). Linton defined status as an individual's position in a family, occupational group, class, and so forth. An individual may have many specialized statuses, and the combination of these is the individual's status within society. Linton identified several criteria that societies use to assign status, including sex, age, family relationships, and birth into a particular group, such as class. Social class supplements, but does not replace, biological factors used in status definition. Also, classes can each have their own internal set of statuses based on age, sex, and biological relationships (Linton 1936:113, 115–116). There is clearly an interplay between status and class, where class can be a means to define status in a society. But class also can be viewed as a hierarchical ranking of statuses based on prestige and power (Goldschmidt 1971:326).

In both contemporary sociology and studies of consumer behavior, the most commonly used social classification is that developed by Warner *et al.* (1960). This system divides the United States into six classes:

1. Upper-Upper: old families, the aristocracy of wealth and birth
2. Lower-Upper: families with new wealth, headed by top executives, high-salaried professionals, or owners of businesses
3. Upper-Middle: professionals, managers, successful businessmen
4. Lower-Middle: white-collar office workers, small business proprietors
5. Upper-Lower: skilled tradesmen, wage earners
6. Lower-Lower: disreputables, unemployed, unskilled workers

The basis for placement in a social class is how members of society regard each other. Assignment of individuals to a social class is quite complex, as it may involve extensive interviews with informants within the community, or it may involve a measurement of more objective factors such as occupation, source of income, residential area, type of dwelling, family background, religious and ethnic affiliation, and so on. Within the six social classes defined by Warner's scheme, there is a range of family incomes, and it is important to emphasize that social class is not determined by income, but by a broad range of factors. Membership in a social class implies consistency in values and life style, and is therefore a concept of a higher order than level of income.

While income has been widely used as a predictor of consumer behavior, the concept of social class has also been widely applied in marketing studies. In studies of mid-twentieth-century consumer behavior by Martineau (1958) and Kassarjian and Robertson (1973), class membership has been linked to differences in spending–saving patterns, expenditures on child rearing and education, preference or taste in certain consumable items, and allocation of expenditures among various classes of goods. Consumption patterns, therefore, serve to define, symbolize, and reinforce class membership.

Research Hypotheses

The preceding review provides a basis for development of a number of specific research hypotheses concerning consumer behavior. The principal area of inquiry will concern the relationship between consumer behavior and the household composition, income strategy, and life cycle:

H1. Consumption patterns will vary according to differences in household composition, particularly with regard to the presence and number of secondary wage earners.

H2. Consumption patterns will vary according to the household life cycle.

Also, there will be an examination of the relationship between consumer behavior and social class or status. Given the difficulty of measuring class or status, particularly for historic populations, occupational categories and income sources will be used as a proxy for these broader concepts:

H3. Consumption patterns will vary according to the social class of the head of household, as measured by occupational group.

The following section provides an overview of the data sets and analytical techniques used to examine these hypotheses.

DATA COLLECTION AND ANALYTICAL METHODS

Historical Research

A diverse set of research techniques was employed in the execution of the historical research. The initial study of the project area included cartographic and deed research as well as consideration of extant tax lists and census records. The map survey provided detailed data on lot partitioning and land use, primarily for the period 1850–1927. Title searches were completed for several of the lots selected for archaeological testing in order to provide data on ownership. Names of owners obtained from the title searches were checked in probate records, city directories, 1816 and 1845 tax assessments, and Orphan's Court records. Owners of industrial properties were checked in the Federal Census of Industries. Because of a gap in information for the eighteenth century, names of owners were cross-checked against the index of manuscripts at the Historical Society of Delaware; this effort resulted in the location of Revolutionary War letters of one of the block's early owners but failed to produce information relevant to the study area in the mid-eighteenth century.

During the data-recovery phase of the project, the historical research focussed on a more detailed consideration of the households, primarily by analysis of the 1840, 1850, and 1860 census manuscripts. Materials postdating 1860 were not subject to comparable analysis as a result of research priorities established by the city and state. Therefore, the 1870 and 1880 censuses were not examined. The census enumeration was taken according to a route, therefore the sequence of names in the list reflects proximity to one another in the city. In order to position the study area in the list, the names of owners believed to reside in the project area, identified by comparison of the city directories with information contained in the deed and tax lists, were identified in the census list. After establishing these "points of reference," several names were taken before and after known names. These were cross-checked again against the city directories and were then used as a sample to represent the study area and vicinity.

Somewhat different data are available in the three schedules. Only the name of the householder, and the age and racial identification of the members of the household were given in 1840. In 1850 and 1860, the census provides the name, age, race, and occupation of each member of the household and the value of the real estate owned. The relationship of members of the household to the head of household was not given, although it could be inferred from the sequence in which names were listed. The householder's name, first and last, were given first. Members of the nuclear family were listed next, although only the first names and ages in reverse chronological order were given. Finally, boarders were listed. If an adult lived with a sibling, this information tended to be obscured, since the order reflected nuclear family and nonnuclear family members of the household.

Households were characterized in terms of the head of household and income sources. Occupation of head of household, in particular, is consistently found to be one of the contributing factors that define class and status, while the income sources provide an indication of household wealth.

Archaeological Investigations

Recent demolition and grading had eliminated the possibility of finding intact yard deposits, therefore archaeological testing was concentrated in areas adjacent to the rear lot lines, where privy features were expected. Virtually the entire one-acre block was available for archaeological investigation, except for the area occupied by a single extant structure. While downcutting of the block had eliminated the possibility of finding intact yard deposits, numerous deep features had been preserved beneath the modern pavement. At the conclusion of field work, a total of thirty-six features had been identified, including privies, wells, foundation walls, cellars, and so on.

During the final field phase of the project, archaeological excavations were focused on the excavation of selected privy-well features. The privy-well features contained eighteenth- and nineteenth-century household deposits with very well-preserved floral and faunal material. Virtually all of the privy-well features had been either truncated by downcutting of the block or partially disturbed by modern intrusive features. In order to allow identification of temporally distinct deposits, privy-well fills were excavated in four-inch levels and according to stratigraphically distinct soil characteristics. All excavated material was water screened and one-liter samples from each stratigraphic unit within each level were retained for flotation processing.

More than 50,000 artifacts and 100,000 floral and faunal specimens were recovered from deposits within the Block 1101 project area. The deposits had a temporal range from the mid-eighteenth century through the late nineteenth century. Materials dating to the period 1736–1790 were fragmentary in nature and not amenable to complex levels of analysis. However, materials dating to the period 1790–1880s were well represented, both in terms of high frequency and state of preservation (i.e., vessel completeness) and were therefore amenable to functional and cost–value analyses

Prior to the derivation of any inferences regarding household behavior, a series of preliminary analyses were undertaken to define the formation proceses that had created the deposits, that is, whether each deposit represented *de facto* refuse, primary refuse, secondary refuse, displaced refuse, and so forth (Schiffer 1972, 1983; South 1977). These included assessment of the soil deposit matrices, dating, calculation of the percentage of vessel completeness, counting minimum number of vessels, identifying vessel crossmends within a feature, and measurement of simple artifact frequencies.

One of the most critical tools for identifying the origin and context of a deposit is the nature of the soil matrix from which the artifacts were recovered. Artifacts within a deposit of building demolition rubble are of a different origin and context than artifacts from a deposit containing night soils. Based on past work in Wilmington (cf. Klein and Garrow 1984) and other cities (Cressey *et al.* 1982), some of the best archaeological contexts for the study of household consumer behavior are artifact-bearing fecal deposits. These deposits can contain large and varied artifact assemblages that are often stratified. As with other fills, understanding the origin of artifacts in fecal deposits is critical in determining their utility for detailed study. Fecal deposits may simply contain displaced refuse placed in the privy in order to seal it. While there are several possible scenarios for the origin of artifacts in fecal fill, prior experience clearly indicates that these deposits often produce the best assemblages for use in studies of household behavior.

The initial tabulation of the assemblages from each feature was done using a format derived from South's (1977) artifact groups and classes; then, specialized analyses were completed for various artifact classes. The proportional representation of the various artifact groups and classes was subsequently used for comparison of the various household deposits.

Ceramics were tabulated by ware and type. After tabulation, ceramic sherds were cross-mended and analyzed to define the minimum number of vessels (MNV) within each feature assemblage. The pattern of mends was graphically portrayed in order to determine which levels and strata within each feature were linked: the pattern of linkages, as defined from ceramic cross-mends, was later used to define discrete depositional units within each feature. MNV's for glass vessels were determined by counting the number of vessel bases in each assemblage rather than cross-mending sherds. Following the work of Beidleman *et al.* (1983) and Klein and Garrow (1984), ceramic and glass vessel forms were sorted into the following categories:

Ceramic Vessels	*Glass Vessels*
Food service	Wine/spirit
Food preparation	Culinary/condiment
Decorative	Tumbler
Hygiene	Glassware
Toy	Soda/mineral water
Beer bottles	Pharmaceutical
Miscellaneous	Personal
Unknown	Miscellaneous
	Unknown

All datable artifacts were used in order to define features and deposit chronology. For ceramics, mean ceramic dates (MCD's) were used in addition to maker's marks. Generally, ceramic wares and types were used for computation of MCD's, but tighter date ranges were occasionally available if the variety were known, such as a particular transfer print pattern. Dating of glass artifacts was based on technological attributes (mold seams, type of finish, type of base and pontil, etc.) as well as various embossments used by known bottlers and druggists.

An important principle used in the dating of deposits was the *terminus post quem* (TPQ). This refers to the earliest possible date of deposition for a particular provenience, based on the beginning date of manufacture for the glass, ceramics, and other artifacts (Noel-Hume 1969). Comparison of deposit dates based on TPQ's versus MCD's produced a better understanding of the depositional processes.

Examination of the level of vessel completeness provided a method to determine whether a deposit originated directly from a household, came from sweepings from within the house, or was derived from existing trash deposits within a yard. This was accomplished by measurement of the percentage of completeness for the ceramic vessels within each deposit's assemblage. Level of completeness was subjectively assigned to one of four percentage of completeness categories: 0 percent to 25 percent, 26 percent to 50 percent, 51 percent to 75 percent, and 76 percent to 100 percent. Then, by computation of a weighted average, an overall vessel completeness index that ranged from 20 to 100 was derived. This index was used to discriminate deposits with nearly whole vessels from deposits with very fragmentary vessels.

Upon completion of the analyses of deposit soil matrices, ceramic cross-mend analysis, dating, and vessel completeness, depositional units were defined that could be linked with historically documented household occupations. In some cases, the preliminary analyses served to discriminate displaced fills from secondary household refuse deposits. In other instances, two or more distinct deposits were identified within the same privy, deposits that could be linked either to successive households on the lot, or to particular occupational periods by the same household.

Economic value analysis of the depositional units was accomplished by application of Miller's (1980) ceramic economic scaling index, as well as analysis of the relative value of the faunal assemblages, which will be discussed later. Miller's scale is based on the index value of certain types of refined wares, expressed in relation to, CC or cream-colored wares, with separate index values computed for cups, plates, and bowls. To facilitate comparison of assemblages, mean index value was computed from the sum of the individual cup, plate, and bowl indices divided by the total number of vessels.

Though very useful, the ceramic value data presented by Miller are often not complete. For example, there is a lack of data for certain years and for various plate sizes, and there is no data for Chinese export porcelain vessels, therefore it was necessary to estimate or extrapolate values for these vessels. Porcelain is a particularly difficult problem area. The majority of the porcelain vessels recovered in this projects were Cantonese export wares, and it was assumed that they were as expensive as the lowest-valued European porcelain published by Miller.

Table 1. Rank Values of Mammal Skeletal Elements

1. Short loin, T-bone, porterhouse	Lumbar vertebrae
2. Sirloin, rib roast	Illium, sacrum, 7–13 thoracic vertebrae, 6–12 ribs proximal
3. Top round, bottom round, sirloin tip, ham, leg of lamb	Distal femoral shaft
4. Rump pot roast	Proximal femoral head, ishium, coccygeal vertebrae
5. Chuck blade, chuck rib, shoulder roast	1–6 thoracic vertebrae, scapula, first five ribs
6. Arm, picnic ham	Distal humerus, 6–12 rib, cut midsection
7. Flank, short plate, brisket	6–12 rib distal end, 3–5 ribs distal end
8. Neck	Cervical vertebrae, atlas, axis
9. Hindshank, foreshank	Tibia/fibula, ulna radius
10. Butchering waste	Manus, pes, cranium, teeth

A number of specialized analyses were undertaken for the floral and faunal assemblages, not only to provide information on overall dietary patterns, but to assist in analysis of household consumer behavior. In general, the privy deposits were characterized by excellent floral and faunal preservation, and provided extremely rich and varied assemblages. In the analysis of dietary patterns, both macro materials (those recovered during excavation) and micro materials (those recovered from flotation sample processing) were considered as complementary components.

Analysis of the relative economic value of the dietary assemblages was accomplished by a ranking of the mammalian skeletal elements of each household assemblage. Because of differences in flavor, tenderness, and nutritional value, various parts of an animal carcass are more highly valued than others. Despite different nineteenth century cooking practices, it is assumed that cultural attitudes concerning these factors have remained somewhat constant. The ranking model used in this analysis incorporates a ranking of "New York" or "Eastern" style butchering practices (Bull 1951), and each identifiable domesticate mammalian element was assigned a value ranking from 1 through 10, according to the classification shown in Table 1. Elements were then consolidated into high (ranks 1, 2, and 3), medium (ranks 4, 5, and 6) and low (ranks 7, 8, and 9) for comparison. Butchering waste (rank 10) was tabulated to determine which species were butchered on site, but was excluded from comparison of dietary assemblage values, with the exception of pig head and foot elements, which were considered dietary elements.

RESULTS

Preliminary analyses defined ten depositional units within the Block 1101 project area that were suitable for analysis of consumer behavior. Of these, eight could be linked to specific households identified in the documentary study. For comparitive purposes, available data from four households in the Wilmington Boulevard Archaeological Project area (Klein and Garrow 1984), three from Alexandria, Virginia (Shephard 1985), and one from the Washington, D.C., Civic Center site (Garrow 1982) were included in some of the analyses. The characteristics of the principal households used in this study are given in Table 2.

All households dating from the early nineteenth century (c. 1800 to 1840) may be classified as upper or upper-middle class. Only one of the Block 1101 households is included in this group, that of John Richardson. Richardson's occupation is not known, however, documentary sources indicate that he was a large land owner in Wilmington and the surrounding county, and that he was a member of a politically prominent family. Deposits dating to the mid- to late nineteenth century (c. 1840 to 1880) are much better represented and include households headed by small business proprietors, skilled tradesmen, and laborers. All of these households may be described as middle or lower class.

Table 2. Characterization of Household Deposits Identified in the Christina Gateway Archaeological Project, Block 1101, Wilmington, Delaware

Household name	Date	Occupation of head of household	Class	Size of household
John Richardson	1810–1816 (?)	Unknown[a]	Upper	?
Jamison–Lansdale	1850–1856 (?)	Painter	Middle	9
James Murdick, Sr.	1850–1860	Livery stable owner	Middle	10
James Murdick, Jr.[b]	1860–1870 1870–1880	Master painter	Middle	9
Mt. Vernon Hotel and owner's household (Christian Krauch)	1850–1870	Hotel keeper and brewer	Middle	7
William Alsentzer household and saloon	1870–1900	Saloon keeper	Middle	10
304–306 King St. households	1880–1900	Shopkeepers, commission merchants, grocers, boarding house keepers	Middle	Variable
Dr. Nicholas Way[c]	c. 1790–1800	Physician	Upper	?
Retail shop[c]	c. 1800–1820s	Shopkeeper	Middle	?
Joseph Dowdall[c] bottling works—domestic deposit	1840s–1850s	Owner or manager of bottling works	Middle	?
Laborer household[c]	1850s	Laborer, blue collar	Lower	?
Laborer household[c]	1860s	Laborer, blue collar	Lower	?
D.C. Civic Center D1 deposit[d]	1840s–1850s	Unknown	Middle (?)	?

[a]John Richardson owned many properties in Wilmington and the surrounding county. He appears to have been wealthy.
[b]Two distinct household deposits have been identified for the Murdick, Jr., household.
[c]Deposit identified in Wilmington Boulevard project (Klein and Garrow 1984).
[d]Deposit identified in the Washington, D.C., Civic Center site (Garrow 1982).

Documentary information for the Block 1101 sample lots showed that land uses through the nineteenth century were primarily residential, with some mixed residential and commercial properties and one industrial property. After 1840, some of the owners appear to have used the properties for both residential and commercial uses. The same overall pattern of development has also been observed in the Wilmington Boulevard project area (Klein and Garrow 1984). In the period prior to 1810, the city's commercial core area contained predominantly upper-middle-class and upper-class households. Subsequent occupants of the area were predominantly small business proprietors.

Composition of the mid-nineteenth-century households in the sample from Wilmington's Block 1101 tended to be complex, and the augmented nuclear family household was the most common form. Census records were sufficiently detailed in 1840, 1850, and 1860 to permit analysis of the composition of the households under investigation. During this twenty-year period, Wilmington's population expanded from 7,000 to 31,000 (Hoffecker 1974), and the mean household size in the Block 1101 sample increased slightly from 6.2 to 7.4 persons per household. While data are less detailed for 1840 than for 1850 and 1860, it appears that the increase in household size was achieved more by the taking in of boarders than by an increase in family size. Only 5 of the 16 sample households in the 1840 sample reported more than one wage earner, while this proportion increased to 9 of 18 households in the 1860 sample and 13 of 21 households in the 1860 sample.

The majority of households in the Block 1101 study area appear to have supplemented the income of the head of household. Keeping of lodgers appears to have been the preferred alternative, although some families included more than one wage earner. It should be noted, however, that none of the secondary family workers were children (i.e., under age fifteen) and, thus, multiple wage earners appear to have been associated with extended families. Comparison of the mean household sizes for owner heads of household versus tenant heads of household shows that slightly larger households were associated with owner heads of household than with tenant heads of household (Figure 2). This suggests that ownership of the home was at least partially supported by the taking in or boarders.

Examination of the age profiles of the boarders and heads of household shows a close articulation of the life cycle to these two household statuses. The mean age of the total population declined slightly during the mid-nineteenth century, from 25.6 in 1840 to 24.6 in 1850 to 22.4 in 1860. Age of the head of household was available for 1850 and 1850; in both samples, the householders were substantially older (46.3 in 1850 and 41.0 in 1860). Boarders were substantially younger than the householders, with a mean age of 24.6 in 1850 and 21.5 in 1860. While there appears to be a linkage between household composition and home ownership, the household life cycle may also influence home ownership, as the departure of children from the household may allow room for additional boarders.

Examination of the relationship between household composition and consumption patterns was accomplished by application of artifact pattern analy-

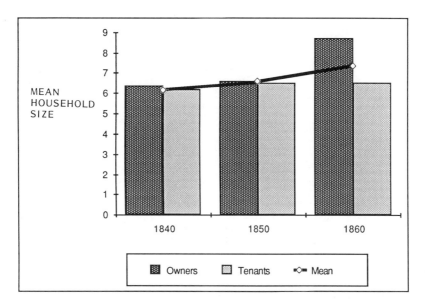

Figure 2. Comparison of mean household size for owner heads of household versus tenant heads of household, 1840–1860, Wilmington Block 1101 households. (Source: Louis Berger & Associates, 1985.)

sis to the household deposits, focusing primarily on the Kitchen Group and Architecture Group artifacts. First, the relative representation of the Kitchen Group and Architecture Group artifacts was examined through a series of regression analyses. Throughout the nineteenth century, a sharp reduction in the Kitchen Group is seen, while the Architecture Group artifacts doubled from 1800 to 1880, with some particularly high values after 1840 (Figures 3 and 4). This is the period when the number of boarders in the study households expanded, and the observed trend may be due to an increase in building construction, renovation, and remodeling to accommodate the larger number of boarders.

Intensive building activity has also been identified in Alexandria, Virginia, post-1860. Cressey *et al.* (1984) maintain that this reflects repair of older houses in the city's commercial core for continued use by the upper-middle class. Unlike Wilmington, the upper-middle class in Alexandria had not migrated from the central core in the early nineteenth century. The intraurban migration in Wilmington coincides with the city's early nineteenth-century industrialization. Alexandria, on the other hand, remained a mercantile city much longer and retained its earlier settlement pattern.

Examination of the proportion of ceramics and bottle glass within the Kitchen Group shows that, in general, bottle glass is more frequent than ceramics in deposits dating after 1870, while in earlier assemblages the ratio of bottle glass and ceramics is reversed (Figure 5). At the Washington, D.C., Civic Center site, the observed increase in bottle glass was attributed to im-

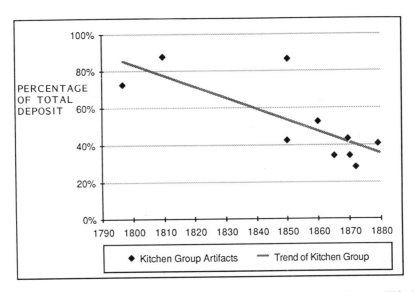

Figure 3. Representation of Kitchen Group artifacts in household deposits. (Source: Wilmington Block 1101 household deposits.)

proved bottle manufacturing technology and lower bottle cost that occurred as the nineteenth century proceeded (Garrow 1982:185–186), but the relatively low correlation coefficients obtained from the Block 1101 deposits indicate that improved bottle manufacturing technology can explain little of the observed variation.

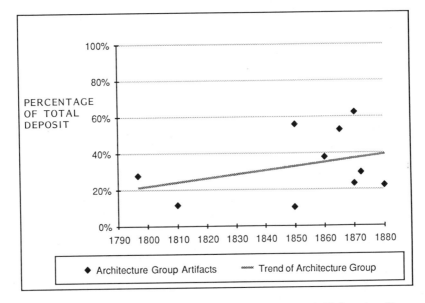

Figure 4. Representation of Architecture Group artifacts in household deposits. (Source: Wilmington Block 1101 household deposits.)

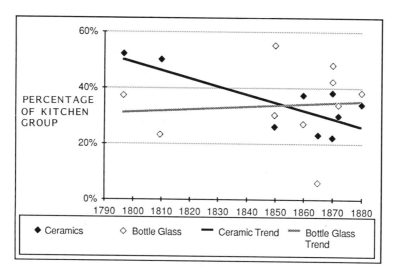

Figure 5. Representation of ceramics and bottle glass in the Kitchen Group. (Source: Wilmington Block 1101 household deposits. Note: One deposit with a TPQ=1850 has equivalent percentages of bottle glass and ceramics in the Kitchen Group.)

The three deposits associated with the Murdick family provide an opportunity to examine the influence of the household developmental cycle and composition on consumer behavior. The three Murdick household deposits were recovered from a single privy at 108 East Fourth Street. The earliest Murdick household deposit is associated with a period when the household was headed by James Murdick, Sr. In the 1840 census, the household consisted of one white man between age 50 and 60, three white men between age 20 and 50, two white women between age 13 and 30, and two free black men between age 10 and 36. At the time of the 1850 enumeration, the household was still headed by James Murdick, Sr. (age 56), and included his son James Murdick, Jr. (age 37), his daughter-in-law Sara (age 40), two granddaughters Mary and Martha aged 17 and 8, four boarders, and a Thomas Murdick (age 48), who is presumed to be a family relative. By 1860, Murdick, Sr., boarded with a neighboring family, and the 108 East Fourth Street household was headed by James Murdick, Jr. The Murdick, Jr., household included his wife Sara, his daughters Mary and Martha, four boarders, and William Murdick, who is presumed to be a relative.

The earliest deposit associated with the Murdick family dates to the 1850s and is associated with a mature phase of the Murdick, Sr., household. The household included ten members and included both the Murdick, Sr., and Murdick, Jr., nuclear families, as well as other wage earners. The second Murdick household deposit dates to the 1860s, a period relatively soon after the departure of Murdick, Sr., when the household included nine members and was headed by James Murdick, Jr. The most recent Murdick family deposit dates to the 1870s, and is presumably associated with a more mature phase of the Murdick, Jr. household.

When analysis of the Kitchen Group artifacts is focused on the sequence of Murdick household deposits, sharp fluctuation is seen, rather than gradual trends. In the mature stages of both the Murdick, Sr., and Murdick, Jr., households, the Kitchen Group contains roughly twice as much bottle glass as ceramics, while this ratio is reversed in the deposit associated with the early stages of the Murdick, Jr., household (Figure 6). This shows that household consumption patterns may be quite variable over time within the same household. Further, this pattern indicates that the Murdick, Jr., household was more conservative in the disposal of bottle glass during the early stage of the household life cycle, leading to the suggestion that they may have reused rather than discarded their glass bottles during this period. An alternate scenario is that the household purchased a lower frequency of bottled goods during the 1860s.

Eight deposits from Block 1101 were selected for comparison of vessel forms, and a total of 1,307 vessels were placed in the various functional categories. The most common vessel form was the food service vessel. Together, food service and food preparation–storage vessels comprise a majority of the ceramic vessels in each of the Block 1101 deposits, a finding that is consistent with the domestic nature of the occupations that produced the deposits. Forms for which at least 50 vessels were identified include food service, wine/spirit, tumblers, glassware, pharmaceuticals, miscellaneous ceramics, miscellaneous glassware, and unknown ceramics. A coefficient of variation was computed for these forms, dividing the standard deviation by the mean percentage occurrence per deposit; the results indicate that, for known vessel forms, wine/spirit bottles exhibit the greatest variability among household deposits. The observed variation in the representation of wine bottles led to the hypothesis

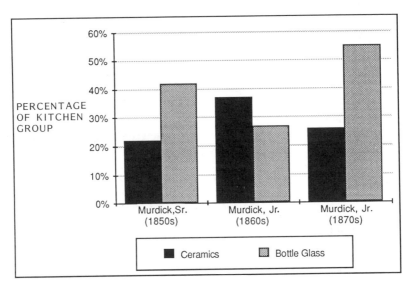

Figure 6. Representation of ceramics and bottle glass in the Kitchen Group, Murdick household deposits.

that wine consumption might be related to household economic position, income strategy, or life cycle. However, the Block 1101 data do not fully support
these expectations, as the two deposits with the greatest proportion of wine
bottles are associated with the Murdick, Sr., and Jamison–Lansdale deposits,
both of which have been assigned to the middle class. The only upper-class
household assemblage examined, that of John Richardson, had the fourth
highest (of eight deposits) percentage of wine/spirit bottles.

The deposits assigned to the Jamison–Lansdale household represent the
domestic component of the mixed industrial-residential occupation at the corner of French and Third Streets in the mid-nineteenth century. Alexander
Jamison, a carriage manufacturer, acquired the property in 1840, and a carriage works at this location is indicated by the available city directories and
the federal census of industries. Recovered materials clearly indicate a domestic occupation assigned to a Mr. Lansdale, who is listed in the 1850 population
schedule and who may have rented the property from Jamison. Lansdale's
household included his wife and seven boarders, but no children. The presence
of multiple wage earners and the lack of children in the Lansdale household
may have elevated the overall household income and permitted a higher level
of discretionary expenditures, and this may be reflected in relatively high
wine consumption.

It should be noted that the greatest representation of wine/spirit bottles
among the three Murdick household deposits is associated with the Murdick,
Sr., household (Figure 7). It was expected that the representation of pharmaceutical vessels might vary according to household life cycle, as modern
studies of consumer behavior have shown that households that include elderly

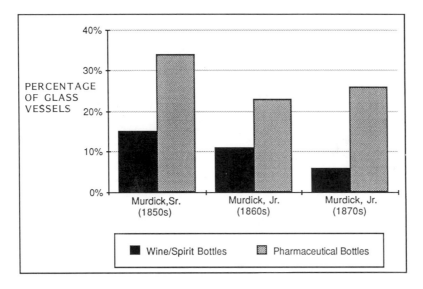

Figure 7. Representation of wine/spirit bottles and pharmaceutical bottles in Murdick household
deposits.

persons or young children are the heaviest buyers of medicines. Again, the
Murdick family provides the only opportunity to test this assumption, since
they represent the only household for which temporally stratified deposits are
available. The greatest representation of pharmaceutical bottles is found in
the deposit associated with the earliest Murdick household, a household that
included elder James Murdick, Sr. (age 56 in 1850) and his granddaughter
Martha (age 8 in 1850). The representation of pharmaceutical bottles declined
during the early Murdick, Jr., household, then rose slightly during the mature
stage of that household (Figure 7).

The economic value of the ceramic assemblages was examined by application of Miller's (1980) ceramic economic index. Figure 8 portrays graphically
the mean index value of the assemblages and the MCD for each deposit. To
expand this important analysis and provide a larger comparative context,
deposits reported by Shephard (1985), Miller (1980), and Garrow (1982) were
included. The results of the Miller analysis differed from what would be expected, given the historical documentation on the households. The position of
the John Richardson household is, as expected, quite high, and this mostly is
attributable to the inclusion of Chinese export porcelain in that assemblage.

Interesting results were also obtained from the Murdick household deposits. The sample size for the Murdick, Sr., deposit was too small for ceramic
economic scaling. The two Murdick, Jr., household deposits have dramatically
different economic values. The earlier deposit, dating to the 1860s, has a much
lower economic value than the later deposit, which dates from the 1870s.

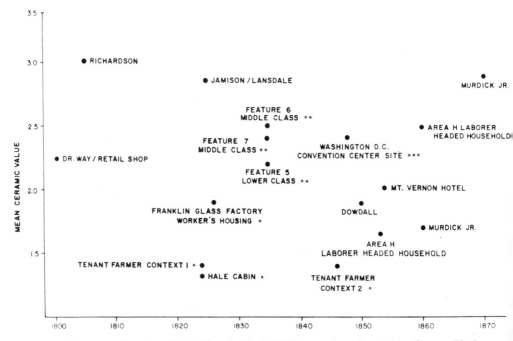

Figure 8. Mean ceramic values derived from Miller's (1980) ceramic scaling index. (Source: Block
1101 household deposits and sites from *Miller 1980; **Shephard 1985; *** Garrow 1982.)

Again, the increase in the economic value of the Murdick, Jr., ceramic assemblages may best be explained by the nature of the household life cycle. The data clearly show that the household used moderately priced ceramics during an earlier stage of household development, and as the household matured, a more expensive set of dishes was purchased. This interpretation is also consistent with the earlier suggestion that the Murdick, Jr., household exhibited different patterns of bottle glass consumption or disposal during the household's early and mature life-cycle stages. The final Murdick, Jr., deposit is at roughly the same level as the Richardson deposit, an upper-class household. This similarity between two households of different documented economic levels may be a result of the "index inflation" noted by Cheek (1984). However, if this process were constant, then the earlier deposit of Murdick, Jr., also should be higher.

The ceramic economic value of the Jamison–Lansdale assemblage was expected to have been much lower, given the assignment of that household to the middle class. The Jamison–Lansdale deposit also contained the highest proportion of wine/spirit bottles of any of the Block 1101 deposits, a fact that may be indicative of more frequent consumption of indulgent goods (cf. Modell 1978:236–237). These findings may be clarified by examination of the composition of household to which the deposit has been assigned. Perhaps the large number of wage earners and the lack of children in the Lansdale househole permitted a level of discretionary expenditure that was considerably higher than other middle-class households with children or with fewer wage earners.

Another unexpected result of the analysis of ceramic economic values is the position of the lower-class households. The two laborer-headed households from Area H of the Wilmington Boulevard project (Klein and Garrow 1984) have strikingly different values. In this case, "index inflation" should not be a problem since the MCD's for the two deposits are only a decade apart. The lower-class households from Alexandria (Shephard 1985) fall in the middle-class range. When compared to the other households, in Figure 8, the differences between the middle-class and lower-class deposits from Alexandria seem minor. Interestingly, an earlier, city-wide study of Alexandria found no class affiliation in terms of ceramic expenditures (Cressey et al. 1982).

Analysis of the household deposits from Wilmington's Block 1101 suggests that, in addition to differences in class, ceramic consumption patterns may be linked to the household life cycle and to the household strategy. Other researchers have demonstrated that several factors influence the measurable economic scaling in a household and, ultimately, in the archaeological record. Changes in ceramic market prices affect the resulting indices, as does the level of access to transportation networks (Cheek 1984; Miller and Hurry 1983; Shephard 1985). Work by Henry et al. (1984) in Phoenix also suggests that the developmental cycle of a household may have an affect on ceramic economic indices. Wise (1985) has shown, following the work of Schiffer et al. (1981), that reuse of secondhand ceramics may lead to a misinterpretation of the Miller indices. Clearly, there is a relationship between the market value of the ceramics in a household deposit, as measured by the Miller index, and the class or status of the household, when measured in terms of occupation of head of household or income level. But this relationship does not appear to be strong enough for the ceramic market value to be used as a proxy or predictor for class or status.

The faunal assemblages were also examined relative to the economic position of the households as predicted from the historical record. It was hypothesized that households of higher economic standing disposed of bone elements of high relative value. The results of the comparison of the deposits are presented in Table 3. The three Murdick household deposits contained statistically equivalent portions of high-quality meat, indicating that the Murdick family used high-quality meats with about the same frequency throughout their occupation. Overall, the Richardson household contains the highest proportion of high-quality meat, a finding consistent with their placement in the upper class. The Richardson deposit contains significantly more high-quality meat than most of the Block 1101 middle-class households, including the Jamison–Lansdale household, but there is no statistically significant difference between the Richardson deposit and the three Murdick deposits. This similarity between the Richardson and Murdick household deposits was unex-

Table 3. Results of Z Scores on Proportion of High-Ranked Bone Elements within Wilmington Block 1101 Households

Household 1[a]	Household 2[a]	Z score[b]	H_0[c]	H_1[c]
Richardson	Murdick, Sr.	1.52	X	
Richardson	Murdick, Jr. (1870s)	.35	X	
Richardson	Murdick, Jr. (1860s)	.36	X	
Richardson	304/306 King St. households	4.28		X
Richardson	Alsentzer saloon	3.50		X
Richardson	Mt. Vernon hotel	4.37		X
Richardson	Jamison–Lansdale	2.11		X
Jamison–Lansdale	Murdick, Sr.	.43	X	
Jamison–Lansdale	Murdick, Jr. (1870s)	1.23	X	
Jamison–Lansdale	Murdick, Jr. (1860s)	1.50	X	
Jamison–Lansdale	304/306 King St. households	1.83	X	
Jamison–Lansdale	Alsentzer saloon	2.00		X
Jamison–Lansdale	Mt. Vernon hotel	2.66		X
Murdick, Sr.	Alsentzer saloon	.75	X	
Murdick, Sr.	Mt. Vernon hotel	.75	X	
Murdick, Jr. (TPQ = 1870)	Alsentzer saloon	2.90		X
Murdick, Jr. (TPQ = 1860)	Alsentzer saloon	3.08		X
Murdick, Jr. (TPQ = 1870)	Mt. Vernon hotel	3.55		X
Murdick, Jr. (TPQ = 1860)	Mt. Vernon hotel	3.36		X

[a]Number of high-ranked elements in total assemblage: Richardson (24/49); Jamison–Lansdale (13/44); Murdick, Sr. (2/9); Murdick, Jr. (1860s 7/14); Murdick, Jr. (1870s, 10/22); Alsentzer saloon (5/37); Mt. Vernon hotel (11/80); 304–306 King St. households (22/116).
[b]Level of Significance for a two-tailed test = 0.05; Z score = 1.96.
[c]H_0: No difference in proportions of high-ranked bone elements between the two households. H_1: Differences in proportion of high-ranked bone elements between the two households.

pected since the Richardson household appears to have been in a higher socioeconomic class, but it may be explained by the Murdick household's income strategy. The taking in of boarders in the Murdick household may have increased the household's per capita income and its overall purchasing power.

CONCLUSION

This examination of Wilmington's Block 1101 has demonstrated the viability of the household as a unit for interdisciplinary research. Archaeological deposits can be assigned to specific household occupations, and research tools are available to discern various stages of the household life cycle. The small number of households included in this study and the lack of comparable information for each household have prevented a systematic examination of the three research hypotheses posited earlier. Notwithstanding a limited data base, however, this study has demonstrated that consumer behavior is related to household composition, life cycle, and income strategy. The study findings suggest that the addition of secondary wage earners to the household may increase overall household income, thereby permitting a higher level of expenditure for dietary elements, basic household goods, and certain classes of discretionary expenditures. The study has also demonstrated that consumer behavior varies according to the household life cycle, particularly with regard to the level of consumption–discard of certain classes of goods as well as the level of expenditure for basic household items. The results of this study suggest that the life-cycle factors that appear to have had the most significant influence on consumer behavior are the presence and ages of children and the presence of elderly or retired persons in the household. The study findings also suggest that home ownership may be related to both the household life cycle and the presence of secondary wage earners in the household. The classification of households as upper, middle, or lower class appears to have limited utility for the prediction of consumer behavior. Rather than distinctive consumption patterns associated with upper-, middle-, and lower-class households, this study has identified broad variations in the consumption patterns of households assigned to these classes, particularly the middle and lower classes.

While this study has produced results similar to those found in previous studies of downtown Wilmington and in other cities, the historical and archaeological analysis of the Block 1101 households has enhanced the current understanding of the consumer behavior of nineteenth-century urban households. The variability in the consumer behavior of lower- and middle-class households examined in this study seems to be more related to the income strategy, developmental stage, and composition of these households. In future studies of consumer behavior, it is suggested that, rather than simply identifying the occupation of the head of household, the character of the household and its consumer behavior should be examined relative to overall household composition, life cycle, and income strategy. This will require more detailed historical research at the household levels as well as analysis of archaeological assemblages that can be associated with relatively short occupation intervals.

The household is the basic economic entity through which individuals are linked to the economic processes of society as a whole. Clearly, more comprehensive analyses of household consumer behavior are necessary to understand the processes by which historic populations have adapted to urban life.

REFERENCES

Beidleman, D. Katherine, Davidson, T. E., Napoli, R., Wheeler, R., and Weiss, P., 1983, Creating a Data Base: The City's Test Square, in: *Approaches to Preserving a City's Past,* Alexandria Urban Archaeology Program, City of Alexandria, Virginia.

Bull, Slater T., 1951, *Meat for the Table,* McGraw-Hill, New York.

Cheek, Charles D., 1984, The Influence of Market Forces on Miller's Ceramic Index, paper presented at the annual meeting of the Eastern States Archaeological Federation, Annapolis, Maryland.

Cressey, Pamela J., Stephens, John F., Shephard, Steven J., and Magid, Barbara H., 1982, The Core/Periphery Relationship and the Archaeological Record in Alexandria, Virginia, in: *Archaeology in Urban America: A Search for Pattern and Process* (Roy S. Dickens, ed.), Academic Press, New York, pp. 143–174.

Cressey, Pamela J., Magid, Barbara H., and Shephard, Steven J., 1984, *Urban Development in North America: Status, Distance, and Material Differences in Alexandria, Virginia,* Office of Historic Alexandria, City of Alexandria, Virginia.

Garrow, Patrick H. (ed.), 1982, Archaeological Investigations on the Washington, D.C., Civic Center Site, report submitted to the Department of Housing and Community Development, District of Columbia, by Soil Systems, Marietta, Georgia.

Glasco, Laurence, 1977, The Life Cycles and Household Structure of American Ethnic Groups: Irish, Germans and Native-Born Whites in Buffalo, New York, 1855, in: *Family and Kin in Urban Communities, 1700–1930* (Tamara K. Hareven, ed.), New Viewpoints, New York, pp. 122–143.

Glasco, Laurence, 1978, Migration and Adjustment in the Nineteenth Century City: Occupation, Property, and Household Structure of Native-Born Whites, Buffalo, New York, 1855, in: *Family and Population in Nineteenth-Century America* (Tamara K. Hareven and Maris Vinovskis, eds.), Princeton University Press, Princeton, New Jersey, pp. 154–178.

Goldin, Claudia, 1979, Households and Market Production of Families in a Late Nineteenth-Century American City, *Explorations in Economic History* 16:111–131.

Goldschmidt, Walter, 1971, *Exploring the Ways of Mankind,* Holt, Rinehart & Winston, New York.

Goody, J. (ed.), 1971, *The Developmental Cycle in Domestic Groups,* Cambridge University Press, New York.

Henry, Susan L., Ritz, Frank, and Hoffman, Kathleen, 1984, Historical Archaeology of an Urban Neighborhood, Part II, in: City of Phoenix: Archaeology of the Murphy Addition (John S. Cable, Susan L. Henry, and David E. Doyel, eds.), report submitted to the City of Phoenix by Soil Systems, Phoenix, Arizona.

Hoffecker, Carol, 1974, *Wilmington, Delaware: Portrait of an Industrial City,* University of Virginia Press, Charlottesville, Virginia.

Kassarjian, Harold H., and Robertson, Thomas S., 1973, Social Class in: *Perspectives in Consumer Behavior* (rev. ed., Harold H. Kassarjian and Thomas S. Robertson, eds.), Scott, Foresman & Co., Glenview, Illinois, pp. 390–400.

Keesing, Roger M., and Keesing, Felix M., 1971, *New Perspectives in Cultural Anthropology,* Holt, Rinehart & Winston, New York.

Klein, Terry, and Garrow, Patrick H. (eds.), 1984, *Final Archaeological Investigation at the*

Wilmington Boulevard Monroe Street to King Street, Wilmington, New Castle County, Delaware, (DELDOT Archaeology Series, Number 29), Delaware Department of Transportation, Dover.

Linton, Ralph, 1936, *The Study of Man: An Introduction,* D. Appleton-Century-Crofts, New York.

Louis Berger & Associates, 1985, Nineteenth Century Wilmington Households: The Christina Gateway Project, report submitted to the City of Wilmington, Delaware, by the Cultural Resource Group, Louis Berger & Associates, East Orange, New Jersey.

Martineau, Pierre, 1958, Social Classes and Spending Behavior, *Journal of Marketing* 23:121–130.

Miller, George L., 1980, Classification and Economic Scaling of 19th Century Ceramics, *Historical Archaeology* 14:1–40.

Miller, George L., and Hurry, Silas D., 1983, Ceramic Supply in an Economically Isolated Frontier Community, Portage County of the Ohio Western Reserve, 1800–1825, *Historical Archaeology* 17:80–92.

Modell, John, 1978, Patterns of Consumption, Acculturation, and Family Income Strategies in Late Nineteenth-Century America, in: *Family and Population in Nineteenth-Century America* (Tamara K. Hareven and Maris Vinovskis, eds.), Princeton University Press, Princeton, New Jersey, pp. 206–242.

Modell, John, and Hareven, Tamara K., 1977, Urbanization and the Malleable Household: An Examination of Boarding and Lodging in American Families, in: *Family and Kin in Urban Communities, 1700–1930* (Tamara K. Hareven, ed.), New Viewpoints, New York, pp. 164–186.

Murdock, George P., 1949, *Social Structure,* Free Press, New York.

Netting, Robert McC., 1982, Some Home Truths on Household Size and Wealth, in: Archaeology of the Household: Building a Prehistory of Domestic Life (Richard R. Wilk and William D. Rathje, eds.), *American Behavioral Scientist* 25:641–662.

Noel-Hume, Ivor, 1969, *Historical Archaeology,* Aflred A. Knopf, New York.

Otto, John S., 1977, Artifacts and Status Differences—A Comparison of Ceramics from Planter, Overseer, and Slave Sites on an Antebellum Plantation, in: *Research Strategies in Historical Archaeology* (Stanley South, ed.), Academic Press, New York, pp. 91–118.

Otto, John S., 1984, *Cannon's Point Plantation, 1794–1860: Living Conditions and Status Patterns in the Old South,* Academic Press, New York.

Schiffer, Michael B., 1972, Archaeological Context and Systemic Context, *American Antiquity* 37:156–165.

Schiffer, Michael B., 1983, Toward the Identification of Formation Processes, *American Antiquity* 48:675–706.

Schiffer, Michael B., Downing, Theodore, E., and McCarthy, Michael, 1981, Waste Not, Want Not: An Ethnoarchaeological Study of Reuse in Tucson, Arizona, in: *Modern Material Culture: The Archaeology of Us* (Richard A. Gould and Michael B. Schiffer, eds.), Academic Press, New York, pp. 67–86.

Shephard, Steven J., 1985, Status Variation in Antebellum Alexandria: An Archaeological Study of Ceramic Tableware, paper presented at the Annual Meeting of the Society for Historical Archaeology, Boston.

South, Stanley, 1977, *Method and Theory in Historical Archaeology,* Academic Press, New York.

Warner, W. Lloyd, with Meeker, M., and Fells, K., 1960, *Social Class in America,* Harper & Row, New York.

Wells, William D., and Gubar, George, 1970, Life Cycle Concept in Marketing Research, in: *Research in Consumer Behavior* (David T. Kollat, Roger D. Blackwell, and James F. Engel, eds.), Holt, Rinehard & Winston, New York, pp. 512–527.

Wilk, Richard R., and Rathje, William D., 1982, Household Archaeology, in: Archaeology of the Household: Building a Prehistory of Domestic Life (Richard R. Wilk and William D. Rathje, eds.), *American Behavioral Scientist* 25:617–640.

Wise, Cara L., 1985, A Tale of Two Privies: Sources of Variability in Working-Class Assemblages, paper presented at the Annual Meeting of the Society for Historical Archaeology, Boston.

12

Adapting to Factory and City

Illustrations from the Industrialization and Urbanization of Paterson, New Jersey

LU ANN DE CUNZO

Introduction

Understanding the cultural history of the United States requires understanding industrialization and urbanization, two processes central to the nation's development. This chapter presents an approach to the investigation of these two phenomena and their impact on the evolution of American culture in the nineteenth century. Specifically, the model deals with the adaptive choices made by individuals, households, and larger social groups in response to an industrializing and urbanizing environment, and the extent and ways economic status influenced these choices.

Industrialization in America, along with the urbanization it promoted, reshaped the physical environment and caused changes in the social and economic structure (Hirsch 1978:xiii). The theories, data sources, and methods of analysis of historical archaeologists are appropriate to the study of these two fundamental elements of the American historical experience, as this study shall illustrate. Methods developed by anthropologically oriented historical archaeologists have made it possible to approach the problem from the perspective of household adaptations to the changes wrought by industrialization and urbanization. Cultural adaptation implies choices—several options or responses may be available. This study is of the series, the patterns, of choices people did make, in Paterson and elsewhere. The theory of industrialization outlined below makes clear how these adaptations involved consumer choices.

Industrialization has been defined as the process of mechanization of production through the exploitation of nonhuman, natural sources of energy and power and the concomitant fragmentation of the production process into series of individual, differentiated tasks (Hirsch 1978:21–22; Klein and Garrow 1984:14; Shephard 1980:4). The process of urbanization, which in the American Northeast was linked closely to industrialization, resulted in high levels of population density, a hierarchical, bureaucratic management system

---

Lu Ann De Cunzo □ Clio Group, 3961 Baltimore Avenue, Philadelphia, PA 19104.

to distribute information, goods, and services and to collect revenues to support its activities, and a population which was socially, economically, and ethnically (in nineteenth-century cities in the American Northeast) diverse (Rothschild and Rockman 1982:8–12; Shephard 1980:3).

Theoretical Orientation

At the theoretical base of this study is the concept of culture—defined as "an organized, integrated system" (White 1949:364) composed of interrelated and interdependent subsystems—specifically: (1) the technological—modes of production and reproduction; (2) the sociological—domestic and political economies; and (3) the ideological—superstructure subsystems (Harris 1979:51–53; White 1949:364). Further, in this theory of culture, because of the interrelationships among the subsystems, change in one subsystem produces, through a cycle of positive feedback, changes in the other subsystems. The three subsystems are not, however, equal, but rather exhibit a hierarchical relationship. The technological-production subsystem is considered to be primary; it determines the form and content of the sociological-domestic and political economy subsystem, which in turn governs the ideological-superstructure subsystem. The feedback relationship among the subsystems means, however, that the socioeconomic subsystem may condition the production subsystem, and that both subsystems may be affected by ideologies. Influence and change are not unidirectional; they are directed (Harris 1979:55; White 1949:365–366). It is within this theoretical context that the process of industrialization—changes in the modes of production—and the responsive changes in the other subsystems, are being considered.

The process of industrialization changed the American cultural system over the course of the nineteenth century. Through identification, comparison, and analysis of individuals' and groups' responses to industrial modes of production at different times and different places, increased understanding of the evolution of the American cultural system will be achieved. This study aspires to contribute in some small way to that understanding.

Research Problem

Industrialization changed the relationship between the means of production and people, specifically the family and household (the basic social units and most fundamental decision-making units of the economy) (Goldin 1981:277). Production, formerly a function of the family–household, was removed to specialized workplaces. The result, admittedly stated somewhat simplistically here, is that the role of the family–household shifted to consumption in the industrial money economy (Hareven 1977:3; Henn 1982:5). Therefore, the study of individuals and groups adapting to urban and industrial change is a study of their consumption patterns and choices. The theory implies that consumer choices will be strongly influenced by the economic means of families–households. As a result, consumer choices, and their relationship to economic status, are focal points of this study.

Through a review of secondary historical and archaeological literature, the following variables were selected for analysis as important areas in which adaptation occurred: settlement patterns, the family and household, ethnic community formation and networking, and consumption patterns. Hypotheses that could be tested in this case study were then developed; these hypotheses state the expected adaptations in each area, their interrelationships, and the hypothesized effects on adaptive choices of economic status and the stage in the industrialization process.

Literature Review

Both archaeological and historical studies of industrialization and urbanization have contributed theoretical models, methodological approaches, and comparative data to this research. Especially significant among the historical works is the rich, varied output of the Philadelphia Social History Project. Despite its title, the project is an "experiment in collaborative, multidisciplinary and interdisciplinary research" (Hershberg 1981:v). The broad goals of the project relate directly to this study—"how the processes of urbanization and industrialization shaped both the development of the nineteenth-century metropolis and the experience of its diverse population groups—what was the dynamic and what were its effects" (Hershberg 1981:vi). Furthermore, project scholars' research has focused on the "material" aspects of the urban–industrial experience—demographic, economic, ecological, technological, and their relationships (Hershberg 1981:xii). Areas of relevance to this study that have been addressed include the relations of work, space utilization (settlement pattern), the family, and ethnic community development (Burstein 1975; Cutler and Gillette 1980; Glassberg 1979; Hershberg 1981; Hershberg and Dockhorn 1976).

In the field of family history, the work of Tamara Hareven and her colleagues has resulted in an increased understanding of the impacts of urbanization and industrialization on the structure and function of the family (Hareven 1977, 1982; Hareven and Vinovskis 1978; Rapp 1979). The perspectives of the labor historian and the student of ethnicity are also relevant to this study of urban, industrial adaptations. In the case of the former, Herbert Gutman and others have emphasized the active role of the worker in the adaptive process, and the resultant potential and importance of working-class history (Gutman 1977; Hirsch 1978). The American Studies Association's 1981 bibliography issue on ethnicity is a useful introduction to the extensive corpus of literature on ethnicity and ethnic history representing the research of historians, sociologists, anthropologists, and archaeologists (American Studies Association 1981). Of importance to this study have been discussions of group boundary maintenance and conflict theory, and their relationship to the traditional culture theory of ethnicity (American Studies Association 1981; Bell 1975; Royce 1982; Ware 1946).

Comparative archaeological study of industrialization and urbanization is hampered by the fact that many urban projects are cultural resource management projects with unpublished final reports that are difficult to access. The hypotheses (South 1977) presented and tested in this study concerning the relationship of consumption to economic level (Klein and Garrow 1984; Shephard 1980; Spencer-Wood and Riley 1981), ethnicity (Praetzellis *et al.* 1981; Schuyler 1980), and the household (Henn 1982) in an urban (Dickens 1982), industrial setting do draw on archaeological as well as historical models. They will be discussed under the heading "Hypotheses."

The subject of this case study is Paterson, New Jersey, a nineteenth-century manufacturing and urban center in northeastern New Jersey, and specifically Paterson's residential district, Dublin, which borders the city's early industrial core. A historical and archaeological research program was designed. The history program included the investigation of secondary sources on Paterson history, comparative analysis of the results of studies by other Paterson historians and archaeologists, and primary historical documentation of the study area in northern Dublin that was also investigated archaeologically. The archaeology program involved the excavation of six nineteenth-century privies, the association of the privy deposits with households, and the analysis of the assemblages to test the proposed hypotheses.

THE RESEARCH PROGRAM

The Strategy and Hypotheses

Research Strategy

The strategy for this project was devised to meet the following research goal: to identify, document, and increase our understanding of people's adaptive responses to the processes of industrialization and urbanization (and thereby our understanding of the processes themselves) through a case study of Paterson, New Jersey. The strategy was as follows:

1. Secondary literature and comparative studies from the fields of historical archaeology, anthropology, history, and allied fields were reviewed for the purposes of (a) identifying areas of the cultural system in which adaptive responses to industrialization and urbanization may be expected, and (b) identifying the expected nature, extent, and interrelationships of the adaptive responses in each area.

2. Based on the results of (1) above, and reflecting the systemic theoretical orientation, testable hypotheses were proposed, stating the expected adaptations in the areas identified.

3. Data were then gathered with which to test the hypotheses, for the city of Paterson as a whole, for three Dublin study areas investigated through primary historical documentation—Mill Street in 1900, the "Ten House Lots study area" on Mill Street, and the Cianci Street block—and for one study

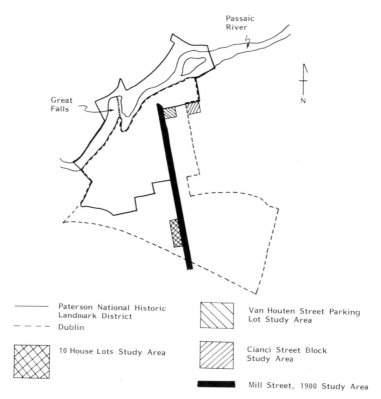

Figure 1. Paterson's historic industrial and residential districts. The city's commercial downtown and upper-class residential neighborhood is to the east of the area shown. The mills lie to the north and west of the Cianci Street and Van Houten Street study areas within the Landmark District. The four study areas are in the Dublin neighborhood. (Based on Edward Rutsch, "Salvage Archaeology Project, Paterson, N.J., 1973–1976," Volume 1, Figure 1, p. 2.)

area investigated both historically and archaeologically—the Van Houten Street Parking Lot block. These study areas were expected to yield information on the urbanization of Paterson because of their nature, location, and the date range of their occupation and use.

4. The proposed hypotheses were tested, utilizing the data gathered.

5. Conclusions were drawn, based on the confirmation and/or refutation of the hypotheses, and the pattern of adaptive responses identified.

6. The research program was evaluated, including the strategy, methods, and data sources employed, and suggestions made for future research.

Hypotheses

In an archaeological study of Sacramento, California, Praetzellis *et al.* (1981) investigated urban adaptation, specifically consumer behavior and its reflection of ethnicity and class. In order to understand consumer behavior as adaptation, they state, it is necessary to understand and control for the factors that govern the behavior—economic factors determining what goods could be acquired by individual households and at what cost; the age, sex, and composition of the family–household; occupational patterns; the nature of property and wealth holding; and ethnic background (Praetzellis *et al.* 1981:33–34). They rightly conclude that "in the absence of a detailed reconstruction of the demographic, economic, social and cultural context of . . . households being observed archaeologically," the recognition of patterns through statistical analysis of artifact assemblages "can shed little light on the manner in which consumer choices reflect the processes of ethnic boundary maintenance and other adaptive strategies" (Praetzellis *et al.* 1981:34).

In other words, information derived from documentary sources gives meaning to the artifact patterns. This does not mean, however, that archaeological data is a mere reflection of documentary data, only that the documents enrich our interpretation of the archaeological record. In this study, for example, the archaeological record has yielded data on the consumption choices of nineteenth-century Paterson residents representing several socioeconomic and ethnic groups, data unavailable from documentary sources. Indeed, increasing understanding of adaptation to industrialization and urbanization shall come only from understanding the complex pattern of relationships among documented and archaeologically analyzed aspects of adaptation.

For this study, a broad program of research into settlement patterns, the nature and composition of the families and households, residence patterns, occupation and income patterns, ethnic community formation and networks, and consumption patterns in the study areas was developed. Detailed reconstruction of the range, types, and costs of the consumer goods available in Paterson from 1830 to 1900 was beyond the means of this study, however, this issue was also addressed.

A basic assumption, or premise, of this study is that the adaptive choices made—social, economic, and consumer choices—were primarily influenced by economic considerations and by the stage in the industrialization and urbanization processes (which also determined the choices available) (Spencer-Wood and Riley 1981:40). Below, expected adaptive choices in settlement, family–household structure, organization, and function, ethnic identification and association, and consumption will be hypothesized and considered in light of the above premise.

Hypothesis 1: Settlement Patterns. The questions raised relating to settlement patterns in this industrializing, urbanizing locale are: How did people decide where to live, and what governed their choices as housing consumers? Several theories have been proposed, and several factors influenced the choices made. A recent theory, accepted by researchers of the Philadelphia Social History Project and others, states that in the initial stage of industrialization, proximity of housing to work opportunities was a fundamental organizing principle of urban, industrial land use (Greenberg 1980:162; Hershberg *et al.* 1981:128, 147; Thomas 1980:85). In this scheme, economics, the stage in the city's development, and later, social status, are primary determinants of settlement choices, while factors such as family, religion, and ethnicity influence choice on the microlevel (Greenberg 1980:162; 1981:225).

The early stage of urban, industrial settlement in nineteenth-century America was characterized by an integrated land use pattern. Manufacturing and commercial establishments were located in close proximity to residential areas, since housing and transportation were limited, and everyone needed to be within walking distance of the workplace and of sources of essential goods and services. Neither were residential neighborhoods segregated along economic, social, ethnic, or religious lines. As the city grew, it was marked by increasing diversity, services such as public transportation were improved, and land use became characterized by functional, economic, and social differentiation. Residential settlement patterns came to reflect socioeconomic stratification. Beginning with the elite, those who were economically able moved away from the central business and industrial districts to new, attractive, socially homogeneous neighborhoods and suburbs connected to the workplace by public transportation lines. The lower-class workers, who could afford neither the housing nor the transportation costs of the new districts, remained in the neighborhoods within walking distance of work opportunities (Hershberg 1981:11, 122; Hershberg et al. 1981:165; Hirsch 1978:98; Klein and Garrow 1984:13, 19–20; Thomas 1980:85). Considerations of proximity to family, ethnic, and religious solidarity influenced housing consumption choices within this broader context (Greenberg 1980:162).

Hypothesis 2: Household and Family Patterns. Before considering their adaptive patterns, it is necessary to distinguish between families and households. Households are residential, and, in industrial society, consumer units. Families are social units constructed from ideological definitions of kinship (Henn 1982:3). Often, household and family units correspond, however, certain adaptive responses to industrialization and urbanization resulted in non-familial households.

Family historians studying family adaptive strategies in urban, industrial contexts believe the family functioned as a corporate economic unit, planning income, expenditures (consumption), and labor force strategies. Michael Anderson considers family relations, especially in the working class, to have been based on economic reciprocity. Parents supported their young children with the expectation they would later contribute to the family income, and ultimately, to the support of the parents (Hareven and Vinovskis 1978:19–20). These and other adaptive strategies to be discussed below were employed because male working-class adults often did not earn sufficient wages to support a family. Families' responses, influenced by employment opportunities, ethnic background, and the stage of the life cycle, included the employment of unmarried children, boarding, and the reduction of expenditures (Glassberg 1979:49, 55).

A major sign of, and response to, inadequate household heads' wages, which shall be an expected adaptive choice in Paterson, is a marriage age in the latter twenties and the employment of unmarried adult children living at home. Other urban researchers have found that sons worked more often than daughters, the elder siblings more often than younger ones, and the children of immigrants more often than the children of native-born parents. Child employment benefited parents still supporting young children, and young workers not yet earning sufficient wages to support themselves (Glasco 1977:124–139; Goldin 1981:284–285, 289–292, 304; Haines 1981:244, 266; Modell 1978:217–222).

Another response which is expected, especially in families with children either too young to work or already married and independent, is boarding. Kin and nonkin, usually single working males, were boarded. Young immigrants from foreign countries and rural American communities comprised a major portion of urban boarders. The experience provided such boarders with a family of "re-orientation" and thereby assisted them in adapting to their new environment and meeting their domestic needs, while providing necessary additional income to the boarding family (Glasco 1977:124–139; Hareven 1982:164).

The third adaptive response of low-income urban families, moderation of consumption, shall be discussed in Hypothesis 4.

Hypothesis 3: Ethnicity. Current theories regard ethnic networking as an adaptive strategy. For immigrants arriving in industrializing, nineteenth-century American cities, ethnicity aided adaptation in two significant ways; it provided the comfort of familiar traditions, values, and social ties in an alien environment, and it offered the strength of group solidarity and organization against the economic conflict and prejudice immigrants faced as competing sources of labor. Ethnicity consists, therefore, of *boundary*-maintaining symbols of identity, and traditional cultural *content* (Royce 1982:7, 26).

In one approach, the development of ethnic consciousness is closely linked to the processes of urban growth and differentiation discussed above. During the early stage of urban settlement, in the absence of social distancing based on spatial segregation, behavioral and material symbols are utilized and manipulated to maintain group identity. As a politicoeconomic adaptive strategy, however, ethnicity functions today in America's postindustrial cities as it did in the nineteenth century. Native discrimination against immigrants, who are considered an economic threat in the labor market, continues to serve as oppositional support of ethnic cohesion (Praetzellis *et al.* 1981:31–32). For the immigrants, the ethnic group provides political leverage to combat discrimination and low wages (Laurie *et al.* 1981:109), as well as providing socioeconomic support for needy group members through the creation of mutual aid societies (Cotz *et al.* 1980:125).

Herbert Gutman and others also see ethnicity as adaptation, however, not out of conflict for resources, but rather as the retention of the familiar and traditional in light of the immigrant's uprooting and introduction to an alien social and cultural environment. Traditions, modes of thought, family and social ties, work behavioral patterns—ethnic cultural content—were tenaciously clung to during the period of industrialization in America (Cotz *et al.* 1980:108–110; Gutman 1977:41, 70, 84; Hareven 1977:4; 1982:5).

The author expects the adaptive strategies of Paterson's nineteenth-century immigrants to include both of these manifestations of ethnicity. The relationship of ethnicity to consumer behavior as adaptation will be discussed in the next section.

Hypothesis 4: Consumer Behavior. Consumption strategies are also adaptive strategies, shaped by need and influenced by economic circumstance, aspirations and values, production and product availability, marketing, tradition, and individual taste.

In the money economy of an industrializing, urbanizing locale like Paterson between 1825 and 1900, the acquisition and disposal of consumer goods should clearly be expected to relate to the family–household's economic circumstances. For example, the average yearly earnings and expenses reported by select New Jersey workers in 1880 suggest that survival for a one-income, working-class family often involved an extreme moderation of consumption. Day laborers spent just over one-half the amount machinists spent on clothing, less than one-half the amount on groceries, and about 70 percent less on sundries (read luxuries) (New Jersey Bureau of Statistics of Labor and Industries 1880). This suggests a direct correspondence between increasing economic status and increases in the quantity, quality, and variety of the ceramics and glassware consumed, for example. Advertising and the capitalist goals and values of upward socioeconomic mobility should also, however, be reflected in consumer behavior. The ceramic and glassware assemblages from deposits associated with working-class households may indicate, therefore, an attempt to approximate the consumption patterns of higher-status families as closely as economic constraints would allow. The methods and techniques of historical archaeologists studying socioeconomic status will be applied to analyze the Paterson privy assemblages as a test of these hypotheses (Miller 1980; Otto 1977).

The processes of industrialization and urbanization themselves influenced production, and therefore, consumption. Mechanization and technological innovations created greater varieties and quantities of goods for the increasingly consumption-oriented (rather than production-oriented) industrial household (Henn 1982:4–6; Shephard 1980:3–4). This development should be evident in a comparison of the domestic assemblages from Paterson dating to various points in the nineteenth century.

Praetzellis *et al.* believe that acculturation and ethnic boundary maintenance strategies are also reflected in consumer behavior (Praetzellis *et al.* 1981:38). Specifically, Rothschild and Rockman (1982:12) suggest that ethnic symbols and traditions, for instance in foodways, are reflected in artifact style and function. This hypothesis will also be tested against data from the Paterson assemblages.

Data Sources and Methods

Documentary Sources

Secondary sources on Paterson history and on the three study areas in the Dublin neighborhood, and primary sources relating to the Van Houten Street Parking Lot study area in Dublin, were consulted.

Secondary Sources—Paterson. Contextual information on the industrial and urban development of Paterson was provided by secondary sources such as nineteenth-century histories (Shriner 1890; Trumball 1882), a more recent thesis, and a dissertation (Carpenter 1947; Garber 1968), and a massive, synthetic report on a 1970s salvage archaeology project in Paterson's early industrial district (Cotz 1975; Cotz *et al.* 1980; Rutsch n.d.).

Secondary Sources—Study Areas.

1. The Ten House Lots. As part of the 1970s salvage archaeology project, ten house lots on southern Mill Street, Paterson, were studied historically, architecturally, and archaeologically. In addition, research was undertaken on the Dublin neighborhood in which the study area was located, in order to understand the house lots in their cultural and historical context (Cotz *et al.* 1980:6). Deeds, the U.S. Census schedules from 1850 to 1880, maps, and city directories provided information on the house lots and their residents; records of the city government, church records, newspapers, and records from voluntary associations yielded supplementary information on the Irish community in Dublin. The research is presented in a journal article (Cotz 1975) and a 381-page, unpublished report (Cotz *et al.* 1980).

2. Mill Street, 1900. This author undertook a computer-assisted analysis of the 1900 U.S. Census schedules for Mill Street, which runs north–south through Dublin. Data on 1222 households were utilized to examine patterns of ethnicity, household and family composition, residence, and the occupational structure of the family–household. The research is reported in a 27-page unpublished paper (De Cunzo 1979).

3. Cianci Street Block. Donald Presa has prepared a 71-page, unpublished paper on the history of the Cianci Street block, located two blocks east of Mill Street at the northern end of Dublin, and now the site of a high-rise municipal garage. Maps, state and U.S. Census data, Historic American Building Survey (HABS) records, city directories, and deeds were examined (Presa 1980).

Primary Sources—The Van Houten Street Parking Lot Study Area. In 1978 and 1979, the Paterson Archaeology Project, under the direction of Dr. Barry Brady, conducted excavations on two blocks at the northern end of Dublin, adjacent to the city's early mill district. The blocks, bounded by Mill Street on the west and Van Houten Street on the north, were to be impacted by a road improvement project and construction of a parking lot. Analysis of the archaeological collections was not complete, and no final report had been prepared when funding for the city project was exhausted in 1981. With the support and cooperation of Dr. Brady, this author undertook preparation of a historical and an archaeological report centering on six nineteenth-century privies excavated in the study area (De Cunzo 1983).

Preliminary research into deeds, maps, architectural reports, photographs, and other graphics was begun prior to the salvage excavations, as most of the structures in the study area had been demolished before 1970. The ten properties associated with the excavated privies formed the focus of this author's research. Emphasis was placed on the "human evolution" of the study area, with information collected on the properties' owners and occupants from private, state, and federal censuses (1824 to 1915), city directories (1855 to 1915), a family genealogy (Mayers 1977), church birth, marriage, and death records, probate records, and county tax records (1907–1908). These sources yielded data on settlement and residence, family and household composition, life cycle, kinship ties, occupational structure, employment, ethnicity, and economic circumstance. Such data lent itself to statistical compilation and pattern recognition; however, diaries, letters, and other papers that would have contributed significant personal observations of life-style, social ties, and daily life were not discovered for any of the individuals and families under study.

Neither were the sources consulted without interpretive problems, especially in the case of the censuses and city directories. Directory entries were often outdated by the time of publication, and were usually incomplete. Census responses were influenced by problems of language, errors in memory, uninformed household members serving as respondents, and purposeful presentation of misinformation in such areas as education, occupation, and employment. There were several discrepancies, for instance, between occupational titles for individuals in the census schedule and directory of the same year. These problems especially plagued analysis of economic circumstance through occupation (in many cases the only economic indicator). Extensive cross-comparison within the samples, understanding of the occupational structure and hierarchy of the appropriate industries, and the use of categories for unspecific occupational listings in the statistical computations (Hershberg and Dockhorn 1976:66–67) helped resolve the problem.

Finally, documentary sources also contributed to the archaeological research. City agency records and newspapers provided information on privy construction, use, and cleaning, trash pickup, and sewer installation. Newspaper and city directory advertisements documented local manufacturing and the availability of the consumer goods selected and deposited by the Dublin households, and subsequently recovered archaeologically.

Archaeological Sources and Methods—The Van Houten Street Parking Lot Privies

The archaeological collections, field notes, drawings, photographs, and preliminary reports were available for study at the Passaic County Historical Society, Paterson. Dr. Brady assisted with the review of the field notes and interpretation of the stratigraphy, alleviating the problems of working with another archaeologist's excavation notes.

The privies had been disturbed and then buried during demolition of the block's structures. In most cases, however, depressions and other features suggested the privies' location. Once the uppermost intact course of stonework was uncovered, the privies' contents were excavated in a combination of natural and three-inch arbitrary levels. Only artifacts and deposits within the intact privy walls and undisturbed by the recent demolition activities were considered in the analysis.

The first step in the analysis consisted of identifying discrete strata and deposits in each privy, solely from the field notes and accompanying documentation. The artifact assemblages from each privy were catalogued by level, and cross-mended within and between levels. Artifacts were then dated, utilizing form, style, decoration, method of manufacture, function, trademarks, patent information, and embossed markings on bottles, as appropriate. The results of the cross-mending and dating were checked against the field observations, and a final stratigraphic depositional sequence defined for each privy. The dated deposits were then associated with the household(s) occupying the house at that time. On the basis of the composition of the assemblages and the percentages of vessel completeness, it has been assumed each deposit represents trash from the associated resident household(s), and was not brought in from off-site for deposition.

Because of a high water table, Paterson privies were shallow. They were cleaned out when filled, often several times during their use-life. The deposits in the six privies reflected this cycle of use and cleaning. Rather than a single, continuous deposit representing fifty to ninety years of accumulation, discrete deposits separated by matrix and temporal discontinuities, or a single deposit dating to after the most recent cleaning episode, were discovered. This made possible analysis of the deposits and assemblages as outlined above.

Descriptions of the artifact assemblages from each deposit—written descriptions, statistical descriptions, line drawings, and photographs—are available (De Cunzo 1983:111–364). For this study, quantitative and qualitative measures, and measures of the variability of the ceramic, bottle, and glassware collections, shall be employed. These measures were computed from basic quantification of the collections—for the ceramics, sherd and minimum-vessel counts were calculated by ware, decoration, and individual functional type; minimum-vessel and sherd counts were also computed for the functional categories tableware, teaware, storage vessels, dairy vessels, and chamberware. For the bottle and glassware collections, sherd counts, minimum-vessel counts, and percentages were calculated for: (1) bottles—beverage (by product), food (by product), medicine, household, personal; and (2) tableware—drinking vessels (tumblers, mugs, stemmed vessels), decorative glassware, decanters. Quantitative measures to be interpreted in this analysis are: (1) the average number of ceramic vessels deposited per year; (2) the average number of bottles and tableware vessels deposited per year; (3) the number of types of glass tableware vessels; and (4) the number of drinking vessels per deposit. Measures of the relative quality of the collections that shall be compared are: (1) the number of decorative patterns represented in the ceramic collection from each deposit, the number of matching sets, and their composition (based on minimum vessel counts); (2) the percentage of the total number of ceramic vessels in each deposit that were porcelain, and the most expensive earthenware represented in the deposit (transfer-printed wares in the earlier deposits, undecorated and molded ironstones in the later deposits); and (3) Miller's Cream Colored Index values (Miller 1980). Finally, variability shall be measured through comparison of: (1) the number of ceramic ware, decorative, and vessel types represented in each deposit; (2) the number of classes of bottles (ie., wine, medicine, household); (3) the number of different products represented by the bottle assemblage; and (4) the number of glass tableware patterns represented in each deposit.

The statistics were computed to aid identification and understanding of the relationships between archaeologically sampled consumption patterns and documentary data on: (1) the number, size, and composition of the household(s) being studied; (2) their socioeconomic status; (3) their ethnic background; and (4) the stage in the industrialization and urbanization process. The questions being asked were: (1) In what ways did the above variables influence the composition of the archaeological deposits? (2) What does understanding of these influences contribute to our understanding of industrialization, urbanization, and the people adapting to an urban, industrial environment?

Findings

Historical Context—The City of Paterson

Paterson, New Jersey, is an ideal subject for a case study of industrialization and urbanization because the reason for its existence and urban development was industrialization. Located in northeastern New Jersey, fourteen miles west of New York City, Paterson was founded in 1791 by the Society for the Establishment of Useful Manufactures. The site was chosen for the first planned manufacturing community, established with the support of the new United States government, because of its proximity to the Passaic River at its fall line—the power source.

By 1815, a workable hydraulic system had been constructed, and successful cotton manufacturing concerns were in operation. Until after mid-century, supported by a textile machinery industry, cotton manufacturing dominated the industrial scene in Paterson. The manufacture of steam locomotives in the city grew out of the textile machine industry, and by 1860 eclipsed cotton manufacturing. In 1840, the first silk mill was opened in Paterson. Proximity to markets, a skilled work force, the established machine industry, an adequate transportation network, affordable land and tax rates, and ample water power contributed to the success of the silk industry in the city. Raw silk was transformed into sewing silk, ribbons, and broad goods, and these products were dyed and finished in Paterson. By 1915, numerous factors relating to labor laws, the labor force, power sources, and synthetic materials had contributed to the decline of the city's third industrial base. No subsequent industry has so dominated Paterson's life and fortunes as cotton, locomotives, and silk did in the nineteenth and early twentieth centuries (Carpenter 1947; Garber 1968; Trumball 1882).

The physical expansion of Paterson, and the growth and diversification of the population, correlate with the industrial history of the site. During the early uncertain years of the 1790s, Paterson's population was as small as 43 persons (Trumball 1882:40), growing to 1,500 by 1814 with the successful establishment of the cotton industry (Cotz *et al.* 1980:49). In 1851, when the City of Paterson was incorporated, its population exceeded 11,000 (U.S. Census 1850). Growth continued throughout the century, with the population increasing another 500 percent by 1900 (Twelfth Census 1901). European immigration contributed significantly to these growth rates, beginning before 1850.

The process of urbanization accompanied the industrial expansion and population growth—the political structure was formalized, city services were expanded, social and economic stratification occurred, and land-use patterns characterized by functional segregation defined the urban, industrial landscape. These developments will be documented in microcosm in the four study areas examined in this chapter.

The Study Areas: Mill Street Ten House Lots, Mill Street 1900, Cianci Street Block and Van Houten Street Parking Lot Block

Census data indicate the Cianci Street and Van Houten Street parking lot study areas were among industrial Paterson's earliest-developed residential blocks. By 1835, for example, four of the ten Van Houten Street parking lot study properties were occupied. Several structures appear to have stood on the Cianci Street block as early as 1820. It was another thirty years, however, before development extended south on Mill Street to the Ten House Lots study area, where the first house was constructed just before 1850.

Data on the study areas' occupants before 1850 is sparse. More complete data is available after 1850, and that which relates to the variables considered in this study—household and family, occupation and economics, and ethnic background—has been quantified and is presented in Tables 1, 2, and 3. The patterns revealed by the data are examined under the heading "Hypothesis Testing," where each variable is analyzed.

Table 4 presents a statistical sketch of the households associated with the Van Houten Street parking lot privy deposits, again focusing on the variables household and family, employment, occupation and economics, and nationality. The households–deposits have been assigned an Economic Rank Order number to facilitate correlation of the documentary and archaeological data on economic position. The ordering has been based exclusively on documentary information on occupation, employment, wages, property ownership, personal property value at death, family size and structure, and stage in the life cycle.

Hypothesis Testing

Hypothesis 1: Settlement Patterns

The Paterson data confirms the hypothesis of the influence of economics, social status, and urban development on settlement pattern, and reflects the principle that housing be accessible to the workplace and essential goods and

Table 1. Household and Family Structure and Composition, Four Dublin Study Areas

Measure	Year	Mill Street ten house lots	Mill Street 1900	Cianci Street block	Van Houten Street parking lot
Number of residents	1850	5	—[a]	—	63
	1860	44	—	275	48
	1870	84	—	267	63
	1880	95	—	317	64
	1885	—	—	293	63
	1895	—	—	313	39
	1900	—	1222	243	90
	1905	—	—	399	—
	1915	—	—	326	—
Average number of	1850	1.0–4	—	—	1.7–5.1
families per house–	1860	1.1–4.8	—	2.3–4.1	1.6–4.4
average family size	1870	1.8–4.6	—	2.2–4.1	1.7–5.3
	1880	2.0–3.9	—	2.6–3.9	1.6–5.8
	1885	—	—	2.1–4.7	1.5–5.3
	1895	—	—	2.3–4.4	1.6–4.9
	1900	—	— –4.6	2.3–4.0	1.8–5.6
	1905	—	—	2.8–4.8	—
	1915	—	—	2.6–5.0	—
Percentage of	1850	20.0–40.0	—	—	11.5–32.8
boarders–	1860	2.3–41.0	—	6.2–36.7	16.7–20.8
percentage of	1870	1.2–32.1	—	13.5–29.6	19.0–17.5
children under 16	1880	10.5–26.3	—	7.3–34.4	10.9–26.6
	1885	—	—	—	22.2–27.0
	1895	—	—	8.6– —	17.9–30.8
	1900	—	6.3–31.9	16.0–31.7	13.3–30.0
	1905	—	—	17.5–34.8	—
	1915	—	—	11.7–38.0	—

[a]— = data not available.

services. Settlement occurred first in the blocks immediately adjacent to the mills. Until the 1850s, this area housed mill owner, manager, and skilled and unskilled worker alike in an integrated environment where manager and worker even coresided in the same house. By 1851, Paterson was a city, and a socially homogeneous, elite residential community was being developed east of the central business district. At the same time, recently arrived Irish famine victims sought employment in the city's mills. With vacant properties still available within walking distance of the mills, the incoming immigrants did not need to displace the English and native workers residing in the older housing. Instead, they built an almost exclusively Irish community to the south. Two decades later, skilled German textile and metal workers arrived, expanding the now working-class neighborhood to the east between the mill and central business districts. By 1900, the streetcar drew upwardly mobile,

Table 2. Occupation and Employment, Four Dublin Study Areas

Measure	Year	Mill Street, ten house lots	Mill Street, 1900	Cianci Street block	Van Houten Street parking lot
Percentage of adult working men–adult working women	1850	50.0–0	—[a]	—	68.2–0
	1860	40.9–9.1	—	53.9–12.9	50.0–15.4
	1870	60.0–25.0	—	63.8–27.1	75.9–35.3
	1880	69.6–20.4	—	65.6–21.0	73.3–32.4
	1885	—	—	—	—
	1895	—	—	—	—
	1900	—	61.1[b]	56.2–10.4	70.2–13.3
	1905	—	—	57.9–10.7	—
	1915	—	—	68.9–16.4	—
Percentage of children under 16 working	1850	0	—	—	5.0
	1860	0	—	3.0	0
	1870	14.8	—	8.9	0
	1880	24.0	—	13.8	17.6
	1885	—	—	—	—
	1895	—	—	—	—
	1900	—	—	10.4	7.4
	1905	—	—	10.1	—
	1915	—	—	2.4	—
Percentage of professional workers–percentage of nonmanual, proprietary	1850	0–0	—	—	0–31.3
	1860	0–9.1	—	2.4–14.6	0–6.2
	1870	0–2.6	—	2.4–16.0	0–5.7
	1880	0–2.1	—	4.6–11.1	0–7.9
	1885	—	—	1.9–17.3	—
	1895	—	—	1.3–23.4	—
	1900	—	6.7[a]	.9–19.6	0–4.9
	1905	—	—	1.6–7.4	—
	1915	—	—	0–11.4	—
Percentage of skilled, semiskilled–percentage of unskilled	1850	50.0–50.0	—	—	56.3–12.4
	1860	45.0–45.5	—	56.1–26.9	87.6–6.2
	1870	43.6–53.8	—	48.0–33.6	60.0–34.3
	1880	53.2–44.7	—	20.9–63.4	47.4–44.7
	1885	—	—	47.1–33.7	—
	1895	—	—	54.5–20.8	—
	1900	—	30.7–9.6	48.2–31.3	65.9–29.2
	1905	—	—	39.5–51.5	—
	1915	—	—	27.9–60.7	—
Percentage working in iron industries–percentage in textile industries	1850	0–0	—	—	50.0–25.1
	1860	27.3–27.3	—	20.7–6.1	43.8–43.8
	1870	23.0–33.3	—	11.2–21.6	42.9–34.3
	1880	25.5–36.2	—	15.7–52.3	26.3–60.5
	1885	—	—	16.3–29.8	—
	1895	—	—	9.1–23.4	—
	1900	—	—–20.6	6.3–33.0	9.5–47.6
	1905	—	—	4.2–42.6	—
	1915	—	—	2.9–42.1	—

[a]— = data not available.
[b]Percentage of total population.

Table 3. National Origin and Ethnicity, Four Dublin Study Areas

Measure	Year	Mill Street, ten house lots	Mill Street, 1900	Cianci Street block	Van Houten Street parking lot
Percentage of foreign	1850	0	—	—	27.0
born	1860	38.6	—	45.1	39.6
	1870	40.0	—	41.0	39.1
	1880	34.7	—	41.2	39.1
	1885	—	—	31.4	31.7
	1895	—	—	42.8	—
	1900	—	38.9	42.4	37.8
	1905	—	—	57.5	—
	1915	—	—	59.5	—
Percentage of	1850	0	—	—	12.7–14.3
British–percentage	1860	6.8–13.6	—	9.4–20.7	22.9–14.5
of Irish	1870	7.1–27.4	—	12.7–14.2	15.9–20.6
	1880	11.6–21.1	—	14.8–9.1	25.4–11.1
	1885	—	—	— –4.9	—
	1895	—	—	— –5.4	—
	1900	—	17.0–41.3	7.0–7.0	2.2–6.7
	1905	—	—	1.8–5.6	—
	1915	—	—	.9–1.2	—
Percentage of	1850	0–0	—	—	0–0
German–percentage	1860	0–0	—	12.0–0	0–0
of Italian	1870	2.4–0	—	12.7–0	0–0
	1880	1.1–0	—	17.0–0	0–0
	1885	—	—	8.8– —	—
	1895	—	—	6.7– —	—
	1900	—	8.8–25.3	9.4–13.1	11.1–14.4
	1905	—	—	5.6–43.2	—
	1915	—	—	2.8–46.3	—

skilled workers and their families away from the dirty, smelly, noisy mill district to new neighborhoods and suburbs. In turn, this movement provided an opportunity for the establishment of a cohesive Italian community in affordable housing adjacent to the mills where community members now worked.

Economics, the development of city services, and social status did determine citywide settlement patterns; within the large working-class community created in Paterson by the interaction of these forces, however, ethnicity and immigration patterns governed the choice of housing.

Hypothesis 2: Household and Family Patterns

It has been proposed that the urban, industrial families being studied in Paterson should be viewed as economic, consumer units, and that the adaptive

Table 4. Characteristics of the Households Associated with Privy Deposits, Van Houten Street Parking Lot

Measure	G1-1 1-4 Van Houten	O1-1 15 Ellison	G1-2 1-2 Van Houten	N1-1 11-13 Ellison	M3-2 9 Ellison	B3 12 Mill	O1-2 15 Ellison
Economic rank	1	2	3	4	5	6	7
Date	1840s–1850s	1850s	1870s–1880s	1830–1835	1850s–1860s	1880s–1890s	1880s–1890s
Number of households	2	2	2	1	1	1	5
Number of residents	11	13	14	8	7	10	29
Household types	1-Nuclear 1-Nuclear, boarders	1-Unknown 1-Extended, boarders	Nuclear	Extended, boarders*	Nuclear	Extended	1-Joint 2-Nuclear 1-Extended, boarders 1-Unknown
Percentage of children under 16	27.3	7.7	50.0	37.5	0	30.0	41.4
Percentage of boarders	27.3	—[a]	0	37.5	0	30.0	0
Number of employed	6	5*[b]	4	1*	4	5	7*
Number male household heads employed	2	2	2	1	1	—	3*

Number of spouses or female household heads employed	0*	—	0	0	1	1	0
Percentage of unmarried children over 16 employed	75.0*	100.0	75.0	0	33.3	100.0	100.0
Percentage of children under 16 employed	0*	0	0	0	0	0	0
Occupations of household heads	1-Blacksmith 1-Mill worker 1-Boilermaker	1-Machinist	1-Machinist	1-Blacksmith	1-Machinist 1-Silk mill foreman	1-Weaver 1-Mill overseer	1-Silk mill manager 1-Paper manufacturer
Occupations of others	3-Silk winders 1-Mill worker*	1-Machinist 4-Mill workers	3-Dress–skirt makers	—	1-Tavern keeper 1-Engineer	1-Carpenter 1-Machinist 1-Gas fitter*	4-Mill workers
House owner-occupied	No	No	Yes	Yes	Yes	Yes	No
Percentage of foreign born	17.2*	30.0	0	—	23.1	21.4	27.3
Percentage of British	0	10.0	0	—	23.1	7.1	9.1
Percentage of Irish	17.2*	20.0	0	—	0	7.1	18.2

[a] — = data not available.
[b] Asterisk (*) = based on available, but incomplete data.

options available to families unable to live on the family head's wages included the employment of other family members, taking in boarders, and moderating consumption.

These residential and employment patterns are, indeed, amply documented in the Paterson study areas. For instance, of the 101 households from the Van Houten Street study area for which data is available for the period 1850 to 1915, 47.5 percent utilized supplementary workers in the family, primarily unmarried children having completed their schooling, and 30.7 percent took in unrelated boarders. The families not employing these income-supplementing techniques were of two types: (1) families whose male head was a mill owner or manager, or (2) families composed solely of a husband and wife or a couple with a few very young children who rented accommodations in a house along with other renting households.

In addition, evidence of a late marriage age and of the predominance of elder children as the family's supplementary wageearners was also recorded. In 1900 on Mill Street, 603 children were living with their parents as opposed to only 94 other relatives. One-third of the children were over 15 years of age, and more than 90 percent of them, male and female, worked outside the home. Wives, on the other hand, were even more consistently, in 94 percent of the cases, not employed outside the home (De Cunzo 1979:12–17).

The household and family patterns of Paterson's working-class inhabitants in the nineteenth and early twentieth centuries did reflect accommodation to the urban, industrial environment rooted, at least in part, in economic circumstance. The consumption patterns of these households will be discussed under Hypothesis 4, and a new element in the interpretation of the household and family patterns will be introduced.

Hypothesis 3: Ethnic Identity and Community Networking

Patterns of residence, occupation, employment, and social relations suggest that ethnic identification and networking also was an adaptive force in Paterson, providing continuity and familiarity through tradition as well as political and economic support, and ultimately, strength.

Residential clusters of three national groups in Dublin—Irish, Germans, and Italians—were evidenced in the study areas. Economic factors, including employment opportunities and wage levels, and prejudice rooted in economic competition, contributed significantly to the development of these immigrant groups into ethnic groups. Irish and Italian immigrants especially filled higher numbers of unskilled positions during their residence in Dublin than members of other groups, and struggled for upward mobility, higher wages, and economic stability (De Cunzo 1979:15; 1983:77).

Ethnic identity and cohesion were manifested, and, at least in part, maintained through the structure of social relations. Cotz has undertaken an in-depth case study of this structure, its purposes, and its forms in the case of Paterson's Dublin Irish community (Cotz *et al.* 1980:103–182). The Irish immigrants' social structure was based on the nuclear family, with its patrilineal tie to the land and an assured place in the community. In industrial Paterson, the agricultural Irish family was forced to reorganize its economic structure, as explained above. The nature of the urban community differed also, as membership and recognition were achieved not through common origin and family ties, but "through a system of social institutions created through social cooperation" (Thomas and Znaniecki 1927:1534; see also Cotz *et al.* 1980:105, 107–110). For Dublin's Irish, the Roman Catholic Church, various voluntary associations, and the political arena constituted the ethnic social system. The Church and affiliated social organizations, schools, and benevolent societies influenced the Irishmen's political, social, and intellectual development, and indeed were the key to the group's successful adaptation (Cotz *et al.* 1980:111). Military clubs and volunteer fire departments provided opportunities for achievement, status, and social interaction for the Irish male (Cotz *et al.* 1980:137–138, 140, 152–153), while political involvement afforded the Irish community leadership and opportunities to improve the group's condition.

Evidence of ethnic traditions and customs, and of boundary-maintaining symbols of identity, will also be sought in the immigrants' consumption patterns, treated in the next section.

Hypothesis 4: Consumer Behavior

Hypothesis 4 states that the consumer behavior of the Paterson households studied was influenced by: (1) economic circumstance; (2) social aspirations and values; (3) marketing; (4) production and product availability, as related to industrial and urban development; (5) cultural tradition and ethnic symbol; and (6) individual taste. The privy assemblages from the Van Houten Street Parking Lot study area were analyzed to determine the nature and extent of the influence of these variables on consumption as reflected in the archaeological record. Emphasis in the artifact analyses is placed on the ceramic and glass assemblages. Table 5 compares the raw numbers of ceramic and glass sherds and vessels being analyzed from each privy deposit.

1. Economic Circumstance. Several artifact measures that historical ar-

Table 5. Summary Statistical Description, Ceramic and Glass Assemblages, Paterson Privy Deposits

	Privy deposit						
Measure	G1-1	G1-2	B3	M3-2	N1-1	O1-1	O1-2
Ceramics: number of sherds	667	320	389	414	1913	892	151
Ceramics: number of vessels	111	74	150	96	279	256	22
Bottles: number of sherds	311	218	155	421	107	280	172
number of bottles	28	60	57	84	39	78	31
Drinking vessels:							
number of sherds	18	98	37	32	88	48	0
number of vessels	6	36	11	7	30	14	0
Other glass tableware:							
number of sherds	6	9	36	58	10	89	1
number of vessels	4	5	13	6	2	22	1

chaeologists have related to economic status were employed in this analysis. Those correlating with the economic ordering based on documentary evidence include: (1) the relative quantities of ceramic tableware, bowls, flatware, and teaware discarded by each household; (2) the percentage of expensive earthenwares discarded by each household; and (3) the size and composition of matching sets of ceramics. Four other measures did not correlate as expected: (1) measures of the size and diversity of the ceramic and glass collections; (2) the percentage of porcelain discarded by each household; (3) the Miller Cream Colored Index value; and (4) the relative quantity and quality of the glassware discarded by each household. The three measures exhibiting positive correlations shall be discussed first.

The types of ceramic vessels used by a household have been shown to reflect economic status (Otto 1977). In Table 6, the types discarded by the study households are quantified. The correlations are weak, as choice of vessel type was affected by the influence of other variables, such as the date of the deposits (which range from c. 1830 to c. 1900). Although the later residents of the neighborhood were generally of lower economic status than the earlier ones, mass production increased their buying power, making it possible for them to acquire more ceramics, and a wider range of forms (including previously "luxury" forms such as tea sets). The positive correlations (although not statistically significant) between flatware and tableware, and economic status, and the negative correlation between bowls and status, do agree with Otto's data from plantation owner, overseer, and slave sites (Otto 1977:102).

A rank ordering of the percentage of highest-priced earthenwares in each deposit (transfer-printed whitewares in the early deposits, ironstones in the later deposits) does correlate with the economic status ranking of the households, as predicted (see Table 7). The ownership of complete ceramic dinnerware sets also correlates with economic status. Only one deposit, that associ-

Table 6. Ceramic Tableware, Bowls, Flatware, and Teaware[a]

Deposit	Economic rank	Percentage of tableware	Percentage of bowls	Percentage of flatware	Percentage of teaware
G1-1	1	56.1	9.3	40.2	24.3
O1-1	2	41.5	12.3	27.1	32.2
G1-2	3	32.4	8.1	18.9	48.7
N1-1	4	51.3	15.2	30.0	28.9
M3-2	5	47.7	12.8	24.5	31.4
B3	6	33.3	9.0	19.4	37.5
O1-2	7	—[b]	—	—	—
Rank order correlation, by economic rank[c]		.37	−.09	.54	.37

[a]Percentages shown here based on minimum vessel counts; rank order correlations not significant using sherd counts, either.
[b]— = insufficient sample size.
[c]Needed for significance at 5 percent level = .786.

Table 7. Percentages Highest Priced Earthenware, Porcelain
Vessels per Deposit[a]

Deposit	Economic rank	Percentage of porcelain	Percentage of highest priced earthenware
G1-1	1	16.2	55.0
O1-1	2	9.8	50.0
G1-2	3	0	91.9
N1-1	4	2.3	42.7
M3-2	5	3.1	30.2
B3	6	18.7	49.4
O1-2	7	—[b]	—

[a]Percentages are of total number of ceramic vessels.
[b]— = insufficient sample size.

ated with a mill owner's and a mill manager's families (G1-1), contained
evidence of dinnerware services (three transfer-printed whiteware sets represented by fragments from at least twenty-seven vessels). The less well-to-do
households in this sample were able in every instance to afford the most up-to-
date in expensive earthenwares, but only if they purchased seconds and/or in
small quantities.

For several possible reasons, as noted in the subsequent discussion, certain artifact measures that other archaeologists have identified as reflecting
economic status did not exhibit a positive correlation in this study. The first of
these are a group of measures of the size and diversity of the ceramic and glass
collections. To compare the sizes of the collections, it was necessary to control
for the differences in the length of time over which each deposit accumulated.
Using the dating methods described in an earlier section, the number of years
of deposition represented by each deposit was approximated. From this, measures of the average numbers of vessels deposited each year could be computed
(see Table 8).

The lack of a correlation between these measures and the documentary
economic ranking (Tables 8, 9, and 10) reflects the complexity and variety of
the variables that determine the composition of these archaeological deposits.
The influence of economic status on consumption has been masked, for example, by the effects of the number, size, and composition of the households
responsible for each deposit, individual taste, and stage in the industrialization and urbanization process (i.e., the date of the deposit).

Wealth does not appear to correlate with ownership of porcelain either
(see Table 7). The household ranked sixth on the economic scale discarded the
largest percentage of porcelain. An 1884 advertisement in *The Paterson Daily
Press* helps explain the apparent inconsistency. The ad, for "Henkel's Baking
Powder," announced the giving away of *free* "Brown Willow Cups and Saucers/
3 line gold band China Cups and Saucers/Elegant Motto Cups and Saucers"
with the purchase of the baking powder (*The Paterson Daily Press* 1884). Eight

Table 8. Number of Ceramic and Glassware Vessels and Bottles Deposited per Year per Deposit

Deposit	Dates	Economic rank	Number of ceramic vessels	Number of bottles	Number of drinking and other glassware vessels
G1-1	1840s–1850s	1	18.5	4.7	1.7
O1-1	1850s	2	32.0	9.7	4.5
G1-2	1872–1880s	3	8.2	6.7	4.5
N1-1	1830–1835	4	55.8	7.8	6.4
M3-2	1850s–1860s	5	16.0	14.0	2.2
B3	1880s–1890s	6	16.7	6.3	2.7
O1-2	1880s–1890s	7	2.3	3.4	.1

of the twenty-three porcelain tableware vessels recovered from this deposit are "3 line gold band China Cups and Saucers"; a brown willow tea cup was also found. For urban sites of the late nineteenth century, the assumption that the consumer choice of porcelain always directly reflects high economic status, may not be valid.

Miller's Ceramic Index values were also computed for the plates, bowls, and tea vessels recovered from each deposit (Table 11). As Table 11 shows, the computed index values do not correlate well with the relative economic positions of the households as determined from documentary evidence. At least two factors affecting the index values computed in part account for this. First is the problem of incomplete ceramic price data. Values were not available for all wares and decorative types represented in each deposit for the appropriate

Table 9. Measures of Diversity by Deposit: Ceramics and Glassware

Deposit	Dates	Economic rank	Number of ceramic vessel types	Number of ceramic ware and decorative types	Number of glassware vessel types
G1-1	1840s–1850s	1	20	17	5
O1-1	1850s	2	26	26	13
G1-2	1872–1880s	3	14	5	8
N1-1	1830–1835	4	26	20	6
M3-2	1850s–1860s	5	16	17	5
B3	1880s–1890s	6	24	17	15
O1-2	1880s–1890s	7	3	3	1
Rank order correlation, by economic rank[a]			.4	.48	.2

[a]Needed for significance at 5 percent level = .786.

Table 10. Rank Order Correlations, Diversity and Deposition Date:
Ceramics, Bottles, Glassware

Measure	Rank order value	Significant
Ceramic vessel types	−.66	No
Ceramic ware and decorative types	−.69	No
Ceramic patterns	−.57	No
Number, bottle classes	.36	No
Number, different products (bottles)	−.03	No
Glassware vessel types	1.00	Yes (at .01 level)
Glassware patterns	—[a]	—

[a]— = insufficient sample size.

year(s); those vessels were not included in the computation. Second, there is the problem illustrated by the baking-powder give-away example. The highest Miller value computed was for the teawares from that assemblage, where at least eight of the procelain vessels had been acquired by the household at no cost. Other researchers using Miller's test in the analysis of late nineteenth-century sites should also consider the possible influences of such marketing techniques on consumer behavior.

The final artifact measures hypothesized as being related to economic status are the quantity and quality of glass tableware (other than drinking vessels) (Table 12). Neither the rank ordering of the number nor the percentage of glass tableware vessels ("luxury" vessels such as spillholders, compotes, covered butter dishes, etc.) correlate directly with the documentary economic ranking. All the glassware is nonlead and American made. The most expensive types present were blown-three-mold, engraved, cut, and early pattern glass prior to 1850, and pressed wares thereafter. Compared to European and even American lead crystals, these wares were relatively inexpensive, supporting the documentary evidence that none of the households was truly wealthy.

Overall, this attempt to correlate documentary and archaeological measures indicative of socioeconomic status, has not been successful. Factors relating to both the documentary and archaeological measures have contributed to the analytical problems encountered. First, there is the problem of the documentary economic rankings themselves. The ranks were ascribed subjectively, based on the evidence collected. The data was neither comparable nor complete for each household, and the problem was exacerbated both by the seventy-year time period involved and the fact that several deposits were associated with more than one household of slightly different economic statuses. In other words, it was difficult, and may just not be possible, to compare the socioeconomic positions of a blacksmith's family in the 1830s town of Paterson with a machinist's family in the 1880s city of Paterson.

With the archaeological data, there is the question of the relationship between wealth and expenditures on ceramics and glassware. The value of a

Table 11. Cream-Colored Index Values[a]

Deposit	Economic rank	Dates of deposit	Index values and index year used		
			Plates	Tea	Bowls
G1-1	1	Late 1840s–early 1850s	1.52 (1846)	1.97 (1846)	2.65 (1846)
O1-1	2	1850s	1.44 (1855)	3.35 (1857)	2.00 (1855)
G1-2	3	c. 1872–early 1880s	2.52 (1874)	2.95 (1874)	—[b]
N1-1	4	c. 1830–1835	2.05 (1833)	2.67 (1814)	1.83 (1833)
M3-2	5	Late 1850s–early 1860s	1.80 (1855)	3.00 (1857)	1.67 (1858)
B3	6	1880s–early 1890s	2.25 (1874)	3.05 (1874), 4.59 (1881)	—
O1-2	7	—	—	—	—
Rank order correlation, by economic rank			−.54	.6	

[a]Note on methods: The index values for the year within or nearest to the deposition period were utilized. If more than one appropriate date was available, the date with values for the most decorative types was used, or in certain cases, values for two years were computed for comparison. If a Miller value was not assigned for a decorative type represented in any assemblage, that type was not included in the computation.
[b]— = insufficient sample size.
[c]Needed for significance at 5 percent level = .886.

Table 12. Glass Tablewares

| Deposit | Economic rank | Glass tablewares | |
		Number of vessels	Percentage of glassware[a]
G1-1	1	4	40.0
O1-1	2	22	61.1
G1-2	3	5	12.2
N1-1	4	2	6.2
M3-2	5	6	46.2
B3	6	13	54.2
O1-2	7	—[b]	—
Rank order correlation by economic rank[c]		.2	.09

[a]Glassware includes tableware and drinking vessels.
[b]— = insufficient sample size.
[c]Needed for significance at 5 percent level = .886.

household's ceramics and glassware generally comprised only a small percentage of the total value of the household's possessions, as nineteenth-century inventories attest. It is therefore possible that expenditures on these items, as reflected in percentages and index values based on the relative amounts of variously priced wares discarded by a household, will not always correlate perfectly with the household's actual economic status. Additionally, there is the bias inherent in the archaeological sample. The privy assemblages compared in this analysis do not contain evidence of all the ceramics and glassware consumed by, or perhaps even discarded by, the households, only that nonrandom portion that was disposed of in the privy. Even the reasons these vessels were discarded are not completely understood. For example, was it only because they happened to have been broken, or were, perhaps, older vessels that were no longer stylish also disposed of?

The main point to be made, however, is that an important reason for the discouraging lack of expected correlations is the number and variability of the factors, besides economic circumstance, also affecting the composition of the deposits, such as the date of deposition (different consumer choices were available in the early and late nineteenth century as a result of mass production), household number, size and composition, ethnic preferences, and individual taste. This is, in fact, a major corollary of this paper, that archaeologists can contribute to an understanding of many aspects of urban, industrial adaptation because archaeological deposits and assemblages reflect many aspects of behavior.

2. *Social Aspirations and Values.* Despite the difficulties encountered in correlating the ceramic and glass assemblages with households' *economic* position, the assemblages did yield important information on *socioeconomic* statuses and aspirations. The assemblages suggest that the study area's working-

Table 13. Commercially Processed Food and Household Products Packaged in Glass Containers

Deposit	Dates	Number of classes of bottles[a]	Number of different products represented[b]
N1-1	1830–1835	5	27
G1-1	1840s–1850s	2	11
O1-1	1850s	5	52
M3-2	1850s–1860s	8	48
G1-2	1872–1880s	9	42
B3	1880s–1890s	9	50
O1-2	1880s–1890s	2	4

[a]Wine, beer, liquor, soda water, other beverages, medicine, toiletry, household, foods.
[b]Only identical bottles counted as containing the same product.

class residents accepted the capitalist ethos and aspired to upward mobility and a middle-class standard of living. All managed to afford the most popular and expensive earthenwares, and at least a minimal amount of porcelain and glass tableware. The mill owners and managers exhibited more buying power than the workers, able to purchase matching sets of ceramics and glassware. However, the presence of nonmatching pieces, possibly used for "everyday," and of American-made, nonlead glassware, suggests a limit to their affluence as well (De Cunzo 1983:438).

3. *Marketing.* The baking-powder give-away example provides corroborating evidence of the workers' social aspirations, documented through product advertising. The goal of marketing is to relate the consumers' own goals, values, and self-image with the product. Henkel, the baking-powder manufacturer, chose highly status-connotative porcelain for a marketing campaign to the aspiring, status-conscious consumer of modest means, and found at least one customer in Dublin's working-class population.

4. *Production and Product Availability.* The interrelated phenomena of industrialization, mass production, and the consumer household also influenced the nature and composition of these domestic archaeological deposits. As Table 13 illustrates, a greater number and variety of commercially processed foods and household products (packaged in glass containers) were consumed by the households occupying the study houses in the latter half of the nineteenth century. In addition, deposits dating from the 1870s through the 1890s did not contain sherds from any ceramic storage jars, crocks, bottles, or jugs, while the earlier deposits included fragments from thirty-five such containers, further evidence of decreasing reliance on home-processed and prepared foods (De Cunzo 1983:391–392).

The size and diversity of the ceramic, bottle, and glass tableware assemblages do not correlate with the deposits' dates, however. In fact, the average numbers of ceramic vessels ($-.95$), bottles ($-.55$), and glass tableware vessels $(-.36)$ deposited each year all exhibit a negative correlation to the date of the respective deposits. Table 10 presents the rank order correlation values for several measures of diversity by date. The deposits were ranked by date, and the diversity measures by frequency value. The rank order correlation, then, compares the frequencies for each measure of diversity statistically to determine whether the deposits' diversity correlates with their date. The only significant correspondence is for the number of different glass tableware patterns, a reflection of the development of the pressing machine and the resulting production of vast numbers and varieties of relatively inexpensive glass tablewares beginning in the 1840s.

    5. *Cultural Tradition and Ethnic Symbol.* The study assemblages were unfortunately not an ideal sample from which to study ethnic adaptation. During the periods represented by the privy deposits, the study house residents were native born, English, and Irish. In the cases of G1-1, G1-2, O1-1, and O1-2, two or more families of different ethnic affiliation produced the deposit. As a result of the blocks' settlement history, the area was not dominated by a single national group until Italian families moved in after 1900. None of the privy deposits, however, date to the period of the Italian occupation.

    Evidence of ethnic associations and patterns was discerned only in the bottle collections. Discard patterns suggest that the Irish preferred to drink beer and soda water at home rather than the wines and liquors consumed by their American and English neighbors (see Table 14). In addition, the consumption of commercial patent medicines was lower among the immigrants in the sample, perhaps reflecting retention of traditional folk medical practices (Table 14).

    Even here, however, other factors may be partly responsible for the patterns, specifically urban, industrial development and economic constraint. Beginning in the 1870s, breweries and soda water firms were established in Paterson in increasing numbers. Almost all of the marked glass soda water bottles and stoneware beer bottles in the collections identify Paterson pro-

Table 14. Glass and Stoneware Bottle Types

		Number of bottles				
Deposit	Ethnicity	Liquor	Beer	Soda water	Medicine	Wine
M3-2	Native	3	2	5	55	6
N1-1	Native	0	0	0	19	5
G1-2	Native–British	3[a]	2	3	35	4
O1-1	Native–Irish	0	0	0	7	11
G1-1	English–Irish	0	0	0	29	21
B3	Irish	6[a]	8	13	15	4
O1-2	Irish	3	19	26	1	0

[a]Samples noted here either liquor or beer bottles.

ducers. These local beverages may have been considerably less expensive than imported wines and liquors, even those only imported from other domestic locations, and the late nineteenth-century Irish residents of the study area (B3—Economic Rank 6, and O1-2—Economic Rank 7) may have favored beer and soda, in part for this reason. The cost of patent medicines may also have contributed to their limited consumption by certain immigrant families.

Identifiable ethnic symbols, such as clay pipes proclaiming support for Irish independence or with an insignia associated with membership in firehouses, military, or other ethnic associations, and evidence of distinctive ethnic foodways or aesthetic tastes, were not reflected in the ceramic and glassware assemblages (De Cunzo 1983:403–408). These findings suggest that ethnicity as adaptation to the industrial, urban environment of Paterson may be more profitably studied through residence and employment patterns, economic conflict, kinship, and social structure and interaction, than through archaeological analysis of consumption and discard patterns.

CONCLUSIONS

The congruence of the patterns of adaptive responses to urbanization and industrialization observed in Paterson with the patterns identified by other researchers in other, similar settings, supports the concept of cultural systemics, and the patterned interrelationships between system components. This was especially true in the areas of settlement pattern, the family and household, and ethnicity, where the Paterson data neatly paralleled the expected, hypothesized behavior. Urban, industrial settlement patterns in Paterson were determined by the industrial production mode, and influenced by urban services, socioeconomic status, and ethnicity. Dublin's families–households did function as economic units striving to improve their condition through their structure, residence, and employment patterns. Ethnicity did make it possible for immigrants to not only survive, but to contribute to and succeed in their new urban, industrial environment.

The analysis of consumer behavior was somewhat more complex, reflecting the nature of the questions being asked, and the two independent data sources being employed, documentary and archaeological. Investigation of consumption patterns in relation to the processes of urbanization and industrialization implies comparison over time and between consumers exhibiting various characteristics, diversity (an urban population is heterogeneous), and change. The operating assumption was that the variables affecting consumer behavior—such as ethnic identification and tradition, the size, structure, and composition of the household, stage in the life cycle, economic circumstances, and date—would be controlled through the documents, and consumption patterns as reflected in discard patterns would be studied in relation to the variables. A problem was encountered, however. Perhaps in part because of the small sample size of seven assemblages, in part because of the nature of the diversity among the households, and in part because more than one household with different characteristics were often associated with a single deposit, it was not possible to fully identify how each variable influenced consumption. It was not possible to say, for instance, that in deposit "x," "a," and "b" reflect the household's economic status, while "c" and "d" reflect ethnicity, and "e" and "f" reflect the extent of urbanization and industrialization as reflected in the deposit's date. Further difficulties were presented by the incompleteness and incomparability of the data available on households' economic circumstances, a critical variable in this study.

Despite these problems, certain tentative conclusions concerning consumer behavior as adaptation were reached. (1) Distinctions in buying power between workers and middle-class mill owners and managers appear in the ability of the latter only to purchase complete ceramic dinner services, rather than in the quantity, variety, or types of ceramics and glassware purchased. (2) The social aspirations of the sampled Paterson workers and a capitalist desire for upward socioeconomic mobility were reflected in their consumption patterns. All of them purchased fashionable dinner and tea wares, and status-connotative porcelains and glass tablewares, although not the most expensive European porcelains and lead glasswares available. The taking in of boarders, employment of elder children, purchase of odd lots and individual pieces, and other consumption strategies (e.g., the baking-power giveaway) were employed in order that the families' consumption could reflect their social values and aspirations as well as economic reality. (3) The influences of technological innovation, mass production, and improved transportation and marketing on foodways and lifestyle were visible through comparison of consumption–discard patterns of households over the course of the nineteenth century. (4) Cultural preferences also appeared to influence consumption, however in close association with other variables. A stronger influence was exerted by ethnicity on social and political organization than on consumption.

The anthropological concept of cultural adaptation has proven to be a useful framework from which to approach the study of industrialization and urbanization. In this approach, consumer behavior is understood as an element of an adaptive strategy, and is investigated in conjunction with, and in the context of, other elements of the strategy, as well as of the circumstances to which the strategy is a response. Economic circumstance is seen as one variable, albeit an important one, that governs consumption strategies, and consumer behavior is viewed as only one area of behavior that is influenced by economic circumstance.

Although this and future studies may benefit from this broad perspective, difficult problems also accompany this approach. Industrialization, urbanization, and adaptation are extremely complex phenomena, and it may not be possible to identify all of the variables affecting the processes. Even in the present study, limited to consideration of only four areas in which adaptation had been documented by other researchers, problems isolating the impact of individual variables and the interrelationships between variables were encountered.

Future research must address these problems, must be interdisciplinary in nature, and must be comparative. This study demonstrated the importance of establishing control of the variables—such as those relating to households and families, ethnic background, the urban and industrial context, and economic status—through historical documentation. Nineteenth-century American cities are, in general, richly documented, and more extensive documentary data need to be collected—especially relating to ethnicity, wages, consumer behavior, product availability, marketing and pricing, foodways, and other aspects of domestic life—than were compiled for this study. The immensity of such a task is, unfortunately, staggering.

In order to conduct research at this level, archaeological deposits must be identifiable with their associated household(s). Ideally, deposits need to be compared for which control can be established over all but one variable, so the influence of single variables on consumption and discard patterns can be isolated and understood. Once the parameters of influence of individual variables in the urban, industrial context have been defined, then analysis of the interrelationships between variables can proceed through comparison of deposits associated with households that differ in respect to more than one variable. Unfortunately, as evidenced by the privies excavated by the Paterson Archaeology Project, archaeologists cannot control the archaeological remains that exist in the way a scientist can control an experiment.

Analytical methods must be designed to measure similarity and diversity within and between deposits quantitatively as well as qualitatively. The correlation of simple proportional measures and more complex tests, such as Miller's index values, have become standard. The choice of appropriate measures for any variable and the accurate, insightful interpretation of the results of such quantifications, should be of utmost concern to future researchers. In addition, guides to the utilization of Miller's test, expansion of the date and price data bases, and the development of new, multivariate tests (such as the Miller test, which correlates date, price, and ware and decorative type) are needed.

This study has also illustrated the relevance of the research of scholars in other fields to archaeological research programs, a fact long recognized by archaeologists. In this case, specific findings and general conclusions of family historians, labor historians, social historians, and students of the city and of ethnicity contributed to the research design and provided comparative analyses. Indeed, comparison is a basis of anthropological and archaeological research. Comparative archaeological data relevant to this research program is not readily available, however, although it is being produced in urban, cultural-resource management projects across the Northeast and beyond. Reports must include raw historical and archaeological data, statistical and qualitative descriptions and analyses of assemblages, and explication of methods, and must be accessible to other researchers; more, comparable research is, of course, also needed.

Archaeologists have voiced similar concerns and offered similar recommendations for many years now, concerns and recommendations that remain relevant today. In this study, evidence of the adaptive choices people make in response to economic limitations, to group conflict, to unfamiliar physical and social environments, and to industrialization and urbanization, has been collected and examined. Without more research, new and refined methods, interdisciplinary cooperation, and comparison, these findings will not be corroborated, nor will alternative patterns be defined. Such studies of America's factories, cities, and people, and more importantly, their comparison and the generation of broader explanations, are one means through which historical archaeologists can contribute to our understanding of culture process and change.

ACKNOWLEDGMENTS

Dr. Barry Brady, then Director of the Paterson Archaeology Project, supervised the excavations at the Van Houten Street Parking Lot and the Ryle-Thompson House sites in 1978 and 1979. I thank him for his professionalism in sharing his data, and for the time he spent reviewing his field notes and documentation with me.

The artifacts from the Paterson Archaeology Project's excavations are now part of the collections of the Passaic County Historical Society in Paterson, New Jersey. Catherine Keene, the director, and her staff furnished me a workplace, guided me through relevant manuscript materials, and sustained me with their friendship during long months of artifact processing and analysis.

I am also indebted to Paterson researchers who preceded me, especially Edward Rutsch, Mary Jane Rutsch, Jo Ann Cotz, and Charles Wilson. Their volumes provided me with both a model and an invaluable resource. The editor of this volume contributed significantly to the final form of this chapter; I thank her for her insightful suggestions during all stages of manuscript preparation and revision. Finally, thanks to my husband, whose patience and tolerance ultimately made this chapter possible.

REFERENCES

American Studies Association, 1981, Bibliography 1981—Ethnicity, *American Quarterly* 33 (3).
Bell, Daniel, 1975, Ethnicity and Social Change, in: Ethnicity: Theory and Experience (N. Glazer and D. Moynihan, eds.), Cambridge: Harvard University Press, pp. 141–174.
Burstein, Alan N., 1975, Residential Distribution and Mobility of Irish and German Immigrants in Philadelphia, 1850–80, Ph.D. dissertation, University of Pennsylvania, Philadelphia.
Carpenter, John A., 1947, The Industrial Development of Paterson, New Jersey: 1791–1913, M.A. thesis, Columbia University, New York.
Cotz, Jo Ann, 1975, A Study of Ten Houses in Paterson's Dublin Area, *Northeast Historical Archaeology* 4 (1,2):44–52.
Cotz, Jo Ann, Rutsch, Mary Jane, and Wilson, Charles, 1980, Salvage Archaeology Project, Paterson, New Jersey, 1973–1976: Paterson's Dublin: An Interdisciplinary Study of Social Structure, Volume 2, unpublished.
Cutler, William W., III, and Gillette, Howard, Jr. (eds.), 1980, *The Divided Metropolis: Social and Spatial Dimensions of Philadelphia, 1800–1975,* Greenwood Press, Westport, Connecticut.
De Cunzo, Lu Ann, 1979, Glimpses of a Working Class Neighborhood: Mill Street, Paterson in 1900, unpublished.

De Cunzo, Lu Ann, 1983, Economics and Ethnicity: An Archaeological Perspective on Nineteenth Century Paterson, New Jersey, Ph.D. dissertation, University of Pennsylvania, University Microfilms International, Ann Arbor.

Dickens, Roy S., Jr. (ed.), 1982, *Archaeology of Urban America: The Search for Pattern and Process,* Studies in Historical Archaeology, Academic Press, New York.

Garber, Morris William, 1968, The Silk Industry of Paterson, New Jersey, 1840–1913: Technology and the Origins, Development and Changes in an Industry, Ph.D. dissertation, Rutgers University, New Brunswick.

Glasco, Laurence A., 1977, The Life Cycles and Household Structure of American Ethnic Groups: Irish, Germans, and Native-born Whites in Buffalo, New York, 1855, in: *Family and Kin in Urban Communities, 1700–1930* (T. Hareven, ed.), New Viewpoints, New York, pp. 122–143.

Glassberg, Eudice, 1979, Work, Wages, and the Cost of Living: Ethnic Differences and the Poverty Line, Philadelphia, 1880, *Pennsylvania History* 46 (1):17–58.

Goldin, Claudia, 1981, Family Strategies and the Family Economy in the Late Nineteenth Century: The Role of Secondary Workers, in: *Philadelphia: Work, Space, Family and Group Experience in the Nineteenth Century, Essays Toward an Interdisciplinary History of the City* (T. Hershberg, ed.), Oxford University Press, New York, pp. 277–310.

Greenberg, Stephanie, W., 1980, The Relationship Between Work and Residence in an Industrializing City: Philadelphia, 1880, in: *The Divided Metropolis: Social and Spatial Dimensions of Philadelphia, 1800–1975* (W. W. Cutler, III, and H. Gillette, Jr., eds.), Greenwood Press, Westport, Connecticut, pp. 141–168.

Greenberg, Stephanie W., 1981, Industrial Location and Ethnic Residential Patterns in an Industrializing City: Philadelphia, 1880, in: *Philadelphia: Work, Space, Family and Group Experience in the Nineteenth Century: Essays Toward an Interdisciplinary History of the City* (T. Hershberg, ed.), Oxford University Press, New York, pp. 204–232.

Gutman, Herbert, 1977, *Work, Culture and Society in Industrializing America: Essays in American Working-Class and Social History,* Vintage, New York.

Haines, Michael, R., 1981, Poverty, Economic Stress, and the Family in a Late Nineteenth Century American City: Whites in Philadelphia, 1880, in: *Philadelphia: Work, Space, Family and Group Experience in the Nineteenth Century: Essays Toward an Interdisciplinary History of the City* (T. Hershberg, ed.), Oxford University Press, New York, pp. 240–276.

Hareven, Tamara (ed.), 1977, *Family and Kin in Urban Communities, 1700–1930,* New Viewpoints, New York.

Hareven, Tamara, 1982, *Family Time and Industrial Time: The Relationship between the Family and Work in a New England Industrial Community,* Cambridge University Press, New York.

Hareven, Tamara, and Vinovskis, Maris A. (eds.), 1978, *Family and Population in Nineteenth Century America,* Princeton University Press, Princeton.

Harris, Marvin, 1979, *Cultural Materialism: The Struggle for a Science of Culture,* Random House, New York.

Henn, Roselle E., 1982, The Changing Role of the Household in Industrial America, paper presented to the Society for Historical Archaeology, Philadelphia.

Hershberg, Theodore (ed.), 1981, *Philadelphia: Work, Space, Family and Group Experience in the Nineteenth Century: Essays Toward an Interdisciplinary History of the City,* (T. Hershberg, ed.), Oxford University Press, New York.

Hershberg, Theodore, and Dockhorn, Robert, 1976, Occupational Classification, *Historical Methods Newsletter* 9 (2,3):59–98.

Hershberg, Theodore, Light, Dale, Jr., Cox, Harold E., and Greenfield, Richard R., 1981, The "Journey to Work": An Empirical Investigation of Work, Residence and Transportation, Philadelphia, 1850 and 1880, in: *Philadelphia: Work, Space, Family and Group Experience in the Nineteenth Century: Essays Toward an Interdisciplinary History of the City* (T. Hershberg, ed.), Oxford University Press, New York, pp. 128–173.

Hirsch, Susan E., 1978, *Roots of the American Working Class: The Industrialization of Crafts in Newark, 1800–1860,* University of Pennsylvania Press, Philadelphia.

Klein, Terry H., and Garrow, Patrick H. (eds.), 1984, *Final Archaeological Investigations at the Wilmington Boulevard, Monroe Street to King Street, Wilmington, New Castle County, Delaware,* (DELDOT Archaeology Series, Number 29) Delaware Department of Transportation.

Laurie, Bruce, Hershberg, Theodore, and Alter, George, 1981, Immigrants and Industry: The Philadelphia Experience, 1850–80, in: *Philadelphia: Work, Space, Family and Group Experience in the Nineteenth Century: Essays Toward an Interdisciplinary History of the City* (T. Hershberg, ed.), Oxford University Press, New York, pp. 93–120.

Mayers, Robert A., 1977, "Mayers Family Genealogy," unpublished paper.

Miller, George, L., 1980, Classification and Economic Scaling of Nineteenth Century Ceramics, *Historical Archaeology* 14:1–41.

Modell, John, 1978, Patterns of Consumption, Acculturation, and Family Income Strategies in Late Nineteenth Century America, in: *Family and Population in Nineteenth-Century America* (T. Hareven and M. Vinovskis, eds.), Princeton University Press, Princeton, pp. 206–227.

New Jersey Bureau of Statistics of Labor and Industries, 1880, *Third Annual Report for the Year Ending October 31, 1880,* Edward B. Porter, Somerville, New Jersey.

Otto, John S., 1977, Artifacts and Status Differences—A Comparison of Ceramics from Planter, Overseer, and Slave Sites on an Antebellum Plantation, in: *Research Strategies in Historical Archaeology* (S. South, ed.), Studies in Archaeology, Academic Press, New York, pp. 91–118.

Paterson Daily Press, The, January 14, 1884.

Praetzellis, Mary, Praetzellis, Adrian, Brown, Marley R., III, and Bragdon, Kathleen, 1981, Test Excavation and Research Strategy on IJ56 Block: Early Chinese Merchant Community in Sacramento, California, Anthropological Studies Center, Sonoma State University, unpublished paper.

Presa, Donald G., 1980, The Development and Demise of the Cianci Street Block, unpublished paper.

Rapp, Rayna, 1979, Examining Family History: Household and Family, *Feminist Studies* 5(1):174–200.

Rothschild, Nan A., and Rockman, Diana di Zerega, 1982, Method in Urban Archaeology: The Stadt Huys Block, in: *Archaeology of Urban America: The Search for Pattern and Process* (R. S. Dickens, ed.), Academic Press, New York, pp. 1–18.

Royce, Anya Peterson, 1982, *Ethnic Identity: Strategies of Diversity,* Indiana University Press, Bloomington.

Rutsch, Edward S., n.d., Salvage Archaeology Project. Paterson, New Jersey 1973–1976, Volume 1, unpublished.

Schuyler, Robert L. (ed.), 1980, *Archaeological Perspectives on Ethnicity in America: Afro-American and Asian American Culture History,* Baywood Publishing, New York.

Shephard, Steven J., 1980, An Archaeological Model: Change in the Nineteenth Century Middle Class, paper presented to the Society for American Archaeology, Philadelphia.

Shriner, Charles A., 1890, *Paterson, New Jersey,* Press Printing and Publishing, Paterson.

South, Stanley, 1977, *Method and Theory in Historical Archaeology,* Academic Press, New York.

Spencer-Wood, Suzanne, and Riley, Richard J., 1981, The Development of an Urban Socio-Economic Model for Archaeological Testing, *Northeast Historical Archaeology* 10:40–50.

Thomas, George E., 1980, Architectural Patronage and Social Stratification in Philadelphia between 1840 and 1920, in: *The Divided Metropolis: Social and Spatial Dimensions of Philadelphia, 1800–1975* (W. W. Cutler III, and H. Gillette, eds.), Greenwood Press, Westport, Connecticut, pp. 85–124.

Thomas, William Isaac, and Florian Znaniecki, 1927, *The Polish Peasant in Europe and America,* A. A. Knopf, New York.

Trumbull, Levi R., 1882, *A History of Industrial Paterson,* Carleton M. Herrick, Paterson, New Jersey.

Twelfth Census of the United States, Taken in the Year 1900: Population, 1901, Part 1, Census Reports, Volume 2, U.S. Census Office, Washington, D.C.

United States Census, 1850, West Ward, Paterson, microfilm of original schedules.

Ware, Caroline, 1946, Ethnic Communities, in: *When Peoples Meet: A Study in Race and Culture Contacts* (rev. ed., A. Locke and B. Stern, eds.), Hinds, Hayden, Eldredge, New York, pp. 474–483.

White, Leslie A., 1949, *The Science of Culture: A Study of Men and Civilization,* 2nd edition, Farrar, Straus & Giroux, New York.

Late Nineteenth- and Twentieth-Century Urban Sites

From the second half of the nineteenth century and into the twentieth century, rapid new growth in industry and urbanism spread from the Northeast to the South, the Midwest, and then the West. Mining industries increased production and developed in new areas (Midwest and West) to provide the energy and raw materials for a number of rapidly growing industries. Technological innovations led to improvements in quantity and quality of products in transportation, agriculture, mining, food processing, and manufacturing industries. Water power was first replaced by steam power, and wood by coal, followed by electricity and the gasoline engine. Some inventions led to the rapid development of entirely new groups of industries, including those related to the manufacture of steel, barbed wire, electric lighting, the telephone, the electric trolley, and the automobile. Businesses and factories became larger in order to gain economies of scale and decrease unit transportation costs. Businesses with high transportation costs for raw materials or finished products agglomerated in large cities where competition between alternative railroad lines kept rates low. Some large businesses developed by forming corporations and decreased competition through the formation of combinations, holding companies, and trusts. As the scale of many factories increased, and railroads increased distribution throughout the country, national scale advertising and marketing developed. Competition on the national scale led to the development of brand names, distinctive packaging, and advertising. More manufacturers distributed their products nationally or internationally as innovations decreased the costs of production and distribution. This resulted in a greater variety of consumer goods becoming available in many areas (Bining and Cochran 1964:427–435, 477–485; Ingle and Ward 1978:283–284; Ratner *et al.* 1979:275–343).

The American business cycle tended to have sequences of relatively rapid boom and bust periods. Rapid growth, prosperity, overexpansion, and overinvestment would lead to inflation, growing interest rates, and rising prices, until investment ceased and bankruptcies quickly followed. The five-year depression starting in 1873 was initiated when economic collapses in England and France led foreigners to decrease their American investments. At the same time, American domestic investment exceeded savings, which resulted in rising interest rates and prices. Despite a recovery in 1878, periods of prosperity were interrupted by downward swings in 1881, 1884, 1890, and by a severe depression from 1893 to 1897 (Bining and Cochran 1964:410–412). In

297

the first half of the twentieth century, major impacts on the economy included World War I, the Great Depression of the 1930s, and World War II.

By the early twentieth century, the primary employment of Americans had shifted from agriculture to industry. Increasing numbers of women and children worked outside the home in factories, offices, and stores in urban areas. Labor laws gradually imposed age and hour restrictions that resulted in decreasing employment of children after 1910. Labor organizations developed both for industrial workers and for farmers. From the mid-nineteenth through the early twentieth centuries, large numbers of European and Asian immigrants arrived in the United States, supplying cheap labor for the growing numbers of large factories and also increasing the market for consumer goods (Bining and Cochran 1964:427, 450, 466, 471–475; Robertson 1973:379–396). Over time, some immigrants became assimilated and increased their status in the American class system, while some formed ethnic enclaves and developed their own social stratification. In Binghamton, New York, Clark found that native-born Americans held more of the supervisory, white-collar, and professional occupations, and were more likely to own a house than were recent immigrants. In the late nineteenth century, municipal, state, and federal governments became increasingly aware of "the public good" as an important political force for clean public water, municipal sewerage systems, city parks, preservation of the natural wonders of the country, and against monopolies and child labor (Bining and Cochran 1964:411; Lebergott 1984:360–363).

In the late nineteenth and early twentieth centuries, some changes developed in regional economies. The Northeast developed the most industry and the largest urban centers. After the Civil War, southern plantations were broken into smaller farms and the sharecropping system became prevalent, in contrast to the antebellum system, as described by Orser in Part I. Many southern whites and blacks migrated to the North or West. Industry also increased in the South, aided by investment by northerners. As railroads expanded in the South and spread to the West, both areas increasingly diversified their crops for eastern city markets, especially after invention of the refrigerator car in the 1870s. Over the century, lumbering, agriculture, mining, industry, and urbanization spread in sequence from the East to the Midwest and then the Far West. Increasing population and the spread of railroads resulted in increasing trade to the West and greater availability there of consumer goods of all types at decreasing prices (Bining and Cochran 1964: 376–387; Higgs 1971:39–43).

In this section, methods are assessed for relating the relative value of archaeologically recovered ceramics, fauna, and gravestones to household socioeconomic status in urban neighborhoods. While most fauna and gravestones would come from American sources, whiteware ceramics were just beginning to be manufactured in quantity in the United States, and many were still imported from England. Branstner and Martin, and Henry contrast distinctions in whiteware and fauna at urban sites. Henry and Spencer-Wood each develop methodological innovations for measuring values of household whiteware. Clark considers the interrelationships among class, ethnicity, and gravestones, while Henry considers the effects of these and some other variables on consumer behavior.

In Branstner and Martin's chapter, late nineteenth-century whiteware and fauna from three features in a Detroit city block are compared and contrasted in order to determine if any distinctions existed among households in a working-class neighborhood. The majority of the whiteware ceramics at all sites were undecorated, but some distinctions among sites were possible in measurements of fauna. Variations among features in frequencies of faunal types, cut values, and range of wild and domestic species were related to possible variations in household status.

In my chapter (Spencer-Wood), correlations between eleven alternative ceramic price-scaling indices and occupational indications of socioeconomic status at five Boston area sites ranged from moderately positive to negative. However, the correlations between cup and saucer indices and occupational indications of status became very positive when one anomalous site was eliminated from these analyses. Among all the ceramic indices, cup and saucer indices were more highly correlated with status than plate or bowl indices, possibly because plates and bowls included utilitarian kitchenware as well as tableware, while tea- and coffeeware served more to display status. Whiteware consumer-choice profiles were developed from Miller's ceramic price-scaling indices by analyzing the relative frequency pattern of alternative whiteware values within each site assemblage. A combination of archaeological and documentary analyses suggest that different whiteware profiles may correspond to high, moderate, and low socioeconomic status groups or classes. Because these profiles do not necessarily produce correspondingly high, moderate, and low ceramic indices, it is suggested that ceramic consumer-choice profiles be used in future analyses to relate patterns in the value of archaeologically deposited whiteware decorative types to patterns of socioeconomic behavior.

Henry analyzed relationships between archaeological samples of whiteware and fauna and associated household socioeconomic status, ethnicity, and life cycle, as well as external economic conditions and market access. She develops a ceramic price-scaling index for the late nineteenth and early twentieth centuries from whiteware decorative type prices in mail order catalogues. Cup index value rankings of fourteen household features, and beef value rankings of nine household features, were found to be moderately correlated with occupational rankings of associated households. She also found that differences in percentage of some faunal types were more strongly related to site ethnic distinctions than to socioeconomic status rankings. For two households, life cycle and changes in income were related to ceramic index values. Some of the variability in whiteware values over time was also related to nationwide changes in economic conditions and market availability. Henry demonstrated that consumer behavior is influenced by the complex interaction of a number of variables, including not only socioeconomic status, but also ethnicity, household life cycle, market availability, economic conditions, and the durable or nondurable nature of commodities.

Clark's chapter is concerned with developing ethnic and class distinctions reflected in aspects of gravestones in Binghamton, New York, in the late nineteenth through mid-twentieth centuries. Clark explores the interrelationships between the maintenance of ethnic boundaries, the development of class differentiation within ethnic groups, assimilation into the dominant culture's class structure, and gravestone distinctions between and within ethnic and occupational groups. Clark found that variations in gravestone choices corresponded most with a combined classification by ethnic/occupational groups. She demonstrates that consumer selections of gravestones from the total variety available was conditioned by the interaction of class and ethnicity within and between social groups.

Chapters in this section are concerned with relating gravestones, or archaeological whiteware and/or faunal assemblages to a number of variables affecting acquisition and deposition of these consumer goods. The relationships between archaeological data and socioeconomic status are not easily measured, but form part of the complex interrelationships among aspects of the cultural system at the household, neighborhood, social group, and pancultural level.

REFERENCES

Bining, Arthur C., and Cochran, Thomas C., 1964, *The Rise of American Economic Life*, Charles Scribner's Sons, New York.

Higgs, R., 1971, *The Transformation of the American Economy 1865–1914,* Wiley, New York.

Ingle, H. L., and Ward, James A., 1978, *American History: A Brief View Through Reconstruction,* Little, Brown, Boston.

Lebergott, S., 1984, *The Americans: An Economic Record,* W. W. Norton, New York.

Ratner, Sidney, Soltow, J. H., and Sulla, R., 1979, *The Evolution of the American Economy,* Basic Books, New York.

Robertson, R. M., 1973, *History of the American Economy,* Harcourt, Brace, Jovanovich, New York.

13

Working-Class Detroit
Late Victorian Consumer Choices and Status

MARK C. BRANSTNER AND
TERRANCE J. MARTIN

INTRODUCTION

The analysis of material culture and faunal remains with an eye towards pattern recognition in historical archaeology has been accused of being only a "form of structural functionalism" (Schuyler 1980:200), due in part to its lack of explanatory underpinnings (Honerkamp *et al.* 1982:2). The search for pattern as espoused by South (1977) and others is a direct product of the nature of sites in the regions where such theoretical orientations were first developed. Nineteenth-century urban archaeology, on the other hand, is often blessed with documentary evidence that obviates concerns of pattern recognition for defining site function, allowing detailed analysis of faunal and material culture in relation to their producers.

Analysis of faunal remains and material culture in relation to socioeconomic status has usually been phrased in terms of differential access to goods and services, or personal preferences reflecting class or ethnicity. In a 1932 study of milk and meat purchasing habits in Pittsburgh, it was suggested that, if the ethnicity variable were eliminated from such considerations, consumption patterns would be seen as most greatly influenced by the neighborhood environment. It was also suggested that "the more homogeneous the neighborhood the greater the facility in isolating significant factors" affecting consumer choices (Cover 1932:2 in Mudar 1978:325). Carrying this supposition further, it is postulated that the presence of a well-documented archaeological population, in a closed context of time, space (neighborhood), socioeconomic status (occupational range), and ethnicity, should allow the recovery of archaeological materials that are representative of the larger population, even when specific proveniences of the individual assemblages are not known. Using archaeologically derived privy lots from a one-block area of a late nineteenth-century, working-class, nonspecific ethnicity neighborhood in Detroit,

Mark C. Branstner ☐ Department of Anthropology, Wayne State University, Detroit, MI 48202. Terrance J. Martin ☐ Anthropology Section, Illinois State Museum, Springfield, IL 62706.

this study will examine the efficacy of small sample archaeological recovery in concert with documentary research for producing socioeconomic analysis generalizable to larger population groups.

Theoretical Orientation

The use of faunal materials for dietary reconstruction in historic archaeology is not an uncommon practice, yet its use as an indicator of socioeconomic status has been limited in scope. One of the first subdisciplines within historical archaeology to recognize the implications of faunal analysis as indicators of status or class was "plantation archaeology." The presumed sharp social, economic, and ethnic distinctions to be found in the slave versus overseer versus upper white site assemblages were ideally suited to such research (Ascher and Fairbanks 1971; Drucker 1981; Fairbanks 1974; Miller 1979; Otto 1977, 1980). Although the results of these studies suggested that social class was a better predictor of faunal diversity than was ethnicity, the faunal component of diet did reflect both differential access and utilization patterns. Following closely patterns of research set forth in the southeast United States, other workers have attempted to document socioeconomic status from the faunal record, often including an ethnic component (Bridges and Salwen 1980; De Cunzo 1982; Langenwalter 1980; Mudar 1978). Most recently, such analysis has assayed socioeconomic status outside the confines of ethnicity, with more emphasis on class attributes or site function in the urban setting (Baugher 1982; Bellantoni *et al.* 1982; Davidson 1982; Martin and Demeter 1985; Schulz and Gust 1983).

The presumed relationship of faunal remains and material culture to socioeconomic status is founded on the assumption of differential access to goods and services. These differences can be seen as the result of a number of factors, including economic constraints or limits, unequal access to distributional systems, or consumer preferences based on less tangible factors such as "taste." In the late 1970s Mudar (1978) sought to test some of these assumptions against a series of faunal assemblages recovered from privies during construction of the Renaissance Center in Detroit, Michigan. Due to the preservation of a detailed 1828 map of the project area and extensive documentary research at the time of the project (Demeter n.d.), these deposits from the 1820s and 1830s could be attributed to individual families, and correlated to both ethnic and socioeconomic variables. Faunal materials were compared to these known social parameters to determine if either variable were apparent within or between faunal assemblages. Mudar's intersite status differences were most sensitively represented by ratios of beef versus pork, or beef versus mutton consumption, rather than in terms of actual cuts of meat being consumed in any single species category.

In 1982 another opportunity arose in Detroit to test the utility of archaeologically recovered faunal materials as correlates of socioeconomic status. In this case the site area and recovered privy assemblages were related to a circa 1870–1900 neighborhood of generalized Anglo-Irish ethnicity. Analysis of resident occupation, residential architecture, and property tax assessment values suggest that socioeconomic ranking within the study area was limited to several strata of laborers, semiskilled and skilled workers. As faunal materials and material culture, specifically ceramics, have been shown to reflect socioeconomic status (Miller 1980; Mudar 1978; Otto 1977 and others), it was postulated that these deposits would also reflect differential access to and utilization of goods and services.

Beyond the given that individual assemblages would reflect the consumer choices of the residents, the conceptualization of the site area as part of a "neighborhood" also predicts certain things about the assemblages in general. First, because of the "neighborliness" of the assemblages and the fact that the same suppliers were potentially available to the residents, it was postulated that there would be certain similarities between assemblages. These might be reflected in terms of what species of animal goods were being utilized, or in what ceramic patterns were being used within the community. Finally, predicated on the concept of "neighborhood," it was expected that any individual privy assemblage would be roughly equivalent to any other assemblage within the community.

CASE STUDY: THE STROH BREWING COMPANY SITE

During the summer and fall of 1982 archaeologists from Caminos Associates of Bay City, Michigan, conducted a Phase I field investigation of a sixteen-block parcel in the near east riverfront area of Detroit. This compliance action was requested in response to the use of various federal funds, and was ultimately administered by Resource Assessment, of Los Angeles, California, and the Community and Economic Development Department of the City of Detroit. An earlier planning document put the general project area into chronological perspective, and identified the major resource concerns (Demeter 1982).

The project area traces its Euro-American settlement history back to the 1730s and includes French, British, and American occupations. Although first settled in the early eighteenth century, land use patterns kept it in agricultural use until well after the American arrival in 1796. With the beginning of the American Settlement period (Branstner and Prahl 1984), the project area came more fully under the sway of development pressures. Baseline data are provided by the 1802 list of taxable property (Campau 1802) and the Private Claim documentation provided by the American State Papers (Lowrie and Clarke 1832). From this point (c. 1808), all property transactions are recorded and are still extant (Wayne County Tract Index). County tax records that enumerate structural development and assessed values are available for the project area from 1858–1870 (Wayne County Archives), as are the city directories from 1837 through most of the twentieth century. These records, in conjunction with the decennial censuses and the post-1884 insurance atlases, provide a fairly comprehensive documentation of Detroit's land-use and demographic trends throughout the nineteenth century. All of these sources are further correlated by the history of Detroit and Wayne County, published first in 1884 by Silas Farmer (Farmer 1890).

The growth of urban Detroit during the early nineteenth century was a slow and deliberate process. The removal of the British in 1796 and the catastrophic burning of Detroit in 1805 severely retarded its economic fortunes. In fact, the population of the urban center during the period from 1805 through about 1820 remained at levels lower than during the preceding colonial period (Farmer 1890; Pilling 1982). It was not until the 1825 opening of the Erie Canal that significant increase, either in trade or population, became an eventuality in Detroit. As late as 1830, the City of Detroit maintained a population of only 2,222 persons. However, between 1830 and 1840, population growth approached nearly 400 percent, reaching 9,102 by 1840. It has been said that in one day in May, 1837, 2,400 passengers disembarked at Detroit (Farmer 1890:335). Although most of these passengers did not remain in Detroit, but traveled into the interior to carve out farms, a substantial number did settle in Detroit. From 1840 until 1870 the population approximately doubled every decade. By 1884 the "metropolis" of Detroit could boast nearly 150,000 residents (Farmer 1890:336).

Along with its growth in population, its increasing significance as a major point of disembarkment for immigrants, and its role as a regional market and redistribution center, Detroit began to develop its industrial and manufacturing base. This was greatly facilitated by Detroit's geographic position on the Great Lakes transportation system, its proximity to the coal fields of Michigan and Pennsylvania, and the iron and copper deposits of the Lake Superior region (Michigan History Division n.d.). This growth in population and industry in the years just preceding the Civil War necessitated the outward expansion of the physical limits of the city. As industrial development was closely linked to Detroit River access, this growth favored the shoreline situation and, by the 1850s, had reached the study area. In 1857 this portion of Hamtramck Township was incorporated into the City of Detroit, resulting in the production of the first property tax rolls for the project area that enumerate structural improvements (Wayne County Archives 1858). Information gained from this baseline documentation suggests that very little structural development had occurred beyond the original agricultural-residential sites. The same documents for 1864 record the arrival of commercial developments along the riverfront, including several sawmills (Wayne County Archives 1864). This secondary building cycle of the 1860s continued through the 1870s and 1880s with the arrival of more and heavier industrial concerns. Major employers in the immediate area included the Michigan Stove Company (1872), the Parke, Davis, and Co. pharmaceutical firm (1873), the Russel Wheel and Foundry Co. (1876), and the Peninsular Car Co. (1880) (Farmer 1890). Although these large firms dominated the local area, many smaller firms were also present, taking advantage of the riverfront and railroad access.

The presence of large numbers of employers fostered a need for housing in close relation to the work sites. The first nearby response appears to have been the Walker Subdivision of 1857, with actual lot development not proceeding until the 1860s (Wayne County Tract Index n.d.). By 1870 about half the residential lots within the project area had been developed with small, frame, single-family dwellings (Wayne County Archives 1870). By the time of the publication of the first insurance atlas for this area the noncommercial land within the project area had become saturated with such housing (Sanborn Map Company 1884) (Figure 1), often within the shadow of the factories that they supported. This property disposition remained constant until the mid-twentieth century, when gradual attrition of the older residential units and competition for parking space from the surrounding commercial-industrial properties finally drove out the remaining residents. Today very little of the original 1860 to 1880 building cycle remains extant.

Phase I archaeological investigations of the entire sixteen-block area addressed a cross section of all major archaeological resource types common to Detroit (Branstner and Prahl 1983a). One block of the project area, Test Area 8, presented an opportunity to examine several problem areas, including (1) the nature of trash disposal patterns in late nineteenth-century Detroit, (2) the reliability of the insurance atlases as predictors of privy locations, and (3) the relationship of a well-documented residential neighborhood to the archaeological deposits produced during their occupation. Test Area 8 encompasses the block bounded on the east and west by McDougall and Joseph Campau

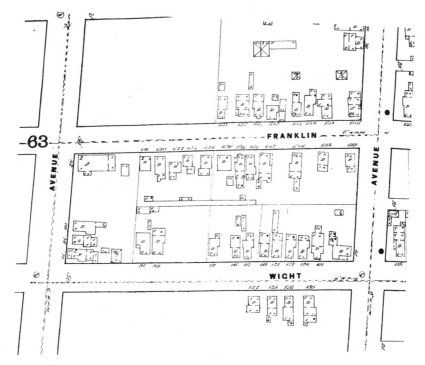

Figure 1. Stroh Brewing Company Test Area 8. (Source: Sanborn Map Company 1884)

avenues, and on the north and south by Franklin and Wight streets. Between 1864 and 1870 the eastern half of the block was subdivided into residential lots, and by 1870 at least ten residences had been built. The ten taxpayers included the following surnames: Quinn, Hawkins, Satiorex, Howie (2), Bullock (2), Robinson, O'Brien, Stone, and Terry (Wayne County Archives 1870). Of the seven names that can be correlated with the Detroit city directory, occupations represented among the taxpayers included laborers (2), a fireman, a carpenter, a painter, a watchman, and a blacksmith (Weeks and Co. 1871). Ethnicity would appear to be generalized Anglo-Irish, and socioeconomic status appears to range from unskilled to skilled. Reflecting this lower-income bracket, the average assessed value of each house was only $60, and lot values averaged only $312 each (Wayne County Archives 1870). Between 1870 and 1884, the remainder of the block was subdivided and by 1884 had been developed with small, single-story frame residences (Sanborn Map Company 1884), as can be seen in Figure 1. This pattern of single-family, working-class, privately owned homes is a characteristic of Detroit throughout the nineteenth and early twentieth centuries. Tenements and apartment houses similar to those of the industrial cities of the East Coast, although known, were not common in Detroit.

The next easy point of access to the residents is after 1891. As our eventual test excavations were confined to the north side and west end of the block, the following list will provide a general picture of the neighborhood and its ethnic-socioeconomic orientation (Polk 1891):

Franklin Street (between Joseph Campau and McDougall)
618 Edward Casse, mounter; wife, dressmaker
    Adeline McQuillen, widow (boarder)
620 Michael Boyle, molder
622 William C. McVay, sailor
624 Oliver LaChance, carpenter
626 George LaChance, foreman
628 Emil Martin, laborer
634 Patrick Prendergast, molder
636 William Lodge, carpenter
624 George Sims, shoemaker
646 Andrew Lehou, tinsmith
    Andrew C. Lehou, vessel mate (boarder)
    Henry Bogin, tinsmith
    Joseph Conroy, molder
654 Lawrence F. Ryan, molder
658 Ann Quinn
       Joseph Campau Avenue (between Franklin and Wight)
 76 Henry T. Cleary, watchman
    Margaret Cleary, grocer (home same)
    Susan Brabyn, widow
 78 Bridget Burke
 92 Elliot and Howell, saloon (proprietors)

Although not an ethnic neighborhood in the classic sense, its generalized An-glo-Irish character and the absence of a non-English-speaking immigrant con-stituent within the neighborhood probably functioned in much the same fash-ion as a more clearly defined ethnic enclave. When considered as an ethnic neighborhood in this sense, the presence of a relatively broad range of work-ing-class household heads correlates well with Zunz's (1982) spatial model of Detroit. In this model the cohesive element of pre-1900 neighborhood struc-ture was the ethnic rather than the socioeconomic variable. According to Zunz, the automobile industry in the post-1900 years led to the dissolution of most ethnicity-based neighborhoods and the formation of community areas formed along ethnicity-crosscutting socioeconomic strata.

The stability of this general land use pattern and the socioeconomic at-tribution of its residents appears to have remained constant until the First World War (Polk 1900, 1910). About this time the residential population was replaced by a Roumanian immigrant group (Polk 1921). While completely changing the ethnic makeup of the neighborhood, the socioeconomic ranking did not appreciably alter with this infusion of a recently arrived immigrant group, deviating from Zunz's (1982) model. The period following their out-migration, during the post–World War II period, corresponds to the gradual attrition of most of the residential units within the study area. At the time of the research project (1982), the entire Test Area 8 consisted of industrial structures and parking lots.

ARCHAEOLOGICAL DATA AND METHODS

Archaeological data recovered within Test Area 8 of the Stroh Brewing Company project area was conducted during the course of the larger Phase I survey program in July and August, 1982, and again during a mitigative salvage effort during December 1982. Due to the presence of three to four feet of rubble and fill over the original ground surface the use of mechanized equipment for all testing and salvage excavations was required. Equipment included a rubber-tired, clam-shell crane, a rubber-tired backhoe, and a Link-Belt trencher. Standard recovery techniques included the monitoring of the excavation of all units until a feature was exposed. Features were taken out by hand with the fill troweled through to recovery cultural materials. In cases where small faunal remains were noted, soil samples were removed for labora-tory processing. During the four weeks of excavation time devoted to Test Area 8, a series of 76 test trenches and units were opened, 20 intact features were encountered, and over 5,600 artifacts were recovered (Branstner and Prahl 1983b).

The recovery strategy employed was a simple one, predicated on the as-sumption that artifact deposition in privy pits, trash features, and middens would be most likely encountered in the rear of the residential lots, adjacent to the alleys. Control excavations along the fronts and through the mid-depths of the lot areas revealed only very thin sheet-midden deposits, and verified con-temporary atlas descriptions of unbasemented structures built on piers. Another area of particular interest to this study was the east–west running alley. The 1884 Sanborn insurance atlas (Sanborn Map Company) illustrated the eastern half of the alley unopened at that date (see Figure 1), as did the 1888–1895 Rascher atlas map (Rascher Map Publishing Company). It does not appear that this alley was opened all the way through the block until sometime after 1897 (Sanborn-Perris Map Company 1897–1919). The Rascher version indicated a series of structures along the right-of-way axis. While not functionally coded in the atlases, it has long been assumed that some of these small wooden structures represent "necessaries." Excavations in Detroit had already noted a direct correlation between an archaeologically recovered privy unit and a mapped atlas location (Demeter and Barnard 1980). As it was known that the alley had been opened post-1895 and had been actively used until the present day, it was hoped that intact privy or trash features would remain *in situ* beneath the modern surface.

Archaeological recovery from Test Area 8 was derived from several sources. The most significant features encountered appear to have been privy pits or vaults secondarily used as trash pits. Cultural deposition in these units ranged from sterile fill of ashes and cinders, to units containing substantial quantities of ceramic, glass, and faunal materials. Due to the disturbed, deep nature of the overburden, and the physical nature of mechanized excavation, it was often difficult to define a feature until a substantial depth had been reached. Feature recovery in such an environment was never 100 percent.

A major problem associated with archaeological analysis in the urban setting is sampling, and the Stroh project area was no exception. Sampling in Test Area 8 was limited to approximately 50 percent of the land surface of the block due to the presence of standing structures on the remainder. Within the remaining test area mechanical trenches and excavation units were placed so as to intersect the most sensitive areas for archaeological recovery, that is, the alleys and the rear twenty feet of the residential lots. Sampling within this more closely defined area approached 100 percent.

The association of specific features to specific households within the study area was also a major concern. Due to the imprecise location of archaeological features in relation to old property lines, particularly in the case of the privy units recovered from the midline of the alley right-of-way, such correlations must also be viewed as imprecise. This is further confounded by the relatively loose chronological placement of any late nineteenth-century archaeological feature and the short-term residency patterns that appear to have been common within the study area. It would appear more appropriate to view the recovered features and archaeological materials as representations of a limited range of socioeconomic strata, anchored in time and space, ranging from unskilled to skilled workers.

ARCHAEOLOGICAL RESULTS

Of the more than twenty identified, discrete features recovered during the Test Area 8 testing and salvage program, only three contained major faunal assemblages in association with temporally diagnostic assemblages of ceramics and glass. The following section will discuss the contents of each of these three features, their temporal significance, and their significance in terms of consumer choices per faunal resources and material culture.

For the purpose of this study we are assuming that consumer choices in the market place are correlates of socioeconomic status. Reflecting on the nature of the study group, that is, a late nineteenth-century working-class population, and the recognition that undecorated white table wares represent the bottom stratum of the ceramic price indices during this period (Miller 1980), it is expected that the representative plain white ironstones will predominate ceramic assemblages within the study area. However, the presence of heads of households within this working-class neighborhood, ranging from unskilled laborers to skilled tradesmen, does indicate a certain socioeconomic stratification within this otherwise working-class group. Again, assuming that socioeconomic status is discernible in the archaeological record, it is assertible that these socioeconomic divisions will be reflected in the recovered assemblages. The presence of the more expensive decorated earthenwares, bone chinas, or porcelains, or the less than strictly utilitarian ceramic and glass items in the household refuse categories, in combination with the ubiquitous white ironstones of the period, may prove capable of sorting these finer-scale socioeconomic strata.

In the same fashion that consumer choices in material goods are a function of socioeconomic status, dietary choices are in large part dependent upon socially and economically based access restrictions. Evidence of these restrictions in faunal resource exploitations should be available in direct terms (i.e., percentage composition of cost-ranked cuts of meat relating to preferred species) and indirectly (i.e., percentage composition of all species within assemblages), relating to the ability of households to acquire preferred species as standard table fare. Therefore, archaeological faunal assemblages potentially reflect body-part and individual-cut preference on the one hand, and species preference on the other.

In this study we have generally accepted the works of Lyman (1979), Mudar (1978), and Schulz and Gust (1983) as more appropriate to faunal analysis in the urban setting than quantification techniques based on faunal recovery in rural or frontier areas, that is, biomass assay. Addressing the question of accurate assemblage representation, Mudar noted that none of the standard quantification techniques (bone counts, bone weights, or minimum number of individuals [MNI]) are without problems. The assumption that most mammal meat is bought by the cut in the urban setting implies that estimations of MNI's as an assessment of dietary importance would greatly overstate the significance of some species (Lyman 1979). For example, assume bones recovered from a privy representing four round steaks can also be shown to represent four individual cattle. There would be little validity in an interpretation that the former residents who deposited the privy assemblage had consumed the biomass of four cattle. By the same token, comparing bone counts between beef and fowl will not present any true ratio of resource preference or utilization between the two species. For these reasons and others, we have assumed that for mammals that were presumably bought by the cut, quantification by butchering units most accurately reflects consumer patterns. Alternatively, fish and birds are quantified by MNI's since the individual animal would have been the normal unit of purchase.

In their respective analyses of urban faunal assemblages, Mudar (1978: 363) and Schulz and Gust (1983:48) have proposed scales of relative value for various beef-butchering units based on late nineteenth-century references. Overall, these scales are quite similar, but because the latter authors' ranking allows for more detailed differentiation of several elements, their classification is used for this study.

Feature A

Besides the several plain unmarked ironstone cups and saucers recovered from this privy unit, there were two marked ceramic pieces that characterize the deposit. The first is an unornamented "Wedgwood and Co." saucer in the "Erie Shape." Although this pattern is an early one, patented in 1850 (Wetherbee 1980:59), the use of the name "Wedgwood and Co." as a successor to Podmore, Walker, and Co. did not appear until after 1860 (Godden 1964: 655). The other marked piece is a plain white plate, bottom-marked "Powell and Bishop." These Staffordshire potters are known to have only operated between 1876–1878 (Godden 1964:509). Other materials recovered from this feature include a dozen French square pharmaceutical bottles, several marked with the logo of the nearby Parke, Davis and Company drug firm, three Detroit aqua soda bottles, and an emerald green "Congress and Empire Spring Co. / Saratoga, NY / Congress Water," commonly produced during the 1870s (McKearin and Wilson 1978:234). This assemblage of ceramics and glass should date to the late 1870s or early 1880s.

More revealing for the socioeconomic analysis of this deposit is the faunal assemblage, which includes 163 identified elements (Table 1). Most noteworthy was the discovery of five bilaterally sawn calf skulls along with mandible fragments, indicating the presence of at least eight calves. In all, 99 of 110 elements identified as cattle were from the calf crania, as probably were most of the 124 unidentified mammal elements. Mature cattle were sparsely represented among the postcranial bones, which, it is important to note, consisted mostly of low-value shank cuts. The significance of calf skulls for insights on socioeconomic status is unclear at this time. Perhaps obtained for the brain or to be processed into headcheese, it may be that the presence of calf skulls represents some variable of individual preference or ethnicity. In addition to a sheep–goat radius and three cervical vertebrate from one chicken, a relatively large and diverse sample of fish remains were uncovered. It is interesting to note that all of the fish species identified in Feature A are available locally. Perhaps more important, the presence of fish such as redhorse and white sucker may reflect the consumption of less than normally desirable fish resources (Mudar 1978; Trautman 1957:461).

Table 1. Species Composition of Feature A

Common name (scientific name)	NISP	(MNI)[a]
Mammals		
Cattle (*Bos taurus*)	110	(9)
Sheep–goat (*Ovis–Capra*)	1	(1)
Unidentified	124	
Birds		
Domestic chicken (*Gallus gallus*)	3	(1)
Fish		
Northern pike (*Esox lucius*)	1	(1)
Redhorse sucker (*Moxostoma* sp.)	35	(4)
White sucker (*Catostomus commersonni*)	1	(1)
Sucker–redhorse (family Catostomidae)	4	
Black bass (*Micropterus* sp.)	1	(1)
Walleye–sauger (*Stizostedion* sp.)	7	(2)
Unidentified	135	
Feature totals	422	(20)

[a]Small scale recovery of faunal remains from a soil sample yielded thirteen scales diagnostic of walleye, sauger, or perch, and three cycloid scales. NISP = number of identified specimens; MNI = minimum number of individuals.

Feature B

This wood-lined privy vault contained an extensive ceramic and glass assemblage, with no apparent stratification within the recovered portion of the feature. The extent of the deposition and its concentration within the feature strongly suggests a single-event "house-keeping episode." The marked ceramics were numerous, yet all but one example were plain white ironstones. The oldest datable piece in the assemblage was a plate with an impressed "Edward Clarke / 5 73" mark. Another piece, a small dessert plate, is bottom-marked in black "Edward Clarke, Tunstall," circa 1865–1877 (Godden 1964:147). Several other pieces of English origin bore varieties of the "J&G Meakin" mark, including several with "England" added to the mark. This addition indicates probable manufacture after the 1891 McKinley Tariff Act, which required the identification of all foreign-produced goods (Godden 1964:11). In addition to the British-produced wares are three pieces of American origin. The first is a fluted serving bowl representing the post-1895 production of John Moses and Co. (the Glasgow Pottery Co.) of Trenton, New Jersey (Barber 1904:50–51), and the remaining two pieces are products of the East Liverpool, Ohio, factories. One is a "Cartwright Brothers," circa 1887–1900, and the other is a product of Homer Laughlin, circa 1877–1900 (Gates and Ormerod 1982:30, 131). As stated earlier, all white wares recovered from Feature B were plain and undecorated, with one exception. This was a seven-inch dessert plate in black transfer-print "Indus" pattern with a registry date of 1877. This piece is a typical example of the open-design, brown-and-black transfer-print revival that was occurring during the late 1870s and early 1880s.

Based on the above ceramic sample, it can be stated that although Feature B included ceramics from the 1870s, it was primarily a product of the 1880s and 1890s, with a terminal date in the latter half of the 1890 decade. The absence of ceramics decorated by the decal technique or marked "Made in England," argues for a pre-1900 closure date.

Also represented were over 100 individual glassware vessels, including canning jars, bottles, flasks, and a number of pressed or molded glass vessels. The quantity present in the assemblage, particularly the pressed and molded serving pieces, reflects the abundance of inexpensive glass being produced in Pennsylvania, Ohio, and Indiana during the late nineteenth century (Measell 1979).

Faunal remains recovered from Feature B numbered thirty-six identified elements and represented at least thirteen individual animals (Table 2). Although the beef sample is small, it shows a bias towards intermediate value cuts, with only three of the 10 elements (two ribs and one rump) representing the higher-value cuts. Perhaps of significance is the absence of any short loins among the beef sample. Seventy percent of the butchering units consisted of arm steaks, cross and/or short ribs, and blade steaks or chuck roasts—cuts that are of middle value. It is also noteworthy that, while yellow perch, rock bass, and whitefish–cisco were available for purchase locally, the proximity of the site area to the Detroit River (less than one-fifth of a mile) gives rise to the

Table 2. Species Composition of Feature B

Common name (scientific name)	NISP	(MNI)[a]
Mammals		
Cattle (*Bos taurus*)	10	(?)
Sheep–goat (*Ovis–Capra*)	1	(1)
Pig (*Sus scrofa*)	9	(2)
Cat (*Felis catus*)	1	(1)
Norway rat (*Rattus norwegicus*)	2	(1)
Unidentified medium and large mammal	3	
Birds		
Duck sp. (tribe anatinae)	1	(1)
Turkey (*Meleagris gallopavo*)	1	(1)
Songbird (order Passeriformes)	2	(1)
Unidentified	4	
Fish		
Whitefish–cisco (*Coregonus* sp.)	3	(2)
Rock bass (*Ambloplites rupestris*)	2	(2)
Yellow perch (*Perca flavescens*)	4	(1)
Unidentified	7	
Feature totals	50	(12+)

[a]Also recovered in a soil sample were three bird eggshell fragments as well as fish scales diagnostic of family Percidae (walleye, sauger, perch) (88), family Coregonidae (whitefish, cisco) (72), and family Cetrarchidae (sunfish) (46). NISP = number of identified specimens; MNI = minimum number of individuals.

suggestion that perch and rock bass may reflect a "cane pole technology" supplementary resource. Alternatively, the net technology required to harvest whitefish most effectively was employed mainly by commercial fishermen; the implication is that whitefish represents a purchased commodity.

Feature C

The general assemblage recovered from Feature C was very similar to those taken from Features A and B. Ceramics included a wide range of white earthenwares, yellow paste earthenwares (both Bennington-decorated and common yellow), salt-glazed stonewares (utility vessels), and a few small porcelain pieces. The whitewares were entirely within the range defined as ironstone for the late nineteenth century and were nearly all plain, unmolded, and devoid of decoration. Molded patterns were limited to the occasional fluted bowl, although one cup was decorated in a "corn" pattern typical of the higher-grade whitewares of the 1860s and 1870s (Wetherbee 1980). Marked whiteware pieces of English production included "J&G Meakin," "Anthony Shaw," "I Meir and Son," and "Hope and Carter" (Godden 1964). Although none of these examples are particularly useful for dating purposes, the fact that none included "England" in their mark argues for a pre-1891 date for the deposit. American pieces include a 1875–1880 "I.Davis" from Trenton, New Jersey (Barber 1904:61), and a "lion and unicorn" over "T.P.C.Co." that was probably a variant of one of the other Trenton potters. The assemblage of marked pieces cited above strongly suggests a Feature C date of between 1880 and 1890.

The faunal assemblage from Feature C contained 162 identified elements, from which a minimum of twenty-five individuals, exclusive of cattle, are represented (Table 3). A positive identification of sheep was made from a metacarpal. The range of birds associated with Feature C was greater than in other features. A single individual lake sturgeon, estimated to have weighed approximately sixty pounds, was the only fish represented. Prior to 1860 lake sturgeon were despised by white fishermen, and Scott and Crossman (1979:88) state that the fish were burned as fuel by steamboats on the Detroit River. After 1860 products from the lake sturgeon, besides caviar and the flesh, included gelatin from the swim bladder, which was used for a variety of commercial and domestic purposes (Scott and Crossman 1979:88). Feature C also contained a right valve of a fresh-water mussel commonly referred to as a "spike" or "lady finger" (*Elliptio dilatata*), a bivalve that prefers strong river currents. Not generally used as food, freshwater mussels were often collected in order to acquire their shells as raw material for shell buttons, or in hopes of obtaining freshwater pearls.

The identification of eighty-seven cow bones furnishes insight into the consumption pattern for the site's former inhabitants. Analysis of eighty-six elements (an unidentified vertebrae fragment excluded) reveals that 38.4 percent of the beef butchering units were from the five highest-valued cuts, 25.6 percent were from cuts of middle value, and 36.0 percent were low-valued shank and neck cuts. Although the relative values of the various butchering

Table 3. Species Composition of Feature C

Common name (scientific name)	NISP	(MNI)[a]
Mammals		
Cattle (*Bos taurus*)	85	(?)
Sheep (*Ovis aries*)	1	(1)
Sheep–goat (*Ovis–Capra*)	10	(2)
Pig (*Sus scrofa*)	32	(10)
Unidentified medium and large mammal	19	
Birds		
Goose sp. (tribe Anserini)	6	(2)
Duck sp. (tribe anatinae)	1	(1)
Turkey (*Meleagris gallopavo*)	11	(3)
Domestic chicken (*Gallus gallus*)	4	(3)
Rock dove (*Columba livia*)	1	(1)
Fish		
Lake sturgeon (*Acipenser fulvescens*)	9	(1)
Mollusks		
Spike–lady finger (*Elliptio dilatata*)	1	(1)
Feature totals	181	(25+)

[a]NISP = number of identified specimens; MNI = minimum number of individuals.

units for pork were more variable and not as well documented as those for beef, pig bones from Feature C were primarily from the picnic shoulder and the shoulder butt, with a complete absence of hams (Table 4). The underrepresentation of such low-valued pig butchering units as feet and jowls may be indicative of a middle-price consumption pattern.

ARCHAEOLOGICAL RESULTS—SUMMARY

White table ceramics recovered from Features A, B, and C generally represent the period between 1875 to 1900, and are highly consistent in both

Table 4. Pork Butchering Units from Feature C[a]

Butchering unit	Number	Percentage
Jowl	0	0
Shoulder butt	5	17.2
Picnic shoulder	21	72.4
Rough back	2	6.9
Rib belly	0	0
Short cut ham	0	0
Feet	1	3.4
Total butchering units	29	99.9

[a]After Lyman (1979).

intrafeature and interfeature terms. The majority of the whitewares present are plain, undecorated ironstones, but they may also represent the softer paste examples of the ironstone range, closer to what might be called CC ware (Miller 1980:30). This subjective evaluation of the wares present is corroborated by the sheer variety of patterns and manufacturers present in any single privy assemblage. Assuming that a privy is the product of a single household, the impression from recovered ceramics is that of miscellaneous table settings rather than sets, suggesting ceramics purchased by the piece or as needed, rather than the purchase of matched sets. This impression was not limited to the features under study, but was consistent across the site. In addition, the recovery of the same wares and patterns produced by major mass-market potters of the late nineteenth century, such as Meakin, Boote, Wedgwood, and others, across the entire site area bespeaks a roughly equivalent access to the ceramics market by the residents. The absence of higher-class ceramics, other than a few transfer-print revival pieces, strongly suggests a ceramics market with restricted access for the Test Area 8 residents. We would suggest that this is directly a consequence of economic criteria.

While the ceramic component recovered from Test Area 8 does not appear to hold potential for discerning between the different socioeconomic strata within this working-class neighborhood, the faunal samples recovered from Features A through C appear to hold promise along these lines. Faunal samples recovered from these three features exhibit considerable variability, both in species composition and in the relative proportions of cost-ranked cuts of meat of individual species held in common by the various features. Remains of domesticated animals, present in all three assemblages, consist of cattle and sheep–goat, with pig absent only from Feature A. Beef is best represented in each feature, although in Feature B pig is nearly equivalent in the number of elements recovered. A diverse pattern for individual consumption patterns of beef is indicated by a predominance of low-value cuts in Feature A, middle cuts in Feature B, and a balance among high-, middle-, and low-value cuts in Feature C (Table 5). Interestingly, the avian assemblages are consistent in that birds from Feature C are most extensive, both in terms of species and in proportion of individuals, whereas Feature A contained only chicken. A contrasting pattern is discernible with fish in that the greatest species diversity and relative proportion by class was obtained from Feature A, whereas Feature C yielded the bones of only one lake sturgeon.

Assuming that the ceramic–glass and faunal assemblages recovered and analyzed from Test Area 8 are representative of the consumption patterns of the former working-class residents in this neighborhood, two conclusions appear appropriate. First, consumption patterns of ceramics and glass at this working-class level, ranging from unskilled laborers to skilled tradesmen, do not produce obviously dissimilar assemblages. Second, faunal assemblages recovered from these same residents do appear to display a degree of variation, perhaps reflective of socioeconomic status differentiation within the test area. Based on the presence of varying species conposition, and varying percentage composition of ranked cuts of meat between features, it appears that the range

Table 5. Butchering Units of Beef from Features A, B, and C, Listed in Descending Order by Price

Butchering unit	Feature A		Feature B		Feature C	
High-value cuts:						
Short loin	0		0		2	2.3
Sirloin	0		0		9	10.5
Ribs	1	9.1	2	20.0	9	10.5
Round	0		0		11	12.8
Rump	0		1	10.0	2	2.3
Medium-value cuts:						
Chuck	0		2	20.0	13	15.1
Arm	0		3	30.0	6	7.0
Cross and short ribs	1	9.1	2	20.0	3	3.5
Plate and brisket	0		0		0	
Low-value cuts:						
Neck	0		0		3	3.5
Foreshank	3	27.3	0		21	24.4
Hindshank	6	54.5	0		7	8.1
Total number of elements	11	100.0	10	100.0	86	100.0

of variation represented does portray individual household socioeconomic status differences, with those residents responsible for Feature A being the least well off financially, and the family or families responsible for Feature C the most affluent. That such differences relate to the range of socioeconomic status within the area, ranging from unskilled to skilled members of the labor force, seems a reasonable conclusion. It is unfortunate that, even with excellent and varied documentary resources, urban neighborhood residency patterns in this case preclude specific attribution of individual assemblages to individual occupants.

The assumption that socioeconomic status should be reflected in dietary access appears to be generally confirmed, although in a somewhat more variable way than access to ceramics would indicate. Although limited as this study is, both in the number and size of the samples available, several characteristics of the working-class households in Test Area 8 are apparent.

1. Cattle, pig, and sheep–goat were consumed in varying numbers by most families residing in the neighborhood, with beef usually being the dominant source of meat. Pork was purchased and consumed in greater amounts by more affluent families.

2. A considerable range was found in the butchering units of beef that were purchased and consumed, and this appears to be an exceptionally useful index in the identification of different income levels within the neighborhood. Refuse from the more affluent households contains a balance among butchered bone that reflects high-, middle-, and low-value cuts. Beef cuts associated with lower-income, working-class families consist mainly of low-value shank

bones. The unexpected discovery of several bilaterally sawn calf skulls from Feature A may also relate to low-income food consumption.

3. Fowl was best represented with higher-income families in the neighborhood, with turkey, chicken, and goose all well represented. On the other end of the continuum, bird remains were limited to a few chicken bones.

4. Fish remains were more plentiful and from more different species when associated with the refuse of low-income families. Species of sucker, especially redhorse, were most prevalent.

5. Imported food items were entirely absent from Test Area 8. This stands in contrast to faunal assemblages from other areas around Detroit, such as the Renaissance Center (Mudar 1978), Millender Center (Martin and Colburn 1984), and sites tested as part of the downtown People Mover project (Martin 1985), where remains of cod (*Gadus callarias*), mackerel (*Scomber scombrus*), oyster (*Crassostrea virginica*), and northern quahog clam (*Mercenaria mercenaria*) have been obtained.

Although the three faunal assemblages from Test Area 8 are interpreted as reflecting different income levels within an otherwise homogeneous working-class neighborhood, the possibility exists that individual food preferences (e.g., for calf skulls) or holiday food consumption (as demonstrated by Davidson 1982) may be involved. Despite this remote possibility, the data from Test Area 8 represents a significant sample of material culture to which other urban archaeological assemblages can be compared and contrasted.

CONCLUSIONS

Analysis of artifacts recovered from Test Area 8 of the Stroh Brewing Company project area indicates that this lower-income, working-class neighborhood of the 1880s and 1890s had significant access to the mass-produced, plain white table ceramics and pressed glass products of both British and American manufacture. Virtually no high-cost wares, such as flow blue with gilt, bone china, or porcelain, were noted in the extensive recovery operation. This suggests that, even though the residents of Detroit had full access to both local, regional, and international markets during the late nineteenth century (Pred 1964), access was clearly limited by socioeconomic status.

Although good, upper-income comparative samples from Detroit have only recently become available (e.g., Martin 1985; Martin and Demeter 1985), analysis of faunal samples from Test Area 8 suggest that a distinct working-class consumption pattern can be defined using butchering units of beef and possibly pork, relative proportions of fowl and fish, and the presence–absence of imported foodstuffs. The appropriateness of Mudar's (1978) earlier approach to the analysis of faunal remains from nineteenth-century urban contexts within Detroit is therefore substantiated.

Both faunal and material culture data acquired during this study illustrate the efficacy of small-scale, isolated feature recovery within areas of well-documented socioeconomic status, even when individual feature provenance is not ascertainable. Currently it appears that faunal analysis may represent a finer-scale analytical tool for discerning individual status differences within a homogeneous, working-class population of this temporal period, than does corresponding ceramic analyses. An extension of Miller's (1980) ceramic price indexing formula to fully cover the wares of the late nineteenth century may reduce this apparent disparity. The study of faunal and material culture assemblages from alternate areas of the urban environment may eventually allow the recognition of "archaeological signatures" for various levels of social stratification in the city setting, ultimately feeding back into and refining the older "pattern recognition" strictures.

ACKNOWLEDGMENTS

Excavations of the Stroh project area were sponsored by the Community and Economic Development Department of the City of Detroit, and the Stroh Brewing Company. Fieldwork was performed by Caminos Associates, of Bay City, Michigan, under the direction of Dr. Earl Prahl. We would like to thank Director C. Kurt Dewhurst and former Director Rollin H. Baker of the Michigan State University Museum for providing laboratory facilities to conduct the faunal analysis. We would also like to thank Dr. Arnold Pilling of Wayne State University for his critical comments on an early draft of this chapter.

REFERENCES

Ascher, R., and Fairbanks, C. H., 1971, Excavation of a Slave Cabin: Georgia, U.S.A., *Historical Archaeology* 5:3–17.
Barber, E. A., 1904, *Marks of American Potters,* Philadelphia, republished Ars Ceramica, 1976, Ann Arbor.
Baugher, S., 1982, Hoboken Hollow: A Nineteenth Century Factory Workers' Housing Site, *Northeast Historical Archaeology* 11:26–38.
Bellantoni, N., Gradie, R. R., III, and Poirier, D., 1982. Zooarchaeology of the Butler-McCook Homestead, Hartford, Connecticut, *Northeast Historical Archaeology* 1:1–8.
Branstner, M. C., and Prahl, E. J., 1983a, A Phase I Archaeological Investigation of the American Natural Resources, Stroh Brewing Company, and Chene Street Project Sites, Detroit, Michigan, Caminos Associates, Bay City, Michigan.
Branstner, M. C., and Prahl, E. J., 1983b, A Phase II Archaeological Investigation of Selected Cultural Components of the American Natural Resources and Stroh Brewing Company Project Areas, Detroit, Michigan, Caminos Associates, Bay City, Michigan.
Branstner, M. C., and Prahl, E. J., 1984, Resource Protection Planning Process: Southeast Michigan: The Late Woodland Context, Caminos Associates, Bay City, Michigan.
Bridges, S. T., and Salwen, B., 1980, Weeksville: The Archaeology of a Black Urban Community, in: *Archaeological Perspectives on Ethnicity in America* (R. L. Schuyler, ed.), Baywood Publishing, New York, pp. 38–47.
Campau, L., 1802, Return of the Taxable Property of the Hamtramck District, In: *Michigan Pioneer and Historical Collections,* Volume 8, 2nd ed., 1907, pp. 530–540.
Cover, J. H., 1932, *Neighborhood Distribution and Consumption of Meat in Pittsburgh,* University of Chicago Press, Chicago.
Davidson, P. E., 1982, Patterns in Urban Foodways: An Example from Early Twentieth Century

Atlanta, in: *Archaeology of Urban America* (R. S. Dickens, ed.), Academic Press, New York, pp. 381–398.

De Cunzo, L., 1982, Households, Economics, and Ethnicity in Patterson's Dublin, 1829–1915: The Van Houten Street Parking Lot Block, *Northeast Historical Archaeology* 11:9–25.

Demeter, C. S., 1982, An Archaeological Evaluation of the Near East Riverfront Area, Detroit, Michigan, Commonwealth Associates, Jackson, Michigan.

Demeter, C. S., n.d., untitled manuscript prepared in conjunction with excavations at the Renaissance Center, Detroit, Michigan.

Demeter, C. S., and Barnard, B., 1980, Archaeological Investigations at the Sheridan Place Development Site, Commonwealth Associates, Jackson, Michigan.

Drucker, L. M., 1981, Socioeconomic Patterning at an Undocumented Late Eighteenth-Century Low Country Site: Spiers Landing, South Carolina, *Historical Archaeology* 15(2):58–68.

Fairbanks, C. H., 1974, The Kingsley Slave Cabins in Duval County, Florida, 1968, in: *Conference on Historic Sites Archaeology Papers 1977* 12:68–86.

Farmer, Silas, 1890, *History of Detroit and Wayne County, Michigan*, S. Farmer, Detroit, republished by Gale Research, 1969, Detroit.

Gates, W. C., and Ormerod, D. E., 1982, The East Liverpool Pottery District: Identification of Manufacturers and Marks, *Historical Archaeology* 16(1–2).

Godden, G. A., 1964, *Encyclopaedia of British Pottery and Porcelain Marks*, Bonanza Books, New York.

Honerkamp, N., Council, R. B., and Will, M. E., 1982, An Archaeological Investigation of the Charleston Convention Center Site, Charleston, South Carolina, University of Tennessee, Chattanooga.

Langenwalter II, P. E., 1980, The Archaeology of Nineteenth Century Subsistence at the Lower China Store, Madera County, California, in: *Archaeological Perspectives on Ethnicity in America* (R. L. Schuyler, ed.), Baywood Publishing, New York, pp. 102–123.

Lowrie, W., and Clarke, M., 1832, *American State Papers, Public Lands,* Volume 1, Gales and Seaton, Washington, D.C.

Lyman, R. L., 1979, Available Meat from Faunal Remains: A Consideration of Techniques, *American Antiquity* 44(3):536–546.

Martin, T. J., 1985, Faunal Remains Associated with Archaeological Sites in the Route of the Downtown People Mover in Detroit, Michigan, Illinois State Museum Society Archaeological Program Technical Report No. 85-234-14, submitted to Gilbert/Commonwealth Inc., Jackson, Michigan.

Martin, T. J., and Colburn, M. L., 1984, Animal Remains from 19th Century Refuse Deposits at the Millender Center in Detroit, Michigan, Illinois State Museum Society Archaeological Program Technical Report No. 84-194-12, submitted to Gilbert/Commonwealth Associates, Inc., Jackson, Michigan.

Martin, T. J., and Demeter, C. S., 1985, Animal Remains from 19th Century Refuse Deposits at the Millender Center in Detroit, Michigan, paper presented at the 18th Annual Meeting of the Society for Historical Archaeology, Boston.

McKearin, H., and Wilson, K. M., 1978, *American Bottles and Flasks and Their Ancestry*, Crown Publishing, New York.

Measell, J., 1979, *Greentown Glass: The Indiana Tumbler and Goblet Company,* Grand Rapids Public Museum, Michigan.

Michigan History Division, n.d., Carp River Forge: A Report, Department of State, Lansing, Michigan.

Miller, G. L., 1980, Classification and Economic Scaling of Nineteenth-Century Ceramics, *Historical Archaeology* 14:1–40.

Miller, H., 1979, Pettus and Utopia: A Comparison of the Faunal Remains from Two Late Seventeenth Century Virginia Households, *Conference on Historic Sites Archaeology Papers 1978* 13:158–179.

Mudar, K., 1978, The Effects of Socio-cultural Variables in Early Nineteenth Century Detroit, *Conference on Historic Archaeology Sites Papers 1977* 12:323–391.

Otto, J. S., 1977, Artifacts and Status Differences—A Comparison of Ceramics from Planter,

Overseer, and Slave Sites on an Antebellum Plantation, in: *Research Strategies in Historical Archaeology* (S. South, ed.), Academic Press, New York, pp. 91–118.

Otto, J. S., 1980, Race and Class on Antebellum Plantations, in: *Archaeological Perspectives on Ethnicity in America* (R. L. Schuyler, ed.), Baywood Publishing, New York, pp. 3–13.

Pilling, A. R., 1982, Detroit: Urbanism Moves West: Pallisaded Fur-Trade Center to Diversified Manufacturing City, *North American Archaeologist* 3(3):225–242.

Polk, R. L. (pub.), 1891–1921, *Detroit City Directory* (various dates), Detroit.

Pred, A., 1964, Toward a Typology of Manufacturing Flows, *The Geographic Review* 54 (January): 65–84.

Rascher Map Publishing Company, 1888–1895, *Rascher's Map of Detroit, Michigan* (1888 publication with paste-on updates through 1895), Chicago.

Sanborn Map Company, 1884, *Insurance Atlas of Detroit, Michigan* Philadelphia.

Sanborn-Perris Map Company, 1897–1919, *Insurance Atlas of Detroit, Michigan,* (1897 publication with paste-on updates through 1919), Philadelphia.

Schulz, P. D., and Gust, S. H., 1983, Faunal Remains and Social Status in Nineteenth Century Sacremento, *Historical Archaeology* 17(1):44–53.

Schuyler, R. L., 1980, review of *Research Strategies in Historical Archaeology,* (S. South, ed.), *American Anthropologist* 82:200–202.

Scott, W. B., and Crossman, E. J., 1979, *Freshwater Fishes of Canada* (3rd printing), Fisheries Research Board of Canada, Ottawa, Ontario.

South, Stanley, 1977, *Method and Theory in Historical Archaeology,* Academic Press, New York.

Trautman, M. B., 1957, *The Fishes of Ohio,* Ohio State University Press, Columbus.

Wayne County Archives, 1839–1870, Wayne County Tax Assessment Rolls, Burton Historical Collection, Detroit Public Library.

Wayne County Tract Index, n.d., City–County Building, County of Wayne, Detroit, Michigan.

Weeks (J. W.) and Co., 1871, *Detroit City Directory for 1871–72,* Detroit.

Wetherbee, J., 1980, *A Look at White Ironstone,* Wallace-Homestead, Des Moines, Iowa.

Zunz, Olivier, 1982, *The Changing Face of Inequality,* University of Chicago Press.

14

Miller's Indices and Consumer-Choice Profiles

Status-Related Behaviors and White Ceramics

SUZANNE M. SPENCER-WOOD

INTRODUCTION: THEORETICAL CONTEXT AND REVIEW OF PREVIOUS RESEARCH

A major area of research in archaeology is concerned with the connections between artifact patterns and sociocultural behavior patterns. Since Binford considered "the study and establishment of correlations between types of social structure classified on the basis of behavioral attributes and structural types of material elements as one of the major areas of anthropological research yet to be developed" (Binford 1962:219), archaeologists have increasingly studied relationships between social and economic stratification and artifact attribute patterns (Flannery and Coe 1968; Hill 1968; Hoffman 1974; Sanders and Webster 1978; Watson 1978). A growing body of research in historical archaeology has contributed analyses of artifact attributes that have been related to social and economic status of site residents (Deagan 1982:164–165, 1983; Drucker 1981; Geismar 1982; Mudar 1978; Otto 1984; Poe 1979; Singer 1985; Schulz and Gust 1983). Miller (1980) recently developed ceramic price scaling indices to measure the mean value of whiteware decorative types in a site ceramic assemblage. Because the attribute of decoration affected whiteware prices, it was hypothesized to be related to socioeconomic status. This research is concerned with the effects of alternative methods for testing the hypothesized relationship between Miller's indices and household participation in consumer behaviors of socioeconomic groups. Perhaps most importantly, a refinement in the use of Miller's indices is proposed, called a consumer choice profile, that involves the analysis of archaeological patterns of whiteware decorative type values in an archaeological assemblage. Beyond establishing relationships between Miller's ceramic price-scaling in-

Suzanne M. Spencer-Wood ☐ Department of Anthropology, University of Massachusetts, Boston, MA 02125

dices[1] and socioeconomic stratification, ceramic consumer-choice profiles delineate archaeological patterns that may permit inferences of status-related
household behavior patterns.

This paper explores the possibility of inferring status-related behavior
patterns from the relationships between archaeological patterns in whiteware
decorative types and documentary indications of socioeconomic status. The
purposes of this research are both substantive and methodological. The substantive goal is to distinguish status-related whiteware acquisition and deposition behaviors by residents of five nineteenth-century Boston area sites. The
methodological goal is to assess the relationship between household socioeconomic status and alternative methods of calculating Miller's price-scaling
ceramic indices (1980). These goals are accomplished by comparing site rankings derived from (1) the documented average value of probate inventories for
site residents' occupational categories with (2) alternative ceramic indices indicating relative mean value of their whiteware assemblages. Miller's ceramic
indices are summary measures representing the weighted mean relative value
of archaeological whiteware samples. In this research, cup and saucer index
rankings had the highest correlations with documentary indications of relative socioeconomic status. This result suggests that teaware and/or coffeeware
was used more for status display than were plates or bowls. Other comparative
site research has yielded similar results for other site locations and for early
nineteenth-century sites (Henry this volume; Spencer-Wood and Heberling,
this volume).

A major finding of the research is that significant information was lost in
using a mean ceramic index by itself. Understanding relationships between
socioeconomic status and alternative patterns in household ceramic deposits
requires detailed analysis of the constituent elements of ceramic indices. Status-related consumer-choice profiles are developed from the relative frequencies of decorative type values within alternative indices. Consumer-choice
profiles describe site archaeological patterns in values of decorative whiteware. For some sites consumer-choice profiles corresponding to high, moderate, and low occupational statuses are different from profiles producing high,
moderate, and low ceramic indices. The site with the highest occupational
status and the highest proportion of ceramic value in porcelain does not necessarily have the highest ceramic index value. Consumer-choice profiles reveal
archaeological patterns in the value distribution of archaeological whiteware
that can be related to status behavior patterns more clearly than the mean
ceramic index measure can be related to socioeconomic status. Consumer-
choice profiles describe patterns in the archaeological data that can be related
to behavior patterns, while the mean price-scaling index can only be correlated
with socioeconomic status. Consumer-choice profiles also permit a detailed

---

[1]Miller's "ceramic" indices are concerned specifically with nineteenth-century white ceramics,
and Miller calls his indices "average CC index values" (Miller 1980: 12–15). In this chapter the
terms "ceramic index" and "consumer-choice profile" are concerned with nineteenth-century
white ceramics, termed whiteware.

explanation of the degree of correspondence between occupational status and alternative ceramic index site rank orders.

Archaeological data at a house site can often be identified with the household living there. Most households in late nineteenth-century America are assumed to have acquired most of their consumer goods from the market economy, although some goods might be acquired second hand or as gifts. Before municipal trash collection, many households, particularly of the working classes, selectively discarded or lost some of their consumer goods in the house yard. If the house yard is clearly separated from other house yards, the household living there could control deposition in the yard. Archaeologists recover partial, biased artifact samples from house yards that can often be associated with particular households and their consumer behavior, including types of goods acquired and selectively lost or discarded at the house site. Within the cultural system, goods may be acquired for an infinite number of reasons within different subsystems (Clarke 1978). Archaeologists can use patterns in archaeological data to investigate reasons for household selection of particular archaeologically deposited goods from the variety available in the market. Household acquisition and discard of goods are conditioned by a number of factors interrelated in the supply–demand dynamic of the market economy. The goods available for acquisition depend on supply, or market access due to site location. The decision to acquire particular goods is conditioned by a number of interrelated variables within the cultural system, including the economic ability to afford those goods, the functional utility of the goods, the use of goods for socioeconomic status display, and behaviors related to ethnicity, political status, religion, family size, and life cycle. Socioeconomic status is an important factor conditioning both acquisition and selective discard of whiteware ceramic decorative types.

Socioeconomic status is indicated by position within a hierarchy of occupational categories. Recently, a number of historical archaeologists have investigated the degree of correspondence between occupation, as a primary documentary indication of socioeconomic status, and the relative quality and price of ceramics that consumers decide to buy and subsequently discard or lose (De Cunzo 1982; Dyson 1982; Exnicios and Pearson 1984; Felton and Shulz 1983; Geismar 1982; Henry this volume; McBride and McBride 1983; Morenon *et al.* 1982; Shephard this volume; Spencer-Wood 1984). Other variables influencing patterns in site assemblages that archaeologists have researched include: (1) the availability of goods due to differential market access (Adams 1976; Miller and Hurry 1983; Riordan 1981; Riordan and Adams, 1985; Schuyler 1980a; Spencer-Wood 1979); (2) ethnicity (Baker 1980; Baugher 1982; Deagan 1983; Otto 1977, 1984; Schuyler 1980b); and (3) family size and structure (De Cunzo this volume; LeeDecker *et al.* this volume). These last two variables often affect consumer choices by impacting socioeconomic status. Site location generally affects the availability of goods from distant markets through transportation costs that increase the price of goods. Thus available status items and their cost, while varying between localities, are comparable between sites in the same town (cf. Spencer-Wood 1984:90), and perhaps even within a larger local area with shared market access. Analyses should attempt to control or take into account the variable of market availability, as well as other variables if possible, in order to focus on the relationship of socioeconomic status to ceramic consumer choices (cf. Spencer-Wood 1984).

This research was conducted with data from five nineteenth-century sites in the Boston metropolitan area, allowing the variable of market access to be considered a constant. The ethnicity variable was also held constant because all site residents were Americans of British or Irish descent. Family size and structure could only be taken into account indirectly through probate inventory values that are affected by this as well as other socioeconomic variables. Most of these sites went through at least one family life cycle during the archaeological assemblage date range of about fifty years. Holding constant the variables of market access, ethnicity, and, to a limited extent, family cycle, this research focused primarily on the relationships between site archaeological patterns in whiteware decorative types and household socioeconomic status.

Socioeconomic status indicates the relationship between economic and social position associated with economic role, particularly occupation. The connection between economic and social status is indicated by the term socioeconomic status. Occupational category is considered the single most objective measure of class and status differences among twentieth-century American groups (Edwards 1939; Hodges 1964:95; Reissman 1959:144). Occupational categories share a level of income, social interaction, leisure time, shared knowledge, and values that form the basis for social classes (Barth and Watson 1967:394; Engel *et al.* 1978:116). Sociological theory considers social class a complex variable resulting from a combination of occupational status, income, education, values, group participation, and approved consumer behavior (Warner *et al.* 1960:3–15). In several studies, occupation was found to the strongest indicator of social status, in conjunction with secondary factors such as type and location of housing, and source of income (Kahl and Davis 1955; Warner *et al.* 1960:168–169). Historians (cf. Hershberg and Dockhorn 1976; Katz 1972) and archaeologists (cf. De Cunzo 1982; Henry, this volume; Orser this volume; Shephard this volume; Spencer-Wood 1984) have also used occupation to indicate membership in a socioeconomic group. In this research, it was assumed that economic status and associated aspects of social status were indicated by occupation in the late nineteenth century as much as they are today. Occupation is considered the major determinant of family wealth and accompanying status-related behavior.

Ceramics serve utilitarian functions in food preparation and consumption, and also can serve to display socioeconomic status. Keynsian economic theory, supported by twentieth-century evidence, holds that nearly all interhousehold variation in amount of consumer expenditures and savings can be accounted for by variations in income (Dusenberry 1971; Heilbroner 1970:230). It seems likely that this economic model would be valid for the relatively developed late nineteenth-century Northeast American economy. Economic anthropologists (cf. Douglas and Isherwood 1979:25, 116–119), as well as economists (Dusenberry 1971; Heilbroner 1970:230) and sociologists (Martineau 1958; Warner *et al.* 1960:168–169), consider income or wealth, usually determined by occupation, as the major factor limiting consumer choices. Comparative research has established that income is more highly related to purchases of many types of consumer goods than is social class (Myers and Mount 1973:71–73). Research involving a large number of variables (occupation, income, education, religion, ethnicity, political affiliation), found the highest correlations among the variables of occupation, income, and education and consumer choices of living-room furniture, a major display of household social status (Laumann and House 1970:Table 1; Myers and Mount 1973:71–73). Since tea was often held in the front living room or parlor, teaware functioned as part of the socioeconomic status display of this room and its furniture.

The relationship among occupational category, income, and value of ceramics and moveable goods has been indicated by research on nineteenth- and twentieth-century data. In research on Quincy inventories from the 1870s, average values of status durables increased in conjunction with rising average total inventory values for a ranked set of four occupational categories (Spencer-Wood and Riley 1981). For the 1840s in St. Mary's County, ceramic values increased proportionately with the increasing value of moveable goods in inventories, until these reached $1,500, after which ceramic values levelled off as moveable goods had reached a "saturation point" (Herman *et al.* 1973: 59–63). A positive relationship was also generally identified between occupational income and degree of expenditure on necessities in contrast to luxury goods in Massachusetts, 1870–1874 (Massachusetts Bureau of Statistics of Labor 1875). For 1926 data, expenditures on dishes and glassware gradually increased with increasing income, although this expense formed a decreasing proportion of income after it reached the $1,800–$2,100 range (Nystrom 1929:394). Economists have developed the concept of decreasing marginal utility to explain the declining investment in consumer goods after a certain level of acquisition has been reached (cf. Peterson 1977:34–39).

Thus wealth or income, usually determined by occupation, is the major limiting factor on consumer choices, even though in some cases wealth is not accompanied by acceptance into high social status groups, or alternatively social status is not accompanied by commensurate income or wealth (Warner *et al.* 1960:21). Among low- to moderate-income occupations, there are very real economic limits on the extent to which any social aspirations can be expressed through consumer choices (Douglas and Isherwood 1979:25; Heilbroner 1970:236–237). In some cases, more expensive ceramics than could be afforded might be inherited or received as gifts, but few of these are expected to be discarded. As wealth increases, the proportion of income spent on ceramics and many other categories of consumer goods decreases, but the total amount increases, resulting in a wider range of possible choices (Heilbroner 1970:234). Beyond a certain income level, consumer choices reflecting status may no longer follow increases in wealth as closely as for those with lower-income occupations. There will also be the occasional eccentric, wealthy individual or family that does not buy consumer items reflecting their economic ability. As the studies discussed above demonstrate, these are few in comparison to those whose consumer appetite increases with wealth, until it nears the limits of status expression possible with ceramics or other categories of consumer goods. While maintaining an awareness of possible deviations from the norm, it was expected that, in most cases, the relative value of archaeological whiteware assemblages would reflect the expected connection between consumer choices, economic status, and associated social status. This was expected because whiteware includes expensive ceramics such as porcelain, ironstone, and transfer printed that are used to display status. Historical archaeologists can test these expectations by contrasting and comparing the results obtained with methods for measuring socioeconomic status and methods for measuring the relative mean value of archaeological whiteware assemblages.

DATA AND FIELD METHODS

Data

Comparisons of documentary indications of socioeconomic status and relative mean value of whiteware decorative types in archaeological samples were made for four house sites in Quincy, Massachusetts, and for one house site in Milton, Massachusetts. The data for this research were excavated in 1981, under my direction, by graduate and undergraduate students, who also supervised local volunteers. The Quincy sites were all located adjacent to each other on the same street, and the Milton site was less than four miles from them. The five sites had very similar market access within the Boston metropolitan area. All the sites were also located in working-class neighborhoods. Each house yard was clearly separated from any adjacent house yards by fences and driveways. The number of adjacent house yards ranged from none to a maximum of two. Since the yards were clearly bounded and controlled by the households living there, it was assumed that each household would have deposited most of the artifacts found in its yard. The analysis ranged from the mid-nineteenth century to the early twentieth century in order to include the house construction dates and the most probable date range of the ceramics. Few artifacts were found that might have been manufactured in the twentieth century because trash collection was initiated early in the century (MAR 1914:342; Milton Record 1915:4; QAR 1900:218, 1925:245).

Documentary data, indicating socioeconomic status, required deed traces to determine property owners, with maps and some deeds indicating approximate dates of house construction. Occupations of household members were determined from manuscript census schedules from 1850, business directories after 1869, and tax records. Personal estates of heads of households were gathered when probate inventories were available, although they often were not. A comparative data base of personal and total estate values corresponding to individuals' occupations was developed from probate records and business directories dating from 1870 to 1900 in Quincy, Massachusetts.

Field Methods

Excavations at the Quincy and Milton sites were conducted with three-foot-square excavation units excavated in three-inch arbitrary levels subdivided by natural and cultural levels. The three-inch arbitrary levels provided subdivisions for large layers without visible divisions. Unfortunately, none of these sites proved to have any temporally distinguishable cultural levels. Artifact dates could not be differentiated within the second half of the nineteenth century to create temporal distinctions among visible layers at any of these sites. This is not unusual, given the similarity of ceramic styles over the last three to four decades of the nineteenth century. Cultural layers of coal ash and artifacts were laid down rapidly in horizontal scatters of sheet refuse, resulting in similar decorative types of ceramics in bottom and top layers in two- to three-foot deep excavation units. The lack of temporally distinguishable stratigraphy or artifacts necessitated consideration of these sites as whole units, because their artifact date ranges were about fifty years. Due to different discard practices, site ceramic sample sizes did not correspond to variations in the number of units excavated. The largest ceramic sample came from four units excavated at the Milton site, while the smallest sample came from five units excavated at Quincy site 27. A larger ceramic sample was obtained from five units excavated at Quincy site 14–16, than from six units excavated at the remaining two sites.

ANALYTICAL METHODS

The methodology used in this research basically involves comparing the rank order of sites obtained using documentary measures of status with rank orders of site assemblage ceramic indices. This section first describes the method of calculating documentary indications of site residents' socioeconomic status from occupational categories and personal estates from probate inventories. Then alternative methods of applying Miller's price-scaling index to sherd and vessel counts are presented. The reasons for using alternative methods of applying Miller's price-scaling index, as well as expected results, are discussed later. Next the method for explaining the degree of correlation between occupational status and alternative ceramic index site rank orders is described. This involves formulating status-related whiteware consumer-choice profiles derived from relative proportions of decorative types contributing to ceramic indices. Finally, possible biases in the archaeological data and their probable effects on alternative ceramic indices are considered.

Occupational categories and personal estates from probate inventories were chosen as documentary indications of socioeconomic status. Average values of probate inventories often have been used to indicate changes in mean wealth (Anderson 1979). While far from perfect, these are particularly appropriate indications of socioeconomic status to relate to archaeological remains of consumer choices. As already discussed, occupation has a strong relationship both to ceramic consumer choices and to social status. Research has established correspondences between occupational categories, average total and personal estate, as well as average value of moveable property, status durables, and value of ceramics and income (Herman *et al.* 1973:59–63; Nystrom 1929:394; Spencer-Wood 1984; Spencer-Wood and Riley 1981).

The six occupational categories in this research were established by distinctions among them in average personal estate values for Quincy 1870–1900 (Table 1). The average personal-estate distinctions between occupational categories result from the larger number of higher personal-estate values in each category than those below it, despite some low inventories for all occupations. Personal estates from probate inventories were chosen to quantify individual and average consumer choices for occupational categories. The entire personal-estate value was used rather than the value for ceramics or other durable status items because a correspondence has been established between these measures. Only the total value of the personal estate was available for an adequate sample size to calculate occupational category averages (cf. Spencer-Wood 1984; Spencer-Wood and Riley 1981).

The socioeconomic status of site residents was measured by their occupations and the value of personal estate in their probate inventories, when available. Because there was no temporally meaningful stratigraphy at these urban sites, an average status index for each site was calculated from the personal estate of each inhabitant, weighted by the number of years in residence at the site. When the actual personal estate was not known, the average value for the individual's occupational category was used (Table 1). The weighted mean personal-estate value was calculated for all site inhabitants, 1850–circa 1900, for whom an actual or average personal-estate value could be determined. Residents of unknown occupation could not be included in the calculation of this status indicator. This summary site index of socioeconomic status is only an average indicator, and is not highly accurate. It has all of the limitations accompanying the use of probate inventories as indicators of wealth (Smith 1975). Yet the occupational categories and their rank order established in this research are similar to those used in other studies of occupations as measures of status by historians (Hershberg and Dockhorn 1976:60, 68; Katz 1972:85, 87), sociologists (Reissman 1959:144–157; Warner *et al.*, 1960:136–142), and archaeologists (Clark this volume; Henry this volume).

Personal estates from probate inventories is a particularly appropriate documentary measure of consumer choices to compare and contrast with archaeological measures. Probate inventories record the value of possessions still retained by an individual at death, while the archaeological data represent consumer goods discarded or lost. Differential discard can be assessed by comparing proportions of whiteware types sampled archaeologically with pro-

Table 1. Quincy Inventory Occupational Categories 1870–1900

	Average[a]		Highest[a]		Lowest[a]		Total number	
	Personal estate	Total estate	Personal estate	Total estate	Personal estate	Total estate	Personal estates	Total estates
Proprietors	22,504	51,315	264,301	1,026,578	75	500	86	72
Farmers	6,845	14,214	89,149	99,849	18	98	44	38
Craftsmen	4,827	11,535	114,202	252,342	25	99	77	53
White-collar employees	4,740	10,049	34,205	41,705	152	652	54	29
Skilled blue-collar employees	1,261	3,583	17,352	31,744	24	186	121	84
Unskilled blue-collar employees	594	2,784	9,200	29,801	16	222	74	47

[a] Amounts in dollars.

portions itemized in detailed probate inventories (cf. Spencer-Wood and Heberling this volume). Miller has used price lists to quantify the relative value of physical attributes accompanying alternative whiteware consumer choices. Ceramic indices yield a mean relative value for a ceramic assemblage that can be contrasted and compared with the site mean value of personal estates in order to assess the relationship between ceramic consumer choices and socioeconomic status.

Miller's indices (1980) are based on prices for decorative types of whiteware cups and saucers, plates, and bowls during the years of their manufacture and primary sale. British potters' and American distributors' price lists were used to calculate ratios representing the cost of other whiteware decorative types relative to undecorated cream-colored ware because the latter was the least expensive type. The price ratios were calculated according to years with records of manufacture and distribution of whiteware types in America, and do not include secondhand or secondary prices far removed from manufacture dates. Separate indices were calculated for cups and saucers, plates, and bowls from price lists in a sequence of years representing nearly every decade from 1770 to 1881 for cups and saucers, from 1787 to 1874 for plates, and from 1802 to 1858 for bowls. Miller's ceramic indices are normally used by selecting an index year and multiplying these ratios of whiteware prices by the quantities of each decorative type recovered archaeologically. Dividing the sum of these products by the total number of vessels yields the weighted mean cost ratio of the archaeological sample.

All of the Boston area archaeological assemblages were within the same temporal range of 1850–1900, and were analyzed using the latest Miller's index year of 1881 for cups and saucers, 1874 for plates, and 1858 for bowls. The latest values were chosen because they best approximated the midpoint of the date ranges of the Quincy sites (MAR 1914:342; Milton Record 1915:4; QAR 1900:218, 1925:245). Unfortunately, all types do not have ratio values for all years, in some cases because they were only manufactured in a certain range of decades in the nineteenth century. The latest value available for each type was used, if no value was given in the latest index year (Table 2). It was decided that more inaccuracies would result from excluding types without values in the last index year than from using the value available from the next latest year. For example, very few years had values for porcelain, but excluding porcelain would drastically affect the index values. With this method all types were included in an index representing the relative weighted mean value of the archaeological whiteware assemblage. Three standard sets of index values were developed to apply to each site's whiteware assemblage of cups and saucers, plates, and bowls (Table 2). This methodology ensures the comparability of the results that is necessary to assess the effects of alternative methods of calculating ceramic indices.

The effect of using values from alternative years in the second half of the nineteenth century was also tested and determined to be minimal because any changes in values affected all assemblages equally. This was the case as long as the relative ranking of values in the index remained the same, which it did

Table 2. Whiteware Decorative-Type Values Used in Ceramic Indices[a]

Decorative types	Cup index[b]		Plate index		Bowl index		CPB mean index value[c]
	Value	Year	Value	Year	Value	Year	
Porcelain	6.00	1881	4.80	1838	0		5.40
Flow-printed	4.00	1860	2.39	1855	2.40	1855	2.93
Transfer-printed	4.00	1860	1.53	1855	2.00	1858	2.51
Ironstone	3.33	1881	2.21	1874	2.00	1858	2.51
Rim-lined	0		1.69	1814	0		1.69
Hand-painted	1.17	1875	2.22	1838	1.30	1855	1.56
Sponged	1.17	1871	1.23	1855	1.10	1855	1.17
Dipped	0		0		1.10	1858	1.10
Edged	0		1.00	1862	0		1.00
Pearlware	1.00[d]		0		1.00[d]		1.64
Cream-colored[e]	1.00	1881	1.00	1874	1.00	1858	1.00

[a]These values of decorative types were used in calculating ceramic indices and percentages of whiteware type values in Tables 5–9.
[b]Cup Index = Miller's cup and saucer index values.
[c]CPB Mean Index Value = Average value of Miller's cup and saucer, plate, and bowl index values, used to calculate combined vessel and sherd indices.
[d]Miller, George L., 1985, personal communication.
[e]Cream-colored includes creamware and common whiteware (Collard 1984:113–114; Miller 1980:27, 31).

for index years in the last quarter of the nineteenth century. The high index values for porcelain were used, although some of the porcelain on late nineteenth century sites may be cheap (Adams 1976; De Cunzo 1982:22). Previous use of Cook's (1982) average values for sherd indices yielded different results because of his unusually high values for transfer-printed and flow-printed wares in 1860, which only represented cups and saucers, rather than the earlier averages of values from all three indices (Spencer-Wood 1984). A lower value more in keeping with values for these wares in other years was obtained by averaging the 1860 high cup and saucer index values with the lower latest values available for plates in 1855 and bowls in 1855 and 1858. A similar procedure was followed in most cases, averaging the values for cup and saucer, plate, and bowl indices to yield an average index value for use with both sherd counts and combined vessel counts of cups and saucers, plates, bowls, and other shapes not included in the three indices (such as pitchers, chamberpots, and tureens). In a few cases, values missing from one or two indices resulted in the use of averages of two index values and in the use of one index in three cases of low-valued whiteware (Table 2).

Miller's indices list small price differences in some years for different-sized plates and for handled versus unhandled and unspecified cups and saucers. Values were averaged for all plate sizes in each type and for all kinds of cups to obtain one value per type for each year of the three vessel indices. This was done because of the difficulty of identifying different types of cups and sizes of plates with the large number of small rims from the Quincy and Milton sites. Price variations among plate sizes and cup types were generally small enough to be averaged without misrepresentation of the range of variation within ware types (Miller 1980:26, 30, 33, Table 2 this chapter). Averaging these values seems more representative of prices than the alternative of arbitrarily using the value for one plate size or one type of cup.

This chapter focuses on the effects of alternative methods of applying Miller's ceramic price-scaling indices to archaeological whiteware assemblages in order to determine their relative value. Specifically, this research concerns the use of vessel versus sherd counts, with Miller's indices and modifications of them. Miller's indices are derived from vessel price lists and therefore were designed for whiteware assemblage vessel counts. However, research has demonstrated a relationship between occupational status and the value of archaeological whiteware assemblages in cases using both vessel counts with Miller's indices (Felton and Shulz 1983; Spencer-Wood and Heberling this volume), as well as sherd counts with modifications of them (Cook 1982; McBride and McBride this volume; Spencer-Wood 1984). This chapter compares and contrasts results obtained for a set of sites where Miller's indices or modifications of them were applied in both vessel and sherd analyses.

Three levels of ceramic indices, from specific to general, were calculated to compare resulting site rank orders with each other and with the site rank order based on occupational categories. At the most specific level, separate vessel indices were calculated for cups and saucers, plates, and bowls. Two combined vessel indices were next calculated: one for these shapes from rims, and one for these and unidentified shapes from distinctive rim and body sherds. The calculation of sherd indices involved the greatest degree of generalization.

Several alternative methods of index calculation were used in order to determine to what extent they would change the rank order obtained for the sites. Vessel ceramic indices were calculated across four categories by two methods. The four categories were cups and saucers, plates, bowls, and the combined vessel count of these three shape categories, or these three categories combined with other or unidentifiable shapes. Two methods of vessel counting were used for each of these four indices. Vessel counts were estimated first from rims, and then from both rims and any other distinctive body sherds. In general, the most conservative vessel count is represented by the number of distinctively colored and/or decorated rims within a type. Using distinctive rims to count vessels usually underrepresents the total variety of vessels within an assemblage. The index values achieved with conservative rim vessel counts were compared and contrasted with vessel counts using both distinctive rims and any body sherds that could not possibly be part of any vessel represented by a rim or any other body sherd. Body sherds representing distinct vessels differed from all rims in body glaze color, color or hue of any decoration, and shape, if identifiable. The distinctive rim and body sherd method of vessel counting yielded a more complete count of assemblage vessel variety than just counting those represented by rims.

To the combined rim and body vessel counts for cups and saucers, plates, and bowls, distinct vessels of other shapes were added to calculate a total vessel index. This method also permitted the inclusion of distinct vessel fragments of unidentifiable shape. The rim and body vessel count represents other vessel shapes, such as knickknacks, teapots, pitchers, and tureens, that indicate status as much as cups and saucers, plates, or bowls. This method tested the hypothesis that it is more accurate to include as many shapes as possible, assuming approximately the same relative values of types as for known shapes, than to completely exclude shapes other than cups and saucers, plates, and bowls. This strategy was supported by the fact that cup and saucer, plate, and bowl indices all had the same basic ranking of types by relative value within each other. Values in these three indices were averaged to form one set of values to apply to vessels of other or unknown shape. Calculations of an average single index for all vessels are compared and contrasted with results of calculating separate indices for plates, bowls, and cups and saucers. This chapter investigates the effects of using such different methods of calculating vessel ceramic indices.

The second analysis compares and contrasts the ranking of sites according to indices calculated from sherd counts rather than vessel counts. The sherd index site rank order was evaluated against site rankings for vessel indices and occupational status. In order to calculate a ceramic index with sherd counts, the index values used for cups and saucers, plates, and bowls were averaged into one set of index values (Table 2). The possibility of using a sherd index is important for those sites where predominantly small archaeological fragments make it difficult or impossible to make a vessel count. If sherd index site rank order corresponds with documented indications of socioeconomic status, then such modifications of Miller's index may permit its application to a broader range of sites.

In order to understand why different site rank orders were produced by alternative ceramic indices, the dynamic interaction of elements comprising indices were analyzed by a method named "consumer-choice profiles." Consumers may decide to select from the market or simply discard more of some decorative types than others. These choices result in the allocation of the whiteware assemblage value among alternative decorative types. The choice of buying and discarding one creamware vessel diminishes the index by the possible alternative selection of a porcelain vessel, which would yield a five-times-higher value for that vessel to contribute to the index. Different relative contributions of decorative types were compared and contrasted within and between indices. Within each index, percentages of decorative types weighted by their relative cost were calculated in order to determine the relative contribution of each decorative type value to the total site index. Comparisons were made between all indices except bowl and plate indices because their site rank orders differed substantially from the documented status ranking of sites. The site percentages of value-weighted decorative types were rank-ordered from highest to lowest proportional contributions to their indices. In this way, the index site rank order was analyzed into the different weightings of decorative types that produced the index values ranking the sites.

The effects of archaeological biases considered in this research included

selectivity of discard and sample representativeness (Schiffer 1976). Within
each site, the effects of selective discard are constant for all alternative ceramic indices, and therefore were not considered as a factor in their different
results. Differential discard between sites due to status level may explain an
unexpectedly low ceramic index ranking for a moderate status household. It
was expected that high-status ceramics, usually whiteware, owned by a moder-
ate- or low-status family would be less frequently used, broken, and discarded
than similar ceramics in high-status households. Such selective behaviors
would result in minimal ceramic index distinctions between low- and moderate-status households, while maximizing differences between high- and moderate-status households. This may explain a haitus or disjunction between the
values for moderate-status households and those at a high status level (Spencer-Wood and Heberling this volume). Because all site residents were working-
class status, few, if any, status distinctions in discard were expected.

A major factor in the explanation of different site rank orders resulting
from alternative ceramic indices concerns the effects of different subsamples
of the total archaeological assemblage. Alternative vessel and sherd counts
form different subsamples, resulting in different index values. For example, it
was expected that sherd indices would include higher counts of undecorated
types than vessel indices because both decorated and undecorated vessels often
produce undecorated sherds. Sherd counts should also include more transfer-
printed body pieces than would be included in vessel counts. Differences in
sherd index values result from the weighing of higher counts for low-valued
types against often higher counts for high-valued porcelain and transfer print.
Vessel rim counts were expected to underrepresent the total number of transfer-printed vessels distinguishable from both rims and bodies. Both rim and
body vessel counts and sherd counts include shapes not identifiable as cups
and saucers, plates, or bowls. This may result in either a higher or lower index,
depending on whether the other vessels and sherds are high-status wares such
as porcelain or transfer-printed, or low-status, undecorated or lightly decorated wares. Analyses of such sample differences obtained from vessel versus
sherd counts were required to explain the differences among alternative ceramic index values. The different ceramic subsamples used to calculate alternative indices yield the differences in index site rank orders discussed in the
results.

HYPOTHESES

Site rank was the primary measurement of relative socioeconomic status.
Hypotheses concerning degree of correspondence between site rank orders for
occupational status and for alternative methods of calculating ceramic indices
were hypothesized from results of previous research. The first two hypotheses
were generated from the comparison of occupational and ceramic index site
rankings for eleven early nineteenth-century sites (Spencer-Wood and Heberling this volume). The third hypothesis was generated from research on sites
in the second half of the nineteenth century that established correspondences

between occupational status and sherd index site rank orders (McBride and McBride 1983; Spencer-Wood 1984).

Hypothesis 1. Site rankings derived from cup and saucer ceramic indices are expected to be more highly correlated with occupationally related status rankings than are plate or bowl index site rank orders. This was expected because teaware served more to display status than did plates or bowls (Miller 1984:47).

Hypothesis 2. Site rankings derived from a combined cup and saucer, plate, and bowl index should be nearly the same as cup and saucer index rank orders because they are more strongly influenced by the consistently higher cup and saucer index values than by the lower plate and bowl index values for all decorative types.

Hypothesis 3. Site rankings derived from sherd ceramic indices should be correlated with occupationally related mean personal-estate site rank orders.

RESULTS

In this section, site rankings derived from documentary indications of status are compared with those derived from alternative ceramic price scaling indices. As described in the methods section, site status rank orders were based on site means of surviving personal estates and occupational category average personal estates for residents without inventories. Although the documentary site rank order is no more definitive than the ceramic index rank orders, it was used initially as a referent to assess the degree of fit between socioeconomic status and alternative index site rank orders. In this section, documentary status site rankings are discussed first, followed by their correlations with both vessel and sherd ceramic indices in order to test the three hypotheses. Of the three hypotheses, the first was supported by the research results. Overall, none of the correlations between site rank orders by any of the ceramic indices and by mean personal-estate value, is highly positive. In exploring explanations for the disparities between site rankings derived from ceramic indices and those derived from mean personal estate values, the analytical tool of the "ceramic consumer-choice profile" was developed. Each consumer choice profile describes the relative weighting of different whiteware value frequencies in the mean ceramic index value. Whiteware consumer-choice profiles corresponding to high, moderate, and low occupational statuses were sometimes markedly different from the ceramic profiles producing high, moderate, and low ceramic indices. The whiteware profile patterns suggested ceramic acquisition and deposition behavior patterns associated with socioeconomic status distinctions that were not necessarily reflected in a ceramic index value. This is because mean ceramic indices do not describe the patterns of relative decorative-type value in a site's whiteware assemblage.

The documentary data indicates that the socioeconomic rank order of sites from highest to lowest are: Q#27, M#6–8, Q#14–16, Q#24, and Q#10–12 (Table 3). The Quincy site rank order is the same as established in previous research (Spencer-Wood 1984). In the present research, occupationally related

Table 3. Average Personal Estates of Site Residents

NCRD deed book/page	Resident	Occupation	Years	Personal estate	Source[a]
		Quincy #27			
154/265	Stephen Penniman	Bootmaker	1845–1864	$102	NCRPI #14276 Walling 1857 USFCQ 1850:276
335/194	Susan Penniman	Widow	1864–1866	$285	NCRPI #27477
345/253	Amos M. Litchfield	Carpenter-builder	1866–1911	Av. $13,666	QD 1868–1911 Sherman 1876
	Total number of years =		66	617,478	= Product
	Residents' average personal estate = $9,356				
		Milton #6–8			
229/133	Thomas Lynes	Laborer	1854–1865	$763	NCRPI #12062 Walling 1858
374/49	Thomas Lynes, Jr.	Teamster	1865–1881	$13,071	NCRPI #45566 NCRPI #12061
374/49	James Lynes	Teamster	1865–1867	$112	NCRPI #33654
532/605	Cornelius Lynes	Teamster	1881–1898	$2,227	Walker 1896
	Total number of years =		44	242,429	= Product
	Residents' average personal estate = $5,510				
		Quincy #14–16			
276/192	James Gallagher	Blacksmith	1859–1874	Av. $4,827	QD 1868–1869
454/236	Mary Gallagher	Widow	1874–1886	$100	NCRPI #24935
	James Gallagher, Jr.	Stonecutter	1874–1886	Av. $1,261	QD 1876; Sherman 1876
569/48	Robert B. Courtney	Granite-cutter	1887–1897	Av. $1,261	QD 1882–1883, 1888–1889, 1897 Robinson 1888
	Total number of years =		37	92,587	= Product
	Residents' average personal estate = $2,502				

Quincy #24

166/70	Ibrahim Bartlett		1846–1853	$242	NCRPI #1125 Walling 1857
429/315	Abigail Bartlett	Widow	1853–1867	$1,602	NCRPI #1108
	Jonathan Tanner	Granite-cutter	1872–1892	Av. $1,261	QD 1882–1904
	Mary Tanner	Widow	1892–1904	$350	NCRPI #39292
	Roger Tanner	Clerk	1892–1904	Av. $1,261	QD 1893–1911
					Sherman 1876
				59,002	= Product

Total number of years = 53

Residents' average personal estate = $1,113

Quincy #10–12

350/288	Abigail Bartlett	Widow	1867–1877	$1,602	NCRPI #1108 Sherman 1876
499/194	Mary Curtis	Milliner	1877–1881	$185	NCRPI #29975
528/502	John W. Brooks	Railroad flagman	1881–1894	$700	NCRPI #30123 Robinson 1888
	Arnold B. Brooks	Blacksmith	1888–1889	Av. $4,827	QD 1888–1889:151
	Richard E. Brooks	Modeler	1888–1892	Av. $1,261	QD 1891–1892:135
	Benjamin A. Brooks	Tool-sharpener	1891–1892	Av. $1,261	QD 1891–1892:135
721/443	Julia A. Brooks	Widow	1894–1900	$200	NCRPI #34937
				29,464	= Product

Total number of years = 33

Residents' average personal estate = $893

mean site personal estate values indicating status were calculated through the last site residents at the turn of the century because trash collection started in the early twentieth century in both Milton and Quincy, and all of the ceramics could date from the nineteenth century. Quincy #27 was inhabited sequentially by a bootmaker, small-scale builders, and carpenters. The first resident, Stephen Penniman, had so many debts when he died that, to pay them, the house had to be sold to the Litchfields. The Pennimans had been excluded in previous estimates of socioeconomic status because their occupational category and personal estates had not been determined. It was found that Stephen Penniman's personal estate was much lower than would be expected from his occupation. Because the Litchfields owned their own business, they had the highest average personal estates, although none of their actual inventories were available. Quincy #27 was ranked highest because it was inhabited for the longest period by the highest occupational category of proprietor. Therefore the ceramic assemblage was expected to represent the forty-five years of proprietor–craftsman status, more than the twenty years of the bootmaker's residence. Milton site #6–8 was occupied by teamsters, whose actual personal estates were average to above-average for this occupational category. Quincy #14–16 included a blacksmith and skilled granite workers, for which averages had to be used, resulting in a lower status rating than the Milton site. Quincy #24 was ranked below #14–16, mostly due to skilled employee averages for stonemasons. Quincy #10–12 was ranked lowest based on a few inventories and average personal estate values for skilled workers. In contrast to Milton #6–8, the small number of actual inventories available for the Quincy sites, mostly for widows, makes this site rank order largely dependent on category averages that reflect the status rank order of occupations.

For each of these five sites, a total of eleven alternative ceramic indices were calculated, including a sherd index, and vessel indices for cups and saucers, plates, and bowls were calculated, first, on the basis of distinctive rims, and secondly, from distinctive rims and other body sherds. Combined cup and saucer, plate, and bowl indices were calculated both from distinctive vessel rims, and as an average of the three indices calculated separately. Total vessel indices were calculated, first, from all distinctive rim and body sherds, and secondly, from the average of cup and saucer, plate, and bowl rim and body vessel indices (Table 4).

The research results only supported the first hypothesis. Of the ceramic indices, cup and saucer index site rank orders correlated most with occupationally related mean personal estate value rankings, possibly because tea- and coffeeware were used more for status display than were other shapes. However, these correlations are not strong. The cup and saucer rim index had the highest Pearson's correlation of .563 (at the .05 level) with the site rank order by mean personal estate value, followed by the cup and saucer rim and body index ($r = .499$ at the .05 level). The higher price ratios for all decorative types of cups and saucers than for plates and bowls results in consistently higher cup and saucer indices, which are more positively correlated with documentary indications of status than are plate or bowl indices. The second hy-

Table 4. Site Mean Personal-Estate and Alternative Ceramic Index Site Rank Orders

	Site mean personal estate[b]	Cup and saucer rim CI[c]	Cup index rims and bodies[d]	All vessels rims and bodies[e]	Mean CPB rims and bodies[f]	CPB rims[g]
Correlations Mean PE & CI's[a] .05 < p < .1		.563	.499	−.55	−.494	−.227
	Q#27	Q#14–16	Q#14–16	Q#14–16	Q#14–16	Q#14–16
	$9,356	3.77	3.78	2.65	2.58	2.73
	M#6–8	Q#27	Q#27	M#6–8	Q#24	Q#10–12
	$5,510	3.70	3.67	2.47	2.37	2.38
	Q#14–16	M#6–8	M#6–8	Q#24	M#6–8	Q#27
	$2,502	3.29	3.46	2.42	2.33	2.37
	Q#24	Q#24	Q#10–12	Q#10–12	Q#10–12	Q#24
	$1,113	3.19	3.39	2.36	2.25	2.33
	Q#10–12	Q#10–12	Q#24	Q#27	Q#27	M#6–8
	$893	3.07	3.20	2.19	2.17	2.26

Mean index CPB rims[h]	Bowl rims[i]	Plate rims and bodies[j]	Plate rims[k]	Bowl index rims and bodies[l]	Sherd index[m]
.047	−.146	−.892	−.578	−.605	−.534
Q#14–16	Q#14–16	Q#14–16	Q#14–16	Q#24	Q#14–16
2.64	2.05	2.07	2.10	1.92	2.65
Q#24	Q#24	Q#24	Q#24	Q#14–16	Q#24
2.41	2.03	1.98	2.01	1.90	2.54
Q#27	Q#27	Q#10–12	Q#10–12	M#6–8	Q#10–12
2.37	1.67	1.91	1.78	1.75	2.24
M#6–8	M#6–8	M#6–8	M#6–8	Q#10–12	Q#27
2.19	1.56	1.78	1.73	1.46	2.20
Q#10–12	Q#10–12	Q#27	Q#27	Q#27	M#6–8
2.06	1.32	1.58	1.73	1.26	2.03

[a]Correlations mean PE and CI's, .05 < p < .1 = Pearson's correlation coefficients between mean personal-estate values and ceramic index values at the .05 significance level.
[b]Site mean personal estate = Mean personal-estate value for each site specified.
[c]Cup rims = Cup and saucer ceramic index based on a vessel count from distinctive rims.
[d]Cup index rims and bodies = Cup and saucer ceramic index based on a vessel count from distinctive rims and other sherds (i.e., complete vessel count).
[e]All vessels rims and bodies = Mean ceramic index for all vessels based on a vessel count from distinctive rims and other body sherds.
[f]Mean CPB rims and bodies = Average ceramic index for cups and saucers, plates, and bowls, based on vessel count from distinctive rims and other sherds (i.e., complete vessel count).
[g]CPB rims = Ceramic index for cups and saucers, plates, and bowls, combined, based on a vessel count from distinctive rims.
[h]Mean index CPB rims = The mean of ceramic indices based on a vessel count from distinctive rims for cups and saucers, plates, and bowls.
[i]Bowl rims = Bowl ceramic index based on a vessel count from distinctive rims.
[j]Plate rims and bodies = Plate ceramic index based on a vessel count from distinctive rim and other body sherds.
[k]Plate rims = Plate ceramic index based on a vessel count from distinctive rims sherds.
[l]Bowl index rims and bodies = Bowl ceramic index based on vessel count from distinctive rim and other body sherds.
[m]Sherd index = Ceramic index based on sherd counts for whiteware decorative types.

pothesis was not supported by research results. The mean cup and saucer, plate, and bowl rim index site rank order had practically no correlation with site mean personal-estate values, and other total vessel indices were negatively correlated with this site status rank order. This suggests that combined vessel indices are more strongly influenced by the plate and bowl indices than the cup and saucer indices, except perhaps for the mean rim indices, for which a weak positive correlation indicated greater influence by cup and saucer index values. The third hypothesis also was not supported by research results. Site rankings produced by sherd indices had negative correlations with occupationally related rankings by mean personal-estate value (Table 4, Figure 1).

These results are only suggestive because the data used in the correlations are only available for five sites. These results are supported by Henry's finding of a similar degree of correlation between occupational status and cup and saucer indices for fourteen domestic site features in Phoenix (this volume). However, completely comparable data are not available from other sites because researchers use a variety of different methods for calculating Miller's indices. In order to more fully test these hypotheses, more comparable data need to be generated for a larger number of sites. This is a strong argument for the adoption of standardized methods for accurately and comparably calculating Miller's indices.

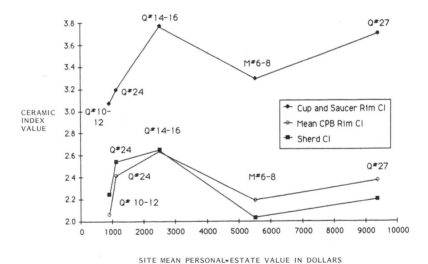

SITE MEAN PERSONAL-ESTATE VALUE IN DOLLARS

Figure 1. Correspondence between ceramic indices and site mean personal-estate values. Cup and saucer rim CI = Miller's cup and saucer ceramic index calculated from vessel counts based on distinctive rim sherds; Mean CPB rim CI = The mean of ceramic indices based on a vessel count from distinctive rims for cups and saucers, plates, and bowls. Sherd CI = Ceramic index calculated from the average values of cup and saucer, plate, and bowl index values, and the total whiteware sherd count; The nearest point is the intersection of the specified ceramic index value and the mean personal-estate value for the specified site.

The fact that only one hypothesis was weakly supported led to further examination of the relationships between site occupational status rankings and the ceramic index site rankings. In order to understand disparities between actual ceramic index site rankings and those expected on the basis of documentary status rankings, the constituent elements of ceramic indices were analyzed, resulting in the development of consumer-choice profiles. Closer analysis of the unexpected ceramic indices into profiles yielded more information than did the weak support of the first hypothesis. Beyond the correlation of site status rankings and cup and saucer ceramic index rankings, consumer-choice profiles permit analyses of site archaeological assemblages into their patterns of relative ceramic value. By delineating these patterns, more may be learned about socioeconomic behavior patterns than is possible solely from a ceramic index.

Disparities between a site's status ranking based on documentary data, and its ceramic index ranking, may be explained by site-specific situations, or through analysis of the index into its ceramic consumer-choice profile. For example, Q#14–16 had the highest value for all but one ceramic index, while its mean personal-estate value ranked third. Without this anomalously high ceramic index, the other four sites' cup and saucer ceramic indices were highly correlated with mean personal estate values. A Pearson's correlation coefficient of .952 at the .05 level was obtained for cup and saucer rim index rankings, and a correlation coefficient of .903 at the .05 level was obtained for cup and saucer rim and body indices. The anomalously high ceramic indices for Q#14–16 could be the result of inheritance and subsequent discard of more expensive whiteware than could otherwise be afforded by the house owner, Mary Gallagher. She was a daughter of Abigail Bartlett, who, in the mid-nineteenth century, owned all of the land on the side of Marsh Street including Q#24, Q#14–16 and Q#10–12. This particular site circumstance might explain the occupationally unexpected high ceramic index values for Q#14–16, and justify their exclusion from the correlations of cup and saucer indices with mean personal-estate values. However, correlation values for other ceramic index rank orders do not become strongly positive even when Q#14–16 is excluded from these analyses. Other sites also have disparities between these index rankings and their occupational status rankings. There are a number of other possible site-specific explanations for disparities between mean personal estate value site rankings and rankings by ceramic indices. However, the analysis of ceramic index constituents into consumer-choice profiles may permit explanations of such disparities in terms of recurring status-related patterns of ceramic value that may not necessarily produce correspondingly status-related ceramic index values. Consumer-choice profiles may be useful in explaining why site Quincy #27, with the highest status occupations of proprietor and craftsmen, did not have the highest cup and saucer ceramic indices. Q#27's second-place ranking among cup and saucer indices suggests that this site's residents archaeologically deposited fewer expensive white ceramics than residents of Q#14–16, who had a higher ceramic index value. However, the Q#27 assemblage in fact had the highest proportions of value in expensive white ceramics, as revealed in its consumer-choice profiles (Figure 2, Tables 5 and 6).

A consumer-choice profile is derived from analysis of the constituent proportions of whiteware decorative-type values contributing to a ceramic index. By analyzing the relative weighting of decorative-type frequencies in ceramic indices, these profiles can suggest reasons for some disparities in site rank orders derived from ceramic indices versus those derived from occupational indications of status. More importantly, consumer-choice profiles corresponding to site occupational status rankings may delineate some regular status-related patterns in ceramic consumer behavior. Consumer decisions result in selecting and archaeologically depositing more of some decorative whiteware types than others. These decisions result in the frequency distribution of decorative-type values that are averaged in the index. The selection and discard of one creamware vessel diminishes the index by the possible alternative choice of a vessel of porcelain, which would yield a five-time-higher value for that vessel to contribute to the index. For each ceramic index subsample of the assemblage, the ceramic consumer-choice profile involves calculation of the different proportions of decorative type values that are averaged in the index. In a consumer-choice profile, the relative proportion of each decorative type value is the percentage formed by that value times its frequency of occurrence, divided by the sum of all such value products. For an explanation, see the addendum at the end of the chapter for Tables 5–9. For cups and saucers, the index value for transfer-printed and flow-printed is the same, so these types were considered as transfer-printed in their combined contribution to the cup

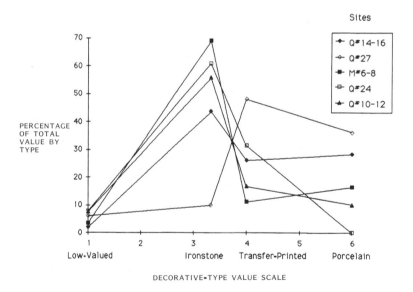

Figure 2. Cup and saucer rim consumer-choice profiles. Low-valued = Whiteware ranging in value from 1 to 1.17 (see Table 2); Transfer-printed = Flow-printed and transfer-printed whiteware are combined because they have the same value in cup and saucer indices.

Table 5. Cup and Saucer Rim Consumer-Choice Profiles: Site Rank Orders by Whiteware-Type Value Percentages[a]

Porcelain	Flow- and transfer-printed[b]	Ironstone	Low-valued whiteware[c]	Cup and saucer rim CI[d]
Q#27[e]	Q#27	M#6–8	Q#14–16	Q#14–16
36.0%[f](2)[g]	48.0%(4)	68.9%(30)	1.9%(6)	3.77(73)
Q#14–16	Q#24	Q#24	M#6–8	Q#27
28.3%(13)	31.3%(3)	60.9%(7)	3.5%(6)	3.70(8)
Q#10–12	Q#14–16	Q#10–12	Q#27	M#6–8
20.1%(4)	26.2%(18)	55.7%(20)	6.0%(2)	3.29(44)
M#6–8	Q#10–12	Q#14–16	Q#10–12	Q#24
16.6%(4)	16.7%(5)	43.6%(36)	7.5%(10)	3.19(12)
Q#24	M#6–8	Q#27	Q#24	Q#10–12
0%(0)	11.0%(4)	10.0%(1)	7.8%(2)	3.07(39)

[a]Cup and saucer rim = Vessel count of cups and saucers based on distinctive rim sherds.
[b]Flow- and transfer-printed = The frequencies of flow-printed and transfer-printed whiteware are combined because they have the same value in the cup and saucer ceramic index.
[c]Low-valued whiteware = Whiteware values ranging from 1.00–1.17 in the cup and saucer ceramic index.
[d]Cup and saucer rim CI = Miller's cup and saucer ceramic index calculated using a vessel count based on distinctive rim sherds.
[e]The site is designated above each relative frequency of whiteware decorative type, rank ordered from highest to lowest percentage for each type.
[f]Each percentage is the relative proportion contributed by the specified decorative type(s) to the total value of the specified site's whiteware subassemblage of cup and saucer rims.
[g]Numbers in parentheses are the frequencies of the specified ceramic vessel types in the specified site's whiteware assemblage.

and saucer indices. In contrast to their different values for cups and saucers, ironstone and transfer-printed have the same value in combined vessel indices. Therefore they have to be treated as one proportional contribution to the index, revealing the relatively low proportions of flow-printed in most indices. Each consumer-choice profile describes the relative weighting of different decorative value frequencies in the mean index value.

Consumer-choice profiles that could correspond to high-, moderate-, and low-status ceramic consumer behavior were suggested by patterns of ceramic value found in the 1840s St. Mary's County, Maryland, probate inventories. As the ceramic value in probate inventories increased, the value of all types of ceramics increased until a value of $8 for white earthenware was reached. After this point, the values of common earthenware and porcelain continued to increase in conjunction with increasing ceramic values, while the value of white earthenware did not. The increasing values of common earthenware among the wealthier inventories could result from servants, boarders, or a large family of children. Wealthy inventories had the highest values, both of porcelain and common earthenware, but proportionally lower values of white earthenware than less wealthy inventories. Common earthenware included both redware and unspecified crockery (Herman *et al.* 1973). While the present research does not include redware, general patterns of ceramic value from the inventory research could be used to hypothesize more detailed whiteware con-

Table 6. Cup and Saucer Rim and Body Consumer-Choice Profiles: Site Rank Orders by Whiteware-Type Value Percentages[a]

Porcelain	Flow- and transfer-printed[b]	Ironstone	Low-valued whiteware[c]	Cup and saucer rim and body CI[d]
Q#27[e]	Q#27	M#6–8	Q#14–16	Q#14–16
32.7%[f](2)[g]	43.6%(4)	56.1%(28)	2.7%(10)	3.78(90)
Q#14–16	Q#10–12	Q#24	Q#10–12	Q#27
31.7%(18)	36.3%(19)	49.5%(10)	4.3%(12)	3.67(10)
M#6–8	Q#24	Q#10–12	M#6–8	M#6–8
25.3%(7)	35.7%(6)	36.5%(23)	4.2%(7)	3.46(48)
Q#10–12	Q#14–16	Q#14–16	Q#27	Q#10–12
22.9%(8)	29.4%(25)	36.2%(37)	5.5%(2)	3.39(62)
Q#24	M#6–8	Q#27	Q#24	Q#24
8.9%(1)	14.4%(6)	18.2%(2)	5.9%(4)	3.20(21)

[a]Cup and saucer rim and body = Vessel count of cups and saucers based on distinctive rim and body sherds.
[b]Flow- and transfer-printed = The frequencies of flow-printed and transfer-printed whiteware are combined because they have the same value in the cup and saucer ceramic index.
[c]Low-valued whiteware = Whiteware values ranging from 1.00–1.17 in the cup and saucer ceramic index.
[d]Cup and saucer rim and body CI = Miller's cup and saucer ceramic index calculated from a vessel count based on distinctive rim and body sherds.
[e]The site is designated above each relative frequency of whiteware decorative type, rank ordered from highest to lowest percentage for each type.
[f]Each percentage is the relative proportion contributed by the specified decorative type(s) to the total value of the specified site's whiteware subassemblage of cups and saucers based on distinctive rim and body sherds.
[g]Numbers in parentheses are the frequencies of the specified ceramic vessel types in the specified site's whiteware assemblage.

sumer-choice profiles corresponding to socioeconomic ranking from high to low occupational status.

Through extrapolation of the St. Mary's County, Maryland, inventory analyses and other research (this volume), comparative proportions of whiteware in consumer-choice profiles can be hypothesized for high- through moderate-, to low-status sites. In comparison to high-moderate statuses, the highest occupational status is expected to produce site assemblages with the largest proportions of ceramic value in porcelain, nearly as large percentages of high-valued white earthenware (i.e., transfer-printed), small proportions of ironstone, and larger proportions of low-valued whiteware than other high- or moderate-status sites. With decreasing status, the proportion of high-valued white earthenware (transfer print) is expected to exceed the proportion of porcelain, while the proportion of ironstone remains small and the proportion of low-valued whiteware remains larger than for moderate-status sites. These whiteware profiles are expected for high-status household assemblages because they are expected to display their status through the most expensive tableware they can afford, replacing ironstone with transfer print or porcelain as much as possible. At the same time, high-status households are expected to deposit more inexpensive ceramics used in the kitchen and/or by live-in servants. In other research, high-status households have exhibited a pattern of archaeologically depositing more inexpensive ceramics and fewer expensive ceramics than expected from documentary data (Baugher and Venables this volume; Spencer-Wood and Heberling this volume).

Moderate-status sites are expected to have a preponderance of ceramic value in ironstone, and moderate proportions of both high- and low-valued whiteware compared with other sites. This profile is expected to result from less kitchenware and fewer servants than high-status households, while ironstone is the most expensive ceramic type that can be afforded in any quantity by the moderate-status working class. In general, low-status household assemblages are expected to have a larger proportion of low-valued whiteware and smaller proportions of ironstone and high-valued ceramics than moderate-status sites. However, all except the lowest-status site assemblages are still expected to have larger proportions of ceramic value in ironstone than do high-status site assemblages. While ironstone remains the most expensive ceramic type that can be afforded in any quantity, low-status profiles are expected to have substitution of lower-valued whiteware for some of the more expensive ironstone. This pattern may result from the presence of more boarders depositing more low-valued whiteware than at moderate-status house sites. Compared with higher-status assemblages, the lowest-status profile is expected to have the largest proportions of low-valued whiteware, and smaller proportions of other decorative types because they are not generally affordable. These consumer choice profiles hypothesize status-related site differences in relative proportions of low-, moderate-, and high-valued whiteware types. The profiles of moderate- and low-status households are expected to be more similar to each other than to high-status profiles because low- and moderate-status households are expected to own, use, and discard fewer high-valued white ceramics than high-status households.

These hypothesized consumer-choice profiles can be tested on comparative-site archaeological assemblages of discarded or lost whiteware. Graphing consumer-choice profiles (Figures 2, 3, and 4) facilitates comparison of decorative-type value proportions, both within an index and between different site indices. Comparisons among sites demonstrates that relatively similar ceramic index values can be derived from quite different consumer-choice profiles, while greater differences in ceramic index values may be derived from more similar-appearing profiles. For example, for cup and saucer rims, the mean index value of Q#27 and Q#14–16 are relatively close, but their consumer-choice profiles are quite different (Figure 2, Table 5). In contrast, these two sites have relatively disparate sherd index values derived from apparently more similar sherd profiles (Figure 4, Table 9).

While the initial impression from the appearance of the cup and saucer profiles is the preponderance of ironstone at most sites, the differences in ceramic index values result from averaging the different proportions of lower-versus higher-valued whiteware (Figure 2, Tables 5 and 6). In combined vessel and sherd profiles, the fact that ironstone and transfer-printed have the same value increases the combined dominance of these two types in the profiles (Figures 3 and 4). The preponderance of ironstone in most site profiles results in index values that vary less from the value of ironstone than might other-

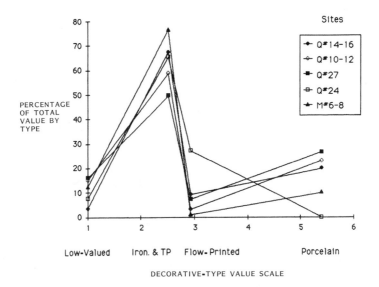

Figure 3. Combined cup and saucer, plate, bowl rim consumer-choice profiles. Low-valued = Whiteware ranging in value from 1 to 1.69 (see Table 2); Iron and TP = Ironstone and transfer-printed whiteware percentages combined, because they have the same average value for combined vessel indices.

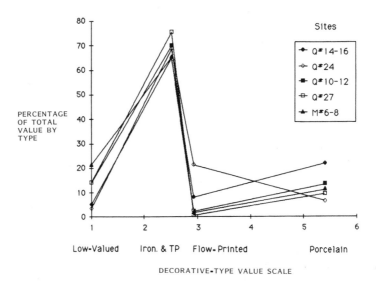

Figure 4. Sherd ceramic consumer-choice profiles. Low-valued = Whiteware ranging in value from 1 to 1.69 (see Table 2); Iron and TP = Ironstone and transfer-printed whiteware percentages combined, because their average value is the same in calculating sherd indices.

wise be the case. Since these site residents were predominantly working-class, skilled employees except for those at Q#27, it was expected that their consumer-choice profiles would be dominated by ironstone rather than more expensive whiteware. At the same time, most sites had relatively small proportions of low-valued ceramics in vessel indices, indicating that these working-class site residents did not have the hypothesized lowest-status profiles. The small proportions of low-valued whiteware from these house sites also correspond well with the lack of documentary records of servants or boarders to contribute low-valued whiteware to the site assemblages. An alternative possibility is that undocumented boarders or servants used ironstone.

The hypothesized status relationship of whiteware consumer choice profiles was borne out best in decorative-type proportions in cup and saucer ceramic indices. While these ceramic indices correlated better with occupational status rankings than did other indices, the consumer-choice profiles explained how averaging decorative-type proportions produced some mean ceramic index rankings that did not correspond with occupational status rankings. For these five sites, the consumer-choice profiles do seem, in general, to represent status-related behavior patterns as hypothesized. However, further tests with more comparable site data are needed to assess the range of site situations for which the hypothesized consumer-choice profiles represent status-related behavior patterns.

The hypothesized whiteware consumer-choice profiles corresponding to high-, moderate, and low occupational status household site assemblages do not necessarily produce correspondingly high, moderate, and low ceramic indices. For example, site rankings by cup and saucer ceramic indices do not completely correspond with occupational status rankings or with associated proportions of decorative-type values in consumer-choice profiles. Quincy #27 had the highest occupational status of proprietor-craftsman, with one low-status skilled employee. Compared to other sites, Q#27 indices had the smallest proportion of ironstone, the largest proportions of porcelain and transfer-printed whiteware, and a relatively large proportion of low-valued whiteware. This pattern corresponds to the hypothesized second-highest status consumer choice profile, because for Q#27 the proportion of transfer-printed is larger than porcelain. However, Q#27 cup and saucer indices only ranked second because its largest proportion of expensive whiteware was weighed against a relatively large proportion of low-valued whiteware and a small proportion of ironstone to produce mean index values (Figure 2, Tables 5 and 6). The relatively large proportion of low-valued whiteware could be due to servants, and/or the relatively low-status, skilled employee who owned Q#27 for twenty years. Although the representativeness of the small Q#27 cup and saucer subsample can be questioned, it is part of a larger total vessel sample, the typical nature of which is indicated by a whiteware value proportion pattern generally similar to those for other sites (Figures 3 and 4). The cup and saucer consumer-choice profile does conform to expectations for high-status ceramic acquisition and deposition behaviors.

In contrast, although the craftsman and skilled employees at Q#14–16 generally had the hypothesized moderate-status consumer-choice profile, the ceramic indices were ranked highest among the sites. Compared to other site cup and saucer profiles, Q#14–16 had the second smallest proportion of its whiteware value in ironstone, with the second largest proportion of porcelain, a moderate proportion of transfer-printed, and the smallest proportion of low-valued whiteware (Figures 2 and 3). In contrast, although M#6–8 had the second largest mean personal-estate value, it ranked third among cup and saucer ceramic indices. However, the occupational status of the skilled employees of M#6–8 did correspond well with its lower-status consumer choice profile and its moderate cup and saucer index ranking. The M#6–8 profile indicates lower status than Q#14–16 because it had the largest proportion of ironstone, slightly larger proportions of low-valued whiteware, and relatively small proportions of high-valued whiteware. The cup and saucer indices and profile of M#6–8 indicate slightly higher status than those for Q#10–12 and Q#24, possibly because of M#6–8's above-average mean personal estate for the occupational category of skilled employees. Compared with other sites, the low cup and saucer indices and skilled employee status for Q#24 and Q#10–12 correspond well with their lower-status profiles, which include comparatively large proportions of low-valued whiteware and sequentially decreasing proportions of ironstone (Figure 2, Tables 5 and 6).

In sum, the present research results suggest a stronger relationship of status-related behavior patterns to whiteware consumer-choice profiles than to mean ceramic index values. The cup and saucer profiles of these five Boston area sites correspond as hypothesized to their relative occupational status rank order, and they also explain how the weighing of expensive against less expensive decorative-type proportions into mean ceramic indices yields site rankings that do not necessarily correspond to the status related, whiteware-value patterns in profiles. Consumer-choice profiles generated from combined cup and saucer, plate, and bowl ceramic indices also generally correspond to those expected from occupational status site rankings (Figure 3, Table 7). Further research may determine the range of site situations for which consumer profiles can be related to socioeconomic behavior patterns.

Some generalizations can be made about consumer-choice profiles implicit in the calculation of high, moderate, and low ceramic indices, in contrast to those corresponding to high, moderate, and low occupational status. The rank orders generated by indices result from the averaging of the relative proportions of low-valued whiteware, ironstone, and high-valued whiteware into a weighted mean. Therefore, a high-status, consumer-choice profile with relatively large proportions of value in both high- and low-valued whiteware, can yield a lower than expected ceramic index. Other things being equal, a larger proportion of low-valued whiteware at one site compared to others, would result in a relatively lower ceramic index value for that site. A much larger proportion of one or two high-valued white ceramics was required to obtain a high index value despite a relatively large proportion of inexpensive whiteware compared to other sites (as for Q#27, Tables 5 to 7). However, the archaeological results of this research and the St. Mary's County inventory study suggests that high-status households use more low-valued ceramics as well as

Table 7. Combined Cup, Plate, Bowl Rim Consumer-Choice Profiles: Site Rank Orders by Whiteware-Type Value Percentages[a]

Porcelain	Flow-printed	Transfer and ironstone[b]	Low-valued ceramics[c]	CPB rim vessel ceramic indices[d]
Q#27[e]	Q#24	M#6–8	Q#14–16	Q#14–16
26.7%[f](2)[g]	27.1%(11)	76.6%(82)	3.3%(11)	2.73(138)
Q#10–12	Q#14–16	Q#14–16	Q#24	Q#10–12
23.0%(8)	9.3%(12)	67.3%(101)	7.6%(9)	2.38(79)
Q#14–16	Q#27	Q#24	M#6–8	Q#27
20.1%(14)	7.3%(1)	65.3%(31)	12.3%(31)	2.37(17)
M#6–8	Q#10–12	Q#10–12	Q#10–12	Q#24
10.0%(5)	3.1%(2)	58.7%(44)	15.2%(25)	2.33(51)
Q#24	M#6–8	Q#27	Q#27	M#6–8
0%(0)	1.1%(1)	49.7%(8)	16.3%(6)	2.26(119)

[a]Combined cup, plate, bowl rim = The total whiteware vessel count for cups and saucers, plates and bowls, based on distinctive rim sherds.
[b]Transfer and ironstone = The frequencies of transfer-printed whiteware and ironstone are combined because they have the same value in the combined vessel rim ceramic index.
[c]Low-valued whiteware = Whiteware values ranging from 1.00–1.69 in the combined vessel ceramic index.
[d]CPB rim vessel ceramic indices = A ceramic index calculated from the average values for cups and saucers, plates, and bowls, and the total vessel count for these shapes, based on distinctive rim sherds.
[e]The site is designated above each relative frequency of whiteware decorative-type, rank ordered from highest to lowest percentage for each type.
[f]Each percentage is the relative proportion contributed by the specified decorative type(s) to the total value of the specified site's whiteware subassemblage of cup and saucer, plate, and bowl rims.
[g]Numbers in parentheses are the frequencies of the specified ceramic vessel types in the specified site's whiteware assemblage.

more high-valued ceramics than do moderate-status households. When the relatively large proportions of both high- and low-valued whiteware are averaged, the resulting moderate index value may not be as high as expected from site residents' documented occupational status. In addition, high status corresponds to smaller proportions of ironstone than does moderate status. Quincy #27 and #14–16 are the only sites among cup and saucer rim indices with smaller proportions of ironstone than higher-valued whiteware, resulting in the two indices with values higher than ironstone. If porcelain had a two- or three-times higher index value, as suggested for 1824 (Miller 1984:48), Q#27 would have had the highest ceramic index.

Ceramic indices tend towards the value of ironstone as proportions of ironstone increase in consumer-choice profiles, especially if there are balanced proportions of low- and high-valued whiteware. In general, lower ceramic indices result from increasing proportions of low-valued whiteware and decreasing proportions of more expensive whiteware. The order of the three lowest ceramic indices correspond to site order by decreasing proportions of ironstone for cup and saucer rim indices, and corresponded to site order by decreasing proportions of porcelain for cup and saucer rim and body indices (Tables 5 and 6).

Since proportions of low-valued whiteware may not indicate status, but are averaged against proportions of higher-valued types in all indices, it may be useful to calculate indices without the low-valued whiteware. Ceramic indices would then measure the mean value of status indicating ceramic decorative types. The different ceramic types indicating status in each time period would need to be determined, possibly through the level of price differentiation from the base value of cream colored. While this procedure might enhance the differentiation of high- and moderate-status site ceramic indices, it might also lessen the differentiation between moderate- and low-status ceramic indices and profiles.

Additional information was suggested by the comparative analysis of general consumer-choice profile differences between cup and saucer and other ceramic indices. Compared with cup and saucer indices, combined cup and saucer, bowl, and plate indices had larger proportions of low-valued whiteware and ironstone and smaller relative value proportions of porcelain in most cases (Figures 2 and 3, Tables 5 to 7). This suggests that plates and bowls include more utilitarian moderate- to low-valued whiteware types and fewer expensive types than do cups and saucers. However, with the addition of unknown shapes in indices calculated for all vessels, Q#10–12, M#6–8, and Q#24 increased their value proportions of porcelain, suggesting some status display at these sites through knickknacks, teapots, pitchers, and other shapes besides cups and saucers, plates, or bowls (Table 8). As anticipated in the methods section, proportions of ceramic decorative-type values in sherd indices differed

Table 8. Total Vessel Consumer-Choice Profiles: Site Rank Orders by Whiteware-Type Value Percentages[a]

Porcelain	Flow-printed	Transfer and ironstone[b]	Low-valued whiteware[c]	Rim and body ceramic indices[d]
Q#10–12[e]	Q#24	Q#24	Q#14–16	Q#14–16
25.5%[f](15)[g]	21.6%(15)	66.7%(54)	5.6%(27)	2.65(195)
M#6–8	Q#14–16	Q#14–16	Q#24	M#6–8
23.2%(24)	6.8%(12)	65.6%(135)	6.4%(13)	2.47(226)
Q#14–16	Q#27	Q#27	Q#10–12	Q#24
22.0%(21)	3.6%(1)	65.0%(21)	10.6%(34)	2.42(84)
Q#27	M#6–8	M#6–8	M#6–8	Q#10–12
13.3%(2)	2.1%(4)	63.0%(140)	11.7%(58)	2.36(135)
Q#24	Q#10–12	Q#10–12	Q#27	Q#27
5.3%(2)	1.5%(7)	62.4%(79)	18.1%(13)	2.19(37)

[a]Total vessel = A count of all whiteware vessels in the assemblage based on distinctive rim and body sherds.
[b]Transfer and ironstone = The frequencies of transfer-printed whiteware and ironstone are combined because they have the same value in the combined vessel ceramic index.
[c]Low-valued whiteware = Whiteware values ranging from 1.00–1.69 in the combined vessel ceramic index.
[d]Rim and body ceramic indices = A ceramic index calculated from a total vessel count based on distinctive rim and body sherds for all shapes, and average values for cups and saucers, plates, and bowls.
[e]The site is designated above each relative frequency of whiteware-decorative type, rank ordered from highest to lowest percentage for each type.
[f]Each percentage is the relative proportion contributed by the specified decorative type(s) to the total value of the specified site's whiteware subassemblage for its total vessel ceramic index.
[g]Numbers in parentheses are the frequencies of the specified ceramic vessel types in the specified site's whiteware assemblage.

Table 9. Sherd Consumer-Choice Profiles: Site Rank Orders by Whiteware-Type Value Percentages[a]

Porcelain	Flow-printed	Transfer and ironstone[b]	Low-valued whiteware[c]	Sherd indices[d]
Q#14–16[e]	Q#24	Q#27	Q#24	Q#14–16
21.9%[f](94)[g]	21.3%(60)	75.5%(119)	3.5%(29)	2.65(875)
Q#10–12	Q#14–16	Q#10–12	Q#14–16	Q#24
13.5%(28)	8.1%(64)	70.1%(312)	5.1%(117)	2.54(324)
M#6–8	Q#10–12	Q#24	Q#10–12	Q#10–12
11.4%(41)	2.4%(9)	68.6%(225)	14.0%(150)	2.24(499)
Q#27	M#6–8	M#6–8	Q#27	Q#27
9.6%(7)	1.8%(12)	65.4%(507)	14.2%(53)	2.20(180)
Q#24	Q#27	Q#14–16	M#6–8	M#6–8
6.6%(10)	.7%(1)	64.9%(600)	21.4%(400)	2.03(960)

[a]Sherd = The total sherd counts for site whiteware assemblages.
[b]Transfer and ironstone = The frequencies of transfer-printed whiteware and ironstone are combined because they have the same value in the combined vessel ceramic index.
[c]Low-valued whiteware = Whiteware values ranging from 1.00–1.69 in the combined vessel ceramic index.
[d]Sherd indices = A ceramic index calculated from the average values for cups and saucers, plates, and bowls, and the total number of sherds in the whiteware assemblage.
[e]The site is designated above each relative frequency of whiteware decorative type, rank ordered from highest to lowest percentage for each type.
[f] Each percentage is the relative proportion contributed by the specified decorative type(s) to the total value of the specified site's whiteware assemblage of sherds.
[g]Numbers in parentheses are the frequencies of the specified sherd types in the specified site's whiteware assemblage.

from those in vessel indices in a variety of ways at different sites, forming no definable status-related pattern (Table 9, Figure 4).

The negative correlations between average personal-estate values for site residents and vessel indices other than cups and saucers suggest some degree of reversal in site rank order by other ceramic indices, resulting in disconfirmation of the second and third hypotheses (Table 4). Consumer-choice profiles describe patterns in the distribution of whiteware decorative-type values that explain these negative correlations. Examination of consumer-choice profiles gives some insight into why some sites with relatively low occupational status rankings have higher-than-expected ceramic index rankings. For the combined vessel and sherd indices analyzed into consumer-choice profiles, some of the sites with relatively low documentary status rankings had larger proportions of expensive whiteware and smaller proportions of low-valued whiteware than did some of the sites with higher-status rankings (Figures 3 and 4, Tables 7 to 9). This may indicate that lower-status households that could not afford to acquire some expensive decorative types of cups and saucers might instead acquire these decorative types in plates, bowls, and other shapes, because decorative types of plates and bowls were always less expensive than the same types of cups and saucers. Low-status households may have been able to afford higher-status display through more expensive decorative types of plates and bowls than they could afford in tea- or coffeeware.

It is, of course, also possible that the archaeological results are due to nonrepresentative archaeological samples of household ceramics, resulting from unknown variations in care and discard of expensive white ceramics. Differential deposition and recovery are always factors influencing ceramic indices, but the predominantly working-class status of these sites does not offer reasons for expecting significant differences among sites. Idiosyncratic variations are possible, although unpredictable. All other things being equal, larger archaeological samples should result in more representative ceramic indices than smaller samples. More representative proportions of the less frequently discarded, expensive status wares should be collected in large rather than small samples, which are likely to include more common wares in proportion to the number of status wares. It is always possible that some small samples could overrepresent decorated types in comparison to undecorated types. Although Q#27's small sample of cups and saucers had two times as much porcelain and transfer-printed as ironstone and low-valued whiteware, cups and saucers were a subset of a larger total sample, with a preponderance of ironstone and low-valued whiteware. For these five Boston area sites, the archaeological results indicate that site consumer-choice profiles and index rankings can be better explained by documented variations in socioeconomic status behaviors than by variations in discard or sampling.

SUMMARY

Historical archaeological research at five Boston area sites produced the following results. Of eleven alternative price-scaling ceramic indices, the cup and saucer index site rank orders had a moderately positive correlation with occupational status site rankings. These results, and consumer-choice profiles, suggest that tea- and coffeeware may have served status display functions more than did plates and bowls. This conclusion is strengthened by similar results obtained for late nineteenth- to twentieth-century sites in Phoenix (Henry this volume), and for ten early nineteenth-century sites (Spencer-Wood and Heberling this volume). The sherd and combined vessel index site rankings and consumer-choice profiles were nearly all negatively correlated with site status rankings. These results suggest the possibility that, while lower-status households acquired and deposited relatively smaller proportions of expensive cups and saucers, they had larger relative proportions of expensive decorative types of other shapes in their assemblages than did moderate- or high-status households. This conclusion was also supported by lower-status site assemblages having larger proportions of porcelain than other decorative types in total vessel profiles, in contrast to cup and saucer profiles. These results suggest that while moderate and high-status households chose to display status through their selection of expensive tea- and/or coffeewares, lower-status households chose to display status by the acquisition of similar decorative types that were less expensive in other shapes.

Consumer-choice profiles were initially constructed in the search to explain disparities between site occupational status rankings and ceramic index rankings in terms of status-related whiteware value patterns rather than site-specific idiosyncracies. By analyzing relative proportions of decorative type values in whiteware assemblages, consumer-choice profiles offer more information about status-related consumer behavior than do ceramic indices. On the basis of other research, consumer choice profiles were hypothesized for high, moderate, and low occupational statuses. These profiles sometimes differed from those producing relatively high, moderate, and low ceramic indices. Because a ceramic index is the weighted mean value of a whiteware assemblage, different consumer-choice profiles can yield similar ceramic index values. It was also found that different ceramic index values could correspond to basically similar consumer-choice profiles. These research results indicate that consumer-choice profiles are more useful than ceramic indices for learning about status-related behaviors of whiteware acquisition and deposition.

Consumer choice profiles for the five Boston area sites suggest consumer behavior patterns distinguishing socioeconomic groups. In a progression from higher- to lower-status households, site profiles showed gradual replacement of more expensive white ceramics with less expensive ones. However, the highest-status consumer-choice profiles had relatively high proportions of both inexpensive and expensive whiteware, possibly as a result of more kitchenware or more servants than in lower-status households. The higher-status households had deposited relatively low proportions of the moderately priced whiteware that was found in greater abundance at sites of lower-status households. Further research might permit a determination of the range of site conditions under which consumer-choice profiles can indicate distinct high-, moderate-, and low-status household behavior patterns. The whiteware profiles generated in this research may only apply in similar urban situations with comparable discard behavior. It may be possible to identify recurring situations in which consumer-choice profiles are related less to status behaviors than to variables such as differential market access, ethnicity, family size and structure, political and religious affiliations, or personal preferences.

In this research, relationships between consumer-choice profiles and status-related behavior patterns have been hypothesized and initially supported. To fully test the hypothesized ceramic profiles, comparable data needs to be generated from more sites. This could be achieved through standardization in methods of analysis and data reporting by archaeologists. Standardization would create an as yet unrealized opportunity for historical archaeologists to share research results more fully, generating a powerful data base to significantly test more broadly applicable hypotheses.

ACKNOWLEDGMENTS

I would like to thank the many graduate and undergraduate students that participated in the field and lab research on the Quincy and Milton sites. In particular I would like to thank graduate students Joan Brown, David Singer, John Tuma, Scott Heberling, Michael Delaney, Sally Goss, and Dick Riley who gave up their weekends in the fall of 1981 to carefully excavate data from the Quincy sites before they were destroyed. David Singer and Joan Brown were the major excavators of the Milton site. In the lab, graduate students Bette Deveuve, Kate Atwood, and Freddy Sperling made major contributions, while Bette, Freddy, David, Shirley Hayden, and undergraduate David Perry gathered documentary data about the sites in Milton and Quincy. A number of undergraduates also contributed to the field and lab work. To all those students who made this research possible, my grateful thanks.

REFERENCES

Adams, William H., 1976, Trade Networks and Interaction Spheres—A View from Silcott, *Historical Archaeology* 10:99–112.

Anderson, Terry L., 1979, Economic Growth in Colonial New England: "Statistical Renaissance," *Journal of Economic History* 39(1):243–257.

Baker, V. G., 1980, Archaeological Visibility of Afro-American Culture: An Example from Black Lucy's Garden, Andover, Massachusetts, in: *Archaeological Perspectives on Ethnicity in America* (R. L. Schuyler, ed.), Baywood Publishing, New York, pp. 29–37.

Barth, Earnest A. T., and Watson, Walter B., 1967, Social Stratification and the Family in Mass Society, *Social Forces* 45:392–402.

Baugher, S., 1982, Hoboken Hollow: A 19th Century Worker's Housing Site, *Northeast Historical Archaeology* 11:26–38.

Binford, Lewis R., 1962, Archaeology as Anthropology, *American Antiquity* 28:217–225.

Clarke, David L., 1978, *Analytical Archaeology*, Columbia University Press, New York.

Collard, E., 1984, *Nineteenth Century Pottery and Porcelain in Canada*, McGill University Press, Montreal.

Cook, L., 1982, Appendix G: Adaptation of Miller's Economic Index for 19th Century Ceramics to the Jere Tabor and Jillson House Sites, in: Morenon, P. E., Cook, L., Callahan, K., Huntington, J., Kroian, C., LaCroix, D., and Stachiw, M., Archaeological Excavations at the Jere Tabor House Site, Triverton, Rhode Island, Public Archaeology Program at Rhode Island College, occasional paper in Anthropology and Geography 9.

Deagan, Kathleen, 1982, Avenues of Inquiry in Historical Archaeology, *Advances in Archaeological Method and Theory* 5:151–178.

Deagan, Kathleen, 1983, *Spanish St. Augustine: The Archaeology of a Colonial Creole Community*, Academic Press, New York.

De Cunzo, L. A., 1982, Households, Economics and Ethnicity in Paterson's Dublin, 1829–1915: The Van Houten Street Parking Lot Block, *Northeast Historical Archaeology* 11:9–25.

Douglas, M., and Isherwood, B., 1979, *The World of Goods*, Basic Books, New York.

Drucker, Lesley M., 1981, Socioeconomic Patterning at an Undocumented Late 18th Century Lowcountry Site: Spiers Landing, South Carolina, *Historical Archaeology* 15(2):58–68.

Dusenberry, J. S., 1971, Income-Consumption Relations and their Implications, in: *Readings in Macroeconomics* (M. G. Mueller, ed.), Holt, Rinehart & Winston, New York, pp. 61–76.

Dyson, S. L., 1982, Material Culture, Social Structure, and Changing Cultural Values: The Ceramics of Eighteenth- and Nineteenth-Century Middletown, Connecticut, in: *Archaeology of Urban America* (R. S. Dickens, Jr., ed.), Academic Press, New York, pp. 361–380.

Edwards, Alba M., 1939, *A Social Economic Grouping of the Gainful Workers of the United States*, U.S. Government Printing Office, Washington, D.C.

Engel, James F., Blackwell, Roger D., and Kollat, David T., 1978, *Consumer Behavior*, Dryden Press, Hinsdale, Illinois.

Exnicios, J. M., and Pearson, Charles, 1984, Nineteenth Century New Orleans: Variability and Pattern in the Archaeological Record, paper presented at the 17th Annual Meeting of the Society for Historical Archaeology, Williamsburg.

Felton, David L., and Schulz, Peter D., 1983, The Diaz Collection: Material Culture and Social Change in Mid-Nineteenth Century Monterey, California Archaeological Report 23, California Department of Parks and Recreation, Sacramento.

Flannery, Kent V., and Coe, Michael D., 1968, Social and Economic Systems in Formative Mesoamerica, in *New Perspectives in Archaeology* (S. R. Binford and L. R. Binford, eds.), Aldine Publishing, Chicago, pp. 103–142.

Geismar, J. H., 1982, *The Archaeology of Social Disintegration in Skunk Hollow, A Nineteenth-Century Rural Black Community,* Academic, New York.

Heilbroner, R. L., 1970, *The Economic Problem,* 2nd ed., Prentice-Hall, Englewood Cliffs, New Jersey.

Herman, Lynne L., Sands, John O., and Schecter, Daniel, 1973, Ceramics in St. Mary's County. Maryland During the 1840's: A Socioeconomic Study, *The Conference on Historic Site Archaeology Papers* 8:52–93.

Hershberg, Theodore, and Dockhorn, Robert, 1976, Occupational Classification, *Historical Methods Newsletter* 9:59–98.

Hill, James N., 1968, Broken K. Pueblo: Prehistoric Social Organization in the American Southwest, *Anthropological Papers of the University of Arizona* No. 18.

Hodges, Harold M., 1964, *Social Stratification: Class in America,* Schenkman Publishing, Cambridge, Massachusetts.

Hoffman, M. A., 1974, The Social Context of Trash Disposal in an Early Dynastic Egyptian Town, *American Antiquity* 39:35–49.

Kahl, Joseph A., and Davis, James A., 1955, A Comparison of Indexes of Socio-economic Status, *American Sociological Review* 20:317–325.

Katz, Michael B., 1972, Occupational Classification in History, *Journal of Interdisciplinary History* 3:63–88.

Laumann, Edward O, and House, James S., 1970, Living Room Styles and Social Attributes: The Patterning of Material Artifacts in a Modern Urban Community, *Sociology and Social Research* 54:321–324.

MAR: City of Milton, 1914, Report of the Board of Health, in *77th Annual Report of Milton Town Report for the Year Ending December 31, 1913,* Poole, Boston.

Massachusetts Bureau of Statistics of Labor, 1875, *Public Document #31: Sixth Annual Report of the Bureau of Statistics of Labor,* Wright & Potter, State Printers, Boston.

Martineau, Pierre, 1958, Social Classes and Spending Behavior, *Journal of Marketing* 23:121–130.

McBride, K. A., and McBride, S. W., 1983, An Examination of Status from Two Perspectives, in: Oral, Historical, Documentary and Archaeological Investigations of Barton and Vinton, Mississippi: An Interim Report on Phase II of the Tombigbee Historic Townsites Project (C. E. Cleland and K. A. McBride, eds.), submitted by Anthropology Divison, Michigan State University, to National Park Service, Mid-Atlantic Region, Philadelphia.

Miller, George L., 1980, Classification and Economic Scaling of 19th Century Ceramics, *Historical Archaeology* 14:1–41.

Miller, George L., 1984, George M. Coates, Pottery Merchant of Philadelphia, *Winterthur Portfolio* 19:37–49.

Miller, George L., and Hurry, Silas D., 1983, Ceramic Supply in an Economically Isolated Frontier Community: Portage County of the Ohio Western Reserve, 1800–1825, *Historical Archaeology* 17(2):80–92.

Milton Record, 1915, Regulation #25 of the Milton Board of Health, April 10, 1915, p. 4.

Morenon, P. E., Cook, L., Callahan, K., Huntington, J., Kroian, C., LaCroix, D., and Stachiw, M., 1982, Archaeological Excavations at the Jere Tabor House Site, Triverton, Rhode Island, Public Archaeology Program at Rhode Island College, occasional paper in Anthropology and Geography 9.

Mudar, K., 1978, The Effects of Socio-cultural Variables on Food Preferences in 19th Century Detroit, *The Conference on Historic Sites Archaeology Papers* 12:323–391.

Myers, James H., and Mount, John F., 1973, More on Social Class vs. Income as Correlates of Buying Behavior, *Journal of Marketing,* 37:71–73.

NCRD (Norfolk County, Massachusetts, Registry of Deeds), 1793–1945, Grantors and Grantees Books, Deed Books.

NCRPI (Norfolk County, Massachusetts, Registry of Probate) 1804–1904, Probate Inventories for Quincy.

Nystrom, Paul H., 1929, *Economic Principles of Consumption,* New York, Ronald Press.

Otto, John S., 1977, Artifacts and Status Differences: A Comparison of Ceramics from Planter, Overseer and Slave Sites on an Antebellum Plantation, in: *Research Strategies in Historical Archaeology* (S. South, ed.), Academic Press, New York, pp. 91–118.

Otto, John S., 1984, *Cannon's Point Plantation, 1794–1860: Living Conditions and Status Patterns in the Old South,* Academic Press, New York.

Peterson, Willis L., 1977, *Principles of Economics: Micro,* Richard D. Irwin, Homewood, Illinois.

Poe, C., 1979, The Manifestation of Status in 18th Century Criollo Culture in Colonial St. Augustine, paper presented at the Society for Historical Archaeology Meetings, Nashville, Tennessee.

QAR, City of Quincy, 1900, Board of Health Report, in: *City of Quincy Annual Report for the Year Ending 1900: City Document #12,* The Advertiser Steam Job Print, Quincy.

QAR, City of Quincy, 1925, Report of the Department of Health, in: *Report of the City of Quincy for 1925: City Document #37,* E. L. Grimes Printing Co., Boston.

QD (Quincy Directory), 1868, *The Dorchester and Quincy Directory for 1868–1869,* Dudley and Greenough, Boston.

QD, 1870, *The Weymouth, Quincy, and Braintree Directory for 1870–1871,* D. Dudley, Boston.

QD, 1873, *The Weymouth, Quincy, and Braintree Directory for 1873–1874,* D. Dudley, Boston.

QD, 1876, *The Quincy, Weymouth, and Braintree Directory for 1876–1877,* C. W. Calkins, Boston.

QD, 1878, *The Quincy, Weymouth, and Braintree Directory for 1878–1879,* C. W. Calkins, Boston.

QD, 1882, *Quincy Directory for 1882–1883,* Green and Prescott, Quincy.

QD, 1888, *1888–1889 Directory and History, Quincy, Massachusetts,* W. F. Richardson, S. Framingham.

QD, 1891, *The Quincy Directory,* W. A. Greenough, Boston.

QD, 1893, *The Quincy Directory, 1893,* E. B. Butterfield, Ayer.

QD, 1895, *The Quincy Directory,* W. A. Greenough, Boston.

QD, 1897, *The Quincy Directory, 1897,* W. A. Greenough: Boston.

QD, 1900, *The Quincy Directory,* W. A. Greenough, Boston.

QD, 1904, *The Quincy Directory,* W. A. Greenough: Boston.

QD, 1911, *The Quincy Directory,* W. A. Greenough, Boston.

Reissman, Leonard, 1959, *Class in American Society,* Free Press, New York.

Riordan, Timothy B., 1981, Commodity Flow Relationships from National Market to the Local Community: Case Studies from Northeastern Mississippi, paper presented at the Fourteenth Annual Meeting of the Society for Historical Archaeology, New Orleans.

Riordan, Timothy B., and Adams, William H., 1985, Commodity Flows and National Market Access, *Historical Archaeology* 19(2):5–18.

Robinson, E., 1888, *Robinson's Atlas of Norfolk County, Massachusetts Compiled from Official Records, Private Plans and Actual Surveys,* E. Robinson, New York.

Sanders, William T., and Webster, David, 1978, Unilinealism, Multilinealism, and the Evolution of Complex Societies, in: *Social Archaeology: Beyond Subsistence and Dating* (C. L. Redman, W. T. Langhorne, Jr., M. J. Berman, E. V. Curtin, N. M. Versaggi, and J. C. Wanser, eds.), Academic Press, New York.

Schiffer, Michael B., 1976, *Behavioral Archeology,* Academic Press, New York.

Schulz, Peter D., and Gust, Sherri M., 1983, Faunal Remains and Social Status in 19th Century Sacramento, *Historical Archaeology* 17(1):44–53.

Schuyler, Robert L., 1980a, Sandy Ground and Archaeology of a 19th Century Oystering Village, in: *Archaeological Perspectives in Ethnicity in America* (Robert L. Schuyler, ed.), Baywood Publishing, New York, pp. 48–59.

Schuyler, Robert L., 1980b, *Archaeological Perspectives on Ethnicity in America,* Baywood Publishing, New York.

Sherman, W. A., 1876, *Atlas of Norfolk County, Massachusetts from Recent and Actual Surveys and Records,* Comstock & Cline, New York.

Singer, David A., 1985, The Use of Fish Remains as A Socio-Economic Measure: An Example from 19th Century New England, *Historical Archaeology* 19(2):110–113.

Smith, Daniel S., 1975, Underregistration and Bias in Probate Records: An Analysis of Data from Eighteenth-Century Hingham, Massachusetts, *William and Mary Quarterly,* 3d ser., 32:100–112.

Spencer-Wood, S., 1979, The National American Market in Historical Archaeology: Urban Versus Rural Perspectives, in: *Ecological Anthropology of the Middle Connecticut River Valley* (R. Paynter, ed.), Research Report 18, Department of Anthropology, University of Massachusetts, Amherst, pp. 117–128.

Spencer-Wood, S., 1984, Status, Occupation, and Ceramic Indices: A Nineteenth Century Comparative Analysis, *Man in the Northeast* 28:87–110.

Spencer-Wood, S., and Riley, Julian A., 1981, The Development of an Urban Socio-economic Model for Archaeological Testing, *Northeast Historical Archaeology* 10:41–51.

USFCQ (United States Census Bureau) 1850, Seventh Census of the U.S.: Manuscript Population Schedules for Quincy, Massachusetts.

Walker, George H., 1896, *Atlas of the Town of Milton, Norfolk County, Massachusetts,* George H. Walker, Boston.

Walling, H. F., 1857, *Map of the Town of Quincy, Norfolk County, Massachusetts,* H. F. Walling.

Warner, W. Lloyd, with Meeker, Marchia, and Eells, Kenneth, 1960, *Social Class in America: A Manual of Procedure for the Measurement of Social Status,* Harper & Row, New York.

Watson, Patty Jo, 1978, Architectural Differentiation in Some Near Eastern Communities, Prehistoric and Contemporary, in *Social Archaeology: Beyond Subsistence and Dating* (C. L. Redman, W. T. Langhorne, Jr., M. J. Berman, E. V. Curtin, N. M. Versaggi, and J. C. Wanser, eds.), Academic Press, New York.

Addendum

Within each site ceramic index, whiteware decorative-type value percentages were calculated as in the following example from Table 5, "Cup and Saucer Rim Consumer-Choice Profiles" under *Porcelain:*

$$Q\#14\text{--}16$$
$$28.3\%(13)$$

The relative proportion contributed by this decorative type (porcelain) to the total value of the Q#14–16 whiteware subassemblage of cups and saucers, counted from distinctive rims, is 28.3%; (13) is the number of porcelain cup and saucer vessels, counted from distinctive rims, in the Q#14–16 site assemblage; 6.00 is the Cup and Saucer Ceramic Index Value for Porcelain, from Table 2.

$$13 \times 6 = 78$$

The product of the number of porcelain cups and saucers (whiteware decorative-type frequency), counted from distinctive rims in the Q#14–16 site assemblage, multiplied three times the porcelain cup and saucer ceramic index value is 78; 78 is 28.3% of the sum of all the whiteware decorative-type frequencies multiplied by their cup and saucer ceramic values, for the Q#14–16 site assemblage.

$$\sum_{i=1}^{n} (f_i \cdot v_i)$$

where f_i = the frequency of each decorative type in a site's whiteware subassemblage used to calculate a ceramic index; v_i = the ceramic index value of each whiteware decorative type; n = the number of decorative types in each site whiteware subassemblage used to calculate a ceramic index.

15

Factors Influencing Consumer Behavior in Turn-of-the-Century Phoenix, Arizona

SUSAN L. HENRY

INTRODUCTION

Socioeconomic status has been put forth as an explanation for some of the variability in the archaeological record: People buy what they do because of their status position in society. This should not come as much of a surprise since it is quite apparent, in the world around us today, that less affluent, "lower-class" people possess different kinds of things than do more affluent, "upper-class" people (consider cars, houses, and clothes, for example). In fact, successful advertising firms and market analysts depend upon this phenomenon to develop advertising campaigns for manufacturers that sell a bewildering array of consumer goods (see Kassarjian and Robertson 1973a; Levy 1973; Martineau 1958). The valuable contribution made by historical archaeological research has been to verify empirically that this phenomenon did in fact occur in the past, and to suggest the degrees to which patterns of material culture varied according to socioeconomic status. While valid as a general explanation, it does not go quite far enough. How does socioeconomic status account for this variability—what are the processes? By looking at a particular kind of human behavior—consumer behavior—and the factors that influence that behavior, we can come closer to understanding why and how the variability covaries with status. If a sufficient data base has been developed, research can focus on analytical units larger than the single site, making comparisons within and between social groups (socioeconomic as well as ethnic). This kind of research could lead toward an understanding of the nature of cultural and social systems in the historic past, the goal toward which we, as anthropologists, are striving to reach.

It is hoped that the research reported here will be a step in that direction. For three years, Soil Systems, Inc. (SSI), under contract to the City of Phoenix, investigated several downtown areas that were undergoing urban redevelopment. Archival and artifactual data from two residential areas are used in the

Susan L. Henry ☐ Heritage Resources Branch, Fairfax County Office of Comprehensive Planning, 2855 Annandale Road, Falls Church, VA 22042.

analyses in this study. As a laboratory for the study of urban growth and human behavior in urban settings, the situation in Phoenix was extremely advantageous. Archival data were readily available and fairly complete; the identification of function and chronology was possible for the majority of artifacts recovered; and in some cases, project area residents were able to provide valuable first-hand information. Yet a major problem remained. Phoenix represents American urban culture of the late nineteenth and early twentieth centuries, a period and site type that has received relatively little intensive attention, even in the West. This has meant that standard analytical techniques used in other urban areas of other time periods were not generally applicable to Phoenix data. Since one major goal of the Phoenix research was to be able to compare its results with those obtained in other urban research projects, several of these analytical techniques were modified slightly (Henry and Garrow 1982). The primary analytical techniques used in addressing questions of consumer behavior are: (1) a hierarchical ranking of occupational titles derived from the work of urban historians studying mid- to late-nineteenth-century Philadelphia (Hershberg and Dockhorn 1976); and (2) an economic scaling of ceramics and butchered food bone developed from Miller's (1980) economic scaling technique. While certain problems have yet to be resolved, these techniques appear to have some use in studying late nineteenth- and early twentieth-century urban consumer behavior.

FACTORS INFLUENCING CONSUMER BEHAVIOR

The primary cultural unit of archaeological analysis is the household (Deetz 1982:717), except in those cases of nondomestic sites such as commercial or industrial complexes and public institutions. A household is a domestic residential group, consisting of the inhabitants of a dwelling or a set of premises and who appear as a discrete group in the documents (e.g., census or tax records) (Laslett and Wall 1972:86). The household is usually coterminous with the family (extended, nuclear, fraternal, etc.), but it may also include nonrelated members, such as boarders and servants. The importance of the household–family in archaeological analysis derives from the fact that the family "functions as the context wherein individuals are brought to an awareness of their culture's rules, and conversely, where those rules are frequently expressed in physical form" (Deetz 1982:718). The patterns of "artifacts and structures that formed the physical focus of family or household activity . . . are reflective of the shared beliefs and behavior of their owners and users, a minimal and understandable level of cultural behavior which nonetheless embodies the world view of the society at large" (Deetz 1982:719).

Not only does the household reflect the society at large, but also various subgroups within that society. A group is defined as a collectivity whose members share common beliefs, values, attitudes, standards of behavior, as well as symbols that represent the group (Kassarjian and Robertson 1973b:292; Vivello 1978:107–108). There are a number of groups to which an individual belongs, such as family, church, school, job, recreation, hobby, neighborhood, ethnic group, and social class. By extension, the household can generally be seen as a member of the groups to which its members belong (particularly neighborhood, ethnic group, and social class).

Some groups have more meaning, for, or exert a greater level of influence on, an individual. These are "reference groups," used by an individual as a "point of reference in determining his judgments, beliefs, and behavior" (Kassarjian and Robertson 1973b:292–293). The individual does not need to be a member of a group to use it as a point of reference (e.g., when an upwardly mobile person aspires to become a member of another group), nor must the reference group function in a positive way (as in the avoidance of the values and behavior standards of a negative reference group) (Kassarjian and Robertson 1973b:293). Nearly every household is a member of two powerful reference groups: social class and ethnic group. This commonality of group membership has important ramifications for archaeological analyses since it permits comparisons of large numbers of households based on consistent measures.

A characteristic of technologically complex industrial societies, such as that in the United States, is social stratification, which is a "system of classifying persons in a hierarchically arranged series of social strata (classes or castes) having differential access to the resources, goods, and skills . . . available to the society as a whole" (Vivello 1978:121). Class systems are open-ended and fluid, permitting movement upward or downward in the hierarchy (Kassarjian and Robertson 1973a:390; Vivello 1978:122). Since the term "class" (as in upper class, middle class, lower class) tends to be defined in many different ways, by different people (researchers, lay public), and in different situations, it lacks a certain precision of meaning. The term "socioeconomic status," as used here, is defined as the position in society occupied by an individual, and, by extension, by a household, based primarily on social and economic factors. Researchers (Coleman and Rainwater 1978; Kassarjian and Robertson 1973a; Warner and Lunt 1941: Willigan and Lynch 1982) note that occupation, income, aggregate wealth, level of education, and religious affiliation are factors that are important in determining socioeconomic status. While income and wealth appear to be the most significant factors in determining status (Coleman and Rainwater 1978:278–283; Warner 1973:404),

> economic factors are not sufficient to predict where a particular family or individual will be [in the status hierarchy] or to explain completely the phenomena of social class. . . . *Money must be translated into socially approved behavior and possessions,* and they [behavior and possessions] in turn must be translated into intimate participation with, and acceptance by, members of a . . . class. (Warner 1973:404; my emphasis)

Each socioeconomic status level, then, constitutes a group, members of which share common beliefs, values, and standards of behavior, including consumption behavior.

A rich man is not simply a poor man with more money (Martineau 1958: 122). The consumer behavior of each reflects the values, attitudes, and lifestyles of the socioeconomic group to which each belongs, since "consuming is ultimately one of the ways in which people implement their values" (Levy 1973:410). In fact, "consumption patterns operate as prestige symbols to define class membership, which is a more significant determination of economic behavior than income" (Martineau 1958:130). Additionally, upwardly mobile individuals tend to purchase external symbols of the status to which they aspire (Martineau 1958:123–124). An individual's style of consumption—what he or she purchases—is a "primary means of asserting and/or validating social status and identity" (Laumann and House 1973:430). Studies have also shown (Kassarjian and Robertson 1973a) that within each status group there is variability in income earned by its members, and those who earn considerably more or considerably less than the average exhibit different consumer behavior than typical members of the group.

Ethnic groups are also influential points of reference for their members, who share a common traditional heritage, which differs from that of the society at large. An ethnic group is therefore a subculture, a minority in the dominant national culture, and may be differentiated on the basis of race, religion, language, or national origin (e.g., blacks, Jews, Italians) (Gordon 1978; Kassarjian and Robertson 1973c; Schuyler 1980). From a review of the literature on class and ethnicity, Gordon (1978:261, 262) notes that "the ethnic factor plays a large role in restricting intimate social relationships not only to members of one's own status level or social class, but to members of one's own ethnic group," and that "the behavioral similarities of social class are more pronounced than those of ethnic group." Thus, it appears that while ethnic group affiliation is a major influence on an individual's behavior, class or socioeconomic status exerts a greater influence.

Other factors also influence consumer behavior. One of these is age, since as the head of the household grows older, there is a general increase in earning power due to accumulated seniority and experience, and a corresponding increase in household income (Wells and Gubar 1970:513–514). Studies have shown, however, that the life cycle of a household is a more accurate indicator of consumption patterns than is age alone (Wells and Gubar 1970). As households pass through the stages in the life cycle, from single unmarried, to newlywed, to a family with children, to older couples whose children have set up their own households, to the elderly single, needs for consumer goods change in quantity and quality (Schiffer *et al.* 1981; Wells and Gubar 1970).

Another factor influencing consumer behavior is the market availability of consumer goods. If a particular item, or type of item, is not to be found in the marketplace, it cannot be purchased (see Gaw 1975). Usually, however, especially in urban areas, there is a variety of consumer goods on the market, differing in type, style, brand name, quality, size, or some other dimension, and the consumer must make choices. In addition to those factors already considered, price of the item influences consumer choice, since if the item is priced beyond the consumer's ability to pay, it will not be purchased. In fact, Miller (1980:3) noted that the "social status of any commodity is related to how much the object costs." The nature of some consumer goods also influences consumer behavior. Studies have shown (Howard and Sheth 1973; Levy 1973; Wells and Gubar 1970) that consumption patterns for durable goods (objects purchased infrequently, such as furniture) are different than those for non-durable goods (items purchased repeatedly and often, such as food).

The artifacts recovered from the excavations in Phoenix represent choices made by Phoenix consumers. It is hypothesized, based on the foregoing discussion, that those choices were influenced primarily by the socioeconomic status position(s) held by those consumers, but that other factors played a role in consumer decision making as well. It is expected that the relative value of durable and nondurable goods, as measured by economic scaling of ceramics and butchered food bone, will vary according to status level, as measured by occupational ranking, and that variability will be due to the influence of other factors. Two separate, but equal, data sets are used to investigate this research problem: archival data and artifactual data.

DATA FROM PHOENIX

Overview of Phoenix History

Pioneers coming into the desert environment of the Salt River Valley of the 1860s encountered the ruins of adobe towns and irrigation canals built by the prehistoric Hohokam (Mawn 1979). Foresighted settlers reexcavated these old canals and successfully grew crops to provision the series of Indian forts then being established in the Arizona Territory. The success of this venture encouraged increased settlement in the valley, which led to the founding of Phoenix in 1870. Named for the mythical bird that was reborn from its own ashes, Phoenix grew rapidly upon the ruins of the Hohokam civilization. The arrival of the railroad in the late 1880s and early 1890s expanded Phoenix's influence as a marketing center. The young city was no longer an isolated, dusty desert town, but was linked efficiently with the rest of the nation by rail. A wider variety of manufactured goods became available to Phoenix consumers, and large numbers of visitors and immigrants came in response to publicity campaigns waged by the Phoenix Chamber of Commerce. The area's agricultural base expanded beyond grain crops to include citrus and fruit orchards, vegetable farms, dairy and livestock herds, and even lucrative ostrich ranches which marketed ostrich feathers to adorn turn-of-the-century ladies' hats. Phoenix quickly grew beyond the boundaries of its Original Townsite, encouraged in part by the construction and expansion of the street-car system after the 1880s.

On the eve of the twentieth century, Phoenix was as modern a city as any of its contemporaries, and could boast multistoried office and commercial buildings; residential suburbs; municipal refuse collection; sewer, water, electric, and gas systems; police and fire departments; mail delivery; telephone service; schools; churches, libraries; and many other social and cultural attractions (Mawn 1979). The completion of the Roosevelt Dam in 1911 guaranteed a dependable, year-round water supply to Phoenix and the surrounding agricultural communities, and the granting of Arizona statehood engendered considerable optimism in the future of Phoenix and the Salt River Valley. The years of World War I were prosperous for the valley in general, as agricultural output was intensified and new industries were established to aid in the war effort. The first 50 years of Phoenix's development saw the city develop into a major Southwestern urban center.

Project Area Descriptions

Soil Systems, Inc., investigated four spatially discrete areas in downtown Phoenix. Data from two of these project areas are used in the analyses here.

The first project area consisted of Blocks 1 and 2 of the Original Townsite, which were initially settled in the 1870s (Henry and Garrow 1982). Intensive settlement occurred during the 1880s and 1890s, influenced by the construction of large homes by the Phoenix elite nearby on the edges of the central business district. Homes in the project area were, however, more modest. In general, residents were shop proprietors, office workers, and tradesmen with Euro-American, Mexican-American, French-Canadian, and Italian surnames. During the 1920s, expansion of the central business district reached Blocks 1 and 2, and some houses were replaced by commercial structures. This pattern of increased commercialization continued until used car lots and gas stations characterized the area in the 1960s.

The second project area was a nine-acre portion of the Murphy Addition to Phoenix, located just outside the eastern boundary of the Original Townsite, and one block southeast of Blocks 1 and 2 (Henry *et al.* 1983). The Murphy Addition was platted in 1884, specifically for residential subdivision, although development occurred gradually over the next twenty to twenty-five years. Until the 1930s, the area was predominantly a Euro-American neighborhood of single-family homes. During the 1930s, the neighborhood changed in character as the older houses were subdivided and new multifamily residences were built. By the late 1940s, the neighborhood was a high-density residential district.

Nature of the Phoenix Data

Two sets of data were used in the Phoenix investigatons: archival and artifactual. Primary documentary sources were particularly rich in information on the project areas. Real estate title records, municipal tax assessment records, city directories, federal manuscript census, photographs, and the Sanborn-Perris Fire Insurance maps provided information on the physical nature of each property lot (location, size, function, construction material, structural alterations) and on the residents of each lot (names of household members, occupations, household composition, and property value). Tax assessment records were, however, of marginal use for wealth data since they are not available after 1912. The federal manuscript censuses are not available after 1910.

The city directories were therefore relied upon to provide most of the information for twentieth-century residents of the project areas. City directories provided information on name, occupation, and address of residence (and sometimes place of work), and were available yearly from 1892 to the present, with only nine missing directories, scattered throughout the series. The level of reporting in the directories is somewhat inconsistent—for example, some individuals or their occupation titles may be omitted from one directory, although present in the directory for a preceding or subsequent year. This is a relatively minor problem, given the fact that this information is available for specific years, while feature depositions can be dated only to a general time period. The problem arises, however, from the very detailed nature of the temporal information provided by the directories. Since each property lot was perceived as a behavioral unit separate from its neighbor, features located within the boundaries of a lot were associated with the household(s) residing on that lot during the period of deposition. Thus, the temporal specificity in the directories permits several households to be associated with one deposit during a short period of time. Unfortunately, it was often not possible to associate only one household with a particular deposit, since none of the features examined here was stratified, either stratigraphically or artifactually. This problem could not be eliminated entirely, and it is doubtful that it ever will be, especially in cases of high tenant turnover; in cases of residential longevity, the problem rarely arises.

The artifactual data used in this study of consumer behavior were recovered from twelve privy pits and three trash deposits. All materials were associated with domestic activities and were discarded between circa 1880 and 1940 (Henry and Garrow 1982; Henry et al. 1983). Deposition of trash in unused privy shafts tended to correspond with the opening of new privy vaults, the construction of septic tanks in some cases (c. 1910–1915), and linking with the municipal sewer system, which was mandatory after 1915 (Mawn 1979: 204, 442). Pits specifically dug to receive trash were not common in the project areas, and the three trash pits which yielded some of the data used here were originally dug for other purposes (in one case, to extract clay for use in making adobe bricks—Henry and Garrow 1982:237, 239). There is little information on municipal trash collection, so its impact on the archaeological record is not clearly understood.

Materials from each feature were treated as a single assemblage, since little stratigraphy was visually evident in the field, and stratigraphic segregation was not observed during ceramic cross-mend analyses. The data from each feature are assumed to be representatives of all the materials originally discarded. A 100 percent recovery rate was not achieved for two reasons: two features (F309 and F2–2) had been partially looted, and nearly all features experienced some minor damage from the backhoe trenching used to locate features during the testing phases of the projects. The impact of these actions on analysis was relatively minor, however, since looters sought only specific, intact items (such as bottles) and disregarded broken materials, and since materials were recovered when the backhoe located features. (Seriously damaged features are not included in this analysis.) In addition, the sizes of the assemblages were large enough in most cases (ranging from 880 to 16,768 in the features used here) to offset the effects of missing materials.

Two types of artifacts are used in this analysis: ceramics and butchered food bone. Ceramics are particularly suitable for this kind of analysis since, as Miller (1980) and other researchers (see Klein and Garrow 1984) have shown, price, and therefore status, are associated with observable ceramic attributes (decoration and ware). The ceramics recovered were in good condition; many had identifiable maker's marks that provided excellent date ranges, decorative techniques were easily distinguished, and vessel types could be identified for the majority of the sherds in the collection. Butchered food bone is also suitable for this analysis, since other researchers (Davidson 1982; Mudar 1978; Reitz and Cumbaa 1983; Schulz and Gust 1983) have shown that differential access to food resources is identifiable archaeologically. Two-thirds of the faunal remains recovered from the two project areas were identifiable (Henry and Garrow 1982; Henry *et al.* 1983). Not all food bone would have survived, however, primarily due to cooking processes, which act to break down the structural properties of the bone (Chaplin, 1971). Additionally, since some meat is retailed without the bone, a household's use of these cuts would leave no evidence in the archaeological record. Therefore, bone data used in this study represents only a part of the total household diet.

Analytical Techniques

Two analytical techniques are used in this study of consumer behavior: hierarchical ranking of occupations held by residents, and economic scaling of ceramics and butchered bone.

Occupational Ranking

Occupational titles for individual residents were obtained from city directory listings and assigned to a hierarchical ranking scale based on that developed and tested on nineteenth-century data by the Philadelphia Social History Project (PSHP) (Hershberg and Dockhorn 1976). The PSHP occupational scale was "neither purely intuitive" (based on status, prestige, or skill), nor entirely empirically derived from wealth, income, or wages (Hershberg and Dockhorn 1976:60). The scale was tested on a portion of the large, computerized data base that PSHP researchers had compiled from mid- to late-nineteenth-century documents, resulting in close correlation between the different rank categories and measurable variables such as level of education, wages, and property owned (Hershberg and Dockhorn 1976:60, 68). This scale is a general one, and does not segregate known variability within rank categories, since PSHP's goal (as well as that of this research) was to understand the behavior of the group rather than that of any individual member of the group (Hershberg and Dockhorn 1976:68).

The ranking scale used here is not inconsistent with that used in analyzing socioeconomic status in Wilmington, Delaware (Klein and Garrow 1984), nor with the scales developed by Katz (1972:85, 87) in studying nineteenth-century Hamilton, Ontario, Canada. Seven occupational categories are used: (1) professional, high white-collar (e.g., banker, lawyer, physician); (2) proprietary and low white-collar (e.g., storekeeper, clerk, teacher); (3) skilled trades (e.g., carpenter, tinsmith, engineer); (4) semiskilled and unskilled (e.g., waiter, teamster, laborer); (5) unclassifiable (job title is unclear or only the work place is listed); (6) unemployed (includes the jobless, as well as students, widows, housewives, and the retired); (7) occupation not recorded. The focus of analysis is upon the first four categories, since the last three yield less information on economic ranking in the absence of more detailed research of other kinds of documents (which was outside the scope of SSI's contract). Within each occupational category, different occupations may have been associated with varying amounts of income and prestige, and individuals holding the occupations ranked here may have perceived status to have been arrayed somewhat differently. These factors are not specifically addressed here, since they are difficult to measure in the present, and even more so in the past.

Economic Scaling

Although many researchers had suggested that variations in ceramic assemblages are associated with socioeconomic status (Miller 1974; Otto 1977; Rathje and McCarthy 1977; Shephard 1980), it was not until Miller (1980) developed his economic scaling technique that archaeologists have been able to measure the nature of the relationship between material culture and socioeconomic level. With this technique, the relative economic value of a ceramic assemblage can be determined, which then provides a means with which to discuss the relative economic level of the households that purchased, used, and discarded the ceramics.

Based on an extensive study of nineteenth-century ceramic price lists, Miller (1980) developed an economic scaling of ceramics based on the cost relationships of variously decorated wares to the cheapest undecorated ware (cream-colored, or CC ware). The values of decorated wares are expressed in relation to a fixed index value of 1.00 for CC ware at specific points in time. For example, transfer-printed tea cups and saucers with an 1860 index value of 4.00 cost four times as much as contemporary undecorated CC tea cups and saucers with an index value of 1.00 (Miller 1980:30). Results obtained from calculating the formula are expressed in terms of adverage relative economic values for cups, plates, and bowls in an assemblage. By summing the products for cups, plates, and bowls, and dividing by the total number of these vessels, a mean economic value for the assemblage is obtained (Klein and Garrow 1984). These mean values can be used to compare the value of one assemblage with that of another.

Miller's (1980) price indices, however, are incomplete for the period after 1870, and nonexistent after 1881. This presented a major problem in applying the technique to the ceramic collections from Phoenix, the majority of which were purchased and discarded after 1880. There appeared to be a solution to this dilemma: a study of ceramic prices listed in seven mail-order catalogues from 1895 through 1927 (Montgomery Ward and Company, 1895, 1922; Sears, Roebuck and Company 1897, 1900, 1902, 1909, 1927) indicated that ceramic prices continued to be linked to various decorative techniques, and that open-stock prices for individual ceramic vessel forms were available on the majority, if not all, of the decorative and ware types offered by these mail-order firms.

Given the availability of ceramic prices for the period during which the two project areas were occupied, a series of price indices were developed for use in discussing the relative economic level of the project area residents. Prices of open-stock cups and saucers, plates, and bowls were collected from the seven mail-order catalogues. From these data, index values were generated based on the price relationships of decorated wares to the cheapest undecorated ware (Miller 1980:11). Miller's cheapest undecorated ware was CC, which was not a ware type identified by name in the catalogues. Therefore, the role filled by CC in Miller's study was filled in this analysis by undecorated "semiporcelain," which was in all cases the least costly. The catalogues also exhibited some variability of prices within each decorative category. Since variability among, rather than within, decorative categories is the sensitive element of this analytical technique, prices within each category were averaged to obtain a single figure, which was used to generate the indices. A combined index value was used for tea and coffee cups since the distinction between them in archaeological collections is not often clear. Likewise, since plate diameters often cannot be determined from sherds, index values for all plate sizes were averaged. Since none of the catalogues included all ranges of, or open-stock prices for, all decorative techniques, data from several catalogues were combined to create indices for a time period, rather than for specific years, as Miller has. A set of mid-1890s indices was generated from data in the 1895 Montgomery Ward and 1897 Sears, Roebuck catalogues, while data from the 1900, 1902, and 1909 Sears catalogues were combined to create indices for the period 1900–1910, and the 1922 Montgomery Ward and 1927 Sears catalogues provided data for a set of indices for the 1920s (Table 1).

The 1890s indices reflect the decoration–price relationships identified by Miller (1980). A new decorative technique appears in the catalogues for the first decade of the twentieth century: Wares decorated by the decalcomania process were offered by the 1902 Sears catalogue. Although only two of the thirteen sets offered were decorated with the new technique, prices for these sets were not inconsistent with those for transfer-printed sets. Not commonly available except on imported European porcelains prior to 1900, decal became the prevalent decorative technique by 1909 (see Sears, Roebuck and Company 1909; Wegars and Carley 1982:7). Given the coexistence of transfer-print and decal designs on ceramics, and since there was little price differentiation between them, these two decorative categories are combined under the term "color" in the listing of index values for the first decade of the twentieth century (Table 1).

Table 1. Ceramic Price Indices

		Average price per dozen			Indices		
Decoration	n	Cups and saucers	Plates	Bowls	Cups and saucers	Plates	Bowls
1895–1897							
Undecorated	1	$1.10	$0.68	$1.00	1.00	1.00	1.00
Molded	2	1.26	0.75	1.15	1.15	1.10	1.15
Transfer	5	1.49	1.00	1.37	1.35	1.47	1.37
Transfer, gilt	10	1.73	1.32	1.94	1.57	1.94	1.94
Porcelain	4	4.12	2.71	2.80	3.75	3.99	2.80
1900–1902–1909							
Undecorated	2	$0.68	$0.50	$0.72	1.00	1.00	1.00
Molded	2	1.07	0.73	0.97	1.57	1.46	1.35
Color, gilt	4	1.70	1.27	1.71	2.50	2.54	2.38
Porcelain	1	2.82	2.01	—	4.15	4.02	4.00[a]
1922–1927							
Undecorated	2	$2.21	$1.50	$1.51	1.00	1.00	1.00
Molded	1	2.52	1.63	1.93	1.14	1.09	1.28
Gilt band	5	3.41	1.70	2.16	1.54	1.13	1.43
Decal	12	4.69	2.36	2.77	2.12	1.57	1.83
Porcelain	7	6.10	4.31	4.02	2.76	2.87	2.66

[a]Estimated value based on the relationship of porcelain to other categories (no bowl prices available).

By the 1920s, shifts in the price relationships among the various decorative and ware categories have occurred. The most startling of these changes is that, in the 1927 Sears catalogue, German porcelain was cheaper than English semiporcelain decorated with decal designs. While German porcelain advertised by Sears over the preceeding years had always been less expensive than French (Haviland) porcelain, it had never before been cheaper than semiporcelain. In the 1922 Montgomery Ward catalogue, however, the only porcelain offered was German-made. Three of the sets were less costly than four semiporcelain sets, and two of the three sets were two to six times as expensive as the French porcelain offered by Sears. This shift in cost relationships may have been associated with post–World War I conditions in Germany, which may have either affected the quality of the ware or influenced its status abroad. Another shift in price relationships was a marked range of prices within each decorative category. For example, a dozen tea cups and saucers decorated with decal and gilt highlights could have been purchased for as little as $1.48 or as much as $8.35. Additionally, within the decorative category of gilt band, there are two separate cost levels, apparently associated with the quality of the gilt applied. In order to mitigate some of the effects of these shifts on the analysis, and so that results would be comparable to earlier periods, several categories were combined in developing the 1920s index values. Prices for decal-decorated ceramics of English and American manufacture were combined, as were those of ceramics with gilt banding, in addition to combining prices for German and French porcelains. The resulting index values (Table 1) are more conducive for use with archaeological collections, in which distinctions are not easily made on gilt quality or on origin of manufacture in the absence of maker's marks.

Data requirements for conducting economic scaling analysis of ceramic collections are an accurate minimum vessel count, an accurate identification of vessel form and decorative-ware type, and an adequate sample. The ceramic collections from fourteen features fulfilled these requirements. The mean ceramic date obtained from each feature guided the selection of which set of indices was appropriate, since the MCD more closely approximated time of purchase than did deposition period. In calculating the values for cups, the minimum number of cups and saucers was used because, with few exceptions, a cup and saucer were sold as a unit. The exception was in the occasional catalogue reference for institutional ("hotel ware") ceramics, which are not included in this analysis.

This economic scaling technique was also adapted for use in analyzing the butchered food bone recovered from the two project areas. Traditional faunal analyses rely upon calculations of minimum number of individual animals, age of animals at death, or weight of edible meat represented by the bones in an assemblage (Jolley 1983). While these kinds of analyses may be appropriate for certain kinds of dietary studies, they provide little useful information in understanding dietary consumer behavior in an urban setting, where most meat was obtained through retail purchase. Since professional butchering techniques have been relatively standard for the past one hundred years (see Schulz and Gust 1983:48), an analysis of the cuts of meat purchased provides results that are more culturally relevant to understanding urban behavior (Henry and Garrow 1982; Henry et al. 1983; Klein and Garrow 1984; Mudar 1978; Schulz and Gust 1983).

The unit of analysis used is the "butchering unit," identified through a study of professional butchering references (Bull 1951; Romans and Ziegler 1977), that indicated the manner in which carcasses were initially divided into wholesale cuts, here termed "butchering units." The wholesale cuts were subsequently butchered into smaller retail cuts, such as steaks and roasts, for household consumption (see Davidson 1982 for a discussion and illustration of the procedures with specific reference to archaeological collections). Bones retrieved from archaeological sites are more readily associated with wholesale units than with the smaller retail cuts.

Studies of late nineteenth- and early twentieth-century butchering guides and meat value relationships (Davidson 1982; Mudar 1978; Schulz and Gust 1983), compared with current relative values and prices (Bayhem et al. 1982; Henry and Garrow 1982; Roberson and Roberson 1966), indicate that the relative values of different butchering units have remained fairly constant over the past one hundred years. It was thus possible to generate a scale of economic indices based on prices of retail meat cuts obtained from five Phoenix markets (Bayham et al. 1982; Henry and Garrow 1982). These indices were developed in the same way as those for ceramics. Indices for the different butchering units for beef, mutton, and pork are presented in Table 2. Meat values for each meat type in a feature, and a mean value for each feature, were calculated in the same way as for ceramics.

A comparison of the meat index values in Table 2 with the ceramic index values in Table 1 indicates a considerable range in the intervals between the upper and lower ends of the scales. This variability is reflected in the results of the index calculations, where, for example, one assemblage yielded a mean meat value of 3.45 and a mean ceramic value of 2.08. In order to be able to determine whether these two values reflect similar or dissimilar levels of expenditures for the two types of consumer goods, the variability evident in the scales had to be mitigated. This was accomplished by subdividing the range for each scale into ten equal parts, creating a decile ranking scale.

Table 2. Average Prices and Index Values for Beef, Mutton, and Pork Butchering Units[a]

Butchering unit	n	Average price per pound	Economic index
Beef			
Hindshank	1	$0.59	1.00
Feet	1	0.69	1.17
Neck	5	0.88	1.49
Plate	5	1.51	2.56
Frontshank	1	1.57	2.66
Chuck	23	1.81	3.07
Tail	3	1.82	3.08
Rump	4	2.32	3.93
Round	14	2.67	4.53
Ribs	7	3.33	5.64
Full loin	18	3.69	6.25
Mutton			
Neck/head	1	$0.69	1.00
Breast	2	1.28	1.86
Leg	5	2.17	3.14
Chuck	4	2.28	3.30
Rack	2	4.17	6.04
Loin	2	4.99	7.23
Pork			
Head/neck	1	$0.49	1.00
Feet	3	0.71	1.45
Picnic shoulder	2	1.49	3.04
Boston butt	9	1.54	3.14
Ribs	3	1.55	3.16
Ham/leg	6	2.14	4.37
Loin	14	2.20	4.49

[a]From Henry and Garrow 1982:347.

Preliminary comparisons using the precision of this scale resulted in little
evident patterning, so pairs of decile ranks were used, with "1" indicating the
highest two tenths of a scale, and "5" indicating the lowest two tenths. These
slightly more general scales are more conducive for use with the general scale
used in ranking occupational titles.

RESULTS

Occupational titles held by members of the households associated with the
fifteen features analyzed were assigned to their appropriate ranking, and
economic values were calculated for the ceramic vessels and butchered food
bone from those features. The results obtained are presented in Table 3.

At first glance, the mean economic values for ceramics and meat appear
quite variable and seem to bear little relationship to occupational ranking.
When the decile-pair ranks for the cermic and meat values are compared,
however, the results seem fairly consistent. In order to measure the strength
of the relationships among the ceramic values, the meat values, and the occupational ranking, Kendall's *tau* statistics for rank–order correlation (Thomas 1976) was calculated. With Kendall's *tau*, a score of plus or minus 1.0
indicates perfect correlation, and a score of 0.0 indicates no correlation. Since
some features were associated with multiple households (Table 3), the occupational rank used was that of the household residing on the lot the longest
during feature deposition. Results indicate a weak correlation between mean
ceramic value and occupational rank (*tau* = 0.256), a somewhat stronger, but
still weak, correlation between mean meat value and occupational rank (*tau* =
0.389), and a very weak correlation between mean value rankings for ceramics
and meat (*tau* = 0.167). Since cups tend to represent social ritual and status
display and therefore should reflect social status, and since the common de-
nominator in all faunal assemblages was beef, economic value ranks of these
two subsets of the ceramic and bone assemblage were compared to occupational rank using the Kendall's *tau* statistic. Results show a moderately strong
correlation between cup value rank and occupational rank (*tau* = 0.487), a
slightly stronger correlation between beef value rank and occupational rank
(*tau* = 0.556), but a very weak correlation between the rankings of beef values
and ceramic values (*tau* = 0.111). These data suggest that, as expected, there is
a correlation between socioeconomic status (as measured by occupation) and
consumer choices for ceramics and meat. However, consumer behavior associated with ceramic purchase bears little relationship to that associated with
meat purchase. This suggests that, although expenditures for both are influenced to some degree by socioeconomic status, that influence affects consumer
choices in different ways. This may be due to the fact that different kinds of
commodities—durable versus nondurable goods—influence different kinds of
consumer choices.

The relationship between status and the values for ceramics and meat is
not, however, an overly strong one. The sample size (fourteen features for

Table 3. Summary of Analysis Results

Feature number	MCD	Deposition date	Ceramic values (rank)[a]				Meat values (rank)[a]				Occupation rank
			Cups	Plates	Bowls	Mean	Beef	Mutton	Pork	Mean	
331	1877.5	1880–1890	1.94(4)	1.00	1.00	1.59(4)	3.29(3)	3.53	2.52	3.22(4)	3
321	1904.1	c.1912	2.04(4)	2.20	1.61	2.02(4)	2.63(4)	0	2.53	2.62(4)	2
327	1920.7	c.1924	1.51(4)	1.70	1.00	1.40(4)	—	—	—	—	2
69/328	1895.0	1903–1910	1.55(5)	2.36	1.00	1.74(4)	—	—	—	—	7
305	1897.2	1907–1915	2.26(3)	1.35	1.76	1.76(4)	3.19(3)	2.38	2.92	3.07(4)	1,2,3,4
310	1916.9	1915–1925	2.08(4)	1.85	2.30	2.05(4)	3.68(3)	2.75	3.31	3.45(4)	2,4
309	1910.7	1911–1915	2.85(3)	2.76	1.89	2.64(3)	—	—	—	—	1,2,3
2-2	1896.1	1902–1927	1.82(4)	1.28	1.05	1.62(4)	—	—	—	—	2
2-3	—	1905–1927	—	—	—	—	4.45(2)[b]	4.05	0	4.25(3)	2
2-4	1898.1	1915–1927	2.00(4)	1.31	1.29	1.73(4)	3.79(3)	3.25	2.26	3.37(4)	2
1-15	1927.3	1913+	2.06(2)	1.75	1.56	1.93(3)	3.71(3)	3.58	3.36	3.48(4)	4
1-132	1924.2	1929+	1.64(4)	1.34	1.65	1.54(4)	—	—	—	—	
3-13	1909.4	1930+	2.12(2)	1.84	2.09	2.04(3)	3.87(3)[b]	3.38	1.30	3.58(3)	2,7
3-14	1919.1	1930+	1.62(4)	1.23	1.66	1.53(4)	—	—	—	—	2,7
4-5	1915.8	1928–1930	3.82(1)	2.46	3.19	3.17(2)	4.35(2)	2.98	3.59	4.09(3)	3,4,7

[a] Numbers in parentheses refer to rank.
[b] Faunal analysis was conducted on remains from combined features associated with the same household(s).

ceramics and nine for meat) has, no doubt, affected the results. Additionally, households at the very upper and very lower ends of the status scale are not represented in the Phoenix data, and all occupational ranks are not equally represented. Eight of the fifteen features are associated with households at the relatively high rank of 2. It is possible that, in dealing on the specific level of individual households, the hierarchical ranking scale is not effective. In fact, historical demographers have recognized that "information on occupation . . . is insufficient by itself for understanding the individual or group experience of occupation" (Willigan and Lynch 1982:100). In other words, just knowing that an individual was a store clerk or a carpenter does not ensure our understanding of that individual's values, aspirations, or lifestyle. Furthermore, there is considerable variability in the economic scaling results that may be due to other factor(s) influencing consumer behavior.

Ethnic group membership may account for some of this variation. It is possible that the Mexican heritage of at least two of the households associated with four features (331, 321, 327, 310) influenced differential consumption patterns reflected in the faunal variability. Since foodways are often the most durable of ethnic traditions (Glassie 1968:206–207, 216, 237), a comparison was made of the extent to which Mexican-American and Euro-American households purchased different kinds of meat. To test the equality of the proportions of beef, mutton, pork, chicken, and wild game consumed by the two groups, the Z statistic was calculated, using the null hypothesis that there is no difference between the frequencies of different meat types associated with both groups (Freund 1973:275–278, 317–320). Table 4 presents the data and results. At the 0.005 level of confidence, results exceed ± 1.96, except for chicken, indicating that for beef, mutton, pork, and wild game, proportions between the two groups are different. Since beef is a major component in all assemblages, the calculations were done again after eliminating the figures for beef (Table 4). Results for mutton and pork again exceed the ± 1.96 range for the 0.005 level of confidence, indicating that proportions of these kinds of meat are different between the groups. There is, however, no significant difference between the groups in the proportions of chicken and wild game. These results suggest that, at least in the case of some meat types, ethnic group membership influences consumer choices.

Changes in household life cycle may account for some of the variability observed in the ceramic and meat values. On Block 1, the Donofrio household increased as five children were born and grew to adulthood, their mother died, and the head of the household experienced financial difficulties with his confectionery business (interview with the youngest son, the late Judge Francis Donofrio). These factors—changes in the family life cycle and business reversals—may explain the decrease in ceramic ceramic values over time (F 321 and F 327 in Table 3). In the Murphy Addition, the Shott household was also passing through stages in the family life cycle as the daughters grew up and married, and their husbands joined the household. The head of the household held positions of respect in the community as city councilman and manager of the Pioneer Band. Additionally, the household experienced an increase in

Table 4. Comparison between Ethnicity and Frequencies of Meat Types

	Mexican-American[a]			Euro-American[b]			Z Scores	
	Number	Percentage	Percentage w/o beef	Number	Percentage	Percentage w/o beef	Z	Z w/o beef
Beef	616	64.1	—	1235	68.2	—	-2.18	—
Mutton	121	12.6	35.1	290	16.0	53.2	-2.39	-5.28
Pork	98	10.2	28.4	70	3.9	12.8	6.58	5.80
Chicken	89	9.3	25.8	172	9.5	31.6	0.17	-1.85
Wild[c]	37	3.9	10.7	73	2.4	7.9	2.24	1.42
Total	961			1810				
Total w/o beef	345			545				

[a]Features 310, 321, 327, 331 (Henry and Garrow 1982).
[b]Features 1–132, 2–2, 2–3, 2–4, 3–13, 3–14, 4–5, 305 (Henry and Garrow 1982; Henry et al. 1983).
[c]Includes duck, quail, dove, pigeon, rabbit, fish.

status as Mr. Shott was promoted from department store salesman to manager of the hardware department in that store. It is likely that household income increased due to the promotion (although both occupations are ranked the same) and due to the contribution of wages of the sons-in-law; the ceramic values indicate an increase in ceramic expenditures over time (F 2–2 and F 2–4 in Table 3).

External economic conditions and market availability may also explain some of the variability observed in the ceramic values. Figure 1 shows the ceramic cup values from fourteen features arrayed in chronological order by mean ceramic date. The decrease in values during the mid-1890s may have been influenced by the economic depression of the early 1890s (Mawn 1979). The general increase during the next decade and a half may represent the

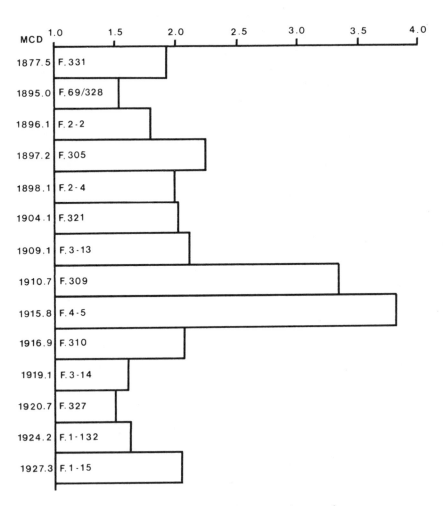

Figure 1. Chronological trends in ceramic cup values.

increased level of prosperity and business activity in Phoenix despite the drought during the early years of 1900 and the economic Panic of 1907 (Mawn 1979). It is appropriate to note that, during this period, Phoenix was enjoying full communication with the rest of the nation via the railroad, and that the Murphy Addition was being actively settled. The decrease in values during and immediately following World War I reflects the presence of fewer French and German porcelains in the archaeological record. European porcelain production was considerably curtailed during the war, and the lower cup values from the mid-teens through the mid-1920s may be due more to availability of supply than to decreasing household expenditures.

Beef values do not reflect a similar chronological trend, although the lowest value occurs during the first decade of the twentieth century, which may reflect the impact of the drought on the area's livestock industry. Several factors may explain why beef (and mean meat) values do not reflect these economic conditions, as do ceramics. Meat was grown and processed locally, so the impact of economic conditions on the manufacture and transport of merchandise was not much of a factor in meat supply. As a durable consumer good, ceramics are purchased infrequently, and in times of economic difficulty, these expenditures can be deferred; food is a nondurable commodity that must be purchased frequently, therefore expenditures cannot be easily deferred. Due to this difference, consumer choices associated with food may also be influenced to a greater degree by individual preferences, by variability in the means of acquisition (retail purchase, poultry raising, hunting), by diversity in culinary practices, and by changes in food storage technology.

The observed values for ceramics from Feature 4–5 are at variance with the rest of the collection. This feature was primarily associated with a widow who owned a fair amount of property elsewhere in the city, according to the latest tax records available (Henry *et al.* 1983). Her status and corresponding level of consumption would have been related to the status of her late husband, about whom no data were available. Additionally, a meatcutter is known to have resided on the property for a period of time during and after 1925. If his household contributed to the deposits in Feature 4–5, this may be reflected in the meat values and frequencies obtained. The meat values for this feature, although high, are not the highest observed, however, except for pork.

Conclusions

The results of these analyses illustrate that many factors, not merely socioeconomic status, influenced consumer behavior in turn-of-the-century Phoenix. Although the household sample size is small, these results indicate that household life cycle, the economic fortunes (or misfortunes) of individual households, external economic conditions, market availability, and the durable or nondurable nature of the commodities themselves affect the decisions consumers had to make. While material culture patterns reflecting consumer behavior are observable in the archaeological record, these patterns are best understood when integrated with data from primary documents and results from research conducted by market analysts, historians, and sociologists.

In conducting these analyses, several problem areas were identified that should be resolved if we are to fully understand urban consumer behavior and the processes involved in consumer decision making. The paramount difficulty is that of defining and measuring socioeconomic status with confidence. Historians, sociologists, and market analysts who study social stratification (see Coleman and Rainwater 1978; Hershberg and Dockhorn 1976; Levy 1973; Warner 1973; Willigan and Lynch 1982) define "class" in terms that are difficult and time-consuming to measure quantifiably. These researchers all point out that occupation alone is an insufficient measure of status position. This situation was reflected in using an occupational ranking scale in these analyses. It is possible that such a scale is useful for certain studies specifically related to the job experience, but it should not be used in the absence of other measures of social stratification. In fact, such a measure does not appear to be a valid technique in comparing individual households, although it may be useful when comparisons of large groups of households are to be made (i.e., when comparing neighborhoods). Additionally, diagnostic characteristics of different social strata and social groups have not been sufficiently identified for archaeologists to determine which patterns of material culture represent which strata or groups (excepting perhaps the social extremes of the very wealthy and the very disadvantaged; see Otto 1977), or why such patterns reflect the strata or groups that they do. Archaeological techniques that address differential social strata, such as economic scaling, should be evaluated in terms of more precise definitions of those strata. The economic scaling of ceramics technique used here needs to be refined, taking into consideration different systems of ceramic pricing and marketing (e.g., discounting; mail-order versus retail store).

Since the household is the appropriate unit of archaeological analysis (Deetz 1982), future research should focus on an identification of the various types of household, on defining household life cycle stages, and on how patterns of material culture vary during the life of a household. The differences between durable and nondurable consumer goods, and the corresponding variations in consumer behavior, are not often recognized by archaeologists, although an eight-year life cycle of the ceramic set postulated by one researcher (Garrow 1982) seems to reflect consumption and use behavior associated with a durable good. Additionally, the effects of commodity supply need to be investigated in more depth.

Given the number of factors that influence consumer behavior, not to mention the effects of individual household idiosyncracies, there is considerable variability in the data, not only in Phoenix, but from other urban areas as well. To offset this so that patterns and processes of consumer behavior can be understood, very large, synchronous samples of households need to be amassed. The quantity of urban areas that have been studied (see Staski 1982) represent a potentially valuable data base of American urban culture that could be used to resolve some of these problems. If the data from all of these urban research projects could be gathered together and analyzed using consistent procedures, we should be able to identify, with a higher level of confidence, material culture patterns associated with consumer behavior and the processes involved in consumer decision making.

References

Bayhem, Frank E., Hatch, Pamela C., and Balsom, Janet, 1982, Interpretation of Faunal Remains from the Original Phoenix Townsite, Blocks 1 and 2, manuscript on file, Soil Systems, Inc., Phoenix, Arizona.

Bull, Sleeter, 1951, *Meat for the Table*, McGraw-Hill, New York.

Chaplin, Raymond, 1971, *The Study of Animal Bones from Archaeological Sites*, Seminar Press, New York.

Coleman, Richard P., and Rainwater, Lee, 1978, *Social Standing in America: New Dimensions of Class*, Basic Books, New York.

Davidson, Paula Edmiston, 1982, Patterns in Urban Food Ways: An Example from Twentieth-Century Atlanta, in: *Archaeology of Urban America: The Search for Pattern and Process* (Roy S. Dickens, ed.), Academic Press, New York, pp. 381–398.

Deetz, James J. F., 1982, Households: A Structural Key to Archaeological Explanation, in: Archaeology of the Household: Building a Prehistory of Domestic Life (Richard R. Wilk and William L. Rathje, eds.), *American Behavioral Scientist* 25:717–724.

Freund, John E., 1973, *Modern Elementary Statistics*, 4th ed., Prentice-Hall, Englewood Cliffs, New Jersey.

Garrow, Patrick H. (ed.), 1982. Archaeological Investigations at the Washington, D.C. Civic Center Site, report prepared for the Historic Preservation Office, Department of Housing and Community Development, Government of the District of Columbia, by Soil Systems, Inc., Marietta, Georgia.

Gaw, Linda P., 1975, The Availability and Selection of Ceramics in Silcott, Washington, 1900–1930, *Northwest Anthropological Research Notes* 9:166–179.

Glassie, Henry, 1968, *Pattern in Material Folk Culture of the Eastern United States*, University of Pennsylvania Press, Philadelphia.

Gordon, Milton M., 1978, *Human Nature, Class, and Ethnicity*, Oxford University Press, New York.

Henry, Susan L., and Garrow, Patrick H., 1982, The Historic Component, Part II, in: The City of Phoenix: Archaeology of the Original Phoenix Townsite, Blocks 1 and 2 (John S. Cable, Susan L. Henry, and David E. Doyel, eds.), *Soil Systems Publications in Archaeology* 1, Professional Service Industries, Inc., Phoenix, Arizona.

Henry, Susan L., Hoffman, Kathleen S., Ritz, Frank, and McKenna, Jeanette A., 1983, The Archaeology of an Early 20th-Century Residential Neighborhood in the Murphy Addition, draft report, Soil Systems, Inc., Professional Service Industries, Phoenix, Arizona.

Hershberg, Theodore, and Dockhorn, Robert, 1976, Occupational Classification, *Historical Methods Newsletter* 9(2–3):59–98.

Howard, John A., and Sheth, Jagdish N., 1973. A Theory of Buyer Behavior, in: *Perspectives in Consumer Behavior* (Harold H. Kassarjian and Thomas S. Robertson, eds.), Scott, Foresman, Glenview, Illinois, pp. 519–540.

Jolley, Robert L., 1983, North American Historic Sites Zooarchaeology, *Historical Archaeology* 17(2):64–79.

Kassarjian, Harold H., and Robertson, Thomas S., 1973a, Social Class, in: *Perspectives in Consumer Behavior* (Harold H. Kassarjian and Thomas S. Robertson, eds.), Scott, Foresman, Glenview, Illinois, pp. 390–400.

Kassarjian, Harold H., and Robertson, Thomas S., 1973b, Social Processes, in: *Perspectives in Consumer Behavior* (Harold H. Kassarjian and Thomas S. Robertson, eds.), Scott, Foresman, Glenview, Illinois, pp. 292–299.

Kassarjian, Harold H., and Robertson, Thomas S., 1973c, Culture and Subcultures, in: *Perspectives in Consumer Behavior* (Harold H. Kassarjian and Thomas S. Robertson, eds.), Scott, Foresman, Glenview, Illinois, pp. 450–465.

Katz, Michael B., 1972, Occupational Classification in History, *Journal of Interdisciplinary History* 3:63–88.

Klein, Terry H., and Garrow, Patrick H. (eds.), 1984, *Final Archaeological Excavations at the Wilmington Boulevard, Monroe Street to King Street, Wilmington, New Castle County, Delaware* (DELDOT Archaeological Series, Number 29), Delaware Department of Transportation, Dover, Delaware.

Laslett, Peter, and Wall, Richard (eds.), 1972, *Household and Family in Past Time,* Cambridge University Press, Cambridge.

Laumann, Edward O., and House, James S., 1973, Living Room Styles and Social Attributes: The Patterning of Material Artifacts in a Modern Urban Community, in: *Perspectives in Consumer Behavior* (Harold H. Kassarjian and Thomas S. Robertson, eds.), Scott, Foresman, Glenview, Illinois, pp. 430–440.

Levy, Sidney J., 1973, Social Class and Consumer Behavior, in: *Perspectives in Consumer Behavior* (Harold H. Kassarjian and Thomas S. Robertson, eds.), Scott, Foresman, Glenview, Illinois, pp. 409–420.

Martineau, Pierre, 1958, Social Classes and Spending Behavior, *Journal of Marketing* 23:121–130.

Mawn, Geoffrey P., 1979, Phoenix Arizona: Central City of the Southwest, 1870–1920, unpublished Ph.D. dissertation, Arizona State University, Tempe.

Miller, George L., 1974, A Tenant Farmer's Tableware: Nineteenth Century Ceramics from Tabb's Purchase, *Maryland Historical Magazine* 69:197–210.

Miller, George L., 1980, Classification and Economic Scaling of 19th Century Ceramics, *Historical Archaeology* 14:1–40.

Montgomery Ward and Company, 1895, *Montgomery Ward and Co. 1894–95 Catalogue and Buyers Guide No. 57,* reprinted in 1969 by Dover Publications, New York.

Montgomery Ward and Company, 1922, *Montgomery Ward and Co. Catalogue No. 97, Fall & Winter, 1922–23,* reprinted in 1969 by H. C. Publishers, New York.

Mudar, Karen, 1978, The Effects of Socio-cultural Variables on Food Preferences in Early 19th Century Detroit, *The Conference on Historic Sites Archaeology Papers 1977* 12:322–391.

Otto, John Solomon, 1977, Artifact and Status Differences—A Comparison of Ceramics from Planter, Overseer, and Slave Sites on an Antebellum Plantation, in: *Research Strategies in Historical Archaeology* (Stanley South, ed.), Academic Press, New York, pp. 91–118.

Rathje, William L., and McCarthy, Michael, 1977, Regularity and Variability in Contemporary Garbage, in: *Research Strategies in Historical Archaeology* (Stanley South, ed.), Academic Press, New York, pp. 261–286.

Reitz, Elizabeth J., and Cumbaa, Stephen L., 1983, Diet and Foodways of Eighteenth-Century Spanish St. Augustine, in: *Spanish St. Augustine: The Archaeology of a Colonial Creole Community* (by Kathleen Deagan), Academic Press, New York, pp. 151–185.

Roberson, John, and Roberson, Marie, 1966, *The Meat Cookbook,* Collier Books, New York.

Romans, John R., and Zeigler, P. Thomas, 1977, *The Meat We Eat,* Interstate Printers and Publishers, Danvill.

Schiffer, Michael B., Downing, Theodore E., and McCarthy, Michael, 1981, Waste Not, Want Not: An Ethnoarchaeological Study of Re-use in Tucson, Arizona, in: *Modern Material Culture: The Archaeology of Us* (Richard A. Gould and Michael B. Schiffer, eds.), Academic Press, New York, pp. 67–86.

Schulz, Peter D., and Gust, Sherri M., 1983, Faunal Remains and Social Status in 19th Century Sacramento, *Historical Archaeology* 17(1):44–53.

Schuyler, Robert L., 1980, Preface, in: *Archaeological Perspectives on Ethnicity in America: Afro-American and Asian American Culture History* (Robert L. Schuyler, ed.), Baywood Publishing, New York, pp. vii–viii.

Sears, Roebuck and Company, 1897, *Sears, Roebuck and Company Consumer Guide, Catalogue No. 104,* reprinted in 1976 by Chelsea House Publishers, New York.

Sears, Roebuck and Company, 1900, *Sears, Roebuck and Co. Consumers Guide, Catalogue No. 110, Fall 1900,* reprinted in 1970 (Joseph J. Schroeder, Jr., ed.) by DBI Books, Northfield, Illinois.

Sears, Roebuck and Company, 1902, *Sears, Roebuck and Company Catalogue No. 111,* reprinted in 1969 by Bounty Books, New York.

Sears, Roebuck and Company, 1909, *Sears, Roebuck and Company Consumers Guide, Catalogue No. 118,* reprinted in 1979 by Ventura Books, New York.

Sears, Roebuck and Company, 1927, *Sears, Roebuck and Company Catalogue,* reprinted in 1970 by Bounty Books, New York.

Shephard, Steven J., 1980, An Archaeological Model: Change in the Nineteenth Century Middle Class, paper presented at the 45th Annual Meeting of the Society for American Archaeology, Philadelphia.

Staski, Edward, 1982, Advances in Urban Archaeology, in: *Advances in Archaeological Method and Theory,* Volume 5 (Michael B. Schiffer, ed.), Academic Press, New York, pp. 97–149.

Thomas, David Hurst, 1976, *Figuring Anthropology: First Principles of Probability and Statistics,* Holt, Rinehart & Winston, New York.

Vivello, Frank Robert, 1978, *Cultural Anthropology Handbook: A Basic Introduction,* McGraw-Hill, New York.

Warner, W. L. 1973, Social Class in America, in: *Perspectives in Consumer Behavior* (Harold H. Kassarjian and Thomas S. Robertson eds.), Scott, Foresman, Glenview, Illinois, pp. 400–409.

Warner, W. L., and Lunt, P. S., 1941, The Social Life of a Modern Community, *Yankee City Series,* Volume 1, Yale University Press, New Haven, Connecticut.

Wegars, Priscilla, and Carley, Caroline E., 1982, "The Very Latest Rage": Design Trends in Twentieth Century Ceramics, paper presented at the 15th Annual Meeting of the Society for Historical Archaeology, Philadelphia.

Wells, William D., and Gubar, George, 1970, Life Cycle Concept in Marketing Research, in: *Research in Consumer Behavior* (David T. Kollat, Roger D. Blackwell, and James F. Engel, eds.), Holt, Rinehart & Winston, New York, pp. 512–527.

Willigan, J. Dennis, and Lynch, Katherine A., 1982, *Sources and Methods of Historical Demography,* Academic Press, New York.

16

Gravestones

Reflectors of Ethnicity or Class?

LYNN CLARK

INTRODUCTION

When we walk through a cemetery, we see in each gravestone the end result of a series of choices made by the individuals who purchased the stones. We see differences in the size, shape, material, and decoration of each gravestone, and we assume that the consumer was able to choose freely from all the available options. All possible choices, however, are not open to every consumer. The complex interaction of the individual's ethnicity and class standing acts as a constraint on the available options. The selections a consumer makes, in turn, modifies the interaction of ethnicity and class. This relationship between ethnicity and class will be explored by studying its effect on the consumer choices available for gravestones.

The ethnic groups dealt with here were found in America as a result of the European immigrations of the nineteenth and early twentieth centuries. Individuals who were not part, or whose ancestors were not part, of those immigrations are considered "nonethnic." Ethnic individuals share customs and a world view that are different from the dominant nonethnic society around them. Many times, they also share lower-class standing (Steinberg 1981).

Class standing is determined by income to a certain extent, but more importantly by status. The prestige associated with life-style, formal education, and occupation all contribute to an individual's standing in others' eyes. According to Weber (Runciman 1978), societies where status is an important consideration are regulated by convention. In a status-based society such as the United States, people are bound to follow the conventionalized rules, hence free choice is limited. In this way, class structures the interaction between individuals and between individuals and material culture.

Problems of ethnicity and class are not new to historical archaeologists. Since the 1970s, researchers have become increasingly interested in delineating the material remains of racial groups and ethnic groups (McGuire 1982; Otto 1977; Schuyler 1980; South 1974). Since members of those racial and

Lynn Clark ☐ Department of Anthropology, State University of New York, Binghamton, NY 13901.

ethnic groups historically have been lower class, several researchers became concerned with separating class from ethnicity in the archaeological record (Baker 1980; McGuire 1982; Otto 1980).

This study goes further by considering how the interaction of ethnicity and class affects material culture. In the first section of this article, ethnicity, class, and their relation to consumer choice will be explored in more detail. After a discussion of specific theories of ethnicity drawn from anthropology and sociology, a series of test implications will be presented. In order to evaluate the test implications, gravestones, as well as written and oral histories, from Broome County, New York, were utilized. The specific research strategy used will be presented, followed by a discussion of the analytical results. The last section of the study will evaluate these results in terms of the proposed theory.

ETHNICITY, CLASS, AND CONSUMER CHOICE

Class limits the number of choices a consumer can make and also provides more options to choose from. One limiting factor, regardless of class, is lower income. Lower income means individuals do not have sufficient disposable income to purchase any memorial they desire. However, this does not mean that individuals with greater income have an unlimited range of alternatives to choose from. As stated earlier, individuals in a status-based society follow conventionalized rules of behavior that limit the consumer choices they can make.

Higher-class individuals follow the socially prescribed rules for more prestigious behavior. If an individual wishes to climb socially, then these same rules are adopted. In this way, lower-class individuals gain status in others' eyes, which equates with greater prestige. Individuals who cannot gain either prestige or income follow an alternate set of behavioral rules (Barth 1969). It is possible, then, for these lower-class individuals to gain a certain amount of prestige in each other's eyes, even though their behavior is not considered prestigious by higher classes.

As more lower-class individuals emulate the behavior of the higher classes, this behavior becomes modified. In order to preserve class distinctions, the upper class must keep its behavior separate from that of the lower classes (Fallers 1973; Miller 1982). Upper-class individuals select new alternatives, thereby opening up additional consumer choices for themselves and for those who will eventually emulate their behavior.

Ethnicity also both limits and expands consumer choices. Traditions brought by immigrants introduced additional alternatives to the field of choice. However, since these new alternatives were associated with immigrant behavior, they were not considered prestigious (Steinberg 1981). These new options were not used by nonethnics for the same reasons upper-class individuals would not choose options associated with lower-class behavior.

Just as lower-class individuals may strive to become upper class, ethnic individuals whose occupations bring increased income may strive to imitate more prestigious nonethnic behavior. Their consumer choices would be the same as those of nonethnics. Since prejudice makes full status equality rare, ethnic individuals may instead decide to maintain ethnic identities, in much the same way lower-class individuals come to follow a different set of behavioral rules than upper-class individuals. The consumer choices made by the ethnic individuals would reflect both their increased buying power and their ethnic ties.

Consumer choice therefore does not imply free choice. Choice is defined by social relations; once choices are made, social relations are either reinforced or redefined.

THEORIES OF ETHNICITY

There are many theories dealing with ethnicity in anthropological and sociological literature. The two presented here were selected because they are concerned with the relation between ethnicity and class in the United States. In addition, Steinberg (1981) looks at European immigrant groups, and McGuire (1982) works specifically with the archaeological record.

Stephen Steinberg (1981) investigates the relation between class and ethnicity in his book *The Ethnic Myth*. He states that immigrant groups came to America in answer to a demand for cheap, unskilled labor. Because of this, they were placed at or near the bottom of the social hierarchy. To escape the attendant social stigma and economic consequences of lower-class life, individuals assimilated. Steinberg asserts that the preservation of ethnic traditions means the preservation of the class distinctions associated with immigrant status.

Randall McGuire (1982) approaches ethnicity from Barth's (1969) theoretical framework of boundaries. Although McGuire introduces the idea of power relations to ethnic boundary maintenance, he never makes a total connection between ethnicity and class. Whereas Steinberg stresses the intertwining of ethnicity, economic status, prestige, and occupation, McGuire sees them as separable units for study in the archaeological record. McGuire's discussion of power relations, however, introduces an important concept to ethnic studies. Where power differences are such that one group monopolizes the prestigious and powerful positions in a society, the weaker group will create a "smaller stage upon which individuals can compete for power, prestige, and wealth" (1982:171).

The theory proposed here is a synthesis of Steinberg's and McGuire's theories. Ethnicity is associated with lower-class status. In order to advance socially, an individual must assimilate. However, because nonethnics in late nineteenth- and early twentieth-century America controlled the prestigious and powerful positions, ethnics were prevented from attaining equal class standing. In this case, they would have created and dominated their own sphere of power relations inside their ethnic community.

In order to examine the proposed theory as evidenced by gravestones, the following test implications were formulated:

A. The gravestones of immigrants and nonethnics will be different if the immigrant group is also lower class.
B. These differences will lessen as the immigrant groups become middle class.
C. As individuals from an ethnic group gain economic advantages, differences will become apparent within the group. Individuals of higher social position will have gravestones more similar to those of nonethnics with comparable social position.
D. Some ethnic individuals may choose to operate in a sphere of relations that is separate from, but contained within, mainstream society. These individuals will have gravestones more similar to others in their ethnic group.

RESEARCH STRATEGY

Broome County seemed a logical choice for a study of ethnicity and class. Gold-domed ethnic churches and ethnic fraternal lodges visibly attest to immigrant activity in the metropolitan areas of Binghamton, Johnson City, and Endicott. In addition, recent exhibits at the Roberson Center for the Arts and Sciences have brought both ethnicity and working-class lives in Broome County to the attention of the public. The projects at Roberson generated written and oral histories that, in addition to other local histories, were consulted to research ethnic group immigration and employment in Broome County.

Before actual recording began, and throughout the recording period, gravestone project workers became familiar with gravestone typology and technology. Monument dealers were interviewed regarding materials used, relative expense, terminology, manufacturing, and decorating techniques (Camarda 1985; Trevor 1982; Welch and Carmien 1985). Pamphlets from the dealers and early twentieth-century monument carvers' manuals also provided useful information (Barre Granite Estimating Guide 1957; Price List of Monumental Marble 1955; Sample 1919; Wyckoff 1923).

Using the interview information and personal observation, a form was created for recording each monument. Gravestone characteristics were grouped into five general categories: locational information, physical description, decoration, individual demographics, and additional text. Each characteristic had several possible choices, which were assigned numerical codes to aid in computer analysis.

Computer analysis of the data was done using the SAS statistical package. Simple frequency charts showed the number of times each characteristic appeared in the sample. Scatter plots charted the changes in continuous variables, such as relative investment and areas of design, over time.

Relative monetary investment was measured by comparing the size of monuments. Differential material costs were accounted for by multiplying size by a factor reflecting the cost difference. Monuments of bronze or colored granite cost from 20 percent to 80 percent more than the same monument of gray Vermont granite. The exact percentage for granite was determined mainly by shipping costs. Some granites came from as far away as India and Africa (Camarda 1985).

Traditionally, a granite monument costs twice as much as a marble monument of the same size (Barre Granite Estimating Guide 1957; Price List of Monumental Marble 1955). Marble is much softer than granite, making carving less time-consuming and therefore less expensive (Camarda 1985; Sample 1919; Wyckoff 1923). Because the Vermont Marble Company ceased to produce marble for monuments in the 1970s, the price of marble has become fairly equal to that of granite in recent years. Marble can be imported from elsewhere in the United States or Italy, but with added shipping expenses (Camarda 1985).

When calculating relative investment, gray granite was taken as the standard. In the case of a marble monument, with marble being half the cost of gray granite, size was multiplied by 0.5. In the case of a black granite monument, because black granite averages 65 percent more than gray granite, size was multiplied by 1.65.

Different family plot arrangements represent different investments for individuals interred in the plot. A multigenerational plot has a large central monument surrounded by smaller individual headstones. In contrast, a husband and wife plot usually has one small monument. To obtain the mean investment per individual, the total investment for each family group was divided by the number of individuals in the group.

Once out of the cemetery, archival research provided data on the individual's ethnicity and occupation. Individuals were assigned to an ethnic group by consulting surname dictionaries or graduate students who possess knowledge of Eastern and Southern European surnames. Occupation was obtained from Binghamton city and suburban directories and the manuscript census.

Following guidelines set forth by the United States Census Bureau in 1960, the occupations were divided into five categories. The first consists of managers and administrators. The second is made up of professionals such as doctors and teachers. Clerical and sales employees make up the third, while the fourth consists of skilled, blue-collar workers such as machinists, painters, tanners, and auto repairmen. Unskilled blue-collar workers, employees with service-oriented jobs, and the unemployed constitute the fifth and final group (Miller 1960).

This classification is not based solely on differences in income, although there is a general increase in income as one proceeds from the unskilled, blue-collar category to the manager and administrator category. The occupation scale, rather than a strict scale of income, was chosen because it incorporates prestige differences between white- and blue-collar workers, thus making it a better indicator of class than income alone. Prestige of occupation is one of the main indicators of status, which, in turn, is one of the main influences on class (Runciman 1978).

Twelve area cemeteries, reflecting the county's ethnic diversity and dating from the 1830s to the present, were chosen for study. Stratified random-sampling techniques were used to obtain a representative sample of 1,117 stones from the cemeteries. The number of stones to be recorded from each cemetery was determined by the cemetery's relative size, the only exception being Vestal Hills, a lawn cemetery, where the sample is smaller.

A field map was created for each cemetery by pacing off its sections. A section is an area bounded by driveways or walkways. A table of random numbers was then used to pick which stones within each section were to be sampled. A map was available for one of the cemeteries so, in this case, a table of random numbers was used to draw lot numbers. Dice were thrown to choose a stone within a lot.

Using random sampling techniques such as these will have predictable consequences for the data collected. The sample obtained approximates a normal distribution, allowing the use of statistics relating to the familiar normal distribution. For the gravestone data, "typical" gravestones are well represented, while certain unusual and therefore highly visible forms appear to be underrepresented. Although the unusual forms were not always present in the sample collected, it will be important to discuss their presence in the following analysis.

RESULTS

Historical Background

Local written and oral histories revealed that the population of Broome County is ethnically mixed as a result of several waves of migrations and immigrations. The area was originally settled in the late eighteenth century by Anglo-Saxon farmers who migrated from New England, eastern New York, and Pennsylvania. Toward the middle of the nineteenth century, German-Jewish merchants from New York City moved into the area. At the same time, Irish laborers migrated from the Pennsylvania coalfields. Later in that century and early in the twentieth, Italians and Eastern Europeans immigrated to Broome County's developing industrial areas, the cities of Binghamton, Johnson City, and Endicott (Bothwell 1983; Immigration History Project 1980–1985; Landmark Society of Broome County 1980; McGuire and Osterud 1980).

Changing Options

The changing options available to gravestone consumers were obtained from monument dealers and monument carvers' manuals. Early in the nineteenth century, gravestones were largely tablet form. The marble slabs were quarried out-of-state and then hand-carved locally. Granite, mainly from Vermont, was introduced in the mid-nineteenth century. Granite is much harder than marble, making it durable yet more difficult to carve, thus decoration would have been limited (Camarda 1985; Sample 1919; Wyckoff 1923).

Technological advances caused changes in the decoration found on monuments. More elaborate carving became possible with the introduction of pneumatic tools sometime before 1920. However, the trend has been to move from local artisans' hand-carved stones toward national manufacturers' stock carvings. This means that, as designs have become more elaborate and cover greater areas of the monument, they have also become fairly standardized and simpler. The simplicity involves a shift from bas-relief carving to flat engraving (Camarda 1985; Sample 1919; Welch and Carmien 1985; Wyckoff 1923).

Mass production has also led to standardization of form and size. Gravestones can be turned out more efficiently if machine specifications are set and many stones are cut, rather than stopping production to change settings every time a stone is cut. The use of robotics for quarrying and carving is the latest step in efficient and standardized monument production. Nonstandard forms can still be made, but at an increased cost. Since the introduction of mass production in the monument industry in the 1930s, consumers have been increasingly limited to buying simplified, smaller, and standardized gravestones (Camarda 1985; Welch and Carmien 1985).

The actual options chosen by consumers were revealed by data collected in the cemeteries and a separate study of Binghamton mausoleums (Roveland 1983). In the mid-nineteenth century, obelisks and pedestal-style family monuments of granite and marble were being used in addition to marble tablet-style headstones. Small beveled or slant-faced individual headstones often clustered around the family monuments.

After the turn of the century, corresponding to the changes in technology, bulky granite forms predominate. There seemed to be great opportunity for experimentation; forms were made to resemble tree stumps, houses, and columns growing out of blocks of granite, only partially smoothed by the carver's chisel. The largest granite form, the family mausoleum, was erected most often between 1900 and 1910 (Roveland 1983).

The Great Depression brought mausoleum sales almost to a complete halt. It also saw the beginning of a trend toward the smaller, standardized forms. This is when the bronze and granite flush markers of lawn cemeteries start appearing. It is also when slant-faced markers and rectangular, small monuments for husband-and-wife pairs start to replace the many-faceted family monuments with their cluster of individual headstones.

In the 1940s and 1950s, the husband-and-wife monuments predominate, and they continue to do so today. Between 1940 and 1960, the area of decoration on gravestones doubled, and the number of stones with decoration increased. Flowers and geometric borders became the main types of decoration for the nonethnic, Irish, and Jewish groups, regardless of occupation. The area of decoration and the number of decorated stones continues to increase to the

present day. Even though smaller, standardized forms predominate, beginning in the 1940s, mausoleums and sarcophagi (similar to mausoleums but
without an interior chamber) have been built regularly, although not as frequently as prior to 1930.

Corresponding to the decrease in monument size, there has been a general
decrease in monument investment, as shown in Figure 1. The peak seen in the
1880s is due to the presence of obelisks in the sample. The peaks in both the
1920s and 1960s are the result of three sarcophagi that were constructed
during those time periods. Investment per individual declines in the same
fashion.

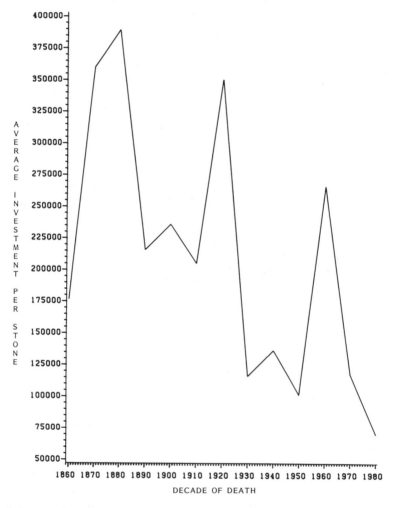

Figure 1. Average investment per gravestone in each decade. Investment equals the size of the
stone in cm³, multiplied by a factor reflecting the cost difference for the material it was made
from.

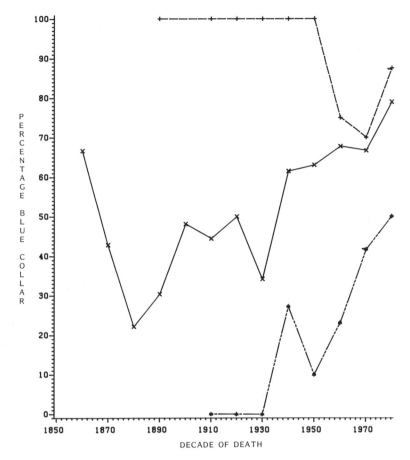

Figure 2. Percentage of blue-collar workers for select ethnic groups in each decade. Surname = (x—x) nonethnic; (+—+) Slovak; (*—*) Jewish.

Ethnicity and Occupation

There are some variations in the options available to, and chosen by, different ethnic and occupation groups, but before these are discussed, it is important to understand the relation between ethnicity and class. This tie is dramatically illustrated by examining the distribution of ethnic groups among the occupation categories. Figure 2 shows the percentage of skilled and unskilled blue-collar workers for selected ethnic groups. Unfortunately, no occupations were obtainable for individuals who died before 1860, and data is generally sparse until 1890. Italians, Slovaks, and Jews do not appear in the sample regularly before 1910, and occupation data for Italians and Slovaks is sparse until the 1930s.

Despite the limitations of the sample, patterns clearly emerge. Italians and Slovaks have always been mainly blue-collar. It is not until the 1950s that

any significant number of Italians start appearing in the white-collar categories. Slovaks do not make this move until the 1960s. The only exception to this
is in the 1920s, when the sample shows only white-collar Italians. In contrast,
Jews have always been mainly white-collar. By 1900, the Irish have settled at
about 50 percent to 65 percent blue-collar. Nonethnics generally had the least
percentage blue-collar workers prior to 1940; afterward they show a slightly
greater percentage than the Irish.

Throughout the following discussion, then, the reader should keep in
mind that when white-collar occupation groups are being discussed, very few,
if any, Italians and Slovaks are represented in those groups.

Different Options for Ethnic and Occupation Groups

The options chosen by white-collar workers helped to reinforce their social
position by displaying their greater consumption of wealth. The average investment per individual is consistently higher for white-collar groups. Perhaps the most prominant display of wealth is in the erection of mausoleums
and sarcophagi. Prior to 1940, the individuals who chose these forms of burial
were either manager-administrators or professionals (Roveland 1983). The
options not chosen by white-collar workers are a more subtle indicator of their
status. The less expensive marble tablets were not used by these individuals
after the turn of the century.

Blue-collar workers either emulated white-collar workers or chose options
according to an alternate set of behavioral rules. Because of the many pos-
sibilities this presented, the unskilled blue-collar group utilized the greatest
number of gravestone forms in the 1920s and 1930s. In addition to forms used
by the white-collar groups, tree stumps, flush markers, marble tablets, and
crosses of both granite and marble were employed. Flush markers and marble
monuments are less expensive forms of memorialization. The other choices
reflect adherence to a different set of conventions than those followed by
white-collar workers.

After the 1930s, as forms became standardized, this variation was chan-
nelled instead into increasingly diversified types and amounts of decoration.
Images of saints and other religious designs, wedding bands, and photographs
became popular with the lower-occupation groups, and the popularity of these
decorations continues today. Emulation is witnessed by the increasing number
of mausoleums and sarcophagi erected by blue-collar workers since the 1940s.

Some choices seem to have been made on the basis of ethnicity. From the
1920s to the 1960s, a pointed monument form was used by Slovaks, Italians,
and Jews irrespective of occupation. Italians and Slovaks incorporated complex religious designs and photographs more often than nonethnics. Italians
also differ from nonethnics and Irish in their utilization of mausoleums and
sarcophagi. Prior to 1940, all but one mausoleum were erected by nonethnics
and Irish. Afterwards they are purchased exclusively by Italians. Jews differ
from nonethnics, and all other groups as well, in their use of epitaphs. Beginning in the 1930s, epitaphs appear less frequently on the gravestones of all

groups except the Jews. Jewish stones increasingly incorporate Hebrew epitaphs of the same basic formula, in addition to English text. The epitaph states the individual's Hebrew name, parentage, the Hebrew month, day, and year of death, and the phrase, "May he or she be bound up in the bond of everlasting life."

These epitaphs act in the same way as the Star of David symbol on Jewish stones and crosses on non-Jewish stones. Cross styles diversified with the influx of Irish, Slovak, and Italian immigrants. These immigrants were mainly Catholic, while nonethnics were mainly Protestant, so the diversity in cross styles can be attributed to religious differences. The use of crosses has increased since the 1930s concomitant with an increase in the use of the Star of David and epitaphs in Hebrew in Jewish cemeteries, all regardless of occupational differences.

It becomes increasingly difficult to visualize the complex relation of material culture, class, and ethnicity if gravestones are analyzed separately in terms of ethnicity and occupation. Overall patterns emerge more clearly when ethnic-occupation groups are considered. Analysis of the gravestones from this point of view shows that, prior to the 1930s, upper-class nonethnics chose to display their wealth by erecting large monuments. German-Jewish and Irish immigrants with higher occupations quickly adopted nonethnic, upper-class buying patterns. Early Slovak and Italian immigrants were unskilled blue-collar, and their stones reflect both their ethnicity and their lower-class standing. Their small and simple stones often had inscriptions in their native language and overall showed a much lower investment per person than nonethnics, Irish, and German Jews.

After the 1920s, it became increasingly unpopular for upper-class nonethnics, Irish, and German Jews to display their position. In contrast, it became increasingly popular for ethnic individuals, whose occupations brought greater income and/or prestige, to invest more per person. It is because of this that investment per individual remained consistently higher for upper-class individuals, even though investment for nonethnics dropped.

Italians in this situation perhaps provide the most interesting look at how consumer choices are affected by the interaction of ethnicity and class. They are the ones who erected large, ornately decorated memorials during the 1950s and 1960s, when prestigious nonethnics had stopped displaying their wealth. They chose to become prestigious in the eyes of their ethnic community rather than in the eyes of the dominant, nonethnic society around them.

CONCLUSIONS

On the basis of the above discussion, the test implications stated earlier can be accepted. The data is best explained by a synthesis of McGuire's and Steinberg's theories. McGuire (1982) points out the importance of understanding the power relations between ethnic groups when trying to determine the effect of ethnicity on material culture. Favorable relations in the late nineteenth century enabled white-collar German Jews and Irish to either have equal prestige as their nonethnic counterparts, or to strive for equal status. The gravestones of these three groups were very similar in size, form, and decoration. Unequal relations between Slovaks, Italians, and nonethnics from that time until World War II prevented most Slovaks and Italians from gaining white-collar occupations. Even in the 1950s and 1960s, when these groups began to gain monetary resources, ethnic prejudice made attainment of equal status difficult. In these cases, ethnic consumers chose to create their own arena for power relations, which operated within mainstream, nonethnic society while remaining separate from it. Italian and Slovak gravestones from this time period show increased investment and diversity of religious decoration, while white-collar workers from other groups decrease their investment and refrain from using great amounts of religious decoration. The most recent trends show Italian and Slovak investment decreasing, which suggests that power relations are balancing.

It is apparent from the previous discussions that ethnicity is tied to class, as Steinberg (1981) stresses. However, ethnicity and class are not synonymous. In their use of increased types and amounts of decoration, lower-class individuals, regardless of ethnicity, are set apart from upper-class individuals. Through their use of photographs and tall, pointed monuments, Slovaks, Italians, and Eastern European Jews are separated from other groups. In the same way, gravestones resembling crosses distinguish Slovaks and Italians.

Ethnic traditions will be preserved only if they do not prevent individuals from operating in the same class as their nonethnic counterparts. If power relations allow ethnics equitable prestige, and these individuals choose to accept upper-class standing, then their consumer choices must be consistent with those of the upper class. Any ethnic traditions, such as ornate religious embellishment, will be dropped if they contradict upper-class norms.

Consumer choices therefore are defined by the social situation: an individual's class standing, ethnicity, and the interaction of the two. A change in any of these variables presents new options to the consumer. It also presents new guidelines to follow when choosing from the available options. The monument chosen reflects the individual's class and ethnicity. Once erected, it also shapes people's perception of the individual's ethnic background and social status. This ability enables individuals to change their social situation by gaining prestige in others' eyes. Italians gained status within their ethnic community during the 1950s and 1960s by erecting mausoleums and sarcophagi. At the end of the nineteenth century, German Jews and Irish gained prestige by purchasing monuments like those of upper-class nonethnics.

A further test of this hypothesis regarding the interrelation of ethnicity and class would be to apply it to burial practices in general. If it were true, one would expect that the forms not dealt with in this study, public mausoleums, cremations, and burial in unmarked graves, would be alternatives associated with specific classes and/or ethnic groups. Those forms that have low status should be used only by lower-class individuals, which would include early immigrants. With forms that have high status, a shift would occur making them the preferred burial practices, as they are used first by upper-class individuals and then by lower-class individuals who emulate their behavior. As with gravestones, ethnics who gain status will choose these alternatives. Ethnics who are denied equal status would instead gain prestige in the eyes of other ethnics by employing more traditional burial practices.

REFERENCES

Baker, V. G., 1980, Archaeological Visibility of Afro-American Culture: An Example from Black Lucy's Garden, Andover, Massachusetts, in: *Archaeological Perspectives on Ethnicity in America* (R. L. Schuyler, ed.), Baywood Publishing, New York, pp. 19–37.

Barre Granite Estimating Guide, 1957, Walter H. Stowell, Barre, Vermont.

Barth, F. (ed.), 1969, *Ethnic Groups and Boundaries,* Little, Brown, Boston.

Bothwell, L., 1983, *Broome County Heritage,* Windsor Publications, Woodland Hills, California.

Camarda, D., 1985, Endicott Artistic Memorial Company, personal communication.

Fallers, L. A., 1973, *Inequality: Social Stratification Reconsidered,* University of Chicago Press, Chicago.

Immigration History Project, 1980–1985, Roberson Center for the Arts and Sciences, Binghamton, New York.

Landmark Society of Broome County, 1980, Susquehanna Urban Cultural Park: Feasibility Study, The Society, Johnson City, New York.

McGuire, R. H., 1982, The Study of Ethnicity in Historical Archaeology, *Journal of Anthropological Archaeology* 1:159–178.

McGuire, R., and Osterud, N. G., 1980, *Working Lives: Broome County, New York 1800–1930,* Roberson Center for the Arts and Sciences, Binghamton, New York.

Miller, D., 1982, Structures and Strategies: An Aspect of the Relationship between Social Hierarchy and Cultural Change, in: *Symbolic and Structural Archaeology* (I. Hodder, ed.), Cambridge University Press, New York.

Miller, H., 1960, Income Distribution in the United States, A 1960 Census Monograph, U.S. Department of Commerce, Bureau of the Census, Washington, D.C.

Otto, J. S., 1977, Artifacts and Status Differences: A Comparison of Ceramics from Planter, Overseer, and Slave Sites on an Antebellum Plantation, in: *Research Strategies in Historical Archaeology* (S. South, ed.), Academic Press, New York.

Otto, J. S., 1980, Race and Class on Antebellum Plantations, in: *Archaeological Perspectives on Ethnicity in America* (R. L. Schuyler, ed.), Baywood Publishing, New York, pp. 3–13.

Price List of Monumental Marble, 1955, Vermont Marble Company, Proctor, Vermont.

Roveland, B. E., 1983, Houses of the Dead, unpublished B.A. thesis, Department of Anthropology, State University of New York at Binghamton, New York.

Runciman, W. G. (ed.), 1978, *Max Weber, Selections in Translation,* Cambridge University Press, New York.

Sample, O., 1919, *Monument Dealers Manual,* Allied Arts Publishing, Chicago.

Schuyler, R. L., 1980, *Archaeological Perspectives on Ethnicity in America,* Baywood Publishing, New York.

South, S. (ed.), 1974, Archaeology of Black Settlements, *Papers of the Conference on Historic Site Archaeology* 7(2).

Steinberg, S., 1981, *The Ethnic Myth,* Beacon Press, Boston.

Trevor, R., 1982, Binghamton–Johnson City Monument Company, personal communication.

Welch, B., and Carmien, J., 1985, E. C. Crooks Memorial Corporation, personal communication.

Wyckoff, J. W. (ed.), 1923, *The Manual of Monumental Lettering,* Monumental News, Chicago.

Epilogue
Middle-Range Theory in Historical Archaeology

MARK P. LEONE AND CONSTANCE A. CROSBY

This essay is based on an observation that could be made about many publications in historical archaeology. After all the work is done, it is not clear what has been discovered that was not known before. It is often asked what historical archaeologists have learned that was not already known from other sources. The answer has come back, time and again, that historical archaeology has great potential but does not yet tell us much that was not already known from the documentary record.

The problem may be one of method, and specifically, with the way in which the relationship between documentary materials and archaeological data is normally conceived.

To address this problem, we want to explore the possibility of giving the written record and the archaeological record differing statuses and then seeing whether they can be related to each other more productively. To do this, we would like to employ our understanding of Lewis R. Binford's use of middle-range theory in prehistoric archaeology, especially through his work on ethnoarchaeology.

Most of the outline of middle-range theory that follows comes from "Researching Ambiguity: Frames of Reference and Site Structure" (Binford 1987). This study uses data from ethnoarchaeological observations on the Alyawara, a group of Central-Desert Australian Aborigines, and from the Nunamiut Eskimos. Binford's specific concern is with understanding hunter–gatherer subsistence strategies, but his general aim is to establish a logically sound method for the use of analogies (Binford 1982, 1983a,b). The paper is long and the use of middle-range theory is not simple, by any means. But we suggest the problem in historical archaeology is serious, and will require a sophisticated solution.

Binford uses primary data on both the Nunamiut Eskimo hunters and the Alyawara. His immediate question is how to understand the scatter of bones

Mark P. Leone ☐ Department of Anthropology, University of Maryland, College Park, MD 20742. **Constance A. Crosby** ☐ Department of Anthropology, University of California, Berkeley, CA 94720.

he mapped at a newly abandoned Alyawara site. How does one make sense of its vis-à-vis the site's former occupants? He begins by pointing out that if the Nunamiut were to be used as an analogy to explain or illuminate the Australian case, the likely result would be a poor fit, with a resulting caveat that analogies are weak ways of learning.

As a starting point, Binford used two different bodies of data, the Nunamiut and Alyawara, and observed that they do not compliment each other, nor is either an analogy for the other. The parallel in historical archaeology, we argue, is between the documentary record and the archaeological record, from the same site. We suggest that most authors use the written record as an identity to understand the archaeological record, and we argue that there is no more necessary a relationship between them than there is between two different hunter–gatherer groups. Not only is there no necessary relationship, but Binford suggests—and we argue too—that if there is to be a relationship at all, it can be created by two very productive logical steps, tied to each other.

Binford suggests that archaeologists, in ethnoarchaeological cases, need to concern themselves with understanding "the organizational frameworks within which . . . events and processes proceeded" (1987:3), as opposed to concerning themselves only with specific event sequences or patterns of artifacts. To employ organizational frameworks from one case to another, he suggests the use of a frame of reference that will define and describe pertinent data. In the Alyawara and Nunamiut cases, where he is concerned with butchered bones and their subsequent treatment, the frame of reference is one he calls economic anatomy and involves the standard description of mammalian skeletal structure, which will allow a uniform comparison of butchering. This is what he means by frame of reference, and there is nothing complicated about this; it allows bones, in many cases, to be identified, counted, and assessed with uniform results so that variation, minimal numbers of whole animals, and other facts can be assembled.

An "organizational framework" is then employed to highlight the fact that different peoples may do similar things but in different ways, and that, in order to discover this archaeologically and to build the needed antecedent models, the context of acts, behavior, customs, series of acts, or repetitive sequences must be understood. An organizational model is a form or part of a social organization with the understanding that an act, event, or custom has meaning, coherence, implication, and so on, and is not a freestanding episode intelligible in and of itself.

The crucial element in middle range theory, as Binford sets it up, is the discrepancy between the expectations produced by using an analogy and the patterns actually found archaeologically. This discrepancy he calls ambiguity; it is one of the keys to distinguishing between the analogy and the situation it is used to illuminate. The ambiguities need to be dealt with, not explained as exceptions, for they provide clues to the context of use and meaning in the case being worked on, and when dealt with, they preserve the integrity of the particular example.

The final step is to use the newly understood case to shape or reshape the general knowledge sought by the archaeological exploration in the first place. For example,

> I am suggesting that there is a generic pattern distinctive to residential sites among the Nunamiut and Alyawara and those similar to them in the past. Basic to this configuration is the fact that domestic space is focal to all other activities. This is not to say that all residential sites are alike in their detail, only that the maintenance of the domestic unit is the primary function of the facilities at the site. The way utilized space is developed during an occupation is a manifestation of planning depth. If one plans to occupy the site for some time and does not care to have the debris from one activity inhibit the performance of another activity one develops special use areas peripherally to the domestic areas. During the course of residential site occupation many different role-specific tasks may be performed at the site and such special "use areas" are generally located peripherally to the domestic space resulting in a kind of generic site "plan". (1987:63)

Within Binford's use of middle-range theory is an important understanding for historical archaeology. While it takes little effort to see that the Nunamiut and Alyawara are epistemologically separate, it is, we argue, more difficult, but equally essential, to see the written documents and archaeologically recovered materials from one culture, and even one site, as epistemologically separate. The data were made by different individuals, at different times, for different purposes. For one set of data—the documents—to be used to understand an independent set of data—the material remains—requires a better method than we possess, for as it now stands, either an object is identified through a record, or is used to verify the record. In neither case is the assumption of identity valid, with very few exceptions.

Our two sources of data—the archaeological and the documentary—are generated by two very different sets of formation processes and dynamics, and therefore two very different sorts of facts are generated. This is so even though historical archaeologists have generally assumed that the same processes that are at work in our own society and culture were operating in the recent, postmedieval past.

To illustrate how we might learn more by using middle-range theory to organize our data, we have chosen one well reported case in this volume (Chapter 8), Steven Shephard's paper on Alexandria, Virginia, and we would like to treat it using our understanding of Binford's learning program. Shephard's is a detailed essay with clear objectives, a more than normally rigorous method, and clear, worthwhile findings. He ends with a call for more testing, and begins with some doubts about the importance of what he is about to undertake. His conclusions leave one convinced of the study's importance, but without specific satisfaction; this is so even though the conclusions have generality. We want to be clear that Shephard's essay is strong and important in its own right. Reworking his data is not meant as criticism.

In order to use middle-range theory to extend Shephard's study and to attempt to make it more secure as an understanding of Alexandria, the first step is the articulation of the contrastive case, the equivalent of Binford's use of the Nunamiut. Our suggestion for historical archaeology is that that contrastive case is to come from the written record of Alexandria itself. But since there is very little material presented by Shephard for Alexandria, except in quantitative form, we will need to draw on less direct information to make an illustration. Shephard does use census and other indexes from Alexandria to create scales of income, professional status, and property ownership. There is no problem with that; it is a crucial step to using Miller's Pricing Index. Nonetheless, our first step is with the organizational framework of a contrastive case.

The clearest element in Shephard's article, where predictions did not match the findings, is in the data from free, urban, black property owners and those who lived with them. He found that they had greater ratios of storage wares to tablewares than the middle-class whites with whom he compared them. The blacks also had a higher ratio of vessel shapes to total number of vessels. To understand this observation, and to take advantage of it to learn more about the past, we recommend building on this legitimate discovery by reading in and learning about Afro-American culture in the area. Drawing from the scholarship in the Chesapeake area, which clearly includes Alexandria, we can build the following sketchy picture. Rhys Isaac (1982:330–346) has pointed out that, throughout the Tidewater of Virginia in the eighteenth century, slaves built a culture that included an extended kinship network, a diffuse but powerful commitment to ecstatic religion, especially in Baptist churches, and, in general, separate foodways, dance, music, language, and attitudes to white masters. Isaac is clear to say that this was not poor consumer behavior; it was a way of life within a political condition that was so different from that of whites, and could be so resistant to whites, that it was feared because it could produce rebellions, created endless runaways, and became a political threat to the planter–owner class. Even though Isaac deals with an earlier century and with slaves, he is dealing with the area that completely surrounded Alexandria and that, once Alexandria was founded in the second half of the eighteenth century, must have included the social relations within it.

Frederick Fausz (1977, 1982, 1983) has traced the condition of slaves and free blacks in Maryland and Virginia. His picture shows that, in the period of initial slave use, one in which Africans were substituted for the dwindling supply of white indentured servants from England, relatively freer conditions existed for slaves. But by about 1705, blacks were barred from owning land, from marrying freely, and even from redeeming their freedom. Lorena Walsh (1984), working in the Chesapeake on the same problem, shows clearly that blacks were harassed more and more as the eighteenth century progressed, in order to restrict their freedom of movement, their access to legal information, their literacy, and in most other areas. In other words, Maryland and Virginia did not begin as deeply stratified societies with a permanent class of legally defined inferiors; they became racist societies as resources dried up, and as wealth became concentrated in from 1 percent to 5 percent of the total population. As this occurred, skin color became the badge of lowest class membership, and freedom for blacks was harder and harder to sustain. All this occurred in and around Alexandria, and its implication is that slaves had developed a separate culture. One would, of course, have to establish that this relationship penetrated Alexandria.

There has always been a debate in and out of anthropology about whether any of Afro-American society held remnants of the African past. That is a debate, or more accurately, a search, that has born relatively little fruit. There are few relics. But what is not debatable is the existence of black culture in the eighteenth and nineteenth centuries in the Chesapeake. And that culture's creation or emergence is likely to have been a function of the changing conditions in which slaves and free blacks lived. In other words, we might expect that, as conditions worsened, the culture—language, religion, art forms, and definitions of whites—deepened, became more defined, and were not only reactive and expressive of poverty, but actively expressed resistance, conflict, and refusal. The culture of free blacks and slaves may be seen as a function of deepening exploitation. Afro-American slave culture should be seen as complete, different, but as an emerging episode, with the episode defined partially by the conditions of existence brought about by white owners and overseers.

In an urban setting like Alexandria, there were both slaves and free blacks. Free blacks, the lower class that Shephard deals with, were almost always workers who were employed for wages. In terms of a view of Alexandria defined by Shephard using censuses, property values, employment lists, and ceramics, there is only one culture—the culture of capitalism—in the city, and blacks participated in it at the lowest end of the single spectrum. There also can be no doubt, on the other hand, that within a wage-labor and industrial-owner society, everything described by historians of Virginia shows the likely existence of a separate culture for the black population.

Binford used a frame of reference called economic anatomy, to sort out bones in both Nunamiut and Alyawara hunter–gatherer cultures. That frame of reference's equivalent is Miller's[1] Pricing Index. A similar frame of reference, useful for different purposes, could be composed using censuses, property lists, or any of the many uniform documents found all over America in the eighteenth and nineteenth centuries. Shephard was particularly innovative in his use of indexes measuring quality, quantity, and variety of ceramics.

The next step in using middle-range theory is the isolation of ambiguity in the archaeological analysis. There are several steps here that can be taken because Shephard has done such a precise analysis. We have what Shephard expected to find, and we have the discrepancy of what he actually found. This discrepancy is the source of ambiguity only when contrasted with the organizational framework we have been building using the interpretation built on the documents. In other words, instead of turning to the historical record for verification or explanation of events that turn out either as expected or, more

---

[1]Our use of George Miller's Pricing Index as a foil for our arguments should not be interpreted as criticism of Miller's continuing work in this area. The ceramic index is a method for measuring the differential cost of ceramic assemblages that allows for the economic scaling of assemblages based on their cost. The questions that remain, after using Miller, are: How do we interpret the observed differences and similarities through time and across space? What do they mean?

usually, as contrary to expectation, one turns to the historical record as though it were from a separate organization, a separate culture, and one looks to it not for corroboration, but for interrelationships between behaviors, events, or organizations—relationships that link artifacts in the archaeological record and their meanings. Such a search will not produce direct knowledge allowing a closer understanding of the archaeological record. It will produce insight into where the archaeological record does not fit the contrastive case. Here, and only here, is where the archaeological record receives both its independence and its centrality to learning about the past.

The places where the archaeological record does not fit the organizational framework comprise its ambiguity. Here we should not search for literary evidence to explain away the ambiguity; rather, we should look to the organizational model derived from the written record for clues to the meaning of the ambiguity. In our case, the organizational model suggests that, as Shephard shows, blacks are clearly on the lowest end of a consumption continuum. They are wage laborers and, as such, we would expect them to be profoundly affected by all the behavioral patterns of mercantile and industrial capitalism. Yet they come from an historically determined setting in which they were regarded by others, and regarded themselves, as different and separate. At the least, they spoke, worshiped, cooked, and ate food differently. Shephard sees them as different in wealth and ethnicity.

That is the least of it, but it is enough to see that blacks are inside Alexandria on one scale and outside it on another. And both are true. We have seen the truth of the first observation by Shephard's using a framework to measure ceramics. And we have seen the truth of the second part of the picture by using an organizational framework derived from a source quite independent of the ceramics.

Binford demonstrates in his article that, for the two hunter–gatherer groups—the Alyawara and the Nuanumit—the butchering, preparation, and consumption of meat, as evidenced by the faunal remains, were structured and organized differently. This may seem self-evident, but in historical archaeology, we frequently make the assumption that the same activities or "events" were organized and structured in similar ways. Our society's mass production and consumption of material culture serves to mask the differences in behavior between various groups. The assumption has been made that consumer behavior in the past, a hundred or two hundred years ago, is the same as today, and that consumer behavior is and was the same for all consumers. We argue that each group has its own rules or guidelines for governing choices and consumption.

Returning to ceramics and the Miller Pricing Index, the "cost" (price or value) of ceramics is only one factor that is relevant to consumer choices. The cost can be considered the minimum criteria; that is, one must have the resources to buy any given item, but having or not having the money to buy transfer-printed wares and tea sets does not tell enough about the ways in which blacks and whites lived.

Where are the ambiguities created by contrasting the archaeological and documentary patterns? They occur in Shephard's measure of ceramic variety. Shephard measures quantity and quality of ceramics, using the idea that, from rich to poor, sites occupied by the better off will have more and costlier ceramics. His findings match his predictions here. Then he measures variety, which means diversity of types, forms, and functions:

> None of the test implications for the variety measure are supported. There is no significant difference between assemblages in proportions of tableware, tea- and coffeeware, serving flatware, serving bowls, or edged flatware. It was predicted that the assemblages of the middle class would have larger proportions of storage wares and larger ratios of number of shapes to total number of vessels as compared to the Gibbon Street [free black] assemblage. Instead, it is the latter [free black] assemblage that has the larger figures.

The initial importance of this finding is established by Shephard when he describes his other results. His first measure is quantity. He found, after ranking three assemblages by upper-middle, middle, and lower class, that: "The assemblages of the middle class contain a significantly greater quantity of refined ware vessels and coarseware vessels . . . as compared to the lower-class assemblage." The middle class also has a greater number of vessels absolutely, more than three times.

Ceramics vary in quality as well: "The ceramic assemblage of the middle class does contain significantly more transfer-printed vessels, and less undecorated ware, as compared to the [free black] assemblage. The value of the ceramic assemblages from . . . [the middle classes is] significantly higher than . . . the lower classes."

Then Shephard summarizes his findings for the middle and lower classes. The middle-class assemblage has more vessels, more expensive wares, such as transfer-printed and porcelain, more matched pieces, and more specialized tableware and storage vessels such as gravy boats, sugar bowls, creamers, ewers, jugs, and milk pans. The ratio of tableware to storageware is also greater, which Shephard attributes to "an emphasis on material display in dining."

The lower-class assemblage has fewer vessels, less expensive wares, such as hand-painted and edge-decorated, less variety in vessel shapes and sizes, and fewer matched pieces or sets. The ratio of storage to tableware is greater. Yet the lower-class assemblage has the same range of ware types as the middle-class assemblage.

The lower-class, free-black assemblage is less expensive, yet it is composed of the same commercial stock, and thus the same range of ceramic forms for cooking, storage, and eating. Shephard was surprised that variety did not function as an indicator of socioeconomic status in the ways that he predicted. This suggests to us that something else needs to be considered: the contexts in which these ceramics were used in the home. What would we see at the table, on display in the cupboard, in the kitchen, and so on? What kinds of foods were prepared and how were they served? Although we do not know what was actually on the table, we can say something about the context in which these vessels were used with the information we have on the middle- and lower-class assemblages.

The middle-class table, arranged with its matched set of transfer-printed dinnerware, forms a striking contrast to the lower-class collection of variously decorated plates and bowls, few of which match. The middle-class table contains a wider range of vessel shapes and forms, with its variety of bowl and plate sizes and specialized serving vessels. Many of the dinnerwares and teawares came in matched sets.

The lower-class table is characterized by a mixture of undecorated and decorated types, including edge-decorated, hand-painted, transfer-printed, and banded. There are fewer functionally specific shapes, like different-sized plates and bowls, and probably fewer vessels overall. Fewer sizes of plates and bowls, along with fewer specialized serving forms, means that any given plate or bowl may be used in a variety of ways. The few matched pieces are cups and saucers.

There is more being communicated here than just a display of one's social position, or lack of one. The lower-class table setting may allow function to remain more fluid and situational since specific vessel shapes and sizes are lacking. The matched set of middle-class tablewares expresses extreme functional specificity in the variety of vessel shapes and sizes used. Differentiation, segmentation, hierarchy, and order are all expressed in the middle-class setting.

Shephard concludes that variety is not a predictor of economic class. But it is if we look to the organizational framework and realize that wage workers are not just consumers. Wage workers must observe time, space, segmentation, rules for orderliness, and all the commodifications of life's ways essential to selling labor and reducing it to surplus value in the form of work done and items or services produced. Shephard focussed on the cost of ceramics, not on the meaning of the ceramics. The meaning comes from use, and that has not disappeared from the record. Use is in serving, and serving involves the etiquette, the rules for eating. Food is served raw or cooked, by color (dark, light, red, green), dry or wet. It is served in segments, on separate dishes, eaten in a prescribed order, with prescribed utensils, according to formulas of what can occur with what, who can eat with whom, and when. Food may be prepared in one place, eaten in another, disposed of in yet another. It is segmented by a set of rules that may be structurally identical to the rules for showing up for work on time, breaking on time, and pacing work to produce expected results. In other words, the world of eating is just like the world of work. Participating in one necessitates participating in the other. And from the point of view of the world of work, the world of eating by "rational" rules and by using both cookbooks and etiquette at dining, makes the world appear more integrated.[2] Thus, Shephard's findings justify his use of universal measures like Miller's

[2]This point was made and explained to the authors by Parker B. Potter, Jr., using ceramics from Annapolis, Maryland.

Pricing Index because free black workers were participating in capitalism. They were obviously making the economy work for them since they owned property. But the cost of ownership is the segmentation or rationalization of cooking–eating in such a way that it mirrors the working world and facilitates it. So, Shephard's data do indeed show that blacks are on the class continuum in a profound way.

Shephard observes that the wealthier whites had fewer pieces of storage ware per unit of tableware. Among blacks, whom he defines principally as poorer, he finds that there are more of these storage vessels in proportion to the rest of the collection from the same group. Shephard suggests that this may reflect dietary differences, or may be a reflection of rural versus urban environment, since the opposite proportion was found in rural, southern plantation contexts.

The fact that poorer people have strikingly different ratios of eating to serving and/or storage vessels is ambiguous. It highlights Isaac's and Walsh's (1984) point that blacks were developing a separate way of life. We know from Otto (1977) and others in eighteenth- and nineteenth-century South Carolina, and from Deetz (1977) and Baker (1978) in New England for the eighteenth and early nineteenth centuries, that black foodways involved more wild foods, more food chopped rather than sawed, more foods stewed in pots rather than cooked separately, and more foods communally eaten from central dishes rather than served in individual portions. The foodways were different. From Shephard's essay, we can pick up nothing of the context of food collection, purchase, preparation, or the etiquette of serving and eating. We are therefore left with an obvious ambiguity that points to a group of poor people who are doing something quite different from the richer people. But we cannot say what that is.

This leaves us with the following specific suggestions. Blacks were obviously employing elements of the industrially prescribed working world. They were segmenting some aspects of their lives. But integrated into their world was a separate pattern, utterly different from that of their bosses or employers. Because we do not have a hold on the organizational framework of food or its social meaning, we cannot say whether a communal pattern survived for some meals, or in some seasons, or whether some other practice is present.

This ambiguity is very important, for by using Miller alone, or any other universal framework, one creates a continuum of rich and poor that fails to recognize that the poor are often not poor in their own eyes, and may also be despised in the eyes of the rich. They are often also an ethnic group, that is, they are not only different, they are sometimes thought of as profoundly other. And the otherness can be an escape as well as a source of integrity amidst exploitation.

The ambiguity of the archaeological record allows us to search for the behavior of the exploited and behaviors attempting to avoid exploitation. Ambiguity will allow us to see what no analogy will ever show and what deference to a written record, with its assumed epistemologically superior status, will never reveal. Ambiguity points out people within Alexandria who were within the system very deeply but who were, at the same time, outside or even beyond it in some crucial ways. Once the ambiguity is utilized fully, a past society can have some of its integrity, and perhaps some of its meaning, retrieved.

Still, a model is needed from some source to understand the integrity of Afro-American culture, including its foodways. An incomplete example comes from the Parting Ways site in Massachusetts. This site is useful in exploring how to use middle-range theory because the blacks at Parting Ways were freed slaves—wage laborers or part-time farmers—dependent on local markets. Although poor, they owned some fine ceramics. Above all, they lived a separate culture. When this picture is compared to that of Alexandria, we may begin to develop a hunch about the meaning of the diversity of ceramic use among Afro-Americans there.

The Parting Ways[3] site (Deetz 1977:138–154) was occupied in the late eighteenth and nineteenth centuries by four freed slaves, their families, and their descendants. The freed slaves had fought in the American Revolution. In poverty, in old age, the veterans were placed by the courts under a guardian's care and received an $8.00-a-month pension from the federal government. Cato Howe's property was valued at $27.00 in 1820, when he applied for a pension. Four years later, at his death, the probate inventory valued his total estate at $61.82 (Deetz 1977:140–141). The men were laborers working at odd jobs, sometimes farmers. Prince Goodwin continued to work for his former master's family in Plymouth.

The documentary record creates a profile of the Parting Ways residents as dominated by, and dependent on, the white community. Yet there is evidence of a desire for independence and of lives whose spheres of interaction extended well beyond the confines of Plymouth. Just after the Revolutionary War, they acquired land and removed themselves physically from the centers of white settlement. Two of Plato Turner's daughters married and lived in Boston on Beacon Hill, participating in the black community's own church and school. A third daughter married a Gay Head Indian from Martha's Vineyard (Crosby 1982).

From the archaeological record, Deetz identified ceramics, architectural remains, and faunal remains where the evidence did not agree with his expectations. This is the ambiguity we would look for. Some of the ceramics were

---

[3]We have chosen Parting Ways as our second case study because, in some ways, it parallels Shephard's comparison of white and black households in Alexandria. In his book *In Small Things Forgotten*, Deetz uses his extensive work on sites in southeastern Massachusetts as his frame of reference for contrasting Parting Ways with Anglo-American patterns of material culture use. In 1977 and 1978, Crosby was research coordinator for a CETA-funded research project conducted under the auspices of Parting Ways, the Museum of Afro-American Ethnohistory, in Plymouth, Massachusetts. In the summer of 1981, Crosby was also part of an NEH-funded research project for the museum. At those and other times, Crosby conducted documentary research on the Parting Ways settlement. In 1982, at the University of California, Crosby prepared "The History of the Parting Ways Settlement" as part of an independent study supervised by Dr. James Deetz. The manuscript is now in the author's possession.

high-quality, hand-painted creamwares and costly Chinese porcelain; the date range of the assemblage was earlier than expected, given the dates of occupation.[4] Deetz proposed that some of the ceramics were probably acquired secondhand, perhaps from their former masters (1977:18,146).

All of the three architectural features excavated, two houses and an outbuilding, were constructed according to a twelve-foot module rather than the expected sixteen-foot module common for Anglo-American sites in the area. To explain the differences, Deetz turned to the work of John Vlach (1976) on Afro-American shotgun houses in the American South and Haiti. Vlach documented the shotgun house as an Afro-American form based on West African antecedents. Deetz argued that the floor plan of the Turner-Burr house more closely approximated the shotgun house in floor plan and living space than the typical Anglo-American hall-and-parlor-house (Deetz 1977:150–151). When the space available inside a house is considered in terms of the proxemics of the house's occupants, there seems to be a different set of rules governing the use of space by Afro-American versus Anglo- or Euro-Americans.[5]

Deetz then considered the faunal remains, on which the butchering marks indicated that chopping rather than sawing was the norm at a time (early nineteenth century) when Anglo-American sites exhibited mostly saw marks on the faunal remains. Sawing allows one to divide meat into discrete individual serving portions, such as steaks and chops. And at Black Lucy's Garden, an early nineteenth-century rural Afro-American site in Massachusetts, Baker found that 82 percent of the faunal remains were chopped rather than sawn[6] (Baker 1978:111).

[4]Subsequent historical research showed that several white families occupied the Turner site in succession from the mid-1750s to 1779, when Plato Turner purchased a house from the last white occupant. The white families were all of small economic means, and therefore were unlikely to have had much access to fine eighteenth-century tablewares (Crosby 1982). However, since the last white family left in 1779, all materials postdating that time can be associated with the black residents, including all the pearlwares (Deetz 1977:18, 146).
The analysis of the archaeological materials from Deetz's work in 1975 and 1976 was completed before Miller published his ceramic index in 1980.
[5]Deetz notes that a twelve foot module provides only 144 square feet of living area while a sixteen foot module offers 256 square feet (1977:150). The Turner-Burr house was built by the Turner family.
[6]Baker discusses the implications of the chopped faunal remains at three sites, including Parting Ways, with respect to the percentage of serving flatware as compared to serving bowls in each assemblage. At Cannon's Point Plantation in Georgia, the faunal remains and documentary evidence both indicate that the planter's family ate mostly roasted meats and vegetables prepared and served separately (Otto 1977:104). In contrast, the assemblages from the overseer and slave middens indicate that both ate primarily stews and pottages; all faunal remains were either chopped or cleaved open. At all three sites, the serving bowls were over 40 percent of the tableware assemblage: 41 percent at Black Lucy's Garden, 44 percent at the slave cabin at Cannon's Point, and 53 percent at Parting Ways (Baker 1978:114). In contrast, serving bowls were only 24 percent of the overseer and 8 percent of the planter assemblages at Cannon's Point (Otto 1977:106). Also, the serving flatware at Cannon's Point was 49 percent of the tableware for the slave, 72 percent for the overseer, and 84 percent for the planter assemblage (Otto 1977:106). At Parting Ways and Black Lucy's Garden, the serving flatware comprised 46 percent and 51 percent of the tableware assemblages, respectively (Baker 1978:114).

The point we wish to emphasize is that the similarities between these three sites do not constitute a universal Afro-American pattern of some sort, nor should we expect to find one. Ira Berlin (1980) has emphasized that different Afro-American societies and cultures developed in the Northern colonies and in the Chesapeake on the one hand, and in the lowland South during the colonial period on the other, in response to different economic and demographic conditions. The people brought from Africa as slaves came from a wide variety of cultures and experiences. Their integration into New World societies varied depending on time and place, thus a search for Africanisms or survivals in the archaeological record is not very fruitful. It is possible, however, to discover how Afro-Americans (and others) employed material culture to resist and oppose the dominant white society and to create meaning in their everyday lives at different times and in different places.

The Parting Ways materials do not conform to the Anglo-American patterns, archaeological or architectural; they also do not exhibit the changes, which Deetz describes throughout his book, in the Anglo-American cultural tradition as it was transformed from "medieval" to Georgian:

> The occupants of the site constructed their house differently, disposed of their trash differently, arranged their community differently. But because the artifacts themselves were so familiar to us, the essential differences were disguised behind them, and only when a more basic consideration of different perceptions of the world was made did the picture come into focus. (Deetz 1977:153)

> While the artifacts available to the members of the Parting Ways settlement were of necessity almost entirely Anglo-American, the rules by which they were put to use in functional combinations might have been more Afro-American. (Deetz 1977:149)

Culture at Parting Ways and at Black Lucy's Garden was quite different from white New England culture. Eating was likely less segmented, less modern, and less focussed on the individuals. What does this tell us about Afro-Americans in Alexandria?

The Massachusetts case is rural and a little earlier than Alexandria. It is probably about people who were a little poorer, compared to free blacks in Alexandria. Three steps need to be taken next, although we do not have enough data to take them in this essay. The ceramic collections we have cited need to be precisely compared to those of Alexandria for ratios so that differences can be clear. Then Alexandria documents need to be read on food preparation, procurement, service, eating, and disposal. Then those documents that have been searched to illuminate the meaning of the ambiguity will have contributed to its meaning. Incidentally, in the search, historical data will be recovered that was not noticed before, or was not understood, or was even misunderstood. Therefore, the documentary record will be given additional meaning.

The last step extends beyond one community and makes a larger hypothesis possible. The larger picture here is that ethnic groups are not free standing; they are not imported whole from anywhere. Ethnicity is partially a product of exploitation, brought into being by it, sustained, lessened, or deep- ened by it, and abolished with it. Ethnicity is an episode, and the terms of ethnicity often place the group low on the economic scale. Ethnicity itself is a definition of subordinates that allows them to be exploited because they either deserve or merit it in local eyes, for it is often thought they merit no better condition for biological, historical, or supernatural reasons. The ethnic group, for its part, may believe some of its imposed inferiority and/or it may reject some of its inferiority by developing its own sense of peculiarity. In both cases, within and outside the group, one major function of ethnicity is to mask the true condition. And the masking can be seen in the ambiguities of the archae- ological record. Blacks in Alexandria bought and used all the same kinds of ceramics, and most of the segmenting forms, but they needed them in very different proportions. If we had the organizational framework of ceramic use, which surely must be researchable, we would have a way of showing how foodways defined and helped to sustain separateness.

To sum up, a truly anthropological historical archaeology may consider separating the documentary from the archaeological records, giving them dif- ferent statuses, and may reconsider assuming whether they are identities. The documentary record can be used to compose an organizational framework, showing in detail the meaning of the items explored in the archaeological record. This means showing the context of food acquisition, service, and dis- posal: food's meaning. This of course assumes one is investigating ceramics, but the procedure would be the same if architecture, glass, pipes, or any other material category were the object of study. The category itself needs to be measured in a precise way, and a frame of reference like Miller's Pricing Index is one such measure. Many others could be created in historical archaeology now (Ross 1983). A precise description of the archaeological record is then matched against the organizational framework in a search for ambiguity, that is, where the two do not fit. The match then provokes, not a flurry to explain away exceptions, but a further exploration of the ethnographic-historical re- cord for what might be there that was not seen or known at first look. Then, as a final step, a proposition or hypothesis can be put forth that attempts to account, not only for the facts of the organizational framework, but for the parts of the archaeological record that now have greater standing for their role in recovering the integrity of other cultures in the past.

ACKNOWLEDGMENTS

Much of our thinking in this essay is based on our understanding of Lewis R. Binford's work on middle-range theory as presented in "Researching Ambi- guity: Frames of Reference and Site Structure," in *Method and Theory for Activity Area Research: An Ethnoarchaeological Approach,* edited by Susan Kent, published by Columbia University Press. Although this volume is pub- lished, our citations are from the manuscript version and permission to use them has been granted by Lewis R. Binford. The attempt to adopt middle-range theory to historical archaeology is ours and we assume full responsibility for any misunderstanding or misuse of Binford's ideas.

We thank Dr. Steven Shephard for commenting fully on our use of his data from Alexandria, Virginia and for lending us a copy of his dissertation. We assume responsibility for any misreading of his data.

REFERENCES

Baker, Vernon G., 1978, *Historical Archaeology at Black Lucy's Garden, Andover, Massachusetts: Ceramics from the Site of a Nineteenth Century Afro-American,* Papers of the Robert S. Peabody Foundation for Archaeology, Volume 8, Phillips Academy, Andover, Massachusetts.
Berlin, Ira, 1980, Time, Space, and the Evolution of Afro-American Society on British Mainland North-America, *American Historical Review* 85(1):44–78.
Binford, Lewis R., 1982, Objectivity–Explanation–Archaeology, in: *Theory and Explanation in Archaeology* (Colin Renfrew, Michael J. Rowlands, and Barbara Abbott Seagraves eds.), Academic, New York, pp. 125–138.
Binford, Lewis R., 1983a, *In Pursuit of the Past: Decoding the Archaeological Record,* Thames and Hudson, New York.
Binford, Lewis R., 1983b, *Working at Archaeology,* Academic Press, New York.
Binford, Lewis R., 1987, Researching Ambiguity: Frames of Reference and Site Structure, in: *Method and Theory for Active Area Research—An Ethnoarchaeological Approach* (Susan Kent, ed.), Columbia University Press, New York.
Crosby, Constance A. 1982, The History of the Parting Ways Settlement, manuscript in the possession of the author.
Deetz, James F., 1977, *In Small Things Forgotten,* Anchor Books, Doubleday, New York.
Fausz, Frederick J., 1977, *The Powhatan Uprising of 1622: A Historical Study of Ethnocentrism and Cultural Conflict,* Ph.D. dissertation, Department of History, College of William and Mary in Virginia.
Fausz, Frederick J., 1982, By Warre Upon Our Enemies, and Kinde Usage of Our Friends: The Beaver Trade and Interest Group Rivalry in the Development of the Early Chesapeake, 1607–1652, paper presented at the October 1982 Colloquium in Colonial American History, Institute of Early American History and Culture. Copy on file at the Institute.
Fausz, Frederick J., 1983, Authority and Opportunity in the Early Chesapeake: The Bay Environment and the English Connection, 1620–1640, paper presented at the 1983 organization of American Historians Annual Meeting, Cincinnati. Copy on file at the Virginia Historical Society, Richmond.
Isaac, Rhys, 1982, *The Transformation of Virginia, 1740–1790,* University of North Carolina Press, Chapel Hill.
Miller, George L., 1980, Classification and Economic Scaling of 19th-Century Ceramics, *Historical Archaeology* 14:1–40.
Otto, John Solomon, 1977, Artifacts and Status Differences—A Comparison of Ceramics from Planter, Overseer, and Slave Sites on an Antebellum Plantation, in: *Research Strategies in Historical Archaeology,* (Stanley South ed.), pp 91–118, Academic Press, New York.
Ross, Lester, 1983, Archaeological Metrology: English, French, American, and Canadian Systems of Weights and Measures for North American Archaeology, *History and Archaeology,* (68), National Historic Parks and Sites Branch, Parks Canada, Ottawa.
Vlach, John, 1976, The Shotgun House: An African Architectural Legacy, *Pioneer America,* Part 1, Vol. 8, No. 1, pp. 47–56; Part 2, Vol. 8, No. 2, pp. 57–70.
Walsh, Lorena, 1984, Changing Work Roles for Slave Labor in Chesapeake Agriculture, 1620–1820, manuscript, Maryland Hall of Records, Annapolis.

Index